1994

MARKETING CLASSICS

MARKETING CLASSICS
A Selection of
Influential Articles
Seventh Edition

BEN M. ENIS
University of Southern California

KEITH K. COX
University of Houston

ALLYN AND BACON
Boston London Toronto Sydney Tokyo Singapore

Series Editor: Henry Reece
Series Editorial Assistant: Katherine Grubbs
Production Coordinator: Lisa Feder
Editorial-Production Service: York Production Services
Cover Administrator: Linda Dickinson
Cover Designer: Suzanne Harbison
Manufacturing Buyer: Louise Richardson

Copyright © 1991, 1988, 1985, 1981, 1977, 1973, 1969 by Allyn and Bacon
A Division of Simon & Schuster, Inc.
160 Gould Street
Needham Heights, Massachusetts 02194

Library of Congress Cataloging-in-Publication Data

Marketing classics : a selection of influential articles / [compiled
  by] Ben M. Enis, Keith K. Cox
    p. cm.
  Includes bibliographical references (p.) and index.
  ISBN 0–205–12924–2
  1. Marketing. I. Enis, Ben M. II. Cox, Keith Kohn.
HF5415.M29748 1991
658.8—dc20   90-45274
                                                        CIP

Printed in the United States of America

10 9 8 7 6 5 4   95 94 93

Contributors

David A. Aaker
Wroe Alderson
Paul F. Anderson
Richard P. Bagozzi
Russell W. Belk
Leonard L. Berry
James R. Bettman
Paul N. Bloom
Booz, Allen and Hamilton, Inc.
Neil H. Borden
Louis P. Bucklin
Robert D. Buzzell
George S. Day
Susan Douglas
Bernard Dubois
Bradley T. Gale
William Gregor
Russell I. Haley
John A. Howard
George Katona
Philip Kotler
Robert Jacobson
Robert J. Lavidge
Theodore Levitt
Sidney J. Levy
Arnold Mitchell
David B. Montgomery

Patrick E. Murphy
William D. Novelli
Alfred R. Oxenfeldt
Thomas J. Peters
Michael E. Porter
Torger Reve
Al Ries
Everett M. Rogers
William Rogers
Robert W. Ruekert
Adrian B. Ryans
Jagdish N. Sheth
Allan D. Shocker
John E. Smallwood
Rajendra K. Srivastava
William A. Staples
Gary A. Steiner
Louis W. Stern
Ralph G.M. Sultan
Gerard J. Tellis
Jack Trout
Orville C. Walker, Jr.
Robert H. Waterman, Jr.
Frederick E. Webster, Jr.
Charles B. Weinberg
Yoram Wind

Contents

Preface

WHEN *MARKETING CLASSICS* was conceived, we commented in the Preface:

> Marketing is that phase of human activity that produces economic want-satisfaction by matching consumers' needs and the resources of business firms. From the firm's point of view, consumer-satisfaction is the result of its marketing strategy. Strategy is based on marketing philosophy and is derived from the analysis of consumers and their functional interrelationships with such market forces as economic conditions, competitors' actions, institutional change, and other environmental factors. This volume is a compilation of articles that provide broad insight into the field of marketing.
>
> The authors consider these works to be among the classics of marketing literature. These articles are generally recognized by marketing scholars as being of enduring significance to marketing thought. They are widely quoted, have led to new directions in marketing research, and reflect the views of influential scholars. Consequently, these are works with which serious marketing students should be familiar and to which they should have ready access. We believe the book will be a useful supplement to advanced undergraduate courses in marketing management and marketing strategy and to graduate courses in marketing fundamentals and marketing theory. The practitioner might also enjoy having these familiar works in his library.
>
> The articles in this volume were chosen on the basis of extensive research in marketing literature, and the authors were fortunate to obtain the suggestions of a number of colleagues. Nevertheless, it would be presumptuous to imply that we have compiled *the* classic works of marketing. Marketing is too rich, too complex, too diverse a discipline to be subsumed in one volume. Our selections reflect our own perceptions of and biases about marketing.

The seventh edition of *Marketing Classics* reflects our continuing attempt to match this concept to the needs of marketing students. Responses to questionnaires sent to some adopters of previous editions revealed that this anthology is used in a variety of courses, ranging from introductory marketing to doctoral-level seminars, in the United States, Canada, Europe, South America, Africa, and the Pacific Rim countries.

This edition includes several new articles that have stood the test of time and deletes a few genuine classics that our research indicates for various reasons are no longer frequently assigned to students.

Again, we are most grateful to the authors and publishers who granted permission to reprint their work. This literally is their book. We appreciate comment and criticism on our selections. Many readers have returned questionnaires or sent letters to us over the years. We particularly thank this time Professors David Stewart and Gerard Tellis, University of Southern California.

The people at Allyn and Bacon, from Executive Editor Henry Reece on down, have been most cooperative and helpful through the years. In spite of all this assistance, errors of omission and/or commission are likely, and differences of opinion as to the nature of marketing classics are inevitable. We are, of course, responsible and would very much appreciate feedback.

B.M.E.
K.K.C.

PART ONE

Marketing Philosophy

Any discipline or area of human inquiry is based on a philosophy, a set of principles that provide the rationale for the existence of the discipline. The articles in Part One present a cross-section of the philosophy of marketing.

Levitt's article sets the stage. Perhaps the discipline's most quoted and reprinted paper vividly demonstrates the need for a broad interpretation of the marketing function; this article is the discipline's single best definitive statement. Levitt's thoughts on the continuing relevance of the paper are also included. Wroe Alderson, in his trenchant style, provides an overview of marketing. He envisions the discipline based in the economics of imperfect competition, composed of the problem-solving activities of consumers and firms, and illuminated by concepts from the social sciences.

Philip Kotler and Sidney Levy began the next decade of marketing through (the 1970s) with the provocative statement that marketing activities were not confined to business firms but had broader applicability to all organizations. Marketing management, they therefore maintain, is a pervasive social activity.

The thinking of Kotler and Levy, illustrated in the article here in Part One as well as several other articles written singly or together, has had a major impact on the marketing discipline. This work was deepened by the rigorous work of their student Bagozzi, who carefully set forth the condition for exchange. A more recent significant contribution to marketing philosophy is Anderson's paper, which links marketing thinking to marketing strategy to marketing planning and the theory of the firm. This is the only paper in *Journal of Marketing* history to win both best-paper awards in the same year.

Marketing Myopia

Theodore Levitt

Every major industry was once a growth industry. But some that are now riding a wave of growth enthusiasm are very much in the shadow of decline. Others which are thought of as seasoned growth industries have stopped growing. In every case the reason growth is threatened, slowed, or stopped is *not* because the market is saturated. It is because there has been a failure of management.

FATEFUL PURPOSES

The failure is at the top. The executives responsible for it, in the last analysis, are

those who deal with broad aims and policies. Thus:

The railroads did not stop growing because the need for passenger and freight transportation declined. That grew. The railroads are in trouble today not because the need was filled by others (cars, trucks, airplanes, even telephones), but because it was *not* filled by the railroads themselves. They let others take customers away from them because they assumed themselves to be in the railroad business rather than in the transportation business. The reason they defined their industry wrong was because they were railroad-oriented instead of transportation-oriented; they were product-oriented instead of customer-oriented.

Hollywood barely escaped being totally ravished by television. Actually, all the established film companies went through drastic reorganizations. Some simply disappeared. All of them got into trouble not because of TV's inroads but because of their own myopia. As with the railroads, Hollywood defined its business incorrectly. It thought it was in the movie business when it was actually in the entertainment business. "Movies" implied a specific, limited product. This produced a fatuous contentment which from the beginning led producers to view TV as a threat. Hollywood scorned and rejected TV when it should have welcomed it as an opportunity—an opportunity to expand the entertainment business.

Today TV is a bigger business than the old narrowly defined movie business ever was. Had Hollywood been customer-oriented (providing entertainment), rather than product-oriented (making movies), would it have gone through the fiscal purgatory that it did? I doubt it. What ultimately saved Hollywood and accounted for its recent resurgence was the wave of new young writers, producers, and directors whose previous success in television had decimated the old movie companies and toppled the big movie moguls.

There are other less obvious examples of industries that have been and are now endangering their futures by improperly defining their purposes. I shall discuss some in detail later and analyze the kind of policies that lead to trouble. Right now it may help to show what a thoroughly customer-oriented management *can* do to keep a growth industry growing, even after the obvious opportunities have been exhausted; and here there are two examples that have been around for a long time. They are nylon and glass—specifically, E.I. duPont de Nemours & Company and Corning Glass Works:

> Both companies have great technical competence. Their product orientation is unquestioned. But this alone does not explain their success. After all, who was more pridefully product-oriented and product-conscious than the erstwhile New England Textile companies that have been so thoroughly massacred? The duPonts and the Cornings have succeeded not primarily because of their product or research orientation but because they have been thoroughly customer-oriented

also. It is constant watchfulness for opportunities to apply their technical know-how to the creation of customer-satisfying uses which accounts for their prodigious output of successful new products. Without a very sophisticated eye on the customer, most of their new products might have been wrong, their sales methods useless.

Aluminum has also continued to be a growth industry, thanks to the efforts of two wartime-created companies which deliberately set about creating new customer-satisfying uses. Without Kaiser Aluminum & Chemical Corporation and Reynolds Metals Company, the total demand for aluminum today would be vastly less than it is.

Error of Analysis

Some may argue that it is foolish to set the railroads off against aluminum or the movies off against glass. Are not aluminum and glass naturally so versatile that the industries are bound to have more growth opportunities than the railroads and movies? This view commits precisely the error I have been talking about. It defines an industry, or a product, or a cluster of know-how so narrowly as to guarantee its premature senescence. When we mention "railroads," we should make sure we mean "transportation." As transporters, the railroads still have a good chance for very considerable growth. They are not limited to the railroad business as such (though in my opinion rail transportation is potentially a much stronger transportation medium than is generally believed).

What the railroads lack is not opportunity, but some of the same managerial imaginativeness and audacity that made them great. Even an amateur like Jacques Barzun can see what is lacking when he says:

> I grieve to see the most advanced physical and social organization of the last century go

down in shabby disgrace for lack of the same comprehensive imagination that built it up. What is lacking is the will of the companies to survive and to satisfy the public by inventiveness and skill.[1]

SHADOW OF OBSOLESCENCE

It is impossible to mention a single major industry that did not at one time qualify for the magic appellation of "growth industry." In each case its assumed strength lay in the apparently unchallenged superiority of its product. There appeared to be no effective substitute for it. It was itself a runaway substitute for the product it so triumphantly replaced. Yet one after another of these celebrated industries has come under a shadow. Let us look briefly at a few more of them, this time taking examples that have so far received a little less attention:

Dry Cleaning. This was once a growth industry with lavish prospects. In an age of wool garments, imagine being finally able to get them safely and easily clean. The boom was on.

Yet here we are 30 years after the boom started and the industry is in trouble. Where has the competition come from? From a better way of cleaning? No. It has come from synthetic fibers and chemical additives that have cut the need for dry cleaning. But this is only the beginning. Lurking in the wings and ready to make chemical dry cleaning totally obsolescent is that powerful magician, ultrasonics.

Electric Utilities. This is another one of those supposedly "no-substitute" products that has been enthroned on a pedestal of invincible growth. When the incandescent lamp came along, kerosene lights were finished. Later the water wheel and the steam engine were cut to ribbons by the flexibility, reliability, simplicity, and just plain easy availability of electric motors. The prosperity of electric utilities continues to wax extravagant as the home is converted into a museum of electric gadgetry. How can anybody miss by investing in utilities, with no competition, nothing but growth ahead?

But a second look is not quite so comforting. A score of nonutility companies are well advanced toward developing a powerful chemical fuel cell which could sit in some hidden closet of every home silently ticking off electric power. The electric lines that vulgarize so many neighborhoods will be eliminated. So will the endless demolition of streets and service interruptions during storms. Also on the horizon is solar energy, again pioneered by nonutility companies.

Who says that the utilities have no competition? They may be natural monopolies now, but tomorrow they may be natural deaths. To avoid this prospect, they too will have to develop fuel cells, solar energy, and other power sources. To survive, they themselves will have to plot the obsolescence of what now produces their livelihood.

Grocery Stores. Many people find it hard to realize that there ever was a thriving establishment known as the "corner grocery store." The supermarket has taken over with a powerful effectiveness. Yet the big food chains of the 1930's narrowly escaped being completely wiped out by the aggressive expansion of independent supermarkets. The first genuine supermarket was opened in 1930, in Jamaica, Long Island. By 1933 supermarkets were thriving in California, Ohio, Pennsylvania, and elsewhere. Yet the established chains pompously ignored them. When they chose to notice them, it was with such derisive descriptions as "cheapy," "horse-and-buggy," "cracker-barrel storekeeping," and "unethical opportunities."

The executive of one big chain announced at the time that he found it "hard to believe that people will drive for miles to shop for foods and sacrifice the personal service chains have perfected and to which Mrs. Consumer is accustomed."[2] As late as 1936, the National Wholesale Grocers convention and the New Jersey Retail Grocers Association said there was nothing to fear. They said that the supers' narrow appeal to the price buyer limited the size of their market. They had to draw from miles around. When imitators came, there would be wholesale liquidations as volume fell. The current high sales of the supers was said to be partly due to their novelty. Basically people wanted convenient neighborhood grocers. If the neighborhood stores "cooperate with their suppliers, pay attention to their costs, and improve their services," they would be able to weather the competition until it blew over.[3]

It never blew over. The chains discovered that survival required going into the supermarket business. This meant the wholesale destruction of their huge investments in corner store sites and in established distribution and merchandising methods. The companies with "the courage of their convictions" resolutely stuck to the corner store philosophy. They kept their pride but lost their shirts.

Self-Deceiving Cycle

But memories are short. For example, it is hard for people who today confidently hail the twin messiahs of electronics and chemicals to see how things could possibly go wrong with these galloping industries. They probably also cannot see how a reasonably sensible businessman could have been as myopic as the famous Boston millionaire who 50 years ago unintentionally sentenced his heirs to poverty by stipulating that his entire estate be forever invested exclusively in electric streetcar securities. His posthumous declaration, "There will always be a big demand for efficient urban transportation," is no consolation to his heirs who sustain life by pumping gasoline at automobile filling stations.

Yet, in a casual survey I recently took among a group of intelligent business executives, nearly half agreed that it would be hard to hurt their heirs by tying their estates forever to the electronics industry. When I then confronted them with the Boston street car example, they chorused unanimously, "That's different!" But is it? Is not the basic situation identical?

In truth, *there is no such thing* as a growth industry, I believe. There are only companies organized and operated to create and capitalize on growth opportunities. Industries that assume themselves to be riding some automatic growth escalator invariably descend into stagnation. The history of every dead and dying "growth" industry shows a self-deceiving cycle of bountiful expansion and undetected decay. There are four conditions which usually guarantee this cycle:

1. The belief that growth is assured by an expanding and more affluent population.
2. The belief that there is no competitive substitution for the industry's major product.
3. Too much faith in mass production and in the advantages of rapidly declining unit costs as output rises.
4. Preoccupation with a product that lends itself to carefully controlled scientific experimentation, improvement, and manufacturing cost reduction.

I should like now to begin examining each of these conditions in some detail. To build my case as boldly as possible, I shall illustrate the points with reference to three industries—petroleum, automobiles, and electronics—particularly petroleum, because it spans more years and more vicissitudes. Not only do these three have excellent reputations with the general public and also enjoy the confidence of sophisticated investors, but their managements have become known for progressive thinking in areas like financial control, product research, and management training. If obsolescence can cripple even these industries, it can happen anywhere.

POPULATION MYTH

The belief that profits are assured by an expanding and more affluent population is dear to the heart of every industry. It takes the edge off the apprehensions everybody understandably feels about the future. If consumers are multiplying and also buying more of your product or service, you can face the future with considerably more comfort than if the market is shrinking. An expanding market keeps the manufacturer from having to think very hard or imaginatively. If thinking is an intellectual response to a problem, then the absence of a problem leads to the absence of thinking. If your product has an automatically expanding market, then you will not give much thought to how to expand it.

One of the most interesting examples of this is provided by the petroleum industry. Probably our oldest growth industry, it has an enviable record. While there are some current apprehensions about its growth rate, the industry itself tends to be optimistic. But I believe it can be demonstrated that it is undergoing a fundamental yet typical change. It is not only ceasing to be a growth industry, but may actually be a declining one, relative to other business. Although there is widespread awareness of it, I believe

that within 25 years the oil industry may find itself in much the same position of retrospective glory that the railroads are now in. Despite its pioneering work in developing and applying the present-value method of investment evaluation, in employee relations, and in working with backward countries, the petroleum business is a distressing example of how complacency and wrong-headedness can stubbornly convert opportunity into near disaster.

One of the characteristics of this and other industries that have believed very strongly in the beneficial consequences of an expanding population, while at the same time being industries with a generic product for which there has appeared to be no competitive substitute, is that the individual companies have sought to outdo their competitors by improving on what they are already doing. This makes sense, of course, if one assumes that sales are tied to the country's population strings, because the customer can compare products only on a feature-by-feature basis. I believe it is significant, for example, that not since John D. Rockefeller sent free kerosene lamps to China has the oil industry done anything really outstanding to create a demand for its product. Not even in product improvement has it showered itself with eminence. The greatest single improvement, namely, the development of tetraethyl lead, came from outside the industry, specifically from General Motors and duPont. The big contributions made by the industry itself are confined to the technology of oil exploration, production, and refining.

Asking for Trouble
In other words, the industry's efforts have focused on improving the *efficiency* of getting and making its product, not really on improving the generic product or its marketing. Moreover, its chief product has contin-

uously been defined in the narrowest possible terms, namely, gasoline, not energy, fuel, or transportation. This attitude has helped assure that:

Major improvements in gasoline quality tend not to originate in the oil industry. Also, the development of superior alternative fuels comes from outside the oil industry, as will be shown later.

Major innovations in automobile fuel marketing are originated by small new oil companies that are not primarily preoccupied with production or refining. These are the companies that have been responsible for the rapidly expanding multipump gasoline stations, with their successful emphasis on large and clean layouts, rapid and efficient driveway service, and quality gasoline at low prices.

Thus, the oil industry is asking for trouble from outsiders. Sooner or later, in this land of hungry inventors and entrepreneurs, a threat is sure to come. The possibilities of this will become more apparent when we turn to the next dangerous belief of many managements. For the sake of continuity, because this second belief is tied closely to the first, I shall continue with the same example.

Idea of Indispensability

The petroleum industry is pretty much persuaded that there is no competitive substitute for its major product, gasoline—or if there is, that it will continue to be a derivative of crude oil, such as diesel fuel or kerosene jet fuel.

There is a lot of automatic wishful thinking in this assumption. The trouble is that most refining companies own huge amounts of crude oil reserves. These have value only if there is a market for products into which oil can be converted—hence the tenacious belief in the continuing competi-

tive superiority of automobile fuels made from crude oil.

This idea persists despite all historic evidence against it. The evidence not only shows that oil has never been a superior product for any purpose for very long, but it also shows that the oil industry has never really been a growth industry. It has been a succession of different businesses that have gone through the usual historic cycles of growth, maturity, and decay. Its over-all survival is owed to a series of miraculous escapes from total obsolescence, of last minute and unexpected reprieves from total disaster reminiscent of the Perils of Pauline.

Perils of Petroleum

I shall sketch in only the main episodes:

First, crude oil was largely a patent medicine. But even before that fad ran out, demand was greatly expanded by the use of oil in kerosene lamps. The prospect of lighting the world's lamps gave rise to an extravagant promise of growth. The prospects were similar to those the industry now holds for gasoline in other parts of the world. It can hardly wait for the underdeveloped nations to get a car in every garage.

In the days of the kerosene lamp, the oil companies competed with each other and against gaslight by trying to improve the illuminating characteristics of kerosene. Then suddenly the impossible happened. Edison invented a light which was totally nondependent on crude oil. Had it not been for the growing use of kerosene in space heaters, the incandescent lamp would have completely finished oil as a growth industry at that time. Oil would have been good for little else than axle grease.

Then disaster and reprieve struck again. Two great innovations occurred, neither originating in the oil industry. The successful development of coal-burning domestic central-heating systems made the space heater obsolescent. While the industry reeled along came its most magnificent boost yet—the internal combustion engine, also invented by outsiders. Then when the prodigious expansion for gasoline finally began to level off in the 1920's, along came the miraculous escape of a central oil heater. Once again, the escape was provided by an outsider's invention and development. And when that market weakened, wartime demand for aviation fuel came to the rescue. After the war the expansion of civilian aviation, the dieselization of railroads, and the explosive demand for cars and trucks kept the industry's growth in high gear.

Meanwhile centralized oil heating—whose boom potential had only recently been proclaimed—ran into severe competition from natural gas. While the oil companies themselves owned the gas that now competed with their oil, the industry did not originate the natural gas revolution, nor has it to this day greatly profited from its gas ownership. The gas revolution was made by newly formed transmission companies that marketed the product with an aggressive ardor. They started a magnificent new industry, first against the advice and then against the resistance of the oil companies.

By all the logic of the situation, the oil companies themselves should have made the gas revolution. They not only owned the gas; they also were the only people experienced in handling, scrubbing, and using it, the only people experienced in pipeline technology and transmission, and they understood heating problems. But, partly because they knew that natural gas would compete with their own sale of heating oil, the oil companies pooh-poohed the potentials of gas.

The revolution was finally started by oil pipeline executives who, unable to persuade their own companies to go into gas, quit and organized the spectacularly successful gas transmission companies. Even after their success became painfully evident to the oil companies, the latter did not go into gas transmission. The multibillion dollar business which should have been theirs went to others. As in the past, the industry was blinded by its narrow preoccupation with a specific product and the value of its reserves. It paid little or no attention to its customers' basic needs and preferences.

The postwar years have not witnessed any change. Immediately after World War II the oil industry was greatly encouraged about its future by the rapid expansion of demand for its traditional line of products. In 1950 most companies projected annual rates of domestic expansion around 6% through at least 1975. Though the ratio of crude oil reserves to demand in the Free World was about 20 to 1, with 10 to 1 being usually considered a reasonable working ration in the United States, booming demand sent oil men searching for more without sufficient regard to what the future really promised. In 1952 they "hit" in the Middle East; the ratio skyrocketed to 42 to 1. If gross additions to reserves continue at the average rate of the past five years (37 billion barrels annually), then by 1970 the reserve ratio will be up to 45 to 1. This abundance of oil has weakened crude and product prices all over the world.

Uncertain Future

Management cannot find much consolation today in the rapidly expanding petrochemical industry, another oil-using idea that did not originate in the leading firms. The total United States production of petrochemicals is equivalent to about 2% (by volume) of the demand for all petroleum products. Although the petrochemical industry is now expected to grow by about 10% per year, this will not offset other drains on the growth of crude oil consumption. Furthermore, while petrochemical products are many and growing, it is well to remember that there are nonpetroleum sources of the basic raw material, such as coal. Besides, a lot of plastics can be produced with relatively little oil. A 50,000-barrel-per-day oil refinery is not considered the absolute minimum size for efficiency. But a 50,000-barrel-per-day chemical plant is a giant operation.

Oil has never been a continuously strong growth industry. It has grown by fits and starts, always miraculously saved by innovations and developments not of its own making. The reason it has not grown in a smooth progression is that each time it thought it had a superior product safe from the possibility of competitive substitutes, the product turned out to be inferior and notoriously subject to obsolescence. Until now, gasoline (for motor fuel, anyhow) has escaped this fate. But, as we shall see later, it too may be on its last legs.

The point of all this is that there is no guarantee against product obsolescence. If a company's own research does not make it obsolete, another's will. Unless an industry is especially lucky, as oil has been until now, it can easily go down in a sea of red figures—just as the railroads have, as the buggy whip manufacturers have, as the corner grocery chains have, as most of the big movie companies have, and indeed as many other industries have.

The best way for a firm to be lucky is to make its own luck. That requires knowing what makes a business successful. One of the greatest enemies of this knowledge is mass production.

PRODUCTION PRESSURES

Mass-production industries are impelled by a great drive to produce all they can. The prospect of steeply declining unit costs as output rises is more than most companies can usually resist. The profit possibilities look spectacular. All effort focuses on production. The result is that marketing gets neglected.

John Kenneth Galbraith contends that just the opposite occurs.[4] Output is so prodigious that all effort concentrates on trying to get rid of it. He says this accounts for singing commercials, desecration of the countryside with advertising signs, and other wasteful and vulgar practices, Galbraith has a finger on something real, but he misses the strategic point. Mass production does indeed generate great pressure to "move" the product. But what usually gets emphasized is selling, not marketing. Marketing, being a more sophisticated and complex process, gets ignored.

The difference between marketing and selling is more than semantic. Selling focuses on the needs of the seller, marketing on the needs of the buyer. Selling is preoccupied with the seller's need to convert his product into cash; marketing with the idea of satisfying the needs of the customer by means of the product and the whole cluster of things associated with creating, delivering, and finally consuming it.

In some industries the enticements of full mass production have been so powerful that for many years top management in effect had told the sales departments, "You get rid of it; we'll worry about profits." By contrast, a truly marketing-minded firm tries to create value-satisfying goods and services that consumers will want to buy. What it offers for sale includes not only the generic product or service, but also how it is made available to the customer, in what form, when, under what conditions, and at what terms of trade. Most important, what it offers for sale is determined not by the seller but by the buyer. The seller takes his cues from the buyer in such a way that the product becomes a consequence of the marketing effort, not vice versa.

Lag in Detroit

This may sound like an elementary rule of business, but that does not keep it from being violated wholesale. It is certainly more violated than honored. Take the automobile industry:

Here mass production is most famous, most honored, and has the greatest impact on the entire society. The industry has hitched its fortune to the relentless requirements of the annual model change, a policy that makes customer orientation an especially urgent necessity. Consequently the auto companies annually spend millions of dollars on consumer research. But the fact that the new compact cars are selling so well in their first year indicates that Detroit's vast researchers have for a long time failed to reveal what the customer really wanted. Detroit was not persuaded that he wanted anything different from what he had been getting until it lost millions of customers to other small car manufacturers.

How could this unbelievable lag behind consumer wants have been perpetuated so long? Why did not research reveal consumer preferences before consumers' buying decisions themselves revealed the facts? Is that not what consumer research is for—to find out before the fact what is going to happen? The answer is that Detroit never really researched the customer's wants. It only researched his preferences between the kinds of things which it had already decided to offer him. For Detroit is mainly product-oriented, not customer-oriented. To the extent that the customer is recognized as having needs that the manufacturer should try to satisfy, Detroit usually acts as if the job can be done entirely by product changes. Occasionally attention gets paid to financing, too, but that is done more in order to sell than to enable the customer to buy.

As for taking care of other customer needs, there is not enough being done to write about. The areas of the greatest unsatisfied needs are ignored, or at best get stepchild attention. These are at the point of sale and on the matter of automotive repair and maintenance. Detroit views these problem areas as being of secondary importance.

That is underscored by the fact that the retailing and servicing ends of this industry are neither owned and operated nor controlled by the manufacturers. Once the car is produced, things are pretty much in the dealer's inadequate hands. Illustrative of Detroit's arm's-length attitude is the fact that, while servicing holds enormous sales-stimulating, profit-building opportunities, only 57 of Chevrolet's 7,000 dealers provide night maintenance service.

Motorists repeatedly express their dissatisfaction with servicing and their apprehensions about buying cars under the present selling setup. The anxieties and problems they encounter during the auto buying and maintenance processes are probably more intense and widespread today than 30 years ago. Yet the automobile companies do not *seem* to listen to or take their cues from the anguished consumer. If they do listen, it must be through the filter of their own preoccupation with production. The marketing effort is still viewed as a necessary consequence of the product, not vice versa, as it should be. That is the legacy of mass production, with its parochial view that profit resides essentially in low-cost full production.

What Ford Put First

The profit lure of mass production obviously has a place in the plans and strategy of business management, but it must always follow hard thinking about the customer. This is one of the most important lessons that we can learn from the contradictory behavior of Henry Ford. In a sense Ford was both the most brilliant and the most senseless marketer in American history. He was senseless because he refused to give the customer anything but a black car. He was brilliant because he fashioned a production system designed to fit market needs. We habitually celebrate him for the wrong reason, his production genius. His real genius was marketing. We think he was able to cut his selling price and therefore sell millions of

$500 cars because his invention of the assembly line had reduced the costs. Actually he invented the assembly line because he had concluded that at $500 he could sell millions of cars. Mass production was the *result* not the cause of his low prices.

Ford repeatedly emphasized this point, but a nation of production-oriented business managers refuses to hear the great lesson he taught. Here is his operating philosophy as he expressed it succinctly:

> Our policy is to reduce the price, extend the operations, and improve the article. You will notice that the reduction of price comes first. We have never considered any costs as fixed. Therefore we first reduce the price to the point where we believe more sales will result. Then we go ahead and try to make the prices. We do not bother about the costs. The new price forces the costs down. The more usual way is to take the costs and then determine the price, and although that method may be scientific in the narrow sense; it is not scientific in the broad sense, because what earthly use is it to know the cost if it tells you that you cannot manufacture at a price at which the article can be sold? But more to the point is the fact that, although one may calculate what a cost is, and of course all of our costs are carefully calculated, no one knows what a cost ought to be. One of the ways of discovering . . . is to name a price so low as to force everybody in the place to the highest point of efficiency. The low price makes everybody dig for profits. We make more discoveries concerning manufacturing and selling under this forced method than by any method of leisurely investigation.[5]

Product Provincialism

The tantalizing profit possibilities of low unit production costs may be the most seriously self-deceiving attitude that can afflict a company, particularly a "growth" company where an apparently assured expansion of demand already tends to undermine a proper concern for the importance of marketing and the customer.

The usual result of this narrow preoccupation with so-called concrete matters is that instead of growing, the industry declines. It usually means that the product fails to adapt to the constantly changing patterns of consumer needs and tastes, to new and modified marketing institutions and practices, or to product developments in competing or complementary industries. The industry has its eyes so firmly on its own specific product that it does not see how it is being made obsolete.

The classical example of this is the buggy whip industry. No amount of product improvement could stave off its death sentence. But had the industry defined itself as being in the transportation business rather than the buggy whip business, it might have survived. It would have done what survival always entails, that is, changing. Even if it had only defined its business as providing a stimulant or catalyst to an energy source, it might have survived by becoming a manufacturer of, say, fanbelts or air cleaners.

What may some day be a still more classical example is again, the oil industry. Having let others steal marvelous opportunities from it (e.g., natural gas, as already mentioned, missile fuels, and jet engine lubricants), one would expect it to have taken steps never to let that happen again. But this is not the case. We are now getting extraordinary new developments in fuel systems specifically designed to power automobiles. Not only are these developments concentrated in firms outside the petroleum industry, but petroleum is almost systematically ignoring them, securely content in its wedded bliss to oil. It is the story of the kerosene lamp versus the incandescent lamp all over again. Oil is trying to improve hydrocarbon fuels rather than to develop *any* fuels best suited to the needs of their users, whether or not made in different ways and with different raw materials from oil.

Here are some of the things which nonpetroleum companies are working on:

Over a dozen such firms now have advanced working models of energy systems which, when perfected, will replace the internal combustion engine and eliminate the demand for gasoline. The superior merit of each of these systems is their elimination of frequent, time-consuming, and irritating refueling stops. Most of these systems are fuel cells designed to create electrical energy directly from chemicals without combustion. Most of them use chemicals that are not derived from oil, generally hydrogen and oxygen.

Several other companies have advanced models of electric storage batteries designed to power automobiles. One of these is an aircraft producer that is working jointly with several electric utility companies. The latter hope to use off-peak generating capacity to supply overnight plug-in battery regeneration. Another company, also using the battery approach, is a medium-size electronics firm with extensive small-battery experience that it developed in connection with its work on hearing aids. It is collaborating with an automobile manufacturer. Recent improvements arising from the need for high-powered miniature power storage plants in rockets have put us within reach of a relatively small battery capable of withstanding great overloads or surges of power. Germanium diode applications and batteries using sintered-plate and nickel-cadmium techniques promise to make a revolution in our energy sources.

Solar energy conversion systems are also getting increasing attention. One usually cautious Detroit auto executive recently ventured that solar-powered cars might be common by 1980.

As for the oil companies, they are more or less "watching developments," as one research director put it to me. A few are doing a bit of research on fuel cells, but almost always confined to developing cells powered by hydrocarbon chemicals. None of them are enthusiastically researching fuel cells, batteries, or solar power plants. None of them are spending a fraction as much on research in these profoundly important areas as they are on the usual run-of-the-mill things like reducing combustion chamber deposit in gasoline engines. One major integrated petroleum company recently took a tentative look at the fuel cell and concluded that although "the companies actively working on it indicate a belief in ultimate success . . . the timing and magnitude of its impact are too remote to warrant recognition in our forecasts."

One might, of course, ask: Why should the oil companies do anything different? Would not chemical fuel cells, batteries, or solar energy kill the present product lines? The answer is that they would indeed, and that is precisely the reason for the oil firms having to develop these power units before their competitors, so they will not be companies without an industry.

Management might be more likely to do what is needed for its own preservation if it thought of itself as being in the energy business. But even that would not be enough if it persists in imprisoning itself in the narrow grip of its tight product orientation. It has to think of itself as taking care of customer needs, not finding, refining, or even selling oil. Once it genuinely thinks of its business as taking care of people's transportation needs, nothing can stop it from creating its own extravagantly profitable growth.

Creative Destruction

Since words are cheap and deeds are dear, it may be appropriate to indicate what this kind of thinking involves and leads to. Let us start at the beginning—the customer. It can be shown that motorists strongly dislike the bother, delay, and experience of buying gasoline. People actually do not buy gasoline. They cannot see it, taste it, feel it, appreciate it, or really test it. What they buy is the right to continue driving their cars. The gas station is like a tax collector to whom people are compelled to pay a periodic toll as the price of using their cars. This makes the gas station a basically unpopular institution. It can never be made popular or pleasant, only less unpopular, less unpleasant.

To reduce its unpopularity completely means eliminating it. Nobody likes a tax collector, not even a pleasant cheerful one. Nobody likes to interrupt a trip to buy a phantom product, not even from a handsome Adonis or a seductive Venus. Hence, companies that are working on exotic fuel substitutes which will eliminate the need for frequent refueling are heading directly into the outstretched arms of the irritated motorists. They are riding a wave of inevitability, not because they are creating something which is technologically superior or more sophisticated, but because they are satisfying a powerful customer need. They are also eliminating noxious odors and air pollution.

Once the petroleum companies recognize the customer-satisfying logic of what another power system can do, they will see that they have no more choice about working on an efficient, long-lasting fuel (or some way of delivering present fuels without bothering the motorist) than the big food chains had a choice about going into the supermarket business, or the vacuum tube companies had a choice about making semiconductors. For their own good the oil firms will have to destroy their own highly profitable assets. No amount of wishful thinking can save them from the necessity of engaging in this form of "creative destruction."

I phrase the need as strongly as this because I think management must make quite an effort to break itself loose from conventional ways. It is all too easy in this day and age for a company or industry to let its sense of purpose become dominated by the economies of full production and to develop a dangerously lopsided product orientation. In short, if management lets itself drift, it invariably drifts in the direction of thinking of itself as producing goods and services, not customer satisfactions. While it probably will not descend to the depths of telling its salesmen, "You get rid of it; we'll worry about profits," it can, without knowing it, be practicing precisely that formula for withering decay. The historic fate of one growth industry after another has been its suicidal product provincialism.

DANGERS OF R&D

Another big danger to a firm's continued growth arises when top management is wholly transfixed by the profit possibilities of technical research and development. To illustrate I shall turn first to a new industry—electronics—and then return once more to the oil companies. By comparing a fresh example with a familiar one, I hope to emphasize the prevalence and insidiousness of a hazardous way of thinking.

Marketing Shortchanged
In the case of electronics, the greatest danger which faces the glamorous new companies in this field is not that they do not pay enough attention to research and development, but that they pay *too much* attention to it. And the fact that the fastest growing electronics firms owe their eminence to their heavy emphasis on technical research is completely beside the point. They have vaulted to affluence on a sudden crest of unusually strong general receptiveness to new technical ideas. Also, their success has been shaped in the virtually guaranteed mar-

ket of military subsidies and by military orders that in many cases actually preceded the existence of facilities to make the products. Their expansion has, in other words, been almost totally devoid of marketing effort.

Thus, they are growing up under conditions that come dangerously close to creating the illusion that a superior product will sell itself. Having created a successful company by making a superior product, it is not surprising that management continues to be oriented toward the product rather than the people who consume it. It develops the philosophy that continued growth is a matter of continued product innovation and improvement.

A number of other factors tend to strengthen and sustain this belief:

1. Because electronic products are highly complex and sophisticated, managements become top-heavy with engineers and scientists. This creates a selective bias in favor of research and production at the expense of marketing. The organization tends to view itself as making things rather than satisfying customer needs. Marketing gets treated as a residual activity, "something else" that must be done once the vital job of product creation and production is completed.

2. To this bias in favor of product research, development, and production is added the bias in favor of dealing with controllable variables. Engineers and scientists are at home in the world of concrete things like machines, test tubes, production lines, and even balance sheets. The abstractions to which they feel kindly are those which are testable or manipulatable in the laboratory, or, if not testable, then functional, such as Euclid's axioms. In short, the managements of the new glamour-growth companies

tend to favor those business activities which lend themselves to careful study, experimentation, and control—the hard, practical, realities of the lab, the shop, the books.

What gets shortchanged are the realities of the *market*. Consumers are unpredictable, varied, fickle, stupid, shortsighted, stubborn, and generally bothersome. This is not what the engineer-managers say, but deep down in their consciousnesses is what they believe. And this accounts for their concentrating on what they know and what they can control, namely, product research, engineering, and production. The emphasis on production becomes particularly attractive when the product can be made at declining unit costs. There is no more inviting way of making money than by running the plant full blast.

Today the top-heavy science-engineering-production orientation of so many electronics companies works reasonably well because they are pushing into new frontiers in which the armed services have pioneered virtually assured markets. The companies are in the felicitous position of having to fill, not find markets; of not having to discover what the customer needs and wants, but of having the customer voluntarily come forward with specific new product demands. If a team of consultants had been assigned specifically to design a business situation calculated to prevent the emergence and development of a customer-oriented marketing viewpoint, it could not have produced anything better than the conditions just described.

Stepchild Treatment

The oil industry is a stunning example of how science, technology, and mass production can divert an entire group of companies from their main task. To the extent the consumer is studied at all (which is not much), the focus is forever on getting information which is designed to help the oil companies improve what they are now doing. They try to discover more convincing advertising themes, more effective sales promotional drives, what the market shares of the various companies are, what people like or dislike about service station dealers and oil companies, and so forth. Nobody seems as interested in probing deeply into the basic human needs that the industry might be trying to satisfy as in probing into the basic properties of the raw material that the companies work with in trying to deliver customer satisfaction.

Basic questions about customers and markets seldom get asked. The latter occupy a stepchild status. They are recognized as existing, as having to be taken care of, but not worth very much real thought or dedicated attention. Nobody gets as excited about the customers in his own backyard as about the oil in the Sahara Desert. Nothing illustrates better the neglect of marketing than its treatment in the industry press:

> The centennial issue of the *American Petroleum Institute Quarterly*, published in 1959 to celebrate the discovery of oil in Titusville, Pennsylvania, contained 21 feature articles proclaiming the industry's greatness. Only one of these talked about its achievements in marketing, and that was only a pictorial record of how service station architecture has changed. The issue also contained a special section on "New Horizons," which was devoted to showing the magnificent role oil would play in America's future. Every reference was ebulliently optimistic, never implying once that oil might have some hard competition. Even the reference to atomic energy was a cheerful catalogue of how oil would help make atomic energy a success. There was not a single apprehension that the oil industry's affluence might be threatened

or a suggestion that one "new horizon" might include new and better ways of serving oil's present customers.

But the most revealing example of the stepchild treatment that marketing gets was still another special series of short articles on "The Revolutionary Potential of Electronics." Under that heading this list of articles appeared in the table of contents:

"In the Search for Oil"
"In Production Operations"
"In Refinery Processes"

Significantly, every one of the industry's major functional areas is listed, *except* marketing. Why? Either it is believed that electronics holds no revolutionary potential for petroleum marketing (which is palpably wrong), or the editors forgot to discuss marketing (which is more likely, and illustrates its stepchild status).

The order in which the four functional areas are listed also betrays the alienation of the oil industry from the consumer. The industry is implicitly defined as beginning with the search for oil and ending with its distribution from the refinery. But the truth is, it seems to me, that the industry begins with the needs of the customer for its products. From that primal position its definition moves steadily backstream to areas of progressively lesser importance, until it finally comes to rest at the "search for oil."

Beginning & End

The view that an industry is a customer-satisfying process, not a goods-producing process, is vital for all businessmen to understand. An industry begins with the customer and his needs, not with a patent, a raw material, or a selling skill. Given the customer's needs, the industry develops backwards, first concerning itself with the physical *delivery* of customer satisfactions. Then it moves back further to *creating* the things by which these satisfactions are in part achieved. How these materials are created is a matter of indifference to the customer, hence the particular form of manufacturing, processing, or what-have-you cannot be considered as a vital aspect of the industry. Finally, the industry moves back still further to *finding* the raw materials necessary for making its products.

The irony of some industries oriented toward technical research and development is that the scientists who occupy the high executive positions are totally unscientific when it comes to defining their companies' over-all needs and purposes. They violate the first two rules of the scientific method—being aware of and defining their companies' problems, and then developing testable hypotheses about solving them. They are scientific only about the convenient things, such as laboratory and product experiments. The reason that the customer (and the satisfaction of his deepest needs) is not considered as being "the problem" is not because there is any certain belief that no such problem exists, but because an organizational lifetime has conditioned management to look in the opposite direction. Marketing is a stepchild.

I do not mean that selling is ignored. Far from it. But selling, again, is not marketing. As already pointed out, selling concerns itself with the tricks and techniques of getting people to exchange their cash for your product. It is not concerned with the values that the exchange is all about. And it does not, as marketing invariably does, view the entire business process as consisting of a tightly integrated effort to discover, create, arouse, and satisfy customer needs. The customer is somebody "out there" who, with proper cunning, can be separated from his loose change.

Actually, not even selling gets much attention in some technologically minded firms. Because there is a virtually guaran-teed market for the abundant flow of their new products, they do not actually know what a real market is. It is as if they lived in a planned economy, moving their products routinely from factory to retail outlet. Their successful concentration on products tends to convince them of the soundness of what they have been doing, and they fail to see the gathering clouds over the market.

CONCLUSION

Less than 75 years ago American railroads enjoyed a fierce loyalty among astute Wall Streeters. European monarchs invested in them heavily. Eternal wealth was thought to be the benediction for anybody who could scrape a few thousand dollars together to put into rail stocks. No other form of transportation could compete with the railroads in speed, flexibility, durability, economy, and growth potentials. As Jacques Barzun put it, "By the turn of the century it was an institution, an image of man, a tradition, a code of honor, a source of poetry, a nursery of boyhood desires, a sublimest of toys, and the most solemn machine—next to the funeral hearse—that marks the epochs in man's life."[6]

Even after the advent of automobiles, trucks, and airplanes, the railroad tycoons remained imperturbably self-confident. If you had told them 60 years ago that in 30 years they would be flat on their backs, broke, and pleading for government subsidies, they would have thought you totally demented. Such a future was simply not considered possible. It was not even a discussable subject, or an askable question, or a matter which any sane person would consider worth speculating about. The very thought was insane. Yet a lot of insane notions now have matter-of-fact acceptance—for example, the idea of 100-ton tubes of metal moving smoothly through the air 20,000 feet above the earth, loaded with 100 sane and solid citizens casually drinking martinis—and they have dealt cruel blows to the railroads.

What specifically must other companies do to avoid this fate? What does customer orientation involve? These questions have in part been answered by the preceding examples and analysis. It would take another article to show in detail what is required for specific industries. In any case, it should be obvious that building an effective customer-oriented company involves far more than good intentions or promotional tricks; it involves profound matters of human organization and leadership. For the present, let me merely suggest what appear to be some general requirements.

Visceral Feel of Greatness

Obviously the company has to do what survival demands. It has to adapt to the requirements of the market, and it has to do it sooner rather than later. But mere survival is a so-so aspiration. Anybody can survive in some way or other, even the skid-row bum. The trick is to survive gallantly, to feel the surging impulse of commercial mastery; not just to experience the sweet smell of success, but to have the visceral feel of entrepreneurial greatness.

No organization can achieve greatness without a vigorous leader who is driven onward by his own pulsing *will to succeed.* He has to have a vision of grandeur, a vision that can produce eager followers in vast numbers. In business, the followers are the customers. To produce these customers, the entire corporation must be viewed as a customer-creating and customer-satisfying organism. Management must think of itself not as producing products but as providing customer-creating value satisfactions. It

must push this idea (and everything it means and requires) into every nook and cranny of the organization. It has to do this continuously and with the kind of flair that excites and stimulates the people in it. Otherwise, the company will be merely a series of pigeonholed parts, with no consolidating sense of purpose or direction.

In short, the organization must learn to think of itself not as producing goods or services but as *buying customers*, as doing the things that will make people *want* to do business with it. And the chief executive himself has the inescapable responsibility for creating this environment, this viewpoint, this attitude, this aspiration. He himself must set the company's style, its direction, and its goals. This means he has to know precisely where he himself wants to go, and to make sure the whole organization is enthusiastically aware of where that is. This is a first requisite of leadership, for *unless he knows where he is going, any road will take him there.*

If any road is okay, the chief executive might as well pack his attaché case and go fishing. If an organization does not know or care where it is going, it does not need to advertise that fact with a ceremonial figurehead. Everybody will notice it soon enough.

1975: RETROSPECTIVE COMMENTARY

Amazed, finally, by his literary success, Isaac Bashevis Singer reconciled an attendant problem: "I think the moment you have published a book, it's not any more your private property. . . . If it has value, everybody can find in it what he finds, and I cannot tell the man I did not intend it to be so." Over the past 15 years, "Marketing Myopia" has become a case in point. Remarkably, the article spawned a legion of loyal partisans, not to mention a host of unlikely bedfellows.

Its most common and, I believe, most influential consequence is the way certain companies for the first time gave serious thought to the question of what business they are really in.

The strategic consequences of this have in many cases been dramatic. The best-known case, of course, is the shift in thinking of oneself as being in the "oil business" to being in the "energy business." In some instances the payoff has been spectacular (getting into coal, for example), and in others dreadful (in terms of the time and money spent so far on fuel cell research). Another successful example is a company with a large chain of retail shoe stores that redefined itself as a retailer of moderately priced, frequently purchased, widely assorted consumer specialty products. The result was a dramatic growth in volume, earnings, and return on assets.

Some companies, again for the first time, asked themselves whether they wished to be masters of certain technologies for which they would seek markets, or be masters of markets for which they would seek customer-satisfying products and services.

Choosing the former, one company has declared, in effect, "We are experts in glass technology. We intend to improve and expand that expertise with the object of creating products that will attract customers." This decision has forced the company into a much more systematic and customer-sensitive look at possible markets and users, even though its stated strategic object has been to capitalize on glass technology.

Deciding to concentrate on markets, another company has determined that "we want to help people (primarily women) enhance their beauty and sense of youthful-ness." This company has expanded its line of cosmetic products, but has also entered the fields of proprietary drugs and vitamin supplements.

All these examples illustrate the "policy" results of "Marketing Myopia." On the operating level, there has been, I think, an extraordinary heightening of sensitivity to customers and consumers. R&D departments have cultivated a greater "external" orientation toward uses, users, and markets—balancing thereby the previously one-sided "internal" focus on materials and methods; upper management has realized that marketing and sales departments should be somewhat more willingly accommodated than before; finance departments have become more receptive to the legitimacy of budgets for market research and experimentation in marketing; and salesmen have been better trained to listen to and understand customer needs and problems, rather than merely to "push" the product.

A Mirror, Not a Window

My impression is that the article has had more impact in industrial-products companies than in consumer-products companies—perhaps because the former had lagged most in customer orientation. There are at least two reasons for this lag: (1) industrial-products companies tend to be more capital intensive, and (2) in the past, at least, they have had to rely heavily on communicating face-to-face the technical character of what they made and sold. These points are worth explaining.

Capital-intensive businesses are understandably preoccupied with magnitudes, especially where the capital, once invested, cannot be easily moved, manipulated, or modified for the production of a variety of products—e.g., chemical plants, steel mills, airlines, and railroads. Understandably, they seek big volumes and operating efficiencies to pay off the equipment and meet the carrying costs.

At least one problem results: corporate power becomes disproportionately lodged with operating or financial executives. If you read the charter of one of the nation's largest companies, you will see that the chairman of the finance committee, not the chief executive officer, is the "chief." Executives with such backgrounds have an almost trained incapacity to see that getting "volume" may require understanding and serving many discrete and sometimes small market segments rather than going after a perhaps mythical batch of big or homogeneous customers.

These executives also often fail to appreciate the competitive changes going on around them. They observe the changes, all right, but devalue their significance or underestimate their ability to nibble away at the company's markets.

Once dramatically alerted to the concept of segments, sectors, and customers, though, managers of capital-intensive businesses have become more responsive to the necessity of balancing their inescapable preoccupation with "paying the bills" or breaking even with the fact that the best way to accomplish this may be to pay more attention to segments, or sectors, and customers.

The second reason industrial-products companies have probably been more influenced by the article is that, in the case of the more technical industrial products or services, the necessity of clearly communicating product and service characteristics to prospects results in a lot of face-to-face "selling" effort. But precisely because the product is so complex, the situation produces salesmen who know the product more than they know the customer, who are more adept at explaining what they have and what it can do than learning what the customer's

needs and problems are. The result has been a narrow product orientation rather than a liberating customer orientation, and "service" often suffered. To be sure, sellers said, "We have to provide service," but they tended to define service by looking into the mirror rather than out the window. They *thought* they were looking out the window at the customer, but it was actually a mirror—a reflection of their own product-oriented biases rather than a reflection of their customers' situations.

A Manifesto, Not a Prescription

Not everything has been rosy. A lot of bizarre things have happened as a result of the article:

- Some companies have developed what I call "marketing mania"—they've become obsessively responsive to every fleeting whim of the customer. Mass production operations have been converted to approximations of job shops, with cost and price consequences far exceeding the willingness of customers to buy the product.
- Management has expanded product lines and added new lines of business without first establishing adequate control systems to run more complex operations.
- Marketing staffs have suddenly and rapidly expanded themselves and their research budgets without either getting sufficient prior organizational support or, thereafter, producing sufficient results.
- Companies that are functionally organized have converted to product, brand, or market-based organizations with the expectation of instant and miraculous results. The outcome has been ambiguity, frustration, confusion, corporate infighting, losses, and finally a reversion to functional arrangements that only worsened the situation.
- Companies have attempted to "serve" cus-

tomers by creating complex and beautifully efficient products or services that buyers are either too risk-averse to adopt or incapable of learning how to employ— in effect, there are now steam shovels for people who haven't yet learned to use spades. This problem has happened repeatedly in the so-called service industries (financial services, insurance, computer-based services) and with American companies selling in less-developed economies.

"Marketing Myopia" was not intended as analysis or even prescription; it was intended as manifesto. It did not pretend to take a balanced position. Nor was it a new idea—Peter F. Drucker, J.B. McKitterick, Wroe Alderson, John Howard, and Neil Borden had each done more original and balanced work on "the marketing concept." My scheme, however, tied marketing more closely to the inner orbit of business policy. Drucker—especially in *The Concept of the Corporation* and *The Practice of Management*—originally provided me with a great deal of insight.

My contribution, therefore, appears merely to have been a simple, brief, and useful way of communicating an existing way of thinking. I tried to do it in a very direct, but responsible, fashion, knowing that few readers (customers), especially managers and leaders, could stand much equivocation or hesitation. I also knew that the colorful and lightly documented affirmation works better than the tortuously reasoned explanation.

But why the enormous popularity of what was actually such a simple preexisting idea? Why its appeal throughout the world

to resolutely restrained scholars, implacably temperate managers, and high government officials, all accustomed to balanced and thoughtful calculation? Is it that concrete examples, joined to illustrate a simple idea and presented with some attention to literacy, communicate better than massive analytical reasoning that reads as though it were translated from the German? Is it that provocative assertions are more memorable and persuasive than restrained and balanced explanations, no matter who the audience? Is it that the character of the message is as much the message as its content? Or was mine not simply a different tune, but a new symphony? I don't know.

Of course, I'd do it again and in the same way, given my purposes, even with what more I now know—the good and the bad, the power of facts and the limits of rhetoric. If your mission is the moon, you don't use a car. Don Marquis's cockroach, Archy, provides some final consolation: "An idea is not responsible for who believes in it."

NOTES

1. Jacques Barzun, "Trains and the Mind of Man," *Holiday* (February 1960), p. 21.
2. For more details see M. M. Zimmerman, *The Super Market: A Revolution in Distribution* (New York, McGraw-Hill Book Company, Inc., 1955), p. 48.
3. Ibid., pp 45–47.
4. *The Affluent Society* (Boston, Houghton-Mifflin Company, 1958), pp. 152–160.
5. Henry Ford, *My Life and Work* (New York, Doubleday, Page & Company, 1923), pp. 146–147.
6. Op. cit., p. 20.

ARTICLE 2

The Analytical Framework for Marketing

Wroe Alderson

My assignment is to discuss the analytical framework for marketing. Since our general purpose here is to consider the improvement of the marketing curriculum, I assume that the paper I have been asked to present might serve two functions. The first is to present a perspective of marketing which might be the basis of a marketing course at either elementary or advanced levels. The other is to provide some clue as to the foundations in the social sciences upon which an analytical framework for marketing may be built.

Economics has some legitimate claim to being the original science of markets. Received economic theory provides a framework for the analysis of marketing functions which certainly merits the attention of marketing teachers and practitioners. It is of little importance whether the point of view I am about to present is a version of economics, a hybrid of economics and sociology, or

the application of a new emergent general science of human behavior to marketing problems. The analytical framework which I find congenial at least reflects some general knowledge of the social sciences as well as long experience in marketing analysis. In the time available I can do no more than present this view in outline or skeleton form and leave you to determine how to classify it or whether you can use it.

An advantageous place to start for the analytical treatment of marketing is with the radical heterogeneity of markets. Heterogeneity is inherent on both the demand and the supply sides. The homogeneity which the economist assumes for certain purposes is not an antecedent condition for marketing. Insofar as it is ever realized, it emerges out of the marketing process itself.

The materials which are useful to man occur in nature in heterogeneous mixtures which might be called conglomerations since these mixtures have only a random relationship to human needs and activities. The collection of goods in the possessions of

Reprinted from Delbert Duncan (ed.), *Proceedings: Conference of Marketing Teachers from Far Western States* (Berkeley: University of California, 1958), pp. 15–28.

22

a household or an individual also constitutes a heterogeneous supply, but it might be called an assortment since it is related to anticipated patterns of future behavior. The whole economic process may be described as a series of transformations from meaningless to meaningful heterogeneity. Marketing produces as much homogeneity as may be needed to facilitate some of the intermediate economic processes but homogeneity has limited significance or utility for consumer behavior or expectations.

The marketing process matches materials found in nature or goods fabricated from these materials against the needs of households or individuals. Since the consuming unit has a complex pattern of needs, the matching of these needs creates an assortment of goods in the hands of the ultimate consumer. Actually the marketing process builds up assortments at many stages along the way, each appropriate to the activities taking place at that point. Materials or goods are associated in one way for manufacturing, in another way for wholesale distribution, and in still another way for retail display and selling. In between the various types of heterogeneous collections relatively homogeneous supplies are accumulated through the process of grading, refining, chemical reduction and fabrication.

Marketing brings about the necessary transformations in heterogeneous supplies through a multiphase process of sorting. Matching of every individual need would be impossible if the consumer had to search out each item required or the producer had to find the users of a product one by one. It is only the ingenious use of intermediate sorts which make it possible for a vast array of diversified products to enter into the ultimate consumer assortments as needed. Marketing makes mass production possible first by providing the assortment of supplies needed in manufacturing and then taking over the successive transformations which ultimately produce the assortment in the hands of consuming units.

To some who have heard this doctrine expounded, the concept of sorting seems empty, lacking in specific behavioral content, and hence unsatisfactory as a root idea for marketing. One answer is that sorting is a more general and embracing concept than allocation, which many economists regard as the root idea of their science. Allocation is only one of the four basic types of sorting, all of which are involved in marketing. Among these four, allocation is certainly no more significant than assorting, one being the breaking down of a homogeneous supply and the other the building up of a heterogeneous supply. Assorting, in fact, gives more direct expression to the final aim of marketing but allocation performs a major function along the way.

There are several basic advantages in taking sorting as a central concept. It leads directly to a fundamental explanation of the contribution of marketing to the overall economy of human effort in producing and distributing goods. It provides a key to the unending search for efficiency in the marketing function itself. Finally, sorting as the root idea of marketing is consistent with the assumption that heterogeneity is radically and inherently present on both sides of the market and that the aim of marketing is to cope with the heterogeneity of both needs and resources.

At this stage of the discussion it is the relative emphasis on assorting as contrasted with allocation which distinguishes marketing theory from at least some versions of economic theory. This emphasis arises naturally from the preoccupation of the market analyst with consumer behavior. One of the most fruitful approaches to understanding what the consumer is doing is the idea that she is engaged in building an assortment, in replenishing or extending an inventory of goods for use by herself and her family. As evidence that this paper is not an attempt to set up a theory in opposition to economics it is acknowledged that the germ of the conception of consumer behavior was first presented some eighty years ago by the Austrian economist Böhm-Bawerk.

The present view is distinguished from that of Böhm-Bawerk in its greater emphasis on the probabilistic approach to the study of market behavior. In considering items for inclusion in her assortment the consumer must make judgments concerning the relative probabilities of future occasions for use. A product in the assortment is intended to provide for some aspect of future behavior. Each such occasion for use carries a rating which is a product of two factors, one a judgment as to the probability of its incidence and the other a measure of the urgency of the need in case it should arise. Consumer goods vary with respect to both measures. One extreme might be illustrated by cigarettes with a probability of use approaching certainty but with relatively small urgency or penalty for deprivation on the particular occasion for use. At the other end of the scale would be a home fire extinguisher with low probability but high urgency attaching to the expected occasion of use.

All of this means that the consumer buyer enters the market as a problem-solver. Solving a problem, either on behalf of a household or on behalf of a marketing organization means reaching a decision in the face of uncertainty. The consumer buyer and the marketing executive are opposite numbers in the double search which pervades marketing; one looking for the goods required to complete an assortment, the other looking for the buyers who are uniquely qualified to use his goods. This is not to say that the behavior of either consumers or executives can be completely characterized as rational problem-solvers. The intention rather is to assert that problem-solving on either side of the market involves a probabilistic approach to heterogeneity on the other side. In order to solve his own problems arising from the heterogeneous demand, the marketing executive should understand the processes of consumer decisions in coping with heterogeneous supplies.

The viewpoint adopted here with respect to the competition among sellers is essentially that which is associated in economics with such names as Schumpeter, Chamberlin, and J. M. Clark and with the emphasis on innovative competition, product differentiation and differential advantage. The basic assumption is that every firm occupies a position which is in some respects unique, being differentiated from all others by characteristics of its products, its services, its geographic location or its specific combination of these features. The survival of a firm requires that for some group of buyers it should enjoy a differential advantage over all other suppliers. The sales of any active marketing organization come from a core market made up of buyers with a preference for this source and a fringe market which finds the source acceptable, at least for occasional purchases.

In the case of the supplier of relatively undifferentiated products or services such as the wheat farmer, differential advantage may pertain more to the producing region than to the individual producer. This more diffused type of differential advantage often becomes effective in the market through such agencies as the marketing cooperative. Even the individual producer of raw materials, however, occupies a position in the sense that one market or buyer provides the customary outlet for his product rather than another. The essential point for the present argument is that buyer and seller are not paired at random even in the marketing of relatively homogeneous products but are related to some scale of preference or priority.

Competition for differential advantage implies goals of survival and growth for the marketing organization. The firm is perenially seeking a favorable place to stand and not merely immediate profits from its operations. Differential advantage is subject to change and neutralization by competitors. In dynamic markets differential advantage can only be preserved through continuous innovation. Thus competition presents an analogy to a succession of military campaigns rather than to the pressures and attrition of a single battle. A competitor may gain ground through a successful campaign based on new product features or merchandising ideas. It may lose ground or be forced to fall back on its core position because of the successful campaigns of others. The existence of the core position helps to explain the paradox of survival in the face of the destructive onslaughts of innovative competition.

Buyers and sellers meet in market transactions, each side having tentatively identified the other as an answer to its problem. The market transaction consumes much of the time and effort of all buyers and sellers. The market which operates through a network of costless transactions is only a convenient fiction which economists adopt for certain analytical purposes. Potentially the cost of transactions is so high that controlling or reducing this cost is a major objective in market analysis and executive action. Among economists John R. Commons has given the greatest attention to the transaction as the unit of collective action.

He drew a basic distinction between strategic and routine transactions which for present purposes may best be paraphrased as fully negotiated and routine transactions.

The fully negotiated transaction is the prototype of all exchange transactions. It represents a matching of supply and demand after canvassing all of the factors which might affect the decision on either side. The routine transaction proceeds under a set of rules and assumptions established by previous negotiation or as a result of techniques of pre-selling which take the place of negotiation. Transactions on commodity and stock exchanges are carried out at high speed and low cost but only because of carefully established rules governing all aspects of trading. The economical routines of self-service in a supermarket are possible because the individual items on display have been presold. The routine transaction is the end-result of previous marketing effort and ingenious organization of institutions and processes. Negotiation is implicit in all routine transactions. Good routines induce both parties to save time and cost by foregoing explicit negotiations.

The negotiated transaction is the indicated point of departure for the study of exchange values in heterogeneous markets. Many considerations enter into the decision to trade or not to trade on either side of the market. Price is the final balancing or integrating factor which permits the deal to be made. The seller may accept a lower price if relieved from onerous requirements. The buyer may pay a higher price if provided with specified services. The integrating price is one that assures an orderly flow of goods so long as the balance of other considerations remains essentially unchanged. Some economists are uneasy about the role of the negotiated transaction in value determination since bargaining power may be controlling within wide bargaining limits. These limits as analyzed by Commons are set by reference to the best alternatives available to either partner rather than by the automatic control of atomistic competition. This analysis overlooks a major constraint on bargaining in modern markets. Each side has a major stake in a deal that the other side can live with. Only in this way can a stable supply relationship be established so as to achieve the economics of transactional routines. Negotiation is not a zero sum game since the effort to get the best of the other party transaction by transaction may result in a loss to both sides in terms of mounting transactional cost.

In heterogeneous markets price plays an important role in matching a segment of supply with the appropriate segment of demand. The seller frequently has the option of producing a stream-lined product at a low price, a deluxe product at a high price or selecting a price-quality combination somewhere in between. There are considerations which exert a strong influence on the seller toward choosing the price line or lines which will yield the greatest dollar volume of sales. Assuming the various classes of consumers having conflicting claims on the productive capacity of the supplier, it might be argued that the price-quality combination which maximized gross revenue represented the most constructive compromise among these claims. There are parallel considerations with respect to the claims of various participants in the firm's activities on its operating revenue. These claimants include labor, management, suppliers of raw materials and stockholders. Assuming a perfectly fluid situation with respect to bargaining among these claimants, the best chance for a satisfactory solution is at the level of maximum gross revenue. The argument becomes more complicated when the claims of stockholders are given priority, but the goal would

still be maximum gross revenue as suggested in a recent paper by William J. Baumol. My own intuition and experience lead me to believe that the maximization of gross revenue is a valid goal of marketing management in heterogeneous markets and adherence to this norm appears to be widely prevalent in actual practice.

What has been said so far is doubtless within the scope of economics or perhaps constitutes a sketch of how some aspects of economic theory might be reconstructed on the assumption of heterogeneity rather than homogeneity as the normal and prevailing condition of the market. But there are issues raised by such notions as enterprise survival, expectations, and consumer behavior, which in my opinion cannot be resolved within the present boundaries of economic science. Here marketing must not hesitate to draw upon the concepts and techniques of the social sciences for the enrichment of its perspectives and for the advancement of marketing as an empirical science.

The general economist has his own justifications for regarding the exchange process as a smoothly functioning mechanism which operates in actual markets or which should be taken as the norm and standard to be enforced by government regulation. For the marketing man, whether teacher or practitioner, this Olympian view is untenable. Marketing is concerned with those who are obliged to enter the market to solve their problems, imperfect as the market may be. The persistent and rational action of these participants is the main hope for eliminating or moderating some of these imperfections so that the operation of the market mechanism may approximate that of the theoretical model.

To understand market behavior the marketing man takes a closer look at the nature of the participants. Thus he is obliged, in my opinion, to come to grips with the organized behavior system. Market behavior is primarily group behavior. Individual action in the market is most characteristically action on behalf of some group in which the individual holds membership. The organized behavior system is related to the going concern of John R. Commons but with a deeper interest in what keeps it going. The organized behavior system is also a much broader concept including the more tightly organized groups acting in the market such as business firms and households and loosely connected systems such as the trade center and the marketing channel.

The marketing man needs some rationale for group behavior, some general explanation for the formation and persistence of organized behavior systems. He finds this explanation in the concept of expectations. Insofar as conscious choice is involved, individuals operate in groups because of their expectations of incremental satisfactions as compared to what they could obtain operating alone. The expected satisfactions are of many kinds, direct or indirect. In a group that is productive activity is held together because of an expected surplus over individual output. Other groups such as households and purely social organizations expect direct satisfactions from group association and activities. They also expect satisfactions from future activities facilitated by the assortment of goods held in common. Whatever the character of the system, its vitality arises from the expectations of the individual members and the vigor of their efforts to achieve them through group action. While the existence of the group is entirely derivative, it is capable of operating as if it had a life of its own and was pursuing goals of survival and growth.

Every organized behavior system exhibits a structure related to the functions it performs. Even in the simplest behavior system there must be some mechanism for decision and coordination of effort if the system is to provide incremental satisfaction. Leadership emerges at an early stage to perform such functions as directing the defense of the group. Also quite early is the recognition of the rationing function by which the leader allocates the available goods or satisfactions among the members of the group.

As groups grow in size and their functions become more complex functional specialization increases. The collection of individuals forming a group with their diversified skills and capabilities is a meaningful heterogeneous ensemble vaguely analogous to the assortment of goods which facilitates the activities of the group. The group, however, is held together directly by the generalized expectations of its members. The assortment is held together by a relatively weak or derivative bond. An item "belongs" to the assortment only so long as it has some probability of satisfying the expectations of those who possess it.

This outline began with an attempt to live within the framework of economics or at least within an economic framework amplified to give fuller recognition to heterogeneity on both sides of the market. We have now plunged into sociology in order to deal more effectively with the organized behavior systems. Meanwhile we attempt to preserve the line of communication to our origins by basing the explanations of group behavior on the quasi-economic concept of expectations.

The initial plunge into sociology is only the beginning since the marketing man must go considerably further in examining the functions and structure of organized behavior systems. An operating group has a power structure, a communication structure and an operating structure. At each stage an effort should be made to employ the intellectual strategy which has already been suggested. That is, to relate sociological notions to the groundwork of marketing economics through the medium of such concepts as expectations and the processes of matching and sorting.

All members of an organized behavior system occupy some position or status within its power structure. There is a valid analogy between the status of an individual or operating unit within the system and the market position of the firm as an entity. The individual struggles for status within the system having first attained the goal of membership. For most individuals in an industrial society, status in some operating system is a prerequisite for satisfying his expectations. Given the minimal share in the power of the organization inherent in membership, vigorous individuals may aspire to the more ample share of power enjoyed by leadership. Power in the generalized sense referred to here is an underlying objective on which the attainment of all other objectives depends. This aspect of organized behavior has been formulated as the power principle, namely, "The rational individual will act in such a way to promote the power to act." The word *promote* deliberately glosses over an ambivalent attitude toward power, some individuals striving for enhancement and others being content to preserve the power they have.

Any discussion which embraces power as a fundamental concept creates uneasiness for some students on both analytical and ethical ground. My own answer to the analytical problem is to define it as control over expectations. In these terms it is theoretically possible to measure and evaluate power, perhaps even to set a price on it. Certainly it enters into the network of imputations in a business enterprise. Management allocates or rations status and recognition as well as or in lieu of material rewards. As for the ethical problem, it does not arise unless the power principle is sub-stituted for ethics as with Machiavelli. Admitting that the power principle is the essence of expediency, the ethical choice of values and objectives is a different issue. Whatever his specific objectives, the rational individual will wish to serve them expediently.

If any of this discussion of power seems remote from marketing let it be remembered that the major preoccupation of the marketing executive, as pointed out by Oswald Knauth, is with the creation or the activation of organized behavior systems such as marketing channels and sales organizations. No one can be effective in building or using such systems if he ignores the fundamental nature of the power structure.

The communication structure serves the group in various ways. It promotes the survival of the system by reinforcing the individual's sense of belonging. It transmits instructions and operating commands or signals to facilitate coordinated effort. It is related to expectations through the communication of explicit or implied commitments. Negotiations between suppliers and customers and much that goes on in the internal management of a marketing organization can best be understood as a two-way exchange of commitments. A division sales manager, for example, may commit himself to produce a specified volume of sales. His superior in turn may commit certain company resources to support his efforts and make further commitments as to added rewards as an incentive to outstanding performance.

For some purposes it is useful to regard marketing processes as a flow of goods and a parallel flow of informative and persuasive messages. In these terms the design of communication facilitates and channels becomes a major aspect of the creation of marketing system. Marketing has yet to digest and apply the insights of the rapidly developing field of communication theory which in turn has drawn freely from both engineering and biological and social sciences. One stimulating idea expounded by Norbert Wiener and others is that of the feedback of information in a control system. Marketing and advertising research are only well started on the task of installing adequate feedback circuits for controlling the deployment of marketing effort.

Social psychology is concerned with some problems of communication which are often encountered in marketing systems. For example, there are the characteristic difficulties of vertical communication which might be compared to the transmission of telephone messages along a power line. Subordinates often hesitate to report bad news to their superiors fearing to take the brunt of emotional reactions. Superiors learn to be cautious in any discussion of the subordinate's status for fear that casual comment will be interpreted as a commitment. There is often a question as to when a subordinate should act and report and when he should refer a matter for decision upstream. Progress in efficiency, which is a major goal in marketing, depends in substantial part on technological improvement in communication facilities and organizational skill in using them.

The third aspect of structure involved in the study of marketing systems is operating structure. Effective specialization within an organization requires that activities which are functionally similar be placed together but properly coordinated with other activities. Billing by wholesaler grocers, for example, has long been routinized in a separate billing department. In more recent years the advances in mechanical equipment have made it possible to coordinate inventory control with billing, using the same set of punch cards for both functions. Designing an operating structure is a special

application of sorting. As in the sorting of goods to facilitate handling, there are generally several alternative schemes for classifying activities presenting problems of choice to the market planner.

Functional specialization and the design of appropriate operating structures is a constant problem in the effective use of marketing channels. Some functions can be performed at either of two or more stages. One stage may be the best choice in terms of economy or effectiveness. Decisions on the placement of a function may have to be reviewed periodically since channels do not remain static. Similar considerations arise in the choice of channels. Some types of distributors or dealers may be equipped to perform a desired service while others may not. Often two or more channels with somewhat specialized roles are required to move a product to the consumer. The product sponsor can maintain perspective in balancing out these various facilities by thinking in terms of a total operating system including his own sales organization and the marketing channels employed.

The dynamics of market organization pose basic problems for the marketing student and the marketing executive in a free enterprise economy. Reference has already been made to the competitive pursuit of differential advantage. One way in which a firm can gain differential advantage is by organizing the market in a way that is favorable to its own operations. This is something else than the attainment of a monopolistic position in relation to current or potential competitors. It means creating a pattern for dealing with customers or suppliers which persists because there are advantages on both sides. Offering guarantees against price declines on floor stocks is one example of market organization by the seller. Attempts to systematize the flow of orders may range from various services offered to customers or suppliers all the way to complete vertical integration. Another dynamic factor affecting the structure of market may be generalized under the term "closure." It frequently happens that some marketing system is incomplete or out of balance in some direction. The act of supplying the missing element constitutes closure, enabling the system to handle a greater output or to operate at a new level of efficiency. The incomplete system in effect cries out for closure. To observe this need is to recognize a form of market opportunity. This is one of the primary ways in which new enterprises develop, since there may be good reasons why the missing service cannot be performed by the existing organizations which need the service. A food broker, for example, can cover a market for several accounts of moderate size in a way that the individual manufacturer would not be able to cover it for himself.

There is a certain compensating effect between closure as performed by new or supplementary marketing enterprises and changes in market organization brought about by the initiative of existing firms in the pursuit of differential advantage. The pursuit of a given form of advantage, in fact, may carry the total marketing economy out of balance in a given direction creating the need and opportunity for closure. Such an economy could never be expected to reach a state of equilibrium, although the tendency toward structural balance is one of the factors in its dynamics. Trade regulation may be embraced within this dynamic pattern as an attempt of certain groups to organize the market to their own advantage through political means. Entering into this political struggle to determine the structure of markets are some political leaders and some administrative officials who regard themselves as representing the consumer's interests. It seem reasonable to believe that the increasing sophistication and buying skill of consumers is one of the primary forces offsetting the tendency of the free market economy to turn into something else through the working out of its inherent dynamic forces. This was the destiny foreseen for the capitalistic system by Schumpeter, even though he was one of its staunchest advocates.

The household as an organized behavior system must be given special attention in creating an analytical framework for marketing. The household is an operating entity with an assortment of goods and assets and with economic functions to perform. Once a primary production unit, the household has lost a large part of these activities to manufacturing and service enterprises. Today its economic operations are chiefly expressed through earning and spending. In the typical household there is some specialization between the husband as primary earner and the wife as chief purchasing agent for the household. It may be assumed that she becomes increasingly competent in buying as she surrenders her production activities such as canning, baking and dressmaking, and devotes more of her time and attention to shopping. She is a rational problem solver as she samples what the market has to offer in her effort to maintain a balanced inventory or assortment of goods to meet expected occasions of use. This is not an attempt to substitute Economic Woman for the discredited fiction of Economic Man. It is only intended to assert that the decision structure of consumer buying is similar to that for industrial buying. Both business executive and housewife enter the market as rational problem solvers, even though there are other aspects of personality in either case.

An adequate perspective on the household for marketing purposes must recognize several facets of its activities. It is an organized behavior system with its aspects of power, communication, and operating structure. It is the locus of forms of behavior other than instrumental or goal-seeking activities. A convenient three-way division, derived from the social sciences, recognizes instrumental, congenial, and symptomatic behavior. Congenial behavior is that kind of activity engaged in for its own sake and presumably yielding direct satisfactions. It is exemplified by the act of consumption as compared to all of the instrumental activities which prepare the way for consumption. Symptomatic behavior reflects maladjustment and is neither pleasure-giving in itself nor an efficient pursuit of goals. Symptomatic behavior is functional only to the extent that it serves as a signal to others that the individual needs help.

Some studies of consumer motivation have given increasing attention to symptomatic behavior or to the projection of symptoms of personality adjustment which might affect consumer buying. The present view is that the effort to classify individuals by personality type is less urgent for marketing than the classification of families. Four family types with characteristically different buying behavior have been suggested growing out of the distinction between the instrumental and congenial aspects of normal behavior. Even individuals who are fairly well adjusted in themselves will form a less than perfect family if not fully adapted to each other.

On the instrumental side of household behavior it would seem to be desirable that the members be well coordinated as in any other operating system. If not, they will not deliver the maximum impact in pursuit of family goals. On the congenial side it would appear desirable for the members of a household to be compatible. That means enjoying the same things, cherishing the same goals, preferring joint activities to solitary pursuits or the company of others.

These two distinctions yield an obvious four-way classification. The ideal is the family that is coordinated in its instrumental activities and compatible in its congenial activities. A rather joyless household which might nevertheless be well managed and prosperous in material terms is the coordinated but incompatible household. The compatible but uncoordinated family would tend to be happy-go-lucky and irresponsible with obvious consequences for buying behavior. The household which was both uncoordinated and incompatible would usually be tottering on the brink of dissolution. It might be held together formally by scruples against divorce, by concern for children, or by the dominant power of one member over the others. This symptomology of families does not exclude an interest in the readjustment of individuals exhibiting symptomatic behavior. Such remedial action lies in the sphere of the psychiatrist and the social worker, whereas the marketer is chiefly engaged in supplying goods to families which are still functioning as operating units.

All of the discussion of consumers so far limits itself to the activities of the household purchasing agent. Actually the term *consumption* as it appears in marketing and economic literature nearly always means consumer buying. Some day marketing may need to look beyond the act of purchasing to a study of consumption proper. The occasion for such studies will arise out of the problems of inducing consumers to accept innovations or the further proliferation of products to be included in the household assortment. Marketing studies at this depth will not only borrow from the social sciences but move into the realm of esthetic and ethical values. What is the use of a plethora of goods unless the buyer derives genuine satisfaction from them? What is the justification of surfeit if the acquisition of goods serves as a distraction from activities which are essential to the preservation of our culture and of the integrity of our personalities?

It has been suggested that a study of consumption might begin with the problem of choice in the presence of abundance. The scarce element then is the time or capacity for enjoyment. The bookworm confronted with the thousands of volumes available in a great library must choose in the face of this type of limitation.

The name *hedonomics* would appear to be appropriate for this field of study suggesting the management of the capacity to enjoy. Among the problems for hedonomics is the pleasure derived from the repetition of a familiar experience as compared with the enjoyment of a novel experience or an old experience with some novel element. Another is the problem of direct experience versus symbolic experience, with the advantages of intensity on the one hand and on the other the possibility of embracing a greater range of possible ideas and sensations by relying on symbolic representations. Extensive basic research will probably be neces-

sary before hedonomics can be put to work in marketing or for the enrichment of human life through other channels.

This paper barely suffices to sketch the analytical framework for marketing. It leaves out much of the area of executive decision-making in marketing on such matters as the weighing of uncertainties and the acceptance of risk in the commitment of resources. It leaves out market planning which is rapidly becoming a systematic discipline centering in the possibilities for economizing time and space as well as resources. It leaves out all but the most casual references to advertising and demand formation. Advertising is certainly one of the most difficult of marketing functions to embrace within a single analytical framework. It largely ignores the developing technology of physical distribution. Hopefully what it does accomplish is to show how the essentially economic problems of marketing may yield to a more comprehensive approach drawing on the basic social sciences for techniques and enriched perspective.

Marketing as Exchange

Richard P. Bagozzi

The exchange paradigm has emerged as a framework useful for conceptualizing marketing behavior. Indeed, most contemporary definitions of marketing explicitly include exchange in their formulations.[1] Moreover, the current debate on "broadening" centers on the very notion of exchange: on its nature, scope, and efficacy in marketing.

This article analyzes a number of dimensions of the exchange paradigm that have not been dealt with in the marketing literature. First, it attempts to show that what marketers have considered as exchange is a special case of exchange theory that focuses primarily on direct transfers of tangible entities between two parties. In reality, marketing exchanges often are indirect, they may involve intangible and symbolic aspects, and more than two parties may participate. Second, the media and

meaning of exchange are discussed in order to provide a foundation for specifying underlying mechanisms in marketing exchanges. Finally, social marketing is analyzed in light of the broadened concept of exchange.

The following discussion proceeds from the assumptions embodied in the generic concept of marketing as formulated by Kotler, Levy, and others.[2] In particular, it is assumed that marketing theory is concerned with two questions: (1) Why do people and organizations engage in exchange relationships? and (2) How are exchanges created, resolved, or avoided? The domain for the subject matter of marketing is assumed to be quite broad, encompassing all activities involving "exchange" and the cause and effect of phenomena associated with it. As in the social and natural sciences, marketing owes its definition to the outcome of debate and competition between divergent views in an evolutionary process that Kuhn terms a "scientific revolution."[3] Although the debate is far from settled, there appears to be a grow-

"Marketing as Exchange," Richard P. Bagozzi, Vol. 39 (October 1975), pp. 32–39. Reprinted from *Journal of Marketing,* published by the American Marketing Association.

ing consensus that exchange forms the core phenomenon for study in marketing. Whether the specific instances of exchange are to be limited to economic institutions and consumers in the traditional sense or expanded to all organizations in the broadened sense deserves further attention by marketing scholars and practitioners. Significantly, the following principles apply to exchanges in both senses.

THE TYPES OF EXCHANGE

In general, there are three types of exchange: restricted, generalized, and complex.[4] Each of these is described below.

Restricted Exchange

Restricted exchange refers to two-party reciprocal relationships which may be represented diagrammatically as A←→B, where "←→" signifies "gives to and receives from" and A and B represent social actors such as consumers, retailers, salesmen, organizations, or collectivities.[5] Most treatments of, and references to, exchanges in the marketing literature have implicitly dealt with restricted exchanges; that is, they have dealt with customer-salesman, wholesaler-retailer, or other such dyadic exchanges.

Restricted exchanges exhibit two characteristics:

> First, there is a great deal of attempt to maintain equality. This is especially the case with repeatable social exchange acts. Attempts to gain advantage at the expense of the other is [sic] minimized. Negatively, the breach of the rule of equality quickly leads to emotional reactions. . . . Secondly, there is a *quid pro quo* mentality in restricted exchange activities. Time intervals in mutual reciprocities are cut short and there is an attempt to balance activities and exchange items as part of the mutual reciprocal relations.[6]

The "attempt to maintain equality" is quite evident in restricted marketing exchanges. Retailers, for example, know that they will not obtain repeat purchases if the consumer is taken advantage of and deceived. The "breach" in this rule of equality—which is a central tenet of the marketing concept—has led to picketing, boycotts, and even rioting. Finally, the fact that restricted marketing exchanges must involve a *quid pro quo* notion (something of value in exchange for something of value) has been at the heart of Luck's criticism of broadening the concept of marketing.[7] However, as will be developed below, there are important exceptions to the *quid pro quo* requirement in many marketing exchanges.

Generalized Exchange

Generalized exchange denotes univocal, reciprocal relationships among at least three actors in the exchange situation. Univocal reciprocity occurs "if the reciprocations involve at least three actors and if the actors do not benefit each other directly but only indirectly."[8] Given three social actors, for instance, generalized exchange may be represented as A⟶B⟶C⟶A, where "⟶" signifies "gives to." In generalized exchange, the social actors form a system in which each actor gives to another but receives from someone other than to whom he gave. For example, suppose a public bus company (B) asks a local department store chain (A) to donate or give a number of benches to the bus company. Suppose further that, after the department store chain (A) gives the benches to the bus company (B), the company (B) then places the benches at bus stops for the convenience of its riders (C). Finally, suppose that a number of the riders (C) see the advertisements placed on the benches by the department store chain (A) and later patronize the store as a result of this exposure. This sequence of exchange, A⟶B⟶C⟶A, is known as generalized exchange; while it fails to conform to the usual notions of *quid pro quo,* it certainly constitutes a marketing exchange of interest.

Complex Exchange

Complex exchange refers to a system of mutual relationships between at least three parties. Each social actor is involved in at least one direct exchange, while the entire system is organized by an interconnecting web of relationships.

Perhaps the best example of complex exchange in marketing is the channel of distribution. Letting A represent a manufacturer, B a retailer, and C a consumer, it is possible to depict the channel as A↔B↔C. Such open-ended sequences of direct exchanges may be designated *complex chain exchanges.*

But many marketing exchanges involve relatively closed sequences of relationships. For example, consider the claim made by Kotler that a "transaction takes place . . . when a person decides to watch a television program."[9] Recently, Carman and Luck have criticized this assertion, maintaining that it may not exhibit an exchange.[10] The differences stem from: (1) a disagreement on whether exchange must consist of transfers of tangible (as opposed to intangible) things of value, and (2) a neglect of the possibility of systems of exchange. Figure 3-1 illustrates the exchange between a person and a television program and how it may be viewed as a link in a system termed *complex circular exchange.*[11] In this system of exchange, the person experiences a direct transfer of intangibles between himself and the program. That is, he gives his attention, support (for example, as measured by the Nielsen ratings), potential for purchase, and so on, and receives entertainment, enjoyment, product information,

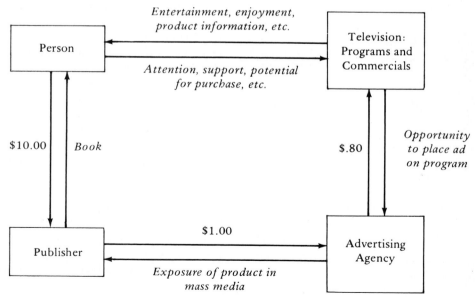

Figure 3-1
An Example of Complex Circular Exchange

and other intangible entities. The person also experiences an indirect exchange with the television program via a sequence of direct, tangible exchanges. Thus, after being informed of the availability of a book through an exchange with the television program and its advertising, a person may purchase it for, say, $10.00. The book's publisher, in turn, may purchase the services of an advertiser, paying what amounts to a percentage of each sale, say, $1.00. Finally, the advertiser receives the opportunity to place a commercial on the air from the television network in exchange for what amounts to a percentage of each sale, say, $.80. In this particular example, the occurrence of the direct intangible exchange was a necessary prerequisite for the development of the series of indirect tangible exchanges. Thus, an exchange *can* occur between a person and a television program.

Complex chain and complex circular exchanges involve predominantly conscious systems of social and economic relationships. In this sense, there is an overt coordination of activities and expectations, which Alderson called an organized behavioral system and which he reserved for the household, the firm, and the channel of distribution.[12] However, it should be evident that the designation "organized" is a relative one and that other exchange systems, such as the one shown in Figure 3-1, also evidence aspects of overt coordination in an economic, social, and symbolic sense.

Generalized and complex exchanges are also present in relatively unconscious systems of social and economic relationships. Thus, a modern economy may experience a covert coordination of activities through exchanges that occur when many individuals, groups, and firms pursue their own self-interest. This is what Adam Smith meant by his reference to an "invisible hand."[13] Similarly, in his analysis of primi-

tive societies and marketing systems, Frazer has shown that exchange and the pursuit of self-interest can be the foundation for the web of kinship, economic, and social institutions.[14] The recent exchange theories of Homans and Blau are also based on this individualistic assumption of self-interest.[15] It should be stressed, however, that the exchange tradition developed by Levi-Strauss is not an individualistic one but rather is built on social, collectivistic assumptions associated with generalized exchange.[16] These differences will become more apparent when social marketing is analyzed below.

THE MEDIA AND MEANING OF EXCHANGE

In order to satisfy human needs, people and organizations are compelled to engage in social and economic exchanges with other people and organizations. This is true for primitive as well as highly developed societies. Social actors obtain satisfaction of their needs by complying with, or influencing, the behavior of other actors. They do this by communicating and controlling the media of exchange which, in turn, comprise the links between one individual and another, between one organization and another. Significantly, marketing exchanges harbor meanings for individuals that go beyond the mere use of media for obtaining results in interactions.

The Media of Exchange
The media of exchange are the vehicles with which people communicate to, and influence, others in the satisfaction of their needs. These vehicles include money, persuasion, punishment, power (authority), inducement, and activation of normative or ethical commitments.[17] Products and ser-

vices are also media of exchange. In consumer behavior research, marketers have extensively studied the effects of these vehicles on behavior. Moreover, it has been suggested that a number of these vehicles be used in conjunction with socio-psychological processes to explain the customer-salesman relationship.[18] It should be noted, however, that marketing is not solely concerned with influence processes, whether these involve manufacturers influencing consumers or consumers influencing manufacturers. Marketing is also concerned with meeting existing needs and anticipating future needs, and these activities do not necessarily entail attempts to influence or persuade.

To illustrate the multivariate nature of media in marketing exchanges, consider the example of the channel of distribution, a complex chain exchange. The firms in a channel of distribution are engaged in an intricate social system of behavioral relationships that go well beyond the visible exchange of products and money.[19] Typically, the traditional channel achieves its conscious coordination of effort through the mutual expectations of profit. In addition, each firm in the channel may influence the degree of cooperation and compliance of its partners by offering inducements in the form of services, deals, or other benefits or by persuading each link in the channel that it is in its own best interest to cooperate. A firm may also affect the behavior of decisions of another firm through the use of the power it may possess. Wilkinson has studied five bases of power in the channel of distribution—reward, coercive, legitimate, referent, and expert power—and has tested aspects of these relationships between firms.[20] Finally, a firm may remind a delinquent member in the channel of its contractual obligations or even threaten the member with legal action for a breach of agreement.

This influence medium is known as the activation of commitments.

The Meaning of Exchange

Human behavior is more than the outward responses or reactions of people to stimuli. Man not only reacts to events or the actions of others but he self-generates his own acts.[21] His behavior is purposeful, intentional. It is motivated. Man is an information seeker and generator as well as an information processor. In short, human behavior is a conjunction of meaning with action and reaction.

Similarly, exchange is more than the mere transfer of a product or service for money. To be sure, most marketing exchanges are characterized by such a transfer. But the reasons behind the exchange—the explanation of its occurrence—lie in the social and psychological significance of the experiences, feelings, and meanings of the parties in the exchange. In general, marketing exchanges may exhibit one of three classes of meanings: utilitarian, symbolic, or mixed.

Utilitarian Exchange. A utilitarian exchange is an interaction whereby goods are given in return for money or other goods and the motivation behind the actions lies in the anticipated use or tangible characteristics commonly associated with the objects in the exchange. The utilitarian exchange is often referred to as an economic exchange, and most treatments of exchange in marketing implicitly rely on this usage. As Bartels notes with regard to the identity crisis in marketing:

> Marketing has initially and generally been associated exclusively with the distributive part of the *economic* institution and function. . . .

The question, then, is whether marketing is identified by the *field* of economics in which the marketing techniques have been developed and generally applied, or by the socalled marketing *techniques,* wherever they may be applied.

If marketing relates to the distributive function of the economy, providing goods and services, that *physical* function differentiates it from all other social institutions.[22]

Most marketers have traditionally conceptualized the subject matter of the discipline in these terms, and they have proceeded from the assumptions embodied in utilitarian exchange.

In general, utilitarian exchange theory is built on the foundation of *economic man.*[23] Thus, it is assumed that:

1. Men are rational in their behavior.
2. They attempt to maximize their satisfaction in exchanges.
3. They have complete information on alternatives available to them in exchanges.
4. These exchanges are relatively free from external influence.

Coleman has developed an elaborate mathematical framework for representing exchange behavior that assumes many of the features of economic man.[24] His model is based on the theory of purposive action, which posits that each "actor will choose that action which according to his estimate will lead to an expectation of the most beneficial consequences."[25] Among other things, the theory may be used to predict the outcomes and degree of control social actors have for a set of collective actions in an exchange system.

Symbolic Exchange. Symbolic exchange refers to the mutual transfer of psychological, social, or other intangible entities between two or more parties. Levy was one of the first marketers to recognize this aspect of behavior, which is common to many everyday marketing exchanges:

> . . . *symbol* is a general term for all instances where experience is mediated rather than direct; where an object, action, word, picture, or complex behavior is understood to mean not only itself but also some *other* ideas or feelings.
>
> The less concern there is with the concrete satisfactions of a survival level of existence, the more abstract human responses become. As behavior in the market place is increasingly elaborated, is also becomes increasingly symbolic. This idea needs some examination, because it means that sellers of goods are engaged, whether willfully or not, in selling *symbols,* as well as practical merchandise. It means that marketing managers must attend to more than the relatively superficial acts with which they usually concern themselves when they do not think of their goods as having symbolic significance. . . . *People buy things not only for what they can do, but also for what they mean.*[26]

Mixed Exchange. Marketing exchanges involve both utilitarian and symbolic aspects, and it is often very difficult to separate the two. Yet, the very creation and resolution of marketing exchanges depend on the nature of the symbolic and utilitarian mix. It has only been within the past decade or so that marketers have investigated this deeper side of marketing behavior in their studies of psycho-graphics, motivation research, attitude and multiattribute models, and other aspects of buyer and consumer behavior. Out of this research tradition has emerged a picture of man in his true complexity as striving for both economic and symbolic rewards. Thus, we see the emergence of *marketing man,* perhaps based on the following assumptions:

1. Man is sometimes rational, sometimes irrational.
2. He is motivated by tangible as well as intangible rewards, by internal as well as external forces.[27]
3. He engages in utilitarian as well as symbolic exchanges involving psychological and social aspects.
4. Although faced with incomplete information, he proceeds the best he can and makes at least rudimentary and sometimes unconscious calculations of the costs and benefits associated with social and economic exchanges.
5. Although occasionally striving to maximize his profits, marketing man often settles for less than optimum gains in his exchanges.
6. Finally, exchanges do not occur in isolation but are subject to a host of individual and social constraints: legal, ethical, normative, coercive, and the like.

The important research question to answer is: *What are the forces and conditions creating and resolving marketing exchange relationships?* The processes involved in the creation and resolution of exchange relationships constitute the subject matter of marketing, and these processes depend on, and cannot be separated from, the fundamental character of human and organizational needs.

SOCIAL MARKETING

The marketing literature is replete with conflicting definitions of *social marketing*. Some have defined the term to signify the *use* of marketing skills in social causes,[28] while others have meant it to refer also to "the *study* of markets and marketing activities within a total social system."[29] Bartels recently muddied the waters with still a new definition that is vastly different from those

previously suggested. For him, social marketing designates "the *application* of marketing techniques to *nonmarketing* fields."[30] Since these definitions cover virtually everything in marketing and even some things outside of marketing, it is no wonder that one author felt compelled to express his "personal confusion" and "uncomfortable" state of mind regarding the concept.[31]

But what is social marketing? Before answering this question, we must reject the previous definitions for a number of reasons. First, we must reject the notion that social marketing is merely the "use" or "application" of marketing techniques or skills to other areas. A science or discipline is something more than its technologies. "Social marketing" connotes what is social and what is marketing, and to limit the definition to the tools of a discipline is to beg the question of the meaning of marketing. Second, social marketing is not solely the study of marketing within the frame of the total social system, and it is even more than the subject matter of the discipline. Rather, the meaning of social marketing—like that of marketing itself—is to be found in the unique *problems* that confront the discipline. Thus, as the philosopher of science, Popper, notes:

> The belief that there is such a thing as physics, or biology, or archaeology, and that these "studies" or "disciplines" are distinguishable by the subject matter which they investigate, appears to me to be a residue from the time when one believed that a theory had to proceed from a definition of its own subject matter. But subject matter, or kinds of things, do not, I hold, constitute a basis for distinguishing disciplines. Disciplines are distinguished partly for historical reasons and reasons of administrative convenience (such as the organization of teaching and of appointments), and partly because the theories which we construct to solve our

problems have a tendency to grow into uni-
fied systems. But all this classification and
distinction is a comparatively unimportant
and superficial affair. *We are not students of
some subject matter but students of problems.*
And problems may cut right across the bor-
ders of any subject matter or discipline.[32]

Social marketing, then, addresses a
particular type of problem which, in turn, is
a subset of the generic concept of marketing.
That is, social marketing is the answer to a
particular question: Why and how are *exchanges* created and resolved in *social* relationships? Social relationships (as opposed
to economic relationships) are those such as
family planning agent–client, welfare agent–
indigent, social worker–poor person, and so
on.[33] Social marketing attempts to determine the dynamics and nature of the exchange behavior in these relationships.

But is there an exchange in a social
relationship? Luck, for example, feels that "a
person who receives a free service is not a
buyer and has conducted no exchange of
values with the provider of the service."[34] It
is the contention in this article that there is
most definitely an exchange in social marketing relationships, but the exchange is not
the simple *quid pro quo* notion characteristic
of most economic exchanges. Rather, social
marketing relationships exhibit what may be
called generalized or complex exchanges.
They involve the symbolic transfer of both
tangible and intangible entities, and they
invoke various media to influence such exchanges.

Figure 3-2 illustrates a typical social
marketing exchange. In this system, society
authorizes government—through its votes
and tax payments—to provide needed social
services such as welfare. In return, the members of society receive social insurance
against common human maladies. Government, in turn, pays the salaries of social

workers, gives them authority to provide
social services, and so on. It also distributes
welfare payments directly to the needy.
These relatively contemporaneous transfers
make this marketing system one of generalized exchange. In addition, a number of
symbolic and delayed transfers occur that
make the system also one of complex exchange. For example, as shown by dotted
lines in the figure, in many cases the needy
and dependent have given to the government
in the past, since they may have paid taxes
and voted. Moreover, members of society
anticipate that they, or a number of their
members, will become dependent and that
social services represent an investment as
well as an obligation. Hence, in one sense
there is a mutual exchange between society
and the needy separated, in part, by the
passage of time. Finally, it should be noted
that there are other tangential exchanges
and forces occurring in this social marketing
system that, depending on their balance,
give it stability or promote change. The
system achieves stability due, first, to the
presence of the exchanges described above,
which create mutual dependencies and univocal reciprocities; and, second, to symbolic
exchanges, which reinforce the overt transfers. For example, the social worker gives to
the needy but also receives back gratitude
and feelings of accomplishment. The system
undergoes change due to the dynamics of
competing interests, as is exemplified in the
efforts of lobbies and pressure groups to
bring their needs to bear on the legislative
process.

Thus, social marketing is really a subset of the generic concept of marketing in
that it deals with the creation and resolution
of exchanges in social relationships. Marketers can make contributions to other areas
that contain social exchanges by providing
theories and techniques for the understanding and control of such transactions. They

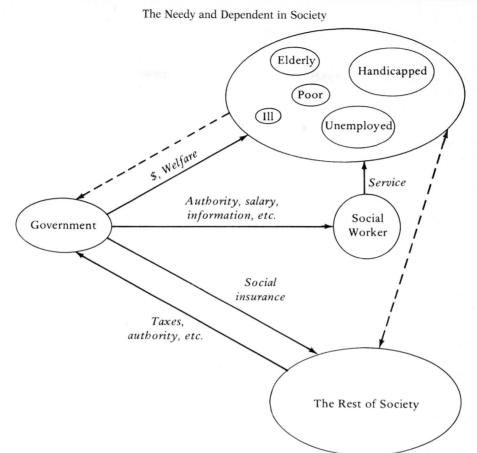

The Needy and Dependent in Society

Elderly

Handicapped

Poor

Ill

Unemployed

$, Welfare

Authority, salary,
information, etc.

Service

Government

Social
Worker

Social
insurance

Taxes,
authority, etc.

The Rest of Society

Figure 3-2
Social Marketing and Exchange

do not usurp the authority of specialists in areas such as social work, but rather they aid and complement the efforts of these social scientists. It is not so much the fact that the subject matter of marketing overlaps with that of other disciplines as it is that the problems of marketing are universal. In answer to Bartels' query, "Is marketing a specific function with general applicability or a general function that is specifically applied?"[35]—one may state that it is neither. Rather, marketing is a general function of universal applicability. It is the discipline of exchange behavior, and it deals with problems related to this behavior.

CONCLUSIONS AND IMPLICATIONS

A number of broad research questions may be posed:

1. Why do marketing exchanges emerge? How do people and organizations satisfy their needs through exchange?

2. Why do some marketing exchanges persist in ongoing relationships while others fall apart?
3. What are the processes leading to changes in marketing exchange relationships? How do the social actors or third parties influence or control an exchange?
4. What are the consequences of imbalances in power, resources, knowledge, and so on, in a marketing exchange? What is an equitable exchange?
5. What are the relationships between conflict, cooperation, competition, and exchange?
6. At what level may marketing exchanges by analyzed? What are the consequences of viewing exchanges as single dyads or complex systems of relationships? What are the consequences of employing the individualistic reductionism of Homans versus the collectivistic orientation of Levi-Strauss for understanding exchange behavior?
7. Is the exchange paradigm universal? Does it apply to the free-enterprise countries of the western world, the planned economies of the communist countries, and the primitive economies of the third world?
8. How well does the exchange paradigm meet the requirements for theory as specified by philosophy of science criteria?

Although marketing seems to defy simple definition and circumspection, it is essential that marketers locate the distinctive focus (or foci) of the discipline. Failure to do so impedes both the growth of the discipline and the character of its performance. Exchange is a central concept in marketing, and it may well serve as the foundation for that elusive "general theory of marketing." This article has attempted to explore some of the key concepts in the exchange paradigm. Future research and discussion must search for specific social and psychological processes that create and resolve marketing exchanges.

NOTES

1. See, for example, Marketing Staff of The Ohio State University, "A Statement of Marketing Philosophy," *Journal of Marketing*, Vol. 29 (January 1965), pp. 43–44; E. Jerome McCarthy, *Basic Marketing*, 5th ed. (Homewood, Ill.: Richard D. Irwin, 1975); Philip Kotler, *Marketing Management*, 2nd ed. (Englewood Cliffs, N.J.: Prentice-Hall, 1972), p. 12; and Ben M. Enis, *Marketing Principles* (Pacific Palisades, Calif.: Goodyear Publishing Co., 1974), p. 21.
2. Philip Kotler, "A Generic Concept of Marketing," *Journal of Marketing*, Vol. 36 (April 1972), pp. 46–54; and Philip Kotler and Sidney J. Levy, "Broadening the Concept of Marketing," *Journal of Marketing*, Vol. 33 (January 1969), pp. 10–15.
3. Thomas S. Kuhn, *The Structure of Scientific Revolutions*, 2nd ed. (Chicago: The University of Chicago Press, 1970).
4. The distinction between restricted and generalized exchange was first made by anthropologist Claude Levi-Strauss in *The Elementary Structure of Kinship* (Boston: Beacon Press, 1969). An extended critical analysis of restricted and generalized exchange may be found in Peter P. Ekeh, *Social Exchange Theory: The Two Traditions* (Cambridge, Mass.: Harvard University Press, 1974), Chap. 3.
5. Ekeh, same reference as footnote 4, p. 50.
6. Ekeh, same reference as footnote 4, pp. 51–52.
7. David J. Luck, "Broadening the Concept of Marketing—Too Far," *Journal of Marketing*, Vol. 33 (January 1969), pp. 10–15; and Luck, "Social Marketing: Confusion Compounded," *Journal of Marketing*, Vol. 38 (October 1974), pp. 70–72.

8. Ekeh, same reference as footnote 4, pp. 48, 50.

9. Kotler, same reference as footnote 2, p. 48.

10. James M. Carman, "On the Universality of Marketing," *Journal of Contemporary Business*, Vol. 2 (Autumn 1973), p. 5; and Luck, "Social Marketing," same reference as footnote 7, p. 72.

11. A form of circular exchange in primitive societies was first suggested by Bonislaw Malinowski in *Argonauts of the Western Pacific* (London: Routledge and Kegan Paul, 1922), p. 93; but in his concept the same physical items were transmitted to all parties, while in complex circular exchange as defined here different tangible or symbolic entities may be transferred.

12. Wroe Anderson, *Dynamic Marketing Behavior* (Homewood, Ill.: Richard D. Irwin, 1965), Chap. 1.

13. For a modern treatment of Adam Smith's contribution to exchange theory, see Walter Nord, "Adam Smith and Contemporary Social Exchange Theory," *The American Journal of Economics and Sociology*, Vol. 32 (October 1974), pp. 421–436.

14. Sir James G. Frazer, *Folklore in the Old Testament*, Vol. 2 (London: Macmillan & Co., 1919).

15. George C. Homans, *Social Behavior: Its Elementary Forms*, rev. ed. (New York: Harcourt Brace Jovanovich, 1974); and Peter M. Blau, *Exchange and Power in Social Life* (New York: John Wiley & Sons, 1964).

16. Levi-Strauss, same reference as footnote 4. See also, Ekeh, same reference as footnote 4, Chaps. 3 and 4.

17. Talcott Parsons, "On the Concept of Influence," *Public Opinion Quarterly*, Vol. 27 (Spring 1963), pp. 37–62; and Parsons, "On the Concept of Political Power," *Proceedings of the American Philosophical Society*, Vol. 107 (June 1963), pp. 232–262. See also, Richard Emerson, "Power Dependence Relations," *American Sociological Review*, Vol. 27 (February 1962), pp. 31–40.

18. Richard P. Bagozzi, "Marketing as an Organized Behavioral System of Exchange," *Journal of Marketing*, Vol. 38 (October 1974), pp. 77–81.

19. See, for example, Louis W. Stern, *Distribution Channels: Behavioral Dimensions* (New York: Houghton Mifflin Co., 1969).

20. Ian Wilkinson, "Power in Distribution Channels," *Cranfield Research Papers in Marketing and Logistics*, Session 1973–1974 (Cranfield School of Management, Cranfield, Bedfordshire, England); and Wilkinson, "Researching the Distribution Channels for Consumer and Industrial Goods: The Power Dimension," *Journal of the Market Research Society*, Vol. 16 (No. 1, 1974), pp. 12–32.

21. This dynamic, as opposed to mechanistic, image of human behavior is described nicely in R. Harré and P. F. Secord, *The Explanation of Social Behavior* (Totawa, N.J.: Littlefield, Adams & Co., 1973).

22. Robert Bartels, "The Identity Crisis in Marketing," *Journal of Marketing*, Vol. 38 (October 1974), p. 75. Emphasis added.

23. For a modern treatment of economic man, see Harold K. Schneider, *Economic Man* (New York: The Free Press, 1974).

24. James S. Coleman, "Systems of Social Exchange," *Journal of Mathematical Sociology*, Vol. 2 (December 1972).

25. James S. Coleman, *The Mathematics of Collective Action* (Chicago: Aldine-Atherton, 1973).

26. Sidney J. Levy, "Symbols for Sale," *Harvard Business Review*, Vol. 37 (July–August 1959), pp. 117–119.

27. It should be stressed that man is motivated by the hope or anticipation of *future* rewards, and these may consist of classes of benefits not necessarily experienced in the past. See Homans's individualistic exchange theory, a learning perspective, same reference as footnote 15; Levi-Strauss's collectivistic, symbolic perspective, same reference as footnote 4; and Ekeh, same reference as footnote 4, pp. 118–124, 163.

28. Philip Kotler and Gerald Zaltman, "Social Marketing: An Approach to Planned Social Change," *Journal of Marketing*, Vol. 35 (July 1971), p. 5.

29. William Lazer and Eugene J. Kelley, eds., *Social Marketing: Perspective and Viewpoints* (Homewood, Ill.: Richard D. Irwin, 1973), p. 4. Emphasis added.

30. Same reference as footnote 22. Emphasis added.

31. Luck, "Social Marketing," same reference as footnote 7, p. 70.

32. Karl R. Popper, *Conjectures and Refutations* (New York: Harper & Row, 1963), p. 67.

33. For a conceptual framework comparing marketing and other social relationships, see Richard P. Bagozzi, "What Is a Marketing Relationship?" *Der Markt,* No. 51, 1974, pp. 64–69.

34. Luck, "Social Marketing," same reference as footnote 7, p. 71.

35. Same reference as footnote 22, p. 73.

Broadening the Concept of Marketing

Philip Kotler and Sidney J. Levy

The term *marketing* connotes to most people a function peculiar to business firms. Marketing is seen as the task of finding and stimulating buyers for the firm's output. It involves product development, pricing, distribution, and communication; and in the more progressive firms, continuous attention to the changing needs of customers and the development of new products, with product modifications and services to meet these needs. But whether marketing is viewed in the old sense of "pushing" products or in the new sense of "customer satisfaction engineering," it is almost always viewed and discussed as a business activity.

It is the authors' contention that marketing is a pervasive societal activity that goes considerably beyond the selling of

toothpaste, soap, and steel. Political contests remind us that candidates are marketed as well as soap; student recruitment by colleges reminds us that higher education is marketed; and fund raising reminds us that "causes" are marketed. Yet these areas of marketing are typically ignored by the student of marketing. Or they are treated cursorily as public relations or publicity activities. No attempt is made to incorporate these phenomena in the body proper of marketing thought and theory. No attempt is made to redefine the meaning of product development, pricing, distribution, and communication in these newer contexts to see if they have a useful meaning. No attempt is made to examine whether the principles of "good" marketing in traditional product areas are transferable to the marketing of services, persons and ideas.

The authors see a great opportunity for marketing people to expand their thinking and to apply their skills to an increasingly interesting range of social activity. The challenge depends on the attention given to

"Broadening the Concept of Marketing," by Philip Kotler and Sidney J. Levy. Reprinted from *Journal of Marketing* (January 1969), pp. 10–15, published by the American Marketing Association. This article received the 1969 Alpha Kappa Psi award as outstanding article of the year.

it; marketing will either take on a broader social meaning or remain a narrowly defined business activity.

THE RISE OF ORGANIZATIONAL MARKETING

One of the most striking trends in the United States is the increasing amount of society's work being performed by organizations other than business firms. As a society moves beyond the stage where shortages of food, clothing, and shelter are the major problems, it begins to organize to meet other social needs that formerly had been put aside. Business enterprises remain a dominant type of organization, but other types of organizations gain in conspicuousness and in influence. Many of these organizations become enormous and require the same rarefied management skills as traditional business organizations. Managing the United Auto Workers, Defense Department, Ford Foundation, World Bank, Catholic Church, and University of California has become every bit as challenging as managing Procter and Gamble, General Motors, and General Electric. These non-business organizations have an increasing range of influence, affect as many livelihoods, and occupy as much media prominence as major business firms.

All of these organizations perform the classic business functions. Every organization must perform a financial function insofar as money must be raised, managed, and budgeted according to sound business principles. Every organization must perform a production function in that it must conceive of the best way of arranging inputs to produce the outputs of the organization. Every organization must perform a personnel function in that people must be hired,

trained, assigned, and promoted in the course of the organization's work. Every organization must perform a purchasing function in that it must acquire materials in an efficient way through comparing and selecting sources of supply.

When we come to the marketing function, it is also clear that every organization performs marketing-like activities whether or not they are recognized as such. Several examples can be given.

The police department of a major U.S. city, concerned with the poor image it has among an important segment of its population, developed a campaign to "win friends and influence people." One highlight of this campaign is a "visit your police station" day in which tours are conducted to show citizens the daily operations of the police department, including the crime laboratories, police lineups, and cells. The police department also sends officers to speak at public schools and carries out a number of other activities to improve its community relations.

Most museum directors interpret their primary responsibility as "the proper preservation of an artistic heritage for posterity."[1] As a result, for many people museums are cold marble mausoleums that house miles of relics that soon give way to yawns and tired feet. Although museum attendance in the United States advances each year, a large number of citizens are uninterested in museums. Is this indifference due to failure in the manner of presenting what museums have to offer? This nagging question led the new director of the Metropolitan Museum of Art to broaden the museum's appeal through sponsoring contemporary art shows and "happenings." His marketing philosophy of museum management led to substantial increases in the Met's attendance.

The public school system in Oklahoma City sorely needed more public support and funds to prevent a deterioration of facilities and exodus of teachers. It recently resorted to television programming to dramatize the work the public schools were doing to fight the high school dropout problem, to develop new teaching techniques, and to enrich the children. Although an expensive medium, television quickly reached large numbers of parents whose response and interest were tremendous.

Nations also resort to international marketing campaigns to get across important points about themselves to the citizens of other countries. The junta of Greek colonels who seized power in Greece in 1967 found the international publicity surrounding their cause to be extremely unfavorable and potentially disruptive of international recognition. They hired a major New York public relations firm and soon full-page newspaper ads appeared carrying the headline "Greece Was Saved From Communism," detailing in small print why the takeover was necessary for the stability of Greece and the world.[2]

An anti-cigarette group in Canada is trying to press the Canadian legislature to ban cigarettes on the grounds that they are harmful to health. There is widespread support for this cause but the organization's funds are limited, particularly measured against the huge advertising resources of the cigarette industry. The group's problem is to find effective ways to make a little money go a long way in persuading influential legislators of the need for discouraging cigarette consumption. This group has come up with several ideas for marketing anti-smoking to Canadians, including television spots, a paperback book featuring pictures of cancer and heart disease patients, and legal research on company liability for the smoker's loss of health.

What concepts are common to these and many other possible illustrations of organizational marketing? All of these organizations are concerned about their "product" in the eyes of certain "consumers" and are seeking to find "tools" for furthering their acceptance. Let us consider each of these concepts in general organizational terms.

Products

Every organization produces a "product" of at least one of the following types:

Physical Products. "Product" first brings to mind everyday items like soap, clothes, and food, and extends to cover millions of *tangible* items that have a market value and are available for purchase.

Services. Services are *intangible* goods that are subject to market transaction such as tours, insurance, consultation, hairdos, and banking.

Persons. Personal marketing is an endemic *human* activity, from the employee trying to impress his boss to the statesman trying to win the support of the public. With the advent of mass communications, the marketing of persons has been turned over to professionals. Hollywood stars have their press agents, political candidates their advertising agencies, and so on.

Organizations. Many organizations spend a great deal of time marketing themselves. The Republican Party has invested considerable thought and resources in trying to develop a modern look. The American Medical Association decided recently that it needed to launch a campaign to improve the image of the American doctor.[3] Many charitable organizations and universities see selling their *organization* as their primary responsibility.

Ideas. Many organizations are mainly in the business of selling *ideas* to the larger society. Population organizations are trying to sell the idea of birth control, and the Women's Christian Temperance Union is still trying to sell the idea of prohibition.

Thus the "product" can take many forms, and this is the first crucial point in the case for broadening the concept of marketing.

Consumers

The second crucial point is that organizations must deal with many groups that are interested in their products and can make a difference in its success. It is vitally important to the organization's success that it be sensitive to, serve, and satisfy these groups. One set of groups can be called the *suppliers. Suppliers* are those who provide the management group with the inputs necessary to perform its work and develop its product effectively. Suppliers include employees, vendors of the materials, banks, advertising agencies, and consultants.

The other set of groups are the *consumers* of the organization's product, of which four subgroups can be distinguished. The *clients* are those who are the immediate consumers of the organization's product. The clients of a business firm are its buyers and potential buyers; of a service organization those receiving the services, such as the needy (from the Salvation Army) or the sick (from County Hospital); and of a protective or a primary organization, the members themselves. The second group is the *trustees* or *directors*, those who are vested with the legal authority and responsibility for the organization, oversee the management, and enjoy a variety of benefits from the "product." The third group is the active *publics* that take a specific interest in the organization. For a business firm, the active publics include consumer rating groups, governmental agencies, and pressure groups of various kinds. For a university, the active publics include alumni and friends of the university, foundations, and city fathers. Finally, the fourth consumer group is the *general public*. These are all the people who might develop attitudes toward the organization that might affect its conduct in some way. Organizational marketing concerns the programs designed by management to create satisfactions and favorable attitudes in the organization's four consuming groups: clients, trustees, active publics, and general public.

Marketing Tools

Students of business firms spend much time studying the various tools under the firm's control that affect product acceptance: product improvement, pricing, distribution, and communication. All of these tools have counterpart applications to nonbusiness organizational activity.

Nonbusiness organizations to various degrees engage in product improvement, especially when they recognize the competition they face from other organizations. Thus, over the years churches have added a host of nonreligious activities to their basic religious activities to satisfy members seeking other bases of human fellowship. Universities keep updating their curricula and adding new student services in an attempt to make the educational experience relevant to the students. Where they have failed to do this, students have sometimes organized their own courses and publications, or have expressed their dissatisfaction in organized protest. Government agencies such as license bureaus, police forces, and taxing bodies are often not responsive to the public because of monopoly status; but even here citizens have shown an increasing readiness to protest mediocre services, and more alert bureaucracies have shown a growing interest in reading a user's needs and developing the required product services.

All organizations face the problem of pricing their products and services so that they cover costs. Churches charge dues, universities charge tuition, governmental agencies charge fees, fund-raising organizations send out bills. Very often specific product charges are not sufficient to meet the organization's budget, and it must rely on gifts and surcharges to make up the difference. Opinions vary as to how much the users should be charged for the individual services and how much should be made up through general collection. If the university increases its tuition, it will have to face losing some students and putting more students on scholarship. If the hospital raises its charges to cover rising costs and additional services, it may provoke a reaction from the community. All organizations face complex pricing issues although not all of them understand good pricing practice.

Distribution is a central concern to the manufacturer seeking to make his goods conveniently accessible to buyers. Distribution also can be an important marketing decision area for nonbusiness organizations. A city's public library has to consider the best means of making its books available to the public. Should it establish one large library with an extensive collection of books, or several neighborhood branch libraries with duplication of books? Should it use bookmobiles that bring the books to the customers instead of relying exclusively on the customers coming to the books? Should it distribute through school libraries? Similarly the police department of a city must think through the problem of distributing its protective services efficiently through the community. It has to determine how much protective service to allocate to different neighborhoods; the respective merits of squad cars, motorcycles, and foot patrolmen; and the positioning of emergency phones.

Customer communication is an essential activity of all organizations although many nonmarketing organizations often fail to accord it the importance it deserves. Managements of many organizations think they have fully met their communication responsibilities by setting up advertising and/or public relations departments. They fail to realize that *everything about an organization talks.* Customers form impressions of an organization from its physical facilities, employees, officers, stationery, and a hundred other company surrogates. Only when this is appreciated do the members of the organization recognize that they all are in marketing, whatever else they do. With this understanding they can assess realistically the impact of their activities on the consumers.

CONCEPTS FOR EFFECTIVE MARKETING MANAGEMENT IN NONBUSINESS ORGANIZATIONS

Although all organizations have products, markets, and marketing tools, the art and science of effective marketing management have reached their highest state of development in the business type of organization. Business organizations depend on customer goodwill for survival and have generally learned how to sense and cater to their needs effectively. As other types of organizations recognize their marketing roles, they will turn increasingly to the body of marketing principles worked out by business organizations and adapt them to their own situations.

What are the main principles of effective marketing management as they appear in most forward-looking business organizations? Nine concepts stand out as crucial in guiding the marketing effort of a business organization.

Generic Product Definition

Business organizations have increasingly recognized the value of placing a broad definition on their products, one that emphasizes the basic customer need(s) being served. A modern soap company recognizes that its basic product is cleaning, not soap; a cosmetics company sees its basic product as beauty or hope, not lipsticks and makeup; a publishing company sees its basic product as information, not books.

The same need for a broader definition of its business is incumbent upon nonbusiness organizations if they are to survive and grow. Churches at one time tended to define their product narrowly as that of producing religious services for members. Recently, most churchmen have decided that their basic product is human fellowship. There was a time when educators said that their product was the three R's. Now most of them define their product as education for the whole man. They try to serve the social, emotional, and political needs of young people in addition to intellectual needs.

Target Groups Definition

A generic product definition usually results in defining a very wide market, and it is then necessary for the organization, because of limited resources, to limit its product offering to certain clearly defined groups within the market. Although the generic product of an automobile company is transportation, the company typically sticks to cars, trucks, and buses, and stays away from bicycles, airplanes, and steamships. Furthermore, the manufacturer does not produce every size and shape of car but concentrates on producing a few major types to satisfy certain substantial and specific parts of the market.

In the same way, nonbusiness organizations have to define their target groups carefully. For example, in Chicago the YMCA defines its target groups as men, women and children who want recreational opportunities and are willing to pay $20 or more a year for them. The Chicago Boys Club, on the other hand, defines its target group as poorer boys within the city boundaries who are in want of recreational facilities and can pay $1 a year.

Differentiated Marketing

When a business organization sets out to serve more than one target group, it will be maximally effective by differentiating its product offerings and communications. This is also true for nonbusiness organizations. Fund-raising organizations have recognized the advantage of treating clients, trustees, and various publics in different ways. These groups require differentiated appeals and frequency of solicitation. Labor unions find that they must address different messages to different parties rather than one message to all parties. To the company they may seem unyielding, to the conciliator they may appear willing to compromise, and to the public they seek to appear economically exploited.

Customer Behavior Analysis

Business organizations are increasingly recognizing that customer needs and behavior are not obvious without formal research and analysis; they cannot rely on impressionistic evidence. Soap companies spend hundreds of thousands of dollars each year researching how Mrs. Housewife feels about her laundry, how, when, and where she does her laundry, and what she desires of a detergent.

Fund raising illustrates how an industry has benefited by replacing stereotypes of donors with studies of why people contribute to causes. Fund raisers have learned that people give because they are getting something. Many give to community chests to relieve a sense of guilt because of their elevated state compared to the needy. Many give to medical charities to relieve a sense of fear that they may be struck by a disease whose cure has not yet been found. Some give to feel pride. Fund raisers have stressed the importance of identifying the motives operating in the marketplace of givers as a basis for planning drives.

Differential Advantages
In considering different ways of reaching target groups, an organization is advised to think in terms of seeking a differential advantage. It should consider what elements in its reputation or resources can be exploited to create a special value in the minds of its potential customers. In the same way Zenith has built a reputation for quality and International Harvester a reputation for service, a nonbusiness organization should base its case on some dramatic value that competitive organizations lack. The small island of Nassau can compete against Miami for the tourist trade by advertising the greater dependability of its weather; the Heart Association can compete for funds against the Cancer Society by advertising the amazing strides made in heart research.

Multiple Marketing Tools
The modern business firm relies on a multitude of tools to sell its product, including product improvement, consumer and dealer advertising, salesmen incentive programs, sales promotions, contests, multiple-size offerings, and so forth. Likewise nonbusiness organizations also can reach their audiences in a variety of ways. A church can sustain the interest of its members through discussion groups, newsletters, news releases, campaign drives, annual reports, and retreats. Its "salesmen" include the religious head, the

board members, and the present members in terms of attracting potential members. Its advertising includes announcements of weddings, births and deaths, religious pronouncements, and newsworthy developments.

Integrated Marketing Planning
The multiplicity of available marketing tools suggests the desirability of overall coordination so that these tools do not work at cross purposes. Over time, the business firms have placed under a marketing vice-president activities that were previously managed in a semi-autonomous fashion, such as sales, advertising, and marketing research. Nonbusiness organizations typically have not integrated their marketing activities. Thus, no single officer in the typical university is given total responsibility for studying the needs and attitudes of clients, trustees, and publics, and undertaking the necessary product development and communication programs to serve these groups. The university administration instead includes a variety of "marketing" positions such as dean of students, director of alumni affairs, director of public relations, and director of development; coordination is often poor.

Continuous Marketing Feedback
Business organizations gather continuous information about changes in the environment and about their own performance. They use their salesmen, research department, specialized research services, and other means to check on the movement of goods, actions of competitors, and feelings of customers to make sure they are progressing along satisfactory lines. Nonbusiness organizations typically are more casual about collecting vital information on how they are doing and what is happening in the marketplace. Universities have been caught off guard by underestimating the magnitude

of student grievance and unrest, and so have major cities underestimated the degree to which they were failing to meet the needs of important minority constituencies.

Marketing Audit

Change is a fact of life, although it may proceed almost invisibly on a day-to-day basis. Over a long stretch of time, it might be so fundamental as to threaten organizations that have not provided for periodic reexaminations of their purposes. Organizations can grow set in their ways and unresponsive to new opportunities or problems. Some great American companies are no longer with us because they did not change definitions of their businesses, and their products lost relevance in a changing world. Political parties become unresponsive after they enjoy power for a while and every so often experience a major upset. Many union leaders grow insensitive to new needs and problems until one day they find themselves out of office. For an organization to remain viable, its management must provide for periodic audits of its objectives, resources, and opportunities. It must reexamine its basic business, target groups, differential advantage, communication channels, and messages in the light of current trends and needs. It might recognize when change is needed and make it before it is too late.

IS ORGANIZATIONAL MARKETING A SOCIALLY USEFUL ACTIVITY?

Modern marketing has two different meanings in the minds of people who use the term. One meaning of marketing conjures up the terms selling, influencing, persuading. Marketing is seen as a huge and increasingly dangerous technology, making it possible to sell persons on buying things, propositions, and causes they either do not want or which are bad for them. This was the indictment in Vance Packard's *Hidden Persuaders* and numerous other social criticisms, with the net effect that a large number of persons think of marketing as immoral or entirely self-seeking in its fundamental premises. They can be counted on to resist the idea of organizational marketing as so much "Madison Avenue."

The other meaning of marketing unfortunately is weaker in the public mind; it is the concept of sensitively *serving and satisfying human needs*. This was the great contribution of the marketing concept that was promulgated in the 1950s, and that concept now counts many business firms as its practitioners. The marketing concept holds that the problem of all business firms in an age of abundance is to develop customer loyalties and satisfaction, and the key to this problem is to focus on the customer's needs.[4] Perhaps the short-run problem of business firms is to sell people on buying the existing products, but the long-run problem is clearly to create the products that people need. By this recognition that effective marketing requires a consumer orientation instead of a product orientation, marketing has taken a new lease on life and tied its economic activity to a higher social purpose.

It is this second side of marketing that provides a useful concept for all organizations. All organizations are formed to serve the interest of particular groups: hospitals serve the sick, schools serve the students, governments serve the citizens, and labor unions serve the members. In the course of evolving, many organizations lose sight of their original mandate, grow hard, and become self-serving. The bureaucratic mentality begins to dominate the original service mentality. Hospitals may become perfunctory in their handling of patients, schools treat their students as nuisances, city bureaucrats behave like petty tyrants toward the citizens, and labor unions try to run instead of serve their members. All of these actions tend to build frustration in the consuming groups. As a result some withdraw meekly from these organizations, accept frustration as part of their condition, and find their satisfactions elsewhere. This used to be the common reaction of ghetto Negroes and college students in the face of indifferent city and university bureaucracies. But new possibilities have arisen, and now the same consumers refuse to withdraw so readily. Organized dissent and protest are seen to be an answer, and many organizations thinking of themselves as responsible have been stunned into recognizing that they have lost touch with their constituencies. They had grown unresponsive.

Where does marketing fit into this picture? Marketing is that function of the organization that can keep in constant touch with the organization's consumers, read their needs, develop "products" that meet these needs, and build a program of communications to express the organization's purposes. Certainly selling and influencing will be large parts of organizational marketing; but, properly seen, selling follows rather than precedes the organization's drive to create products to satisfy its consumers.

CONCLUSION

It has been argued here that the modern marketing concept serves very naturally to describe an important facet of all organizational activity. All organizations must develop appropriate products to serve their sundry consuming groups and must use modern tools of communication to reach their consuming publics. The business heritage of marketing provides a useful set of concepts for guiding all organizations.

The choice facing those who manage nonbusiness organizations is not whether to market or not to market, for no organization can avoid marketing. The choice is whether to do it well or poorly, and on this necessity the case for organizational marketing is basically founded.

NOTES

1. This is the view of Sherman Lee, Director of the Cleveland Museum, quoted in *Newsweek*, Vol. 71 (April 1, 1968), p. 55.
2. "PR for Colonels," *Newsweek*, Vol. 71 (March 18, 1968), p. 70.
3. "Doctors Try an Image Transplant," *Business Week*, No. 2025 (June 22, 1968), p. 64.
4. Theodore Levitt, "Marketing Myopia," *Harvard Business Review*, Vol. 38 (July–August, 1960), pp. 45–56.

Marketing, Strategic Planning and the Theory of the Firm

Paul F. Anderson

Would you tell me, please, which way I ought to go from here? asked Alice.
That depends a good deal on where you want to get to, said the Cat.
I don't much care where, said Alice.
Then it doesn't matter which way you go, said the Cat.
   Lewis Carroll—*Alice's Adventures in Wonderland*

The obvious wisdom of the Cheshire's statement reveals an important fact concerning strategic planning: without a clear set of objectives, the planning process is meaningless. Two authorities on the subject refer to strategy as "the major link between the goals and objectives the organization wants to achieve and the various functional area policies and operating plans it uses to guide its day-to-day activities" (Hofer and Schendel

Paul F. Anderson, "Marketing Strategic Planning and the Theory of the Firm," Vol. 46 (Spring 1982), pp. 15–26. Reprinted from *Journal of Marketing*, published by the American Marketing Association.

1978, p. 13). Other strategy experts generally agree that the process of goal formulation must operate prior to, but also be interactive with, the process of strategy formulation (Ackoff 1970, Ansoff 1965, Glueck 1976, Newman and Logan 1971). Given the growing interest of marketers in the concept of strategic planning, it would appear fruitful to assess the current state of knowledge concerning goals and the goal formulation process.

Over the years, this general area of inquiry has fallen under the rubric of the "theory of the firm." One objective of this paper is to review some of the major theories of the firm to be found in the literature. The extant theories have emerged in the disciplines of economics, finance and management. To date, marketing has not developed its own comprehensive theory of the firm. Generally, marketers have been content to borrow their concepts of goals and goal formulation from these other disciplines. Indeed, marketing has shown a strange ambivalence toward the concept of corporate goals. The recent marketing literature pays scant attention to the actual content of corporate goal hierarchies. Even less attention is focused on the normative issue of what firm goals and objectives ought to be. Moreover, contemporary marketing texts devote little space to the subject. Typically, an author's perspective on corporate goals is revealed in his/her definition of the marketing concept, but one is hard pressed to find further development of the topic. There is rarely any discussion of how these goals come about or how marketing may participate in the goal formulation process.

This is not to say that received doctrine in marketing has been developed without regard for corporate objectives. The normative decision rules and procedures that have emerged always seek to attain one or more objectives. Thus it could be said that these marketing models implicitly assume a theory of the firm. However, the particular theory that serves as the underpinning of the model is rarely made explicit. More importantly, marketing theorists have devoted little attention to an exploration of the nature and implications of these theories. For example, the product portfolio (Boston Consulting Group 1970, Cordoza and Wind 1980), and PIMS (Buzzell, Gale and Sultan 1975) approaches that are so much in vogue today implicitly assume that the primary objective of the firm is the maximization of return on investment (ROI). This objective seems to have been accepted uncritically by many marketers despite its well-documented deficiencies (e.g., its inability to deal with timing, duration and risk differences among returns and its tendency to create behavioral problems when used as a control device; Hopwood 1976, Van Horne 1980). However, the concern expressed in this paper is not so much that marketers have adopted the wrong objectives, but that the discipline has failed to appreciate fully the

nature and implications of the objectives that it has adopted.

As a result, in the last sections of the paper the outline of a new theory of the firm will be presented. It will be argued that the theories of the firm developed within economics, finance and management are inadequate in varying degrees as conceptual underpinnings for marketing. It is asserted that the primary role of a theory of the firm is to act as a kind of conceptual backdrop that functions heuristically to guide further theory development within a particular discipline. As such, the proposed model is less of a theory and more a Kuhnian-style paradigm (Kuhn 1970). Moreover, for a theory of the firm to be fruitful in this respect it must be congruent with the established research tradition of the field (Laudan 1977). It will be demonstrated, for example, that the theories emerging from economics and finance are inconsistent with the philosophical methodology and ontological framework of marketing. However, the proposed model is not only fully consonant with marketing's research tradition, but, unlike existing theories, it explicitly considers marketing's role in corporate goal formulation and strategic planning. Thus it is hoped that the theory will be able to provide a structure to guide future research efforts in these areas.

ECONOMIC THEORIES OF THE FIRM

In this section three theories of the firm are reviewed. The first, the neoclassical model, provides the basic foundation of contemporary microeconomic theory. The second, the market value model, performs a similar function with financial economics. Finally, the agency costs model represents a modification of the market value model to allow a divergence of interests between the owners and managers of the firm. In this sense, it operates as a transitional model between the economically oriented theories of this section and the behavioral theories of the section to follow. However, all three may be classified as economic models since they share the methodological orientation and conceptual framework of economic theory. Note that each postulates an economic objective for the firm and then derives the consequences for firm behavior under different assumption sets.

The Neoclassical Model

The neoclassical theory of the firm can be found in any standard textbook in economics. In its most basic form the theory posits a single product firm operating in a purely competitive environment. Decision making is vested in an owner-entrepreneur whose sole objective is to maximize the dollar amount of the firm's single period profits. Given the standard assumptions of diminishing returns in the short run and diseconomies of scale in the long run, the firm's average cost function will have its characteristic U-shape. The owner's unambiguous decision rule will be to set output at the point where marginal costs equal marginal revenues. The introduction of imperfections in the product market (such as those posited by the monopolistically competitive model) represent mere elaborations on the basic approach. The objective of the firm remains single period profit maximization.

The neoclassical model is well known to marketers. Indeed, it will be argued below that the profit maximization assumption of neoclassical economics underlies much of the normative literature in marketing management. It will be shown that this is true despite the fact that neoclassical theory is inconsistent with the basic research tradition of marketing. Moreover, the neoclassi-

cal model suffers from a number of limitations.

For example, the field of finance has challenged the profit maximization assumption because it fails to provide the business decision maker with an operationally feasible criterion for making investment decisions (Solomon 1963). In this regard, it suffers from an inability to consider risk differences among investment alternatives. When risk levels vary across projects, decision criteria that focus only on profitability will lead to suboptimal decisions (Copeland and Weston 1979, Fama and Miller 1972, Van Horne 1980). As a result of these and other problems, financial economists have generally abandoned the neoclassical model in favor of a more comprehensive theory of the firm known as the market value model.

The Market Value Model

Given the assumptions that human wants are insatiable and that capital markets are perfectly competitive, Fama and Miller (1972) show that the objective of the firm should be to maximize its present market value. For a corporation this is equivalent to maximizing the price of the firm's stock. In contrast to the profit maximization objective, the market value rule allows for the consideration of risk differences among alternative investment opportunities. Moreover, the model is applicable to owner-operated firms as well as corporations in which there is likely to be a separation of ownership and control.

The existence of a perfectly competitive capital market allows the firm's management to pursue a single unambiguous objective despite the fact that shareholders are likely to have heterogeneous preferences for current versus future income. If, for example, some stockholders wish more income than the firm is currently paying in dividends, they can sell some of their shares to make up the difference. However, if other shareholders prefer less current income in favor of more future income, they can lend their dividends in the capital markets at interest. In either case shareholder utility will be maximized by a policy that maximizes the value of the firm's stock.

The value maximization objective is implemented within the firm by assessing all multiperiod decision alternatives on the basis of their risk-adjusted net present values (Copeland and Weston 1979, Fama and Miller 1972, Van Horne 1980):

$$NPV_j = \sum_{i=1}^{n} \frac{A_i}{(1 + k_j)^i} \qquad (1)$$

where NPV_j equals the net present value of alternative j, A_i equals the net after-tax cash flows in year i, n is the expected life of the project in years, and k_j is the risk-adjusted, after-tax required rate of return on j. In the absence of capital rationing, the firm should undertake all projects whose net present values are greater than or equal to zero. Assuming an accurate determination of k_j, this will ensure maximization of the firm's stock price. The discount rate k_j should represent the return required by the market to compensate for the risk of the project. This is usually estimated using a parameter preference model such as the capital asset pricing model or (potentially) the arbitrage model (Anderson 1981). However, it should be noted that there are serious theoretical and practical difficulties associated with the use of these approaches (Anderson 1981; Meyers and Turnbull 1977; Roll 1977; Ross 1976, 1978).

From a marketing perspective this approach requires that all major decisions be treated as investments. Thus the decision to introduce a new product, to expand into new territories, or to adopt a new channel of distribution should be evaluated on the basis of its risk-adjusted net present value. While similar approaches have been suggested in marketing (Cravens, Hills and Woodruff 1980; Dean 1966; Howard 1965; Kotler 1971; Pessemier 1966), it has generally not been recognized that this implies the adoption of shareholder wealth maximization as the goal of the firm. Moreover, these approaches are often offered in piecemeal fashion for the evaluation of selected decisions (e.g., new products), and are not integrated into a consistent and coherent theory of the firm.

Despite the deductive logic of the market value model, there are those who question whether corporate managers are motivated to pursue value maximization. An essential assumption of the market value theory is that stockholders can employ control, motivation and monitoring devices to ensure that managers maximize firm value. However, in the development of their agency theory of the firm, Jensen and Meckling (1976) note that such activities by shareholders are not without cost. As a result, it may not be possible to compel managers to maximize shareholder wealth.

The Agency Costs Model

The separation of ownership and control in modern corporations gives rise to an agency relationship between the stockholders and managers of the firm. An agency relationship may be defined as "a contract under which one or more persons (the principal(s)) engage another person (the agent) to perform some service on their behalf which involves delegating some decision making authority to the agent" (Jenson and Meckling 1976, p. 308). In any relationship of this sort, there is a potential for the agent to expend some of the principal's resources on private pursuits. As such, it will pay the principal to provide the agent with incentives and to incur monitoring costs to encourage a convergence of interests between the objectives of the principal and those of the agent. Despite expenditures of this type, it will generally be impossible to ensure that all of the agent's decisions will be designed to maximize the principal's welfare. The dollar value of the reduction in welfare experienced by the principal along with the expenditures on monitoring activities are costs of the agency relationship. For corporate stockholders these agency costs include the reduction in firm value resulting from management's consumption of nonpecuniary benefits (perquisites) and the costs of hiring outside auditing agents.

The tendency of managers of widely held corporations to behave in this fashion will require the stockholders to incur monitoring costs in an effort to enforce the value maximization objective. Unfortunately, perfect monitoring systems are very expensive. Thus the stockholders face a cost-benefit trade-off in deciding how much to spend on monitoring activities. Since it is unlikely that it will pay the shareholders to implement a "perfect" monitoring system, we will observe corporations suboptimizing on value maximization even in the presence of auditing activities. This leads to implications for managerial behavior that are quite different from those predicted by the market value model. For example, the Fama-Miller model predicts that managers will invest in all projects that will maximize the present value of the firm. However, the agency costs model suggests that management may actually invest in suboptimal projects and may even forego new profitable investments (Barnea, Haugen and Senbet 1981).

The recognition that a firm might not pursue maximization strategies is a relatively new concept to the literature of financial economics. However, in the middle 1950s and early 1960s, various economists and management specialists began to question the neoclassical assumption of single objective maximization on the basis of their observations of managerial behavior. This led directly to the development of the behavioral theory of the firm.

BEHAVIORAL THEORIES OF THE FIRM

In this section two behaviorally oriented theories of the firm will be reviewed. While other approaches could also be included (Bower 1968, Mitzberg 1979), these models will lay the foundation for the development of a constituency-based theory in the last sections of the paper. The first approach is the behavioral model of the firm that emerged at the Carnegie Institute of Technology. The behavioral model can best be understood as a reaction against the neoclassical model of economic theory. The second approach is the resource dependence model of Pfeffer and Salancik (1978). The resource dependence perspective builds on a number of ideas contained in the behavioral model. For example, both approaches stress the coalitional nature of organizations. Moreover, both models emphasize the role of behavioral rather than economic factors in explaining the activities of firms.

The Behavioral Model
The behavioral theory of the firm can be found in the writings of Simon (1955, 1959, 1964), March and Simon (1958), and especially in Cyert and March (1963). The behavioral theory views the business firm as a coalition of individuals who are, in turn, members of subcoalitions. The coalition members include "managers, workers, stockholders, suppliers, customers, lawyers, tax collectors, regulatory agencies, etc." (Cyert and March 1963, p. 27).

The goals of the organization are determined by this coalition through a process of quasi-resolution of conflict. Different coalition members wish the organization to pursue different goals. The resultant goal conflict is not resolved by reducing all goals to a common dimension or by making them internally consistent. Rather, goals are viewed as "a series of independent aspiration-level constraints imposed on the organization by the members of the organizational coalition" (Cyert and March 1963, p. 117).

As Simon (1964) points out, in real world decision making situations acceptable alternatives must satisfy a whole range of requirements or constraints. In his view, singling out one constraint and referring to it as the goal of the activity is essentially arbitrary. This is because in many cases, the set of requirements selected as constraints will have much more to do with the decision outcome than the requirement selected as the goal. Thus he believes that it is more meaningful to refer to the entire set of constraints as the (complex) goal of the organization.

Moreover, these constraints are set at aspiration levels rather than maximization levels. Maximization is not possible in complex organizations because of the existence of imperfect information and because of the computational limitations faced by organizations in coordinating the various decisions made by decentralized departments and divisions. As a result, firm behavior concerning goals may be described as satisficing rather than maximizing (Simon 1959, 1964).

Cyert and March (1963) see decentralization of decision making leading to a kind of local rationality within subunits of the organization. Since these subunits deal only with a small set of problems and a limited number of goals, local optimization may be possible, but it is unlikely that this will lead to overall optimization. In this regard, the firm not only faces information processing and coordination problems but is also hampered by the fact that it must deal with problems in a sequential fashion. Thus organizational subunits typically attend to different problems at different times, and there is no guarantee that consistent objectives will be pursued in solving these problems. Indeed, Cyert and March agree that the time buffer between decision situations provides the firm with a convenient mechanism for avoiding the explicit resolution of goal conflict.

Thus in the behavioral theory of the firm, goals emerge as "independent constraints imposed on the organization through a process of bargaining among potential coalition members" (Cyert and March 1963, p. 43). These objectives are unlikely to be internally consistent and are subject to change over time as changes take place in the coalition structure. This coalitional perspective has had a significant impact on the development of management thought. Both Mintzberg (1979) and Pfeffer and Salancik (1978) have developed theories of the firm that take its coalitional nature as given. In the following section the resource dependence approach of Pfeffer and Salancik is outlined.

The Resource Dependence Model

Pfeffer and Salancik (1978) view organizations as coalitions of interest which alter their purposes and direction as changes take place in the coalitional structure. Like Mintzberg (1979) they draw a distinction between internal and external coalitions, although they do not use these terms. Internal coalitions may be viewed as groups functioning within the organization (e.g., departments and functional areas). External coalitions include such stakeholder groups as labor, stockholders, creditors, suppliers, government and various interested publics. Pfeffer and Salancik place their primary emphasis on the role of environmental (i.e., external) coalitions in affecting the behavior of organizations. They believe that "to describe adequately the behavior of organizations requires attending to the coalitional nature of organizations and the manner in which organizations respond to pressures from the environment" (Pfeffer and Salancik 1978, p. 24).

The reason for the environmental focus of the model is that the survival of the organization ultimately depends on its ability to obtain resources and support from its external coalitions. Pfeffer and Salancik implicitly assume that survival is the ultimate goal of the organization and that to achieve this objective, the organization must maintain a coalition of parties willing to "legitimize" its existence (Dowling and Pfeffer 1975, Parsons 1960). To do this, the organization offers various inducements in exchange for contributions of resources and support (Barnard 1938, March and Simon 1958, Simon 1964).

However, the contributions of the various interests are not equally valued by the organization. As such, coalitions that provide "behaviors, resources and capabilities that are most needed or desired by other organizational participants come to have more influence and control over the organization" (Pfeffer and Salancik 1978, p. 27). Similarly, organizational subunits (departments, functional areas, etc.) which are best able to deal with critical contingencies related to coalitional contributions are able to enhance their influence in the organization.

A common problem in this regard is that the various coalitions make conflicting demands on the organization. Since the satisfaction of some demands limits the satisfaction of others, this leads to the possibility that the necessary coalition of support cannot be maintained. Thus organizational activities can be seen as a response to the constraints imposed by the competing demands of various coalitions.

In attempting to maintain the support of its external coalitions, the organization must negotiate exchanges that ensure the continued supply of critical resources. At the same time, however, it must remain flexible enough to respond to environmental contingencies. Often these objectives are in conflict, since the desire to ensure the stability and certainty of resource flows frequently leads to activities limiting flexibility and autonomy. For example, backward integration via merger or acquisition is one way of coping with the uncertainty of resource dependence. At the same time, however, this method of stabilizing resource exchanges limits the ability of the firm to adapt as readily to environmental contingencies. Pfeffer and Salancik suggest that many other activities of organizations can be explained by the desire for stable resource exchanges, on the one hand, and the need for flexibility and autonomy on the other. They present data to support their position that joint ventures, interlocking directorates, organizational growth, political involvement and executive succession can all be interpreted in this light. Other activities such as secrecy, multiple sourcing and diversification can also be interpreted from a resource dependence perspective.

Thus the resource dependence model views organizations as "structures of coordinated behaviors" whose ultimate aim is to garner the necessary environmental support for survival (Pfeffer and Salancik 1978, p. 32). As in the behavioral model, it is recognized that goals and objectives will emerge as constraints imposed by the various coalitions of interests. However, the resource dependence model interprets these constraints as demands by the coalitions that must be met in order to maintain the existence of the organization.

RESEARCH TRADITIONS AND THE THEORY OF THE FIRM

In reflecting on the various theories of the firm presented herein, it is important to recognize that one of their primary roles is to function as a part of what Laudan calls a "research tradition" (Laudan 1977). A research tradition consists of a set of assumptions shared by researchers in a particular domain. Its main purpose is to provide a set of guidelines for theory development. In so doing it provides the researcher with both an ontological framework and a philosophical methodology.

The ontology of the research tradition defines the kinds of entities that exist within the domain of inquiry. For example, in the neoclassical model such concepts as middle management, coalitions, bureaucracy and reward systems do not exist. They fall outside the ontology of neoclassical economics. Similarly, the concepts of the entrepreneur, diminishing returns and average cost curves do not exist (or at least are not used) in the resource dependence model. The ontology of the research tradition defines the basic conceptual building blocks of its constituent theories.

The philosophical methodology, on the other hand, specifies the procedure by which concepts will be used to construct a theory. Moreover, it determines the way in which the concepts will be viewed by theorists working within the research tradition. For example, the neoclassical, market value and agency costs models have been developed in accordance with a methodology that could be characterized as deductive instrumentalism. The models are deductive in that each posits a set of assumptions or axioms (including assumptions about firm goals) from which implications for firm behavior are deduced as logical consequences (Hempel 1965, p. 336). The models are also

instrumentalist in that their component concepts are not necessarily assumed to have real world referents. Instrumentalism views theories merely as calculating devices that generate useful predictions (Feyerabend 1964, Morgenbesser 1969, Popper 1963). The reality of a theory's assumptions or its concepts is irrelevant from an instrumentalist point of view.

It is essentially this aspect of economic instrumentalism that has drawn the most criticism from both economists and noneconomists. Over 30 years ago concerns for the validity of theory among economists emerged as the famous "marginalism controversy" which raged in the pages of the *American Economic Review* (Lester 1946, 1947; Machlup 1946, 1947; Stigler 1946, 1947). More recently, much of the criticism has come from proponents of the behavioral theory of the firm (Cyert and March 1963, Cyert and Pottinger 1979). Perhaps the most commonly heard criticism of the neoclassical model is that the assumption of a rational profit-maximizing decision maker who has access to perfect information is at considerable variance with the real world of business management (Cyert and March 1963, Simon 1955). Moreover, these critics fault the "marginalists" for concocting a firm with "no complex organization, no problems of control, no standard operating procedures, no budget, no controller [and] no aspiring middle management" (Cyert and March 1963, p. 8). In short, the business firm assumed into existence by neoclassical theory bears little resemblance to the modern corporate structure.

Concerns with the realism of assumptions in neoclassical theory have been challenged by Friedman (1953) and Machlup (1967). In Friedman's classic statement of the "positivist" viewpoint, he takes the position that the ultimate test of a theory is the correspondence of its predictions with reality. From Friedman's perspective the lack of realism in a theory's assumptions is unrelated to the question of its validity.

Machlup, in a closely related argument, notes that much of the criticism of neoclassical theory arises because of a confusion concerning the purposes of the theory (1967). He points out that the "firm" in neoclassical analysis is nothing more than a theoretical construct that is useful in predicting the impact of changes in economic variables on the behavior of firms in the aggregate. For example, the neoclassical model performs well in predicting the *direction* of price changes in an industry that experiences an increase in wage rates or the imposition of a tax. It does less well, however, in explaining the complex process by which a particular firm decides to implement a price change. Of course, this is to be expected since the theory of the firm was never intended to predict the real world behavior of individual firms.

Thus the question of whether corporations really seek to maximize profits is of no concern to the economic instrumentalist. Following Friedman, the only consideration is whether such assumptions lead to "sufficiently accurate predictions" of real world phenomena (1953, p. 15). Similarly, the financial economist is unmoved by criticism related to the lack of reality in the market value and agency cost models. The ultimate justification of the theory from an instrumental viewpoint comes from the accuracy of its predictions.

In contrast to the instrumentalism of the first three theories of the firm, the behavioral and resource dependence models have been developed from the perspective of realism. The realist believes that theoretical constructs should have real world analogs and that theories should describe "what the world is really like" (Chalmers 1978, p. 114). Thus, it is not unexpected that these models

are essentially inductive in nature. Indeed, in describing their methodological approach Cyert and March state that they "propose to make detailed observations of the procedures by which firms make decisions and to use these observations as a basis for a theory of decision making within business organizations" (1963, p. 1).

Thus it can be seen that the theories of the firm that have been developed in economics and financial economics emerged from a very different research tradition than the behaviorally oriented theories developed in management. This fact becomes particularly significant in considering their adequacy as a framework for marketing theory development. For example, the discipline of marketing appears to be committed to a research tradition dominated by the methodology of inductive realism, yet it frequently employs the profit maximization paradigm of neoclassical economic theory. Despite the recent trend toward the incorporation of social objectives in the firm's goal hierarchy, and the recognition by many authors that firms pursue multiple objectives, profit or profit maximization figures prominently as the major corporate objective in leading marketing texts (Boone and Kurtz 1980, p. 12; Markin 1979, p. 34; McCarthy 1978, p. 29; Stanton 1978, p. 13). More significantly perhaps, profit maximization is the implicit or explicit objective of much of the normative literature in marketing management. While the terms may vary from return on investment to contribution margin, cash flow or cumulative compounded profits, they are all essentially profit maximization criteria. Thus such widely known and accepted approaches as product portfolio analysis (Boston Consulting Group 1970), segmental analysis (Mossman, Fischer and Crissy 1974), competitive bidding models (Simon and Freimer 1970), Bayesian pricing procedures (Green 1963), and many others all adhere to the profit maximization paradigm. It may seem curious that a discipline that drifted away from the research tradition of economics largely because of a concern for greater "realism" (Hutchinson 1952, Vaile 1950) should continue to employ one of its most "unrealistic" assumptions. In effect, marketing has rejected much of the philosophical methodology of economics while retaining a significant portion of its ontology.

It would seem that what is required is the development of a theory of the firm that is consistent with the existing research tradition of marketing. Such a theory should deal explicitly with the role of marketing in the firm and should attempt to explicate its relationship with the other functional areas (Wind 1981) and specify its contribution to the formation of corporate "goal structures" (Richards 1978). In this way it would provide a framework within which marketing theory development can proceed. This is particularly important for the development of theory within the area of strategic planning. It is likely that greater progress could be made in this area if research is conducted within the context of a theory of the firm whose methodological and ontological framework is consistent with that of marketing.

TOWARD A CONSTITUENCY-BASED THEORY OF THE FIRM

The theory of the firm to be outlined in this section focuses explicitly on the roles performed by the various functional areas found in the modern corporation. There are basically two reasons for this. First, theory development in business administration typically proceeds within the various academic disciplines corresponding (roughly) to the functional areas of the firm. It is felt that a theory explicating the role of the functional areas will be of greater heuristic value in providing a framework for research within these disciplines (and within marketing in particular).

Second, a theory of the firm that does not give explicit recognition to the activities of these functional subunits fails to appreciate their obvious importance in explaining firm behavior. As highly formalized internal coalitions operating at both the corporate and divisional levels, they often share a common frame of reference and a relatively consistent set of goals and objectives. These facts make the functional areas an obvious unit of analysis in attempting to explain the emergence of goals in corporations.

The proposed theory adopts the coalitional perspectives of the various behaviorally oriented theories of the firm and relies especially on the resource dependence model. As a matter of analytical convenience, the theory divides an organization into both internal and external coalitions. From a resource dependence perspective, the task of the organization is to maintain itself by negotiating resource exchanges with external interests. Over time the internal coalitions within corporate organizations have adapted themselves to enhance the efficiency and effectiveness with which they perform these negotiating functions. One approach that has been taken to accomplish this is specialization. Thus certain coalitions within the firm may be viewed as specialists in negotiating exchanges with certain external coalitions. By and large these internal coalitions correspond to the major functional areas of the modern corporate structure.

For example, industrial relations and personnel specialize in negotiating resource exchanges with labor coalitions; finance, and to a lesser extent, accounting specialize in negotiating with stockholder and creditor groups; materials management and purchasing specialize in supplier group exchanges; and, of course, marketing specializes in negotiating customer exchanges. In addition, public relations, legal, tax and accounting specialize to a greater or lesser extent in negotiating the continued support and sanction of both government and public coalitions. In most large corporations the production area no longer interacts directly with the environment. With the waning of the production orientation earlier in this century, production gradually lost its negotiating functions to specialists such as purchasing and industrial relations on the input side and sales or marketing on the output side.

The major resources that the firm requires for survival include cash, labor and material. The major sources of cash are customers, stockholders and lenders. It is, therefore, the responsibility of marketing and finance to ensure the required level of cash flow in the firm. Similarly, it is the primary responsibility of industrial relations to supply the labor, and materials management and purchasing to supply the material necessary for the maintenance, growth and survival of the organization.

As Pfeffer and Salancik point out, external coalitions that control vital resources have greater control and influence over organizational activities (1978, p. 27). By extension, functional areas that negotiate vital resource exchanges will come to have greater power within the corporation as well. Thus, the dominance of production and finance in the early decades of this century may be attributed to the fact that nearly all vital resource exchanges were negotiated by these areas. The ascendance, in turn, of such subunits as industrial relations and personnel (Meyer 1980), marketing (Keith 1960),

purchasing and materials management (Keith 1960), purchasing and materials management (*Business Week* 1975) and public relations (Kotler and Mindak 1978) can be explained in part by environmental changes which increased the importance of effective and efficient resource exchanges with the relevant external coalitions. For example, the growth of unionism during the 1930s did much to enhance the role and influence of industrial relations departments in large corporations. Similarly, the improved status of sales and marketing departments during this same period may be linked to environmental changes including the depressed state of the economy, the rebirth of consumerism, and a shift in demand away from standardized "Model-T type products" (Ansoff 1979, p. 32). More recently, the OPEC oil embargo, the institutionalization of consumerism, and the expansion of government regulation into new areas (OSHA, Foreign Corrupt Practices Act, Affirmative Action, etc.) has had a similar impact on such areas as purchasing, public relations and legal.

Thus the constituency-based model views the major functional areas as specialists in providing particular resources for the firm. The primary objective of each area is to ensure an uninterrupted flow of resources from the appropriate external coalition. As functional areas tend to become specialized in dealing with particular coalitions, they tend to view these groups as constituencies both to be served and managed. From this perspective, the chief responsibility of the marketing area is to satisfy the long-term needs of its customer coalition. In short, it must strive to implement the marketing concept (Keith 1960, Levitt 1960, McKitterick 1957).

Of course, in seeking to achieve its own objectives, each functional area is constrained by the objectives of the other departments. In attempting to assure maximal consumer satisfaction as a means of maintaining the support of its customer coalition, marketing will be constrained by financial, technical and legal considerations imposed by the other functional areas. For example, expenditures on new product development, market research and advertising cut into the financial resources necessary to maintain the support of labor, supplier, creditor and investor coalitions. When these constraints are embodied in the formal performance measurement system, they exert a significant influence on the behavior of the functional areas.

In this model, firm objectives emerge as a series of Simonian constraints that are negotiated among the various functions. Those areas that specialize in the provision of crucial resources are likely to have greater power in the negotiation process. In this regard, the marketing area's desire to promote the marketing concept as a philosophy of the entire firm may be interpreted by the other functional areas as a means of gaining bargaining leverage by attempting to impress them with the survival value of customer support. The general failure of the other areas to embrace this philosophy may well reflect their belief in the importance of their own constituencies.

Recently, the marketing concept has also been called into question for contributing to the alleged malaise of American business. Hayes and Abernathy (1980) charge that excessive emphasis on marketing, research and short-term financial control measures has led to the decline of U.S. firms in world markets. They argue that American businesses are losing more and more of their markets to European and Japanese firms because of a failure to remain technologically competitive. They believe that the reli-

ance of American firms on consumer surveys and ROI control encourages a low-risk, short run investment philosophy, and point out that market research typically identifies consumers' current desires but is often incapable of determining their future wants and needs. Moreover, the short run focus of ROI measures and the analytical detachment inherent in product portfolio procedures tends to encourage investment in fast payback alternatives. Thus Hayes and Abernathy believe that American firms are reluctant to make the higher risk, longer-term investments in new technologies necessary for effective competition in world markets. They feel that the willingness of foreign firms to make such investments can be attributed to their need to look beyond their relatively small domestic markets for success. This has encouraged a reliance on technically superior products and a longer-term payoff perspective.

From a resource dependence viewpoint the Hayes and Abernathy argument seems to suggest that the external coalitions of U.S. firms are rather myopic. If the survival of the firm is truly dependent on the adoption of a longer-term perspective, one would expect this to be forced on the firm by its external coalitions. Indeed, there is ample evidence from stock market studies that investor coalitions react sharply to events affecting the longer run fortunes of firms (Lev 1974, Lorie and Hamilton 1973). Moreover, recent concessions by government, labor and supplier coalitions to Chrysler Corporation suggest a similar perspective among these groups.

However, the real problem is not a failure by internal and external coalitions in recognizing the importance of a long run investment perspective. The real difficulty lies in designing an internal performance measurement and reward system that balances the need for short run profitability against long-term survival. A number of factors combine to bias these reward and measurement systems in favor of the short run. These include:

- Requirements for quarterly and annual reports of financial performance.
- The need to appraise and reward managers on an annual basis.
- The practical difficulties of measuring and rewarding the long-term performance of highly mobile management personnel.
- Uncertainty as to the relative survival value of emphasis on short run versus long run payoffs.

As a result of these difficulties, we find that in many U.S. firms the reward system focuses on short run criteria (Ouchi 1981). This naturally leads to the use of short-term financial control measures and an emphasis on market surveys designed to measure consumer reaction to immediate (and often minor) product improvements. In some cases the marketing area has adopted this approach in the name of the marketing concept.

However, as Levitt (1960) noted more than two decades ago, the real lesson of the marketing concept is that successful firms are able to recognize the fundamental and enduring nature of the customer needs they are attempting to satisfy. As numerous case studies point out, it is the *technology* of want satisfaction that is transitory. The long-run investment perspective demanded by Hayes and Abernathy is essential for a firm that focuses its attention on transportation rather than trains, entertainment rather than motion pictures, or energy rather than oil. The real marketing concept divorces strategic thinking from an emphasis on contemporary technology and encourages investments in research and development with

long-term payoffs. Thus, the "market-driven" firms that are criticized by Hayes and Abernathy have not really embraced the marketing concept. These firms have simply deluded themselves into believing that consumer survey techniques and product portfolio procedures automatically confer a marketing orientation on their adopters. However, the fundamental insight of the marketing concept has little to do with the use of particular analytical techniques. The marketing concept is essentially a state of mind or world view that recognizes that firms survive to the extent that they meet the real needs of their customer coalitions. As argued below, one of the marketing area's chief functions in the strategic planning process is to communicate this perspective to top management and the other functional areas.

IMPLICATIONS FOR STRATEGIC PLANNING

From a strategic planning perspective, the ultimate objective of the firm may be seen as an attempt to position itself for long run survival (Wind 1979). This, in turn, is accomplished as each functional area attempts to determine the position that will ensure a continuing supply of vital resources. Thus the domestic auto industry's belated downsizing of its product may be viewed as an attempt to ensure the support of its customer coalition in the 1980s and 1990s (just as its grudging acceptance of the UAW in the late 1930s and early 1940s reflected a need to ensure a continuing supply of labor).

Of course, a firm's functional areas may not be able to occupy all of the favored long run positions simultaneously. Strategic conflicts will arise as functional areas (acting as units at the corporate level or as subunits at the divisional level) vie for the financial resources necessary to occupy their optimal long-term positions. Corporate management as the final arbiter of these disputes may occasionally favor one area over another, with deleterious results. Thus, John De Lorean, former group executive at General Motors, believes that the firm's desire for the short run profits available from larger cars was a major factor in its reluctance to downsize in the 1970s (Wright 1979). He suggests that an overwhelming financial orientation among GM's top executives consistently led them to favor short run financial gain over longer-term marketing considerations. Similarly, Hayes and Abernathy (1980) believe that the growing dominance of financial and legal specialists within the top managements of large U.S. corporations has contributed to the slighting of technological considerations in product development.

Against this backdrop marketing must realize that its role in strategic planning is not preordained. Indeed, it is possible that marketing considerations may not have a significant impact on strategic plans unless marketers adopt a strong advocacy position within the firm (Mason and Mitroff 1981). On this view, strategic plans are seen as the outcome of a bargaining process among functional areas. Each area attempts to move the corporation toward what it views as the preferred position for long run survival, subject to the constraints imposed by the positioning strategies of the other functional units.

This is not to suggest, however, that formal-analytical procedures have no rule to play in strategic planning. Indeed, as Quinn's (1981) research demonstrates, the actual process of strategy formulation in large firms is best described as a combination of the formal-analytical and power-behavioral approaches. He found that the formal planning system often provides a kind of infrastructure that assists in the strategy development and implementation process, although the formal system itself rarely generates new or innovative strategies. Moreover, the study shows that strategies tend to emerge incrementally over relatively long periods of time. One reason for this is the need for top management to obtain the support and commitment of the firm's various coalitions through constant negotiation and implied bargaining (Quinn 1981, p. 61).

Thus, from a constituency-based perspective, marketing's role in strategic planning reduces to three major activities. First, at both the corporate and divisional levels it must identify the optimal long-term position or positions that will assure customer satisfaction and support. An optimal position would reflect marketing's perception of what its customers' wants and needs are likely to be over the firm's strategic time horizon. Since this will necessarily involve long run considerations, positioning options must be couched in somewhat abstract terms. Thus the trend toward smaller cars by the domestic auto industry represents a very broad response to changing environmental, social and political forces and will likely affect the industry well into the 1990s. Other examples include the diversification into alternate energy sources by the petroleum industry, the movement toward "narrowcasting" by the major networks, and the down-sizing of the single family home by the construction industry. The length of the time horizons involved suggests that optimal positions will be determined largely by fundamental changes in demographic, economic, social and political factors. Thus strategic positioning is more likely to be guided by long-term demographic and socioeconomic research (Lazer 1977) than by surveys of consumer attitudes.

Marketing's second major strategic

planning activity involves the development of strategies designed to capture its preferred positions. This will necessarily involve attempts to gain a competitive advantage over firms pursuing similar positioning strategies. Moreover, the entire process is likely to operate incrementally. Specific strategies will focus on somewhat shorter time horizons and will be designed to move the firm toward a particular position without creating major dislocations within the firm or the marketplace (Quinn 1981). Research on consumers' current preferences must be combined with demographic and socioeconomic research to produce viable intermediate strategies. For example, Detroit's strategy of redesigning all of its subcompact lines has been combined with improved fuel efficiency in its larger cars (*Business Week* 1980).

Finally, marketing must negotiate with top management and the other functional areas to implement its strategies. The coalition perspective suggests that marketing must take an active role in promoting its strategic options by demonstrating the survival value of a consumer orientation to the other internal coalitions.

Marketing's objective, therefore, remains long run customer support through consumer satisfaction. Paradoxically, perhaps, this approach requires marketers to have an even greater grasp of the technologies, perspectives and limitations of the other functional areas. Only in this way can marketing effectively negotiate the implementation of its strategies. As noted previously, the other functional areas are likely to view appeals to the marketing concept merely as a bargaining ploy. It is the responsibility of the marketing area to communicate the true long run focus and survival orientation of this concept to the other interests in the firm. However, this cannot be accomplished if the marketing function itself does not understand the unique orientations and decision methodologies employed by other departments.

For example, the long run investment perspective implicit in the marketing concept can be made more comprehensive to the financial coalition if it is couched in the familiar terms of capital budgeting analysis. Moreover, the marketing area becomes a more credible advocate for this position if it eschews the use of short-term ROI measures as its sole criterion for internal decision analysis. At the same time, an appreciation for the inherent limitations of contemporary capital investment procedures will give the marketing area substantial leverage in the negotiation process (Anderson 1981).

In the final analysis, the constituency model of the firm suggests that marketing's role in strategic planning must be that of a strong advocate for the marketing concept. Moreover, its advocacy will be enhanced to the extent that it effectively communicates the true meaning of the marketing concept in terms that are comprehensible to other coalitions in the firm. This requires an intimate knowledge of the interests, viewpoints and decision processes of these groups. At the same time, a better understanding of the true nature of the constraints imposed by these interests will allow the marketing organization to make the informed strategic compromises necessary for firm survival.

REFERENCES

Ackoff, Russell (1970), *A Concept of Corporate Planning,* New York: John Wiley & Sons.

Anderson, Paul F. (1981), "Marketing Investment Analysis," in *Research in Marketing,* 4, Jagdish N. Sheth, ed., Greenwich, CT: JAI Press, 1–37.

Ansoff, Igor H. (1965), *Corporate Strategy,* New York: McGraw-Hill.

———(1979), "The Changing Shape of the Strategic Problem," in *Strategic Management: A View of Business Policy and Planning,* Dan E.

Schendel and Charles W. Hofer, eds., Boston: Little Brown and Company, 30–44.

Barnard, Chester I. (1938), *The Functions of the Executive,* London: Oxford University Press.

Barnea, Amir, Robert A. Haugen and Lemma W. Senbet (1981), "Market Imperfections, Agency Problems and Capital Structure: A Review," *Financial Management,* 10 (Summer), 7–22.

Boone, Louis E. and David L. Kurtz (1980), *Foundations of Marketing,* 3rd ed., Hinsdale, IL: Dryden Press.

Boston Consulting Group (1970), *The Product Portfolio,* Boston: The Boston Consulting Group.

Bower, Joseph L. (1968), "Descriptive Decision Theory from the 'Administrative' Viewpoint," in *The Study of Policy Formation,* Raymond A. Bauer and Kenneth J. Gergen, eds., New York: Collier-Macmillan, 103–148.

Business Week (1975), "The Purchasing Agent Gains More Clout," (January 13), 62–63.

———-(1980), "Detroit's New Sales Pitch," (September 22), 78–83.

Buzzell, Robert D., Bradley T. Gale and Ralph G. M. Sultan (1975), "Market Share: A Key to Profitability," *Harvard Business Review,* 53 (January–February), 97–106.

Cardozo, Richard and Yoram Wind (1980), "Portfolio Analysis for Strategic Product—Market Planning," working paper, The Wharton School, University of Pennsylvania.

Chalmers, A. F. (1978), *What Is This Thing Called Science?* St. Lucia, Australia: University of Queensland Press.

Copeland, Thomas E. and J. Fred Weston (1979), *Financial Theory and Corporate Policy,* Reading, MA: Addison-Wesley Publishing Company.

Cravens, David W., Gerald E. Hills and Robert B. Woodruff (1980), *Marketing Decision Making,* rev. ed., Homewood, IL: Richard D. Irwin.

Cyert, Richard M. and James G. March (1963), *A Behavioral Theory of the Firm,* Englewood Cliffs, NJ: Prentice-Hall.

———and Garrel Pottinger (1979), "Towards a Better Microeconomic Theory," *Philosophy of Science,* 46 (June), 204–222.

Dean, Joel (1966), "Does Advertising Belong in the Capital Budget?" *Journal of Marketing,* 30 (October), 15–21.

Dowling, John and Jeffrey Pfeffer (1975), "Orga-

nizational Legitimacy," *Pacific Sociological Review,* 18 (January), 122–36.

Fama, Eugene and Merton H. Miller (1972), *The Theory of Finance,* Hinsdale, IL: Dryden Press.

Feyerabend, Paul K. (1964), "Realism and Instrumentalism: Comments on the Logic of Factual Support," in *The Critical Approach to Science and Philosophy,* Mario Bunge, ed., London: The Free Press of Glencoe, 280–308.

Friedman, Milton (1953), "The Methodology of Positive Economics," in *Essays in Positive Economics,* Chicago: University of Chicago Press.

Glueck, William (1976), *Policy, Strategy Formation and Management Action,* New York: McGraw-Hill.

Green, Paul E. (1963), "Bayesian Decision Theory in Pricing Strategy," *Journal of Marketing,* 27 (January), 5–14.

Hayes, Robert H. and William J. Abernathy (1980), "Managing Our Way to Economic Decline," *Harvard Business Review,* 58 (July–August), 67–77.

Hempel, Carl G. (1965), *Aspects of Scientific Explanation,* New York: Macmillan Publishing Co.

Hofer, Charles W. and Dan Schendel (1978), *Strategy Formulation: Analytical Concepts,* St. Paul, MN: West Publishing Company.

Hopwood, Anthony (1976), *Accounting and Human Behavior,* Englewood Cliffs, NJ: Prentice-Hall.

Howard, John A. (1965), *Marketing Theory,* Boston: Allyn and Bacon.

Hutchinson, Kenneth D. (1952), "Marketing as a Science: An Appraisal," *Journal of Marketing,* 16 (January), 286–93.

Jensen, Michael C. and William H. Meckling (1976), "Theory of the Firm: Managerial Behavior, Agency Costs and Ownership Structure," *Journal of Financial Economics,* 3 (October), 305–60.

Keith, Robert J. (1960), "The Marketing Revolution," *Journal of Marketing,* 24 (January), 35–38.

Kotler, Philip (1971), *Marketing Decision Making,* New York: Holt, Rinehart and Winston.

———and William Mindak (1978), "Marketing and Public Relations," *Journal of Marketing,* 42 (October), 13–20.

Kuhn, Thomas S. (1970), *The Structure of Scien-*

tific Revolutions, 2nd ed., Chicago: University of Chicago Press.

Laudan, Larry (1977), *Progress and Its Problems,* Berkeley, CA: University of California Press.

Lazer, William (1977), "The 1980's and Beyond: A Perspective," *MSU Business Topics,* 25 (Spring), 21–35.

Lester, R. A. (1946), "Shortcomings of Marginal Analysis for Wage-Employment Problems," *American Economic Review,* 36 (March) 63–82.

——— (1947), "Marginalism, Minimum Wages, and Labor Markets," *American Economic Review,* 37 (March), 135–48.

Lev, Baruch (1974), *Financial Statement Analysis: A New Approach,* Englewood Cliffs, NJ: Prentice-Hall.

Levitt, Theodore (1960), "Marketing Myopia," *Harvard Business Review,* 38 (July–August), 24–47.

Lorie, James H. and Mary T. Hamilton (1973), *The Stock Market: Theories and Evidence,* Homewood, IL: Richard D. Irwin.

Machlup, Fritz (1946), "Marginal Analysis and Empirical Research," *American Economic Review,* 36 (September), 519–54.

——— (1947), "Rejoinder to an Antimarginalist," *American Economic Review,* 37 (March), 148–54.

——— (1967), "Theories of the Firm: Marginalist, Behavioral, Managerial," *American Economic Review,* 57 (March), 1–33.

March, James G. and Herbert A. Simon (1958), *Organizations,* New York: John Wiley & Sons.

Markin, Rom (1979), *Marketing,* New York: John Wiley & Sons.

Mason, Richard O. and Ian I. Mitroff (1981), "Policy Analysis as Argument," working paper, University of Southern California.

McCarthy, E. Jerome (1978), *Basic Marketing,* 6th ed., Homewood, IL: Richard D. Irwin.

McKitterick, J. B. (1957), "What Is the Marketing Management Concept?" in *Readings in Marketing 75/76,* Guilford, CT: Dushkin Publishing Group, 23–26.

Meyer, Herbert E. (1980), "Personnel Directors Are the New Corporate Heros," in *Current Issues in Personnel Management,* Kendrith M. Rowland et al., eds., Boston: Allyn & Bacon, 2–8.

Meyers, Stewart C. and Stuart M. Turnbull (1977), "Capital Budgeting and the Capital Asset Pricing Model: Good News and Bad News," *Journal of Finance,* 32 (May), 321–336.

Mintzberg, Henry (1979), "Organizational Power and Goals: A Skeletal Theory," in *Strategic Management,* Dan E. Schendel and Charles W. Hofer, eds., Boston: Little, Brown and Company.

Morgenbesser, Sidney (1969), "The Realist-Instrumentalist Controversy," in *Philosophy, Science and Method,* New York: St. Martin's Press, 200–18.

Mossman, Frank H., Paul M. Fischer and W. J. E. Crissy (1974), "New Approaches to Analyzing Marketing Profitability," *Journal of Marketing,* 38 (April), 43–48.

Newman, William H. and James P. Logan (1971), *Strategy, Policy and Central Management,* Cincinnati: South-Western Publishing Company.

Ouchi, William G. (1981), *Theory Z,* Reading, MA: Addison-Wesley.

Parsons, Talcott (1960), *Structure and Process in Modern Societies,* New York: Free Press.

Pessemier, Edgar A. (1966), *New-Product Decisions: An Analytical Approach,* New York: McGraw Hill.

Pfeffer, Jeffrey and Gerald R. Salancik (1978), *The External Control of Organizations,* New York: Harper and Row.

Popper, Karl R. (1963), *Conjectures and Refutations,* New York: Harper & Row.

Quinn, James Brian (1981), "Formulating Strategy One Step at a Time," *Journal of Business Strategy,* 1 (Winter), 42–63.

Richards, Max D. (1978), *Organizational Goal Structures,* St. Paul: West Publishing Company.

Roll, Richard (1977), "A Critique of the Asset Pricing Theory's Tests: Part I," *Journal of Financial Economics,* 4 (March), 129–76.

Ross, Stephen A. (1976), "The Arbitrage Theory of Capital Asset Pricing," *Journal of Economic Theory,* 13 (December), 341–360.

——— (1978), "The Current Status of the Capital Asset Pricing Model (CAPM)," *Journal of Finance,* 33 (June), 885–901.

Simon, Herbert A. (1955), "A Behavioral Model of Rational Choice," *Quarterly Journal of Economics,* 69 (February), 99–118.

———(1959), "Theories of Decision Making in Economics and Behavioral Science," *American Economic Review*, 49 (June), 253–83.

———(1964), "On the Concept of Organizational Goal," *Administrative Science Quarterly*, 9 (June), 1–22.

Simon, Leonard S. and Marshall Freimer (1970), *Analytical Marketing*, New York: Harcourt, Brace & World.

Solomon, Ezra (1963), *The Theory of Financial Management*, New York: Columbia University Press.

Stanton, William J. (1978), *Fundamentals of Marketing*, 5th ed., New York: McGraw-Hill.

Stigler, G. J. (1946), "The Economics of Minimum Wage Legislation," *American Economic Review*, 36 (June), 358–65.

———(1947), "Professor Lester and the Marginalists," *American Economic Review*, 37 (March), 154–57.

Vaile, Roland S. (1950), "Economic Theory and Marketing," in *Theory in Marketing*, Reavis Cox and Wroe Alderson, eds., Chicago: Richard D. Irwin.

Van Horne, James C. (1980), *Financial Management and Policy*, 5th ed., Englewood Cliffs, NJ: Prentice-Hall.

Wind, Yoram (1979), "Product Positioning and Market Segmentation: Marketing and Corporate Perspectives," working paper, The Wharton School, University of Pennsylvania.

———(1981), "Marketing and the Other Business Functions," in *Research in Marketing*, 5, Jagdish N. Sheth, ed., Greenwich, CT: JAI Press, 237–64.

Wright, Patrick J. (1979), *On a Clear Day You Can See General Motors*, Grosse Pointe, MI: Wright Enterprises.

PART TWO

Buyer Behavior

The marketing objectives of any firm are to identify potential customers and to convince them that the firm's products will satisfy their needs. These objectives imply an understanding of human behavior, especially the behavioral role of a buyer, as it relates to production, resale, or consumption. The articles in Part Two represent some of marketing's most significant attempts to analyze buyer behavior.

The normative framework for analyzing the buyer, as Alderson pointed out in Part One, is provided by economic theory. However, marketing scholars have never been satisfied with the sterility of economics. Katona led the movement to integrate economic theory and the behavioral sciences. His early paper remains the best overview of what has come to be known as "the new theory of consumer economics."

A number of marketing scholars have elaborated, with comprehensive conceptualizations, on the economic foundations of buyer behavior. Two of the best articles are included in Part Two. "The Theory of Buyer Behavior," by Howard and Sheth, presents the most widely acknowledged general model of buyer behavior; it has been extensively debated and subjected to numerous empirical tests. Webster and Wind offer an essentially similar construct but focus on the behavior of the organizational buyer rather than of the consumer. Bettman focuses on the role of memory in buyer behavior. This seminal paper has stimulated much subsequent research.

Marketing scholars are increasingly recognizing the influence of people and other factors not directly involved in the exchange transaction on its participants. Belk provides an overview of situational effects on buyer behavior.

Murphy and Staples have reconceptualized the traditional family life to bring that framework more into line with changing social trends. Similarly, Rogers' lifetime of work in the diffusion of innovations focuses attention on the dynamics of behavioral change over time. These papers have added precision to our thinking about the contexts within which buyer behavior occurs in marketing.

One of the most compelling reasons for studying buyer behavior is to group buyers with like behavior patterns into market segments. Bridging the gap between the more traditional buyer behavior work and the segmentation focus is Mitchell's report of the VALS (Values and Lifestyles) research conducted by the Stanford Research Institute. The classic segmentation work from a strategic perspective is Haley's "Benefit Segmentation" which combines various types of buyer behavior information. Finally, Trout and Reis link buyer behavior to marketing strategy through their pioneering concept of product positioning.

Rational Behavior and Economic Behavior

George Katona

While attempts to penetrate the boundary lines between psychology and sociology have been rather frequent during the last few decades, psychologists have paid little attention to the problems with which another sister discipline, economics, is concerned. One purpose of this paper is to arouse interest among psychologists in studies of economic behavior. For that purpose it will be shown that psychological principles may be of great value in clarifying basic questions of economics and that the psychology of habit formation, of motivation, and of group belonging may profit from studies of economic behavior.

A variety of significant problems, such as those of the business cycle or inflation, of consumer saving or business investment, could be chosen for the purpose of such demonstration. This paper, however,

will be concerned with the most fundamental assumption of economics, the principle of rationality. In order to clarify the problems involved in this principle, which have been neglected by contemporary psychologists, it will be necessary to contrast the most common forms of methodology used in economics with those employed in psychology and to discuss the role of empirical research in the social sciences.

THEORY AND HYPOTHESES

Economic theory represents one of the oldest and most elaborate theoretical structures in the social sciences. However, dissatisfaction with the achievements and uses of economic theory has grown considerably during the past few decades on the part of economists who are interested in what actually goes on in economic life. And yet leading sociologists and psychologists have recently declared, "Economics is today, in a theoretical sense, probably the most highly elabo-

Reprinted from *Psychological Review* (September, 1953), pp. 307–318. Copyright 1953 by the American Psychological Association.

rated, sophisticated, and refined of the disciplines dealing with action."[1]

To understand the scientific approach of economic theorists, we may divide them into two groups. Some develop an a priori system from which they deduce propositions about how people *should* act under certain assumptions. Assuming that the sole aim of businessmen is profit maximization, these theorists deduce propositions about marginal revenues and marginal costs, for example, that are not meant to be suited for testing. In developing formal logics of economic action, one of the main considerations is elegance of the deductive system, based on the law of parsimony. A wide gap separates these theorists from economic research of an empirical-statistical type which registers what they call aberrations or deviations, due to human frailty, from the norm set by theory.

A second group of economic theorists adheres to the proposition that it is the main purpose of theory to provide hypotheses that can be tested. This group acknowledges that prediction of future events represents the most stringent test of theory. They argue, however, that reality is so complex that it is necessary to begin with simplified propositions and models which are known to be unreal and not testable.[2] Basic among these propositions are the following three which traditionally have served to characterize the economic man or the rational man:

1. The principle of complete information and foresight. Economic conditions—demand, supply, prices, etc.—are not only given but also known to the rational man. This applies as well to future conditions about which there exists no uncertainty, so that rational choice can always be made. (In place of the assumption of certainty of future developments, we find nowadays more frequently the assumption that risks prevail but the probability of occurrence of different alternatives is known; this does not constitute a basic difference.)

2. The principle of complete mobility. There are no institutional or psychological factors which make it impossible, or expensive, or slow, to translate the rational choice into action.

3. The principle of pure competition. Individual action has no great influence on prices because each man's choice is independent from any other person's choice and because there are no "large" sellers or buyers. Action is the result of individual choice and is not group-determined.

Economic theory is developed first under these assumptions. The theorists then introduce changes in the assumptions so that the theory may approach reality. One such step consists, for instance, of introducing large-scale producers, monopolists, and oligopolists, another of introducing time lags, and still another of introducing uncertainty about the probability distribution of future events. The question raised in each case is this: Which of the original propositions needs to be changed, and in what way, in view of the new assumptions?

The fact that up to now the procedure of gradual approximation to reality has not been completely successful does not invalidate the method. It must be acknowledged that propositions were frequently derived from unrealistic economic models which were susceptible to testing and stimulated empirical research. In this paper, we shall point to a great drawback of this method of starting out with a simplified a priori system and making it gradually more complex and more real—by proceeding in this way one tends to lose sight of important problems and to disregard them.

The methods most commonly used in psychology may appear at first sight to be quite similar to the methods of economics which have just been described. Psychologists often start with casual observations, derive from them hypotheses, test those through more systematic observations, reformulate and revise their hypotheses accordingly, and test them again. The process of hypotheses-observations-hypotheses-observations often goes on with no end in sight. Differences from the approach of economic theory may be found in the absence in psychological research of detailed systematic elaboration prior to any observation. Also, in psychological research, findings and generalizations in one field of behavior are often considered as hypotheses in another field of behavior. Accordingly, in analyzing economic behavior[3] and trying to understand rationality, psychologists can draw on (a) the theory of learning and thinking, (b) the theory of group belonging, and (c) the theory of motivation. This will be done in this paper.

HABITUAL BEHAVIOR AND GENUINE DECISION MAKING

In trying to give noneconomic examples of "rational calculus," economic theorists have often referred to gambling. From some textbooks one might conclude that the most rational place in the world is the Casino in Monte Carlo where odds and probabilities can be calculated exactly. In contrast, some mathematicians and psychologists have considered scientific discovery and the thought processes of scientists as the best examples of rational or intelligent behavior.[4] An inquiry about the possible contributions of psychology to the analysis of rationality may then begin with a formulation of the differences between (a) associative learning and habit formation and (b) problem solving and thinking.

The basic principle of the first form of behavior is repetition. Here the argument of Guthrie holds: "The most certain and dependable information concerning what a man will do in any situation is information concerning what he did in that situation on its last occurrence."[5] This form of behavior depends upon the frequency of repetition as well as on its recency and on the success of past performances. The origins of habit formation have been demonstrated by experiments about learning nonsense syllables, lists of words, mazes, and conditioned responses. Habits thus formed are to some extent automatic and inflexible.

In contrast, problem-solving behavior has been characterized by the arousal of a problem or question, by deliberation that involves reorganization and "direction," by understanding of the requirements of the situation, by weighing of alternatives and taking their consequences into consideration and, finally, by choosing among alternative courses of action.[6] Scientific discovery is not the only example of such procedures; they have been demonstrated in the psychological laboratory as well as in a variety of real-life situations. Problem solving results in action which is new rather than repetitive; the actor may have never behaved in the same way before and may not have learned of any others having behaved in the same way.

Some of the above terms, defined and analyzed by psychologists, are also being used by economists in their discussion of rational behavior. In discussing, for example, a manufacturer's choice between erecting or not erecting a new factory, or raising or not raising his prices or output, reference is usually made to deliberation and to taking the consequences of alternative choices into consideration. Nevertheless, it is not justified to identify problem-solving behavior with rational behavior. From the point of view of an outside observer, habitual behavior may prove to be fully rational or the most appropriate way of action under certain circumstances. All that is claimed here is that the analysis of two forms of behavior—habitual versus genuine decision making—may serve to clarify problems of rationality. We shall proceed therefore by deriving six propositions from the psychological principles. To some extent, or in certain fields of behavior, these are findings or empirical generalizations to some extent, or in other fields of behavior, they are hypotheses.

1. Problem-solving behavior is a relatively rare occurrence. It would be incorrect to assume that everyday behavior consistently manifests such features as arousal of a problem, deliberation, or taking consequences of the action into consideration. Behavior which does not manifest these characteristics predominates in everyday life and in economic activities as well.

2. The main alternative to problem-solving behavior is not whimsical or impulsive behavior (which was considered the major example of "irrational" behavior by nineteenth-century philosophers). When genuine decision making does not take place, habitual behavior is the most usual occurrence: people act as they have acted before under similar circumstances, without deliberating and choosing.

3. Problem-solving behavior is recognized most commonly as a deviation from habitual behavior. Observance of the established routine is abandoned when in driving home from my office, for example, I learn that there is a parade in town and choose a different route, instead of automatically taking the usual one. Or, to mention an example of economic behavior: Many businessmen have rules of thumb concerning the timing for reorder of merchandise; yet sometimes they decide to place new orders even though their inventories have not reached the usual level of depletion (for instance, because they anticipate price increases), or not to order merchandise even though that level has been reached (because they expect a slump in sales).

4. Strong motivational forces—stronger than those which elicit habitual behavior—must be present to call forth problem-solving behavior. Being in a "crossroad situation," facing "choice points," or perceiving that something new has occurred are typical instances in which we are motivated to deliberate and choose. Pearl Harbor and the Korean aggression are extreme examples of "new" events; economic behavior of the problem-solving type was found to have prevailed widely after these events.

5. Group belonging and group reinforcement play a substantial role in changes of behavior due to problem solving. Many people become aware of the same events at the same time; our mass media provide the same information and often the same interpretation of events to groups of people (to businessmen, trade union members, sometimes to all Americans). Changes in behavior resulting from new events may therefore occur among very many people at the same time. Some economists[7] argued that consumer optimism and pessimism are unimportant because usually they will cancel out; in the light of sociopsychological principles, however, it is probable, and has been confirmed by recent surveys, that a change from optimistic to pessimistic attitudes, or vice versa,

sometimes occurs among millions of people at the same time.

6. Changes in behavior due to genuine decision making will tend to be substantial and abrupt, rather than small and gradual. Typical examples of action that results from genuine decisions are cessation of purchases or buying waves, the shutting down of plants or the building of new plants, rather than an increase or decrease of production by 5 or 10 percent.[8]

Because of the preponderance of individual psychological assumptions in classical economics and the emphasis placed on group behavior in this discussion, the change in underlying conditions which has occurred during the last century may be illustrated by a further example. It is related—the author does not know whether the story is true or fictitious—that the banking house of the Rothschilds, still in its infancy at that time, was one of the suppliers of the armies of Lord Wellington in 1815. Nathan Mayer Rothschild accompanied the armies and was present at the Battle of Waterloo. When he became convinced that Napoleon was decisively defeated, he released carrier pigeons so as to transmit the news to his associates in London and reverse the commodity position of his bank. The carrier pigeons arrived in London before the news of the victory became public knowledge. The profits thus reaped laid, according to the story, the foundation to the outstanding position of the House of Rothschild in the following decades.

The decision to embark on a new course of action because of new events was then made by one individual for his own profit. At present, news of a battle, or of change of government, or of rearmament programs, is transmitted in short order by press and radio to the public at large. Businessmen—the manufacturers or retailers of steel or clothing, for instance—usually receive the same news about changes in the price of raw materials or in demand, and often consult with each other. Belonging to the same group means being subject to similar stimuli and reinforcing one another in making decisions. Acting in the same way as other members of one's group or of a reference group have acted under similar circumstances may also occur without deliberation and choice. New action by a few manufacturers will, then, frequently or even usually not be compensated by reverse action on the part of others. Rather the direction in which the economy of an entire country moves—and often the world economy as well—will tend to be subject to the same influences.

After having indicated some of the contributions which the application of certain psychological principles to economic behavior may make, we turn to contrasting that approach with the traditional theory of rationality. Instead of referring to the formulations of nineteenth-century economists, we shall quote from a modern version of the classical trend of thought. The title of a section in a recent article by Kenneth J. Arrow is "The Principle of Rationality." He describes one of the criteria of rationality as follows: "We can imagine the individual as listing, once and for all, all conceivable consequences of his actions in order of his preference for them."[9] We are first concerned with the expression "all conceivable consequences." This expression seems to contradict the principle of selectivity of human behavior. Yet habitual behavior is highly selective since it is based on (repeated) past experience, and problem-solving behavior likewise is highly selective since reorganization is subject to a certain direction instead of consisting of trial (and error) regarding all possible avenues of action.

Secondly, Arrow appears to identify rationality with consistency in the sense of repetition of the same choice. It is part and parcel of rational behavior, according to Arrow, that an individual "makes the same choice each time he is confronted with the same set of alternatives."[10] Proceeding in the same way on successive occasions appears, however, a characteristic of habitual behavior. Problem-solving behavior, on the other hand, is flexible. Rationality may be said to reflect adaptability and ability to act in a new way when circumstances demand it, rather than to consist of rigid or repetitive behavior.

Thirdly, it is important to realize the differences between the concepts, action, decision, and choice. It is an essential feature of the approach derived from considering problem-solving behavior that there is action without deliberate decision and choice. It then becomes one of the most important problems of research to determine under what conditions genuine decision and choice occur prior to an action. The three concepts are, however, used without differentiation in the classical theory of rationality and also, most recently, by Parsons and Shils. According to the theory of these authors, there are "five discrete choices (explicit or implicit) which every actor makes before he can act;" before there is action "a decision must always be made (explicitly or implicitly, consciously or unconsciously)."[11]

There exists, no doubt, a difference in terminology, which may be clarified by mentioning a simple case: Suppose my telephone rings: I lift the receiver with my left hand and say, "Hello." Should we then argue that I made several choices, for instance, that I decided not to lift the receiver with my right hand and not to say, "Mr. Katona speaking"? According to our use of the terms *decision* and *choice*, my action was habitual and did not involve "taking consequences into consideration."[12] Parsons and Shils use the terms *decision* and *choice* in a different sense, and Arrow may use the terms *all conceivable consequences* and *same set of alternatives* in a different sense from the one employed in this paper. But the difference between the two approaches appears to be more far-reaching. By using the terminology of the authors quoted, and by constructing a theory of rational action on the basis of this terminology, fundamental problems are disregarded. If every action by definition presupposes decision making, and if the malleability of human behavior is not taken into consideration, a one-sided theory of rationality is developed and empirical research is confined to testing a theory which covers only some of the aspects of rationality.

This was the case recently in experiments devised by Mosteller and Nogee. These authors attempt to test basic assumptions of economic theory, such as the rational choice among alternatives, by placing their subjects in a gambling situation (a variation of poker dice) and compelling them to make a decision, namely, to play or not to play against the experimenter. Through their experiments the authors prove that "it is feasible to measure utility experimentally,"[13] but they do not shed light on the conditions under which rational behavior occurs or on the inherent features of rational behavior. Experiments in which making a choice among known alternatives is prescribed do not test the realism of economic theory.

MAXIMIZATION

Up to now we have discussed only one central aspect of rationality—means rather than ends. The end of rational behavior, according to economic theory, is maximization of profits in the case of business firms and maximization of utility in the case of people in general.

A few words, first, on maximizing profits. This is usually considered the simpler case because it is widely held (*a*) that business firms are in business to make profits and (*b*) that profits, more so than utility, are a quantitative, measurable concept.

When empirical research, most commonly in the form of case studies, showed that businessmen frequently strove for many things in addition to profits or in place of profits, most theorists were content with small changes in their systems. They redefined profits so as to include long-range profits and what has been called nonpecuniary or psychic profits. Striving for security or for power was identified with striving for profits in the more distant future; purchasing goods from a high bidder who was a member of the same fraternity as the purchaser, rather than from the lowest bidder— to cite an example often used in textbooks— was thought to be maximizing of nonpecuniary profits. Dissatisfaction with this type of theory construction is rather widespread. For example, a leading theorist wrote recently:

> If *whatever* a business man does is explained by the principle of profit maximization—because he does what he likes to do, and he likes to do what maximizes the sum of his pecuniary and nonpecuniary profits—the analysis acquires the character of a system of definitions and tautologies, and loses much of its value as an explanation of reality.[14]

The same problem is encountered regarding maximization of utility. Arrow defines rational behavior as follows: "... among all the combinations of commodities an individual can afford, he chooses that combination which maximizes his utility or satisfaction"[15] and speaks of the "traditional identification of rationality with maximization of some sort."[16] An economic theorist has recently characterized this type of definition as follows:

> The statement that a person seeks to maximize utility is (in many versions) a tautology: it is impossible to conceive of an observational phenomenon that contradicts it. . . . What if the theorem is contradicted by observation: Samuelson says it would not matter much in the case of utility theory; I would say that it would not make the slightest difference. For there is a free variable in his system: the tastes of consumers. . . . Any contradiction of a theorem derived from utility theory can always be attributed to a change of tastes, rather than to an error in the postulates or logic of the theory.[17]

What is the way out of this difficulty? Can psychology, and specifically the psychology of motivation, help? We may begin by characterizing the prevailing economic theory as a single-motive theory and contrast it with a theory of multiple motives. Even in case of a single decision of one individual, multiplicity of motives (or of vectors or forces in the field), some reinforcing one another and some conflicting with one another, is the rule rather than the exception. The motivational patterns prevailing among different individuals making the same decision need not be the same; the motives of the same individual who is in the same external situation at different times may likewise differ. This approach opens the way (*a*) for a study of the relation of different motives to different forms of behavior and (*b*) for an investigation of changes in motives. Both problems are disregarded by postulating a single-motive theory and by restricting empirical studies to attempts to confirm or contradict that theory.

The fruitfulness of the psychological approach may be illustrated first by a brief reference to business motivation. We may rank the diverse motivational patterns of businessmen by placing the striving for high immediate profits (maximization of short-run profits, to use economic terminology; charging whatever the market can bear, to use a popular expression) at one extreme of the scale. At the other extreme we place the striving for prestige or power. In between we discern striving for security, for larger business volume, or for profits in the more distant future. Under what kinds of business conditions will motivational patterns tend to conform with the one or the other end of the scale? Preliminary studies would seem to indicate that the worse the business situation is, the more frequent is striving for high immediate profits, and the better the business situation is, the more frequent is striving for nonpecuniary goals.[18]

Next we shall refer to one of the most important problems of consumer economics as well as of business-cycle studies, the deliberate choice between saving and spending. Suppose a college professor receives a raise in his salary or makes a few hundred extra dollars through a publication. Suppose, furthermore, that he suggests thereupon to his wife that they should buy a television set while the wife argues that the money should be put in the bank as a reserve against a "rainy day." Whatever the final decision may be, traditional economic theory would hold that the action which gives the greater satisfaction was chosen. This way of theorizing is of little value. Under what conditions will one type of behavior (spending) and under what conditions will another type of behavior (saving) be more frequent? Psychological hypotheses according to which the strength of vectors is related to the immediacy of needs have been put to a test through nationwide surveys over the past six years.[19] On the basis of survey findings the following tentative generalization was established: Pessimism, insecurity, expectation of income declines or bad times in the near future promote saving (putting the extra money in the bank), while optimism, feeling of security, expectation of income increases, or good times promote spending (buying the televison set, for instance).

Psychological hypotheses, based on a theory of motivational patterns which change with circumstances and influence behavior, thus stimulated empirical studies. These studies, in turn, yielded a better understanding of past developments and also, we may add, better predictions of forthcoming trends than did studies based on the classical theory. On the other hand, when conclusions about utility or rationality were made on an a priori basis, researchers lost sight of important problems.[20]

DIMINISHING UTILITY, SATURATION, AND ASPIRATION

Among the problems to which the identification of maximizing utility with rationality gave rise, the measurability of utility has been prominent. At present the position of most economists appears to be that while interpersonal comparison of several consumers' utilities is not possible, and while cardinal measures cannot be attached to the utilities of one particular consumer, ordinal ranking of the utilities of each individual can be made. It is asserted that I can always say either that I prefer A to B, or that I am indifferent to having A or B, or that I prefer

B to *A*. The theory of indifference curves is based on this assumption.

In elaborating the theory further, it is asserted that rational behavior consists not only of preferring more of the same goods to less ($2 real wages to $1, or two packages of cigarettes to one package, for the same service performed) but also of deriving diminishing increments of satisfaction from successive units of a commodity.[21] In terms of an old textbook example, one drink of water has tremendous value to a thirsty traveler in a desert; a second, third, or fourth drink may still have some value but less and less so; an *n*th drink (which he is unable to carry along) has no value at all. A generalization derived from this principle is that the more of a commodity or the more money a person has, the smaller are his needs for that commodity or for money, and the smaller his incentives to add to what he has.

In addition to using this principle of saturation to describe the behavior of the rational man, modern economists applied it to one of the most pressing problems of contemporary American economy. Prior to World War II the American people (not counting business firms) owned about 45 billion dollars in liquid assets (currency, bank deposits, government bonds) and these funds were highly concentrated among relatively few families; most individual families held no liquid assets at all (except for small amounts of currency). By the end of the year 1945, however, the personal liquid-asset holdings had risen to about 140 billion dollars and four out of every five families owned some bank deposits or war bonds. What is the effect of this great change on spending and saving? This question has been answered by several leading economists in terms of the saturation principle presented above. "The rate of saving is . . . a diminishing function of the wealth the individual

holds"[22] because "the availability of liquid assets raises consumption generally by reducing the impulse to save."[23] More specifically: a person who owns nothing or very little will exert himself greatly to acquire some reserve funds, while a person who owns much will have much smaller incentives to save. Similarly, incentives to increase one's income are said to weaken with the amount of income. In other words, the strength of motivation is inversely correlated with the level of achievement.

In view of the lack of contact between economists and psychologists, it is hardly surprising that economists failed to see the relevance for their postulates of the extensive experimental work performed by psychologists on the problem of levels of aspiration. It is not necessary in this paper to describe these studies in detail. It may suffice to formulate three generalizations as established in numerous studies of goal-striving behavior:[24]

1. Aspirations are not static, they are not established once for all time.
2. Aspirations tend to grow with achievement and decline with failure.
3. Aspirations are influenced by the performance of other members of the group to which one belongs and by that of reference groups.

From these generalizations hypotheses were derived about the influence of assets on saving which differed from the postulates of the saturation theory. This is not the place to describe the extensive empirical work undertaken to test the hypotheses. But it may be reported that the saturation theory was not confirmed; the level-of-aspiration theory likewise did not suffice to explain the findings. In addition to the variable "size of liquid-asset holdings," the studies had to consider such variables as income level, income change, and saving habits. (Holders of large liquid assets are primarily people who have saved a high proportion of their income in the past!)[25]

The necessity of studying the interaction of a great number of variables and the change of choices over time leads to doubts regarding the universal validity of a one-dimensional ordering of all alternatives. The theory of measurement of utilities remains an empty frame unless people's established preferences of *A* over *B* and of *B* over *C* provide indications about their probable future behavior. Under what conditions do people's preferences give us such clues and under what conditions do they not? If at different times *A* and *B* are seen in different contexts—because of changed external conditions or the acquisition of new experiences—we may have to distinguish among several dimensions.

The problem may be illustrated by an analogy. Classic economic theory postulates a one-dimensional ordering of all alternatives; Gallup asserts that answers to questions of choice can always be ordered on a yes-uncertain (don't know)-no continuum; are both arguments subject to the same reservations? Specifically, if two persons give the same answer to a poll question (e.g., both say "Yes, I am for sending American troops to Europe" or "Yes, I am for the Taft-Hartley Act") may they mean different things so that their identical answers do not permit any conclusions about the similarity of their other attitudes and their behavior? Methodologically it follows from the last argument that yes-no questions need to be supplemented by open-ended questions to discern differences in people's level of information and motivation. It also follows that attitudes and preferences should be ascer-

tained through a multi-question approach (or scaling) which serves to determine whether one or several dimensions prevail.

ON THEORY CONSTRUCTION

In attempting to summarize our conclusions about the respective merits of different scientific approaches, we might quote the conclusions of Arrow which he formulated for social science in general rather than for economics:

> To the extent that formal theoretical structures in the social sciences have not been based on the hypothesis of rational behavior, their postulates have been developed in a manner which we may term *ad hoc*. Such propositions . . . depend, of course, on the investigator's intuition and common sense.[26]

The last sentence seems strange indeed. One may argue the other way around and point out that such propositions as "the purpose of business is to make profits" or "the best businessman is the one who maximizes profits" are based on intuition or supposed common sense, rather than on controlled observation. The main problem raised by the quotation concerns the function of empirical research. There exists an alternative to developing an axiomatic system into a full-fledged theoretical model in advance of testing the theory through observations. Controlled observations should be based on hypotheses, and the formulation of an integrated theory need not be delayed until all observations are completed. Yet theory construction is part of the process of hypothesis-observation-revised hypothesis and prediction-observation, and systematization should rely on some empirical research. The proximate aim of scientific research is a body of empirically validated generalizations and not a theory that is valid under any and all circumstances.

The dictum that "theoretical structures in the social sciences must be based upon the hypothesis of rational behavior" presupposes that it is established what rational behavior is. Yet, instead of establishing the characteristics of rational behavior a priori, we must first determine the conditions a^1, b^1, c^1 under which behavior of the type x^1, y^1, z^1, and the conditions a^2, b^2, c^2 under which behavior of the type x^2, y^2, z^2 is likely to occur. Then, if we wish, we may designate one of the forms of behavior as rational. The contributions of psychology to this process are not solely methodological; findings and principles about noneconomic behavior provide hypotheses for the study of economic behavior. Likewise, psychology can profit from the study of economic behavior because many aspects of behavior, and among them the problems of rationality, may be studied most fruitfully in the economic field.

This paper was meant to indicate some promising leads for a study of rationality, not to carry such study to its completion. Among the problems that were not considered adequately were the philosophical ones (rationality viewed as a value concept), the psychoanalytic ones (the relationships between rational and conscious, and between rational and unconscious), and those relating to personality theory and the roots of rationality. The emphasis was placed here on the possibility and fruitfulness of studying forms of rational behavior, rather than the characteristics of *the* rational man. Motives and goals that change with and are adapted to circumstances, and the relatively rare but highly significant cases of our becoming aware of problems and attempting to solve them, were found to be related to behavior that may be called truly rational.

NOTES

1. T. Parsons and E. A. Shils, (Editors), *Toward a General Theory of Action* (Cambridge, Mass.: Harvard University Press, 1951).

2. A variety of methods used in economic research differ, of course, from those employed by the two groups of economic theorists. Some research is motivated by dissatisfaction with the traditional economic theory; some is grounded in a systematization greatly different from traditional theory (the most important example of such systematization is national income accounting); some research is not clearly based on any theory; finally, some research has great affinity with psychological and sociological studies.

3. The expression "economic behavior" is used in this paper to mean behavior concerning economic matters (spending, saving, investing, pricing, etc.). Some economic theorists use the expression to mean the behavior of the "economic man," that is, the behavior postulated in their theory of rationality.

4. Reference should be made first of all to Max Wertheimer who in his book *Productive Thinking* uses the terms "sensible" and "intelligent" rather than "rational." Since we are mainly interested here in deriving conclusions from the psychology of thinking, the discussion of psychological principles will be kept extremely brief. See M. Wertheimer, *Productive Thinking* (New York: Harper, 1945); G. Katona, *Organizing and Memorizing* (New York: Columbia University Press, 1940); and G. Katona, *Psychological Analysis of Economic Behavior* (New York: McGraw-Hill, 1951), especially Chapters 3 and 4.

5. E. R. Guthrie, *Psychology of Learning* (New York: Harper, 1935), p. 228.

6. Cf. the following statement by a leading psychoanalyst: "Rational behavior is behavior that is effectively guided by an understanding of the situation to which one is reacting." French adds two steps that follow the choice between alternative goals, namely, commitment to a goal and commit-

ment to a plan to reach a goal. See T. M. French, *The Integration of Behavior* (Chicago: University of Chicago Press, 1952).

7. J. M. Keynes, *The General Theory of Employment, Interest and Money* (New York: Harcourt, Brace, 1936), p. 95.

8. Some empirical evidence supporting these six propositions in the area of economic behavior has been assembled by the Survey Research Center of the University of Michigan. See G. Katona, "Psychological Analysis of Business Decisions and Expectations," *American Economic Review* (1946), pp. 44–63.

9. K. J. Arrow, "Mathematical Models in the Social Sciences," in D. Lerner and H. D. Lasswell (Editors), *The Policy Sciences* (Stanford: Stanford University Press, 1951), p. 135.

10. In his recent book Arrow adds after stating that the economic man "will make the same decision each time he is faced with the same range of alternatives": "The ability to make consistent decisions is one of the symptoms of an integrated personality." See K. J. Arrow, *Social Choice and Individual Values* (New York: Wiley, 1951), p. 2.

11. T. Parsons and E. A Shils, *op. cit.*

12. If I have reason not to make known that I am at home, I may react to the ringing of the telephone by fright, indecision, and deliberation (should I lift the receiver or let the telephone ring?) instead of reacting in the habitual way. This is an example of problem-solving behavior characterized as deviating from habitual behavior. The only example of action mentioned by Parsons and Shils, "a man driving his automobile to a lake to go fishing," may be habitual or may be an instance of genuine decision making.

13. F. Mosteller and P. Nogee, "An Experimental Measurement of Utility," *Journal of Political Economy* (1951), pp. 371–405.

14. F. Machlup, "The Marginal Analysis and Empirical Research," *American Economic Review* (1946), p. 526.

15. K. J. Arrow, *op cit.*

16. K. J. Arrow, *Social Choice and Individual Values* (New York: Wiley, 1951). The quotation refers specifically to Samuelson's definition but also applies to that of Arrow.

17. G. J. Stigler, "Review of P. A. Samuelson's Foundations of Economic Analysis," *Journal of American Statistical Association* (1984), p. 603.

18. G. Katona, *Psychological Analysis of Economic Behavior* (New York: McGraw-Hill, 1951), pp. 193–213.

19. In the Surveys of Consumer Finances, conducted annually since 1946 by the Survey Research Center of the University of Michigan for the Federal Reserve Board and reported in the *Federal Reserve Bulletin*. See a forthcoming publication of the Survey Research Center on consumer buying and inflation during 1950–52.

20. It should not be implied that the concepts of utility and maximization are of no value for empirical research. Comparison between maximum utility as determined from the vantage point of an observer with the pattern of goals actually chosen (the "subjective maximum"), which is based on insufficient information, may be useful. Similar considerations apply to such newer concepts as "minimizing regrets" and the "minimax."

21. This principle of diminishing utility was called a "fundamental tendency of human nature" by the great nineteenth century economist, Alfred Marshall.

22. G. Haberler, *Prosperity and Depression*, 3rd ed. (Geneva: League of Nations, 1941), p. 199.

23. The last quotation is from the publication of the U.S. Department of Commerce, *Survey of Current Business*, May 1950, p. 10.

24. K. Lewin et al., "Level of Aspiration," in J. Hunt (Editor), *Personality and the Behavior Disorders* (New York: Ronald, 1944).

25. The empirical work was part of the economic behavior program of the Survey Research Center under the direction of the author.

26. K. J. Arrow, "Mathematical Models in the Social Sciences," in D. Lerner and H. D. Lasswell (Editors), *The Policy Sciences* (Stanford: Stanford University Press, 1951), p. 137.

A Theory of Buyer Behavior

John A. Howard and Jagdish N. Sheth

In the last fifteen years, considerable research on consumer behavior both at the conceptual and empirical levels has accumulated. This can be gauged by reviews of the research.[1] As a consequence we believe that sufficient research exists in both the behavioral sciences and consumer behavior to attempt a comprehensive theory of buyer behavior. Furthermore, broadly speaking, there are two major reasons at the basic research level which seem to have created the need to take advantage of this opportunity. The first reason is that a great variety exists in today's effort to understand the consumer, and unfortunately there is no integration of this variety. The situation resembles the seven blind men touching different parts of the elephant and making inferences about the animal which differ,

and occasionally contradict one another. A comprehensive theory of buyer behavior would hopefully not only provide a framework for integrating the existing variety but also would prepare the researcher to adopt appropriate research designs which would control sources of influences other than those he is immediately interested in. The difficulty of replicating a study and the possibility of getting contradictory findings will be minimized accordingly.

The second major basic research reason for a comprehensive theory is the potential application of research in buying behavior to human behavior in general. In asserting the need to validate psychological propositions in a real world context Sherif has repeatedly and eloquently argued for applied research.[2] Also, McGuire argues that social psychology is moving toward theory-oriented research in *settings* because a number of forces are encouraging the movement away from laboratory research, and he cites the current work in buyer behavior as one of these forces.[3]

Reprinted from Reed Moyer (ed.), *Changing Marketing Systems . . . Consumer, Corporate and Government Interfaces: Proceedings of the 1967 Winter Conference of the American Marketing Association*, 1967, published by the American Marketing Association.

Again, one way that we can contribute to "pure" areas of behavioral science is by attempting a comprehensive theory which would help to identify and to iron out our own inconsistencies and contradictions. Such an attempt looks ambitious on the surface, but after several years of work and drawing upon earlier work,[4] we are confident that it can be achieved.

A BRIEF SUMMARY OF THE THEORY

Before we describe each component of the theory in detail, it will be helpful to discuss briefly the essentials of our view of the consumer choice process.

Much of buying behavior is more or less repetitive brand choice decisions. During his life cycle, the buyer establishes purchase cycles for various products which determine how often he will buy a given product. For some products, this cycle is very lengthy, as for example in buying durable appliances, and, therefore, he buys the product quite infrequently. For many other products, however, the purchase cycle is short and he buys the product frequently as is the case for many grocery and personal care items. Since there is usually the element of repeat buying, we must present a theory which incorporates the dynamics of purchase behavior over a period of time if we wish to capture the central elements of the empirical process.

In the face of repetitive brand choice decisions, the consumer simplifies his decision process by storing relevant information and routinizing his decision process. What is crucial, therefore, is to identify the elements of decision making, to observe the structural or substantive changes that occur in them over time due to the repetitive nature, and show how a combination of the decision elements affect search processes and the incorporation of information from the buyer's commercial and social environment.

The buyer, having been motivated to buy a product class, is faced with a brand choice decision. The elements of his decision are: (1) a set of motives, (2) several courses of action, and (3) decision mediators by which the motives are matched with the alternatives. Motives are specific to a product class, and they reflect the underlying needs of the buyer. The alternative courses of actions are the purchase of one of the various brands with their potential to satisfy the buyer's motives. There are two important notions involved in the definition of alternatives as brands. First, the brands which are alternatives of the buyer's choice decision at any given time are generally a small number, collectively called his "evoked set." The size of the evoked set is only two or three, a fraction of the brands he is aware of and still smaller fraction of the total number of brands actually available in the market. Second, any two consumers may have quite different alternatives in their evoked sets.

The decision mediators are a set of rules that the buyer employs to match his motives and his means of satisfying those motives. They serve the function of ordering and structuring the buyer's motives and then ordering and structuring the various brands based on their potential to satisfy these ordered motives. The decision mediators develop by the process of learning about the buying situation. They are, therefore, influenced by information from the buyer's environment and even more importantly by the actual experience of purchasing and consuming the brand.

When the buyer is just beginning to purchase a product class such as when a purchase is precipitated by a change in his life cycle, he lacks experience. In order, therefore, to develop the decision mediators, he *actively seeks information* from his commercial and social environments. The information that he either actively seeks or accidentally receives is subject to perceptual processes which not only limit the intake of information (magnitude of information is affected) but modify it to suit his own frame of reference (quality of information is affected). These modifications are significant since they distort the neat "marketing stimulus-customer response" relation.

Along with active search for information, the buyer may, to some extent, generalize from past similar experiences. Such generalization can be due to physical similarity of the new product class to the old product class. For example, in the initial purchases of Scotch whiskey, the buyer may generalize his experiences in buying of gin. Generalization can also occur even when the two product classes are physically dissimilar but have a common meaning such as deriving from a company-wide brand name. For example, the buyer could generalize his experiences in buying a refrigerator or range to his first purchase of a dishwasher of the same brand.

Whatever the source, the buyer develops sufficient decision mediators to enable him to choose a brand which seems to have the best potential for satisfying his motives. If the brand proves satisfactory, the potential of that brand to satisfy his motives is increased. The result is that the probability of buying that brand is likewise increased. With repeated satisfactory purchases of one or more brands, the buyer is likely to manifest a routinized decision process whereby the sequential steps in buying are well structured so that some event which triggers the process may actually complete the choice decision. Routinized purchasing implies that his decision mediators are well established and that the buyer has strong brand preferences.

The phase of repetitive decision making, in which the buyer reduces the complexity of a buying situation with the help of information and experience, is called the *psychology of simplification*. Decision making can be divided into three stages and used to illustrate the psychology of simplification: Extensive Problem Solving, Limited Problem Solving and Routinized Response Behavior. The further he is along in simplifying his environment, the less is the tendency toward active search behavior. The environmental stimuli related to the purchase situation become more meaningful and less ambiguous. Furthermore, the buyer establishes more cognitive consistency among the brands as he moves toward routinization and the incoming information is then screened both with regard to its magnitude and quality. He becomes less attentive to stimuli which do not fit his cognitive structure and he distorts those stimuli which are forced upon him.

A surprising phenomenon, we believe, occurs in many instances of frequently purchased products such as in grocery and personal care items. The buyer, after attaining routinization of his decision process, may find himself in too simple a situation. He is likely to feel the monotony or boredom associated with such repetitive decision making. It is also very likely that he is dissatisfied with even the most preferred brand. In both cases, he may feel that all existing alternatives including the preferred brand are unacceptable. He therefore feels a need to *complicate* his buying situation by considering new brands, and this process can be called the *psychology of complication*. The new situation causes him to identify a new brand, and so he begins again to simplify in the manner described earlier. Thus with a frequently purchased item buying is a continuing process with its ups and downs in terms of information seeking analogous to the familiar cyclical fluctuations in economic activity.

ELEMENTS OF THEORY

Any theory of human behavior needs some means for explaining individual differences. The marketing manager also is interested in differentiated masses of buyers. He wants to understand and separate individual differences so that he can classify or segment the total market based upon individual differences. By understanding the psychology of the individual buyer we may achieve this classification. Depending on the internal state of the buyer, a given stimulus may result in a given response. For example, one buyer who urgently needs a product may respond to the ad of a brand in that product class by buying it whereas another buyer who does not need the product may simply notice the ad and store the information or ignore the ad. A construct such as "level of motivation" will then explain the divergent reactions to the same stimulus. Alternatively, two buyers may both urgently need a product, but they buy two different brands. This can be explained by another construct: predisposition toward a brand.

Figure 7-1 represents the theory of buyer behavior. The central rectangular box isolates the various internal state variables and processes which combined together show the state of the buyer. The inputs to the rectangular box are the stimuli from the marketing and social environments. The outputs are a variety of responses that the buyer is likely to manifest based on the interaction between the stimuli and his internal state. Besides the inputs and outputs, there are a set of seven influences which affect the variables in the rectangular box.[5] These variables appear at the top of the diagram and are labelled "exogenous variables." Their function is to provide a means of adjusting for the interpersonal differences discussed above. The variables within the rectangular box serve the role of endogenous variables in the sense that changes in them are explained but they are something less than endogenous variables. They are not well defined and hence are not measurable. They are hypothetical constructs. Their values are inferred from relations among the output intervening variables. Several of the exogenous variables such as personality, social class and culture have traditionally been treated as part of the endogenous variables. We believe that they affect more specific variables, and by conceptualizing their effect as via the hypothetical constructs, we can better understand their role.

Thus it will be seen that the theory of buyer behavior has four major components; the stimulus variables, the response variable, the hypothetical constructs and the exogenous variables. We will elaborate on each of the components below both in terms of their substance and their interrelationships.

Stimulus Variables

At any point in time, the hypothetical constructs which reflect the buyer's internal state are affected by numerous stimuli from the environment. The environment is classified as Commercial or Social. The commercial environment is the marketing activities of various firms by which they attempt to communicate to the buyer. From the buyer's point of view, these communications basically come either via the physical brands themselves or some linguistic or pictorial representations of the attributes of the brands. If the elements of the brands such as price, quality, service, distinctiveness or availability are communicated through the physical brands (significates) then the stimuli are defined and classified as significative

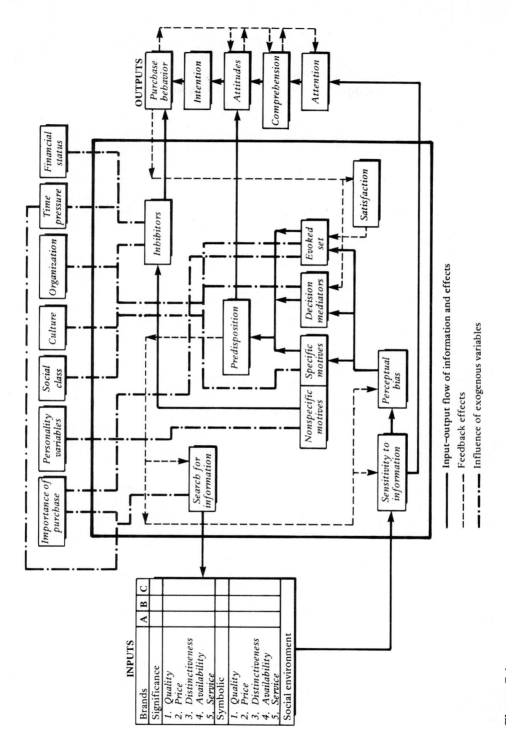

Figure 7-1
A Theory of Buyer Behavior

stimuli. If, on the other hand, the attributes are communicated in linguistic or pictorial symbols such as in mass media, billboards, catalogs, salesmen, etc., then the stimuli from commercial stores are classified as symbolic stimuli. We view the marketing mix as the optimum allocation of funds between the two major channels of communication—significative or symbolic—to the buyer.

Each commercial input variable is hypothesized to be multivariate. Probably the five major dimensions of a brand—price, quality, distinctiveness, availability and service—summarize the various attributes. The same dimensions are present in both significative or symbolic communication which become the input stimuli for the buyer. However, certain dimensions may be more appropriately conveyed by significative rather than symbolic communication and vice versa. For example, price is easily communicated by both channels; shape may best be communicated by two-dimensional pictures rather than verbal communication. Finally, size may not be easily communicated by any symbolic representation: the physical product (significate) may be necessary.

The third stimulus input variable is social stimuli. It refers to the information that the buyer's social environment provides regarding a purchase decision. The most obvious is word of mouth communication.

The inputs to the buyer's mental state from the three major sources are then processed and stored by their interaction with a series of hypothetical constructs, and the buyer may react immediately or later.

Hypothetical Constructs

The hypothetical constructs and their interrelationships are the result of an integration of Hull's learning theory,[6] Osgood's cognitive theory,[7] and Berlyne's theory of exploratory behavior[8] along with other ideas.

We may classify the constructs into two classes: (i) those that have to do with perception, and (ii) those having to do with learning. Perceptual constructs serve the function of information processing while the learning constructs serve the function of concept formation. It is interesting that, after years of experience in advertising, Reeves has a very similar classification:[9] his "penetration" is analogous to perceptual variables and his "unique selling propositions" is analogous to learning variables. We will at first describe the learning constructs since they are the major components of decision making; the perceptual constructs which serve the important role of obtaining and processing information are more complex and will be described later.

Learning Constructs. The learning constructs are labeled as: (1) Motives—Specific and Nonspecific, (2) Brand Potential of Evoked Set, (3) Decision Mediators, (4) Predisposition toward the brands, (5) Inhibitors, and (6) Satisfaction with the purchase of the brand.

Motive is the impetus to action. Motives or goals may be thought of as constituting a means-end chain and hence, as being general or specific depending upon their position in the chain. Motives can refer to the buyer's specific goals in purchasing a product class. The buyer is motivated by the expectation or anticipation due to past learning of outcome from the purchase of each of the brands in his evoked set.

The specific motives—lower level motives in the means-end chain—are very closely anchored to the attributes of a product class and in this way they become purchase criteria. Examples of specific motives for buying a dietary product such as Metrecal or Sego are low calories, nutrition, taste, and value.

Very often, several specific motives are nothing more than indicators of some underlying more general motive, that is, some motive that is higher in the means-end chain. In the above example, the specific motives of nutrition and low calories might be merely indicators of the common motive of good health.

Motives also serve the important function of raising the buyer's general motivational state or arousal and thereby tuning up the buyer, causing him to pay attention to environmental stimuli. Examples of nonspecific motives are probably anxiety, fear, many of the personality variables such as authoritarianism, exhibitionism, aggressiveness, etc., and social motives of power, status, prestige, etc. Although they are nonspecific, they are not innate, but rather learned, mostly due to acculturation. The nonspecific motives also possess a hierarchy within themselves. For example, anxiety is considered to be the source of another motive, that of the need of money.[10]

Brand Potential of Evoked Set is the second learning construct. A buyer who is familiar with a product class has an evoked set of alternatives to satisfy his motives. The elements of his evoked set are some of the brands that make up the product class. The concept is important because for this buyer the brands in his evoked set constitute competition for the seller.

A brand is, of course, a class concept like many other objects or things. The buyer attaches a *word* to this concept—a label—which is the brand name such as "Campbell's Tomato Soup." Whenever he sees a can of Campbell's Tomato Soup or hears the phrase, the image conveys to him certain satisfactions, procedures for preparation, etc. In short, it conveys certain meaning including its potential to satisfy his motives.

Various brands in the buyer's evoked set will generally satisfy the goal structure differently. One brand may possess potential to the extent that it is an ideal brand for the buyer. Another brand, on the other hand, may satisfy motives just enough to be part of his evoked set. By the process of learning the buyer obtains and stores knowledge regarding each brand's potential and then rank orders them in terms of their want-satisfying potential. The evoked set, in short, is a set of alternatives with each alternative's payoff. Predisposition mentioned below enables the buyer to choose one among them.

Decision-Mediator is the third learning construct and it brings together motives and alternatives. The brand potential of each of the brands in his evoked set are the decision alternatives with their payoffs. Decision mediators are the buyer's mental rules for matching the alternatives with his motives, for rank-ordering them in terms of their want-satisfying capacity. As mental rules, they exhibit reasons wherein the cognitive elements related to the alternatives and the motives are structured. The words that he uses to describe these attributes are also the words that he thinks with and that he finds are easy to remember. The criterial attributes are important to the manufacturer because if he knows them he can deliberately build into his brand and promotion those characteristics which will differentiate his brand from competing brands.

The decision mediators thus represent enduring cognitive rules established by the process of learning, and their function is to obtain meaningful and congruent relations among brands so that the buyer can manifest goal-directed behavior. The aim of the theory of buyer behavior is not just the identification of motives and the respective brands but to show their structure as well. It is the decision mediators which provide this structure.

In view of the fact that decision mediators are learned, principles of learning become crucial in their development and change over time. There are two broad sources of learning: (1) actual experiences, and (2) information. Actual experiences can be either with the *same* buying situation in the past or with a *similar* buying situation. The latter is generally labelled as generalization as discussed earlier. Similarly, information as a source of learning can be from: (1) the buyer's commercial environment, or (2) his social environment. Later, we will elaborate on each of the sources of learning.

Predisposition, the fourth construct, is the summary effect of the previous three constructs. It refers to the buyer's preference toward brands in his evoked set. It is, in fact, an aggregate index which is reflected in attitude which, in turn, is measured by attitude scales. It might be visualized as the "place" where brands in Evoked Set are compared with Mediator's choice criteria to yield a judgment on the relative contribution of the brands to the buyer's motives. This judgment includes not only an estimate of the value of the brand to him but also an estimate of the confidence with which he holds that position. This uncertainty aspect of Predisposition can be called "brand ambiguity," in that, the more confident he holds it, the less ambiguous is the connotative meaning of the brand to the buyer and the more likely he is to buy it.[11]

Inhibitors, the fifth learning construct, are forces in the environment which create important disruptive influences in the actual purchase of a brand even when the buyer has reasoned out that that brand will best satisfy his motives. In other words, when the buyer is both predisposed to buy a brand and has the motivation to buy some brand in the product class, he may not buy it because several environmental forces inhibit its purchase and prevent him from satisfying his preferences.

We postulate at least four types of inhibitors. They are: (1) high price of the brand; (2) lack of availability of the brand, (3) time pressure on the buyer, and (4) the buyer's financial status. The first two are part of the environmental stimuli, and therefore, they are part of the input system. The last two come from the two exogenous variables of the same name. It should be pointed out that social constraints emanating from other exogenous variables may also create temporary barriers to the purchase of a brand.

An essential feature of all inhibitors is that they are *not internalized* by the buyer because their occurrence is random and strictly situational. However, some of the inhibitors may persist systematically over time as they concern a given buyer. If they persist long enough, the buyer is likely to incorporate them as part of his decision mediators and thus to internalize them. The consequence is that they may affect even the structure of alternatives and motives.

Satisfaction, the last of the learning constructs, refers to the degree of congruence between the actual consequences from purchase and consumption of a brand and what was expected from it by the buyer at the time of purchase. If the actual outcome is adjudged by the buyer as *at least* equal to the expected, the buyer will feel satisfied. If, on the other hand, the actual outcome is adjudged as less than what he expected, the buyer will feel dissatisfied and his attitude will be less favorable. Satisfaction or dissatisfaction with a brand can exist with respect to any one of the different attributes. If the brand proves more satisfactory than he expected, the buyer has a tendency to enhance the attractiveness of the brand. Satisfaction will, therefore, affect the reordering of the brands in the evoked set for the next buying decision.

Relations among Learning Constructs.
Underlying Predisposition toward the brands and related variables, several important notions are present. The simplest way to describe them is to state that we may classify a decision process as either Extensive Problem Solving, Limited Problem Solving or Routinized Response Behavior depending on the strength of Predisposition toward the brands. In the early phases of buying, the buyer has not yet developed decision mediators well enough; specifically his product class concept is not well formed and predisposition is low. As he acquires information and gains experience in buying and consuming the brand, Decision Mediators become firm and Predisposition toward a brand is generally high.

In Extensive Problem Solving, Predisposition toward the brands is low. None of the brands is discriminated enough based on their criterial attributes for the buyer to show greater brand preference toward any one brand. At this state of decision making, brand ambiguity is high with the result that the buyer actively seeks information from his environment. Due to greater search for information, there exists a greater *latency of response*—the time interval from the initiation of a decision to its completion. Similarly, deliberation or reasoning will be high since he lacks a well-defined product class concept which is the denotative aspect of mediator. He is also likely to consider many brands as part of Evoked Set, and stimuli coming from the commercial environment are less likely to trigger any immediate purchase reaction.

When Predisposition toward the brands is moderate, the buyer's decision process can be called Limited Problem Solv-ing. There still exists brand ambiguity since the buyer is not able to discriminate and compare brands so that he may prefer one brand over others. He is likely to seek information but not to the extent that he seeks it in Extensive Problem Solving. More importantly, he seeks information more on a relative basis to compare and discriminate various brands rather than to compare them absolutely on each of the brands. His deliberation or thinking is much less since Decision Mediators are tentatively well defined. Evoked Set will consist of a small number of brands, each having about the same degree of preference.

In Routinized Response Behavior, the buyer will have a high level of Predisposition toward brands in his evoked set. Furthermore, he has now accumulated sufficient experience and information to have little brand ambiguity. He will in fact discriminate among brands enough to show a strong preference toward one or two brands in the evoked set. He is unlikely to actively seek any information from his environment since such information is not needed. Also, whatever information he passively or accidentally receives, he will subject it to selective perceptual processes so that only congruent information is allowed. Very often, the congruent information will act as "triggering cues" to motivate him to manifest purchase behavior. Much of impulse purchase, we believe, is really the outcome of a strong predisposition and such a facilitating commercial stimulus as store display. The buyer's evoked set will consist of a few brands toward which he is highly predisposed. However, he will have greater preference toward one or two brands in his evoked set and less toward others.

As mentioned earlier, Predisposition is an aggregate index of decision components. Thus, any changes in the components due to learning from experience or information imply some change in Predisposition. The greater the learning, the more the predisposition toward the brands in the evoked set. The exact nature of learning will be described later when we discuss the dynamics of buying behavior.

Perceptual Constructs. Another set of constructs serves the function of information procurement and processing relevant to a purchase decision. As mentioned earlier, information can come from any one of the three stimulus inputs—significative commercial stimuli, symbolic commercial stimuli, and social stimuli. Once again we will here only describe the constructs; their utilization by the buyer will be explained when we discuss the dynamics of buying behavior. The perceptual constructs in Figure 7–1 are: (a) Sensitivity to Information, (b) Perceptual Bias, and (c) Search for Information.

A perceptual phenomenon implies either ignoring a physical event which could be a stimulus, seeing it attentively or sometimes imagining what is not present in reality. All perceptual phenomena essentially create some change in quantity or quality of objective information.

Sensitivity to Information refers to the opening and closing of sensory receptors which control the intake of information. The manifestation of this phenomenon is generally called perceptual vigilance (paying attention) or perceptual defense (ignoring the information). Sensitivity to Information, therefore, primarily serves as a gatekeeper to information entering into the buyer's mental state. It thus controls the quantity of information input.

Sensitivity to Information, according to Berlyne,[12] is a function of the degree of ambiguity of the stimuli to which the buyer is exposed. If the stimulus is very familiar or too simple, the ambiguity is low and the buyer will not pay attention unless he is predisposed to such information from past learning. Furthermore, if ambiguity of the stimulus continues to be low, the buyer feels a sense of monotony and actually seeks other information, and this act can be said to *complicate* his environment. If the stimulus is very complex and ambiguous, the buyer finds it hard to comprehend and, therefore, he ignores it by resorting to perceptual defense. Only if the stimulus is in the moderate range of ambiguity is the buyer motivated to pay attention and to freely absorb the objective information.

In a single communication, the buyer may at first find the communication complex and ambiguous and so he will resort to perceptual defense and tend to ignore it. As some information enters, however, he finds that it is really at the medium level of ambiguity and so pays attention. On the other hand, it might be that the more he pays attention to it, the more he finds the communication too simple and, therefore, ignores it as the process of communication progresses.

A second variable which governs Sensitivity to Information is the buyer's predisposition toward the brand about which the information is concerned. The more interesting the information, the more likely the buyer is to open up his receptors and therefore to pay attention to the information. Hess has recently measured this by obtaining the strength of pupil dilation.

Perceptual Bias is the second perceptual construct. The buyer not only selectively attends to information, but he may actually distort it once it enters his mental state. In other words, quality of information can be altered by the buyer. This aspect of the perceptual process is summarized in Perceptual Bias. The buyer may distort the cognitive elements contained in information to make them congruent with his own frame of reference as determined by the amount of information he already has stored. A series of cognitive consistency theories have been recently developed to explain how this congruency is established and what the consequences are in terms of the distortion of information we might expect.[13] Most of the qualitative change in information arises because of feedback from various decision components such as Motives, Evoked Set and Decision Mediators. These relations are too complex, however, to describe in the summary.

The perceptual phenomena described above are likely to be less operative if the information is received from the buyer's social environment. This is because: (i) the source of social information, such as a friend, is likely to be favorably regarded by the buyer and therefore proper, undistorted reception of information will occur, and (ii) the information itself is modified by the social environment (the friend) so that it conforms to the needs of the buyer and, therefore, further modification is less essential.

Search for Information is the third perceptual construct. During the total buying phase which extends over time and involves several repeat purchases of a product class, there are stages when the buyer *actively* seeks information. It is very important to distinguish the times when he passively receives information from the situations where he actively seeks it. We believe that perceptual distortion is less operative in the latter instances and that a commercial communication, therefore, at that stage has a high probability of influencing the buyer.

The active seeking of information occurs when the buyer senses ambiguity of the brands in his evoked set. As we saw earlier, this happens in the Extensive Problem Solving and Limited Problem Solving phases of the decision process. The ambiguity of brand exists because the buyer is not certain of the outcomes from each brand. In other words, he has not yet learned enough about the alternatives to establish an expectancy of potential of the brands to satisfy his motives. This type of brand ambiguity is essentially confined to initial buyer behavior which we have called Extensive Problem Solving. However, ambiguity may still exist despite knowledge of the potential of alternative brands. This ambiguity is with respect to his inability to discriminate because his motives are not well structured: he does not know how to order them. He may then seek information which will resolve the conflict among goals, a resolution that is implied in his learning of the appropriate product class aspect of decision mediators that we discussed earlier.

There is yet another stage of total buying behavior in which the buyer is likely to seek information. It is when the buyer has not only routinized his decision process but he is so familiar and satiated with repeat buying that he feels bored. Then, all the existing alternatives in his evoked set including the most preferred brand become unacceptable to him. He seeks change or variety in that buying situation. In order to obtain this change, he actively searches for information on other alternatives (brands) that he never considered before. At this stage, he is particularly receptive to any information about new brands. Incidentally, here is an explanation for advertising in a highly stable industry. This phenomenon has long baffled both the critics and defenders of the institution of advertising. Newcomers to the market and forgetting do not provide a plausible explanation.

We have so far described the stimulus input variables and the hypothetical constructs. Now we proceed to describe the output of the system—the responses of the buyer.

Response Variables

The complexity of buyer behavior does not stop with the hypothetical constructs. Just as there is a variety of inputs, there exists a variety of buyer responses which become relevant for different areas of marketing strategy. This variety of consumer responses can be easily appreciated from the diversity of measures to evaluate advertising effectiveness. We have attempted to classify and order this diversity of buyer responses in the output variables. Most of the output variables are directly related to some and not other constructs. Each output variable serves different purposes both in marketing practice and fundamental research. Let us at first describe each variable and then provide a rationale for their interrelationships.

Attention. Attention is related to Sensitivity to Information. It is a response of the buyer which indicates the magnitude of his information intake. Attention is measured continuously during the time interval when the buyer receives information. There are several psychophysical methods of quantifying the degree of attention that the buyer pays to a message. The pupil dilation is one.

Comprehension. Comprehension refers to the store of knowledge about the brand that the buyer possesses at any point in time. This knowledge could vary from his simply being aware of a single brand's existence to a complete description of the attributes of the product class of which the brand is an element. It reflects the denotative meaning of the brand and in that sense it is strictly in the cognitive realm. It lacks the motivational aspects of behavior. Some of the standard measures of advertising effectiveness such as awareness, aided or unaided recall, and recognition may capture different aspects of the buyer's comprehension of the brand.

Attitude toward a Brand. Attitude toward a brand is the buyer's evaluation of the brand's potential to satisfy his motives. It, therefore, includes the connotative aspects of the brand concept: it contains those aspects of the brand which are relevant to the buyer's goals. Attitude is directly related to Predisposition and so it consists of both the evaluation of a brand in terms of the criteria of choice from Mediator and the confidence with which that evaluation is held.

Intention to Buy. Intention to buy is the buyer's forecast of his brand choice some time in the future. Like any forecast, it involves assumptions about future events including the likelihood of any perceived inhibitors creating barriers over the buyer's planning horizon. Intention to buy has been extensively used in the purchases of durable goods with some recent refinements in terms of the buyer's confidence in his own forecast; these studies are in terms of broadly defined product classes.[14] We may summarize this response of the buyer as something short of actual purchase behavior.

Purchase Behavior. Purchase Behavior refers to the overt act of purchasing a brand. What becomes a part of a company's sales or what the consumer records in a diary as a panel member, however, is only the terminal act in the sequence of shopping and buying. Very often, it is useful to observe the complete movement of the buyer from his home to the store and his purchase in the store. Yoell, for example, shows several case histories where a time and motion study of consumers' purchase behavior has useful marketing implications.[15] We think that at times it may be helpful to go so far as to incorporate the act of consumption into the definition of Purchase Behavior. We have, for example, developed and used the technique of sequential decision making where the buyer verbally describes the sequential pattern of his purchase behavior in a given buying situation. Out of this description a "flow chart" of decision making is obtained which reveals the number and the structure of the decision rules that the buyer employs.

Purchase Behavior is the overt manifestation of the buyer's Predisposition in conjunction with any Inhibitors that may be present. It differs from Attitude to the extent that Inhibitors are taken into consideration. It differs from Intention to the extent that it is the actual manifestation of behavior which the buyer only forecasted in his intention.

Several characteristics of Purchase Behavior become useful if we observe the buyer in a repetitive buying situation. These include the incidence of buying a brand, the quantity bought, and the purchase cycle. Several stochastic models of brand loyalty, for example, have been developed in recent years.[16] Similarly, we could take the magnitude purchased and compare light buyers with heavy buyers to determine if heavy buyers are more loyal buyers.

Interrelationship of Response Variables.
In Figure 7–1, it will be seen that we have ordered the five response variables to create a hierarchy. The hierarchy is similar to the variety of hierarchies used in practice such as AIDA (Attention, Interest, Desire and Action), to the Lavidge and Steiner hierarchy of advertising effectiveness,[17] as well as to the different mental states that a person is alleged by the anthropologists and sociologists to pass through when he adopts an innovation.[18] There are, however, some important differences which we believe will clarify certain conceptual and methodological issues raised by Palda and others.[19]

First, we have added a response variation called Attention which is crucial since it reflects whether a communication is received by the buyer. Secondly, several different aspects of the cognitive realm of behavior such as awareness, recall, recognition, etc., are lumped into one category called Comprehension to suggest that they all are varying indicators of the buyer's storage of information about a brand which can be extended to *product class*, and in this way we obtain leverage toward understanding buyer innovation. Third, we have defined Attitude to include both affective and conative aspects since anyone who wants to establish causal relations between attitude and behavior must bring the motivational aspects into attitude. Furthermore, we separate the perceptual and the preference maps of the buyer into Comprehension and Attitude respectively. Fourth, we add another variable, Intention to Buy, because there are several product classes in both durable and semidurable goods where properly defined and measured intentions have already proved useful. To the extent that Intention incorporates the buyer's forecast of his inhibitors, it might serve the useful function of informing the firm how to remove the inhibitors before the actual purchase behavior is manifested.

Finally, and most importantly, we have incorporated several feedback effects which were described when we discussed the hypothetical constructs. We will now show the relations as direct connections among response variables but the reader should bear in mind that these "outside" relations are merely the reflection of relations among the hypothetical constructs. For example, Purchase Behavior via Satisfaction entails some consequences which affect Decision Mediators and brand potential in Evoked Set; any change in them can produce change in Predisposition. Attitude is related to Predisposition and, therefore, it can also be changed in the period from prepurchase to post-purchase. In incorporating this feedback, we are opening the way to resolving the controversy whether Attitude causes Purchase Behavior or Purchase Behavior causes Attitude. Over a period of time, the relation is interdependent, each affecting the other. Similarly, we have a feedback from Attitude to Comprehension and Attention, the rationale for which was given when we described the perceptual constructs.

DYNAMICS OF BUYING BEHAVIOR

Let us now explain the changes in the hypothetical constructs which occur due to learning.

The learning constructs are, of course, directly involved in the change that we label "learning." Since some of the learning constructs indirectly govern the perceptual constructs by way of feedbacks, there is also an indirect effect back upon the learning constructs themselves. As mentioned earlier, learning of Decision Mediators which structure Motives and Evoked Set of Brands which contain brand potentials can occur from two broad sources: (i) past experience and (ii) information. Experience can be further classified as having been derived from buying a specified product or buying some similar product. Similarly, information can come from the buyer's commercial environment or his social environment, and if commercial, it can be significative or symbolic.

We will look at the development and change in learning constructs as due to: (i) generalization from similar buying situations, (ii) repeat buying of the same product class, and (iii) information.

Generalization from Similar Purchase Situations

Some decision mediators are common across several product classes because many motives are common to a wide variety of purchasing activity. For example, a buyer may satisfy his health motive from many product classes by looking for nutrition. Similarly, many product classes are all bought at the same place which very often leads to spatial or contiguous generalization. The capacity to generalize provides the buyer with a truly enormous range of flexibility in adapting his purchase behavior to the myriad of varying market conditions he faces.

Generalization refers to the transfer of responses and of the relevance of stimuli from past situations to new situations which are similar. It saves the buyer time and effort in seeking information in the face of uncertainty that is inevitable in a new situation. Generalization can occur at any one of the several levels of purchase activity, but we are primarily interested in generalization of those decision mediators which only involve brand choice behavior in contrast to store choice or choice of shopping time and day. In other words, we are concerned with brand generalization.

Repeat Purchase Experiences

Another source of change in the learning constructs is the repeated purchase of the same product class over a period of time.

In Figure 7–1 the purchase of a brand entails two types of feedbacks, one affecting the decision mediators and the other affecting the brand potential of the evoked set. First, the experience of buying with all its cognitive aspects of memory, reasoning, etc., has a learning effect on the decision mediators. This occurs irrespective of which specific brand the buyer chooses in any one purchase decision because the decision mediators like the motives are product-specific and not limited to any one brand. Hence every purchase has an incremental effect in firmly establishing the decision mediators. This is easy to visualize if we remember that buying behavior is a series of mental and motor steps while the actual choice is only its terminal act.

Purchase of a brand creates certain satisfactions for the buyer which the consumer compares with his expectations of the brand's potential and this expectation is the basis on which he made his decision in the first place. This comparison of expected and actual consequences causes him to be satisfied or dissatisfied with his purchase of the brand. Hence, the second feedback from Purchase Behavior to Satisfaction changes the attractiveness of the brand purchased. If the buyer is satisfied with his consumption, he enhances the potential of the brand and this is likely to result in greater probability of its repeat purchase. If he is dissatisfied, the potential of the brand is diminished, and its probability of repeat purchase is also similarly reduced.

If there are no inhibitory forces which influence him, the buyer will continue to buy a brand which proves satisfactory. In the initial stages of decision making he may show some tendency to oscillate between brands in order to formulate his decision mediators. In other words, he may learn by trial-and-error at first and then settle on a brand and therefore he may buy the brand with such regularity to suggest that he is brand loyal. Unless a product is of very high risk, however, there is a limit as to how long this brand loyalty will continue: he may become bored with his preferred brand and look for something new.

Information as a Source of Learning

The third major source by which the learning constructs are changed is information from the buyer's (i) commercial environment consisting of advertising, promotion, salesmanship and retail shelf display of the competing companies, and (ii) his social environment consisting of his family, friends, reference group and social class.

We will describe the influence of information at first as if the perceptual constructs were absent. In other words, we assume that the buyer receives information with perfect fidelity as it exists in the environment. Also, we will discuss separately the information from the commercial and social environments.

Commercial Environment. The company communicates about its offerings to the buyers either by the physical brand (significates) or by symbols (pictorial or linguistic) which represent the brand. In other words, significative and symbolic communication are the two major ways of interaction between the sellers and the buyers.

In Figure 7–1, the influence of information is shown on Motives, Decision Mediators, Evoked Set, and Inhibitors. We believe that the influence of commercial information on motives (specific and nonspecific) is limited. The main effect is primarily to *intensify* whatever motives the buyer has rather than to create new ones. For example, physical display of the brand may intensify his motives above the threshold levels which combined with strong predisposition can result in impulse (unplanned) purchase. A similar reaction is possible when an ad creates sufficient intensity of motives to provide an impetus for the buyer to go to the store. A second way to influence motives is to show the *perceived instrumentality* of the brand and thereby make it a part of the buyer's defined set of alternatives. Finally, to a very limited extent, marketing stimuli may change the *content of the motives*. The general conception both among marketing men and laymen is that marketing stimuli change the buyer's motives. However, on a closer examination it would appear that what is changed is the *intensity* of buyer's motives already provided by the social environment. Many dormant or latent motives may become stimulated. The secret of success very often lies in identifying the change in motives created by social change and intensifying them as seems to be the case in the recent projection of youthfulness in many buying situations.

Marketing stimuli are also important in determining and changing the buyer's evoked set. Commercial information tells him of the existence of the brands (awareness), their identifying characteristics (Comprehension plus brand name) and their relevance to the satisfaction of the buyer's needs (Attitude).

Marketing stimuli are also important in creating and changing the buyer's decision mediators. They become important sources for learning decision mediators when the buyer has no prior experience to rely upon. In other words, when he is in the extensive problem-solving (EPS) stage, it is marketing and social stimuli which are the important sources of learning. Similarly, when the buyer actively seeks information because all the existing alternatives are unacceptable to him, marketing stimuli become important in *changing* his decision mediators.

Finally, marketing stimuli can unwittingly create inhibitors. For example, a company feels the need to emphasize price-quality association, but it may result in high-price inhibition in the mind of the buyer. Similarly, in emphasizing the details of usage and consumption of a product, the communication may create the inhibition related to time pressure.

Social Environment. The social environment of the buyer—family, friends, reference groups—is another major source of information in his buying behavior. Most of the inputs are likely to be symbolic (linguistic) although at times the physical product may be shown to the buyer.

Information from his social environment also affects the four learning constructs: Motives, Decision Mediators, Evoked Set and Inhibitors. However, the effect on these constructs is different from that of the commercial environment. First, the information about the brands will be considerably modified by the social environment before it reaches the buyer. Most of the modifications are likely to be in the nature of adding connotative meanings to brand descriptions, and of the biasing effects of the communication's perceptual variables like Sensitivity to Information and Perceptual Bias. Second, the buyer's social environment will probably have a very strong influence on the content of his motives and their ordering to establish a goal structure. Several research studies have concentrated on such influences.[20] Third, the social environment may also affect his evoked set. This will be particularly true when the buyer lacks experience. Furthermore, if the product class is important to the buyer and he is technically incompetent or uncertain in evaluating the consequences of the brand for his needs, he may rely more on the social than on the marketing environment for information. This is well documented by several studies using the perceived risk hypothesis.[21]

Exogenous Variables
Earlier we mentioned that there are several influences operating on the buyer's deci-

sions which we treat as exogenous, that is, we do not explain their formation and change. Many of these influences come from the buyer's social environment and we wish to separate the effects of his environment which have occurred in the past and are not related to a specific decision from those which are current and directly affect the decisions that occur during the period the buyer is being observed. The inputs during the observation period provide information to the buyer to help his current decision making. The past influences are already imbedded in the values of the perceptual and learning constructs. Strictly speaking, therefore, there is no need for some of the exogenous variables which have influenced the buyer in the past. We bring them out explicitly, however, for the sake of research design where the research may control or take into account individual differences among buyers due to such past influences. Incorporating the effects of these exogenous variables will reduce the size of the unexplained variance or error in estimation which it is particularly essential to control under field conditions. Figure 7–1 presents a set of exogenous variables which we believe provide the control essential to obtaining satisfactory predictive relations between the inputs and the outputs of the system. Let us briefly discuss each of the exogenous variables.

Importance of Purchase refers to differential degrees of ego-involvement or commitment in different product classes. It, therefore, provides a mechanism which must be carefully examined in interproduct studies. Importance of Purchase will influence the size of the Evoked Set and the magnitude of Search for Information. The more important the product class, the larger the Evoked Set.

Time Pressure is a current exogenous variable and, therefore, specific to a decision situation. It refers to the situation when a buyer feels pressed for time due to any of several environmental influences and so must allocate his time among alternative uses. In this process a re-allocation unfavorable to the purchasing activity can occur. Time pressure will create inhibition as mentioned earlier. It will also unfavorably affect Search for Information.

Financial Status refers to the constraint the buyer may feel because of lack of financial resources. This affects his purchase behavior to the extent that it creates a barrier to purchasing the most preferred brand. For example, a buyer may want to purchase a Mercedes-Benz but lacks sufficient financial resources and, therefore, he will settle for some low-priced American automobile such as a Ford or Chevrolet. Its effect is via Inhibitor.

Personality Traits take into consideration many of the variables such as self-confidence, self-esteem, authoritarianism and anxiety which have been researched to identify individual differences. It will be noted that these individual differences are "topic free" and, therefore, are supposed to exert their effect across product classes. We believe their effect is felt on: (i) nonspecific Motives and (ii) Evoked Set. For example, the more anxious a person, the greater the motivational arousal; dominant personalities are more likely by a small margin to buy a Ford instead of a Chevrolet; the more authoritarian a person, the narrower the category width of his evoked set.

Social and Organizational Setting (Organization) takes us to the group, to a higher level of social organization than the individual. It includes both the informal social organization such as family and reference groups which are relevant for *consumer behavior* and the formal organization which constitutes much of the environment for *industrial purchasing*. Organizational variables are those of small group interaction such as power, status and authority. We believe that the underlying process of intergroup conflicts in both industrial and consumer buying behavior are in principle very similar and that the differences are largely due to the formalization of industrial activity. Organization, both formal and social, is a crucial variable because it influences all the learning constructs.

Social Class refers to a still higher level of social organization, the social aggregate. Several indices are available to classify people into various classes. The most common perhaps is the Warner classification of people into upper-upper, lower-upper, upper-middle, lower-middle, upper-lower, and lower-lower classes. Social class mediates the relation between the input and the output by influencing: (i) specific Motives, (ii) Decision Mediators, (iii) Evoked Set, and (iv) Inhibitors. The latter influence is more important particularly in the adoption of innovations.

Culture provides an even more comprehensive social framework than social class. Culture consists of patterns of behavior, symbols, ideas and their attached values. Culture will influence Motives, Decision Mediators, and Inhibitors.

CONCLUSIONS

In the preceding pages we have summarized a theory of buyer brand choice. It is complex. We strongly believe that complexity is essential to adequately describe buying behavior, from the point of view of both marketing practice and public policy.

We hope that the theory can provide new insights into past empirical data and guide future research so as to instill with coherence and unity current research which now tends to be atomistic and unrelated. We are vigorously pursuing a large research program aimed at testing the validity of the theory. The research was designed in terms of the variables specified by the theory and our most preliminary results cause us to believe that it was fruitful to use the theory in this way. Because it specifies a number of relationships, it has clearly been useful in interpreting the preliminary findings. Above all, it is an aid in communication among the researchers and with the companies involved.

Finally, a number of new ideas are set forth in the theory, but we would like to call attention to three in particular. The concept of evoked set provides a means of reducing the noise in many analyses of buying behavior. The product class concept offers a new dimension for incorporating many of the complexities of innovations and especially for integrating systematically the idea of innovation into a framework of psychological constructs. Anthropologists and sociologists have been pretty much content to deal with peripheral variables in their investigations of innovation. The habit-perception cycle in which perception and habit respond inversely offers hope for explaining a large proportion of the phenomenon that has long baffled both the critics and defenders of advertising: large advertising expenditures in a stable market where, on the surface, it would seem that people are already sated with information.

NOTES

1. Jagdish N. Sheth, "A Review of Buyer Behavior," *Management Science*, Vol. 13 (August 1967), pp. B718–B756; John A. Howard, *Marketing Theory* (Boston, Mass.: Allyn and Bacon, 1965).
2. Musafer Sherif and Carolyn Sherif, "Interdisciplinary Coordination as a Validity

Check: Retrospect and Prospects," in M. Sherif (ed.), *Problems of Interdisciplinary Relationships in the Social Sciences* (Chicago: Aldine Publishing Company, 1968).

3. William J. McGuire, "Some Impending Reorientations in Social Psychology," *Journal of Experimental Social Psychology,* Vol. 3 (1967), pp. 124–139.

4. Patrick Suppes, *Information Processing and Choice Behavior* (Technical Paper No. 9: Institute for Mathematical Studies in the Social Sciences, Stanford University, January 31, 1966), p. 27; John A. Howard, *op. cit.*

5. Terminology in a problem area that cuts across both economics and psychology is different because each discipline has often defined its terms differently from the other. We find the economists definitions of exogenous versus endogenous, and theory versus model more useful than those of the psychologist. The psychologist's distinction of hypothetical constructs and intervening variables, however, provides a helpful breakdown of endogenous variables. Finally, for the sake of exposition we have often here not clearly distinguished between the theory and its empirical counterparts. Although this practice encourages certain ambiguities, and we lay ourselves open to the charge of reifying our theory, we believe that for most readers it will simplify the task of comprehending the material.

6. Clark C. Hull, *Principles of Behavior* (New York: Appleton-Century-Crofts, Inc., (1943); Clark C. Hull, *A Behavior System* (New Haven: Yale University Press, 1952).

7. Charles E. Osgood, "A Behavioristic Analysis of Perception and Meaning as Cognitive Phenomena," *Symposium on Cognition, University of Colorado, 1955* (Cambridge, Harvard University Press, 1957), pp. 75–119; Charles E. Osgood, "Motivational Dynamics of Language Behavior," in J. R. Jones (ed.), *Nebraska Symposium on Motivation, 1957* (Lincoln: University of Nebraska Press, 1957), pp. 348–423.

8. D. E. Berlyne, "Motivational Problems Raised by Exploratory and Epistemic Behavior," in Sigmund Koch (ed.), *Psychology: A Study of a Science,* Vol. 5 (New York: McGraw-Hill Book Company, 1963).

9. Rosser Reeves, *Reality in Advertising* (New York: Alfred A. Knopf, Inc., 1961).

10. J. S. Brown, *The Motivation of Behavior* (New York: McGraw-Hill Book Company, 1961).

11. George S. Day, "Buyer Attitudes and Brand Choice Behavior," Unpublished Ph.D. Dissertation, Graduate School of Business, Columbia University, 1967.

12. Berlyne, *op. cit.*

13. S. Feldman (ed.), *Cognitive Consistency: Motivational Antecedents and Behavioral Consequents* (Academic Press, 1966); Martin Fishbein (ed.), *Readings in Attitude Theory and Measurement* (New York: John Wiley & Sons, 1967).

14. Thomas F. Juster, *Anticipations and Purchases: An Analysis of Consumer Behavior* (Princeton University Press, 1964).

15. William Yoell, *A Science of Advertising through Behaviorism.* Unpublished manuscript, December, 1965.

16. Sheth, *op. cit.*

17. R. J. Lavidge and G. A. Steiner, "A Model for Predictive Measurements of Advertising Effectiveness," *Journal of Marketing* (October, 1961), pp. 50–68.

18. Everett M. Rogers, *The Diffusion of Innovations* (New York: Free Press, 1962).

19. Kristian S. Palda, "The Hypothesis of a Hierarchy of Effects: A Partial Evaluation," *Journal of Marketing Research* (February, 1966), pp. 13–24.

20. Sheth, *op. cit.*

21. Donald F. Cox, *Risk Taking and Information Handling in Consumer Behavior* (Boston, Mass.: Graduate School of Business Administration, Harvard University, 1967).

A General Model for Understanding Organizational Buying Behavior

Frederick E. Webster, Jr., and Yoram Wind

Industrial and institutional marketers have often been urged to base their strategies on careful appraisal of buying behavior within key accounts and in principal market segments. When they search the available literature on buyer behavior, however, they find virtually exclusive emphasis on consumers, not industrial buyers. Research findings and theoretical discussions about consumer behavior often have little relevance for the industrial marketer. This is due to several important differences between the two purchase processes. Industrial buying takes place in the context of a formal organization influenced by budget, cost, and profit considerations. Furthermore, organizational (i.e., industrial and institutional) buying usually involves many people in the decision process with complex interactions among

people and among individual and organizational goals.

Similar to his consumer goods counterpart, the industrial marketer could find a model of buyer behavior useful in identifying those key factors influencing response to marketing effort. A buyer behavior model can help the marketer to analyze available information about the market and to identify the need for additional information. It can help to specify targets for marketing effort, the kinds of information needed by various purchasing decision makers, and the criteria that they will use to make these decisions. A framework for analyzing organizational buying behavior could aid in the design of marketing strategy.

The model to be presented here is a *general* model. It can be applied to all organizational buying and suffers all the weaknesses of general models. It does not describe a specific buying situation in the richness of detail required to make a model operational, and it cannot be quantified. However, generality offers a compensating

"A General Model for Understanding Organizational Buying Behavior," Frederick E. Webster, Jr., and Yoram Wind, Vol. 36 (April 1972), pp. 12–19. Reprinted from *Journal of Marketing*, published by the American Marketing Association.

set of benefits. The model presents a comprehensive view of organizational buying that enables one to evaluate the relevance of specific variables and thereby permits greater insight into the basic processes of industrial buying behavior. It identifies the *classes* of variables that must be examined by any student of organizational buying, practitioner, or academician. Although major scientific progress in the study of organizational buying will come only from a careful study of specific relationships among a few variables within a given class, this general model can help to identify those variables that should be studied. It can be useful in generating hypotheses and provides a framework for careful interpretation of research results that makes the researcher more sensitive to the complexities of the processes he is studying.

TRADITIONAL VIEWS

Traditional views of organizational buying have lacked comprehensiveness. The literature of economics, purchasing, and, to a limited degree, marketing has emphasized variables related to the buying task itself and has emphasized "rational," economic factors. In these economic views, the objective of purchasing is to obtain the minimum price or the lowest total cost-in-use (as in the materials management model[1]). Some of the models focussing on the buying task have emphasized factors that are not strictly economic such as reciprocal buying agreements[2] and other constraints on the buyer such as source loyalty.[3]

Other traditional views of organizational buying err in the opposite direction, emphasizing variables such as emotion, personal goals, and internal politics that are involved in the buying decision process but not related to the goals of the buying task.

This "nontask" emphasis is seen in models which emphasize the purchasing agent's interest in obtaining personal favors,[4] in enhancing his own ego,[5] or in reducing perceived risk.[6] Other nontask models have emphasized buyer-salesman interpersonal interaction[7] and the multiple relationships among individuals involved in the buying process over time.[8] The ways in which purchasing agents attempt to expand their influence over the buying decision have also received careful study.[9] These views have contributed to an understanding of the buying process, but none of them is complete. To the extent that these models leave out task or nontask variables they offer incomplete guidelines for the industrial market strategist and researcher. The tendency in interpreting research results based on these simple models is to overemphasize the importance of some variables and to understate or ignore the importance of others.

AN OVERVIEW OF A GENERAL MODEL

The fundamental assertion of the more comprehensive model to be presented here is that organizational buying is a decision-making process carried out by individuals, in interaction with other people, in the context of a formal organization.[10] The organization, in turn, is influenced by a variety of forces in the environment. Thus, the four classes of variables determining organizational buying behavior are *individual, social, organizational* and *environmental*. Within each class, there are two broad categories of variables: Those directly related to the buying program, called *task* variables; and those that extend beyond the buying problem, called *nontask* variables. This classification of variables is summarized and illustrated in Table 8–1.

Table 8-1
Classification and Examples of Variables Influencing Organizational Buying Decisions

	Task	Nontask
Individual	Desire to obtain lowest price	Personal values and needs
Social	Meetings to set specifications	Informal, off-the-job interactions
Organizational	Policy regarding local supplier preference	Methods of personnel evaluation Political climate in an election year
Environmental	Anticipated changes in prices	

The distinction between task and nontask variables applies to all of the classes of variables, and subclasses, to be discussed below. It is seldom possible to identify a given set of variables as exclusively task or nontask; rather, any given set of variables will have both task and nontask dimensions although one dimension may be predominant. For example, motives will inevitably have both dimensions—those relating directly to the buying problem to be solved and those primarily concerned with personal goals. These motives overlap in many important respects and need not conflict; a strong sense of personal involvement can create more effective buying decisions from an organizational standpoint.

Organizational buying behavior is a complex *process* (rather than a single, instantaneous act) and involves many persons, multiple goals, and potentially conflicting decision criteria. It often takes place over an extended period of time, requires information from many sources, and encompasses many interorganizational relationships.

The organizational buying process is a form of problem-solving, and a *buying situation* is created when someone in the organization perceives a problem—a discrepancy between a desired outcome and the present situation—that can potentially be solved through some buying action. Organizational buying behavior includes all activities of organizational members as they define a buying situation and identify, evaluate, and choose among alternative brands and suppliers. The *buying center* includes all members of the organization who are involved in that process. The roles involved are those of user, influencer, decider, buyer, and gatekeeper (who controls the flow of information into the buying center). Members of the buying center are motivated by a complex interaction of individual and organizational goals. Their relationships with one another involve all the complexities of interpersonal interactions. The formal organization exerts its influence on the buying center through the subsystems of tasks, structure (communication, authority, status, rewards, and work flow), technology, and people. Finally, the entire organization is embedded in a set of environmental influences including economic, technological, physical, political, legal, and cultural forces. An overview of the model and a diagrammatic presentation of the relationships among these variables are given in Figure 8–1.

ENVIRONMENTAL INFLUENCES

Environmental influences are subtle and pervasive as well as difficult to identify and

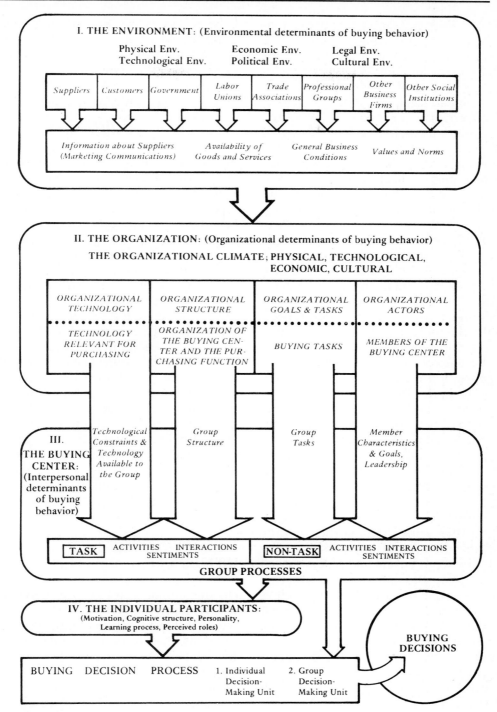

Figure 8-1
A Model of Organizational Buying Behavior

to measure. They influence the buying process by providing information as well as constraints and opportunities. Environmental influences include physical (geographic, climate, or ecological), technological, economic, political, legal, and cultural factors. These influences are exerted through a variety of institutions including business firms (suppliers, competitors, and customers), governments, trade unions, political parties, educational and medical institutions, trade associations, and professional groups. The nature of these institutional forms will vary significantly from one country to another, and such differences are critical to the planning of multinational marketing strategies.

As Figure 8–1 illustrates, environmental influences have their impact in four distinct ways. First, they define the availability of goods and services. This function reflects especially the influence of physical, technological, and economic factors. Second, they define the general conditions facing the buying organization including the rate of economic growth, the level of national income, interest rates, and unemployment. Economic and political forces are the dominant influences on general business conditions. Some of these forces, such as economic factors, are predominantly (but not exclusively) task variables whereas others such as political variables may be more heavily nontask in nature. Third, environmental factors determine the values and norms guiding interorganizational and interpersonal relationships between buyers and sellers as well as among competitors, and between buying organizations and other institutions such as governments and trade associations. Such values and norms may be codified into laws, or they may be implicit. Cultural, social, legal, and political forces are the dominant sources of values and norms. Finally, environmental forces influence the information flow into the buying organization. Most important here is the flow of marketing communications from potential suppliers, through the mass media and through other personal and impersonal channels. Information flows reflect a variety of physical, technological, economic, and cultural factors.

The marketing strategist, whose customers are organizations, must carefully appraise each set of environmental factors and identify and analyze the institutions that exert those influences in each of the market segments served. This kind of analysis is especially important in entering new markets. For example, economic factors as revealed in measures of general business conditions must be continually assessed where market prices fluctuate and buyers make decisions to build or reduce inventories based on price expectations. Similarly, the impact of technological change in markets served must be considered as the basis for strategic decisions in the areas of product policy and promotion. The necessity of analyzing institutional forms is most readily apparent when markets are multinational in scope and require specific consideration of government policies and trade union influences. Environmental factors are important determinants of organizational buying behavior, but they can be so basic and pervasive that it is easy, and dangerous, to overlook them in analyzing the market.

ORGANIZATIONAL INFLUENCES

Organizational factors cause individual decision makers to act differently than they would if they were functioning alone or in a different organization. Organizational buying behavior is motivated and directed by the organization's goals and is constrained by its financial, technological, and human resources. This class of variables is primarily task-related. For understanding the influence of the formal organization on the buying process, Leavitt's classification of variables is most helpful.[11] According to Leavitt's scheme, organizations are multivariate systems composed of four sets of interacting variables:

Tasks—the work to be performed in accomplishing the objectives of the organization.
Structure—subsystems of communication, authority, status, rewards, and work flow.
Technology—problem-solving inventions used by the firm including plant and equipment and programs for organizing and managing work.
People—the actors in the system.

Each of these subsystems interacts with, and is dependent upon, the others for its functioning. Together, these four interacting sets of factors define the information, expectations, goals, attitudes, and assumptions used by each of the individual actors in their decision making. This general model defines four distinct but interrelated sets of variables that must be carefully considered in the development of marketing strategies designed to influence that process: buying tasks, organization structure, buying technology, and the buying center.

Buying Tasks

Buying tasks are a subset of organizational tasks and goals that evolves from the definition of a buying situation. These are pure task variables by definition. The specific tasks that must be performed to solve the buying problem can be defined as five stages in the buying decision process. (1) Identification of need; (2) establishment of specifications; (3) identification of alternatives; (4) evaluation of alternatives; and (5) selection of suppliers.[12] Buying tasks can be further defined according to four dimensions:

1. The *organizational purpose* served—e.g., whether the reason for buying is to facilitate production, or for resale, or to be consumed in the performance of other organizational functions.
2. The *nature of demand*, especially whether demand for the product is generated within the buying organization or by forces outside of the organization (i.e., "derived" demand) as well as other characteristics of the demand pattern such as seasonal and cyclical fluctuations.
3. The *extent of programming*, i.e., the degree of routinization at the five stages of the decision process.
4. The *degree of decentralization* and the extent to which buying authority has been delegated to operating levels in the organization.

Each of these four dimensions influences the nature of the organizational buying process and must be considered in appraising market opportunities. At each of the five stages of the decision process, different members of the buying center may be involved, different decision criteria are employed, and different information sources may become more or less relevant. Marketing strategies must be adjusted accordingly. There are rich research opportunities in defining the influence of different members of the buying center at various stages of the buying process.[13]

Organizational Structure

The formal organizational structure consists of subsystems of communication, authority, status, rewards, and work flow, all of which have important task and nontask dimensions. Each of these subsystems deserves careful study by researchers interested in organizational buying. The marketing literature does not include studies in this area. A beginning might be several rigorous observational or case studies.

The *communication* subsystem performs four essential functions: (1) information; (2) command and instruction; (3) influence and persuasion; and (4) integration.[14] The marketer must understand how the communication system in customer organizations *informs* the members of the buying center about buying problems, evaluation criteria (both task and nontask related), and alternative sources of supply. He must appraise how *commands* and *instructions* (mostly task-related) flow through the hierarchy defining the discretion and latitude of individual actors. The pattern of *influence* and *persuasion* (heavily nontask in nature) defines the nature of interpersonal interactions within the buying center. Organizational members may differ in the extent to which they prefer either commands and instructions or more subtle influence and persuasion to guide the actions of subordinates. The *integrative* functions of communication become critical in coordinating the functioning of the buying center and may be one of the primary roles of the purchasing manager.

The *authority* subsystem defines the power of organizational actors to judge, command, or otherwise act to influence the behavior of others along both task and nontask dimensions. No factor is more critical in understanding the organizational buying process because the authority structure determines who sets goals and who evaluates (and therefore determines rewards for) organizational performance. The authority structure interacts with the communication structure to determine the degree of decentralization in the decision process.

The *status* system is reflected in the organization chart and defines the hierarchical structure of the formal organization. It also expresses itself in an informal structure. Both the formal and the informal organization define each individual's position in a hierarchy with respect to other individuals. Job descriptions define positions within the organization and the associated dimensions of responsibility and authority. Knowing the responsibility, authority, and the position in the internal status hierarchy of each member of the buying center is a necessary basis for developing an account strategy for the organizational customer. A complete theory of organizational buying will permit accurate predictions of an organizational actor's influence based upon his position and role.

The *rewards* system defines the payoffs to the individual decision maker. It is intimately related to the authority system which determines the responsibilities of organizational actors for evaluating other individuals. Here is the mechanism for relating organizational task accomplishment to individual nontask objectives. Persons join organizations in anticipation of the rewards given by the organization and agree to work toward organizational objectives in return for those rewards. A careful analysis of the formal and social reward structure of the organization as it affects and is perceived by the members of the buying center can be most helpful in predicting their response to marketing effort. The key fact is that people work for organizations in order to earn rewards related to personal goals, both economic and noneconomic.[15]

Every buying organization develops task-related procedures for managing the *work flow* of paperwork, samples, and other items involved in the buying decision process. The flow of paperwork also has nontask aspects which reflect the composition of the buying center as well as the authority and communication subsystems of an organizational structure. Needless to say, marketers must understand the mechanical details of buying procedures. Such procedures also provide documentation of the buying process that can provide useful data for the academic researcher.

Buying Technology

Technology influences both what is bought and the nature of the organizational buying process itself. In the latter aspect, technology defines the management and information systems that are involved in the buying decision process, such as computers and management science approaches to such aspects of buying as "make or buy" analysis. More obviously, technology defines the plant and equipment of the organization, and these, in turn, place significant constraints upon the alternative buying actions available to the organization. It is a common failing of industrial marketing strategy, especially for new product introductions, to underestimate the demands that will be placed upon existing technology in customer organizations.[16] A new material, for example, may require new dies and mixing equipment, new skills of production personnel, and substantial changes in methods of production.

Buying Center

The buying center is a subset of the organizational actors, the last of the four sets of variables in the Leavitt scheme. The buying center was earlier defined as consisting of five roles: users, influencers, deciders, buyers, and gatekeepers. Since people operate as part of the total organization, the behavior of members of the buying center reflects the influence of others as well as the effect of the buying task, the organizational structure, and technology.

This interaction leads to unique buying behavior in each customer organization. The marketing strategist who wishes to influence the organizational buying process

must, therefore, define and understand the operation of these four sets of organizational variables—tasks, structure, technology, and actors—in each organization he is trying to influence. The foregoing comments provide only the skeleton of an analytical structure for considering each of these factors and its implications for marketing action in a specific buying situation. The marketer's problem is to define the locus of buying responsibility within the customer organization, to define the composition of the buying center, and to understand the structure of roles and authority within the buying center.

SOCIAL (INTERPERSONAL) INFLUENCES

The framework for understanding the buying decision process must identify and relate three classes of variables involved in group functioning in the buying center. First, the various roles in the buying center must be identified. Second, the variables relating to interpersonal (dyadic) interaction between persons in the buying center and between members of the buying center and "outsiders" such as vendors' salesmen must be identified. Third, the dimensions of the functioning of the group as a whole must be considered. Each of these three sets of factors is discussed briefly in the following paragraphs.

Within the organization as a whole only a subset of organizational actors is actually involved in a buying situation. The buying center includes five roles:

Users—those members of the organization who use the purchased products and services.
Buyers—those with formal responsibility and authority for contracting with suppliers.

Influencers—those who influence the decision process directly or indirectly by providing information and criteria for evaluating alternative buying actions.

Deciders—those with authority to choose among alternative buying actions.

Gatekeepers—those who control the flow of information (and materials) into the buying center.

Several individuals may occupy the same role; e.g., there may be several influencers. Also, one individual may occupy more than one role; e.g., the purchasing agent is often both buyer and gatekeeper.

To understand interpersonal interaction within the buying center, it is useful to consider three aspects of role performance: (1) Role *expectations* (prescriptions and prohibitions for the behavior of the person occupying the role and for the behavior of other persons toward a given role); (2) role *behavior* (actual behavior in the role); and (3) role *relationships* (the multiple and reciprocal relationships among members of the group). Together, these three variables define the individual's *role set*. An awareness of each of these dimensions is necessary for the salesman responsible for contacting the various members of the buying center. It is especially important to understand how each member expects the salesman to behave toward him and the important ongoing relationships among roles in the buying center.

As illustrated in Figure 8–1, the nature of group functioning is influenced by five classes of variables—the individual members' goals and personal characters, the nature of leadership within the group, the structure of the group, the tasks performed by the group, and external (organizational and environmental) influences. Group processes involve not only activities but also interactions and sentiments among members, which have both task and nontask dimensions. Finally, the output of the group is not only a task-oriented problem solution (a buying action) but also nontask satisfaction and growth for the group and its members.

In analyzing the functioning of the buying center, it helps to focus attention on the buyer role, primarily because a member of the purchasing department is most often the marketer's primary contact point with the organization. Buyers often have authority for managing the contacts of suppliers with other organizational actors, and thus also perform the "gatekeeper" function. While the buyer's authority for selection of suppliers may be seriously constrained by decisions at earlier stages of the decision process (especially the development of specifications), he has responsibility for the terminal stages of the process. In other words, the buyer (or purchasing agent) is in most cases the final decision maker and the target of influence attempts by other members of the buying center.

In performing their task, purchasing agents use a variety of tactics to enhance their power which vary with the specific problems, the conditions of the organization, and the purchasing agent's personality. The tactics used by purchasing agents to influence their relationships with other departments can be viewed as a special case of the more general phenomenon of "lateral" relationships in formal organizations—those among members of approximately equal status in the formal organizational hierarchy.[17] These include *rule-oriented* tactics (e.g., appealing to the boss for the enforcement of organizational policy; appealing to rules and formal statements of authority); *rule-evading* tactics (e.g., compliance with requests from users that violate organizational policies); *personal-political* tactics (e.g., reliance on informal relationships and friendships to get decisions made and an exchange of favors with other members of the buying center); *educational* tactics (e.g., persuading other members of the organization to think in purchasing terms and to recognize the importance and potential contribution of the purchasing function); and finally, *organizational-interactional* tactics (e.g., change the formal organizational structure and the pattern of reporting relationships and information flows).

Buyers who are ambitious and wish to extend the scope of their influence will adopt certain tactics and engage in bargaining activities in an attempt to become more influential at earlier stages of the buying process. These tactics or bargaining strategies define the nature of the buyer's relationships with others of equal organizational status and structure the social situation that the potential supplier must face in dealing with the buying organization. An understanding of the nature of interpersonal relationships in the buying organization is an important basis for the development of marketing strategy.

THE INFLUENCE OF THE INDIVIDUAL

In the final analysis, all organizational buying behavior is individual behavior. Only the individual as an individual or a member of a group can define and analyze buying situations, decide, and act. In this behavior, the individual is motivated by a complex combination of personal and organizational objectives, constrained by policies and information filtered through the formal organization, and influenced by other members of the buying center. The individual is at the center of the buying process, operating within the buying center that is in turn bounded by the formal organization which is likewise embedded in the influences of the broader environment. It is the specific individual who is the target for marketing effort, not the abstract organization.

The organizational buyer's personality, perceived role set, motivation, cognition, and learning are the basic psychological processes which affect his response to the buying situation and marketing stimuli provided by potential vendors. Similar to consumer markets, it is important to understand the organizational buyer's psychological characteristics and especially his predispositions, preference structure, and decision model as the basis for marketing strategy decisions. Some initial attempts to develop categories of buying decision makers according to characteristic decision styles ("normative" and "conservative") have been reported.[18] Cultural, organizational, and social factors are important influences on the individual and are reflected in his previous experiences, awareness of, attitudes and preference toward particular vendors and products and his particular buying decision models.

The organizational buyer can, therefore, be viewed as a constrained decision maker. Although the basic mental processes of motivation, cognition, and learning as well as the buyer's personality, perceived role set, preference structure, and decision model are uniquely individual; they are influenced by the context of interpersonal and organizational influences within which the individual is embedded. The organizational buyer is motivated by a complex combination of individual and organizational objectives and is dependent upon others for the satisfaction of these needs in several ways. These other people define the role expectations for the individual, they determine the payoffs he is to receive for his performance, they influence the definition of the goals to be pursued in the buying decision, and they provide information with which the individual attempts to evaluate risks and come to a decision.

Task and Nontask Motives

Only rarely can the organizational buyer let purely personal considerations influence his buying decisions: In a situation where "all other things are equal," the individual may be able to apply strictly personal (nontask) criteria when making his final decision. In the unlikely event that two or more potential vendors offer products of comparable quality and service at a comparable price, then the organizational buyer may be motivated by purely personal, nontask variables such as his personal preferences for dealing with a particular salesman, or some special favor or gift available from the supplier.

The organizational buyer's motivation has both task and nontask dimensions. Task-related motives relate to the specific buying problem to be solved and involve the general criteria of buying "the right quality in the right quantity at the right price for delivery at the right time from the right source." Of course, what is "right" is a difficult question, especially to the extent that important buying influencers have conflicting needs and criteria for evaluating the buyer's performance.

Nontask-related motives may often be more important, although there is frequently a rather direct relationship between task and nontask motives. For example, the buyer's desire for promotion (a nontask motive) can significantly influence his task performance. In other words, there is no necessary conflict between task and nontask motives and, in fact, the pursuit of nontask objectives can enhance the attainment of task objectives.

Broadly speaking, nontask motives can be placed into two categories: achievement motives and risk-reduction motives. Achievement motives are those related to personal advancement and recognition. Risk-reduction motives are related, but somewhat less obvious, and provide a critical link between the individual and the organizational decision-making process. This is also a key component of the behavior theory of the firm[19] where uncertainty avoidance is a key motivator of organizational actors.

The individual's perception of risk in a decision situation is a function of uncertainty (in the sense of a probabilistic assessment) and of the value of various outcomes. Three kinds of uncertainty are significant: Uncertainty about available alternatives; uncertainty about the outcomes associated with various alternatives; and uncertainty about the way relevant other persons will react to various outcomes.[20] This uncertainty about the reaction of other persons may be due to incomplete information about their goals or about how an outcome will be evaluated and rewarded.

Information gathering is the most obvious tactic for reducing uncertainty, while decision avoidance and lowering of goals are means of reducing the value of outcomes. A preference for the status quo is perhaps the most common mode of risk reduction, since it removes uncertainty and minimizes the possibility of negative outcomes. This is one explanation for the large amount of source loyalty found in organizational buying and is consistent with the "satisficing" postulate of the behavioral theory of the firm.

The individual determinants of organizational buyer behavior and the tactics which buyers are likely to use in their dealing with potential vendors must be clearly understood by those who want to affect their behavior.

SUMMARY

This article has suggested the major dimensions and mechanisms involved in the complex organizational buying process. The framework presented here is reasonably complete although the details clearly are lacking. It is hoped that these comments have been sufficient to suggest a general model of the organizational buying process with important implications for the development of effective marketing and selling strategies as well as some implicit suggestions for scholarly research. The model is offered as a skeleton identifying the major variables that must be appraised in developing the information required for planning strategies. Hopefully, the model has also suggested some new insights into an important area of buying behavior presently receiving inadequate attention in the marketing literature.

NOTES

1. Dean S. Ammer, *Materials Management* (Homewood, Illinois: Richard D. Irwin, Inc., 1962), pp. 12 and 15.

2. Dean S. Ammer, "Realistic Reciprocity," *Harvard Business Review*, Vol. 40 (January–February, 1962), pp. 116–124.

3. Yoram Wind, "Industrial Source Loyalty," *Journal of Marketing Research*, Vol. 7 (November, 1970), pp. 450–457.

4. For a statement of this view, see J. B. Matthews, Jr., R. D. Buzzell, T. Levitt, and R. Frank, *Marketing: An Introductory Analysis* (New York: McGraw-Hill Book Company, Inc., 1964), p. 149.

5. For an example, see William J. Stanton, *Fundamentals of Marketing*, Second Ed. (New York: McGraw-Hill Book Company, Inc., 1967), p. 150.

6. Theodore Levitt, *Industrial Purchasing Behavior: A Study of Communications Effects* (Boston: Division of Research, Graduate School of Business Administration, Harvard University, 1965).

7. Henry L. Tosi, "The Effects of Expectation Levels and Role Consensus on the Buyer-Seller Dyad," *Journal of Business*, Vol. 39 (October, 1966), pp. 516–529.

8. Robert E. Weigand, "Why Studying the Purchasing Agent Is Not Enough," *Journal of Marketing*, Vol. 32, (January, 1968), pp. 41–45.

9. George Strauss, "Tactics of Lateral Relationship," *Administrative Science Quarterly*, Vol. 7 (September, 1962) pp. 161–186.

10. The complete model is presented and discussed in detail in Frederick E. Webster, Jr. and Yoram Wind, *Organizational Buying Behavior* (Englewood Cliffs, New Jersey: Prentice-Hall, Inc., in press).

11. Harold J. Leavitt, "Applied Organization Change in Industry: Structural, Technical, and Human Approaches," in *New Perspectives in Organizational Research*, W. W. Cooper, H. J. Leavitt, and M. W. Shelly, II, eds. (New York: John Wiley and Sons, Inc., 1964), pp. 55–71.

12. A modified version of this model is presented in P. J. Robinson, C. W. Faris, and Y. Wind, *Industrial Buying and Creative Marketing* (Boston: Allyn & Bacon, Inc., 1967), p. 14.

13. For research on the influence of organizational actors and information sources at various stages of the decision process, see Urban B. Ozanne and Gilbert A. Churchill, "Adoption Research: Information Sources in the Industrial Purchasing Decision," in *Marketing and the New Science of Planning*, Robert L. King, ed. (Chicago, Ill.: American Marketing Association, Fall, 1968), pp. 352–359; and Frederick E. Webster, Jr., "Informal Communication in Industrial Markets," *Journal of Marketing Research*, Vol. 7 (May, 1970), pp. 186–189.

14. Lee Thayer, *Communication and Communication Systems* (Homewood, Ill.: Richard D. Irwin, Inc., 1968), pp. 187–250.

15. Yoram Wind, "A Reward-Balance Model of

Buying Behavior in Organizations," in *New Essays in Marketing Theory*, G. Fisk ed. (Boston: Allyn & Bacon, 1971).

16. Frederick E. Webster, Jr., "New Product Adoption in Industrial Markets: A Framework for Analysis," *Journal of Marketing*, Vol. 33 (July, 1969), pp. 35–39.

17. Same reference as footnote 9.

18. David T. Wilson, H. Lee Mathews, and Timothy W. Sweeney, "Industrial Buyer Segmentation: A Psychographic Approach," paper presented at the Fall, 1971 Conference of the American Marketing Association. See also Richard N. Cardozo, "Segmenting the Industrial Market," in *Marketing and the New Science of Planning*, Robert L. King ed. (Chicago: American Marketing Association, 1969), pp. 433–440.

19. Richard M. Cyert and James G. March, *A Behavioral Theory of the Firm* (Englewood Cliffs, N.J.: Prentice-Hall, 1963).

20. Donald F. Cox, ed., *Risk Taking and Information Handling in Consumer Behavior* (Boston: Division of Research, Graduate School of Business Administration, Harvard University, 1967).

Memory Factors in Consumer Choice: A Review

James R. Bettman

Memory plays a major role in consumer choice. The specific inferences drawn by consumers from product stimuli, advertising, word of mouth, and other sources of product-related information are heavily dependent upon what data are in memory and how they are organized. Important questions to which research on consumer memory can contribute insights include (a) What is remembered from an advertisement or a product-related conversation; (b) Under what conditions do consumers tend to emphasize information on packages or stored in memory when they are in the store; (c) How much time is necessary for consumer to learn some piece of information from an ad; (d) How many repetitions are needed before a consumer can remember a piece of information; (e) What can be done to facilitate in-store recognition of a brand by con-

sumers; and (f) What types of new information, claims, and so on are easier for consumers to remember, given their current knowledge about a product.

Despite its potential importance, research on consumer memory is a relatively neglected area. The purpose of this paper is to present a survey of the literature on the structure and operation of memory and some implications of the memory principles uncovered by the survey (see Olson 1978b for another review of memory notions as related to consumer choice).

OVERVIEW

One concept of memory that recently has been very influential is the multiple-store approach. It is postulated that there are different types of memory storage systems, each with different functions and properties. A typical model of this type hypothesizes a

"Memory Factors in Consumer Choice: A Review," James R. Bettman, Vol. 43 (Spring 1979), pp. 37–53. Reprinted from *Journal of Marketing,* published by the American Marketing Association.

119

set of sensory stores (SS), a short-term memory store (STS), and a long-term store (LTS) (Atkinson and Shiffrin 1968).

In the basic processing sequence, information passes from the sense organs to the appropriate sensory store which is hypothesized to be very short-lived, losing information within fractions of a second unless the information is further processed (i.e., unless attention is allocated to the stimulus). If the information is attended to and processed, it is transferred to the STS. The STS has a limited capacity and information can be kept active in it by further processing. Information which is active in the STS can be retrieved quickly and almost automatically. Information in the LTS may be brought into the STS as needed to interpret the input information. Thus the STS is the locus of current processing activity, where information from the sense organs and long-term memory can be brought together and processed. Finally, a portion of that information, if adequately processed (a discussion of the meaning of "adequate" in this context is given below), can be transferred to the LTS which is hypothesized to be essentially unlimited in capacity and a permanent repository of information. Although the above discussion, if taken literally, implies that there are several physically distinct memory stores, the separate *functions* of these are the crucial element of the multiple-store viewpoint.

In addition to this characterization of the basic structure of memory, one must also consider how individuals *use* memory. Individuals have various strategies for how and what to process, for what to store in long-term memory and how to store it, and for how to retrieve information from long-term memory. Such strategies are often called control processes (Atkinson and Shiffrin 1968). Although in many cases, storage of and access to items in memory may be

nearly automatic, retrieval and storage also can be involved and difficult processes.

In consumer choice there is an *external* memory, in many cases, where information is available without needing to be stored in the consumer's memory. Package information, shopping lists, buying guides, or ads clipped out by the consumer and brought to the store are part of this external memory system.

Thus there is a memory system and a set of control processes which can be used to interact with that system. In general, two very basic kinds of memory usage occur. In one case, information which is currently in long-term storage or external memory must be retrieved *from* the memory to be used in interpreting incoming information or in current processing. In the second case, incoming information is processed and stored *in* memory for later use. These two functions are, of course, not independent; they simultaneously occur at almost all times.

Some basic memory concepts are now presented in more detail: multiple store and other views of memory, control processes; properties of short-term and long-term memory, and the impact of different types of consumer choice tasks on memory usage. In examining memory research, one general caveat should be considered. Much of the experimental research studies situations where individuals are *trying* to memorize (for texts which review this research, see Loftus and Loftus 1976; Crowder 1976; Norman 1976). Consumers also may deliberately try to remember things at times, but in many situations what consumers remember may be incidental rather than deliberate. This difference needs to be considered in attempting to apply any experimental results, and suggests that future research on consumer memory might emphasize incidental memory (McLaughlin 1965; Postman 1975).

BASIC CONCEPTS OF MEMORY

Multiple Store and Other Approaches to Memory

As noted above, one prevalent view of memory is the multiple-store view. However, recent research has begun to cast doubt on the strict interpretation of this concept, particularly the distinction between the LTS and the STS as separate memories. Postman (1975) provides a thorough and critical summary of the evidence and concludes that the distinction is not well supported. Other conceptions of memory have been advanced which do not postulate separate multiple stores.

Craik and Lockhart (1972) propose that individuals have limited processing capacity which can be allocated to processing incoming information. In particular, they argue that capacity can be allocated to yield various *levels of processing* which might range from simple sensory analysis (e.g., noting that the information is printed in red type) to more complex semantic and cognitive elaborations of the information (e.g., relating it to other information in memory and seeing how it fits with previous beliefs). Presumably the "lower" levels of processing (e.g., sensory analyses) would require less allocation of capacity than the "higher" or "deeper" levels (e.g., semantic analyses). It is then hypothesized that the level of processing attained determines the future retention of the information. In particular, "deeper" levels of processing (and hence greater use of processing capacity) are hypothesized to be associated with more elaborate and longer lasting memory for the information. For example, consumers who only process an advertisement's sensory features (e.g., a waterfall, a pretty scene, or a well-dressed spokesperson), without processing the semantic information in the ad and relating it to what they know about the product category, presumably will not recall the claims presented when they attempt to make a choice. In that sense, advertisements can err in actually *encouraging* sensory rather than semantic processing by their very nature (i.e., the "background" of the ad may divert attention from the message). Although this issue of background diversion is not new, examining it from the viewpoint of research on memory can suggest approaches for studying such diversion—researching which parts of an ad are processed, and with what degree of elaboration; and what information, images, and reactions to the various parts of the ad are stored in memory after exposure.

Since there is limited overall processing capacity to be allocated, only a small amount of information can be processed in depth at any one time. Rather than postulating several distinct memories, the levels of processing theory assumes one memory, an overall processing capacity, and the ability to engage in different levels of processing. Although this theory is quite provocative, it also has some serious problems. Some have suggested that *spread* of processing (i.e., the degree of elaboration used in coding the information) is more important than depth alone (Craik and Tulving 1975). Others note that there is a substantial problem with measuring depth of processing in some a priori and independent fashion (Nelson 1977; Baddeley 1978). Most research simply uses types of processing that seem intuitively to differ in depth, without attempting any formal measure of depth. These critics are quite persuasive, so the fate of levels of processing approaches is not clear at present, although research continues (Jacoby, Bartz, and Evans 1978; Saegert 1979; Seamon and Virostek 1978; Cermak and Craik 1978). Until these problems are resolved, however, this approach might best be regarded with caution.

Another general conception of memory which does not require multiple stores is the activation model. In this model, there is one memory store, but only limited portions of that store can be activated at any one time. Only the activated portion can be used for current processing. Activation is temporary and will die out unless further effort is devoted to maintaining it. The exact nature of activation is typically unspecified; however, the concept is one of rate or intensity. Therefore, notions of effort (Kahneman 1973) or allocation of processing capacity also can be viewed as concepts of activation. A general model of this type is outlined by Collins and Loftus (1975) and considered in more detail below. The limited capacity for dealing with incoming information which led to postulation of the STS is thus handled in this model by the limitation on total amount of activation.

The three models described to this point, multiple-store, levels of processing, and activation, do not seem incompatible. The multiple-store theories do not strictly require that there be physiologically separate stores; the *functions* of each store are important. Shiffrin and Atkinson (1969, pp. 179–180) note that their system is "equally as consistent with the view that stores are separate physiological structures as with the view that the short-term store is simply a temporary activation of information permanently stored in the long-term store." Bower (1975) makes the same point. Thus, the multiple-store model can be viewed as an activation model. A liberal view of the Craik and Lockhart (1972) model also allows it to be viewed as an activation approach, since the allocation of processing capacity is a major mechanism of the model.

It seems that all three models of memory are consistent with the principles of a limited processing capacity and a single memory store with allocations of that capacity to the processing of incoming information. The phenomena of the limited STS seem perfectly explainable in these terms, since there is a limitation on the total amount of processing capacity available for allocation. In examining the properties of memory below, the terminology of short-term memory (STM) and long-term memory (LTM) will be utilized to escape from the notion of separate stores, rather than defining new terms for the currently activated portion of memory and the entire memory itself. These terms are to be understood in the light of the above discussion.

As noted above, external memory devices ranging from package information to detailed shopping check lists are often available. The presence of an external memory can serve to reduce the burden on the consumer's internal memory. That is, both internal memory and external memory can be viewed functionally as sources of information. In some cases, it may be easier to encode and process information from a package when making product comparisons than to try to retrieve and process these same data, perhaps fallibly, from internal memory. The consumer also may not try to store complex data internally if these data are available in external memory. The use of information in internal memory may be necessary to interpret such externally available data when they are processed, of course, but overall the burden on internal memory seems smaller if an external memory exists. Thus, the availability of external memory in any particular choice situation can be an important characterizing factor.

Memory Control Processes

Memory control processes are the strategies used by humans to control the flow of information in and out of memory (Atkinson and Shiffrin 1968). These processes can be under the active control of the individual. There are certainly many habitual, nearly automatic processes used by individuals in inputting and outputting information. However in some cases, such conscious decisions are made, so an understanding of the strategies involved is important. In the following, several such strategies are discussed.

Rehearsal. After a stimulus has entered short-term memory, processing effort, called rehearsal, may be needed to further analyze it. The two roles usually assigned to rehearsal are maintenance of information (keeping it activated) in the STM and ultimate transfer of information to the LTM.

The initial concept of rehearsal was that of rote repetition of the information in STM, usually verbal in memory experiments. That is, the individual was viewed as silently repeating the information being considered. Retention in LTM was postulated to be a direct function of the amount of time spent in rehearsal. However many studies have shown that retention in LTM does not necessarily vary directly with amount of rehearsal time. Instead, retention can vary with the form of the rehearsal itself (Woodward, Bjork, and Jongeward 1973; Postman 1975), whether mere repetition (less retention) or more detailed analysis (more retention). Thus, rehearsal can probably best be characterized as allocation of processing capacity, which will be done in accordance with the goals of the individual and the requirements of the task at hand. For example, consumers may remember a price or the value of some other product attribute not so much by rote repetition of the attribute value to themselves, but by mentally relating the value to what they already know (e.g., this price is a few cents more than the cost of my regular brand).

Coding. Coding refers to the way the individual *structures* information for rehearsal.

It is now well known that subjects in verbal learning studies use mnemonics, associations, images, and many other strategies of encoding the inputs received to facilitate memory (Bower 1970; Reitman 1970). In attempting to remember the name of a new brand from an ad, the consumer may also associate the brand name with some mental image that suggests that name. For example, a consumer may remember Autumn margarine by associating it with a fall scene. The ads for this margarine use such scenes to try to encourage this process (see Lutz and Lutz, 1977).

Transfer. A third control process is the transfer process which governs *what* is stored in memory and the form in which it is stored. Information which is important for attaining goals and/or easily stored is likely to be given highest priority (Shiffrin and Atkinson 1969). These properties need not coincide; that is, information needed for goals may be difficult to process. For example, a consumer may be very interested in nutritional information, but may not be able to store USRDA ratings. Trade-offs must be made in such a case, with the consumer perhaps only attempting to store whether or not the food is basically nutritious.

What is to be stored and the form of storage will thus depend on what the individual expects to do with the information, if such expectations are present. More or less detail may be required depending upon the task to be performed when the information will be used. If the individual plans to compare foods on nutritional content in the store using package information, then only the brands to be compared need be put into memory. However, if the information is presented in an ad and not on the package, the consumer may put more into memory. In situations where individuals do not have firm expectations about how the information will be used, the easiest transfer strategy will probably be used. Events which are surprising, novel, inconsistent with expectations, and so on will often be given priority for processing and storage (e.g., a new price may be stored).

Placement.   Placement deals with where an element is stored. This depends upon the existing organization of memory and the particular associations utilized in coding the item. In this sense, the "where" question does not refer to a physical location, but the association structure developed when the item was processed. This structure is affected by the context of presentation: for example, if words are presented in categories, recall tends to be grouped by those same categories (Bower 1970). The importance of the placement decision is that later retrieval may depend upon the likelihood that the particular placement strategy can be reconstructed. In addition, a placement decision may lead to *reorganization* of a portion of memory.

Retrieval.   Retrieval of items from memory is a crucial control process. Retrieval processes can range from almost immediate access for familiar items to involved problem solving search processes for other items. The control processes discussed above interact with retrieval. If the basis used for coding, transfer, and placement cannot be retrieved, the item itself may not be accessible. Forgetting is seen, in light of the permanence of the LTM, as a failure of the retrieval process rather than a decay or loss of items. The basic underlying notion can be best seen intuitively by considering cases where an item cannot be remembered, and then some event occurs which gives the "clue" needed to immediately retrieve the item. For example, a consumer may remember needing some item not on his/her shopping list, but

not the item itself. While in the store, the item or a related product may trigger remembrance. This retrieval problem is of course central to disputes over the definition of impulse purchases.

Such phenomena imply that the correct retrieval strategy just could not be found at first. Failure of the retrieval process may result from searching in the wrong "part" of memory (i.e., in the wrong set of associations), running out of time to perform the search, or losing one's place in the search. This latter possibility reflects the limited capacity for STM which may result in one's not being able to keep track of one's place in a complex search for a hard to retrieve item (Olshavsky 1971). Use of some external device (e.g., paper and pencil) as a memory aid is often tried by individuals in such cases.

Response Generation.   A final control process is response generation. Many theorists view remembering as a constructive process where items are reconstructed from memory. Partial recollections are used as the basis for reconstructing what "must have been." Items are *not* stored in memory exactly as they were entered and aroused in toto when desired. Neisser (1967, pp. 285–86) calls this latter view the "reappearance hypothesis," and rejects it in favor of a constructive approach: "The present proposal is, therefore, that we store traces of earlier cognitive acts. . . . The traces are not simply 'revived' or 'reactivated' in recall; instead the stored fragments are used as information to support a new construction." Jenkins (1974) and Cofer (1973) summarize research supporting the constructive approach. This view implies that memory may be subject to biases, since reconstructions will be based partly on what was and partly on individuals' expectations or schemes for what "must have been" (D'Andrade 1974). A consumer may not remember the actual details of an interaction with a salesperson, for example, but may decide that there "must have been" deceptive statements if he/she is not pleased with a purchase.

Properties of Short-Term Memory

Properties fall into two major categories: capacity and the times needed to transfer information to LTM.

Capacity. As discussed above, the STM is of limited capacity.[1] Miller (1956) first formulated the hypothesis that STM was limited, and reviewed evidence showing that approximately seven chunks of information could be processed at any one time. The number of items is limited because the attention or processing capacity necessary to rehearse these items is limited. Recent evidence (Simon 1974) suggests that a four- or five-chunk capacity seems more likely. A chunk was defined as a configuration that was familiar to an individual and could be manipulated as a unit, in essence an organized, cognitive structure that could grow as information is integrated into it.[2] For example, a brand name can summarize a good deal of more detailed information for a consumer familiar with that brand, hence the name and all it stands for can be thought of as a chunk. The actual amount of underlying material that can be processed simultaneously can be expanded by formation of larger chunks (e.g., by associating several attributes with a brand name so that the mere mention of the name elicits an entire "gestalt"), although the consumer may presumably reach a point where he or she is unable to further expand a chunk due to difficulties in dealing with more and more complex configurations of information or other factors.

This notion of a capacity for chunks is consistent with a memory model where the constraint is on processing capacity or amount of activation if the assumption is made that the processing capacity needed to manipulate a chunk is independent of its size. That seems to be the essence of the chunking concept; it is the organization of the chunk that allows for ease in processing.

The capacity of STM is lowered if other processing demands are made. This follows immediately from the notion of the limits on STM as processing capacity limits. If part of total capacity must be used for another task, that leaves less for processing chunks of information. The normal capacity may be reduced to a capacity of two or three chunks if other tasks are undertaken simultaneously (see Newell and Simon 1972).

Transfer Times. Another property of STM concerns the amount of time required to transfer an item from STM to LTM, assuming suitable processing is performed (i.e., if the type of coding needed to allow retention in LTM is performed, or if the form of rehearsal leads to retention, as discussed above). Simon (1969, pp. 35–42) and Newell and Simon (1972, pp. 793–96) cite evidence that suggests that approximately five to 10 seconds are required to fixate one chunk of information in LTM if one must later *recall* it. If only *recognition* is required, two to five seconds may be needed (Simon 1969, p. 39; Shepard 1967). This task difference follows from the fact that for recognition, only discrimination of the item from others is needed, not reconstruction of the information. The times above are rough guides rather than precise estimates, and refer to deliberate rather than incidental learning.

If information is not rehearsed at all, it is lost from STM in about 30 seconds or less (Shiffrin and Atkinson 1969). Whether this loss is due to decay or displacement by new items is still under debate (Postman 1975).

Properties of Long-Term Memory

The LTM is hypothesized to be an essentially unlimited, permanent store with semantic and some auditory and visual storage. The basic properties of LTM are the types of elements stored and the organization of that storage.

Elements in Long-Term Memory. There seems to be some agreement that an important part of what is stored in LTM are semantic concepts and the associations among them (e.g., Quillian 1968; Anderson and Bower 1973). Concepts may include events, objects, processing rules, and attributes of objects and events. Underwood (1969) particularly emphasizes that various attributes of objects and events, such as temporal sequence information, spatial aspects information, modality through which the information was obtained (e.g., audio, visual, smell, etc.), affective data, and contextual data, potentially can be stored. This notion of contextual data, particularly time context, has been suggested by several authors (Russo and Wisher 1976; Hintzman and Block 1970). Such time-line memory is essentially similar to Tulving's (1972) notion of episodic memory—memory for past episodes and events.

Another important type of information in memory, related to chunks, is memory schemata. A schema is "an internal structure, developed through experience with the world, which organizes incoming information relative to previous experience" (Mandler and Parker 1976, p. 39). Thus it is an organized pattern of expectations about the environment. One might have schemata about what salespeople are like or how various product attributes interrelate. These schemata can obviously play a powerful role in how consumers perceive the events in their environment. Abelson (1976) considers the related notion of scripts, expectations about how various types of events will unfold (see Wyer and Srull 1979).

Processing rules also are elements of LTM. Newell and Simon (1972) hypothesize that processing rules can be stored in the memory data base and operated on and activated like any other type of information in memory. In addition to memory for semantic concepts, there is substantial memory for visual images and auditory events in LTM, but the mechanisms are currently not well understood (Paivio 1975).

The Structure of Long-Term Memory. There is also general agreement on the structure of the storage of semantic information in LTM. This storage is thought to be organized as a network of nodes and links between nodes, with the nodes representing concepts and the links denoting relationships among concepts; or as some organization which is structurally equivalent to a network formulation (Frijda 1972).[3]

Collins and Loftus (1975) present a network model, originally based on Quillian's (1968) work, in which there are nodes representing concepts and several links between concepts. Each link has a strength corresponding to how essential it is to the meaning of the concept. Processing a concept corresponds to activating the node corresponding to it with activation spreading through the network along the links. Collins and Loftus (1975) show how the theory can explain results on the effects of perceptual set and other data. Anderson and Bower (1973) also see memory as a network of nodes interconnected by associations and use the notion of activation. Finally, within the marketing literature, Nakanishi (1974) proposed a contiguous retrieval model. In this model, concepts are stored in clusters rather than in lists. Their retrieval is based upon their closeness of association or contiguity in the cluster. This model is essentially equivalent to the Collins and Loftus (1975) model, in that the cluster of concepts can be defined by nodes and links, with the notion of closeness or contiguity being modeled by the strength of the links.

Other models also have been proposed, but they can be viewed as equivalent to network models. Newell and Simon (1972) see memory as an organization of list structures (a list whose elements can also be lists). A list structure can be transformed into an equivalent network. Smith, Shoben, and Rips (1974) present a set-theoretical model where concepts are described by a set of features or properties. As Hollan (1975) points out, their model also can be reduced to a network model. (See Smith 1978 for a more detailed discussion of theories of semantic memory.)

In network models, new information is integrated by developing a configuration of links between the new concept and already stored concepts, or by adding links to already existing concepts. Also, inferences can be made by following paths of links and nodes. Such inferences allow us to construct responses and test inputs for consistency with what we already know.

Such models can be extremely important for understanding consumer choice because they imply that consumers have organized systems of concepts related to various brands, ads, stores, and so on. The particular concepts included and the relationships among them can have a powerful effect on the inferences made by consumers based on these concepts (Olson 1978a). For example, if a ballpoint pen has an ultra-fine point, and a consumer links the ultra-fine point with greater writing effort, that consumer may infer that the pen requires greater writing effort and not purchase it, even if in fact greater effort is not required. Also, the inferences underlying the price-quality relationship have been studied a great deal in con-

sumer research (Olson 1977). Thus, studying what concepts are in consumers' memories and exactly how they are linked can be extremely important for understanding consumer responses to products. This type of insight is one benefit of adopting a network view of memory, which provides a framework for *systematically* exploring the contents and interconnections in consumer memory.

Consumer Choice Tasks and Memory

The range of choice tasks performed by consumers is very broad, with decisions not only being made at many levels (save vs. spend, trade-offs among attributes, store, and brand), but in very different task environments, ranging from reading *Consumer Reports* to watching television commercials, ordering from a catalog, or searching through a supermarket. There may also be great differences across tasks in the availability of external memories (e.g., store displays) and their usage. Such factors complicate the examination of memory research, since in general the results are specific to the type of task performed. Therefore, understanding what parts of the memory literature are most relevant for understanding consumer choice requires some notion of what consumer tasks are to be considered. In general, this notion of *task analysis* is important. Newell and Simon (1972) argue that a thorough task analysis yields a great deal of knowledge about how behavior must be structured to adapt to that task environment. Particular tasks impose particular constraints on the processing needed to perform them. Hence, a limited and brief view of some important consumer tasks is presented below, with particular emphasis on the areas of memory research implicated. This task analysis is limited to retail-outlet shopping situations, to some major types of tasks performed outside of the store environment, and to some major types of tasks performed in the store. The specific tasks considered were chosen because they seemed most closely related to consumer choice processes.

Tasks Performed outside the Store. We consider three of the main types of tasks that may be carried on outside the store environment: receipt and processing of information, formation of rules or strategies for weighting attributes, and choice of an alternative.

The consumer receives information outside of the store from many sources, including commercials on television, advertisements, and word of mouth. This information may be presented to the consumer or may be sought by him/her. Important questions relative to the memory component are whether or not the information is stored, and if so, what is stored. Whether or not information can be stored may be in large part a function of not only the consumer's interest in the information, but also of how easy the information is to process. Factors impacting ease of processing include the organization of the information processed, the sheer amount of information presented, and any competing activities carried out while the information is presented (e.g., a consumer is talking while a television commercial is being shown). Competing activities may have less impact for print ads or for conversations where the consumer has some control over the rate of processing required, than for television or radio where such control is lacking. Finally, the modality of information presentation, visual versus auditory, and the amount of information repetition may impact degree of retention, since these factors also effect ease of processing.

What information is stored may depend in large part on the use, if any, to which the consumer intends to put it. The consumer may wish to use the information as a reminder of something when in the store, such as a brand, which implies that recognition of that brand on the shelf suffices. On the other hand, the consumer may want to decide before arriving at the store, so that recall will be required. An individual difference variable, the degree to which prior planning outside of the store and in-store decision making are used, may greatly influence the type of memory needed, whether for recognition or for recall.

A second out-of-store task considered is the formation of rules or strategies for weighting attributes. Formation of such rules requires information on attributes and the trade-offs among them. Information relevant for developing strategies may be obtained from such sources as ads, family members, product testing magazines, or friends. However, rules for weighting attributes seem to require recall more than recognition, since the rules per se are not usually found explicitly stated in the shopping environment. Thus, recall of evaluative and belief information from memory may be necessary, particularly recall of the rules for combining that information.

Finally, a third out-of-store task is choice of an alternative. As discussed above, the degree to which this occurs out of the store may be an individual difference variable. Choice in the store also occurs, probably more frequently. However, if choice outside the store is carried out, it may involve recall in matching brands against criteria, particularly if the matching is done incrementally as ads or other pieces of information are received. Such an incremental process may require at the very least a recall of the current stage of the process or the operations necessary to reconstruct that stage. In addition, how attribute and evaluative information is stored in memory can be important, since this can affect how alternatives are compared (i.e., whether information is recalled by attribute, across brands; or by brand, across attributes). Finally, external memory can be a factor for choice outside of the store if a display of information such as that in a *Consumer Reports'* table is available. Such displays might ease the need for recall of properties of the alternatives, but recall of factors relevant to weighting attributes might still be necessary.

Tasks Performed inside the Store. One basic feature that characterizes the in-store environment as a task environment is the external memory it provides. Brands are available for inspection, values for various attributes (e.g., price, nutrition) can be obtained from the package, displays may be available, and so on. Within this environment, two basic tasks are considered: formation of rules or strategies for weighting attributes and choice of an alternative.

As noted above, formation or usage of rules for weighting attributes seems to involve mainly recall, since such rules are not normally directly available in the external memory to be recognized. There can be some recognition component, in that examination of packages may remind the consumer of criteria to be used, but recall seems to be the major memory mechanism involved.

A second major in-store task is the choice of an alternative. Here the level of prior experience may be important. In a simple, habitual response situation, the consumer need only recognize what was bought previously, and may very well recall it. At the other extreme is extensive problem solving (Howard and Sheth 1969; Howard 1977), where weights for attributes are developed and processed in some detail. The discussion that follows is not as relevant for the habitual response case, but rather is more suited to decisions involving some problem solving.

Processing alternatives in the store may involve memory only to the extent of recognition of those brands to be processed further from some larger set of brands. However, some recall is probably involved. The particular product class being processed also will have an influence on use of recall versus recognition, since the completeness of the attribute information on the package varies over product classes. If little information is available from the external memory, recall may be more heavily implicated. Also, if no brands are known previously, then recall of information relevant to rules may be necessary. The type of decision being made, whether a choice between product classes or brands within a product class, may also influence use of recognition versus use of recall. For a choice between product classes, the physical setup of the store (e.g., the product classes are probably physically separated) implies that the external memory cannot be relied upon exclusively. Also, more abstract criteria may need to be developed and applied for choice among product classes than for choice among brands within a product class (Howard 1977). Thus recall may become relatively more important than recognition in choice among product classes. Finally, the context of the original learning about the brand is important, in that recognition or recall may be affected if the context in the store differs from the original learning context.

Thus, the major factors affecting memory involved in in-store tasks are the distinction between recognition and recall, and the effects of differences in context between receipt and attempted retrieval of information. This brief, simplified analysis of typical consumer choice tasks shows the complexity that rapidly arises in attempting to characterize task properties. It also points up the need for a systematic classification or taxonomy of consumer choice tasks, rather than the ad hoc scheme used here.[4] This is an important area for future research. Despite the limitations, several areas of memory research that seem particularly relevant for consumer choice are identified:

- Factors differentially affecting recognition and recall
- Organization of information when received by the consumer
- Effects of a difference in context between the receipt of and attempted retrieval of information
- Form of coding and storage for objects in memory
- Effects of total processing load on the individual
- Memory for rules and operations
- Effects of the modality of information presentation
- Effects of repetition of information

Before turning to a discussion of each of these areas, some perspective on the implications of this research should be given. The problems studied in memory research are often simplistic and narrowly focused, using digits, letters, nonsense syllables, or words as stimuli. As Wright (1974) notes, this research is deficient as far as being directly applicable to consumer research problems in the simplicity of the stimuli and the fact that the responses studied are not evaluative. Reitman (1970) also points out that humans outside the laboratory do not often deliberately rehearse and attempt to memorize items, and that laboratory tasks attempt (with limited success) to decouple the study of memory from the strategies people typically use to remember. These strategies, of course, are of great interst for understanding how consumers make real-life decisions. Thus, the results to be presented below should be taken as *indications* of how various processes operate and should

raise issues to be considered in the consumer research context. Actual applications of the results might require new research examining the relevant issues in more realistic consumer choice settings.

MORE DETAILED MEMORY CONCEPTS

Factors Differentially Affecting Recognition and Recall

In the following discussion, the focus is upon differences between recognition and recall. It has been noted above that recognition is in some sense "easier" than recall. Also, the tasks of recognition and recall differ in the basic type of processing that leads to effective performance. To recognize a stimulus from among a set of distracting stimuli, information allowing one to *differentiate* or *discriminate* the previously encountered stimulus is necessary. In recall, however, information allowing one to *reconstruct* the stimulus is required, since the stimulus itself is not present. This distinction between discrimination and reconstruction is implicated again and again in the findings discussed below.

Frequency of Occurrence of Stimuli. Words with low frequency of occurrence in normal text seem to be recognized better than words of high frequency, whereas the reverse is true for recall (Kintsch 1970; Shepard 1967; however, see Goldin 1978 for some contradictory evidence for visual stimuli—chess positions). This finding can be explained by noting that low frequency words, being unusual, are easier to discriminate from others; high frequency words, being familiar, are easier to reconstruct.

This could have implications for the types of brands chosen, depending upon whether choice is guided by recognition (e.g., in-store) or recall (e.g., planning outside of the store). A less frequently seen brand, even if attractive, might be chosen less frequently in the out-of-store situation (recall) relative to the in-store situation (recognition), with the reverse true for more frequently seen brands.

Plans for Learning in Recognition and Recall.

The *plans for learning,* or how subjects go about the task, appear to differ between recognition and recall. Given the difference in the tasks themselves, with discrimination required for recognition and reconstruction for recall, this difference in plans should be expected if humans adapt to the task environment (Newell and Simon 1972). Subjects have been shown to encode information differently and to have different levels of recall and recognition accuracy depending upon whether they expected a recall or recognition task (Eagle and Leiter 1964; Tversky 1973).

Thus, the learning plans of the subject may be a function of expected task requirements, and effective plans may *differ* for recall and recognition. The consumer may encode incoming information with some task in mind. This may imply that in some cases the expectation of using recall or recognition procedures in shopping is set a priori, that consumers make this decision at the time of encoding. Since the learning plans may differ depending upon these task expectations and may influence how effectively information is processed, empirical study of this assumption of prior task expectations is desirable. Of course, an alternative hypothesis to setting expectations about use of recognition or recall a priori would be that the task itself determines whether recall or recognition is used, particularly the degree of difficulty involved. Simple tasks may stimulate more use of recall, and more complex tasks may lead to greater use of recognition.

Rehearsal and Transfer Times.

Rehearsal may effect recognition and recall differently, although the research results to date are mixed. As noted above, rehearsal can vary from rote repetition to semantic elaboration. Woodward, Bjork, and Jongeward (1973) found that rote repetition rehearsal could improve recognition, but had no effect on recall. However, Chabot, Miller, and Juola (1976) and Nelson (1977) found improvements for recall as well. As noted above, the rough guide for the time required for transfer of a chunk of information to LTM differs for recognition (two to five seconds) and recall (five to 10 seconds). Thus, communications to consumers, particularly in the case of television or radio commercials where the consumer cannot control the rate of information presentation, may have very different effects depending upon whether recognition or recall is attempted.

Effects of Arousal Level.

A final factor which may differentially affect recognition and recall is the level of arousal at the time the desired information is to be retrieved from memory (Eysenck 1976). This factor can be important for consumer choice in that arousal (defined by Eysenck 1976, p. 389 as "some elevated state of bodily function") may be characteristic of high time pressure or high conflict choice situations. Eysenck hypothesizes that high arousal may lessen the difficulty of retrieving readily accessible information, but increase the difficulty of retrieving less accessible information. Eysenck then argues that a recognition task, by providing the subject with the item, which then must be judged "old" (recognized) or "new" (not recognized) involves in general more accessible information than a recall task. He summarizes research results which show, as predicted, that under high arousal recognition response speeds are facilitated, but recall response speeds are hindered. These findings could be important for consumer choice, since consumers who tend to use recall may be less able to operate effectively under time pressure or conflict than those who tend to use recognition. Perhaps, on the other hand, consumers choose to rely on either recall or recognition adaptively, choosing recognition more in situations where they feel time pressure, conflict, or some other source of arousal, and recall more for less demanding choice tasks.

Organization of Information
Input

In tasks for which recall is the focus, subjects given instructions to recall as much as possible have been consistently shown to use memory strategies which concentrate on organizing, associating, and grouping together the items to be learned (Bower 1970; Buschke 1976). If groupings are already present in the materials to be learned, then this can greatly facilitate recall (Bower et al. 1969).

However, the effects of organization in the input may only be beneficial if this organization *corresponds* to the rules subjects might normally use to group the data. If the groupings or chunks in the input do not match those usually used by subjects in organizing their own memories, the input groupings may hinder recall performance (Bower and Springston 1970). The implication is that if an advertisement is to present information which is already "chunked" or "grouped" for the consumer, whether that structuring is helpful to the consumer or not will depend upon how consumers group or would tend to group the information.

Effects of Context

The role of context has been investigated in memory studies. The encoding specificity hypothesis states that no context, even if strongly associated with a particular item or event, can be effective in aiding retrieval for that item or event *unless* the item or event was originally encoded in terms of that context (Thomson and Tulving 1970). Many studies have shown, for both recognition and recall, that changes in context are associated with poorer performance (e.g., Thomson 1972; Thomson and Tulving 1970). Although information may be *available* (in memory), in the wrong context it can be *inaccessible*.

Such effects of the relationship of the context at memory input to that when memory is to be accessed have not been specifically studied in consumer research. However, advertisements present information in a particular context which very often does not match the in-store context. Perhaps information usage, usage of particular attributes as criteria, or even recognition of brands is influenced by the degree to which the context posed in the ad is present in the actual choice situation. Thus, if in-store recognition is desired, the package should be shown in the advertisement. In one case, a cereal (Life) with a very powerful commercial (the "Mikey" commercial) ingeniously put a scene from the commercial on the front of the package.

Form of Coding and Storage of Objects in Memory

A series of research studies has examined whether encoding and memorization of properties of objects are easier if all the attribute values of one object are presented at one time (object coding or brand coding), or if all the values on a particular attribute for the set of objects under study are presented at one time (dimension coding or attribute coding). Haber (1964) used a brief presentation (¹⁄₁₀ second) of cards portraying stimuli which varied along three dimensions, one of which was emphasized to the subjects as being important. Some subjects were instructed to use object coding, while others were instructed to use dimension coding. Haber found that dimension coders were slower and less accurate in recalling unemphasized dimensions. Lappin (1967) used different stimuli, again with three dimensions, and did not instruct his subjects on coding schemes. Rather, he tested recall by objects and dimensions. He found better recall for the three dimensions of each object than for the same dimension over three objects. Montague and Lappin (1966) found, in a replication of Haber's (1964) results, that object coding was faster than dimension coding. However, they did not find differences in accuracy, contrary to Haber's results. Johnson and Russo (1978) found that subjects tended to store information in the form it was presented to them, whether by object (brand) or by dimension (attribute). However, they did not find differences in time or accuracy depending upon the organization of the input. Thus, there is mixed support for the notion that when inputting data, coding by objects may be more effective for later recall.

Effects of Processing Load

Studies cited earlier have shown that the effective capacity of STM is a function of the total processing load on the individual. If processing capacity is required for some activity which competes with a memory task, less capacity is available for memory processing. In addition, there may be task effects on memory processing. That is, the information input rate characteristic of a task or the processing rate required in performing that task may affect memory. Seibel, Christ, and Teichner (1965) assert that the rate of incoming information itself is not the critical factor, but rather the rate of internal processing the task requires in analyzing and transferring the information into memory, in interaction with this presentation rate. This is completely congruent with a capacity allocation theory of memory. In this view, it is not the presentation rate per se that requires capacity, but the task to be performed. Thus, the more processing required by the task in a limited time period, the greater the effects on memory performance. If the tasks of monitoring and processing the incoming data are not demanding, high input rates may be tolerable.

Since the tasks involved in consumer choice differ greatly across situations, the above considerations may be quite important for consumer choice. If advertisements presenting a great deal of information per unit time are shown to consumers, memory performance may depend upon what is required of consumers in processing the ad. For example, whether recall or recognition is used could be important. Recognition might be less affected by presentation rate than recall, since forming associations and other strategies for recall may require more effort than analyzing a single item for later recognition. Also, if a consumer is processing an ad by looking to see if certain elements are above a threshold (e.g., does this product have at least 25% of the U.S. Recommended Daily Allowance of vitamin C) this may be much easier than attempting to comprehend and learn actual parameters (e.g., 30% of the USRDA for vitamin C).

Memory for Rules and Operations

In judging alternatives, consumers may combine evaluations on various attributes.

The rules for combining evaluations are thus important aspects of the choice process. There are very few studies that examine memory for such rules. Dosher and Russo (1976) and Russo and Wisher (1976) show that in mental arithmetic tasks, memory for sequences of operations and intermediate processing details is better than memory for the actual original numbers comprising the arithmetic task. For example, intermediate subtotals in an addition and subtraction task are recognized, but the original numbers are not.

Johnson (1978), in an initial test of the impact of decision processes on consumer memory, used recall reaction times to study similar issues. His results resembled those noted above: final outcomes and intermediate processing results were recalled faster than the original data on the alternatives used. It is clear that more research is needed before any confident statements about consumer memory for rules and operations can be made.

Effects of Input Modality

There is a great deal of research on differences in memory as a function of the sensory modality of the input (e.g., visual versus auditory). The findings have shown that for simple stimuli such as series of digits or numerals, there are modality effects on STM, but *not* on LTM. Penney (1975) reviews this research in some detail. The findings show that there consistently has been better short-term recall of auditory input, particularly for the most recently presented items. For lists where auditory and visual presentations are mixed, recall tends to be organized by modality of the input, and auditory recall is better. Recall performance is best when the initial presentation and test are in the same modality. When auditory and visual tasks compete in a mixed situation, the auditory task seems to have priority

(Penney 1975). These findings, although based upon a great deal of research, may not be too applicable to consumer choice because of their emphasis on simple stimuli and STM phenomena. However, some ads may use simple digit stimuli (e.g., nutritional ratings) and the findings can serve as a source of hypotheses to be examined in a consumer context. For example, the notion that competing audio and visual portions of an ad will lead to downgraded recall of the visual information could be quite important for understanding the effects of proposals for presenting visual nutritional information in ads with competing audio portions (Bettman 1975). Also, the notion that the modes at presentation and at test should coincide may imply that points should be made visually that relate to in-store aspects of choice.

Although the above findings can serve as a source of hypotheses, they differ drastically from research involving more complex stimuli. Several authors have noted the powerful beneficial effects on memory of forming visual images involving the input stimuli (see Paivio 1971). Lutz and Lutz (1977) demonstrated such effects of visual imagery using advertisements as stimuli. In addition, Shepard (1967) demonstrated humans' remarkable recognition memory for pictures. Shepard used many ads for stimuli and found that subjects recognized, from a series of about 600 pictures, 96.7%, 99.7%, 92%, 87%, and 57.7% at test delays of zero, two hours, three days, seven days, and 120 days respectively. Finally, Rossiter (1976) shows that visual memory of the package may be quite important in children's cereal choices, and may also be important for adults. He found that cereal preferences assessed visually by using a drawing task differed from preferences assessed verbally.[5] Paivio (1975) argues that in general there is a dual coding system in memory—an imagery system that deals with nonverbal information, and a verbal system that deals with semantic concepts. Depending upon the task requirements, either or both systems may be utilized (other theorists do not subscribe to this view; see Kieras 1978 for a review and model of imagery effects). The nonverbal imagery system needs more research to determine its impact on consumer choice processes, as most research has concentrated on the verbal concept system (see Lutz and Lutz 1978).

Effects of Repetition

One of the oldest notions in the memory literature is that repeated exposure to a stimulus enhances future recall or recognition of that stimulus. Most of the work on the effects of repetition has involved a passive view of human learning, with repetition serving to "stamp in" an item, to increase the strength of that item's memory trace. This research will be briefly reviewed and then the implications of viewing man as a more "active" learner are discussed.

Sawyer (1974) presents a good summary of the effects of repetition as related to marketing phenomena. The basic findings are that recall and recognition increase as a function of presentation frequency and that there are decreasing increments in memory performance as repetition increases (i.e., later exposures appear to add less and less to performance). Even rote repetition without more elaborative processing may improve recognition or recall (Chabot, Miller, and Juola 1976; Nelson 1977). Finally, for single series of stimuli, it has been shown that recall performance is better when a given number of repetitions is spaced or distributed rather than massed (Postman 1975, pp. 316–18). Zielske (1959), in a classic study in marketing, showed that for final level of recall, distributed presentation was better than massed presentation, but noted that the

amount of final retention may not be the relevant criterion for the marketer. If maximum temporary response is desired, massed presentation may be better; if maximum average exposure is desired, distributed presentation was better.

This view of repetition ignores the notion of man as an active processor governed by plans and goals. In several studies cited above, it was noted that memory performance may depend upon the learning plans formed by the consumer. Krugman (1972) points this out, and rejects the notion that the effects of learning must be through "practice" alone. He asserts that the presence of interest or involvement is important, i.e., that the consumer has some plan or need for using the information in the ad. He then claims that three repetitions are enough: the first evokes a "What is It?" response, with a preliminary decision about whether the ad is of any use or interest; the second generates more detailed evaluative responses and planning for future actions if the preliminary decision was favorable; and the third becomes the reminder to carry out any plan formed in the second. Most people may screen out ads at the first exposure; however, if later an interest in the product category or brand is present, the person may see an ad for the 23rd time, but process it as if it were their *second* exposure (Krugman 1972, p. 13). Thus, for group data, different levels of interest in a product over time could lead to gradually increasing curves of response to repetition (because with increased repetition, the odds that someone who is interested would have had the first "What is It?" exposure increase), even though for the individual the response was in some sense more rapid. Goldberg and Gorn (1974) offer evidence consistent with Krugman's general notion, in that exposure to one commercial affects children's attitudes toward a toy and their persistence at a task to obtain the toy.

However, an increase to three exposures did not change either attitude or persistence beyond the initial effect of the first exposure.

While the specific mechanisms and numbers of exposures proposed by Krugman may be debated, there may be a strong component of active planning and assessment in human learning. If an ad is seen as useful based upon interests, future choice tasks expected, or other factors, then consumers may use the information in the ad to generate partial plans for choice (e.g., "check this brand," "look at this new attribute in my decision," and so forth).[6] The important question then becomes whether sheer repetition has an effect on this process of forming plans, or functions solely to make sure information is available at the relevant time, when needed.

At this point, the evidence seems to be that both processes operate. As Krugman (1965) himself notes, low and high involvement learning may be governed by different processes. For low involvement learning, sheer repetition may have effects, particularly if recognition rather than recall is involved (Woodward, Bjork, and Jongeward 1973; Chabot, Miller, and Juola 1976; Nelson 1977; Postman 1975, p. 303). For learning under higher involvement, more elaborate and focused processing may ensue. (For some recent research on the kinds of processing which occur for different levels of involvement, see Gardner, Mitchell, and Russo 1978.)

IMPLICATIONS FOR MARKETING

The following discussion emphasizes some selected implications of memory principles for promotional decisions. (For further implications, see Bettman 1979, Chapters 10 and 11, particularly for discussion of the effects of the organization of information by brand or by attribute.) In the presentation below, factors influencing *where* and *how* to present information are emphasized.

It is necessary, before discussing these questions, to briefly consider the type of processing characterizing certain consumer decisions, since where and how to present information can depend upon the type of processing used. It has been hypothesized (Bettman 1979) that where consumers have little prior knowledge or experience or where the decision is difficult for some other reason, they will tend to process information in the store and use recognition rather than recall. Consumers with a good deal of experience or for whom the choice is easy will tend to process outside of the store environment and use recall. The basic reasoning behind these hypotheses is that consumers will only be *able* to recall information and make choices outside of the store where the choice is easy and familiar. For difficult choices, attempting to use recall or process outside of the store may be too hard. It should be noted that these hypotheses are speculative and greatly in need of empirical research. However, they seem plausible and are utilized in the following discussion.

Where Information Should Be Provided

Presentation of information in the store (on the package or through various forms of point-of-purchase displays) and presentation of information out of the store (television, radio, print, billboards) may in general have very different properties. In particular, the types of memory processing necessary for consumers to use the information may differ.

Provision of Information in the Store. One of the most salient features of providing information in the store is that the information on packages or other displays can serve as an external memory for the consumer allowing him/her to simply recognize rather than recall various pieces of information. A second characteristic of in-store information provision is that there may be more time available for processing the information, unlike radio or television advertising where there is limited processing time. Finally, it may be easier for consumers to make detailed comparisons among brands if information is provided on packages in the store than to compare brands using memory for the information presented in television advertising, for example.

Given these characteristics, under what conditions might the marketer wish to present information in the store? As noted above, consumers may tend to process in the store for decisions where they have little previous experience or knowledge or where the decision is difficult. Thus, a marketer of a product class characterized by low levels of consumer experience or by difficulty in choice might concentrate to a greater extent on in-store, point-of-purchase information displays or on greater amounts of package information. Even if consumers do have experience, the marketer may wish to encourage comparison of the product with others in the store, if it is a new brand or is believed to have some differential advantage, for example. Comparing package information is easier than making internal memory comparisons. Thus if the marketer feels consumers are processing in the store or wishes to encourage such processing, in-store information provision is needed.

Provision of Information outside the Store. Presenting information outside the store may require the consumer to rely on his or her own memory to a greater extent. Although print ads can provide an external memory device (by clipping the ad), televi-

sion, radio, and billboards do not provide an easy external memory aid.

The conditions under which marketers might wish to concentrate on presenting information outside of the store would tend to be the opposite of those for in-store presentation. In general, consumers may process outside the store for product classes where the choice is easy and they have a good deal of experience. Thus a marketer with a brand in a product class where consumers have a good deal of experience might concentrate more on out-of-store and less on in-store activity, since consumers will tend to decide outside of the store. Note that these prescriptions refer to the emphasis which might be appropriate for the marketer. It is not suggested that either the in-store or out-of-store method be used exclusively. Consumers will vary in their degree of prior experience, and the in- and out-of-store methods have different properties, so some combination of approaches will, in most cases, be the best strategy.

How Information Should Be Provided

In the following, two aspects of how to provide information are presented: facilitating use of recognition or recall, and how memory research can help in presenting information to special groups of consumers.

Facilitating Use of Recognition or Recall.
Since consumers may attempt to use recognition more often in the store, the external memory provided by packages and in-store displays is a crucial consideration. Use of recognition presupposes some earlier presentation of information, with later recognition of that information. Therefore, in general there may be some out-of-store presentation, with recognition cued by the package or display in the store. This implies that the information on the package or dis-

play should be the same or nearly the same as that presented in the out-of-store advertising. One typical method for ensuring this match is to show the package in the advertisement (if visual information can be presented, as for television and billboards). This need not be the only method, however. In the Life cereal case noted above, a scene from an ad was placed on the front of the cereal package, thus bringing the context of the commercial into the store. For radio commercials, either descriptions of the package ("Look for the red and yellow box") or slogans which would be repeated on the package might be used. Finally, if the marketer wishes to have particular claims recognized, they should be presented in the store on the package or in a display, as well as in the advertisement. Although the information on the package may trigger recall of associated information from memory, there is no guarantee that any particular claim will be recalled in this fashion.

For the consumer to use recall, the information presented should be relatively simple and congruent with what consumers know. Recall will tend to be used for familiar choice situations, so the consumer will attempt to fit the new information into an existing set of beliefs about the product class. As noted above, different modes of information presentation can affect the ease of recall of that information. For example, use of visual imagery is often a good way to enhance recall. Lutz and Lutz (1977) show that recall of brand names is higher for advertisements using certain types of visual imagery.

Whether consumers use recall or recognition, the ease with which the information presented can be processed will affect later usage. A general principle is that the amount of information which can be assimilated is a function of the time available for processing. For example, if recall is used,

then the research on transfer speeds from short- to long-term memory (cited above) implies that roughly five to 10 seconds of time is required to memorize one chunk of information for later recall. Thus, the feasibility of processing the information and recalling it depends upon the amount of information presented relative to the time available for processing, and the ability of the consumer to organize the information into chunks. For example, if there are 15 seconds available for processing the information and capacity is fully allocated to that processing, perhaps two or three chunks could be recalled at a later time. For recognition, the transfer speeds are on the order of two to five seconds per chunk, so perhaps as many as eight chunks of information could be recognized later after a 15 second presentation.

Thus, the amount of information which may be acquired during the limited time available in a television commercial depends upon the ability of the consumer to chunk the information provided. The degree of chunking possible may depend largely upon the organization of the information in the ad and the degree of the consumer's prior knowledge and interest in it. If information is prechunked for the consumer by the way the ad is designed *and* if these chunks are consistent with the way the consumer categorizes, then "larger" chunks and hence more information could be processed per unit time. Also, if the individual has prior knowledge related to the information presented, so it can be integrated meaningfully with the existing knowledge, then more information in the ad can perhaps be chunked and processed per unit time. Therefore, there is a great effect on memory of the size of the "vocabulary" of chunks in memory. The greater the number of such chunks, the faster information can be processed.

The time available for processing can

thus have important effects. For media where the time available for processing is limited (television or radio), the amount of information which can be presented may also be limited. For cases where the marketer wishes to present large amounts of information, or where the information is complex, either media which do not limit the time available for processing should be used (print, in-store), or the time given for processing should be expanded to meet processing needs.

Presenting Information to Special Groups of Consumers. In some cases, marketers may wish to present information to special groups of consumers such as children or the elderly. Such groups may be characterized by different memory properties which must be understood in order to present information effectively.

For example, research on the information processing characteristics of the elderly has tended to focus on memory abilities. Several studies have compared the abilities of groups of differing ages on various memory tasks, and have found that the groups of older subjects (generally over 60) performed less well than the younger subjects (generally in their 20s). These memory findings may have implications for the choice processing of the elderly. First, the elderly appear to have difficulties in making shifts in search (Welford 1962, p. 337) and difficulties in recall (Craik 1971). This may imply that attempting to make choices between product classes by recall would be more difficult for them. Second, tasks requiring rapid processing (e.g., viewing of television commercials which present a great deal of information) may be harder for older subjects due to their slower memory and visual search speeds (Anders and Fozard 1973; Chiang and Atkinson 1976). Finally, tasks where distraction is likely to be present

(e.g., viewing television commercials) would probably be difficult (Broadbent and Heron 1962). These findings may suggest greater use of in-store displays or print ads in communicating to elderly consumers, since these methods do not limit processing time and may facilitate use of recognition memory rather than use of recall (see Phillips and Sternthal 1977, for similar arguments).

DIRECTIONS FOR FUTURE RESEARCH

It is obvious from the above that there is an enormous amount we do not know about consumer memory. However, certain areas seem to be of higher research priority. Basic information on what consumers have in memory and how it is organized is a high priority. As noted above, clarifying the "networks" of concepts and interrelations among them can have many implications for understanding consumer reactions to products. In addition, determining the "vocabulary" of chunks and schemas consumers use would be extremely helpful in addressing other issues, such as how rapidly consumers can process the information contained in ads and how the information in ads can best be organized for consumers. Current research on memory schemas (Markus 1977; Clary, Tesser, and Downing 1978; Kintsch 1978; Wyer and Srull 1979) may be helpful in attacking these issues.

A second major priority is analysis of the properties of various consumer choice tasks, particularly those affecting memory processing. Such factors as the extent of external memory available, time pressure, the organization of available information, and so on might be very relevant. As stated earlier, however, one major factor whose effect should be studied is whether the consumer is trying deliberately to memorize or is remembering items incidentally. Much of the research surveyed studied deliberate memorization. Future research should include studies carried out in consumer settings without explicit instructions to memorize to ascertain whether the conclusions of this prior research still hold.

Finally, research on when consumers use recognition or recall seems very important, since the properties of recognition and recall and the implications for how to present information differ. Thus, knowledge of consumer memory is important for both theoretical and pragmatic reasons. There are many issues to be investigated and work in these areas should be strongly encouraged.

NOTES

1. The notion of the STM as a "box" with a fixed number of "slots" has also been used, but is rejected on the basis of the arguments above denying the need for the distinction between the long-term and short-term stores.

2. Bower (1975) points out that this definition is circular: a chunk is something that can be processed as a unit, and the capacity of STM is inferred from examining units of information that are processed, which units are then called chunks.

3. Wyer and Srull (1979) propose a content-addressable bin model of memory which departs somewhat from these network approaches.

4. The concept of a task analysis seems somewhat different from the recent work on situational factors in consumer choice (Belk 1975). Belk (1975, p. 158) defines situational factors to be roughly those factors which are not inherent properties of the individuals or stimuli of interest. Within the context of this definition, task analyses are in some respects more narrow and in some ways more broad than research on situational factors. The task analysis notion is more narrow in the types of situational factors considered, with particular emphasis being placed upon those situational factors which will influence the type of information processing carried out. Thus, the situational factors considered in task analyses are a relatively circumscribed area within the broad range of factors one might consider. In addition, some factors important in performing task analyses may be properties of stimuli (e.g., how many attributes there are for brands in a product class, or the medium through which a particular piece of information is propagated), and hence would not be considered situational factors by Belk's definition. Thus task analyses are more broad in this sense than research on situational impacts alone.

5. Rossiter (1975) also found that musical imagery (jingles, songs in ads) was important for children.

6. Of course, even when the consumer is trying actively to learn the information contained in an ad, if there is a great deal of information a number of repetitions may be necessary before the consumer can learn that information. Thus, the number of repetitions necessary for the consumer to carry out plans for learning may vary as a function of the information load in the ad.

REFERENCES

Abelson, Robert P. (1976), "Script Processing in Attitude Formation and Decision Making," in *Cognition and Social Behavior*, John S. Carroll and John W. Payne, eds., Hillsdale, NJ: Lawrence Erlbaum, 33–45.

Anders, Terry R. and James L. Fozard (1973), "Effects of Age Upon Retrieval from Primary and Secondary Memory," *Developmental Psychology*, 9, 411–415.

Anderson, John R. and Gordon H. Bower (1973), *Human Associative Memory*, Washington, D.C.: Winston.

Atkinson, R.C. and R.M. Shiffrin (1968), "Human Memory: A Proposed System and Its Control

Processes," in *The Psychology of Learning and Motivation: Advances in Research and Theory,* Volume 2, K. W. Spence and J. T. Spence, eds., New York: Academic Press, 89–195.

Baddeley, Alan D. (1978), "The Trouble with Levels: A Reexamination of Craik and Lockhart's Framework for Memory Research," *Psychological Review,* 85 (May), 139–152.

Belk, Russell W. (1975), "Situational Variables and Consumer Behavior," *Journal of Consumer Research,* 2 (December), 157–164.

Bettman, James R. (1975), "Issues in Designing Consumer Information Environments," *Journal of Consumer Research,* 2 (December), 169–177.

———(1979), *An Information Processing Theory of Consumer Choice,* Reading, MA: Addison-Wesley.

Bower, Gordon H. (1970), "Organizational Factors in Memory," *Cognitive Psychology,* 1 (January), 18–46.

———(1975), "Cognitive Psychology: An Introduction," in *Handbook of Learning and Cognitive Processes,* Volume 1, William K. Estes, ed., Hillsdale, NJ: Lawrence Erlbaum, 25–80.

———, Michael C. Clark, Alan M. Lesgold, and David Winzenz (1969), "Hierarchical Retrieval Schemes in Recall of Categorized Word Lists," *Journal of Verbal Learning and Verbal Behavior,* 8, 323–343.

———, and Fred Springston (1970), "Pauses as Recoding Points in Letter Series," *Journal of Experimental Psychology,* 83, 421–430.

Broadbent, D.E. and Alastair Heron (1962), "Effects of a Subsidiary Task on Performance Involving Immediate Memory by Younger and Older Men," *British Journal of Psychology,* 53, 189–198.

Buschke, Herman (1976), "Learning is Organized by Chunking," *Journal of Verbal Learning and Verbal Behavior,* 15, 313–324.

Cermack, L.S. and F. I. M. Craik, eds. (1978), *Levels of Processing and Human Memory,* Hillsdale, NJ: Lawrence Erlbaum.

Chabot, Robert J., Timothy J. Miller, and James F. Juola (1976), "The Relationship Between Repetition and Depth of Processing," *Memory and Cognition,* 4, 677–682.

Chiang, Alice and Richard C. Atkinson (1976),

"Individual Differences and Interrelationships Among a Select Set of Cognitive Skills," *Memory and Cognition,* 4, 661–672.

Clary, E. Gil, Abraham Tesser, and Leslie L. Downing (1978), "Influence of a Salient Schema on Thought-induced Cognitive Change," *Personality and Social Psychology Bulletin,* 4 (Winter), 39–43.

Cofer, Charles N. (1973), "Constructive Processes in Memory," *American Scientist,* 61 (September-October), 537–543.

Collins, Allan M. and Elizabeth F. Loftus (1975), "A Spreading-Activation Theory of Semantic Processing," *Psychological Review,* 82, 407–428.

Craik, Fergus I.M. (1971), "Age Differences in Recognition Memory," *Quarterly Journal of Experimental Psychology,* 23, 316–323.

———, and Robert S. Lockhart (1972), "Levels of Processing: A Framework for Memory Research," *Journal of Verbal Learning and Verbal Behavior,* 11, 671–684.

———, and Endel Tulving (1975), "Depth of Processing and the Retention of Words," *Journal of Experimental Psychology: General,* 1, 268–294.

Crowder, Robert G. (1976), *Principles of Learning and Memory,* Hillsdale, NJ: Lawrence Erlbaum.

D'Andrade, Roy G. (1974), "Memory and the Assessment of Behavior," in *Measurement in the Social Sciences,* H.M. Blalock Jr., ed., Chicago: Aldine, 159–186.

Dosher, Barbara Anne and J. Edward Russo (1976), "Memory for Internally Generated Stimuli," *Journal of Experimental Psychology: Human Learning and Memory,* 2 (November), 633–640.

Eagle, Morris and Eli Leiter (1964), "Recall and Recognition in Intentional and Incidental Learning," *Journal of Experimental Psychology,* 68, 58–63.

Eysenck, Michael W. (1976), "Arousal, Learning, and Memory," *Psychological Bulletin,* 83 (May), 389–404.

Frijda, Nico H. (1972), "Simulation of Human Long-Term Memory," *Psychological Bulletin,* 77 (January), 1–31.

Gardner, Meryl P., Andrew A. Mitchell, and J. Edward Russo (1978), "Chronometric Analysis: An Introduction and an Application to Low

Involvement Perception of Advertisements," in *Advances in Consumer Research,* Volume 5, H. Keith Hunt, ed., Chicago: Association for Consumer Research, 581–589.

Goldberg, Marvin E. and Gerald J. Gorn (1974), "Children's Reactions to Television Advertising: An Experimental Approach," *Journal of Consumer Research,* 1 (September), 69–75.

Goldin, Sarah E. (1978), "Memory for the Ordinary: Typicality Effects in Chess Memory," *Journal of Experimental Psychology: Human Learning and Memory,* 4 (November), 605–616.

Haber, Ralph N. (1964), "Effects of Coding Strategy on Perceptual Memory," *Journal of Experimental Psychology,* 68 (November), 357–362.

Hintzman, Douglas L. and Richard A. Block (1970), "Memory Judgments and the Effects of Spacing," *Journal of Verbal Learning and Verbal Behavior,* 9, 561–566.

Hollan, James D. (1975), "Features and Semantic Memory: Set Theoretic or Network Model?" *Psychological Review,* 82, 154–155.

Howard, John A. (1977), *Consumer Behavior: Application of Theory,* New York: McGraw-Hill.

———, and Jagdish N. Sheth (1969), *The Theory of Buyer Behavior,* New York: John Wiley and Sons.

Jacoby, Larry L., Wayne H. Bartz, and James D. Evans (1978), "A Functional Approach to Levels of Processing," *Journal of Experimental Psychology: Human Learning and Memory,* 4 (July), 331–346.

Jenkins, James J. (1974), "Remember That Old Theory of Memory? Well, Forget It!" *American Psychologist,* 29 (November), 785–795.

Johnson, Eric J. (1978), "What Is Remembered About Consumer Decisions," unpublished manuscript, Pittsburgh: Department of Psychology, Carnegie-Mellon University.

———, and J. Edward Russo (1978), "The Organization of Product Information in Memory Identified by Recall Times," in *Advances in Consumer Research,* Volume V, H. Keith Hunt, ed., Chicago: Association for Consumer Research, 79–86.

Kahneman, Daniel (1973), *Attention and Effort,* Englewood Cliffs, NJ: Prentice-Hall, Inc.

Kieras, David (1978), "Beyond Pictures and Words: Alternative Information-Processing Models for Imagery Effects in Verbal Memory," *Psychological Bulletin,* 85 (May), 532–554.

Kintsch, Walter (1970), "Models for Free Recall and Recognition," in *Models of Human Memory,* Donald A. Norman, ed., New York: Academic Press, 331–373.

———(1978), "Comprehension and Memory of Text," in *Handbook of Learning and Cognitive Processes,* Volume 6: *Linguistic Functions in Cognitive Theory,* W.K. Estes, ed., Hillsdale, NJ: Lawrence Erlbaum.

Krugman, Herbert E. (1965), "The Impact of Television Advertising: Learning Without Involvement," *Public Opinion Quarterly,* 29 (Fall), 349–356.

———(1972), "Why Three Exposures May Be Enough," *Journal of Advertising Research,* 12 (December), 11–14.

Lappin, Joseph S. (1967), "Attention in the Identification of Stimuli in Complex Visual Displays," *Journal of Experimental Psychology,* 75 (November), 321–328.

Loftus, Geoffrey R. and Elizabeth F. Loftus (1976), *Human Memory: The Processing of Information,* Hillsdale, NJ: Lawrence Erlbaum.

Lutz, Kathy A. and Richard J. Lutz (1977), "Effects of Interactive Imagery on Learning: Application to Advertising," *Journal of Applied Psychology,* 62 (August), 493–498.

———, and ———(1978), "Imagery-Eliciting Strategies: Review and Implications of Research," in *Advances in Consumer Research,* Volume 5, H. Keith Hunt, ed., Chicago: Association for Consumer Research, 611–620.

Mandler, Jean M. and Richard E. Parker (1976), "Memory for Descriptive and Spatial Information in Complex Pictures," *Journal of Experimental Psychology: Human Learning and Memory,* 2 (January), 38–48.

Markus, Hazel (1977), "Self-Schemata and Processing Information About the Self," *Journal of Personality and Social Psychology,* 35 (February), 63–78.

McLaughlin, Barry (1965), " 'Intentional' and 'Incidental' Learning in Human Subjects: The Role of Instructions to Learn and Motivation," *Psychological Bulletin,* 63, 359–376.

Miller, George A. (1956), "The Magical Number Seven, Plus or Minus Two: Some Limits on Our

Capacity for Processing Information," *Psychological Review*, 63, 81–97.

Montague, William S. and Joseph S. Lappin (1966), "Effects of Coding Strategy on Perceptual Memory," *Journal of Experimental Psychology*, 72 (November), 777–779.

Nakanishi, Masao (1974), "Decision Net Models and Human Information Processing," in *Buyer/Consumer Information Processing*, G. David Hughes and Michael L. Ray, eds., Chapel Hill, NC: University of North Carolina Press, 75–88.

Neisser, Ulric (1967), *Cognitive Psychology*, New York: Appleton-Century-Crofts.

Nelson, Thomas O. (1977), "Repetition and Depth of Processing," *Journal of Verbal Learning and Verbal Behavior*, 16, 151–171.

Newell, Allan and Herbert A. Simon (1972), *Human Problem Solving*, Englewood Cliffs, NJ: Prentice-Hall, Inc.

Norman, Donald A. (1976), *Memory and Attention: An Introduction to Human Information Processing*, 2nd Ed., New York: John Wiley and Sons.

Olshavsky, Richard W. (1971), "Search Limits As a Function of Tree Size and Storage Requirements," *Organizational Behavior and Human Performance*, 6, 336–344.

Olson, Jerry C. (1977), "Price as an Informational Cue: Effects on Product Evaluations," in *Consumer and Industrial Buying Behavior*, Arch G. Woodside, Jagdish N. Sheth, and Peter D. Bennett, eds., New York: North Holland, 267–286.

———(1978a), "Inferential Belief Formation in the Cue Utilization Process," in *Advances in Consumer Research*, Volume 5, H. Keith Hunt, ed., Chicago: Association for Consumer Research, 706–713.

———(1978b), "Theories of Information Encoding and Storage: Implications for Consumer Research," in *The Effect of Information on Consumer and Market Behavior*, Andrew Mitchell, ed., Chicago: American Marketing Association, 49–60.

Paivio, Allan (1971), *Imagery and Verbal Processes*, New York: Holt, Rinehart, and Winston.

——— (1975), "Perceptual Comparisons Through the Mind's Eye," *Memory and Cognition*, 3, 635–647.

Penney, Catherine G. (1975), "Modality Effects in Short-Term Verbal Memory," *Psychological Bulletin*, 82 (January), 68–84.

Phillips, Lynn W. and Brian Sternthal (1977), "Age Differences in Information Processing: A Perspective on the Aged Consumer," *Journal of Marketing Research*, 14 (November), 444–457.

Postman, Leo (1975), "Verbal Learning and Memory," *Annual Review of Psychology*, 26, 291–335.

Quillian, M.R. (1968), "Semantic Memory," in *Semantic Information Processing*, M. Minsky, ed., Cambridge, MA: The MIT Press, 216–270.

Reitman, Walter R. (1970), "What Does It Take to Remember?" in *Models of Human Memory*, Donald A. Norman, ed., New York: Academic Press, 469–509.

Rossiter, John R. (1975), "Cognitive Phenomena in Contemporary Advertising," paper presented at the 1975 Conference on Culture and Communication, Temple University, March.

———(1976), "Visual and Verbal Memory in Children's Product Information Utilization," in *Advances in Consumer Research* Volume III, Beverlee B. Anderson, ed., Chicago: Association for Consumer Research, 523–527.

Russo, J. Edward and Robert A. Wisher (1976), "Reprocessing as a Recognition Cue," *Memory and Cognition*, 4 (November), 683–689.

Saegert, Joel (1979), "A Demonstration of Levels-of-Processing Theory in Memory for Advertisements," in *Advances in Consumer Research*, Volume 6, William L. Wilkie, ed., Miami: Association for Consumer Research.

Sawyer, Alan G. (1974), "The Effects of Repetition: Conclusions and Suggestions about Experimental Laboratory Research," in *Buyer/Consumer Information Processing*, G. David Hughes and Michael L. Ray, eds., Chapel Hill: University of North Carolina Press, 190–219.

Seamon, John G. and Susan Virostek (1978), "Memory Performance and Subject-Defined Depth of Processing," *Memory and Cognition*, 6 (May), 283–287.

Seibel, Robert, Richard E. Christ, and Warren E. Teichner (1965), "Short-Term Memory Under Work Load Stress," *Journal of Experimental Psychology*, 70, 154–162.

Shepard, Roger N. (1967), "Recognition Memory for Words, Sentences, and Pictures," *Journal of*

Verbal Learning and Verbal Behavior, 6, 156–163.

Shiffrin, Richard M. and R.C. Atkinson (1969), "Storage and Retrieval Processes in Long-Term Memory," *Psychological Review,* 76, 179–193.

Simon, Herbert A. (1969), *The Sciences of the Artificial,* Cambridge, MA: The MIT Press.

———(1974), "How Big is a Chunk?" *Science,* 183 (February), 482–488.

Smith, Edward E. (1978), "Theories of Semantic Memory," in *Handbook of Learning and Cognitive Processes,* Volume 6: *Linguistic Functions in Cognitive Theory,* W.K. Estes, ed., Hillsdale, NJ: Lawrence Erlbaum.

———, Edward J. Shoben, and Lance J. Rips (1974), "Structure and Process in Semantic Memory: A Featural Model for Semantic Decisions," *Psychological Review,* 81, 214–241.

Thomson, Donald M. (1972), "Context Effects in Recognition Memory," *Journal of Verbal Learning and Verbal Behavior,* 11, 497–511.

——— and Endel Tulving (1970), "Associative Encoding and Retrieval; Weak and Strong Cues," *Journal of Experimental Psychology,* 86, 255–262.

Tulving, Endel (1972), "Episodic and Semantic Memory," in *Organization of Memory,* Endel Tulving and W. Donaldson, eds., New York: Academic Press, 381–403.

Tversky, Barbara (1973), "Encoding Processes in Recognition and Recall," *Cognitive Psychology,* 5 (November), 275–287.

Underwood, Benton J. (1969), "Attributes of Memory," *Psychological Review,* 76, 559–573.

Welford, A.T. (1962), "On Changes of Performance with Age," *Lancet,* (February 17), 335–339.

Woodward, Addison E. Jr., Robert A. Bjork, and Robert H. Jongeward Jr. (1973), "Recall and Recognition as a Function of Primary Rehearsal," *Journal of Verbal Learning and Verbal Behavior,* 12, 608–617.

Wright, Peter L. (1974), "Analyzing Media Effects on Advertising Responses," *Public Opinion Quarterly,* 38, 192–205.

Wyer, Robert S., and Thomas K. Srull (1979, forthcoming), "The Processing of Social Stimulus Information: A Conceptual Integration," in *Person Memory and Encoding Processes,* R. Hastie, E. Ebbeson, T.M. Ostrom, R.S. Wyer, D.L. Hamilton, and D.E. Carlston, eds., Hillsdale, NJ: Lawrence Erlbaum.

Zielske, Hubert A. (1959), "The Remembering and Forgetting of Advertising," *Journal of Marketing,* 23 (January), 239–243.

Situational Variables and Consumer Behavior

Russell W. Belk

Growing recognition of limitations in the ability of individual consumer characteristics to explain variation in buyer behavior has prompted a number of appeals to examine situational influences on behavior. Ward and Robertson argued that "situational variables may account for considerably more variance than actor-related variables" (1973, p. 26). Lavidge (1966) cautioned that many buyer behaviors may be enacted only under specific conditions and necessitate situational investigations of intra-individual variability. Engel, Kollat, and Blackwell (1969) urged that *both* individual and situational factors must be considered in order to explain consumer choices. Nevertheless, these and other suggestions to include situational variables in research on consumer behavior have gone largely unheeded. The primary obstacle has been the absence of an adequate conception of the variables which

comprise a situation. It is the purpose of the following discussion to explore such concepts and to suggest directions for the study of situational influence in consumer behavior.

CONSUMER SITUATIONS AND RELATED CONCEPTS

Situations, Behavioral Settings, and Environments

As a starting point for a definition, most theoreticians would agree that a situation comprises a point in time and space (Belk, 1975). For students of human behavior, a discrete time and place occupied by one or more persons identifies a situation of potential interest. A somewhat larger alternative unit of analysis would be Barker's (1968) "behavioral setting." A behavioral setting is not only bounded in time and space, but also by a complete sequence of behavior or an "action pattern." For example, a basketball

Reprinted by permission from *Journal of Consumer Research* (December 1975), pp. 157–164.

game or a piano lesson is a behavioral setting because each involves an interval in time and space in which certain behaviors can be expected regardless of the particular persons present. But such patterns of behavior require stretching the time and place dimensions to broader and more continuous units than those defining a situation. While a behavioral setting might be a store which is open from 8:00 AM to 6:00 PM (Barker, 1968, p. 19), the current perspective would recognize a number of discrete situations which may occur within this setting.

The concept of an "environment" extends the time, place, and behavioral dimensions still further. Although there is less agreement as to what bounds and defines an environment,[1] it is clear that situations and behavioral settings are subunits within an environment. In one of his early formulations Lewin pointed out that an environment may be thought of as the chief characteristics of a more or less permanent "situation" (Lewin, 1933). In this sense situations represent momentary encounters with those elements of the total environment which are available to the individual at a particular time. Environment is also broader in terms of the geographic area over which it applies. For example, while the "legal environment" may be described to consist of laws, legal institutions, and interpretive tendencies within a governmental territory, and the behavioral setting may refer to a certain courtroom, the specific experience of individual A being cross-examined by attorney G during trial M in city R at 4:00 on day X, can only be described from a narrower situational perspective. It is this latter view of the conditions for experiences and the effect of these conditions on specific behavioral outcomes which the current perspective seeks to develop.

**Situational Versus
Non-Situational Determinants
of Consumer Behavior**

A second group of concepts from which situations must be distinguished are the nonsituational determinants of a particular consumer behavior. Figure 10–1 shows a familiar stimulus-organism-response paradigm which has been modified to divide the stimulus into an object and a situation. This split is analogous to the perceptual distinctions between figure and ground or focal and contextual cues (Helson, 1964). That is, because behavior with respect to a product or service object is of primary significance in consumer behavior, the object to which the consumer is directly responding will be re-

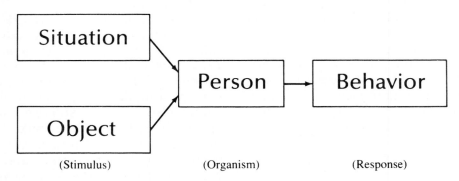

(Stimulus)   (Organism)   (Response)

Figure 10–1
A Revised S–O–R Paradigm

garded as a unique source of behavioral influence. In not including personal and object characteristics within the concept of the situation there is also a purposeful departure from Lewin's (1935) formulation of the life space. The rationale for this more limited view of situation is the greater possibility of operationalizing a construct which has an existence apart from the individual's total consciousness. For there to be hope of really adding to the ability to explain consumer behavior, this separate existence is essential.[2]

It might seem that a clear distinction may be made between persons, objects, and situations as separate sources of influence on behavior, but some potential for confusion exists in attempting to separate the characteristics of each determinant. R. L. Thorndike's (1947) concept of "lasting and general characteristics of the individual" is a useful device in distinguishing personal and situational characteristics. These individual features, including personality, intellect, sex, and race, are stable over times and places of observation and may therefore be attributed consistently to the individual. Where the feature is more transitory, such as having a headache, it must be considered to be at least partly a function of the situation. It is necessary to impose similar constraints on the conception of object characteristics in order to categorize a description such as a brand of soda being 10¢ less than competing brands. In cases where the characteristic tends to be a lasting and general feature of the brand it may be attributed to the object. Where the characteristic is specific to a time and place (e.g., a special sale) it should be regarded as a characteristic of the situation.

Characteristics of Consumer Situations

Consistent with the previous distinctions, a consumer situation may be viewed as com-

prising ". . . all those factors particular to a time and place of observation which do not follow from a knowledge of personal (intra-individual) and stimulus (choice alternative) attributes and which have a demonstrable and systemic effect on current behavior" (Belk, 1974a). The greatest problem in operationalizing this view lies in defining "all those factors." Several attempts have been made to develop comprehensive taxonomies of situational characteristics. Using general guidelines suggested by Sherif and Sherif (1956), Sells (1963) constructed a subjective classification of over 200 situational variables including gravity, temperature, group structure, role requirements, and novelty of the situation in relation to prior experiences. Unfortunately, from the point of view of the current conception of situation, Sells' classification also includes some characteristics of the individual (e.g., age, sex, race) and environment (e.g., sources of food, erosion, language), and excludes certain descriptors of the physical locale (e.g., noises, colors, room or area size). Classification attempts by Bellows (1963), Wolf (1966), and Moos (1973), are less complete and suffer from similar drawbacks. Although also incomplete and parochial in its focus, a limited taxonomy by Allen (1965) of the situational factors found to affect conformity highlights several important social dimensions (e.g., public/private, interdependence of participants) and task dimensions (e.g., difficulty, importance) of the situation. These features contrast sharply with the taxonomy of 66 bipolar adjectival scales constructed by Kasmar (1970) to measure situations. From an initial list of 300 characteristics generated through room description protocols obtained from architecture students, scales were developed to describe 13 aspects of the situation; size, volume, scale, mood, color, texture, function, illumination, esthetic quality, climate, color, acoustical quality, and miscellaneous. Such characteristics provide a comprehensive description of the design features of the situation, but they completely neglect the social and task attributes which Allen's review (1965) emphasized. Furthermore a higher order factor analysis of data from Kasmar's scales has shown them to be highly redundant in terms of an underlying affective dimension (Mehrabian and Russel, 1974). Mehrabian and Russell's own (1974) attempt to develop three comprehensive situational descriptors (pleasure, arousal, and dominance) is also not very satisfying to depict the array of possible situational dimensions. However, by selectively combining features suggested in the various taxonomies cited, a skeletal notion of what is meant by "all those factors" comprising a situation may be offered. The following five groups of situational characteristics represent the general features from these taxonomies which are consistent with the current definition of situation.

1. *Physical Surroundings* are the most readily apparent features of a situation. These features include geographical and institutional location, decor, sounds, aromas, lighting, weather, and visible configurations of merchandise or other material surrounding the stimulus object.

2. *Social Surroundings* provide additional depth to a description of a situation. Other persons present, their characteristics, their apparent roles, and interpersonal interactions occurring are potentially relevant examples.

3. *Temporal Perspective* is a dimension of situations which may be specified in units ranging from time of day to season of the year. Time may also be measured relative to some past or future event for the situational participant. This allows conceptions such as time since last purchase, time since or until meals or payday, and time constraints imposed by prior or standing commitments.

4. *Task Definition* features of a situation include an intent or requirement to select, shop for, or obtain information about a general or specific purchase. In addition, task may reflect different buyer and user roles anticipated by the individual. For instance, a person shopping for a small appliance as a wedding gift for a friend is in a different situation than he would be in shopping for a small appliance for personal use.

5. *Antecedent States* make up a final group of features which characterize a situation. These are momentary moods (such as acute anxiety, pleasantness, hostility, and excitation) or momentary conditions (such as cash on hand, fatigue, and illness) rather than chronic individual traits. These conditions are further stipulated to be immediately antecedent to the current situation in order to distinguish states which the individual brings to the situation from states of the individual which results from the situation. For instance, a person may select a certain motion picture because he feels depressed (an antecedent state and a part of the choice situation), but the fact that the movie causes him to feel happier is a response to the consumption situation.[3] This altered state may then become antecedent for behavior in the next choice situation encountered, such as passing a street vendor on the way out of the theater.

Given a conception of the dimensions characterizing a situation, the final element of the definition of a situation requiring clarification is the requirement that these features have a "demonstrable and systematic effect on current behavior." To a greater extent than the problem of situational dimensions, this is an empirical question which has been the subject of some research. The following section reviews this research and examines the extent to which situational knowledge can be expected to add to our ability to explain consumer behavior.

ASSESSMENTS OF SITUATIONAL EFFECTS ON CONSUMER BEHAVIOR

Inventory Evidence

In the past six or seven years a small but growing number of empirical tests of situational influence in consumer behavior have been conducted using inventories of situational scenarios and choice alternatives. These inventories ask subjects to rate the likelihood that they would choose each of several alternative products or services under each of several sets of situational conditions. Summary descriptions of seven of these inventories are provided in the Appendix. It may well be argued that the situations investigated in these studies do not constitute random samples of possible situations and do not always reflect the full range of situational dimensions just outlined. Despite

the fact that most of the inventories have relied on pretests to generate familiar situations, the argument is undoubtedly valid. Even so, any demonstration that behavior differs widely between the situations specified is evidence that there are important situational determinants for the class of choices considered.

Results comparing the relative influence from persons, products (responses), situations, and their interactions are presented in Table 10–1 for the six product categories that have been examined.[4] For all inventories the effects explaining the smallest proportions of variance are those which reflect superfluous response styles. For instance, a sizable interaction term for persons by situations would only indicate that some subjects view using any of the products in certain situations as more likely than do other subjects. Similarly, sizable main ef-

Table 10–1
Analysis of Consumer Behavior Variance[a] (percents of total variance)

	Response Category[b]					
Source	Beverage Products	Meat Products	Snack Products A	Fast Foods[c]	Leisure Activities[d]	Motion Pictures
Persons (P)	0.5%	4.6%	6.7%	8.1%	4.5%	0.9%
Situations (S)	2.7%	5.2%	0.4%	2.2%	2.0%	0.5%
Products (Responses: R)	14.6%	15.0%	6.7%	13.4%	8.8%	16.6%
R × S	39.8%	26.2%	18.7%	15.3%	13.4%	7.0%
P × S	2.7%	2.9%	6.1%	2.2%	4.0%	1.9%
P × R	11.8%	9.7%	22.4%	20.1%	21.2%	33.7%
P × S × R	—[e]	—[e]	3.4%	—[e]	—[e]	—[e]
Residual	27.8%[f]	36.4%	35.6%	38.7%	46.1%	39.4%
Total	100.0%	100.0%	100.0%	100.0%	100.0%	100.0%

[a]Components of variance analyses for mixed effects model with subjects random. For computational details, see Gleser, Chronbach and Rajaratnam (1965) and Endler and Hunt (1966).
[b]Inventories are described in Appendix.
[c]Variance components from this inventory have not previously been presented.
[d]Means of four samples.
[e]Not obtained due to single presentations of each situation-response combination.
[f]Incorrectly reported as entirely P × S × R.

fects for persons or situations would have little meaning since they do not involve preference differences by product. A more dominant influence is the responses by situations interaction, especially for the meat and beverage inventories. This is the variance component which directly reflects the influence of systemic situational differences in product preferences. Furthermore, the lower contributions from the responses main effect in all inventories except motion pictures, suggest that general product popularity is a substantially less important determinant of consumer preferences than are situational conditions. For the meat and beverage inventories the small interaction terms for persons by responses reveal that in these categories situational influence also outstrips *individual* product preferences. For other inventories, again excepting motion pictures, the effects of situational and individual influences are jointly dominant. Motion pictures is the only category examined in which situational effects appear to be minimal. In this case individual preferences appear to be the consistent choice determinant with the general popularity of the movies following in importance.

A recent challenge to the validity of these inventory-based findings has been presented by Lutz and Kakkar (1975). They argued that the experimental procedure of having subjects rate the same choice alternatives under all situational conditions may have spuriously inflated the situations by products interaction term. In order to test this possibility they replicated Belk's (1974a) snack product inventory, but exposed each subject to only one level of the situation factor (see Appendix for a description of their experiment). Their analysis obtained a contribution of less than 6 percent for the situations by products interaction, with a residual term which accounted for over 86 percent of the variance.[5] Unfortunately,

their analysis assumed an inappropriate completely randomized factorial design rather than the split plot factorial design which was actually employed (Winter, 1971, pp. 366–371, Kirk, 1968, pp. 245–318). This problem renders their analysis meaningless and leaves the question of artifactual situational influence open. By altering the numbers of situations or responses by a factor of one half, Belk (1974b) has shown the variance component estimates of this inventory to be relatively stable across the resulting formats. Comparable results have been found by Endler and Hunt (1969) for a similar anxiety inventory. However, since these examinations do not reduce the number of situations to one per subject, the possibility that situational influence has been overestimated by these inventories still exists.

Other Evidence

Evidence of the importance of consumer situations has been found using other approaches which lend additional credence to a conclusion that situational influence is a pervasive factor in consumer behavior. Using multidimensional scaling Green and Rao (1972) found that consumer perceptions of and preferences for various bread and pastry items changed markedly over differing meal and menu situations. In a series of experimental choice simulations Hansen (1972) found that selection of a hairdryer as a gift depended upon characteristics of the supposed recipient, and that information seeking and choices from a fixed menu varied according to the description of the restaurant. Grønhaug (1972) found that buyers of tableware utilized different types and sources of information depending upon whether the purchase was for personal use or for a gift. By having subjects reconstruct word of mouth incidents, Belk (1971) found that one-third of the conversations about a new freeze dried coffee took place where the prior conversation concerned food, and that another third of the conversations began while drinking coffee. Sandell (1968b) was able to condition choice of specific cigarette brands to either stressful or boring situations and to consumption of a specific brand of beer.

From the variety of methods employed in these studies it appears that situational effects can be demonstrated both descriptively and experimentally. Although the amount of research specifically focused on situational influence is still quite small, a number of instances have been found in which situations can be shown to affect consumer behavior systematically. There is further encouragement for situational research from the refreshing fact that analyses of the behavioral inventories specifying situations have been able to explain the majority of variance encountered.

SITUATIONAL RESEARCH IN CONSUMER BEHAVIOR

Despite the substantial promise and appeal of research which employs situational vari-

ables to explain consumer choice behavior, several basic issues require resolution before this potential can be fully realized. Foremost among the issues which this research must address is the question of the most appropriate means of measuring situations. Two alternative perspectives proposed have been labeled "psychological" (Lutz and Kakkar, 1975) and "objective" (Belk, 1975) measurements. Psychological measurements of situations rely on the subjects' perceptions of the situation and are an extension of sociological inquiry into the "situation as defined" (Thomas, 1927). The premise for such measurements is that the way an individual construes a situation should be more important to behavior than the inherent features of that situation. Objective measurements of situations restrict themselves to features of the situation as it exists before subjects' interpretations. The primary rationale for this perspective is that it removes the idiosyncrasies of perception which may otherwise limit aggregation and manipulation of consumer situations. The possibility has also been raised that some situational influences, such as subtle cueing effects, may operate without the subject's perceptual awareness. Without some sort of hybrid measurement which merges these perspectives, it appears that situational research must utilize both types of measurements.

A related issue concerns the most appropriate means of manipulating situations in experimental research. Both psychologically and objectively defined situations may be manipulated by assigning subjects to different times, places, and conditions, although successful manipulations of psychologically defined situations may need to be more clever or elaborate. However, this sort of research is costly and is best limited to the investigation of one or two situational dimensions at a time. Alternatively, and more commonly, the projective use of situational scenarios may continue to be used. Typically these scenarios have ranged from a one phrase to one paragraph written description of situational conditions. Photographs, motion pictures, and video tapes are possible refinements of stimulus input in this procedure, but these methods favor visual cues and may unnaturally focus attention and control the *rate* of experience. Perhaps the best means of manipulation, short of actually modifying situational conditions, is to couple written descriptions of features such as temporal perspective, task definition, and antecedent states, with visual and auditory input of physical and social surroundings. Comparisons of results using each alternative means of manipulation will be needed to assess their relative adequacy.

Whether the existence of a particular situational effect has been determined under simulated or actual conditions, interpretation of the importance of this effect requires knowledge of the frequency of occurrence of these conditions. Because consumers can selectively seek or avoid many of the situations they encounter and because all unanticipated situations are not equally common, descriptive evidence of the frequency of situational occurrences is needed. A number of time budget studies based on consumer diaries (e.g., Szali, 1973) are available which provide general records of the times and places of consumer activities. But even the most detailed consumer accounts (e.g., Muse, 1946) seldom go beyond "shopping" in their descriptions of purchase situations. Nevertheless activity diaries appear to be a useful approach to gathering relevant data on situational occurrences. In addition to providing data on relevant situational variables, this approach may simultaneously measure individual characteristics and behavioral outcomes which can be cross tabulated with situations to obtain a picture of individual differences in situational expo-

sure and susceptibility to situational influence.

The ultimate problem for all future situational research is the lack of a comprehensive taxonomy of situational characteristics and normal combinations of these characteristics. Hopefully this discussion has made some headway in establishing a general conceptualization of consumer situations, but obviously greater detail is necessary. It is a false hope at this point to expect that we can systematically investigate a complete list of situational characteristics, because no such list exists. Only by continuing to conceptualize and research situational characteristics under a guiding understanding of the scope and criteria for situations can such a summary ever be achieved.

APPENDIX: SUMMARY DETAILS FOR SEVEN SITUATIONAL INVENTORIES

1. *Beverages.* Sandell (1968a) presented 31 student subjects with ten beverages (e.g., coffee, water, beer) which they rated in seven situations (e.g., when alone, feeling sleepy in the afternoon, reading the paper in the morning) using a seven-point scale from "extremely unwilling" to "extremely willing" (to try). Situations and beverages tested were apparently chosen subjectively, although five subjects who did not appear to view the products as alternatives were eliminated.

2. *Leisure Activities.* Bishop and Witt (1970) investigated the effect of ten situations (e.g., returning from studying at a noisy library, relaxing Friday afternoon following a busy week, waking up fresh and rested on a Saturday morning) on the likelihood of engaging in each of

13 leisure activities (e.g., go shopping for clothes, watch television, visit a friend) using a five-point scale from "almost certainly" to "I would not feel like" (doing this). Situations were selected based on five alternative theories of leisure behavior, and leisure activities were based on their frequency of occurrence in previous community surveys. Subjects were male and female students at two colleges and totalled 141.

3. *Meat Products.* Belk (1974a) examined choices of 11 different meat products (e.g., hamburger, steak, chicken) in nine different situations (e.g., party for friends, meal on a weekday evening, at a nice restaurant with friends) using five-point scales from "extremely likely" to "not at all likely," administered to 100 members of a community. Situations and meat products were chosen from protocols and familiarity pretests.

4. *Motion Pictures.* Belk (1974b) had 100 students rate 12 hypothetical motion pictures (e.g., The Motorcycle Freaks, Summer of Dreams, Only Fools are Sad) described in mock advertisements, in nine situations (e.g., on a weeknight with friends of the same sex, just for something to do, together with spouse or date at their request) on a five-point scale. Situations were selected via protocols and pretests based on familiarity, and motion pictures were structured to parallel currently popular themes.

5. *Snack Products A.* Belk (1974b) varied ten different situations (e.g., while watching television with family, going on a long automobile trip, an urge for a between meal snack) and had 100 students subjects rate the likelihood of choosing each of ten snack products (e.g., potato chips, pastries, ice cream) on two occasions (two weeks apart) using five-point scales. Situations and

products were chosen as in the meat inventory.

6. *Snack Products B.* Lutz and Kakkar (1975) replicated Belk's snack product inventory except that subjects in each of ten groups of from 24 to 36 students responded within only one of the situations and on only one occasion. Each group rated products in a different situation and a total of 306 subjects were employed.

7. *Fast Foods.* Using data collected by Leo Burnett U.S.A., Belk (1975) analyzed the effect of ten different situations (e.g., too tired to cook dinner, unexpected dinner guests, having a few friends over for a casual get-together) on responses to a six-point likelihood scale for each of ten (confidential) fast food outlets and related meal choices. Subjects were 98 housewives in a single community.

NOTES

1. A great deal of the effort in the emerging discipline of environmental or ecological psychology has been spent in debating boundaries. See for example Barker (1963), Craik (1970), Proshansky, Ittelson, and Rivlin (1970), Ittelson (1973), and Rivlin (1973).

2. This point is elaborated by Belk (1975). Mausner (1963) captured the argument in stating that "if one specifies the stimulus in terms of the nature of the receiver, lawfulness becomes impossible."

3. Hansen (1972) distinguishes between purchase, consumption, and communication situations. Comments in this paper concentrate primarily on consumer purchase choices.

4. The research reported generally employed a situations by products by persons repeated measures experimental design. While nearly all main effects and two way interactions

yielded significant *F*-ratios, proportions of variance accounted for by each effect are more revealing (Belk, 1974a).

5. Hays' Omega squared statistic (Hays, 1964) was employed to derive these estimates. Since this statistic assumed a completely fixed effects model, results are not strictly comparable to those of the mixed effects components of variance method employed in the other studies reported.

REFERENCES

Albaum, G. "Exploring Interaction in a Marketing Situation," *Journal of Marketing Research*, 4 (May, 1967), 168–72.

Allen, B. L. "Situational Factors in Conformity," in Leonard Berkowitz, *Advances in Experimental Social Psychology*, Vol. 2, New York: Academic Press, 1965.

Barker, R. G. *The Stream of Behavior*. New York: Appleton-Century-Crofts, 1963.

———. *Ecological Psychology: Concepts and Methods for Studying the Environment of Human Behavior*, Stanford University Press, 1968.

Belk, R. W. "Occurrence of Word of Mouth Buyer Behavior as a Function of Situation and Advertising Stimuli," *Proceedings*, American Marketing Association Fall Conference, 1971, 419–22.

———. "An Exploratory Assessment of Situational Effects in Buyer Behavior," *Journal of Marketing Research*, 11 (May, 1974a), 156–163.

———. "Application and Analysis of the Behavior Differential Inventory for Assessing Situational Effects in Consumer Behavior," in Scott Ward and Peter Wright (eds.), *Advances in Consumer Research*, Vol. 1. Urbana: Association for Consumer Research, 1974b.

———. "The Objective Situation as a Determinant of Consumer Behavior," in Mary Jane Schlinger (ed.) *Advances in Consumer Research*, Vol. 2. Chicago: Association for Consumer Research, 1975.

Bell, G. D. "Self-Confidence and Persuasion in Car Buying," *Journal of Marketing Research*, 4 (February, 1967), 46–52.

Bellows, R. "Towards a Taxonomy of Social Situations," in Stephen B. Sells (ed.), *Stimulus Determinants of Behavior*, New York: Ronald, 1963.

Bishop, D. W. and P. A. Witt, "Sources of Behavioral Variance During Leisure Time," *Journal of Personality and Social Psychology*, 16 (October, 1970), 352–60.

Craik, K. H. "Environmental Psychology," in Kenneth H. Craik, et al. *New Directions in Psychology*, Vol. 4, New York: Holt, Rinehart and Winston, 1970.

Endler, N. S. and J. McV. Hunt. "Sources of Behavioral Variance as Measured by the S–R Inventory of Anxiousness," *Psychological Bulletin*, 65 (1966), 336–46.

Engel, J. F., D. T. Kollat, and R. D. Blackwell. "Personality Measures and Market Segmentation," *Business Horizons*, 12 (June, 1969), 61–70.

Gleser, G. L., L. J. Cronbach and N. Rajaratnam. "Generalizability of Scores Influenced by Multiple Sources of Variance," *Psychometricka*, 30 (1965), 395–418.

Green, P. E. and V. R. Rao, "Configural Synthesis in Multidimensional Scaling," *Journal of Marketing Research*, 9 (February, 1972), 65–68.

Grønhaug, K. "Buying Situation and Buyer's Information Behavior," *European Marketing Research Review*, 7 (September, 1972), 33–48.

Hansen, F. *Consumer Choice Behavior*. New York: The Free Press, 1972.

Hays, W. L. *Statistics for Psychologists*. New York: Rinehart and Winston, 1964.

Helson, H. "Current Trends and Issues in Adaptation-Level Theory," *American Psychologist*, 19 (1964), 26–38.

Ittelson, W. H. *Environment and Cognition*. New York: Seminar Press, 1973.

Kasmar, J. V. "The Development of a Usable Lexicon of Environmental Discriptors," *Environment and Behavior*, 2 (1970), 133–169.

Kirk, R. E. *Experimental Design: Procedures for the Behavior Sciences*, Belmont, California: Wadsworth Publishing, 1968.

Lavidge, R. J. "The Cotton Candy Concept: Intra-Individual Variability," in Lee Adler and Irving Crespi, *Attitude Research at Sea*, Chicago: American Marketing Association, 1966, 39–50.

Lewin, K. "Environmental Forces in Child Behavior and Development," in Carl C. Murchison,

Handbook of Child Psychology, second edition, revised. Worcester, Massachusetts: Clark University Press, 1933, 94–127.

Lewin, K. *A Dynamic Theory of Personality*. New York: McGraw-Hill, 1935.

Lutz, R. J. and P. K. Kakkar. "The Psychological Situation as a Determinant of Consumer Behavior," in Mary Jane Schlinger (ed.), *Advances in Consumer Research*, Vol. 2. Chicago: Association for Consumer Research, 1975.

Mausner, B. M. "The Specification of the Stimulus Situation in a Social Interaction," in Stephen B. Sells, *Stimulus Determinants of Behavior*. New York: Ronald, 1963.

Mehrabian, A. and J. A. Russell. *An Approach to Environmental Psychology*. Cambridge: M.I.T. Press, 1974.

Moos, R. H. "Conceptualizations of Human Environments," *American Psychologist*, 28 (1973), 652–663.

Muse, M. "Time Expenditures in Homemaking Activities in 183 Vermont Farm Homes," *Vermont Agricultural Experimental Station Bulletin*, No. 530, 1946.

Nisbett, R. E. and D. E. Kanouse, "Obesity, Food Deprivation and Supermarket Shopping Behavior," *Journal of Personality and Social Psychology*, 12 (August, 1969), 289–94.

Pennington, A. L. "Customer-Salesman Bargaining Behavior in Retail Transactions," *Journal of Marketing Research*, 5 (August, 1965), 255–62.

Proshansky, H. M., W. H. Ittelson, and L. G. Rivlin. (eds.) *Environmental Psychology*, New York: Holt, Rinehart and Winston, 1970.

Sandell, R. G. "Effects of Attitudinal and Situational Factors on Reported Choice Behavior," *Journal of Marketing Research*, 4 (August, 1968a), 405–08.

———. "The Effects of Attitude Influence and Representational Conditioning on Choice Behavior," Stockholm: The Economic Research Institute, Stockholm School of Economics, 1968b.

Sells, S. B. "Dimensions of Stimulus Situations Which Accounts for Behavioral Variance," in Stephen B. Sells (ed.), *Stimulus Determinants of Behavior*, New York: Ronald, 1963.

Sherif, M. and C. W. Sherif. *An Outline of Social Psychology*, Rev. Ed. New York: Harper and Row, 1956.

Spence, H. E., J. R. Engel, and Roger D. Blackwell. "Perceived Risk in Mail-Order and Retail Store Buying," *Journal of Marketing Research*, 7 (August, 1970), 364–69.

Szali, A. et al. (eds) *The Use of Time*. The Hague: Mouten, 1973.

Thomas, W. I. "The Behavior Pattern and the Situation," *Proceedings*, Twenty-second Annual Meeting, American Sociological Society, 22 (1927), 1–13.

Thorndike, R. L. *Research Problems and Techniques*. Washington: U.S Government Printing Office, Report No. 3 AAF Aviation Psychology Program, 1947.

Ward, S. and T. S. Robertson. "Consumer Behavior Research: Promise and Prospects," in Scott Ward and Thomas S. Robertson, *Consumer Behavior: Theoretical Sources*. Englewood Cliffs: Prentice-Hall, 1973, 3–42.

Wells, W. D. and A. LoSciuto. "A Direct Observation of Purchasing Behavior," *Journal of Marketing Research*, (August, 1966), 227–33.

Winer, B. J. *Statistical Principles in Experimental Design*, Second Edition. New York: McGraw-Hill, 1971.

Wolf, R. "The Measurement of Environments," in Anne Anastasi (ed.), *Testing Problems in Perspective*, Washington, D.C.: American Council on Education, 1966, 491–503.

A Modernized Family Life Cycle

Patrick E. Murphy and William A. Staples

The family has been one of the hallmarks of American society. However, events in recent years, including rising divorce rates, falling fertility figures, and widespread use of contraceptives, have begun to bring about changes in family structure. It might be argued that the revolution of the 70's is occurring within the home rather than on college campuses or in central cities.

Certain writers (Bernard 1975; Cooper 1970; Davids 1971; Keller 1971; Toffler 1970) have conjectured that families today, and especially those of the future, will not resemble those of the past. Others (Bane 1976; Kerchoff 1976; Olson 1972) believe that family formation and dissolution is much the same today as it was in the past. The position taken in this paper falls between those extremes. It appears that certain changes have occurred that affect family life and consumption behavior, but the institution of the family will undoubtedly survive.

Reprinted by permission from *Journal of Consumer Research* (June 1979), pp. 12–22.

One aspect of the family that has been studied by sociologists and consumer and marketing researchers is the "family life cycle" (FLC). It has been shown to be a valuable concept for these three groups of researchers (Lansing and Kish 1957; Rich and Jain 1968; Spanier, Lewis, and Cole 1975). Unfortunately, the life cycle has not been examined in light of current demographic trends. The purpose of this paper is to review the family life cycle concept, discuss prior research concerning its impact on consumer behavior, and suggest a new, more appropriate FLC with research implications.

THE TRADITIONAL FAMILY LIFE CYCLE

Approach and Eras

The family life cycle is derived from the "developmental" approach to studying the family (Hill and Rodgers 1964; Hill 1970; Rodgers 1964; Rodgers 1973), an interdisciplinary approach drawing from rural and urban sociology, child psychology, and human development. Consequently, alternative views have been expressed about the number, as well as the determinants, of the "stages" in the FLC.

Before examining these viewpoints, other points need to be clarified. A few researchers have argued that the terms "cycle" and "stage" are not appropriate. Specifically, Rodgers (1962) proposed substituting "career" for cycle and "category" for stage. Applying this conceptualization, Feldman and Feldman (1975) suggested four subcareers of a lifetime family career: (1) sexual experience, (2) marital, (3) parental, and (4) adult-parent. Although these ideas have generally not been adopted, it is important to recognize that the FLC terminology has not received universal support.

Family life cycles can be characterized as ranging from simple to complex. Table 11–1 shows three distinct eras of FLC development.[1] The first one is called the "foundation era" because the concept began to be seriously studied by several writers simultaneously. Although Rowntree (1903) is credited with originating the FLC notion as a method to study poverty patterns in England, it was not until the 30's that family researchers began systematic evaluation of it. In one of the earliest FLC articles, Sorokin, Zimmerman, and Galpin (1931) identified four stages based on the changing family member constellation. Another four-stage FLC developed by Kirkpatrick and others (1934) viewed FLC in terms of the children's position in the educational system, i.e., preschool, grade school, high school, and adult. In examining the differences between rural and urban families, Loomis (1936) also delineated a four-stage cycle using the children's age as the criterion variable.

During the "expansion era" of FLC research depicted in Table 11–1, the number of stages identified tended to increase. Bigelow (1942) utilized school placement in a cycle he demarked in seven stages. Similarly, Glick (1947) postulated a seven-stage FLC determined by the birth and marriage of the first and last child, and the husband or wife's death. For the National Conference on Family Life in 1948, another seven-stage FLC was developed using multiple factors to separate stages (Duvall and Hill 1948).

In recent years, further refinements in FLC stages have occurred. Consequently, this period is labeled the "refinement era" (Table 11–1). The most complex breakdown to date was a twenty-four stage FLC proposed by Rodgers (1960). Although suggested outside the family literature, Wells and Gubar's (1966) nine-stage FLC, based on the ages of parents and children and employment status, has been accepted by family and consumer researchers. Duvall (1971) identified eight FLC stages using both children's and parents' ages to determine the stages.

This review of the chronological eras of the FLC reveals its strong foundation in the sociological literature. Despite the differences in number of stages and the factors causing movement through them, agreement exists on one central idea—each family progresses through a number of distinct phases from point of formation to death of both spouses.

Research over Stages

Considerable attention has been devoted to consumer behavior over the various FLC stages. The first such concerted effort was undertaken in 1954 in a conference entitled "The Life Cycle and Consumer Behavior." Several papers investigated the topic from different perspectives (Clark 1955). Lansing and Morgan (1955) analyzed the family financial situation across the FLC stages, in-

Table 11-1
Alternative Views of the Family Life Cycle

Author(s)/stages	Author(s)/stages	Author(s)/stages

Foundation era

Sorokin, Zimmerman, and Galpin (1931)	Kirkpatrick, Cowles, and Tough (1934)	Loomis (1936)
1. Married couples just starting their independent economic existence 2. Couples with one or more children 3. Couples with one or more adult self-supporting children 4. Couples growing old	1. Preschool family 2. Grade school family 3. High school family 4. All adult family	1. Childless couples of childbearing age 2. Families with children (eldest under 14) 3. Families with oldest child over 14 and under 36 4. Old families

Expansion era

Bigelow (1942)	Glick (1947)	Duvall and Hill (1948)
1. Establishment 2. Child-bearing and preschool period 3. Elementary school period 4. High school period 5. College 6. Period of recovery 7. Period of retirement	1. First marriage 2. Birth of first child 3. Birth of last child 4. Marriage of first child 5. Marriage of last child 6. Death of husband or wife 7. Death of spouse	1. Childless 2. Expanding (birth of first to last child) 3. School age 4. Stable (birth of last child to launching) 5. Contracting (first launched to last launched) 6. Aging companions (no children at home) 7. One partner deceased

Refinement era

Rodgers (1962)	Rodgers (1962) cont.	Wells and Gubar (1966)

1. Beginning families (defined as childless couples)
2. Families with infants (all children less than 36 months old)
3. Preschool families
  a. With infants (oldest child 3–6 years; youngest child, birth to 36 months)
  b. All children 3–6 years
4. School-age families
  a. With infants (oldest child, 6–13 years; youngest child, birth to 36 months)
  b. With preschoolers (oldest, 6–13 years; youngest, 3–6 years)
	7. Launching families
	  a. With infants (first child launched; youngest, birth to 36 months)
	  b. With preschoolers (first child launched; youngest 3–6)
	  c. With school-agers (first child launched; youngest, 6–13)
	  d. With teen-agers (first child launched; youngest, 13–20)
	  e. With young adults (first child launched; youngest, over 20)
	8. Middle years (all children launched to retirement of breadwinner)
		1. Bachelor stage (young single people not living at home)
		2. Newly married couples (no children)
		3. Full nest I (youngest child under 6)
		4. Full nest II (youngest child 6 or over)
		5. Full nest III (older married couples with dependent children)
		6. Empty nest I (no children living at home, head in labor force)
		7. Empty nest II (head retired)
		8. Solitary survivor (in labor force)

Table 11-1
Alternative Views of the Family Life Cycle (continued)

Author(s)/stages	Author(s)/stages	Author(s)/stages
c. All children 6–13 years 5. Teen-age families 　a. With infants (oldest, 13–20; youngest, birth to 36 months) 　b. With preschoolers (oldest, 13–20; youngest, 6–13) 　c. With school-aged (oldest 13–20; youngest 6–13) 　d. All children 13–20 years 6. Young adult families 　a. With infants (oldest, over 20; youngest, birth to 36 months) 　b. With preschoolers (oldest, over 20; youngest, 3–6) 　c. With school-agers (oldest, 13–20; youngest, 6–13) 　d. With teen-agers (oldest, over 20; youngest, 6–13) 　e. All over 20	9. Aging couple (retirement to death of one spouse) 10. Widowhood (death of first spouse to death of survivor)	9. Solitary survivor (retired) Duvall (1971) 1. Married couples (without children) 2. Childbearing families (oldest child under 30 months) 3. Families with pre-school children (oldest, 2½–6) 4. Families with school children (oldest, 6–13) 5. Families with teen-agers (oldest, 13–20) 6. Families as launching centers (first child gone to last child's leaving home) 7. Middle-aged parents (empty nest to retirement) 8. Aging family members (retirement to death of both spouses)

cluding its relationship to the purchase of durable goods. In another paper at the same conference, Barton (1955) studied the consumption of nondurable goods. Further, Miller (1955) examined the impact of advertising over the FLC and found stage inversely related to advertising effectiveness. In addition, Fisher (1955) exhorted consumer researchers to conduct more longitudinal family studies and to identify social and psychological factors influencing the FLC stages.

The most comprehensive research relating to the FLC stages was presented by Wells and Gubar (1966). They discussed several of the aforementioned conference papers in detail and supplemented them with data from a then recent *Survey of Consumer Finances* and a *Life* magazine study. In this manner, they were able to develop a thorough profile of financial and consumption behavior across the FLC stages they identified (Table 11–1).

Several other researchers have concentrated on individual stages of the FLC. Wortzel (1977) studied the "young singles," and concluded that their activities are increasingly oriented toward personal growth and enriching experience rather than mate searching and marriage preparation. Specifically, he found purchases decreasingly sex-related and a greater tendency toward buying household durables as an expression of a person's individuality and accomplishments. In an analysis of a "newly forming families" stage, Wattenberg (1974) discussed the demographic make-up of married couples of recent years, contrasted them with married couples of previous times, and indicated their importance as consumers. Earlier studies (Berey and Polley 1968; Ward and Wackman 1972) determined that children have varying influence on family decision-making. Finally, Ward (1974) analyzed "consumer socialization" and the family's pervasive effect on it, especially in the childhood and adolescent ages.

The manner in which decisions are made over the FLC stages has also been treated in the literature. Kenkel (1961) found that joing involvement in decision-making decreases with the presence of children. Furthermore, the fact that joint spouse involvement decreases over the family life cycle is well documented (Blood and Wolfe 1960; Granbois 1963; and Wolgast 1958).

The applicability of the FLC concept to consumer research is evident from these studies. In fact, a recent text (Reynolds and Wells 1977) adopted a developmental level (i.e., early, middle, and later adulthood), or life cycle approach, to the study of consumer behavior.

Criticisms of the Family Life Cycle

Critics of the FLC, to date, have been few in number. Glick and Parke (1965) attempted to revise and update the lengths of the various stages, using the most recent census data. They examined family social and economic characteristics at each stage, but did not posit any new stages. In discussing marriage and family trends, the same two authors (Parke and Glick 1967) suggested that men and women are now being married at closer ages, teen-age marriages are on the decline, and there are more young women than men living in the U.S. However, their speculations that the frequency of divorce would decline because of reductions in poverty and general improvements in the population's socioeconomic status have not proven accurate. They also did not foresee the declining birth rate.

In two other recent articles with almost identical titles, Norton (1974) and Glick (1977) stipulated that the FLC needed to be "updated." Both stated that the length of time within the stages is changing because women are beginning and completing childbearing sooner and the number of children per family is declining. Specifically, Glick said that a couple now entering marriage has the prospect of jointly surviving for 13 years after the last child's departure. Norton mentioned that rising divorce rates could have profound effects of future FLC studies.

Trost (1974) was more adamant in his criticism of the FLC. After reviewing several of the more popular FLC formulations, he listed their major weaknesses. He pointedly stated that they exclude those couples who never have children, do not account for one parent families, place undue emphasis on the ages of the children, and place stress on the importance of the changing role of the father/husband but not that of the mother/wife.

These criticisms in themselves probably are not sufficient to warrant a revision of the concept. However, when they are considered in light of significant events in recent years, the need for a modernized version of the FLC is more compelling. The following trends suggest that the traditional FLC conceptualization has diminished applicability.

CHANGES IN FAMILY COMPOSITION AND LIFESTYLE

A number of recent demographic shifts have altered the composition of the "typical"

American family and, in some cases, changed its life style significantly. One of the most influential factors is the overall decline in the average family size. The fertility rate by 1976 had decreased to 1.8 children per woman.[2] With the number of children in the family declining and likely born within a few years of one another, the middle FLC stages (i.e., those with children present) will tend to last fewer years. Therefore, the time with children living at home may no longer be the predominant portion of the FLC.

A related trend is the tendency for delay of time of first marriage. The annual rate of first marriages has declined almost continuously for two decades. Postponement of marriage has been especially prominent among women in their early 20's. The proportion of women still single at ages 20 to 24 has increased by nearly one-half since 1960, from 28 percent to 43 percent. Continuation of this trend would indicate an increase in the amount of time women and, as a result, men spend in the single FLC stage.

A third important demographic development affecting the FLC is increasing incidence of divorce in the United States. From 1965 to 1976 the divorce rate doubled, from 2.5 to 5.0 per 1,000 population. Also, initial divorces are occurring about six months to one year earlier than they did ten years ago, and those who remarry are doing so sooner. Clearly, marital events are being compressed into a shorter span of years.

Although in 1975 four of every five divorced persons remarried by middle age, the decrease in remarriages since 1972 suggests that the proportion may decline in the near future. For example, for persons 35 to 54 years old, the proportion of persons currently divorced increased by one-third between 1970 and 1975. It appears, then, that the middle and older age segments of the family life cycle may be increasingly composed of divorced individuals who are living alone or with children. Divorce projections indicate further increases in the divorce rate. Among women in their 20's today, 40 percent can expect their first marriage to end in divorce. Although it cannot be stated with certainty that this high rate of divorce will proceed unabated, these statistics emphasize the current necessity of recognizing "divorce" as an option within the FLC.

A MODERNIZED FAMILY LIFE CYCLE

Before delineating the steps of the proposed family life cycle, a few exceptions that will not be taken into account in this revised concept need recognition. Although cohabitation as an alternative to marriage is becoming increasingly popular with some segments of society and is beginning to draw research attention (Danzier and Greenwald 1977; Satow 1977), less than one percent of all couples are living together and maintaining a quasi-familial relationship out of marriage (Carter and Glick 1976).

In addition, women who have never been married but are raising a family are also excluded. Individuals who remain single throughout their life are by definition not included in forming a family. Furthermore, married couples who are separated are not explicitly dealt with in this revised FLC. It appears, however, that most persons who separate eventually divorce because it is now easier to afford, and the social stigma of divorce is rapidly lifting (Glick and Norton 1977, p. 15). Finally, young and middle-aged widowed husbands and wives and their families are not taken into account.

Table 11–2 presents the modernized (i.e., revised) family life cycle; it contains five major stages with 13 subcategories. To provide a sense of continuity for the following elaboration, Figure 11–1 depicts the flow of families through the revised FLC stages. The viability of this FLC conceptualization is

Table 11-2
Comparison of Population Distributions across the Stages of Two Family Life Cycles, 1970[a]

Murphy and Staples			Wells and Gubar		
Stage	*No. individuals or families (000's)*	*% Total U.S. population*[b]	*Stage*	*No. individuals or families (000's)*	*% Total U.S. population*[b]
1. Young single	16,626	8.2	1. Bachelor	16,626	8.2
2. Young married without children	2,958	2.9	2. Newly married couples	2,958	2.9
3. Other young			3. Full nest I	11,433	24.2
a. Young divorced without children	277	0.1	4. Full nest II	6,547	13.2
b. Young married with children Infant[c] Young (4–12 years old)[c] Adolescent[c]	8,082	17.1	5. Full nest III	6,955	14.7
			6. Empty next I	5,627	5.5
			7. Empty next II	5,318	5.2
c. Young divorced with children Infant Young (4–12 years old) Adolescent	1,144	1.9	8. Solitary survivor—in labor force	428	0.2
			9. Solitary survivor— retired	3,510	2.0
4. Middle-aged	4,815	4.7	All other[d]	46,738	23.3
a. Middle-aged married without children				203,210[e]	
b. Middle-aged divorced without children	593	0.3			
c. Middle-aged married with children Young Adolescent	15,574	33.0			
d. Middle-aged divorced with children Young Adolescent	1,080	1.8			
e. Middle-aged married without dependent children	5,627	5.5			
f. Middle-aged divorced without dependent children	284	0.1			

Table 11–2
Comparison of Population Distributions across the Stages of Two Family Life Cycles, 1970[a]
(continued)

Murphy and Staples			Wells and Gubar		
Stage	No. individuals or families (000's)	% Total U.S. population[b]	Stage	No. individuals or families (000's)	% Total U.S. population[b]
5. Older					
a. Older married	5,318	5.2			
b. Older unmarried	3,510	2.0			
Divorced					
Widowed					
All other[d]	34,952	17.2			
	203,210[e]				

[a]Figures for this table were taken or derived from U.S. Bureau of the Census 1973, Tables 2 and 9.
[b]As there are single and divorced individuals in some of the stages, the numbers were calculated as a percentage of the entire population, not just the number of families. Also, the percentages of the total for families were determined by multiplying the number of families by 2.3 (average number of children per family in 1970) and adding the parents (or parent, in divorced instances) to the number. For example, the 17.1 percent in the young married with children was computed as follows:

$$\frac{8,082 \ (2.3 \ \text{children}) + 16,164 \ (\text{parents})}{203.210} = 17.1\%.$$

[c]As many families have children at more than one of these age levels, it is not meaningful to compute the numbers for each of these ages independently.
[d]Includes all adults and children not accounted for by the family life cycle stages.
[e]Source: U.S. Bureau of the Census 1970. The numbers do not add to this total because of the calculations explained in Footnote *b*.

supported by comparison of the number of American families in each of these stages with those in Wells and Gubar's FLC (Table 11–2). Specifically, 11.8 million more people are accounted for by the inclusion of the divorced and middle-aged married without children stages in the modernized FLC version. As the figures in Table 11–2 were derived from 1970 census data, the growing percentage of divorced persons (4.3 percent in 1970 to 6.6 percent in 1975, U.S. Bureau of the Census 1975) and the declining family size would tend to magnify the differences between these two FLCs today.

Further support for the proposed FLC is provided by Uhlenberg (1974). He compared the number of females in different age groups who followed the "preferred" or traditional FLC path with those who deviated from it because of early death, remaining childless or single or experiencing a broken marriage. Although he detected a trend toward the preferred life cycle course for women born in the early 1900s, census data utilized in his study revealed that this pattern is not continuing. He stated that for both white and nonwhite women:

> Upon reaching the age category 25–29, the 1940–44 cohort, compared to the earlier one, had a larger percent still single and, among those who were ever-married, a larger percent childless and a smaller percent with their first marriage intact. The movement

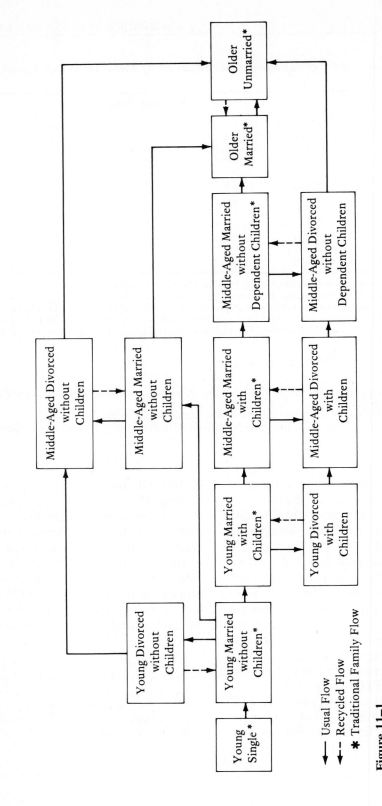

Figure 11–1
Family Life Cycle Flows

164

toward later marriage, delayed childbearing, and increased marital instability initiated by the 1940–44 cohort is continuing among more recent cohorts. These recent cohort changes have been reflected in the highly publicized decreasing annual birth rates and increasing divorce rates during the 1960's and early 1970's. If continued, these changes will reduce the number of women in younger cohorts who follow a preferred life cycle course (p. 288).

The efficacy of this revised family life cycle should not be judged exclusively by the absolute numbers of people that it accounts for, but rather by its ability to reflect changing demographic trends. Wells and Gubar (1966) and other traditional FLC formulations do not take into account the divorced or childless families and, therefore, are not reflective of recent major demographic shifts. Even if the divorce rate subsides somewhat and family size increases in the future, the modernized FLC sufficiently covers these potential changes.

Young Stages
Although "young single" is not technically a family stage, almost everyone passes through it before beginning a family. For most individuals, this stage would begin at about 18 years of age or the time they graduate from high school. Those who marry at 18 or before will skip this stage, but the number of teen-age marriages has been declining (Glick 1977). One study (Bomball, Primeaux, and Pursell 1975) found that as the number of college graduates increases, marriage is temporarily postponed. College enrollments, especially on the part of women, are continuing to grow (VanDusen and Sheldon 1976). Therefore, with the postponement of marriage until the mid-twenties by more individuals, young singles will establish some amount of financial independence and may experience several life styles, e.g., student, employee, dropout.

The second FLC stage is the young (under 35) marrieds without children. Research generally indicates that spouses tend to be alike in age, religion, ethnic group, social origin, and educational level (Kerckhoff 1976). This period of establishment, or "honeymoon" stage, was traditionally rather short, lasting less than two years before the first child was born (Glick and Parke 1965, p. 190). Currently, because of the widespread use of contraception, changing attitudes toward parenthood, and more working wives for financial or career reasons, this stage may be extended for several years. This decision usually allows the young married to establish a degree of financial security.

In addition to those who consciously decide not to have children, there are two options for the next stage of the revised FLC. One option is "young divorced." According to recent statistics, one of every three marriages will end in divorce, and, as mentioned previously, divorces are occurring at earlier points in the marriage (Glick and Norton 1977, pp. 25–6). Historically, blacks (United States Bureau of Census 1972) and lower socioeconomic status couples (Udry 1966) have experienced higher divorce rates than more affluent whites. Life styles of divorced individuals may revert back to the single stage, but sometimes they are psychologically unprepared to begin the "mating game" again. Both are usually financially worse off, unless the wife received a large alimony settlement or has a career of her own. As most men and women remarry after an early divorce, they would then "recycle" through the young married stage again.

The stage that traditionally follows young married without children is young married with children (Table 11–1). As shown in Table 11–2, the subsections of this stage are infant, young (4–12 years old), and adolescent children. The existence of children usually alters drastically the life style and financial situation within the family. Commitment to child rearing in terms of years will probably not be as extensive as in earlier generations.

Divorce within the young-married-with-children FLC stage, although traumatic, is becoming more prevalent. In fact, over 60 per cent of divorces in 1976 occurred when the woman was under age 30, and in about two-thirds of these cases children were present (Glick and Norton 1977). Whether the divorce happens when the children are in the infant, young, or adolescent subcategory, both life style and financial implications are significant. Almost always the wife retains custody of the children and, although child support is usually required of the husband, it is frequently inadequate. The wife must then look for employment—sometimes several years after being out of the labor force. The cost of maintaining a separate household leaves many men without much discretionary income.

Middle-Aged Stages

As shown in Table 11–2, the middle-aged stages contain six possibilities. The range for this category is approximately 35–64 years of age for the family head.[3] One possibility within the middle-aged group is marriage without children. Although this group has historically been a very small segment, it will likely increase in the future because more couples are making a conscious decision not to have children. Urban highly-educated women (Kerckhoff 1976), who are presently growing in number, show the greatest tendency to remain childless. The life style of middle-aged couples without children will probably not be as hectic as when they were younger, but the freedom will remain. If the couple is healthy and financially comfort-

able, these families could be characterized as occupying the "carefree stage."

The middle-aged divorced situation without children (stage 4b in Table 11–2) may occur at this time in the family development, or as a continuation of those in young divorced stage not remarrying. A divorce in this stage is less common (Kerckhoff 1976), and when it occurs may present a major life style adjustment for both the spouses. The financial condition of the divorced individual is likely dependent on occupation and socioeconomic status. For some it may be quite comfortable, but for others financially strained. These persons may remarry (Figure 11–1), but the likelihood that they would ever have children is small.

The more traditional middle-aged group (stage 4c in Table 11–2) comprises those with young and adolescent children. The number of families in this stage is large and will continue to be significant. The predominant family life style is one that revolves around the children and their school activities. However, the father's and/or mother's career and its concomitant social and time obligations may alter this life style. Today's family in this stage is better off financially because a larger percentage of the wives are working. Sometimes, it is necessary for the wife to work to meet family financial needs (Oppenheimer 1974).

Middle-aged divorced with children (4d in Table 11–2) can be arrived at either by a divorce occurring at this time or an extension of the young-divorced-with-children stage. If divorce takes place at this time, life style changes are significant. Both parents and children must adapt. This may mean that the wife and often the children have to take on additional responsibilities for the family's livelihood. On the other hand, families that have experienced a divorce at an earlier stage have likely undergone the adaptive process and are settled in this life style. The procedure for getting to this stage makes little difference in financial terms, however. The divorced father has financial constraints as long as the children are still eligible for child support. Likewise, the mother with children present is saddled with financial burdens.

The final two categories within the middle-aged group are married without dependent children (4e in Table 11–2) and divorced without dependent children (4f). These represent what Wells and Gubar (1966) and others have described as the "empty nest" stage. Since the age at which children are born is lower for nonwhites and those of lesser education, income, and job status (United States Census 1974), these families or divorced individuals would probably experience a longer empty nest period. The trend toward smaller families in all socioeconomic levels may mean more time in this stage for middle and upper socioeconomic classes in the future, also (Glick 1977). In any event, once the children are on their own the married couple or the divorced man and woman not only experience financial relief, but also many life style options become available.

Older Stages

The final FLC stages (Table 11–2) are simply labeled "older." The family head's age is about 65 years old, and this category begins at retirement. It might happen at age 60, 62, 65, or possibly later. The recent legislation postponing mandatory retirement may defer this category for some. As retirement represents a major life style and financial change for most, it seems logical that the older stages would start here.

The two major distinctions within the older category are married or unmarried, i.e., divorced or widowed. Older retired couples have few time commitments, but also may have to reduce their standard of living. Those with past savings and good health may have an active retirement, e.g., travel and recreation; others less financially solvent or with infirmities will probably experience an unpleasant final stage.

The "solitary survivor" stage (5b in Table 11–2), like the young single, is not technically part of the "family" life cycle, but is included to complete the process. For the previously divorced individual, this stage represents only an occupational and possibly a life style change, but not an emotional one. However, the person who was married for most of his/her lifetime may experience emotional as well as physical and financial hardships when losing his/her spouse. Of course, it is possible that an older widowed or divorced person will remarry (Figure 11–1).

The major stages and their subsections shown in Table 11–2 attempt to depict a more thorough conceptualization of the modern American family's life cycle. It is possible to follow the flow through the stages as shown in Figure 11–1. For instance, the "typical" family would progress through stage 1, 2, 3b, 4c, and 4e, and 5a and 5b (see Table 11–2). On the other hand, a woman divorced at age 30 with one child and not remarried would follow the sequence 1, 2, 3b, 3c, 4d, and later 4f and 5b. Those divorced individuals who remarry may recycle through one or more stages, depicted by the dotted lines in Figure 11–1.

RESEARCH IMPLICATIONS

The objective of this section is to specify areas that may be studied by family sociologists and consumer and marketing researchers. For each of these groups, topics that may be researched, as suggested by recent demographic trends, are examined—e.g., postponement of marriage and declining family size. These might be analyzed by either the traditional or modernized FLC. More significantly, two important areas (divorced persons and childless couples) can be studied using only the revised FLC categories.

Family Sociologists

Although these researchers have extensively investigated family behavior as it relates to the traditional FLC, one issue that needs further analysis is the life cycle squeeze. According to the literature (Estes and Wilensky 1978; Gove, Grimm, Motz, and Thompson 1973; Oppenheimer 1974), the life cycle squeeze occurs in the stages where children are present and family income does not adequately meet family needs. The current trend toward smaller families may reduce the amount of time this squeeze is operable.

Two other topics that deserve attention are marital satisfaction and marital dissolution. Marital satisfaction, according to the traditional FLC stages, has been widely studied (Bossard and Ball 1955; Paris and Luckey 1966; Rollins and Feldman 1970). However, satisfaction within the various "divorced" stages should be measured and compared to the corresponding married stages over time. The modernized FLC would also provide a new context for applying the conceptual framework of marital dissolution developed by Levinger (1976). Moreover, the study of marital dissolution is a subject that could be related to the new FLC.[5] Also, marital satisfaction and dissolution in the revised stages need to be related to social class membership, racial background, and other relevant social factors.

Consumer Researchers

Family decision-making patterns have been extensively analyzed by consumer researchers using the decision process (i.e., problem recognition, search, evaluation, purchase, and postpurchase behavior) and family role structure (i.e., initiator, decider, buyer, etc.) approaches (Davis 1976; Davis and Rigaux 1974; Ferber and Lee 1974). These approaches can be applied in both the traditional and modernized FLC context. In examining the age of family members, the earlier findings (Blood and Wolfe 1960; Granbois 1963; Wolgast 1958) that joint involvement in decision making decreases over the stages of life cycle might be reexamined. For example, those not marrying until the middle or late twenties could have already established strong decision-making patterns or time constraints that may preclude young husbands and wives from extensive joint decision making. Furthermore, those couples spending an extended time in the empty nest stage might become more oriented to joint decision making again.

Another important research area that can be best analyzed by employing the revised FLC concerns family size. For instance, the differences in husband and wife influence in families with children may no longer follow Kenkel's (1961) findings that joint decision-making involvement decreases with the presence of children. Young, middle-aged, or older married couples *without* children might currently differ substantially from families with children, with respect to husband and wife influence in the decision process stages and/or the extent of role specialization. Joint decision making of couples never having children could be analyzed over the revised FLC stages.

The area of future FLC research most obvious from the modernized family life cycle, and most absent in the literature, is a comparison between the decision-making patterns of traditional and nontraditional (those headed by a divorced parent) households. Specifically, does that divorced person engage in more or less external search than married couples? Possible role structure differences in families of married versus divorced parents with one or more children deserve attention. In addition, the role children play in household decision making in divorced families appears to be an important research topic. For example, is the teen-age daughter the primary supermarket products decision-maker? The degree of husband, wife, or child dominance could vary widely depending on the family composition or the stage in the revised family life cycle. Also, the "gatekeeper" effect for information acquisition and purchase deliberation may not be operable in divorced families.

Marketing Researchers

Those engaged in marketing products and services will be interested in how consumption is affected by the FLC. In fact, Cox (1975) found the traditional FLC stage superior to "length of marriage" in determining consistency between husbands' and wives' attitudes toward automobiles. Hisrich and Peters (1974) also determined that life cycle stage was more significantly correlated with the use or nonuse of several entertainment activities than age or social class.

The changing family size and age profile of the United States population implies that researchers using either the traditional or modernized FLC should investigate the marketing implications of these trends. For example, declining family size affects marketers who sell products appealing to large families, such as station wagons, several-bedroom homes and large size packages. In addition, the quantities of products purchased by families in stages containing children will likely decline. The extended "empty nest" stage identified by Glick (1977) may also be a segment for marketers to study and cultivate. Even if the family is not wealthy, the length of this stage may allow couples to save for vacations, better furniture, and possibly a different home.

The young divorced stage might be a promising segment for marketers of small appliances rather than large ones, because the individual may view this stage as temporary. Within the service area, personal enhancement services, such as health spas and tennis clubs, would seem to be in demand by the more affluent in this group. Also, life insurance marketers may find the divorced woman interested in buying insurance for herself and possibly the children. Moreover, most divorced women with children from middle and lower social classes would probably be seeking inexpensive clothing for herself and the children.

In the middle-aged categories of the revised FLC, those who remain childless may represent a good market for luxury goods, e.g., expensive restaurants, extended vacation packages, high quality furniture. Divorced individuals who hold good jobs and have no dependents may also be classified as part of this same market. Middle-aged divorced parents, on the other hand, would seem to be seeking more low-priced and functional products, such as used cars, inexpensive furniture, and fast food restaurants.

CONCLUDING COMMENT

Although the traditional family life cycle has proven to be a valuable tool for researchers, recent changes in family composition and life style suggest that a revision of the concept is needed. The modernized FLC proposed in this paper utilizes the age of household head, marital status, and, to a less extent, children's ages to determine the length of the stages. Recognition of divorce and remaining childless as options (Table 11–2) are its major distinguishing features.

An explanation of life style and financial characteristics for each stage is given to clarify this conceptualization, and research implications are drawn for family sociologists and consumer and marketing researchers.

NOTES

1. The labels applied to the family life cycle development eras are generic. In other words, they could be used to describe the evolution of most major concepts.
2. The statistics reported in this section were taken or derived from Glick and Norton (1977).
3. The U.S. Bureau of the Census divides ages ending in the digit five according to ten-year intervals (i.e., 25–34, 35–44, etc.). Therefore, the lower limit of middle-age was set at 35 to correspond with these data. Reasons for the upper limit are provided in the "older stages" section.
4. Of course, race, socioeconomic status, and occupation may affect the degree to which this stage may be characterized as carefree.
5. For a thorough discussion of this topic, see *Journal of Social Issues*, Winter 1976 (Vol. 32, No. 1), which is devoted to research on divorce and separation.

REFERENCES

Bane, Mary Jo (1976), *Here To Stay*, New York: Basic Books, Inc.

Barton, S. G. (1955), "The Life Cycle and Buying Patterns," in *Consumer Behavior*, Vol. 2, ed. Lincoln H. Clark, New York: New York University Press, 53–7.

Berey, Lewis, A., and Pollay, Richard W. (1968), "The Influencing Role of the Child in Family Decision-Making," *Journal of Marketing Research*, 5, 70–2.

Bernard, Jessie (1975), "Notes on Changing Life Styles, 1970–1974," *Journal of Marriage and the Family*, 37, 582–600.

Bigelow, Howard F. (1942), "Money and Marriage," in *Marriage and Family*, eds. Howard Becker and Reuben Hill, Boston: Heath and Company, 382–6.

Blood, Robert O., Jr., and Wolfe, Donald M. (1960), *Husbands and Wives: The Dynamics of Married Living*, New York: The Free Press, pp. 41–4.

Bomball, Mark R., Primeaux, Walter J., and Pursell, Donald E. (1975), "Forecasting Stage 2 of the Family Life Cycle," *Journal of Business*, 48, 65–73.

Bossard, James H. S., and Boll, Eleanor S. (1955), "Marital Unhappiness in the Life Cycle of Marriage," *Marriage and Family Living*, 17, 10–4.

Carter, Hugh, and Glick, Paul C. (1976), *Marriage and Divorce: A Social and Economic Study*, 2nd ed., Cambridge MA.: Harvard University Press.

Clark, Lincoln H. (1955), ed., *Consumer Behavior*, Vol. 2, New York: New York University Press.

Cooper, David (1970), *The Death of the Family*, New York: Pantheon Books.

Cox, Eli P. III (1975), "Family Purchase Decision Making and the Process of Adjustment," *Journal of Marketing Research*, 12, 189–95.

Danziger, Carl, and Greenwald, Mathew (1977), "An Overview of Unmarried Heterosexual Cohabitation and Suggested Marketing Implications," in *Advances in Consumer Research*, Vol. 4, ed. William D. Perreault, Jr., Atlanta: Association for Consumer Research, pp. 330–4.

Davids, Leo (1971), "North American Marriage: 1990," *The Futurist*, 5, October, 190–4.

Davis, Harry L. (1976), "Decision Making within The Household," *Journal of Consumer Research*, 2, 241–60.

———, and Rigaux, Benney P. (1974), "Perception of Marital Roles in Decision Processes," *Journal of Consumer Research*, 1, 51–62.

Duvall, Evelyn M. (1971), *Family Development*, 4th ed., Philadelphia: J. B. Lippincott Company, pp. 106–32.

———, and Hill, Reuben (1948), "Report of the Committee on the Dynamics of Family Interaction," Washington, D.C.: National Conference on Family Life, mimeographed.

Estes, Richard J., and Wilensky, Harold L. (1978), "Life Cycle Squeeze and the Morale Curve," *Social Problems*, 25, 277–92.

Feldman, Harold, and Feldman, Margaret (1975), "The Family Life Cycle: Some Suggestions for Recycling," *Journal of Marriage and the Family*, 37, 277–84.

Ferber, Robert, and Lee, Lucy C. (1974), "Husband-Wife Influence in Family Purchasing Behavior," *Journal of Consumer Research*, 1, 43–50.

Fisher, Janet A. (1955), "Family Life Cycle Analysis in Research on Consumer Behavior," in *Consumer Behavior*, Vol. 2., ed. Lincoln H. Clark, New York: New York University Press, pp. 28–35.

Glick, Paul C. (1947), "The Family Cycle," *American Sociological Review*, 12, 164–74.

———, (1977), "Updating the Life Cycle of the Family," *Journal of Marriage and the Family*, 39, 5–13.

———, and Norton, Arthur J. (1977), "Marrying, Divorcing, and Living Together in the U.S. Today," *Population Bulletin*, 32, Washington, D.C.: Population Reference Bureau, Inc.

———, and Parke, Robert, Jr. (1965), "New Approaches in Studying the Life Cycle of the Family," *Demography*, 2, 187–202.

Gove, Walter R., Grimm, James W., Motz, Susan C., and Thompson, James D. (1973), "The Family Life Cycle: Internal Dynamics and Social Consequences," *Sociology and Social Research*, 57, 182–95.

Granbois, Donald H. (1963), "The Role of Communication in the Family Decision-Making Process," in *Proceedings*, ed. S. Greyser, Chicago: American Marketing Association, pp. 44–57.

Hill, Reuben (1970), *Family Development in Three Generations*, Cambridge, MA: Schenkman Publishing Company, Inc.

———, and Rodgers, Roy H. (1964), "The Developmental Approach," in *Handbook of Marriage and the Family*, ed. Harold T. Christensen, Chicago: Rand McNally and Company, pp. 171–211.

Hisrich, Robert D., and Peters, Michael P. (1974), "Selecting the Superior Segmentation Correlate," *Journal of Marketing*, 38, July, 60–3.

Keller, Suzanne (1971), "Does the Family Have a Future? *Journal of Comparative Family Studies*, 2, 1–14.

Kenkel, William F. (1961), "Family Interaction in Decision Making on Spending," in *Household Decision-Making*, ed. Nelson N. Foote, New York: New York University Press, pp. 140–64.

Kerckhoff, Alan C. (1976), "Patterns of Marriage and Family Formation and Dissolution," *Journal of Consumer Research*, 2, 261–75.

Kirkpatrick, Ellis L., Cowles, Mary, and Tough, Roselyn (1934), "The Life Cycle of the Farm Family in Relation to Its Standard of Living," *Research Bulletin No. 121*, Madison, WI: University of Wisconsin Agricultural Experiment Station.

Lansing, John B., and Kish, Leslie (1957), "Family Life Cycle As an Independent Variable," *American Sociological Review*, 22, 512–9.

———, and Morgan, James N. (1955), "Consumer Finances over the Life Cycle," in *Consumer Behavior*, Vol. 2, ed. Lincoln H. Clark, New York: New York University Press, pp. 36–51.

Levinger, George (1976), "A Social Psychological Perspective on Marital Dissolution," *Journal of Social Issues*, 32, 21–47.

Loomis, Charles P. (1936), "The Study of the Life Cycle of Families," *Rural Sociology*, 1, 180–99.

Miller, Donald L. (1955), "The Life Cycle and the Impact of Advertising," in *Consumer Behavior*, Vol. 2, ed. Lincoln H. Clark, New York: New York University Press.

Norton, Arthur J. (1974). "The Family-Life Cycle Updated: Components and Uses," in *Selected Studies in Marriage and the Family*, eds. Robert F. Winch and Graham B. Spanier, New York: Holt, Rinehart and Winston, pp. 162–7.

Olson, Daniel H. (1972), "Marriage of the Future: Revolutionary or Evolutionary Change?" *The Family Coordinator*, 21, 383–93.

Oppenheimer, Valerie K. (1974), "The Life Cycle Squeeze: The Interaction of Men's Occupational and Family Life Cycles," *Demography*, 11, 227–45.

Paris, Bethel L., and Luckey, Eleanore B. (1966), "A Longitudinal Study of Marital Satisfaction," *Sociology and Social Research*, 50, January, 212–23.

Parke, Robert, Jr., and Glick, Paul C. (1967), "Prospective Changes in Marriage and the

Family," *Journal of Marriage and the Family*, 29, 249–56.

Rainwater, Lee (1974), *What Money Buys: Inequality and the Social Meanings of Income*, New York: Basic Books, Inc.

Reynolds, Fred D., and Wells, William D. (1977), *Consumer Behavior*, New York: McGraw-Hill Book Company.

Rich, Stuart U., and Jain, Subhash C. (1968), "Social Class and Life Cycle as Predictors of Shopping Behavior," *Journal of Marketing Research*, 5, 41–9.

Rodgers, Roy H. (1962), "Improvements in the Construction and Analysis of Family Life Cycle Categories," unpublished Ph.D. thesis, University of Minnesota.

————, (1960), "Proposed Modification of Duvall Family Life Cycle Stages," paper presented at the American Sociological Association meetings, New York City.

————, (1973), "The Family Life Cycle Concept—Past, Present, and Future," paper presented at Thirteenth International Family Research Seminar, Committee on Family Research, International Sociological Association, Paris, France.

————, (1964), "Toward a Theory of Family Development," *Journal of Marriage and the Family*, 26, 262–70.

Rollins, Boyd C., and Feldman, Harold (1970), "Marital Satisfaction over the Family Life Cycle," *Journal of Marriage and the Family*, 32, February, 20–8.

Rowntree, Benjamin S. (1903), *Poverty: A Study of Town Life*, London: Macmillan.

Satow, Kay (1977), "Some Comments on Changing Life Styles among Single Young Adults," in *Advances in Consumer Research*, Vol. 4, ed. William D. Perreault, Jr., Atlanta: Association for Consumer Research, pp. 335–6.

Sorokin, Pitirim A., Zimmerman, Carle C., and Galpin, Charles J., (1931), *A Systematic Sourcebook in Rural Sociology*, Vol. 2, Minneapolis: University of Minnesota Press.

Spanier, Graham B., Lewis, Robert A., and Cole, Charles L. (1975), "Marital Adjustment over the Family Life Cycle: The Issue of Curvilinearity," *Journal of Marriage and the Family*, 37, 263–75.

Toffler, Alvin (1970), "The Fractured Family," in *Future Shock*, New York: Random House, pp. 211–30.

Trost, Jan (1974), "This Family Life Cycle—An Impossible Concept?" *International Journal of Sociology of the Family*, Spring, 37–47.

Udry, J. Richard (1966), "Marital Instability by Race, Sex, Education, and Occupation Using 1960 Census Data," *American Journal of Sociology*, 22, September, 203–9.

Uhlenberg, Peter (1974), "Cohort Variations in Family Life Cycle Experiences of U.S. Females," *Journal of Marriage and the Family*, 36, 284–92.

U.S. Bureau of the Census (1970), *Census of the Population*, Washington, D.C.: U.S. Government Printing Office.

————, (1973), *Family Composition*, Subject Report of 1970 Census, Washington, D.C.: Government Printing Office.

————, (1974), *Fertility Histories and Birth Expectations of American Women: June 1971*. Current Population Reports, Population Characteristics, Series P-20, No. 263, Washington, D.C.: U.S. Government Printing Office.

————, (1975), *Marital Status and Living Arrangements*, Current Population Reports, Population Characteristics, Washington, D.C.: U.S. Government Printing Office.

————, (1972), *Marriage, Divorce, and Remarriage by Year of Birth: June 1971*, Current Population Reports, Population Characteristics, Series P-20, No. 239, Washington, D.C.: U.S. Government Printing Office.

Van Dusen, Roxann A., and Sheldon, Eleanor B. (1976), "The Changing Status of American Women: A Life Cycle Perspective," *American Psychologist*, February, 106–16.

Ward, Scott (1974), "Consumer Socialization," *Journal of Consumer Research*, 1, 1–14.

————, and Wackman, Daniel B. (1972), "Children's Purchase Influence Attempts and Parental Yielding," *Journal of Marketing Research*, 9, 316–9.

Wattenberg, Ben J. (1975), "The Forming-Families: The Spark in the Tinder, 1975–1985," in *1974 Combined Proceedings*, ed. Ronald C.

Curhan, Chicago: American Marketing Association, pp. 51–62.

Wells, William C., and Gubar, George (1966), "Life Cycle Concept in Marketing Research," *Journal of Marketing Research,* 3, 355–63.

Wolgast, Elizabeth H. (1958), "Do Husbands or Wives Make the Purchasing Decisions?" *Journal of Marketing,* 23, 151–8.

Wortzel, Lawrence H. (1977), "Young Adults: Single People and Single Person Households," in *Advances in Consumer Research,* Vol. 4, ed. William D. Perreault, Jr., Atlanta: Association for Consumer Research, pp. 321–9.

New Product Adoption and Diffusion

Everett M. Rogers

The studies of the diffusion of innovations, including the part played by mass communication, promise to provide an empirical and quantitative basis for developing more rigorous approaches to theories of social change.

Melvin L. De Fleur (1966, p. 138)

Diffusion of innovations has the status of a bastard child with respect to the parent interests in social and cultural change: too big to ignore but unlikely to be given full recognition.

Frederick C. Fliegel and Joseph E. Kivlin (1966, p. 235n)

Diffusion research is thus emerging as a single, integrated body of concepts and generalizations, even though the investigations are conducted by researchers in several scientific disciplines.

Everett M. Rogers (1971, p. 47)

Reprinted from Everett M. Rogers, "New Product Adoption and Diffusion," *Journal of Consumer Research*, Vol. 2 (March 1976), published by The Journal of Consumer Research, Inc.

The purposes of this paper are (1) to summarize what we have learned from research on the diffusion of innovations that contributes to our understanding of new product adoption and diffusion, (2) to discuss how the academic history and the intellectual structuring of the diffusion field have affected its contributions and its shortcomings, and (3) to indicate future research priorities on the diffusion on innovations.

Our focus here is especially on the last 10-year period and on the diffusion of a particular type of innovation (new products), but for historical and comparative purposes, we also must briefly deal with the origins of diffusion research.

Since about the mid-1960s, there has been considerable interest in diffusion research on the part of consumer researchers and a certain degree of integration of diffusion frameworks and research findings into the literature on consumer behavior. For example, the leading textbook on consumer behavior today features a chapter on the diffusion and adoption of innovations. Many marketing texts these days have a chapter on diffusion, or at least give considerable coverage to such topics as the innovation-decision process, adopter categories, opinion leadership, and the S-shaped diffusion curve.

Further, about 8 percent of the 1,800 publications dealing with empirical research on the diffusion of innovations, available to date, were authored by researchers associated with the field of marketing. These studies, mostly conducted since the mid-1960s, focus on new products as innovations. The present paper deals not only with these 8 percent of all diffusion publications but also with the other 92 percent, since I believe that the findings, methodologies, and theoretic frameworks from research on various types of innovations has applicability to consumer's adoption of new products. The adoption of most innovations entails the purchase of a new product, although this fact has often not been recognized by diffusion scholars.

THE RISE OF DIFFUSION RESEARCH AS AN INVISIBLE COLLEGE

From Revolutionary Paradigm to Classical Model

The origins of research on the diffusion of innovations trace from (1) the German-Austrian and the British schools of diffusionism in anthropology (whose members claimed that most changes in a society resulted from the introduction of innovations from other societies) and (2) the French sociologist Gabriel Tarde (1903), who pioneered the proposing the S-shaped diffusion curve and the role of opinion leaders in the process of "imitation." But the "revolutionary paradigm" for diffusion research occurred in the early 1940s when two sociologists, Bryce Ryan and Neal Gross (1943), published their seminal study of the diffusion of hybrid seed corn among Iowa farmers.

Any given field of scientific research begins with a major breakthrough or reconceptualization that provides a new way of looking at some phenomenon (Kuhn, 1962). This revolutionary paradigm typically sets off a furious amount of intellectual effort as promising young scientists are attracted to the field, either to advance the new conceptualization with their research or to disprove certain of its aspects. Gradually, a scientific consensus about the field is developed, and perhaps after several generations of academic scholars, the "invisible college" (composed of researchers on a common topic who are linked by communication ties) declines in scientific interest as fewer findings of an exciting nature are turned up. These are the usual stages in the normal growth of science, Kuhn (1962) claims.

Research on the diffusion of innovations has followed these rise-and-fall stages rather closely, although the final stage of demise has not yet begun (Crane, 1972). The hybrid corn study set forth a new approach to the study of communication and change that was soon followed up by an increasing number of scholars in a wide variety of scientific fields. Within 10 years (by 1952), over 100 diffusion researches were completed; during the next decade (by 1962), another 450; and by the end of 1974, another 1,250. So today there are over 2,700 publications about the diffusion of innovations, including about 1,800 empirical research reports and 900 other writings (Figure 12–1).[1] The amount of scientific activity in investigating the diffusion of innovations has increased at an exponential rate (doubling almost every two years) since the revolutionary paradigm appeared 32 years ago, as Kuhn's (1962) theory of the growth of science would predict.

The main elements in the "classical

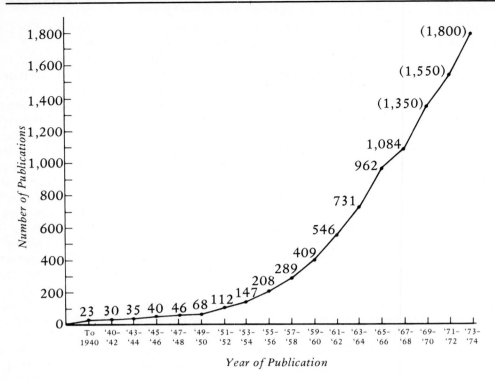

Figure 12–1
*Cumulative Number of Empirical Diffusion
Research Publications, by Year of Publication*

model" of the diffusion of new ideas that emerged are (1) the *innovation,* defined as an idea, practice, or object perceived as new by an individual or other relevant unit of adoption, (2) which is *communicated* through certain *channels* (3) over *time* (4) among the members of a *social system.* The Ryan and Gross (1943) study focused on hybrid corn, one of the most important innovations in midwestern agriculture. Data were gathered by personal interviews with all the Iowa farmers in two communities. The rate of adoption of the agricultural innovation followed an S-shaped, normal curve when plotted on a cumulative basis over time. The first farmers to adopt (the

innovators) were more cosmopolite (indicated by traveling more frequently to Des Moines) and of higher socioeconomic status than later adopters. The typical Iowa farmer first heard about the innovation from a seed corn salesman, but interpersonal communication with peers was the most frequent channel leading to persuasion. The innovation process from awareness/knowledge to final adoption averaged about nine years, indicating that considerable time was required for adoption to occur.

Diffusion research is a particular type of communication research, but it began outside the academic field of communication. This was mostly a matter of timing, since the Ryan and Gross (1943) study preceded the first university centers or departments on communication by a good dozen years. Research of persuasion and attitude change, on nonverbal communication, and on most of the other important topics for communication research also began in psychology, anthropology, sociology, or other social sciences and then came to flower in the hands of communication scholars. The diffusion research approach was taken up in a variety of fields: education, anthropology, medical sociology, marketing, geography, and, most of all, rural sociology. Each of these disciplines pursued diffusion research in its specialized way and, for some time, without much interchange with the other diffusion research traditions.

The Intellectual Watershed of 1960

The year 1960 was in several respects a turning point for research on the diffusion of innovations. For one thing, the old disciplinary boundaries began to break down, and diffusion research began to emerge as "a single, integrated body of concepts and generalizations" (Rogers, 1971, p. 47). This emergence did not necessarily mean that all diffusion scholars completely agreed on definitions of concepts or on the most appropriate methods of inquiry, but at least the scholars generally recognized that they were investigating the same basic type of human behavior. Evidence of this recognition is shown in the works cited in their publications, as well as in the methods and models that they followed.

Second, researchers in the academic field of mass communication began to engage in diffusion research, at first by investigating the diffusion of major news events carried by the mass media: Alaskan statehood, the launching of Sputnik, and President Kennedy's assassination. The most

noted news-event diffusion study, itself representing a "mini-revolutionary paradigm," was by Deutschmann and Danielson (1960). Today there are over 100 such news-event diffusion studies. Communication scholars soon began to study many types of other innovations, including technological innovations in agriculture, health, and family planning, especially in the developing nations of Latin America, Africa, and Asia.[2]

The early 1960s marked the beginning of a sharp takeoff in the number of diffusion studies in developing countries. Pioneering ventures in this direction by S. A. Rahim (1961) in Bangladesh and by Paul J. Deutschmann and Orlando Fals Borda (1962a, b) in Colombia suggested that new ideas spread among peasants in villages in a generally similar pattern to their diffusion in more media-saturated settings like the United States and Europe. The diffusion process, and the concepts and models utilized to analyze it, seemed to be cross-culturally valid, at least in the sense that comparable results were found in the new settings.

There were compelling reasons for the fast growth of diffusion studies in developing countries after 1960. Technology was assumed to be at the heart of development, at least in the dominant paradigm of development popular until very recent years.[3] In fact, innovativeness was thought to be the best single indicant of the multifaceted dimension called "modernization," the individual-level equivalent of development at the societal or system level (Rogers, 1969). Therefore, microlevel investigations of the diffusion of technological innovations among villagers were of direct relevance to development planners and other government officials in developing nations. These research results, and the general framework of diffusion, provided development agencies with both a kind of theoretical approach and an evaluation procedure.

The number of diffusion researches in developing nations totaled only about 54 in 1960 (13 percent of all diffusion studies), but rose steeply to over 800 or so by 1975, when about half of all diffusion studies were conducted in Latin America, Africa, and Asia. The major developing country of study is India, with over 450 of the 800 diffusion researches in developing countries.

An important boost to the internationalization of the diffusion field was the rise of KAP surveys in developing countries during the 1960s. KAP studies are sample surveys of knowledge (K), attitudes (A), and practice (P)—that is, adoption—of family planning innovations. K, A, and P are the logical dependent variables in evaluations of family planning communication campaigns, and, as national family planning programs arose after 1960 in many developing nations (especially in Asia) to cope with the population problem, KAP-type diffusion researches blossomed on all sides. Over 500 such KAP surveys were conducted in 72 nations by 1973 (Rogers, 1973, p. 377); India alone was the location for over half these investigations.

With the exception of the Taichung experiment in Taiwan (Freedman and Takeshita, 1969), the intellectual contribution of these KAP surveys "to scientific understanding of human behavior change has been dismal" (Rogers, 1973, p. 378). However, the KAP studies have provided a useful function by generally showing that most parents in developing countries want fewer children than they actually have, and that the majority desire a government family planning program. Even the harshest critic of KAP studies, Professor Philip M. Hauser (1967, p. 405), stated: "KAP survey results, erroneous or not, have helped to persuade prime ministers, parliaments, and the general population to move in a desirable direc-

tion and have provided family planning program administrators with 'justification' for budgets and programs."

Intellectually speaking, the family planning diffusion studies were generally disappointing, although several modifications in the "classical diffusion model" (such as the payment of incentives to promote diffusion and the use of nonprofessional change agent aides to help overcome the taboo nature of family planning communication) did emerge when family planning programs found the model wanting (Rogers, 1973). Also, the family planning diffusion studies gave a boost to field experimental research designs,[4] for over a dozen such experiments in various nations followed the Taichung study (Rogers and Agarwala-Rogers, 1975).

The rise of these field experiments, in place of one-shot survey designs, helped to overcome some of the methodological difficulties of diffusion studies in coming to grips with the "overtime" aspects of the communication of new ideas.

MARKETING RESEARCH ON DIFFUSION

While many of the field experimental designs in the diffusion field were conducted in developing nations and were concerned with family planning innovations, a number of other field experiments were carried out in the United States by marketing researchers.

The marketing tradition of diffusion research has come on strong since the early 1960s. Marketing managers of firms have long been concerned with how to launch new products more efficiently. One reason for this interest is the high failure rate of new consumer products, estimated at 92 percent of the approximately 6,000 new consumer items introduced each year (Connor, 1964).

The adoption of most innovations involves sale of a new product, of course, and it was easy for commercial firms of conceive of their new products as innovations and to adapt the theoretical and methodological framework of diffusion research to marketing problems. University faculty members in graduate schools of business led the way into diffusion research (Zaltman, 1965), to be followed soon after by marketing researchers in the employ of commercial firms. Unfortunately, a large proportion of these research reports lie only in the secret files of the sponsoring companies because of competitive threat, and they are thus unavailable to attempts at academic synthesis and the progress of scientific understanding of the diffusion process.

Much of the diffusion research in the marketing field was conducted either by the commercial manufacturers of the new product or by university professors with the sponsorship, or at least the cooperation, of the manufacturers. One advantage of this close relationship was that the diffusion researchers in the field of marketing often had some degree of control over the diffusion strategies that were used to promote the new products. This is a particularly important ingredient in the conduct of field experiments on diffusion. In fields other than marketing, diffusion scholars have seldom been able to manipulate the "treatment" variables, and it has therefore been impossible to conduct field experiments.

Perhaps a somewhat typical illustration of the field experimental approach by marketing researchers is provided by Arndt's (1967) study of the diffusion of a new food product. A letter about this innovation, enclosing a coupon allowing its purchase at one-third price, was sent to 495 housewives living in a married-student apartment complex. Personal interviews were carried out with these consumers 16 days after the diffusion campaign was launched. Arndt found that interpersonal communication about the new product frequently led to its initial purchase. Housewives who perceived the innovation as risky were more likely to seek the advice of their neighborhood opinion leaders about it. Naturally, this type of field experiment allowed determination of the impact of the reduced-price sample offer; the measure of impact was the rate of adoption (that is, purchase) of the new food product.

The diffusion research tradition of marketing has displayed an especially strong bias toward producing research results of use to the innovation's source (that is, the manufacturer of the new product) rather than to the consumers. This pro-innovation and pro-source orientation is also characteristic of other branches of diffusion research (a point to which we shall return), but less so than in the field of marketing.

One cannot help but wonder how the research approach (and the understandings that were obtained) might have been different if the Ryan and Gross (1943) hybrid corn study had been sponsored by the Iowa Farm Bureau Federation rather than by the Iowa Agricultural Extension Service and if the Coleman, Katz, and Menzel (1966) investigation of a new medical drug had been conducted under the auspices of the American Medical Association rather than Pfizer Drug Company. Perhaps "diffusion" research would have been called something like "innovation-seeking" or the "evaluation of innovations" had the receivers been in control (Rogers, 1971, p. 79).

The source-bias in marketing research on diffusion is especially surprising since this scientific specialty is often called "*consumer* research" in graduate schools of marketing, and it is often inspired by the "marketing concept," an approach that puts the consumer in control of the marketing process, at least in principle (Kotler and Zaltman, 1971). In diffusion researches following the marketing concept, the customer has often been studied, but usually to the advantage of the seller of the new product or service.

Even though the studies were usually commissioned by the selling agencies, consumers have often benefited from the diffusion researches in which they were respondents if their needs were met by the new products that emerged from such diffusion researches. These investigations *can* put the consumer in the driver's seat regarding new products, especially through a variant of diffusion inquiry called "acceptability research," in which the consumers' desires are determined and then a new product is designed to meet these previously unmet needs. Acceptability research began at the hands of marketing researchers and is now also followed in wider contexts. For example, the World Health Organization is currently involved in a research program in which the desired qualities of contraceptives are determined for the fertile audience in Latin America, Africa and Asia to guide WHO biomedial researchers in the invention and development of future methods of family planning. This acceptability approach puts the potential consuming couples in the position, via survey research, of helping design more acceptable contraceptives.

Nevertheless, certain basic consumer-oriented research questions have not been asked in diffusion research, such as, How can the consumer be protected against the influence of advertising (or other promotional) messages? What information does the consumer need to know in order to make intelligent innovation decisions?

LACK OF A PROCESS ORIENTATION

We shall now consider the first of three important conceptual/methodological biases in diffusion research, which also characterize other types of communication research:

1. Lack of a process orientation.
2. A pro-innovation bias (and an associated ignoring of causality).
3. A psychological orientation, leading to shortchanging structure.

Every textbook definition of the concept of communication either states or directly implies that it is a *process*.[5] Thus, one might expect an overwhelming emphasis in research and theory on the conceptualization of communication as process. However, a recent analysis by Arundale (1971) shows that the research designs and measurements of communication almost never allow analysis of the over-time aspects of communication that would be necessary to explore process adequately. Very little communication research includes data at more than one observation point, and almost none at more than two such points in time. Therefore, almost all communication research is unable to trace the change in a variable over time; it deals only with the present tense of behavior. Communication thus becomes, in the actuality of communication research, an artificially halted snapshot.

Why has communication research not dealt more adequately with the change-over-time aspects of process?

1. We lack concepts and propositions that reflect a process orientation.
2. Time-series data are expensive to gather, unless one depends on respondent re-

call, a procedure that is often less than satisfactory.

3. Data gathering repeated over time leads to problems of respondent sensitization (unless one uses unobtrusive and nonreactive measurement methods), since communication research itself is a communication process.

4. Communication researchers are often pressured by research sponsors, doctoral requirements, and other logistic forces to produce immediate results; this is a strong discouragement to over-time research designs.

Thus, unfortunately, we define communication as process, but then proceed in communication research to treat communication as a one-shot affair.

Diffusion research is only slightly "less bad" in this respect than other types of communication research. Because *time* is one of the four essential elements in the diffusion process, and thus receives more explicit attention than in other types of communication research, it should be stressed in the research designs utilized in diffusion research.

These designs consist mainly of correlational analyses of cross-sectional data gathered in one-shot surveys of the respondents, thus following exactly the method pioneered by Ryan and Gross (1943). By 1968 (the last time a tabulation was made of the methodologies used in diffusion studies), only 65 of the then 1,084 empirical diffusion publications (about 6 percent) reported results from field experiments, and most of these field experiments had been done since 1960 (our turning-point year in the diffusion field, as mentioned earlier). Even allowing for the 67 diffusion publications (another 6 percent) that reported longitudinal panel studies at two or more points in time, the vast majority (about 88 percent)

of all diffusion researches are one-shot surveys permitting only cross-sectional data analysis. Such research designs cannot tell us very much about the *process* of diffusion over time other than what can be reconstructed from recall data.

Diffusion studies are particularly able to rely on "moving pictures" of behavior rather than on "snapshots" because of their unique capacity to trace the sequential flow of an innovation through a social system. However, diffusion researchers mainly have relied on their respondents' ability to recall their date of awareness or adoption of a new idea. Essentially, the respondent is asked to look back over his shoulder and mentally reconstruct his past history of innovation experiences. This hindsight ability is not very accurate and undoubtedly varies on the basis of (1) the innovations' salience to the respondents; (2) the length of time over which recall is requested; and (3) individual differences in education, mental ability, etc.

Future diffusion research ought to develop improved methods for tracer studies, in which alternative sources of data are used to provide validity checks on recall data over time.[6] Much greater use should be made of field experiments and longitudinal panel studies, which, by their research designs, are able to take "moving pictures" of the diffusion process.

THE PRO-INNOVATION BIAS AND CAUSALITY

The second important bias found in most diffusion research is an inherent pro-change bias, which assumes that the innovations studied are "good" and should be adopted by everyone. Undoubtedly hybrid corn was profitable for each of the Iowa farmers in the Ryan and Gross (1943) study, but most other innovations that have been studied do not have this high degree of relative advantage. Many individuals, for their own good, should *not* adopt then.

The pro-innovation bias, coupled with the unfortunate and overwhelming dependence on survey research designs, means that diffusion research has mostly studied "what is" instead of "what could be" about diffusion processes. Therefore, method has followed the assumption that innovation is good, that the present process of diffusion is satisfactory and needs only minor tune-up rather than a major overhauling. Röling, Ascroft, and Chege (1974) have heavily scored diffusion research on this count, arguing that it has often led to increased inequity; field experimental designs are needed to test alternatives to current practice instead of replicating more surveys of "what is."

The pro-innovation bias in diffusion research, and its overwhelming reliance on correlational analysis of survey data, often led in the past to avoiding or ignoring the issue of causality. We often speak of "independent" and "dependent" variables in diffusion research, having taken these terms from experimental designs and then used them rather loosely with correlational analysis. A dependent variable thus means little more than the main variable in which the investigator is interested. In about 60 percent of all diffusion researches, the dependent variable is *innovativeness,* defined as the degree to which a responding unit is relatively earlier in adopting an innovation than other units in the system. It is implied that the independent variables "lead to" innovativeness, although it is often unstated or uncertain whether this really means that an independent variable *causes* innovativeness.

In order for variable X to be the cause of variable Y, (1) X must precede Y in time order, (2) they must be related or covary, and

(3) X must have a "forcing quality" on Y. Most diffusion researches have only determined that various independent variables covary with innovativeness; correlational analysis of one-shot survey data does not allow the determination of time order. Diffusion research has tarried too long at step 3 in Table 12–1 and should move on to step 4.

Correlational studies face a particular problem of time order that might be called "yesterday's innovativeness": In most diffusion surveys, innovativeness is measured "today" with recall data about past adoption behavior, while the independent variables are measured in the present tense. It is obviously impossible for an individual's attitudes, formed and measured now, to cause his adoption of an innovation three years previously (this would amount to X following Y in time order, thus making it impossible for X to cause Y).

So again we see the importance of research designs that allow us to learn the overtime aspects of diffusion. Field experiments are ideally suited to the purpose of assessing the effect of various independent variables (the treatments) on the dependent variable of innovativeness.

In order for X to cause Y, they must covary. If such covariance is very low, X is probably not a cause of Y. If their common variance is high, X *may* be a cause of Y. Diffusion research has specialized in determining the correlates of innovativeness.

Forcing quality, the way in which X acts on Y, is a theoretical rather than an empirical issue. The theoretical reasoning why certain variables might have a forcing quality on others needs to be given much greater attention in diffusion research. Theoretical approaches from other fields of communication study may have application to conceptualizing the forcing quality of certain independent variables on innovativeness and other dependent variables.

Table 12-1
A Classification of Stages in Social Science Research

Research Stages	Research Purpose	Research Method
1. Problem delineation	To define what we are looking for, and the extent to which it is a social problem	Qualitative analysis, such as case studies, observation, unstructured interviews, and literature review
2. Variable identification	To define variables which might be linked to the problem, and to describe possible interconnections between these variables	Exploratory case studies, and other qualitative methods that are low on structure
3. Determination of relationships among the variables	To determine the clusters of relevant variables required for prediction, and to analyze their patterns of relationships	Cross-sectional, correlational analysis of quantitative survey data
4. Establishment of causality among the variables	To determine which factors are critical in promoting or inhibiting the problem	Longitudinal studies, and small-scale experiments with (1) over-time data, (2) in which at least one variable changes prior to the others, so as to determine time order
5. Manipulation of causal variables for policy-formation purposes	To determine the correspondence between a theoretical problem solution and the manipulative factors	Field experiments
6. Evaluation of alternative policies/programs	To assess the expected, as well as the unanticipated consequences of various programs/policies before and after they are applied on a large scale, and to determine the effectiveness of such programs in overall program solution	Controlled field comparisons, such as the interrupted time-series field experiment

Source: Based on Gordon, MacEachron, and Fisher, "A Contingency Model for the Design of Problem-Solving Research Problems," *Millbank Memorial Fund Quarterly*, Spring 1974, p. 193. Permission for use granted by the Millbank Memorial Fund.

THE PSYCHOLOGICAL BIAS THAT SHORT-CHANGES STRUCTURE

The psychological bias in diffusion research stems from (1) its historical roots in academe and (2) the researchers' acceptance of how social problems are defined. Several early communication scholars came from psychological backgrounds, and it was only natural that their models of communication (and diffusion) largely ignored social-structural variables that affect communication. The transactional and relational nature of human communication tended to be overlooked, and this shortcoming was also characteristic of diffusion research, at least until fairly recently.

The Individual as the Unit of Analysis

The overwhelming focus on the *individual* as the unit of analysis in communication research (while largely ignoring the importance of communication *relationships* between sources and receivers) is often due to the assumption that the individual, as the unit of response, must consequently be the unit of analysis (Coleman, 1958–59). The monadic view of human behavior determined that "the kinds of substantive problems on which such research focused tended to be problems of 'aggregate psychology,' that is *within*-individual problems, and never problems concerned with relations between people" (Coleman, 1958–59, p. 28). The use of survey methods in communications research has "destructured" behavior:

> Using random sampling of individuals, the survey is a sociological meatgrinder, tearing the individual from his social context and guaranteeing that nobody in the study interacts with anyone else in it. It is a little like a biologist putting his experimental animals through a hamburger machine and looking at every hundredth cell through a microscope; anatomy and physiology get lost; structure and function disappear and one is left with cell biology. [Barton, 1968, p. 1]

The main focus in diffusion research on the individual as the unit of analysis has only recently shifted to the dyad, clique, network, or system of individuals, centering on the communication relationships between individuals rather than on the individuals themselves. Encouraging attempts to overcome the psychological bias in diffusion research are provided by network analysis and by the open-systems approach.

These conceptual/methodological approaches suggest that even when the individual is the unit of response, the communication relationship (even though *it* can't "speak") can be the unit of analysis via some type of sociometric measurement. Sampling and data analysis procedures for relational analysis are being worked out,[7] but we still lack relational concepts and theories linking these concepts. Until diffusion scholars begin to think in relational terms, there will not be much relational analysis.

Person-Blame

The second reason for the artificially "destructured" psychological bias in communication research is the acceptance of a *person-blame-causal-attribution* definition of the social problems that we study: Individual-blame is the tendency to hold an individual responsible for his problems. Obviously, what is done about a social problem, including research, depends on how it is defined. Since communication scientists seldom participate in the identification and definition of social problems, they borrow or accept these definitions from alarmists, government officials, and other scientists.

Many illustrations of individual-blame can be cited in behavioral research. Caplan and Nelson (1973) found a high degree of individual-blame in psychological research on such problems as highway safety and race relations. They asked, "Why do we constantly study the poor rather than the nonpoor in order to understand the origins of poverty?"

An example of individual-blame is the poster produced by a pharmaceutical manufacturer: "LEAD PAINT CAN KILL!" The poster blamed mothers for allowing their children to eat paint. In New Haven, Connecticut, with the highest reported rates of lead paint poisoning of children in the U.S., landlords are legally prohibited from using lead paint on the inside of residences (W.

Ryan, 1971). But the poster blames the mother, not the paint manufacturers or the landlords. And this tendency toward stressing individual-blame rather than system-blame is very common in communication research.

Diffusion research was originally (and for many years) as guilty as other types of communication research in following an individual-blame approach:

> We note an assumption in diffusion writings that the rate of adoption should be speeded up, that the innovation should be adopted by receivers, etc. [This is a consequence of the pro-innovation bias of diffusion research.] Seldom is it implied in diffusion documents that the source or the channels may be at fault for not providing more adequate information, for promoting inadequate or inappropriate innovations, etc. (Rogers, 1971, p. 79)

This psychological bias in diffusion research began with the hybrid seed corn study. Strangely, Ryan and Gross (1943) did not gather sociometric data about the interpersonal diffusion of the innovation within their two Iowa communities of study even though (1) they found that interpersonal communication from neighbors was essential in clinching adoption decisions and (2) their sampling design of a complete census of farmers in the two communities was ideal for gathering relational data for network-analysis purposes.

RESTORING SOCIAL STRUCTURE TO DIFFUSION RESEARCH

The refocusing of diffusion researches had to wait until later investigations, especially the drug study among medical doctors by Coleman et al. (1966). Then it became a common procedure for diffusion scholars to ask their respondents sociometric questions of the general form, "From whom in this system did you obtain information that led you to adopt this innovation?" The sociometric dyad represented by each answer to this question could consequently be punched on an IBM card (including data on the characteristics of the seeker *and* the sought), which then became the unit of analysis.

The relational data thus obtained were utilized to provide deeper insight into the role of opinion leaders in the two-step flow of communication, a conceptualization that was originated by Lazarsfeld, Berelson, and Gaudet (1944) prior to most diffusion research. Later research showed that the two-step flow hypothesis was mainly a gross oversimplification, since the flow of communication may actually have any number of steps, but the concept of opinion leadership has much theoretical and practical utility. Diffusion researches were able to advance understandings of opinion leadership because of their unique capacity to focus on the *flow* of innovations, new messages (to the receiver) that seem to leave deeper (and hence more recallable) scratches on men's minds. The tracer quality of an innovation's diffusion pathways aids the investigation of the flow of communication messages, and especially the role of certain individuals such as opinion leaders in this flow. For instance, the complicated relationship of leadership and group norms, first raised theoretically by George Homans (1961, p. 339), has received rather definite empirical elucidation by diffusion scholars, resulting in the proposition: *"When the system's norms favor change, opinion leaders are more innovative, but when the norms are traditional, opinion leaders are not especially innovative"* (Rogers, 1971, p. 219).

Network Analysis of Diffusion

Most communication research has largely ignored the effect of social structure on communication behavior, as we pointed out earlier, and diffusion research to date has only partly realized its full potential in this regard. *Network analysis* is a method of research for identifying the communication structure of a system in which sociometric data about communication flows or patterns are analyzed by using interpersonal relationships as the units of analysis (Rogers and Agarwala-Rogers, 1976). This tool promises to capitalize on the unique ability of diffusion inquiry to reconstruct specific message flows in a system and then to overlay the social structure of the system on these flows. The innovation's diffusion brings life to the otherwise static nature of the structural variables; network analysis permits understanding the social structure as it channels the process of diffusion. About the only other place in communication research where network analysis has been used to restore social structure to the communication process is in a few recent investigations of organizational communication.

The first, and very partial, attempts toward network analysis of the diffusion process simply identified opinion leaders in a system and determined their mass media and interpersonal communication behavior. This approach was only a slight extension of the usual monadic analysis, moving toward a relation type of analysis.

Next, diffusion scholars began to plot sequential-over-time sociograms of the diffusion of an innovation among the members of a system. Tentative steps were taken toward using communication relationships (such as sociometric dyads) as the units of analysis. The advance allowed data analysis of a "who-to-whom" communication matrix and facilitated inquiry into the identification (1) of cliques within the total system[8] and

how such structural subgroupings affected the diffusion of an innovation and (2) of specialized communication roles such as liaisons, bridges, and isolates,[9] thus allowing communication research to proceed far beyond the relatively simpler issue of studying just opinion leadership. Further, the measurement of various structural indexes (such as system connectedness and system openness[10]) for individuals, cliques, or entire systems (such as organizations or communities) now became possible. Generally, system innovativeness is positively related to connectedness and to system openness.

These network analyses necessitated a new kind of sampling, as well as a shift to relational units of analysis. Instead of random samples of scattered individuals in a large population, the network studies usually depended on gathering data from *all* the eligible respondents in a system (such as a village) or a sample of such systems (Table 12–2). Usually these sample designs meant less emphasis on the ability to generalize the research results, which was traded off for a greater focus on understanding the role of social structures on diffusion flows. If such research were to study social structure, it had to sample intact social structures, or at least the relevant parts of them.

The Strength of Weak Ties

Out of the network analysis of interpersonal diffusion grew a research issue that came to be called "the strength of weak ties" (Granovetter, 1973; Liu and Duff, 1972).[11] The proposition summarizing this research is, *The informational strength of dyadic communication relationships is inversely related to the degree of homophily (and the strength of the attraction) between the source and the receiver.* Or, in other words, an innovation is diffused to a larger number of individuals and traverses a greater social distance when

Table 12-2
Comparison of Monadic and Relational Analysis in Research on the Diffusion of Innovations

Characteristics of the Research Approach	Type of Diffusion Research Approach	
	Monadic Analysis	*Relational Analysis*
1. Unit of analysis	The individual	The communication relationship between two (or more) individuals
2. Most frequent sample design	Random samples of scattered individuals in a large sample (in order to maximize the generalizability of the research results)	Complete census of all eligible respondents in a system (such as a village), or a sample of such intact systems
3. Type of data utilized	Personal and social characteristics of individuals, and their communication behavior	Same as for monadic analysis, plus sociometric data about communication relationships
4. Main type of data analysis methods	Correlational analysis of cross-sectional survey data	Various types of network analysis of cross-sectional survey data
5. Main purpose of the research	To determine the variables (usually characteristics of individuals) related to innovativeness	To determine how social-structural variables affect diffusion flows in a system

passed through weak ties rather than strong ones (Granovetter, 1973).

For any given topic, each individual operates in his/her particular communication environment consisting of a number of friends and acquaintances with whom the topic is discussed most frequently. These friends are usually highly homophilous (or similar) with the individual and with each other, and most of the individual's friends are friends of each other, thus constituting an "interlocking network" (Laumann, 1973; Rogers, 1973). This homophily and close attraction facilitate effective communication, but they act as a barrier preventing new ideas from entering the network. There is thus not much informational strength in the interlocking network; some heterophilous ties into the network are needed to give it more openness. These "weak ties" enable innovations to flow from clique to clique via

liaisons and bridges. There is a cohesive power to the weak ties.

Laumann (1973) found important differences in political behavior, organizational participation, and consumer behavior between Detroit men with interlocking networks and those with radial networks. Thus the nature of these personal communication networks is perhaps one important way to distinguish consumers, at least in their receptivity to innovations. Innovators have more radial personal networks, and interlocking networks are more likely centered on later adopters.

Network analysis of the diffusion of the IUD in the Philippines demonstrated this strength of weak ties: The innovation spread most easily within interlocking cliques among housewives of very similar social status (Liu and Duff, 1972). But heterophilous flows were necessary to link these cliques; usually these "weak ties" connected two women who were not close friends and allowed the IUD to travel from a higher-status to a somewhat lower-status housewife. Therefore, at least occasional heterophilous dyadic communication in a network was a structural prerequisite for effective diffusion.

The case of network analysis on the strength of weak ties illustrates an important recent trend in diffusion research: The concepts used in this analysis are *relational* constructs. Perhaps we are seeing the real beginning of relational thinking in communication research.

CONCLUSIONS

Our quick tour of the past 32 years of diffusion research provides many examples of Thorstein Veblen's concept of "trained incapacity": By being taught to "see" innovativeness, opinion leadership, and other aspects of the classical model of diffusion, we failed to "see" much else. Acceptance of a revolutionary paradigm by scholars in a field enables them to cope with uncertainty and information overload through the simplification of reality that the paradigm represents. It also imposes and standardizes a set of assumptions and conceptual biases that, once begun, are difficult to recognize and overcome.

In my opinion the research designs, concepts, and measurement procedures of diffusion research have been very stereotyped. This similarity has facilitated the synthesis of diffusion findings, a task to which I have contributed; in fact, all diffusion studies look a good deal alike. But such standardization of research approaches has also greatly limited the contribution of diffusion research to more effective social programs and to furthering the scientific understand-

ing of communication and human behavior change. Presumably this indictment is what one dean of a U.S. school of communication had in mind when he characterized the diffusion field as "a mile and an inch deep."

Nevertheless, I believe that *research on the diffusion of innovations has played an important role in helping put social structure back in the communication process.* Focus on structural variables has increasingly characterized diffusion research in the past decade, and the techniques of network analysis promise exciting further steps in this direction. Eventually this trend may help communication research shed its psychological bias and person-blame orientation.

For network analysis to fulfill its potential, however, I feel we must improve the methods of data gathering and measurement. Sociometric questions about communication behavior leave much to be desired; adequate evidence of their accuracy and stability over time are presently lacking. Unobtrusive, nonreactive measures are needed to provide validity checks on sociometry, leading to a multiple-measurement approach. At present, I believe our data-analysis techniques for rational analysis of communication behavior have far outrun the quality of our measurement.

Longitudinal panel designs for network analysis of diffusion processes are also needed; along with field experiments, they help secure the necessary data to illuminate the over-time process aspects of diffusion (and communication) and to facilitate exploration of the causal relationships involved in communication behavior.

Time is an explicit element in all diffusion research. But the measurement of time is one of the most egregious methodological weaknesses of past diffusion inquiry through its overwhelming dependence on recall data.

Thus network analysis of over-time

data and field experiments are robust tools offering promise for research on the diffusion of innovations in the years ahead.

Consumer researchers have already made important contributions to understanding the diffusion of innovations, and the diffusion model has extended the scope of investigations of the consumption of new products.

NOTES

1. All of these 1,800 empirical research publications, plus another 900 nonempirical, publications (bibliographies, theoretical works, etc.), are held in the Diffusion Documents Center in the Department of Population Planning at the University of Michigan. A bibliography of these 2,700 items (Rogers and Thomas, 1975) is available from the Department at no cost.

2. Detail on the convergence of diffusion research with communication research is provided by Katz (1960) and Rogers (1967).

3. In addition to assuming that capital-intensive technology was the vital ingredient in development, the dominant paradigm assumed that a nation had to pass through an industrial revolution en route to development, and that economic growth (guided by central planning agencies and quantified in aggregate terms like GNP) largely constituted the nature of development. After the paradigm shift, the newer conceptions of development stressed (1) the *equality* of distribution, (2) popular *participation* in decentralized development planning and execution, (3) *self-reliance* and independence in development, and (4) *integration* of traditional with modern systems (Rogers, 1975a).

4. A *field experiment* is an active intervention by an experimenter who administers a treatment (in the form of a program, project, or activity) to randomly selected respondents arranged in groups that are equivalent in the way they are chosen, with at least one treatment group and one control group (who do not receive the treatment).

5. A common definition of *communication* is the process by which an idea is transferred from a source to a receiver with the intent to change his/her behavior.

6. For example, in a study of the diffusion of a new drug among medical doctors, the physicians' recall data were checked against pharmacists' sales records for each doctor (Coleman et al., 1966).

7. *Relational analysis* is a research approach in which the unit of analysis is a relationship between two or more individuals (Rogers and Bhowmik, 1970–71).

8. A *clique* is a subsystem whose elements interact with each other relatively more frequently than with other members of the communication system.

9. A *liaison* is an individual who interpersonally connects two or more cliques within a system, without belonging to any clique. A *bridge* is an individual who is a member of a communication clique and has a link to an individual who is a member of a different communication clique. An *isolate* is an individual who has few communication contacts with the rest of the system.

10. *System connectedness* is the degree to which the members of a system as a whole are linked with each other in communication flows. *System openness* is the degree to which a system exchanges information with its environment.

11. These two sets of authors independently discovered the diffusion strength of weak sociometric ties, and although approaching the issue in somewhat different ways, they published articles with virtually identical titles within a few months of each other in 1972–73. Professors Liu, Duff, and Granovetter were well read in the diffusion literature but had not previously published on this topic, and their articles showed a relatively fresh approach to analyzing diffusion networks. Perhaps this relative newness in working with the classical diffusion model was one requisite for the originality of their contribution.

REFERENCES

Arndt, J. "Role of Product-Related Conversations in the Diffusion of a New Product," *Journal of Marketing Research,* 4 (August 1967), 291–95.

Arundale, R. B. *The Concept of Process in Human Communication Research.* Unpublished doctoral dissertation, Michigan State University, 1971.

Barton, A. H. "Bringing Society Back In: Survey Research and Macro-Methodology," *American Behavioral Scientist,* 12 (November–December 1968), 1–9.

Caplan, N. and S. D. Nelson. "On Being Useful: The Nature and Consequences of Psychological Research on Social Problems," *American Psychologist,* 28 (March 1973), 199–211.

Coleman, J. S. "Relational Analysis: The Study of Social Organization with Survey Methods," *Human Organization,* 17, (Winter 1958–59), 28–36.

Coleman, J. S., E. Katz, and H. Menzel, *Medical Innovation: A Diffusion Study.* Indianapolis: Bobbs-Merrill, 1966.

Connor, J. T. "Needed: New Economics for a New Era," *Printer's Ink,* 287 (May 29, 1964), 35–37.

Crane, D. *Invisible Colleges: Diffusion of Knowledge in Scientific Communities.* Chicago: University of Chicago Press, 1972.

De Fleur, M. L. *Theories of Mass Communication.* New York: McKay, 1966.

Deutschmann, P. J. and O. F. Borda. *Communication and Adoption Patterns in an Andean Village.* San José, Costa Rica: Programa Interamericano de Información Popular and Facultad de Sociologia, Universidad Nacional de Colombia, 1962a.

Deutschmann, P. J. and O. F. Borda. *La Comunicación de las Ideas entre-los-Campesinos Colombianos: Un Análisis Socio-Estadistico. Monografias Sociologicas* 14. Bogota: Universidad Nacional de Colombia, 1962b.

Deutschmann, P. J. and W. A. Danielson. "Diffusion of Knowledge of the Major News Story," *Journalism Quarterly,* 37 (Summer 1960), 345–55.

Fliegel, F. C. and J. E. Kivlin. "Attributes of Innovations as Factors in Diffusion," *American Journal of Sociology,* 72 (November 1966), 235–48.

Freedman, R. and J. Y. Takeshita. *Family Planning in Taiwan: An Experiment in Social Change.* Princeton: Princeton University Press, 1969.

Gordon, G., A. E. MacEachron, and G. L. Fisher. "A Contingency Model for the Design of Problem-Solving Research Problems: A Perspective on Diffusion Research," *Milbank Memorial Fund Quarterly/Health and Society,* 52 (Spring 1974) 185–220.

Granovetter, M. "The Strength of Weak Ties," *American Journal of Sociology,* 78 (May 1973), 1360–80.

Hauser, P. M. "'Family Planning and Population Programs': A Book Review Article," *Demography,* 4 (no. 1, 1967), 397–414.

Homans, G. C. *Social Behavior: Its Elementary Forms.* New York: Harcourt, Brace and World, 1961.

Katz, E. "Communication Research and the Image of Society: Convergence of Two Traditions," *American Journal of Sociology,* 65 (March 1960), 435–40.

Kotler, P., and G. Zaltman. "Social Marketing: An Approach to Planned Social Change," *Journal of Marketing,* 35 (July 1971), 3–12.

Kuhn, T. K. *The Structure of Scientific Revolutions.* Chicago: University of Chicago Press, 1962.

Laumann, E. O. *Bonds of Pluralism: The Form and Substance of Urban Social Networks.* New York: Wiley, 1973.

Lazarsfeld, P. F., B. Berelson, and H. Gaudet. *The People's Choice.* New York: Duell, Sloan, and Pearce, 1944.

Liu, W. T. and R. W. Duff. "The Strength in Weak Ties," *Public Opinion Quarterly,* 36 (Fall 1972), 361–66.

Rahim, S. A. *Diffusion and Adoption of Agricultural Practices: A Study of Pattern of Communication, Diffusion and Adoption of Improved Agricultural Practice in a Village in East Pakistan.* Technical publication no. 7. Comilla, Pakistan: (Bangledesh) Academy for Village Development, 1961.

Robertson, T. S. *Innovative Behavior and Communication.* New York: Holt, Rinehart & Winston, 1971.

Rogers, E. M. "Mass Communication and the Diffusion of Innovations: Conceptual Convergence of Two Research Traditions." Paper presented at the Association for Education in Journalism, Boulder, Colorado, 1967.

————. *Modernization among Peasants:The Impact of Communication.* New York: Holt, Rinehart & Winston, 1969.

————. *Communication of Innovations: A Cross-Cultural Approach.* (2nd ed.) New York: Free Press, 1971.

————. *Communication Strategies for Family Planning.* New York: Free Press, 1973.

————. "The Anthropology of Modernization and the Modernization of Anthropology," *Reviews in Anthropology,* 2 (August 1975a), 345–58.

————. "Where We Are in Understanding Innovation." Paper presented at the East-West Communication Institute Conference on Communication and Change: Ten Years After, Honolulu, January 12–17, 1975b.

Rogers, E. M. and R. Agarwala-Rogers, eds. *Evaluation Research on Family Planning Communication.* UNESCO Technical Report. Paris: UNESCO, 1975.

Rogers, E. M. and R. Agarwala-Rogers. *Communication in Organizations.* New York: Free Press, 1976.

Rogers, E. M. and D. K. Bhowmik. "Homophily-Heterophily: Relational Concepts for Communication Research," *Public Opinion Quarterly,* 34 (Winter 1970–71), 523–38.

Rogers, E. M. and P. C. Thomas, *Bibliography on the Diffusion of Innovations.* Ann Arbor: Department of Population Planning, University of Michigan, 1975.

Röling, N., J. Ascroft, and F. Chege. "Innovation and Equity in Rural Development." Paper presented at the World Congress of Sociology, Toronto, 1974.

Ryan, B. and N. C. Gross. "The Diffusion of Hybrid Seed Corn in Two Iowa Communities," *Rural Sociology,* 8 (March 1943), 15–24.

Ryan, W. *Blaming the Victim.* New York: Pantheon, 1971.

Tarde, G. *The Laws of Imitation.* Trans. by E. C. Parsons. New York: Holt, 1903.

Zaltman, G. *Marketing Contributions for the Behavioral Sciences.* New York: Harcourt, Brace and World, 1965.

The VALS Typology

Arnold Mitchell

More than anything else, we are what we believe, what we dream, what we value. For the most part we try to mold our lives to make our beliefs and dreams come true. And in our attempts to reach our goals, we test ourselves again and again in diverse ways, and in doing so we grow. With this growth comes change, so that new goals emerge, and in support of these new goals come new beliefs, new dreams, and new constellations of values. Some unusual people grow and change many times throughout their lives. Others change hardly at all with the decades. Most experience one or two periods when what is most important, most compelling, most beautiful shifts from one comprehensive pattern to another. These are the times when a person's values change—and lifestyles are transformed.

Further, studies made by developmental psychologists indicate that change is not random; it progresses step by step from relatively simple, immature states toward more complex, wider-ranging, more balanced states. Human growth can be thought of as an ordered sequence—a hierarchy—advancing in response to changing drives from the undeveloped toward the developed.

The values and lifestyles (VALS) typology that is the subject of this book incorporates the above concepts. In addition it rests upon data obtained in a major mail survey conducted by VALS in 1980. The Appendix describes this survey in detail and gives selected demographic, attitudinal, and financial data drawn from it. The survey asked over 800 specific questions on a great range of topics. Sample size exceeded 1,600. Respondents constituted a national probability sample of Americans aged eighteen or over living in the forty-eight contiguous states. Statistical analysis of survey results quantified and enriched the basic concepts of the VALS typology and enabled us to provide detailed quantitative and human portraits of the VALS types, together with

Reprinted with permission from Arnold Mitchell, *The Nine American Lifestyles*, Chapter 1. Warner Books, 1983.

their activities and consumption patterns. Essentially all of the specific data presented in this book are derived from this survey, although we have space to touch only on highlights.

The VALS typology comprises four comprehensive groups that are subdivided into nine lifestyles, each intended to describe a unique way of life defined by its distinctive array of values, drives, beliefs, needs, dreams, and special points of view:

Need-Driven Groups
    Survivor lifestyle
    Sustainer lifestyle
Outer-Directed Groups
    Belonger lifestyle
    Emulator lifestyle
    Achiever lifestyle
Inner-Directed Groups
    I-Am-Me lifestyle
    Experiential lifestyle
    Societally Conscious lifestyle
Combined Outer- and Inner-Directed Group
    Integrated lifestyle

Each of these groups is characterized in the pages that follow.

NEED-DRIVEN GROUPS

At the lowest levels of the lifestyles typology come the Need-Driven groups, called Survivors and Sustainers. The two groups are very different, but they share the burden of being poverty-stricken, so that their lives are driven by need. The luxury of choice in many economic matters is a relative rarity. This means, in effect, that they are less able to express their values in everyday living in the contemporary American society than are more affluent people. This overwhelming fact shows up dramatically in the activity and consumption patterns of the Need-Driv-

ens: Their poverty forces them into patterns that deviate greatly from national averages, and the greater the poverty, the larger the deviations. One might say, then, that the Need-Drivens are, from an economic perspective, a values-based group more in the sense of denial of values than of expression of them. But happily there are many exceptions. Thus, many Need-Drivens occasionally splurge—accounting, for example, for many color TVs and splendid automobiles in "poor" neighborhoods. More significantly, many activities—such as gardening, or baking—and virtually all the emotional and spiritual aspects of life do not involve appreciable income, and in these the Need-Drivens are as able as others to find rewards and self-expression.

Much evidence shows that the Need-Drivens are the farthest removed from the cultural mainstream of any of the VALS groups. They are the least flexible psychologically and least aware of the events of our times. They tend to be distrustful, rebellious, left out, and to think things are changing too fast. Hopelessness causes many to lead shrunken lives with little sensitivity to the wants of others and little vision of what can be.

Survivors

Located at the foot of the lifestyles typology, the nation's 6 million Survivors are the least favored segment of the population. Terrible poverty marks them. Only 22 percent of Survivor households made over $5,000 per year in 1979, and none made over $7,500. And the direction is down. Very few Survivors experienced improved finances in the 1977–1980 period, and only about 12 percent expected to be able to keep up with inflation in the years ahead. Many are old—the median age is sixty-six. Many are ill, without the energy to fend for themselves. Most are poorly educated—over a third haven't gone beyond eighth grade, and half have not graduated from high school—and hence find it difficult to take advantage of whatever opportunities come their way to better their positions. Not surprisingly, Survivors tend to be despairing, depressed, withdrawn, mistrustful, rebellious about their situation, lacking in self-confidence, and finding little satisfaction in any aspect of their lives. Their focus is on the elemental needs of survival and security; the aim is less to get ahead than not to slip backward. For many, existence has shriveled to the bleak reality of the moment and the fantasy world of television. As a group, Survivors are traditional, conservative, conventional. Of all the segments of the U.S. population, they are the most likely to think things are changing too fast.

There appear to be at least two rather distinct classes of Survivors. One consists largely of those ensnared in the culture of poverty. Generation and generation are born, live, and die in unchanging, paralyzing poverty. Few expect to escape, and even fewer do, for the experience of these people shows there is little reason to put out the enormous mental and social effort of trying to move upward through classic means—education, work, leadership. Those who do achieve financial success usually chose other channels, such as athletics, or drugs, or various rackets that can pay off hugely. The proportion of minorities in this class of Survivors is very high. Most live in urban ghettoes and some in rural backwaters of the South. In general, minority group Survivors are younger than other Survivors, probably less well educated, and certainly farthest (but not wholly) removed from the trends and ideas that power the society.

The other class of Survivor is less likely to have been born into the predicament; rather, through bad luck, lack of enterprise, or the onslaughts of old age, they have slipped back into the Survivor lifestyle, after following most of a lifetime spent as a Sustainer or Belonger. This, the largest group of Survivors, tends to be older than the other and is more likely to be white, to be in better touch with the events of the world, and to have larger resources, especially a home. Some live in city slums and ghettoes, but many inhabit the aging frame houses of small towns or the porches and shuttered rooms of old folks' homes.

For most of these people, the years of ambition and achievement have passed. Life has become a waiting game. Television is their main entertainment. Their homes are filled with mementoes of the past. Most are retired, and at least 80 percent are widows. They lead lives full of echoes, for most of their friends are dead or have moved to places unknown.

Sustainers

Sustainers are angry, distrustful, rebellious, anxious, combative people who often feel left out of things—but, unlike Survivors, they have not given up hope. Their life problem is less merely to survive than to secure and sustain hard-earned gains and, if possible, to move ahead to a better life. They live at the edge of poverty, probably with erratic incomes, for over a fourth are looking for work or work only part-time. Average income of Sustainers in 1979 was about $11,000, with only 22 percent exceeding $15,000. Few get much satisfaction from their jobs, which are heavily skewed to machine, manual, and service occupations. It is not surprising to find that Sustainers are the least satisfied of any lifestyle group with their financial status and the most anxious to get ahead economically.

Sustainers have the largest families despite the fact that over 25 percent are divorced, separated, or living together unmarried. They contain the highest fraction of minorities—13 percent are of Hispanic origin and 21 percent are black. More than any other group Sustainers see themselves as having low social status. Only a relative handful have gone beyond high school. They rank second lowest of the lifestyle segments in self-evaluation of overall happiness.

Mistrust of the system goes deep. Sustainers have less confidence in elected officials and corporate leaders than any other groups. They are least likely to think products are getting better or safer or that labeling is improving. More than any other group they think the energy crisis is imaginary. They also rank high in thinking things are changing too fast.

Despite all this, Sustainers see themselves as financially expert—probably a reflection of their adroitness in stretching a dollar and, perhaps, their ability to operate in the so-called underground economy. Over 80 percent look forward to better things. And many support some contemporary social trends—for example, unmarried sex and legalization of marijuana. At the same time, deep insecurities seem evident in the high need Sustainers express to have social status and to feel part of a group.

There appear to be several distinct types of Sustainers. First is the street-smart operator of urban slums and ghettoes, where much organized and disorganized crime originates. Sometimes of minority descent, these Sustainers know the ropes of the illicit economy—dope, liquor, gambling, prostitution, and the like. Extreme violence, threats, payoffs, and gang agreements are common. Business is done in cash; the spoken word is the only record. Life is dangerous and uncertain but often spectacularly rewarding.

Far more common and less dramatic is the crafty Sustainer, who makes ends meet through barter, side jobs done for cash, and, sometimes, adroit manipulation of the welfare system. This variety of Sustainer is likely to be other than the hard-crime type, less systematic, less urbanized, less exclusively male. They may think of themselves as taking advantage of a system that asks for it, but they do not see themselves as criminals.

A very different kind of Sustainer is found in the impoverished family struggling to keep going on minimal wages supplemented sometimes by food stamps, sometimes welfare. The lone mother, divorced or separated, with several children is frequently a Sustainer. So, too, are members of the family whose wage earners are frequently unemployed or whose income is minimal. Because they are subject to intense ups and downs financially, these people often consider that they're in the grip of temporary hard times, and they promise themselves the revved-up muscle car and the new TV as soon as the corner has been turned.

A final type of Sustainer, less common today than early in the century, is the recent immigrant trying to make a go of it in a new world. Without much English, without appropriate skills, without sophistication, sometimes without real friends or family, this individual finds that only substandard jobs are available. But these are enterprising, hard-working, ambitious people with faith in the system and drive sufficient to keep striving. Many of them will not escape from the Sustainer pattern, but their children may do so, driven by the conviction that here indeed is the land of opportunity.

Psychologically, Sustainers are more advanced than Survivors in that they ask much more of their world. They do more planning, are more self-confident, and expect more of the future than Survivors. At the same time, like Survivors, they are not trusting of people, they are unhappy, and in particular they often feel left out. Although many are unemployed, it is clear that they seek work and place enormous importance on financial security. Many Sustainers will move up to Belonger or, more likely, Emulator levels in the years ahead. These are people learning the ways of outer-directed America; indeed, many would qualify as outer-directed except that their resources remain so restricted as to force them into need-driven living patterns.

OUTER-DIRECTED GROUPS

The Outer-Directeds make up middle America. It is a huge category, including about two-thirds of the adult population, or well over 100 million people. It is also highly diverse, consisting of three distinct lifestyles we call Belongers, Emulators, and Achievers. Belongers, at about 57 million adults, are the largest group in the typology. They are followed in size by Achievers at about 35 million, and about 16 million Emulators.

The common denominator of these three groups is what we call Outer-Direction. Outer-directed people respond intensely to signals, real or fancied, from others. They conduct themselves in accord with what they think others will think. Since "out there" is paramount, this tends to create ways of life geared to the visible, tangible, and materialistic.

Attributes shared (especially by Belongers and Achievers) include a sense that most people are honest, a lack of rebelliousness, a sense of being "with it," conventional behavior, and insistence that the family is the most important thing in their lives.

Outer-Directedness is a major step forward psychologically from the need-driven state in that the perspective on life has broadened enormously to include real concern for other people, affiliation with a host of institutions, a developed sense of the nation, and an array of personal values and options far more diverse and complex than those available to the Need-Drivens. Because they dominate the economy, the Outer-Directeds have much greater control over the events of their lives than do the Need-Drivens, and hence they are far less despairing, less suspicious, and less fearful. In general, the Outer-Directeds seem to be the happiest of Americans, being well attuned to the cultural mainstream—a fact that does not surprise because, in truth, they are the mainstream.

Belongers

Belongers typify what is generally regarded as middle-class America. Traditional, conforming, conservative, "moral," nonexperimental, family-oriented, Belongers are a mighty force for stability in a world of tumbling change. As a group, Belongers prefer the status quo if not the ways of yesteryear. Old-fashioned values still shine bright: patriotism, home and family, sentimentality. These are people who above all cherish shared institutions such as the family, church, and loyalty to nation, job, and old associations.

The key drive of Belongers is to fit in, not to stand out. Their world is well posted, and they follow the rules. About 95 percent are white. Most are middle-aged or older and have middle incomes and middle levels of education. Women, largely housewives, predominate; in fact, 30 percent are housewives, the highest fraction of any values group. Belongers tend to live in small towns or the open country and to shun big cities. They are not much interested in sophistication or intellectual affairs. All the evidence suggests that Belongers lead contented, happy lives relatively little vexed by the stresses and mercurial events that swirl around them.

Belonging as a lifestyle in the United States is almost always associated with the "middle middle" class. Belongers are the people for whom soap operas and romance magazines are created to fill their emotional needs. The needs of Belongers reflect the fact that many were exposed to much rejection or ridicule in their formative years, resulting in an excessive need for acceptance. Family mores were usually conventional; as children Belongers often were criticized for unusual ideas or punished for experimental actions (which often were called "bad" or, worse, "deviant"). Dependency and conformity were cultivated in family life through reward and punishment. The usual message was that the parents (or the church) knew what was right.

People brought up this way tend to be puritanical, conventional, dependent, sentimental, nostalgic, mass-oriented, outer-directed, xenophobic. Most Belongers have exceptionally strong matriarchal feelings because the first belonging relationship for most people is with their mothers, and mothers provide the classic image of the most unselfish, forgiving, nurturing, belonging symbol.

Belongers see safety in numbers; they think it is important to be an insider; alikeness, togetherness, and agreement are important measures. But closeness with others tends to be quite formalized; open emotionalism and sensuality are embarrassing. Tolerance for ambiguity is low. They feel the system should reward "virtue." They prefer to follow rather than to lead; to avoid hostility they will accept the lowest common denominator. They are threatened by the aberrant. Adherence to tradition and the status quo is essential. "Should" and "ought" are dominant words.

Belonging of this sort has the strength and virtue of providing a reference point, a sense of stability and often tradition, a set of agreed-upon rules, a charted road, a nest. At the same time, unalloyed belonging tends to exclude unaccustomed ways and in that sense is prejudiced, authoritarian, and closed. The Belonger thus tends to be accepting and following within the group and rejecting of anything outside it. Group interests and concerns come first; the individual tends to be suppressed. The world the Belonger feels more comfortable in is a well-posted, well-lighted place whose outer limits are in view at all times.

Belongers are easily the most old-fashioned and traditional of the VALS groups. This stance is taken against a background of much happiness and intermediate levels of satisfaction and trust in people. Although they are not particularly affluent and their financial progess is not above average, Belongers are satisfied with their situation. Generally they seem a contented, unambitious group. Traditional values emerge clearly in their opposition to "women's liberation," moral and sexual freedom, and rights for blacks. Belongers feel strongly that obedience is a prime virtue in children and that the military deserves much confidence. They tend, relatively, to abstain from alcohol; they are heavy TV watchers. This description is to a degree overdrawn, yet it captures the sense of the Belonger seeking security through avoidance of surprise, comfort through being surrounded by the familiar, and happiness through acceptance by the group.

In terms of psychological maturity Belongers are ahead of the Need-Drivens in many ways. Their concerns extend to a wide range of institutions and people; they plan for the years ahead; they match their consumption to their means; they are much more trusting of people and less rebellious. They feel better attuned to events around them and find more satisfaction in job, hobbies, and friends; and they are markedly more supportive of military leaders, elected officials, and corporate leaders.

Emulators

The outer-directed world of the Emulator is totally different from that of Belongers. Emulators are intensely striving people, seeking to be like those they consider richer and more successful than they are—that is, Achievers. They are more influenced by the values of others than any other lifestyle group. Whether man or woman, they tend to be ambitious, competitive, ostentatious, unsubtle, "macho." They are also hardworking, supportive of contemporary social trends, and fairly successful. Despite a relatively young median age of twenty-seven, Emulator households in 1979 had an average income of over $18,000. But they are spenders and tend to be in debt. The problem for Emulators is that they do not really understand the values and lifestyle of those they emulate. Nor are their life patterns very similar. The important area of occupation illustrates the mismatch: 29 percent of Achievers hold professional or technical jobs, but only 9 percent of Emulators do; 17 percent of Achievers are managers or administrators vs. 6 percent of Emulators.

Emulators are more likely than any other group to have attended technical school. Unusually large numbers have one or two years of college but have not graduated. Self-assessed social class is strongly skewed to the low side, although the Sustainer pattern is more extreme. On the other hand, educational patterns of the fathers of Emulators are surprisingly high—higher, in fact, than those of Survivors, Sustainers, or Belongers, even when age differences are taken into account. Our data provide some support for the hypothesis that the Emulator stage is a key resting place for many upwardly mobile members of minority groups. Blacks and Hispanics both are materially overrepresented in the group, but not as much as they are among Sustainers. Despite this, Emulators appear to include many raised in favored circumstances but who, for one reason or another, have conjured up ambitions inappropriate for their achievements and perhaps for their abilities. Although many surely sense this—witness their anger at and mistrust of "the Establishment"—they seem unable, or unwilling, to realign their goals.

The information that Emulators have about Achievers tends to be secondhand—from movies, romanticized magazines, gossip columns. The result, naturally, is that they experience much rejection, inevitably generating a pervasive sense of anger, mistrust of individuals, and little faith that "the system" will give them a break. Emulators wind up with a poor self-image: for example, only 5 percent (vs. 41 percent for Achievers) regard themselves as upper-class; many often feel left out of things; they are below average in considering the inner self more important than fame or power; they rank next to lowest (after Survivors) in their self-confidence; they are unable to get much satisfaction from job or friends; their levels of confidence in institutional leaders are low, and they distrust information coming from institutional sources. It comes as no surprise to find that Emulators rank near the bottom of the lifestyle groups in overall self-ratings of happiness.

Although Emulators are probably the most upwardly ambitious of the lifestyle groups, it appears likely that most of them will not make it to Achiever status. One reason is that their blind upward striving seems to force many into leading lives of deception—lives filled with acts calculated to mislead others. Hence Emulators tend to be "operators" and to embrace conspicuous consumption, follow the voguish fashion, and spend only where it shows. This profoundly secondhand or imitative lifestyle accounts for the extraordinary lack of differentiation of Emulator activity and consumption patterns from those of other lifestyles. Thus Emulators seem in some sense to lead hollow lives—solid in appearance on the outside, empty inside.

Psychologically, Emulators represent a turbulent transition stage between the established, solid, self-confident, well-adjusted lifestyles of Belongers and Achievers. Scornful of the first, Emulators have not yet attained the second emotionally, intellectually, economically, or socially. Emulators, nonetheless, are psychologically a step ahead of Belongers in the sense that they ask more of themselves and the system and have taken on greater responsibility for getting ahead, instead of drifting with events in the style of many Belongers.

Achievers

Achievers are at the top—at the pinnacle of Outer-Direction. They are the driving and driven people who have built "the system" and are now at the helm. Including almost one-fourth of the adult population, they are a diverse, gifted, hard-working, self-reliant, successful, and happy group.

Achievers come in many shapes and forms. The ambitious, competitive, effective corporate executive is one familiar type. But there is also the skilled professional—lawyer, doctor, scientist—the adroit politician, the money-oriented athlete or entertainer, and the artist whose goal is fame and "the big life." Then there is the vicarious Achiever—the individual who expresses his or her achievement needs through others as much as through personal attainment.

To some, Achievers typify the stereotype of the wealthy, successful American. To social critics, Achievers represent the Establishment. But more than anything else Achievers have learned to live the comfortable, affluent, affable, outer-directed life,

and in so doing they have set the standard for much of the nation.

In things material Achievers are far in the vanguard among the lifestyle groups. Average household income in 1979 exceeded $31,000; over 20 percent were self-employed, and two and one-half times as many Achievers as any other VALS group held managerial or administrative jobs. Almost half had total household assets of over $100,000 in 1979, compared with 31 percent for the next highest lifestyle group. Life appears to be comfortable; almost half of the Achievers live in the suburbs, 87 percent own their own homes, and they top the lifestyle groups in recent financial improvement.

Importantly, this success enables Achievers to feel good about themselves; 94 percent rate themselves as "very happy." They lead all groups in trusting people, in considering themselves upper-class, in having self-confidence, in not feeling rebellious or left out of things, and in supporting many national issues, such as encouraging industry growth, spending on the military, and supporting U.S. involvement in world affairs. They are more satisfied with their financial situation than any other group. They feel that products are getting better and safer. They support technology and go for the "new and improved" product. Achievers are staunchly Republican and conservative. Politically they do not want radical change. After all, much of the culture is of their making; they are on top, and radical change might shake them off.

The demographics of Achievers show them to have a mean age in the early forties, but with a wide spread. Over 95 percent are Caucasian and only 2 percent black. A third are college graduates, and many went on to attend graduate school. Contrary to popular impression, the evidence is that they are more happily married (that is, with fewer broken marriages) than any group other than Belongers. It is clear from data on their fathers' educational attainment that Achievers tend to be self-made people. Regionally they are a bit underrepresented in the South and overrepresented in the West.

No doubt because they are leaders, Achievers tend to be conservative, not only politically, but socially as well. Only Belongers rate themselves as more conservative in their general behavior. Specifically, they are far down the list in support of such issues as sex between unmarried people, working women also being good mothers, legalization of marijuana, or air pollution as a world danger. But they are not full of resentments. Indeed, Achievers show their psychological maturity by their success in bringing their ambitions into good alignment with reality.

But Achievers have contributed to the development of American values in a fashion they did not anticipate. By building an economic system of unprecedented affluence in the years following World War II, they made possible the emergence of postmaterial values. Further, it was largely the children of Achievers who spearheaded this change toward valuing the nonmaterial in the 1960s and 1970s. We are referring, of course, to the advent of inner-directed values, especially as expressed by members of what we have called the I-Am-Me lifestyle.

INNER-DIRECTED GROUPS

The Inner-Directeds are so named because the principal driving forces of their lives are internal, not external. That is, what is most important is what is "in here," not what is "out there." This extends to attitudes toward job, personal relationships, spiritual matters, and the satisfaction to be derived from everyday pursuits. Inner growth—sometimes sought through the great Western religious or analytic techniques, but often through transcendental meditation, yoga, Zen, or other Eastern spiritual practice—is central to many of the Inner-Directeds. Most seek intense involvement in whatever they are doing; the secondhand and vicarious are anathema. Their sensitivity to their own feelings enables them to be sensitive to others and to events around them. Many are active in social movements such as consumerism, conservation, or environmentalism, while others express their concerns more privately in artistic pursuits. As a group the Inner-Directeds are highly self-reliant and notably indifferent to social status. Money is of relatively little concern to them. They are powerfully supportive of such modern trends as women working, sex between unmarried people, or legalization of marijuana. They tend to be self-expressive, individualistic, concerned with people, impassioned, diverse, complex. (It should be noted that the term "inner-directed" was made famous by Riesman, Glazer, and Denney in *The Lonely Crowd*[1] some thirty years ago. Although we have borrowed the expression, our use of the phrase is quite different from Riesman's; he used it to mean selfish rather than self-aware. Employed that way, the term applies better to Survivors and Sustainers than to other groups in our typology.)

Most Inner-Directeds are members of the postwar generation. Most have excellent educations and hold good jobs, often of a professional or technical nature. Except for the most youthful among them, incomes average around $25,000 per year. Politically, the Inner-Directeds are heavily independent.

Essentially all Inner-Directeds were raised in the predominantly outer-directed society of the United States—especially in Achiever families. As children and adolescents they learned and internalized outer-directed parental and societal values, but at some point, usually in mid- or late adolescence, Outer Directedness began to seem less than the way to live a lifetime. Their family affluence was such that money and materialism no longer had to dominate existence as it has for almost everyone else in industrial societies. Relieved of incessant economic pressures, prosperous parents tended to raise their children permissively, perhaps thinking thus to improve upon their own upbringing. A natural effect was to emphasize noneconomic aspects of life, and this aspect became the focus of many of the most socially favored youths of the 1960s and '70s. In dramatic distinction to strictly raised Belonger children, the offspring of most Achiever families were freed (if not invited) to reject the economic values of the society. And so, in a sense as a result of the success of the U.S. economic system, a new class of lifestyles was born—lifestyles focused on the inner world rather than the external world of tangibles. Inner-Direction, of course, has always been part of the American romantic tradition—witness Emerson and Thoreau—but until the past twenty years it has been confined to a relative few. Today it is a mass movement. And it is assuredly one of the most significant sociological phenomena of the post–World War II period, although it is remarkably little noted in these terms.

If the Inner-Directeds tend to be the children of prosperous, outer-directed families, one implication is that inner-directed people tend *not* to come from need-driven or even inner-directed families. The best explanation is that some measure of satiation with the pleasures of external things seems to be required before a person can believe in—or take deep satisfaction from—the less visible, incorporeal pleasures of Inner-Direction. This does not mean that the joys of the outer world disappear (our typology is a nested model), but that inner needs become more imperious than the outer.

We have identified three inner-directed lifestyles, which we call I-Am-Me, Experiential, and Societally Conscious. Emerging as a major trend in the early and mid-1960s (when the first big wave of the postwar generation was reaching age eighteen), Inner-Direction has now reached major proportions. Survey results for 1980 indicate that about 20 percent of American adults are now more Inner-Directed than Outer-Directed or Need-Driven. This amounts to over 30 million individuals, the majority of whom are in their twenties or thirties with their years of greatest influence as citizens, parents, and consumers still ahead of them.

In the American culture Inner-Direction represents a psychological advance over Outer-Direction in that it adds another "layer" of values to the old, offering the individual new options for self-expression, new perspectives to consider, new ways in which to find satisfaction. In inner-directed cultures, such as those of India or old Japan, the psychological advance would clearly be represented by a switch from Inner- to Outer-Direction, for that would add the missing dimension. Hence it is not possible to say that Inner-Direction is "better" than Outer-Direction, or vice versa, any more than one can say a dog is "better" than a cat or age twenty is "better" than age forty. They are simply different. It may be, however, that one lifestyle is more effective than another for certain purposes, just as a dog is a better guard and a cat is a better mouser.

I-Am-Mes[2]

This is a stage of tumultuous transition from an outer-directed way of life to Inner-Direction. It is usually short-lived—no more than a few years—and marked by spectacular emotional ups and downs and sidewise veerings. It is a stage of much anxiety brought on by fear of losing the old and uncertainty concerning the new. As a frantic result,

I-Am-Mes are both contrite and aggressive, demure and exhibitionistic, self-effacing and narcissistic, conforming and wildly innovative. To give the appearance of solidity and direction, they have developed whims of iron.

The immediate shift is usually from the comfortable, established, well-defined, deeply outer-directed lifestyle of Achiever parents to the evanescent, fanciful, mercurial, flighty styles of I-Am-Me peers and contemporaries. The change is powered by both love and hate, admiration and disgust, envy and resentment of outer-directed ways of life. The stage thus is not only I-Am-Me but also I-Am-Not-You. Clearly it is a time full of confusions, contradictions, uncertainties, excesses, and protean changes. But the style also involves genuine inventiveness, for the shift from the outer to the inner dimension often brings with it the discovery of new interests and new interior rewards that redirect life goals. It is this aspect of the I-Am-Me lifestyle that is of central significance, not the accompanying flamboyance expressed through conspicuous dress, spectacular behavior, or the famed insolence of the modern teenager toward parents.

The picture we have, then, is of youths raised in favored circumstances seeking out—often ungraciously and noisily, to be sure—a new way of life for themselves. Average age is about twenty-one, and almost none are over thirty. The majority are students, and only a few have been married. Many still live with their parents and identify strongly with them—a fact that complicates their sense of personal identity. Interestingly, in 1980 only 36 percent of I-Am-Mes were found to be female, in contrast to a majority of women ten or fifteen years earlier. Because the I-Am-Mes learned to understand Outer-Direction as children and adolescents, they can afford to leave it behind as adults. The evidence is that the new way of

life, once found, is a permanent change. The I-Am-Mes of ten and more years ago retain the essence of their old values. But the I-Am-Mes of the 1980s appear in many ways to be less extreme than the I-Am-Mes of yesterday.

As a lifestyle, the I-Am-Me mode is expressed more through activities and demographics than through attitudes. Indeed, many I-Am-Mes appear not to have thought in great depth about many societal issues, but they have no problem in being and acting. Their actions mark them as energetic, enthusiastic, daring, and seeking the new. Intellectual and cultural activities attract them as well as social pursuits and physically demanding games. Overall, in fact, I-Am-Mes display the most distinctive activity patterns in any group in the values typology save the Survivors. I-Am-Mes represent the zippy, high-energy, enthusiastic end of the lifestyle spectrum, Survivors the withdrawn, despairing, weary end.

Experientials

Next in the typology of American values and lifestyles come the Experientials, the name deriving from the fact that above all these people seek direct, vivid experience. For some what matters most is deep personal involvement in ideas or issues, for others it is intense hedonism; for some it is the challenge and excitement of great physical exertion, like rock climbing; for many the quest of inner exploration is all-important; for a few the core of existence is a lifestyle of voluntry simplicity—what Emerson called "plain living and high thinking." For most of the Experientials life at one moment is a noisy parade and at the next a journey, often touched with the mystic, through the silent inner domains of thought, feeling, and spirit. For them, the secondhand, the inhibited, the unfeeling is not living. Action and interaction with people, events, and ideas—pure and strong—is the essence of life.

Most such people passed a few years earlier through the chaotic, exhibitionistic I-Am-Me stage. A few years hence many will extend their perspectives to the society—perhaps even the globe—and become more activist and mission-oriented. But for now it is not things that count, but emotion. The intangible and evanescent is likely to loom larger than the plain and visible. Experientials tend to be artistic people attuned to subtlety and nuance. "Right-brained," they will often follow the dictates of the sudden tear or prickled skin in preference to logic and the reasoned advice of others.

Psychologically, the Experientials have the most inner-directed of the lifestyles. Their independence and self-reliance goes deep, enabling them to try anything once, if only for the experience of it. So this inventive, experimental group is given to the unusual, the one-of-a-kind, the daring, the dramatic, the impulsive, the quaint. Their self-understanding makes the Experientials excellent judges of what is authentic and decisive about rejecting what comes across to them as fraudulent. Energetic, they engage in many social activities ranging from vigorous outdoor sports, to the van life, to wine tasting, to participating in artistic events.

Experientials are youthful—mostly in their late twenties—excellently educated and with income averaging between $23,000 and $24,000 annually. Many hold technical and professional jobs. They are happy, self-assured, well-adjusted people with faith in the trustworthiness of others and great assurance that they are on top of things. They tend to be liberal politically and highly supportive of such phenomena as the women's movement, unmarried sex, legalization of marijuana, conservation, consumer movements, and limits to industrial growth. Many are intensely opposed to spending on military armaments (for they are part of the "Vietnam generation") and have little faith in institutional leaders.

Most Experientials have a deep sense of the natural and a belief in the innate rightness of nature. As a result they prefer natural products to the synthetic; almost as much as Belongers, they like to grow their own flowers and vegetables. Many preserve their own food or shop in organic food stores. Many have much faith in holistic medicine. It is they who do most of the rock climbing and backpacking. It is they who love above all to get out away from it all, where the signs of civilization are few.

Finally, one of the powerful forces in the lives of most Experientials is a feel for the mystic. Usually this is not connected with the formal Western religions, but is more likely to reflect personal insight and perhaps the study of Zen, Yoga, and the *Tao Te Ching* or other ancient Eastern works. For some Experientials, marijuana and other drugs play an important role in mystic experience; for others the way lies through transcendental meditation; for still others self-hypnosis or learned deep introspection works best.

The Experientials tend to be happy individuals, not because they don't have their depressions and frustrations, but because they feel they are growing and changing and any day may bring a fresh new insight—a peak experience—to illuminate all that has gone before. In its way, the Experiential phase is an untroubled time, not in the sense of being motionless (it is far from that), but in the sense that most of what happens is considered self-induced and is welcomed as one more step on the very long road of life—a road that many of the Experientials think may, in fact, be eternal.

From the psychological standpoint the Experiential lifestyle is much less self-centered than I-Am-Me, is concerned with a broader range of issues, is more participative, is more self-assured. Experientials are notably self-reliant, whereas I-Am-Mes, being in transition to Inner-Direction, are more dependent on peer support and social status for their self-image. The Experientials appear quite able to risk a wide range of inner-exploration techniques. They have begun to leave their flamboyance and aggressively conspicuous behavior and are moving on to more spiritual, intellectual, and artistic preoccupations.

Societally Conscious

The focus of the inner-directed drives of some 13 million Americans is not rejection of other lifestyles (as in the I-Am-Mes) or intense personal experience (as in the Experientials) but concern with societal issues, trends, and events.

The range of concerns and the styles of dealing with them are great. Consumer issues are foremost for some people, who become leaders or supporters of movements concerned with such issues as pricing, additives, labeling, and advertising. Other individuals concentrate on conservation; their concerns range from national lands to energy, packaging, and a host of practices regarded as wasteful. Other concerns are with issues of product safety, environmental pollution, protection of wildlife. Stylistically the Societally Conscious range from aggressive political antagonism, to the more muted collaborative resistance of networks with a common interest, to withdrawal to lives of voluntary simplicity.

As a group the Societally Conscious are successful, influential, mature. They are, in a sense, the inner-directed equivalent of outer-directed Achievers, but they differ attitudinally in fundamental ways. Most Societally Conscious people share some key beliefs: that humanity should live in harmony with nature and not try to dominate it; that nature has its own wisdom; that small is usually beautiful; that this truly is one world; that nonmaterial aspects of life are in some sense "higher" than the material; that each person can, and should, help remedy societal problems; that outer simplicity often goes with inner richness; that simplicity may be the most powerful lifestyle of the future.[2]

Few of the Societally Conscious live fully the life of voluntary simplicity, but all act on at least some aspects of it (although, of course, they are not the only ones who do). Thus, for example, they may ride a bicycle or drive an economy car, insulate their home or install solar heating, eat only foods grown without pesticides or prepared without additives.

As a group the Societally Conscious are a sophisticated and politically effective lot. At an average age of almost forty, they have arrived at positions of influence in their jobs and communities. An extraordinary 39 percent have attended graduate school and, even more extraordinary, 59 percent hold professional or technical jobs. Average income in 1979 exceeded $27,000. These outward trappings of success combine with a consistent attitudinal pattern to create a high degree of political activism. Most try to lead lives that conserve, protect, heal. Their confidence in outer-directed leadership is minimal. They have returned unsatisfactory products or complained to a store more than any other group. They are much worried about air pollution, support more spending to protect the environment, believe industrial growth should be limited, and feel more than most that military spending is too high. Societally conscious people place a high importance on energy conservation in the home—more than any other group they have looked into solar heating—and, again leading the groups, they believe the energy crisis is real.

The fact—and action—of societal awareness is of course the psychological hallmark of this lifestyle. Although numbering only 8 or 9 percent of the adult population (but rapidly expanding), the Societally Conscious have had, and are having, a very substantial political and corporate impact on the country. They more than any other group have used the powerful technique known as "single-issue politics"—a technique that has enabled tiny percentages of the population to block causes supported by far larger numbers. The style of the Societally Conscious has often been aggressively confrontational, reflecting the assuredness of the group. In corporate areas they have spearheaded consumer issues and have powered attacks on corporate practices ranging from investment policies to product safety to more diverse representation on corporate boards.

The overall picture is of a well-educated, prosperous, politically liberal group driven by social ideals they they take with high seriousness.

COMBINED OUTER- AND INNER-DIRECTED GROUP

Integrateds

Maturity, balance, and a sense of what is "fitting" are prime characteristics of the Integrateds. These are people who have put together the decisiveness of Outer-Direction with the penetration of Inner-Direction. To these rare individuals Outer-Direction and Inner-Direction are equally good, powerful, useful, and needed; the two styles are simply different, each appropriate in its own place. Psychologically mature, the Integrateds have an unusual ability to weigh consequences, to consider subtlety along with flamboyance, to see the small within the large and the potential within what has gone wrong.

These qualities of mind and spirit enable Integrateds, we think, often to pluck the best from opposing views and combine them into a solution that subsumes both perspectives. Abraham Lincoln—surely an Integrated human being in his later years—was able to do this in trying to mend the wounds of the Civil War. Such tasks are not easy but the Integrated person is unusual, seeing things from a perspective hidden from all but a few. And so it was that Lincoln (and countless heretics and pioneers over the centuries) was excoriated by many on one side and slain by the other.

Such people elude the common ways, hence are recognized less by exterior measures than are members of the other categories. Most of us know some few people who seem to have a kind of inner completeness, a kind of deep-core certainty, that commands respect, admiration, sometimes awe, and not infrequently love. These are people one truly trusts and seeks to be like. These are people who seem to have more wisdom than the rest of us. Very likely these people are Integrateds.

Because of the elusiveness of the Integrated lifestyle, we have not yet been able to identify Integrateds on the basis of the demographic and attitudinal items we have used to categorize the other eight lifestyle groups. One reason is that there are not many people who have attained a truly integrated outlook on life. Our estimate for the fraction of American adults that qualify is 2 percent. If this is correct, our main survey should have included thirty-three Integrateds—not a large enough number to identify with confidence. A second and more compelling reason is that Integrateds undoubtedly are highly diverse, subtle in their responses, complex in their outlook. The "golden mean" characterizes many of their reactions. These attributes make it exceptionally difficult to capture such people in the agree/disagree terms of our survey. A third and very real problem is that the issues and problems of greatest concern to Integrateds involve subtleties and perspectives (as in the case of Lincoln) that either are not understook at all or are badly misinterpreted by people of other lifestyles. The latter may respond to a questionnaire item in the same fashion as the Integrateds yet mean something wholly different—a fact that the data analyst cannot determine. Work in the Values and Lifestyle program at SRI International is continuing in an effort to find means of defining the Integrateds through the development of more discriminating items, but as of now reliable results are not available.

Our sense is that Integrated people adapt easily to most conventions and mores but are powerfully mission-oriented on matters about which they feel strongly. They are people able to lead when action is required and able to follow when that seems appropriate. They usually possess a deep sense of what is fitting and appropriate. They tend to be open, self-assured, self-expressive, keenly aware of nuance and shadings, and often possessed of a world perspective. Our guess is that they are able to do their best, to be satisfied with the result, and to move on to what is next. We would expect them to be quick with laughter and generous with tears, to have found ways to meld work and play, to combine close relationships with people with the drive to accomplish (rather than visibly achieve). We think they are both makers and movers, observers and creators—people who believe in themselves and in what they are doing.

Our surmise is that Integrated individuals score high both as Achievers and as Societally Conscious types. If this surmise is correct, we can draw some inferences concerning the demographics, attitudes, and financial status of the group.

We would expect more Integrateds to be people of middle or upper-middle years, many of whom have lived decades as successful Achievers or Societally Conscious. They find it wise or necessary to move from those ways of life to the integrated pattern usually as a result of changing basic values as to what is important. A smaller but particularly interesting group consists of much younger people, in their thirties or even twenties, who have had the good luck, the means, and the gifts to find themselves early in life.

Reflecting Achievers and the Societally Conscious, we would expect Integrateds to be slightly more male than female, generally married, heavily Caucasion, very well educated, working in well-paying occupations, with average incomes of $30,000 or more. They probably would be less conservative than Achievers and less liberal than the Societally Conscious.

The Integrateds probably would not feel rebellious or express much need for social status—although they would have it. Our sense is that they might remain quite divided on controversial social questions that now distinguish Achievers from the Societally Conscious. These probably would include issues such as legalization of marijuana, industrial growth, military and environmental spending. We would expect them to draw closer together, however, on more personal issues such as women working, unmarried sex, trust in organizational leaders, or most consumer trends.

We also believe the Integrateds play a unique and crucial role in the operation of our society.

NOTES

1. Riesman, Glazer, and Denney. (1950). *The Lonely Crowd,* Yale University Press, New Haven, CT.

2. We use the colloquial phrase as more appropriate despite the command of grammar that this be I-Am-I!

Benefit Segmentation: A Decision-Oriented Research Tool

Russell I. Haley

Market segmentation has been steadily moving toward center stage as a topic of discussion in marketing and research circles. Hardly a conference passes without at least one session devoted to it. Moreover, in March the American Management Association held a three-day conference entirely concerned with various aspects of the segmentation problem.

According to Wendell Smith, "segmentation is based upon developments on the demand side of the market and represents a rational and more precise adjustment of product and marketing effort to consumer or user requirements."[1] The idea that all markets can be profitably segmented has now received almost as widespread acceptance as the marketing concept itself. However, problems remain. In the extreme, a marketer can divide up his market in as many ways as he can describe his prospects. If he wishes, he can define a left-handed segment, or a blue-eyed segment, or a German-speaking segment. Consequently, current discussion revolves largely around which of the virtually limitless alternatives is likely to be most productive.

SEGMENTATION METHODS

Several varieties of market segmentation have been popular in the recent past. At least three kinds have achieved some degree of prominence. Historically, perhaps the first type to exist was geographic segmentation. Small manufacturers who wished to limit their investments, or whose distribution channels were not large enough to cover the entire country, segmented the U.S. market, in effect, by selling their products only in certain areas.

However, as more and more brands became national, the second major system

Reprinted from *Journal of Marketing*, published by the American Marketing Association. Russell I. Haley, "Benefit Segmentation: A Decision-Oriented Research Tool," *Journal of Marketing*, Vol. 32, pp. 30–35, July 1968.

of segmentation—demographic segmentation—became popular. Under this philosophy targets were defined as younger people, men, or families with children. Unfortunately, a number of recent studies have shown that demographic variables such as age, sex, income, occupation and race are, in general, poor predictors of behavior and consequently, less than optimum bases for segmentation strategies.[2]

More recently, a third type of segmentation has come into increasing favor—volume segmentation. The so-called "heavy half" theory, popularized by Dik Twedt of the Oscar Mayer Company,[3] points out that in most product categories one-half of the consumers account for around 80% of the consumption. If this is true, the argument goes, shouldn't knowledgeable marketers concentrate their efforts on these high-volume consumers? Certainly they are the most *valuable* consumers.

The trouble with this line of reasoning is that not all heavy consumers are usually available to the same brand—because they are not all seeking the same kinds of benefits from a product. For example, heavy coffee drinkers consist of two types of consumers— those who drink chain store brands and those who drink premium brands. The chain store customers feel that all coffees are basically alike and, because they drink so much coffee, they feel it is sensible to buy a relatively inexpensive brand. The premium brand buyers, on the other hand, feel that the few added pennies which coffees like Yuban, Martinson's Chock Full O'Nuts, and Savarin cost are more than justified by their fuller taste. Obviously, these two groups of people, although they are both members of the "heavy half" segment, are not equally good prospects for any one brand, nor can they be expected to respond to the same advertising claims.

These three systems of segmentation have been used because they provide helpful guidance in the use of certain marketing tools. For example, geographic segmentation, because it describes the market in a discrete way, provides definite direction in media purchases. Spot TV, spot radio, and newspapers can be bought for a geographical segment selected for concentrated effort. Similarly, demographic segmentation allows media to be bought more efficiently since demographic data on readers, viewers, and listeners are readily available for most media vehicles. Also, in some product categories demographic variables are extremely helpful in differentiating users from non-users, although they are typically less helpful in distinguishing between the users of various brands. The heavy-half philosophy is especially effective in directing dollars toward the most important parts of the market.

However, each of these three systems of segmentation is handicapped by an underlying disadvantage inherent in its nature. All are based on an ex post facto analysis of the kinds of people who make up various segments of a market. They rely on *descriptive* factors rather than *causal* factors. For this reason they are not efficient predictors of future buying behavior, and it is future buying behavior that is of central interest to marketers.

BENEFIT SEGMENTATION

An approach to market segmentation whereby it is possible to identify market segments by causal factors rather than descriptive factors, might be called "benefit segmentation." The belief underlying this segmentation strategy is that the benefits which people are seeking in consuming a given product are the basic reasons for the existence of true market segments. Experience with this approach has shown that benefits sought by consumers determine their behavior much more accurately than do demographic characteristics or volume of consumption.

This does not mean that the kinds of data gathered in more traditional types of segmentation are not useful. Once people have been classified into segments in accordance with the benefits they are seeking, each segment is contrasted with all of the other segments in terms of its demography, its volume of consumption, its brand perceptions, its media habits, its personality and life-style, and so forth. In this way, a reasonably deep understanding of the people who make up each segment can be obtained. And by capitalizing on this understanding, it is possible to reach them, to talk to them in their own terms, and to present a product in the most favorable light possible.

The benefit segmentation approach is not new. It has been employed by a number of America's largest corporations since it was introduced in 1961.[4] However, case histories have been notably absent from the literature because most studies have been contracted for privately, and have been treated confidentially.

The benefit segmentation approach is based upon being able to measure consumer value systems in detail, together with what the consumer thinks about various brands in the product category of interest. While this concept seems simple enough, operationally it is very complex. There is no simple straightforward way of handling the volumes of data that have to be generated. Computers and sophisticated multivariate attitude measurement techniques are a necessity.

Several alternative statistical approaches can be employed, among them the so-called "Q" technique of factor analysis, multi-dimensional scaling, and other dis-

tance measures.[5] All of these methods relate the ratings of each respondent to those of every other respondent and then seek clusters of individuals with similar rating patterns. If the items related are potential consumer benefits, the clusters that emerge will be groups of people who attach similar degrees of importance to the various benefits. Whatever the statistical approach selected, the end result of the analysis is likely to be between three and seven consumer segments, each representing a potentially productive focal point for marketing efforts.

Each segment is identified by the benefits it is seeking. However, it is the *total configuration* of the benefits sought which differentiates one segment from another, rather than the fact that one segment is seeking one particular benefit and another a quite different benefit. Individual benefits are likely to have appeal for several segments. In fact, the research that has been done thus far suggests that most people would like as many benefits as possible. However, the *relative* importance they attach to individual benefits can differ importantly and, accordingly, can be used as an effective lever in segmenting markets.

Of course, it is possible to determine benefit segments intuitively as well as with computers and sophisticated research methods. The kinds of brilliant insights which produced the Mustang and the first 100-millimeter cigarette have a good chance of succeeding whenever marketers are able to tap an existing benefit segment.

However, intuition can be very expensive when it is mistaken. Marketing history is replete with examples of products which someone felt could not miss. Over the longer term, systematic benefit segmentation research is likely to have a higher proportion of successes.

But is benefit segmentation practical? And is it truly operational? The answer to both of these questions is "yes." In effect, the crux of the problem of choosing the best segmentation system is to determine which has the greatest number of practical marketing implications. An example should show that benefit segmentation has a much wider range of implications than alternative forms of segmentation.

An Example of Benefit Segmentation

While the material presented here is purely illustrative to protect the competitive edge of companies who have invested in studies of this kind, it is based on actual segmentation studies. Consequently, it is quite typical of the kinds of things which are normally learned in the course of a benefit segmentation study.

The toothpaste market has been chosen as an example because it is one with which everyone is familiar. Let us assume that a benefit segmentation study has been done and four major segments have been identified—one particularly concerned with

decay prevention, one with brightness of teeth, one with the flavor and appearance of the product, and one with price. A relatively large amount of supplementary information has also been gathered (Table 14–1) about the people in each of these segments.

The decay prevention segment, it has been found, contains a disproportionately large number of families with children. They are seriously concerned about the possibility of cavities and show a definite preference for fluoride toothpaste. This is reinforced by their personalities. They tend to be a little hypochondriacal and, in their life-styles, they are less socially-oriented than some of the other groups. This segment has been named The Worriers.

The second segment, comprised of people who show concern for the brightness of their teeth, is quite different. It includes a relatively large group of young marrieds. They smoke more than average. This is where the swingers are. They are strongly social and their life-style patterns are very active. This is probably the group to which

Table 14-1
Toothpaste Market Segment Description

Segment Name:	The Sensory Segment	The Sociables	The Worriers	The Independent Segment
Principal benefit sought:	Flavor, product appearance	Brightness of teeth	Decay prevention	Price
Demographic strengths:	Children	Teens, young people	Large families	Men
Special behavioral characteristics:	Users of spear-mint-flavored toothpaste	Smokers	Heavy users	Heavy users
Brands dispro-portionately favored:	Colgate, Stripe	Macleans, Plus White, Ultra Brite	Crest	Brands on sale
Personality characteristics:	High self-involvement	High sociability	High hypo-chondriasis	High autonomy
Life-style characteristics:	Hedonistic	Active	Conservative	Value-oriented

toothpastes such as Macleans or Plus White or Ultra Brite would appeal. This segment has been named the Sociables.

In the third segment, the one which is particularly concerned with the flavor and appearance of the product, a large portion of the brand deciders are children. Their use of spearmint toothpaste is well above average. Stripe has done relatively well in this segment. They are more ego-centered than other segments, and their life-style is outgoing but not to the extent of the swingers. They will be called The Sensory Segment.

The fourth segment, the price-oriented segment, shows a predominance of men. It tends to be above average in terms of toothpaste usage. People in this segment see very few meaningful differences between brands. They switch more frequently than people in other segments and tend to buy a brand on sale. In terms of personality, they are cognitive and they are independent. They like to think for themselves and make brand choices on the basis of their judgment. They will be called The Independent Segment.

Marketing Implications of Benefit Segmentation Studies

Both copy directions and media choices will show sharp differences depending upon which of these segments is chosen as the target—The Worriers, The Sociables, The Sensory Segment, or The Independent Segment. For example, the tonality of the copy will be light if The Sociable Segment or The Sensory Segment is to be addressed. It will be more serious if the copy is aimed at The Worriers. And if The Independent Segment is selected, it will probably be desirable to use rational, two-sided arguments. Of course, to talk to this group at all it will be necessary to have either a price edge or some kind of demonstrable product superiority.

The depth-of-sell reflected by the copy will also vary, depending upon the segment which is of interest. It will be fairly intensive for The Worrier Segment and for The Independent Segment, but much more superficial and mood-oriented for The Sociable and Sensory Segments.

Likewise, the setting will vary. It will focus on the product for The Sensory Group, on socially-oriented situations for The Sociable Group, and perhaps on demonstration or on competitive comparisons for The Independent Group.

Media environments will also be tailored to the segments chosen as targets. Those with serious environments will be used for The Worrier and Independent Segments, and those with youthful, modern and active environments for The Sociable and The Sensory Groups. For example, it might be logical to use a large proportion of television for The Sociable and Sensory Groups, while The Worriers and Independents might have heavier print schedules.

The depth-of-sell needed will also be reflected in the media choices. For The Worrier and Rational Segments longer commercials—perhaps 60-second commercials—would be indicated, while for the other two groups shorter commercials and higher frequency would be desirable.

Of course, in media selection the facts that have been gathered about the demographic characteristics of the segment chosen as the target would also be taken into consideration.

The information in Table 14–1 also has packaging implications. For example, it might be appropriate to have colorful packages for The Sensory Segment, perhaps aqua (to indicate fluoride) for The Worrier Group, and gleaming white for The Sociable segment because of their interest in bright white teeth.

It should be readily apparent that the kinds of information normally obtained in the course of a benefit segmentation study have a wide range of marketing implications. Sometimes they are useful in suggesting physical changes in a product. For example, one manufacturer discovered that his product was well suited to the needs of his chosen target with a single exception in the area of flavor. He was able to make a relatively inexpensive modification in his product and thereby strengthen his market position.

The new product implications of benefit segmentation studies are equally apparent. Once a marketer understands the kinds of segments that exist in his market, he is often able to see new product opportunities or particularly effective ways of positioning the products emerging from his research and development operation.

Similarly, benefit segmentation information has been found helpful in providing direction in the choice of compatible point-of-purchase materials and in the selection of the kinds of sales promotions which are most likely to be effective for any given market target.

Generalizations from Benefit Segmentation Studies

A number of generalizations are possible on the basis of the major benefit segmentation studies which have been conducted thus far. For example, the following general rules of thumb have become apparent:

- It is easier to take advantage of market segments that already exist than to attempt to create new ones. Some time ago the strategy of product differentiation was heavily emphasized in marketing textbooks. Under this philosophy it was believed that a manufacturer was more or less able to create new market segments at will by making his product somewhat different from those of his competitors. Now it is generally recognized that fewer costly

errors will be made if money is first invested in consumer research aimed at determining the present contours of the market. Once this knowledge is available, it is usually most efficient to tailor marketing strategies to existing consumer-need patterns.

- No brand can expect to appeal to all consumers. The very act of attracting one segment may automatically alienate others. A corollary to this principle is that any marketer who wishes to cover a market fully must offer consumers more than a single brand. The flood of new brands which have recently appeared on the market is concrete recognition of this principle.

- A company's brands can sometimes cannibalize each other but need not necessarily do so. It depends on whether or not they are positioned against the same segment of the market. Ivory Snow sharply reduced Ivory Flakes' share of the market, and the Ford Falcon cut deeply into the sales of the standard size Ford because, in each case, the products were competing in the same segments. Later on, for the same companies, the Mustang was successfully introduced with comparatively little damage to Ford; and the success of Crest did not have a disproportionately adverse effect on Gleem's market position because, in these cases, the segments to which the products appealed were different.

- New and old products alike should be designed to fit *exactly* the needs of some segment of the market. In other words, they should be aimed at people seeking a specific combination of benefits. It is a marketing truism that you sell people one at a time—that you have to get *someone* to buy your product before you get *anyone* to buy it. A substantial group of people must be interested in your specific set of benefits before you can make progress in a market.

Yet, many products attempt to aim at two or more segments simultaneously. As a result, they are not able to maximize their appeal to any segment of the market, and they run the risk of ending up with a dangerously fuzzy brand image.

- Marketers who adopt a benefit segmentation strategy have a distinct competitive edge. If a benefit segment can be located which is seeking exactly the kinds of satisfactions that one marketer's brand can offer better than any other brand, the marketer can almost certainly dominate the purchases of that segment. Furthermore, if his competitors are looking at the market in terms of traditional types of segments, they may not even be aware of the existence of the benefit segment which he has chosen as his market target. If they are ignorant in this sense, they will be at a loss to explain to success of his brand. And it naturally follows that if they do not understand the reasons for his success, the kinds of people buying his brand, and the benefits they are obtaining from it, his competitors will find it very difficult to successfully attack the marketer's position.

- An understanding of the benefit segments which exist within a market can be used to advantage when competitors introduce new products. Once the way in which consumers are positioning the new product has been determined, the likelihood that it will make major inroads into segments of interest can be assessed, and a decision can be made on whether or not counteractions of any kind are required. If the new product appears to be assuming an ambiguous position, no money need be invested in defensive measures. However, if it appears that the new product is ideally suited to the needs of an important segment of the market, the manufacturer in question can introduce a new competitive product of his own, modify the physical properties of existing brands, change his advertising strategy, or take whatever steps appear appropriate.

Types of Segments Uncovered through Benefit Segmentation Studies

It is difficult to generalize about the types of segments which are apt to be discovered in the course of a benefit segmentation study. To a large extent, the segments which have been found have been unique to the product categories being analyzed. However, a few types of segments have appeared in two or more private studies. Among them are the following:

The Status Seeker a group which is very much concerned with the prestige of the brands purchased.

The Swinger a group which tries to be modern and up to date in all of its activities. Brand choices reflect this orientation.

The Conservative a group which prefers to stick to large successful companies and popular brands.

The Rational Man a group which looks for benefits such as economy, value, durability, etc.

The Inner-Directed Man a group which is especially concerned with self-concept. Members consider themselves to have a sense of humor, to be independent and/or honest.

The Hedonist a group which is concerned primarily with sensory benefits.

Some of these segments appear among the customers of almost all products and services. However, there is no guarantee that a majority of them or, for that matter, any of them exist in any given product category. Finding out whether they do and, if so, what should be done about them is the purpose of benefit segmentation research.

CONCLUSION

The benefit segmentation approach is of particular interest because it never fails to provide fresh insight into markets. As was indicated in the toothpaste example cited earlier, the marketing implications of this analytical research tool are limited only by the imagination of the person using the information a segmentation study provides. In effect, when segmentation studies are conducted, a number of smaller markets emerge instead of one large one. Moreover, each of these smaller markets can be subjected to the same kinds of thorough analyses to which total markets have been subjected in the past. The only difference—a crucial one—is that the total market was a heterogeneous conglomeration of subgroups. The so-called average consumer existed only in the minds of some marketing people. When benefit segmentation is used, a number of relatively homogeneous segments are uncovered. And, because they are homogeneous, descriptions of them in terms of averages are much more appropriate and meaningful as marketing guides.

NOTES

1. Wendell R. Smith, "Product Differentiation and Market Segmentation as Alternative Product Strategies," *Journal of Marketing,* Vol. XXI (July, 1956), pp. 3–8.
2. Ronald E. Frank, "Correlates of Buying Behavior for Grocery Products," *Journal of Marketing,* Vol. 31 (October, 1967), pp. 48–53; Ronald E. Frank, William Massey, and Harper W. Boyd, Jr., "Correlates of Grocery Product Consumption Rates," *Journal of Marketing Research,* Vol. 4 (May, 1968), pp. 184–190; and Clark Wilson, "Homemaker Living Patterns and Marketplace Behavior—A Psychometric Approach," in John S. Wright and Jac L. Goldstucker, Editors, *New Ideas for Successful Marketing,* Proceedings of 1966 World Congress (Chicago: American Marketing Association, June, 1966), pp. 305–331.
3. Dik Warren Twedt, "Some Practical Applications of the 'Heavy Half' Theory" (New York: Advertising Research Foundation 10th Annual Conference, October 6, 1964).
4. Russell I. Haley, "Experimental Research on Attitudes toward Shampoos," an unpublished paper (February, 1961).
5. Ronald E. Frank and Paul E. Green, "Numerical Taxonomy in Marketing Analysis: A Review Article," *Journal of Marketing Research,* Vol. V (February, 1968), pp. 83–98.

Positioning Cuts through Chaos in Marketplace

Jack Trout and Al Ries

As far as advertising is concerned, the good old days are gone forever.

As the president of a large consumer products company said recently, "Count on your fingers the number of successful new national brands introduced in the last two years. You won't get to your pinky."

Not that a lot of companies haven't tried. Every supermarket is filled with shelf after shelf of "half successful" brands. The manufacturers of these me-too products cling to the hope that they can develop a brilliant advertising campaign which will life their offspring into the winner's circle.

Meanwhile, they hang in there with coupons, deals, point of purchase displays. But profits are hard to come by and that "brilliant" advertising campaign, even if it comes, doesn't ever seem to turn the brand around.

No wonder management people turn skeptical when the subject of advertising comes up. And instead of looking for new ways to put the power of advertising to work, management invents schemes for reducing the cost of what they are currently doing. Witness the rise of the house agency, the media buying service, the barter deal.

ADS DON'T WORK LIKE THEY USED TO

The chaos in the marketplace is a reflection of the fact that advertising just doesn't work like it used to. But old traditional ways of doing things die hard. "There's no reason that advertising can't do the job" say the defenders of the status quo, "as long as the product is good, the plan is sound and the commercials are creative."

But they overlook one big, loud reason. The marketplace itself. The noise level today is far too high. Not only the volume of advertising, but also the volume of products and brands.

To cope with this assault on his or her mind, the average consumer has run out of brain power and mental ability. And with a rising standard of living the average consumer is less and less interested in making the "best" choice. For many of today's more affluent customers, a "satisfactory" brand is good enough.

Advertising prepared in the old, traditional ways has no hope of being successful in today's chaotic marketplace.

In the past, advertising was prepared in isolation. That is, you studied the product and its features and then you prepared advertising which communicated to your customers and prospects the benefits of those features.

It didn't make much difference whether the competition offers those features or not. In the traditional approach, you ignored competition and made every claim seem like a preemptive claim. Mentioning a competitive product, for example, was considered not only bad taste, but poor strategy as well.

In the positioning era, however, the rules are reversed. To establish a position, you must often not only name competitive names, but also ignore most of the old advertising rules as well.

In category after category, the prospect already knows the benefits of using the product. To climb on his product ladder, you must relate your brand to the brands already there.

AVIS TOOK 'AGAINST' POSITION

In today's marketplace, the competitor's image is just as important as your own. Sometimes more important. An early success in the positioning era was the famous Avis campaign.

The Avis campaign will go down in marketing history as a classic example of establishing the "against" position. In the case of Avis, this was a position against the leader.

"Avis is only Number 2 in rent-a-cars, so why go with us? We try harder."

For 13 straight years, Avis lost money. Then they admitted they were No. 2 and have made money every year since. Avis was able to make substantial gains because they recognized the position of Hertz and didn't try to attack them head-on.

VW MADE "UGLY" POSITION WORK

A company can sometimes be successful by accepting a position that no one else wants. For example, virtually all automobile manufacturers want the public to think they make cars that are good looking. As a result, Volkswagen was able to establish a unique position for themselves. By default.

The strength of this position, of course, is that it communicates the idea of reliability in a powerful way. "The 1970 VW will stay ugly longer" was a powerful statement because it is psychologically sound. When an advertiser admits a negative, the reader is inclined to give them the position.

A similar principle is involved in Smucker's jams and jellies. "With a name like Smucker's," says the advertising, "you know it's got to be good."

BATTLE OF THE COLAS

The advantage of owning a position can be seen most clearly in the soft drink field. Three major cola brands compete in what is really not a contest. For every ten bottles of Coke, only four bottles of Pepsi and one bottle of Royal Crown are consumed.

While there may be room in the market for a No. 2 cola, the position of Royal Crown is weak. In 1970, for example, Coca-Cola's sales increase over the previous year (168,000,000 cases) was more than Royal Crown's entire volume (156,000,000 cases).

Obviously, Coke has a strong grip on the cola position. And there's not much room left for the other brands. But, strange as it might seem, there might be a spot for a reverse kind of product. One of the most interesting positioning ideas is the one currently being used by Seven-Up. It's the "Un-Cola" and it seems silly until you take a closer look.

"Wet and Wild" was a good campaign in the image era. But the "Un-Cola" is a great program in the positioning era. Sales jumped something like 10 percent the first year the product was positioned against the cola field. And the increases have continued.

The brilliance of this idea can only be appreciated when you comprehend the intense share of mind enjoyed by the cola category. Two out of three soft drinks consumed in the U.S. are cola drinks.

A somewhat similar positioning program is working in the media field. This is the "third newsweekly" concept being used by *Sports Illustrated* to get into the mind of the media buyer.

It obviously is an immensely successful program. But what may not be so obvious, is why it works. The "third newsweekly" certainly doesn't describe *Sports Illustrated*. (As the Un-Cola doesn't describe Seven-Up.)

What it does do, however, is to relate the magazine to a media category that is uppermost in the prospect's mind (as the Un-Cola relates to the soft drink category that is uppermost in the mind).

Both the Seven-Up and the *Sports Illustrated* programs are dramatic reminders that positioning is not something you do with the product. Positioning is something you do with the mind. That is, you position the product in the mind of the prospect.

YOU CAN REPOSITION COMPETITOR

In order to position your own brand, it's sometimes necessary to reposition the competitor.

In the case of Beck's beer, the repositioning is done at the expense of Lowenbrau: "You've tasted the German beer that's the most popular in America. Now taste the German beer that's the most popular in Germany."

This strategy works because the prospect had assumed something about Lowenbrau that wasn't true.

The current program for Raphael aperitif wine also illustrates this point. The ads show a bottle of "made in France" Raphael and a bottle of "made in U.S.A." Dubonnet. "For $1.00 a bottle less," says the headline, "you can enjoy the imported one." The shock, of course, is to find that Dubonnet is a product of the U.S.

PLIGHT OF AIRLINE X

In the positioning era, the name of a company or product is becoming more and more important. The name is the hook that allows the mind to hang the brand on its product ladder. Given a poor name, even the best brand in the world won't be able to hang on.

Take the airline industry. The big four domestic carriers are United, American, TWA and an airline we'll call Airline X.

Like all airlines, Airline X has had its ups and downs. Unfortunately, there have been more downs than ups. But unlike some of its more complacent competitors, Airline X has tried. A number of years ago, it brought in big league marketing people and pushed in the throttle.

Airline X was among the first to "paint the planes," "improve the food" and "dress up the stewardesses" in an effort to improve its reputation.

And Airline X hasn't been bashful when it comes to spending money. Year after year, it has one of the biggest advertising budgets in the industry. Even though it advertises itself as "the second largest passenger carrier of all the airlines in the free world," you may not have guessed that Airline X is Eastern. Right up there spending with the worldwide names.

For all that money, what do you think of Eastern? Where do you think they fly? Up and down the East Coast, to Boston, Washington, Miami, right? Well, Eastern also goes to St. Louis, New Orleans, Atlanta, San Francisco, Acapulco. But Eastern has a regional name and their competitors have broader names which tell the prospect they fly everywhere.

Look at the problem from just one of Eastern's cities, Indianapolis. From Indianapolis, Eastern flies *north* to Chicago, Milwaukee and Minneapolis. And *south* to Birmingham and Mobile. They just don't happen to fly *east*.

And then there is the lush San Juan run which Eastern has been serving for more than 25 years. Eastern used to get the lion's share of this market. Then early last year American Airlines took over Trans Caribbean. So today, who is number one to the San Juan sun? Why American, of course.

No matter how hard you try, you can't hang "The Wings of Man" on a regional name. When the prospect is given a choice, he or she is going to prefer the national airline, not the regional one.

B. F. GOODRICH HAS IDENTITY CRISIS

What does a company do when its name (Goodrich) is similar to the name of a much larger company in the same field (Goodyear)?

Goodrich has problems. They could reinvent the wheel and Goodyear would get most of the credit.

If you watched the Super Bowl last January, you saw both Goodrich and Goodyear advertise their "American-made radial-ply tires." But which company do you think got their money's worth at $200,000 a pop?

We haven't seen the research, but our bet would be on Goodyear, the company that owns the tire position.

BEWARE OF THE CO-NAME TRAP

But even bad names like Eastern and Goodrich are better than no name at all.

In *Fortune's* list of 500 largest industrials, there are now 16 corporate nonentities. That is, 16 major American companies have legally changed their names to meaningless initials.

How many of these companies can you recognize: ACF, AMF, AMP, ATO, CPC, ESB, FMC, GAF, NVF, NL, PPG, RCA, SCM, TRW, USM and VF?

These are not tiny companies either. The smallest of them, AMP, has more than 10,000 employees and sales of over $225,000,000 a year.

What companies like ACF, AMF, AMP and the others fail to realize is that their initials have to stand for something. A prospect must know your name first before he or she can remember your initials.

GE stands for General Electric. IBM stands for International Business Machines. And everyone know it. But how many people knew that ACF stood for American Car & Foundry?

Furthermore, now that ACF has legally changed its name to initials, there's presumably no way to even expose the prospect to the original name.

An exception seems to be RCA. After all, everyone knows that RCA stands for, or rather used to stand for, Radio Corp. of America.

That may be true today. But what about tomorrow? What will people think 20 years from now when they see those strange initials. Roman Catholic Archdiocese?

And take Corn Products Co. Presumably it changed its name to CPC International because it makes products out of lots of things besides corn, but you can't remember "CPC" without bringing Corn Products Co. to mind. The tragedy is CPC made the change to "escape" the past. Yet the exact opposite occurred.

LINE EXTENSION CAN BE TRAP, TOO

Names are tricky. Consider the Protein 21/29 shampoo, hair spray, conditioner, concentrate mess.

Back in 1970, the Mennen Co. introduced a combination shampoo conditioner called "Protein 21." By moving rapidly with a $6,000,000 introductory campaign (followed by a $9,000,000 program the next year), Mennen rapidly carved out a 13 per-cent share of the $3,000,000 shampoo market.

Then Mennen hit the line extension lure. In rapid succession, the company introduced Protein 21 hair spray, Protein 29 hair spray (for men), Protein 21 conditioner (in two formulas), Protein 21 concentrate. To add to the confusion, the original Protein 21 was available in three different formulas (for dry, oily and regular hair).

Can you imagine how confused the prospect must be trying to figure out what to put on his or her head? No wonder Protein 21's share of the shampoo market has fallen from 13 percent to 11 percent. And the decline is bound to continue.

FREE RIDE CAN BE COSTLY

Another similar marketing pitfall recently befell, of all companies, Miles Laboratories.

You can see how it happens. A bunch of the boys are sitting around a conference table trying to name a new cold remedy.

"I have it," says Harry. "Let's call it Alka-Seltzer Plus. That way we can take advantage of the $20,000,000 we're already spending to promote the Alka-Seltzer name."

"Good thinking, Harry," and another money-saving idea is instantly accepted.

But lo and behold, instead of eating into the Dristan and Contac market, the new product turns around and eats into the Alka-Seltzer market.

And you know Miles must be worried. In every TV commercial, the "Alka-Seltzer" gets smaller and smaller and the "Plus" gets bigger and bigger.

Related to the free-ride trap, but not exactly the same, is another common error of judgment called the "well known name" trap.

Both General Electric and RCA thought they could take their strong positions against IBM in computers. But just because a company is well known in one field doesn't mean it can transfer that recognition to another.

In other words, your brand can be on top of one ladder and nowhere on another. And the further apart the products are conceptually, the greater the difficulty of making the jump.

In the past when there were fewer companies and fewer products, a well-known name was a much greater assets than it is today. Because of the noise level, a "well-known company" has tremendous difficulty trying to establish a position in a different field than the one in which it build its reputation.

YOU CAN'T APPEAL TO EVERYONE

A human emotion called "greed" often leads an advertiser into another error. American Motors' introduction of the Hornet is one of the best examples of the "everybody" trap.

You might remember the ads, "The little rich car. American Motors Hornet: $1,994 to $3,589."

A product that tries to appeal to everyone winds up appealing to no one. People who want to spend $3,500 for a car don't buy the Hornet because they don't want their friends to think they're driving a $1,900 car. People who want to spend $1,900 for a car don't buy the Hornet because they don't want a car with $1,600 worth of accessories taken off of it.

AVOID THE F.W.M.T.S. TRAP

If the current Avis advertising is any indication, the company has "forgotten what made them successful."

The original campaign not only related No. 2 Avis to No. 1 Hertz, but also exploited the love that people have for the underdog. The new campaign (Avis is going to be No. 1) not only is conventional "brag and boast" advertising, but also dares the prospect to make the prediction not come true.

Our prediction: Avis ain't going to be No. 1. Further prediction: Avis will lose ground to Hertz and National.

Another company that seems to have fallen into the forgotten what made them successful trap is Volkswagen.

"Think small" was perhaps the most famous advertisement of the sixties. Yet last year VW ran an ad that said, "Volkswagen introduces a new kind of Volkswagen. Big."

O.K., Volkswagen, should we think small or should we think big?

Confusion is the enemy of successful positioning. Prediction: Rapid erosion of the Beetle's position in the U.S. market.

The world seems to be turning faster.

Years ago, a successful product might live 50 years or more before fading away. Today, a product's life cycle is much shorter. Sometimes it can be measured in months instead of years.

New products, new services, new markets, even new media are constantly being born. They grow up into adulthood and then slide into oblivion. And a new cycle starts again.

Yesterday, beer and hard liquor were campus favorites. Today it's wine.

Yesterday, the well-groomed man had his hair cut every week. Today, it's every month or two.

Yesterday, the way to reach the masses was the mass magazines. Today, it's network TV. Tomorrow, it could be cable.

The only permanent thing in life today is change. And the successful companies of tomorrow will be those companies that have learned to cope with it.

The acceleration of "change" creates enormous pressures on companies to think in terms of tactics rather than strategy. As one respected advertising man commented, "The day seems to be past when long-range strategy can be a winning technique."

But is change the way to keep pace with change? The exact opposite appears to be true.

The landscape is littered with the debris of projects that companies rushed into in attempting to "keep pace." Singer trying to move into the boom in home appliances. RCA moving into the boom of computers. General Foods moving into the boom in fast-food outlets. Not to mention the hundreds of companies that threw away their corporate identities to chase the passing fad to initials.

While the programs of those who kept at what they did best and held their ground have been immensely successful. Maytag selling their reliable appliances. Walt Disney selling his world of fantasy and fun. Avon calling.

And take margarine. Thirty years ago the first successful margarine brands positioned themselves against butter. "Tastes like the high-priced spread," said a typical ad.

And what works today? Why the same strategy. "It isn't nice to fool Mother Nature," says the Chiffon commercial, and sales go up 25 percent. Chiffon is once again the best selling brand of soft margarine.

LONG-RANGE THINKING IMPORTANT

Change is a wave on the ocean of time. Short-term, the waves cause agitation and confusion, but long-term the underlying currents are much more significant.

To cope with change, it's important to take a long-range point of view. To determine your basic business. Positioning is a concept that is cumulative. Something that takes advantage of advertising's long-range nature.

In the seventies a company must think even more strategically than it did before. Changing the direction of a large company is like trying to turn an aircraft carrier. It takes a mile before anything happens. And if it was a wrong turn, getting back on course takes even longer.

To play the game successfully, you must make decisions on what your company will be doing not next month or next year, but in five years, ten years. In other words, instead of turning the wheel to meet each fresh wave, a company must point itself in the right direction.

You must have vision. There's no sense building a position based on a technology that's too narrow. Or a product that's becoming obsolete. Remember the famous *Harvard Business Review* article entitled "Marketing Myopia?" It still applies.

If a company has positioned itself in the right direction, it will be able to ride the currents of change, ready to take advantage of those opportunities that are right for it. But when an opportunity arrives, a company must be ready to move quickly.

Because of the enormous advantages that accure to being the leader, most companies are not interested in learning how to *compete* with the leader. They want to be the leader. They want to be Hertz rather than Avis. *Time* rather than *Newsweek*. General Electric rather than Westinghouse.

Historically, however, product leadership is usually the result of an accident, rather than a preconceived plan.

The xerography process, for example, was offered to 32 different companies (including IBM and Kodak) before it wound up at the old Haloid Co. Renamed Haloid Xerox and then finally Xerox, the company has since dominated the copier market. Xerox now owns the copier position.

Were IBM and Kodak stupid to turn down xerography? Of course not. These companies reject thousands of ideas every year.

Perhaps a better description of the situation at the time was that Haloid, a small manufacturer of photographic supplies, was desperate, and the others weren't. As a result, it took a chance that more prudent companies couldn't be expected to take.

When you trace the history of how leadership positions were established, from Hershey in chocolate to Hertz in rent-a-cars, the common thread is not marketing skill or even product innovation. The common thread is seizing the initiative before the competitor has a chance to get established. In someone's oldtime military terms, the marketing leader "got there firstest with the mostest." The leader usually poured in the marketing money while the situation was still fluid.

IBM, for example, didn't invent the computer. Sperry Rand did. But IBM owns the computer position because they built their computer fortress before competition arrived.

And the position that Hershey established in chocolate was so strong they didn't need to advertise at all, a luxury that competitors like Nestle couldn't afford.

You can see that establishing a leadership position depends not only on luck and timing, but also upon a willingness to "pour it on" when others stand back and wait.

Yet all too often, the product leader makes the fatal mistake of attributing its success to marketing skill. As a result, it thinks it can transfer that skill to other products and other marketing situations.

Witness, for example, the sorry record of Xerox in computers. In May of 1969, Xerox exchanged nearly 10,000,000 shares of stock (worth nearly a billion dollars) for Scientific Data Systems Inc. Since the acquisition, the company (renamed Xerox Data Systems) has lost millions of dollars, and without Xerox's support would have probably gone bankrupt.

And the mecca of marketing knowledge, International Business Machines Corp., hasn't done much better. So far, the IBM plain-paper copier hasn't made much of a dent in Xerox's business. Touché.

The rules of positioning hold for all types of products. In the packaged goods area, for example, Bristol-Myers tried to take on Crest toothpaste with Fact (killed after $5,000,000 was spent on promotion). Then they tried to go after Alka-Seltzer with Resolve (killed after $11,000,000 was spent). And according to a headline in the February 7 [1972] issue of *Advertising Age*, "Bristol-Myers will test Dissolve aspirin in an attempt to unseat Bayer."

The suicidal bent of companies that go head-on against established competition is hard to understand. They know the score, yet they forge ahead anyway. In the marketing war, a "charge of the light brigade" happens every day. With the same predictable result.

ONE STRATEGY FOR LEADER

Successful marketing strategy usually consists of keeping your eyes open to possibilities and then striking before the product leader is firmly fixed.

As a matter of fact, the marketing leader is usually the one who moves the ladder into the mind with his or her brand nailed to the one and only rung. Once there, what can a company do to keep its top-dog position?

There are two basic strategies that should be used hand in hand. They seem contradictory, but aren't. One is to ignore competition, and the other is to cover all bets.

As long as a company owns the position, there's no point in running ads that scream "We're No. 1." Much better is to enhance the product category in the prospect's mind. Notice the current IBM campaign that ignores competition and sells the value of computers. All computers, not just the company's types.

Although the leader's advertising should ignore the competition, the leader shouldn't. The second rule is to cover all bets.

This means a leader should swallow his or her pride and adopt every new product development as soon as it shows signs of promise. Too often, however, the leader pooh-poohs the development, and doesn't wake up until it's too late.

ANOTHER STRATEGY FOR NON-LEADERS

Most companies are in the No. 2, 3, 4 or even worse category. What then?

Hope springs eternal in the human breast. Nine times out of ten, the also-ran sets out to attack the leader, à la RCA's assault on IBM. Result: Disaster.

Simply stated, the first rule of positioning is this: You can't compete head-on against a company that has a strong, established position. You can go around, under or over, but never head-to-head.

The leader owns the high ground. The No. 1 position in the prospect's mind. The top rung of the product leader.

The classic example of No. 2 strategy is Avis. But many marketing people misread the Avis story. They assume the company was successful because it tried harder.

Not at all. Avis was successful because it related itself to the position of Hertz. Avis preempted the No. 2 position. (If trying harder were the secret of success, Harold Stassen would be president.)

Most marketplaces have room for a strong No. 2 company provided they position themselves clearly as an alternative to the leader. In the computer field, for example, Honeywell has used this strategy successfully.

"The other computer company vs. Mr. Big," says a typical Honeywell ad. Honeywell is doing what none of the other computer companies seems to be willing to do. Admit that IBM is, in fact, the leader in the computer business. Maybe that's why Honeywell and Mr. Big are the only large companies reported to be making money on computers.

SOME 'STRONG' POSITIONS AREN'T

Yet there are positions that can be taken. These are positions that look strong, but in reality are weak.

Take the position of Scott in paper products. Scott has about 40 percent of the $1.2 billion market for towels, napkins, toilet tissues and other consumer paper products. But Scott, like Mennen with Protein 21, fell into the line-extension trap.

ScotTowels, ScotTissue, Scotties, Scottkins, even BabyScott. All of these items undermined the Scott foundation. The more products hung on the Scott name, the less meaning the name had to the average consumer.

When Procter & Gamble attacked with Mr. Whipple and his tissue-squeezers, it was no contest. Charmin is now the No. 1 brand in the toilet-tissue market.

In Scott's case, a large "share of market" didn't mean they owned the position. More important is a large "share of mind." The housewife could write "Charmin, Kleenex, Bounty and Pampers" on her shopping list and know exactly what products she was going to get. "Scott" on a shopping list has no meaning. The actual brand names aren't much help either. Which brand, for example, is engineered for the nose, Scotties or ScotTissue?

In positioning terms, the name "Scott" exists in limbo. It isn't firmly ensconced on any product ladder.

ELIMINATE EGOS FROM DECISION MAKING

To repeat, the name of the hook that hangs the brand on the product ladder in the prospect's mind. In the positioning era, the brand name to give a product is probably a company's single, most important marketing decision.

To be successful in the positioning era, advertising and marketing people must be brutally frank. They must try to eliminate all ego from the decision making process. It only clouds the issue.

One of the most critical aspects of "positioning" is being able to evaluate objectively products and how they are viewed by customer and prospects.

As a rule, when it comes to building strong programs, trust no one, especially managers who are all wrapped up in their products. The closer people get to products, the more they defend old decisions or old promises.

Successful companies get their information from the marketplace. That's the place where the program has to succeed, not in the product manager's office.

A company that keeps its eye on Tom, Dick and Harry is going to miss Pierre, Hans and Yoshio.

Marketing is rapidly becoming a worldwide ball game. A company that owns a position in one country now finds that it can use that position to wedge its way into another.

IBM has 62 percent of the German computer market. Is this fact surprising? It shouldn't be. IBM earns more than 50 percent of its profits outside the U.S.

As companies start to operate on a worldwide basis, they often discover they have a name problem.

A typical example is U.S. Rubber, a worldwide company that marketed many products not made of rubber. Changing the name to Uniroyal created a new corporate identity that could be used worldwide.

CREATIVITY TAKES BACK SEAT

In the seventies, creativity will have to take a back seat to strategy.

Advertising Age itself reflects this fact. Today you will find fewer stories about individual campaigns and more stories about what's happening in an entire industry. Creativity alone isn't a worthwhile objective in an era where a company can spend millions of dollars on great advertising and still fail miserably in the marketplace.

Consider what Harry McMahan calls the "Curse of Clio." In the past, the American Festival has made special awards to "Hall of Fame Classics." Of the 41 agencies that won these Clio awards, 31 have lost some or all of these particular accounts.

But the cult of creativity dies hard. One agency president said recently, "Oh, we do positioning all the time. But after we develop the position, we turn it over to the creative department." And too often, of course, the creativity does nothing but obscure the positioning.

In the positioning era, the key to success is to run the naked positioning statement unadorned by so-called creativity.

ASK YOURSELF THESE QUESTIONS

If these examples have moved you to want to apply positioning thinking to your own company's situation, here are some questions to ask yourself:

1. What position, if any, do we already own in the prospect's mind?

Get the answer to this question from the marketplace, not the marketing manager. If this requires a few dollars for research, so be it. Spend the money. It's better to know exactly what you're up against now than to discover it later when nothing can be done about it.

2. What position do we want to own?

Here is where you bring out your crystal ball and try to figure out the best position to own from a long-term point of view.

3. What companies must be outgunned if we are to establish that position?

If your proposed position calls for a head-to-head approach against a marketing leader, forget it. It's better to go around an obstacle rather than over it. Back up. Try to select a position that no one else has a firm grip on.

4. Do we have enough marketing money to occupy and hold the position?

A big obstacle to successful positioning is attempting to achieve the impossible. It takes money to build a share of mind. It takes money to establish a position. It takes money to hold a position once you've established it.

The noise level today is fierce. There are just too many "me-too" products and too many "me-too" companies vying for the mind of the prospect. Getting noticed is getting tougher.

5. Do we have the guts to stick with one consistent positioning concept?

With the noise level out there, a company has to be bold enough and consistent enough to cut through.

The first step in a positioning program normally entails running fewer programs, but stronger ones. This sounds simple, but actually runs counter to what usually happens as corporations get larger. They normally run more programs, but weaker ones. It's this fragmentation that can make many large advertising budgets just about invisible in today's media storm.

6. Does our creative approach match our positioning strategy?

Creative people often resist positioning thinking because they believe it restricts their creativity. And it does. But creativity isn't the objective in the seventies. Even "communications" itself isn't the objective.

The name of the marketing game in the seventies is "positioning." And only the better players survive.

RETROSPECTIVE COMMENTARY

THE POSITIONING ERA: A VIEW TEN YEARS LATER

If one word could be said to have marked the course of advertising in the decade of the '70s it is the word "positioning." Positioning

---

has become the buzzword of advertising and marketing people, not only in this country, but around the world.

It was just 10 years ago that the word and the concept were introduced for the first time to the advertising community in the pages of *Industrial Marketing* and *Advertising Age*.

The article, written by Jack Trout, named names and made predictions, all based on the "rules" of a game Jack called positioning.

On positioning's 10th anniversary, it might be interesting to look back at that 1969 article and see what changes have taken place.

> Today's marketplace is no longer responsive to strategies that worked in the past. There are just too many products, too many companies and too much marketing noise. We have become an overcommunicated society. (1969)

The question most frequently asked us is "why"? Why do we need a new approach to advertising and marketing?

The answer today is the same as it was then. We have become an overcommunicated society. With only 5% of the world's population, America consumes 57% of the world's advertising output. The per capita consumption of advertising in the U.S. today is about $200 a year.

If you spend $1,000,000 a year on advertising, you are bombarding the average consumer with less than ½ ¢ of advertising, spread out over 365 days—a consumer who is already exposed to $200 worth of advertising from other companies.

In our overcommunicated society, to talk about the "impact" of advertising is to seriously overstate the potential effectiveness of your messages. It's an egocentric view that bears no relationship to the realities of the marketplace itself.

In the communication jungle out there, the hope to score big is to be selective, to concentrate on narrow targets, to practice segmentation. In a word, "positioning" is still the name of the game today.

> The mind, as a defense against the volume of today's communications, screens and rejects much of the information offered it. In general, the mind accepts only that which matches prior knowledge or experience. (1969)

Millions of dollars have been wasted trying to change minds with advertising. Once a mind is made up, it's almost impossible to change it. Certaintly not with a weak force like advertising.

The average person can tolerate being told something about which he or she knows nothing. (This is why "news" is an effective advertising approach.) But the average person can't tolerate being told he or she is "wrong." Mindchanging is the road to advertising disaster.

Back in 1969, Jack used the computer industry as an example of the folly of trying to change minds.

Company after company tried to tell people its computers were "better" than IBM's. Yet that doesn't "compute" in the prospect's mind. "If you're so smart," says the prospect, "how come you're not rich like IBM?"

The computer "position" in the minds of most people is filled with the name of a company called "IBM." For a competitive company manufacturer to obtain a favorable position in the prospect's mind, he or she must somehow relate the company to IBM's position.

In other words, don't try to change the prospect's mind at all. Accept what's up there and work around it. It's the only hope in today's overcommunicated society.

> Positioning is a game where the competitor's image is just as important as your own. Sometimes more important. (1969)

The classic example is the famous Avis campaign.

"Avis is only No. 2 in rent-a-cars. So why go with us? We try harder." This program was extremely successful for Avis until corporate egos got in the way. Then the company launched a campaign which said "Avis is going to be No. 1."

No way.

Be honest. In the last 15 years, Avis has run many different advertising campaigns. "The wizard of Avis." "You don't have to run through airports." Etc. But what is the single theme that leaps into your mind when someone mentions Avis?

Of course, "Avis is only No. 2., etc." Yet Avis in the last few years has consistently ignored this No. 2 concept.

We call this the "F.W.M.T.S." trap. (Forgot What Made Them Successful.)

If you want to be successful today, you can't ignore the competitor's position. Nor can you walk away from your own. In the immortal words of Woody Allen, "Play it where it lies."

Another advertiser that fell into the F.W.M.T.S. trap is Seven-Up. With the "Un-cola" campaign, the company successfully positioned its 7UP drink as an alternative to Coke and Pepsi. (Almost two-thirds of all the soft drinks consumed in the U.S. are cola drinks.)

But the current campaign says, "America is turning 7UP." American is doing no such thing, Seven-Up is advertising its aspirations. No different conceptually than the "Avis is going to be No. 1" campaign. And no more effective.

> In the positioning era, the name of your company or product is becoming more and more important. (1969)

No aspect of positioning has proved as controversial as the "importance of the name."

Our 1969 example was Eastern Airlines. Among the four largest domestic airlines, Eastern consistently ranks at the bottom on passenger surveys.

Why? Eastern has a "regional" name that puts them in a different category than the big nationwide carriers (American, United, Trans World Airlines). The name Eastern puts the airline in the same category with Southern, North Central, Piedmont, Allegheny. The regional airline category.

After 10 years of effort, Eastern still ranks at the bottom of the big four.

You see what you expect to see. The passenger who has a bad experience on American or United says, "It just was one of those things." An exception to the good service he or she was expecting.

The passenger who has a bad experience on Eastern says, "It's that darn Eastern Airlines again." A continuation of the bad service he or she was expecting.

One prime objective of all advertising is to heighten expectations. To create the illusion that the product or service will perform the miracles you expect. And presto, it does.

Recently, Allegheny Airlines has seen the light. The new name: USAir. Now watch them take off.

Yes, but that's consumer advertising and the industrial customer buys on reason, not emotion. On logic and facts.

As IBM's competitors. Or Xerox's or General Electric's.

Especially for high technology, high visibility products like computers and copiers, the average industrial customer tends to be far more economical than your average Charmin-squeezing housewife. (Who, more than often than not, is downright practical.)

Industrial customers are also cursed by a "play it safe" attitude.

You can't blame them. No housewife ever got fired for buying the wrong brand of coffee. But plenty of industrial buyers have been in deep trouble over a high-technology buy that went sour. (Babcock & Wilcox will have trouble pushing its nuclear power plants in the future no matter how "superior" its specs are.)

The trend in industrial products is toward more sophistication, more use of integrated circuits, fiber optics, lasers, etc. So you can expect the industrial buyer to buy more on feelings, hunches and especially reputation. And less on objective production comparisons.

Which is why "factual expository copy" is getting less important in industrial advertising and "positioning" more important.

Your program has to go beyond just establishing a name. Too many programs start there and end there. To secure a worthwhile position for a corporate name, you need a thought to go with it. (1969)

Ten years ago, the Olin campaign was getting a lot of creative kudos. And the ads were beautifully done. But what is Olin? What is its position.

Even today, these questions have no clear-cut answer in the mind of the prospect.

Line Extension Trap

You can't hand a company on a name. You need an idea. Of all the positioning concepts suggested by the 1969 article, this one has proved to be the most useful. It led directly to what we call "the line extension trap."

When the marketing history of the '70s is written, the single most significant trend will have to be "line extension." Line extension has swept through the marketing community like Sherman through Georgia. And for some very sound reasons.

Logic is on the side of line extension. Arguments of economists. Trade acceptance. Customer acceptance. Lower advertising costs. Increased income. Reduced costs. The corporate image.

As we said, logic is on the side of line extension. Truth, unfortunately, is not. The paradox of marketing is that conventional wisdom is almost always wrong.

Xerox went out and bought a computer company with a perfectly good name. Scientific Data Systems.

And what was the first thing they did? They changed the name to Xerox Data Systems. Then they ran an ad that said. "This Xerox machine can't make a copy."

Any Xerox machine that couldn't make a copy was headed for trouble, believe us.

When Xerox folded their computer operations, it cost another $84,000,000 to sweep up the mess.

Singer went out and did the same thing with the old, respected Friden name. One of their introductory ads said, "Singer Business Machines introduces Touch & Know."

Get it? Touch and know, touch and sew.

This is the ultimate positioning mistake. To try to transfer a generic brand name to a different product sold to a different market. And then, to top it all off, to knock off your own sewing machine slogan.

Touch and Go would have been more appropriate. When they folded this operation, Singer set a record. They recorded one of the largest one quarter write-offs ever reported by any company anywhere in the world—$341,000,000.

If your corporate name is inappropriate for the new product you intend to market, create a new one. And a new position.

> One thing that's worse than a 'just a name' program is one without a name. That sounds like it could never happen, doesn't it? Well, it does when companies use initials instead of a name. (1969)

This idea was later developed into what we call "The no-name trap." Of all the positioning concepts outlined back in 1969, this one generated the most instant acceptance. The superiority of a name over a meaningless set of initials could generally be documented by market research.

The initialitus that struck American business in the late '60s and early '70s abated. Some companies even went back to their original names.

> A company has no hope to make progress head-on against the position that IBM has established. (1969)

This is perhaps the most quoted sentence from the original article—so true today as it was then.

IBM has an overwhelming position in the broad middle range of computers. So, how do you compete against IBM in computers? The 1969 article had a suggestion on how to do it.

> It's almost impossible to dislodge a strongly dug-in leader who owns the high ground. You're a lot better off to open up a new front or position—that is, unless you enjoy being shot-up. (1969)

A New Front

The big computer successes in the '70s were the companies that avoided going head-to-head with IBM—Digitial Equipment Corp.

and Data General, in particular, at the low end of the market.

Even Apple and Radio Shack have done profitable computer business, in the home market.

This "new front" idea has been developed in our marketing warfare seminars into a concept called "flanking warfare." You avoid the competitor's high-ground by outflanking them.

> Another problem that occurs fairly often is represented by the one B.F. Goodrich faces. What do you do when your name (Goodrich) is similar to the name of a larger company in the same field [Goodyear]? (1969)
>
> Goodrich has problems. Our research indicates that they could reinvent the wheel and Goodyear would get the most of the credit. If ever a company could benefit from a name change, they're one. (1969)

In 1968, Goodyear had sales of $2,926,000,000 while B.F. Goodrich's sales were $1,340,000,000. A ratio of 2.2 to 1.

Ten years later, in 1978, Goodyear had sales of $7,489,000,000 while B.F. Goodrich had sales of $2,594,000,000. A ratio of 2.9 to 1.

So the rich get richer. Fair enough.

But what is odd is that the loser's advertising continues to get all the publicity. "We're the other guys" got a lot of favorable attention in the press. But not a lot of favorable attention from the tire-buying public.

The Real Reckoning

But what really rattled the cages of the Madison Ave. mavens was positioning's implied attack on "creativity."

Even though creativity was not mentioned in the 1969 article, we didn't hesitate to attack it later on. By 1972, we were saying,

"Creativity is dead. The name of the advertising game in the '70s is positioning."

In truth, the decade of the '70s might well be characterized as a "return to reality." White knights and black eyepatches gave way to such positioning concepts as Lite Beer's "Everything you've always wanted in a great beer. And less."

Poetic? Yes. Artful? Yes. But also a straightforward, clearly defined explanation of the basic positioning premise.

On the occasion of positioning's 10th anniversary, it might be appropriate to ask, where do we go from here?

If creativity belonged to the '60s and positioning to the '70s, where will we be in the '80s?

Would you believe us if we told you in the next decade we will be burying the marketing concept?

Probably not, but we'll tell you anyway.

For at least 50 years now, astute advertising people have preached the marketing gospel. "The customer is king," said the marketing moguls. Over and over again, they used their wondrous presentations to warn top management that to be "production" oriented instead of "customer" oriented was to flirt with disaster.

But it's beginning to look like "King Customer" is dead. And that they're selling a corpse to their management.

Plenty of companies who have dutifully followed their marketing experts have seen millions of dollars disappear in valiant but disastrous customer-oriented efforts.

Who do you suppose masterminded those classic positioning mistakes? Not amateurs, but full-fledged marketing professionals with briefcases full of credentials.

General Electric in computers. Singer in business machines. Sara Lee in frozen dinners.

Of course, these marketing executives had excuses. "Product problems." "Not enough capital." Or the ever popular, "Not enough distribution" were often cited to explain these failures.

Can it be that marketing, itself, is the problem?

Many managers are beginning to realize that something is wrong—that the traditional definition of marketing (to be customer-oriented) is becoming an obsolete concept.

A New Perspective

To get a better perspective of the situation, you have to go back to the '20s, when industry started its dramatic march forward. It was then that business first became production oriented. This was the heyday of Henry Ford and his Model T.

You could have any color you wanted as long as it was black. Mr. Ford was more interested in keeping his production lines rolling (and his prices down) than in keeping his customers satisfied.

You might think that advertising was an unnecessary luxury in a production-oriented economy. Quite the contrary.

Advertising was an important ingredient in the scheme of things. Advertising's first commandment was "Mass advertising creates mass demand which makes mass production possible."

Neat. Except that General Motors tooled up its production lines to please its prospects rather than its production engineers and quickly grabbed the sales leadership from Ford.

Things haven't been the same since.

In the aftermath of World War II, business became customer-oriented with a vengeance.

The marketing man was in charge, no doubt about it, and his prime minister was marketing research.

But today, every company has become marketing oriented. Knowing what the customer wants isn't too helpful if a dozen other companies are already serving his or her wants.

American Motors' problem is not the customer. American Motors' problem is General Motors, Ford and Chrysler.

To be successful today, a company must be "competitor" oriented. It must look for weak points in the positions of its competitors and then launch marketing attacks against those weak points. For example, while others were losing millions in the computer business, DEC was making millions by exploiting IBM's weakness in small computers.

Similarly, Savin established a successful beachhead in small, inexpensive copiers. A weak point in the Xerox lineup.

And from out of nowhere came a product called Bubble Yum to take a big bite out of the bubble gum market. By exploiting the competitions' weakness of being hard to chew, they over-ran some strongly entrenched brands that had been around for years.

There are those who would say that competitors are always considered in a well-thought-out marketing plan. Indeed they are. Usually towards the back of the book under a heading entitled "Competitive Evaluation." Almost as an afterthought.

Upfront with prominence is the major part of the plan. The details of marketplace, the various demographic segments and a myriad of "customer" research statistics carefully gleaned from endless focus groups, test panels, concept and market tests.

The Battle Plan

The future marketing plan won't look like this. In fact, it won't be called a marketing plan at all. But a competitive plan, or a battle plan.

In the battle plan of the future, many more pages will be dedicated to the competition. The plan will carefully dissect each participant in the marketplace. It will develop a list of competitive strengths and weaknesses as well as a plan of action to either exploit or defend against them.

There might even come a day when this plan will contain a dossier on each of the competitors' key management people which will include their favorite tactics and style of operation. (Not unlike those Germans kept on the Allied commanders in World War II.)

And we're not talking about the distant future. Already the first signs of this trend are starting to appear in the professional journals.

In the August, 1978, issue of *Management Review*, is a report entitled, "Customer or competitor: Which guideline for marketing?" In the article, Alfred R. Oxenfeldt and William L. Moore spell out six "weaknesses" that can make a firm vulnerable to an attack from a competitor. The article's basic premise was that switching to a competitor orientation can provide a better payoff.

In the August, 1978, issue of *Business Horizons*, William S. Sachs and George Benson state the issue more directly: "Is it time to discard the marketing concept?"

These articles point out that a small, but growing, number of experts believe that the customer isn't what he or she used to be.

Confusion has set in. In many categories, customers no longer perceive any large differences in products. Thus brand choice will not be based on a rational search of all brands in the category but on a brand that was previously tried. Or the leader. Or the one positioned to the prospect's segment.

Once buying patterns are established, it has become more and more difficult to change them. The customer doesn't really want to accept any more information on a category that he or she has already cataloged in the mind. No matter how dramatically or how creatively this information is presented.

What does all this portend for the marketing people of the '80s? Or whatever they are going to be called.

In simple terms, it means that they have to be prepared to wage marketing warfare. Successful marketing campaigns will have to be planned like military campaigns.

Strategic planning will become more and more important. Companies will have to learn how to attack, defend and flank their competition. And when to resort to guerrilla warfare.

They will need better intelligence on how to anticipate competitive moves.

On the personal level, successful marketing people will have to exhibit many of the same virtues that make a great general—courage, boldness, loyalty and perseverance.

The winners in the marketing battles of the future will be those men and women who have best learned the lessons of military history—the marketing people who have learned to plan like Alexander the Great, maneuver like Napoleon Bonaparte and fight like George S. Patton.

They will also be the marketing people who know their competitors better than they know their own customers.

PART THREE

Marketing Strategy

No doubt the dominant trend in the marketing discipline during the last ten to fifteen years has been the increasing emphasis on strategic analysis and planning. Articles in Part Three present some of the discipline's best scholarly thinking about marketing strategy.

The overview is provided by an excerpt from one of the best selling business books of all times, Peters and Waterman's *In Search of Excellence.* Much of this and subsequent work by these two authors focuses on the importance of marketing strategy. Abell's discussion of strategic windows highlights the importance of participating and responding to changes in the market place. Porter's article provides a useful framework for thinking about competitors.

The next set of papers relates the marketplace to product decisions. Day describes the classic Boston Consulting Group's growth/-share matrix for product portfolio planning. Buzzell, Gale and Sultan, using the PIMS empirical database, demonstrate the significant connections among marketing strategy, market share, and profitability. Their now classic work has been extended, refined and criticized. Perhaps the most thoughtful criticism is offered by Jacobson and Aaker.

The role of information in marketing strategy is well-illustrated by the next two articles. Day, Shocker and Srivastava provide a rigorous overview of empirical market definition. Their work is complemented by the more general information systems framework offered by Montgomery and Weinberg.

Successful American Companies

Thomas J. Peters and Robert H. Waterman, Jr.

The Belgian Surrealist René Magritte painted a series of pipes and entitled the series *Ceci n'est pas une pipe (This is not a pipe)*. The picture of the thing is not the thing. In the same way, an organization chart is not a company, nor a new strategy an automatic answer to corporate grief. We all know this; but like as not, when trouble lurks, we call for a new strategy and probably reorganize. And when we reorganize, we usually stop at rearranging the boxes on the chart. The odds are high that nothing much will change. We will have chaos, even useful chaos for a while, but eventually the old culture will prevail. Old habit patterns persist.

At a gut level, all of us know that much more goes into the process of keeping a large organization vital and responsive than the policy statements, new strategies, plans, budgets, and organization charts can possi-

Reprinted with permission from Thomas J. Peters and Robert H. Waterman, *In Search of Excellence*, Chapter 1. Harper and Row, 1982.

bly depict. But all too often we behave as though we don't know it. If we want change, we fiddle with the strategy. Or we change the structure. Perhaps the time has come to change our ways.

Early in 1977, a general concern with the problems of management effectiveness, and a particular concern with the nature of the relationship between strategy, structure, and management effectiveness, led us to assemble two internal task forces at McKinsey & Company. One was to review our thinking on strategy, and the other was to go back to the drawing board on organizational effectiveness. It was, if you like, McKinsey's version of applied research. We (the authors) were the leaders of the project on organizational effectiveness.

A natural first step was to talk extensively to executives around the world who were known for their skill, experience, and wisdom on the question of organizational design. We found that they, too, shared our disquiet about conventional approaches. All were uncomfortable with the limitations of

237

the usual structural solutions, especially the latest aberration, the complex matrix form. Yet they were skeptical about the usefulness of any known tools, doubting they were up to the task of revitalizing and redirecting billion-dollar giants.

In fact, the most helpful ideas were coming from the strangest places. Way back in 1962, the business historian Alfred Chandler wrote *Strategy and Structure,* in which he expressed the very powerful notion that structure follows strategy. And the conventional wisdom in 1977, when we started our work, was that Chandler's dictum had the makings of universal truth. Get the strategic plan down on paper and the right organization structure will pop out with ease, grace, and beauty. Chandler's idea *was* important, no doubt about that; but when Chandler conceived it everyone was diversifying, and what Chandler most clearly captured was that a strategy of broad diversification dictates a structure marked by decentralization. Form follows function. For the period following World War II through about 1970, Chandler's advice was enough to cause (or maintain) a revolution in management practice that was directionally correct.

But as we explored the subject, we found that strategy rarely seemed to dictate unique structural solutions. Moreover, the crucial problems in strategy were most often those of execution and continuous adaptation: getting it done, staying flexible. And that to a very large extent meant going far beyond strategy to issues of organizing—structure, people, and the like. So the problem of management effectiveness threatened to prove distressingly circular. The dearth of practical additions to old ways of thought was painfully apparent. It was never so clear as in 1980, when U.S. managers, beset by obvious problems of stagnation, leaped to adopt Japanese management practices, ignoring the cultural difference, so much

wider than even the vast expanse of the Pacific would suggest.

Our next step in 1977 was to look beyond practicing businessmen for help. We visited a dozen business schools in the United States and Europe (Japan doesn't have business schools). The theorists from academe, we found, were wrestling with the same concerns. Our timing was good. The state of theory is in refreshing disarray, but moving toward a new consensus; some few researchers continue to write about structure, particularly that latest and most modish variant, the matrix. But primarily the ferment is around another stream of thoughts that follows from some startling ideas about the limited capacity of decision makers to handle information and reach what we usually think of as "rational" decisions, and the even lesser likelihood that large collectives (i.e., organizations) will automatically execute the complex strategic design of the rationalists.

The stream that today's researchers are tapping is an old one, started in the late 1930s by Elton Mayo and Chester Barnard, both at Harvard. In various ways, both challenged ideas put forward by Max Weber, who defined the bureaucratic form of organization, and Frederick Taylor, who implies that management really can be made into an exact science. Weber had pooh-poohed charismatic leadership and doted on bureaucracy; its rule-driven, impersonal form, he said, was the one way to assure long-term survival. Taylor, of course, is the source of the time and motion approach to efficiency: if only you can divide work up into enough discrete, wholly programmed pieces and then put the pieces back together in a truly optimum way, why then you'll have a truly top-performing unit.

Mayo started out four-square in the mainstream of the rationalist school and ended up challenging, de facto, a good bit of it. On the shop floors of Western Electric's Hawthorne plant, he tried to demonstrate that better work place hygiene would have a direct and positive effect on worker productivity. So he turned up the lights. Productivity went up, as predicted. Then, as he prepared to turn his attention to another factor, he routinely turned the lights back down. Productivity went up again! For us, the very important message of the research that these actions spawned, and a theme we shall return to continually in the book, is that it is *attention to employees*, not work conditions per se, that has the dominant impact on productivity. (Many of our best companies, one friend observed, seem to reduce management to merely creating "an endless stream of Hawthorne effects.") It doesn't fit the rationalist view.

Chester Barnard, speaking from the chief executive's perspective (he had been president of New Jersey Bell), asserted that a leader's role is to harness the social forces in the organization, to shape and guide values. He described good managers as value shapers concerned with the informal social properties of organization. He contrasted them with mere manipulators of formal rewards and systems, who dealt only with the narrower concept of short-term efficiency.

Barnard's concept, although quickly picked up by Herbert Simon (who subsequently won a Nobel prize for his efforts), lay otherwise dormant for thirty years while the primary management disputes focused on structure attendant to postwar growth, the burning issue of the era.

But then, as the first wave of decentralizing structure proved less than a panacea for all time and its successor, the matrix, ran into continuous troubles born of complexity, Barnard and Simon's ideas triggered a new wave of thinking. On the theory side, the exemplars were Karl Weick of Cornell and James March of Stanford, who attacked the rational model with a vengeance.

Weick suggests that organizations learn and adapt v-e-r-y slowly. They pay obsessive attention to habitual internal cues, long after their practical value has lost all meaning. Important strategic business assumptions (e.g., a control versus a risk-taking bias) are buried deep in the minutiae of management systems and other habitual routines whose origins have long been obscured by time. Our favorite example of the point was provided by a friend who early in his career was receiving instruction as a bank teller. One operation involved hand-sorting 80-column punched cards, and the woman teaching him could do it as fast as lightning. "Bzzzzzzt" went the deck of cards in her hands, and they were all sorted and neatly stacked. Our friend was all thumbs.

"How long have you been doing this?" he asked her.

"About ten years," she estimated.

"Well," said he, anxious to learn, "what's that operation for?"

"To tell you the truth"—Bzzzzzzt, another deck sorted—"I really don't know."

Weick supposes that the inflexibility stems from the mechanical pictures of organizations we carry in our heads; he says, for instance: "Chronic use of the military metaphor leads people repeatedly to overlook a different kind of organization, one that values improvisation rather than forecasting, dwells on opportunities rather than constraints, discovers new actions rather than defends past actions, values arguments more highly than serenity and encourages doubt and contradiction rather than belief."

March goes even further than Weick. He has introduced, only slightly facetiously, the garbage can as organizational metaphor. March pictures the way organizations learn and make decisions as streams of problems, solutions, participants, and choice opportunities interacting almost randomly to carry the organization toward the future. His observations about large organizations recall President Truman's wry prophecy about the vexations lying in wait for his successor, as recounted by Richard E. Neustadt. "He'll sit here," Truman would remark (tapping his desk for emphasis), "and he'll say, 'Do this! Do that!' And nothing will happen. Poor Ike—it won't be a bit like the army. He'll find it very frustrating."

Other researchers have recently begun to accumulate data that support these unconventional views. The researcher Henry Mintzberg, of Canada's McGill University made one of the few rigorous studies of how effective managers use their time. They don't regularly block out large chunks of time for planning, organizing, motivating, and controlling, as most authorities suggest they ought. Their time, on the contrary, is fragmented, the average interval devoted to any one issue being *nine minutes*. Andrew Pettigrew, a British researcher, studied the politics of strategic decision making and was fascinated by the inertial properties of organizations. He showed that companies often hold on to flagrantly faulty assumptions about their world for as long as a decade, despite overwhelming evidence that that world has changed and they probably should too. (A wealth of recent examples of what Pettigrew had in mind is provided by the several American industries currently undergoing deregulation—airlines, trucking, banks, savings and loans, telecommunications.)

Among our early contacts were managers from long-term top-performing companies: IBM, 3M, Procter & Gamble, Delta Airlines. As we reflected on the new school of theoretical thinking, it began to dawn on us that the intangibles that those managers described were much more consistent with Weick and March than with Taylor or Chandler. We heard talk of organizational cultures, the family feeling, small is beautiful, simplicity rather than complexity, hoopla associated with quality products. In short, we found the obvious, that the individual human being still counts. Building up organizations that take note of his or her limits (e.g., information-processing ability) and strengths (e.g., the powerflowing from commitment and enthusiasm) was their bread and butter.

CRITERIA FOR SUCCESS

For the first two years we worked mainly on the problem of expanding our diagnostic and remedial kit beyond the traditional tools for business problem solving, which then concentrated on strategy and structural approaches.

Indeed, many friends outside our task force felt that we should simply take a new look at the structural question in organizing. As decentralization had been the wave of the fifties and sixties, they said, and the so-called matrix the modish but quite obviously ineffective structure of the seventies, what then would be the structural form of the eighties? We chose to go another route. As important as the structural issues undoubtedly are, we quickly concluded that they are only a small part of the total issue of management effectiveness. The very word "organizing," for instance, begs the question, "Organize for what!" For the large corporations we were interested in, the answer to that question was almost always to build some sort of major new corporate capability—that is, to become more innovative, to be better marketers, to permanently improve labor relations, or to build some other skill which that corporation did not then possess.

An excellent example is McDonald's. As successful as that corporation was in the

United States, doing well abroad meant more than creating an international division. In the case of McDonald's it meant, among other things, teaching the German public what a hamburger is. To become less dependent on government sales, Boeing had to build the skill to sell its wares in the commercial marketplace, a feat most of its competitors never could pull off. Such skill building, adding new muscle, shucking old habits, getting really good at something new

to the culture, is difficult. That sort of thing clearly goes beyond structure.

So we needed more to work with than new ideas on structure. A good clue to what we were up to is contained in a remark by Fletcher Byrom, chairman and chief executive of Koppers: "I think an inflexible organization chart which assumes that anyone in a given position will perform exactly the same way his predecessor did, is ridiculous. He won't. Therefore, the organization ought

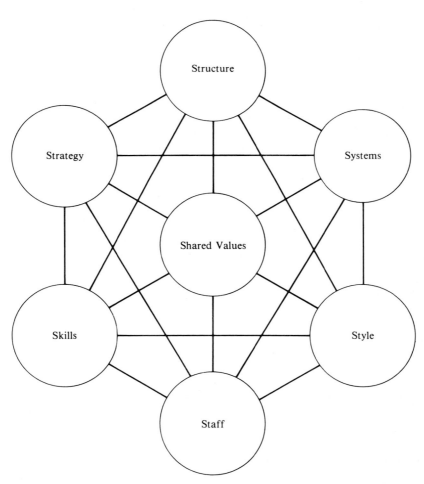

Figure 16–1
Mckinsey 7-S Framework©

to shift and adjust and adapt to the fact that there's a new person in the spot." There is no such thing as a good structural answer apart from people considerations, and vice versa. We went further. Our research told us that any intelligent approach to organizing had to encompass, and treat as interdependent, at least seven variables: structure, strategy, people, management style, systems and procedures, guiding concepts and shared values (i.e., culture), and the present and hoped-for corporate strengths or skills. We defined this idea more precisely and elaborated what came to be known as the McKinsey 7-S Framework (see Figure 16–1). With a bit of stretching, cutting, and fitting, we made all seven variables start with the letter S and invented a logo to go with it. Anthony Athos at the Harvard Business School gave us the courage to do it that way, urging that without the memory hooks provided by alliteration, our stuff was just too hard to explain, too easily forgettable.

Hokey as the alliteration first seemed, four years' experience throughout the world has borne out our hunch that the framework would help immeasurably in forcing explicit thought about not only the hardware—strategy and structure—but also about the software of organization—style, systems, staff (people), skills, and shared values. The framework, which some of our waggish colleagues have come to call the happy atom, seems to have caught on around the world as a useful way to think about organizing.[1] Richard Pascale and Anthony Athos, who assisted us in our concept development, used it as the conceptual underpinning for *The Art of Japanese Management.* Harvey Wagner, a friend at the University of North Carolina and an eminent scholar in the hard-nosed field of decision sciences, uses the model to teach business policy. He said recently, "You guys have taken all the mystery out of my class. They (his students) use the framework and all the issues in the case pop right to the surface."

In retrospect, what our framework has really done is to remind the world of professional managers that "soft is hard." It has enabled us to say, in effect, "All that stuff you have been dismissing for so long as the intractable, irrational, intuitive, information organization *can* be managed. Clearly, it has as much or more to do with the way things work (or don't) around your companies as the formal structures and strategies do. Not only are you foolish to ignore it, but here's a way to think about it. Here are some tools for managing it. Here, really, is the way to develop a new skill."

But there was still something missing. True, we had expanded our diagnostic tool kit by quantum steps. True, we had observed managers apparently getting more done because they could *pay attention* with seven S's instead of just two. True, by recognizing that real change in large institutions is a function of at least seven hunks of complexity, we were made appropriately more humble about the difficulty of changing a large institution in any fundamental way. But, at the same time, we were short on practical design ideas, especially for the "soft S's." Building new corporate capability wasn't the simple converse of describing and understanding what's not working, just as designing a good bridge takes more than understanding why some bridges fail. We now had far better mental equipment for pinpointing the cause of organizational malaise, which was good, and we had enhanced our ability to determine what was working despite the structure and ought to be left alone, which was even better. But we needed to enrich our "vocabulary" of design patterns and ideas.

Accordingly, we decided to take a look at management excellence itself. We had put that item on the agenda early in our project, but the real impetus came when the managing directors of Royal Dutch/Shell Group asked us to help them with a one-day seminar on innovation. To fit what we had to offer with Shell's request, we chose a double meaning for the word "innovation." In addition to what might normally be thought of—creative people developing marketable new products and services—we added a twist that is central to our concern with change in big institutions. We asserted that innovative companies not only are unusually good at producing commercially viable new widgets; *innovative companies are especially adroit at continually responding to change of any sort in their environments.* Unlike Andrew Pettigrew's inertial organizations, when the environment changes, these companies change too. As the needs of their customers shift, the skills of their competitors improve, the mood of the public perturbates, the forces of international trade realign, and government regulations shift, these companies tack, revamp, adjust, transform, and adapt. In short, as a whole culture, they innovate.

That concept of innovation seemed to us to define the task of the truly excellent manager or management team. The companies that seemed to us to have achieved that kind of innovative performance were the ones we labeled excellent companies.

We gave our presentation to Royal Dutch/Shell Group on July 4, 1979, and if this research has a birthday, that was it. What fascinated us even more than the effort in The Netherlands, however, was the reaction we subsequently got from a few companies like HP and 3M that we had contacted in preparation for our discussions with Shell. They were intrigued with the subject we were pursuing and urged us on.

Largely because of that, several months later we put together a team and undertook a full-blown project on the subject of excellence as we had defined it—

continuously innovative big companies. This was mainly funded by McKinsey, with some support from interested clients. At that point we chose seventy-five highly regarded companies, and in the winter of 1979–80 conducted intense, structured interviews in about half these organizations. The remainder we initially studied through secondary channels, principally press coverage and annual reports for the last twenty-five years; we have since conducted intensive interviews with more than twenty of those companies. (We also studied some underachieving companies for purposes of comparison, but we didn't concentrate much on this, as we felt we had plenty of insight into underachievement through our combined twenty-four years in the management consulting business.)

Our findings were a pleasant surprise. The project showed, more clearly than could have been hoped for, that the excellent companies were, above all, brilliant on the basics. Tools didn't substitute for thinking. Intellect didn't overpower wisdom. Analysis didn't impede action. Rather, these companies worked hard to keep things simple in a complex world. They persisted. They insisted on top quality. They fawned on their customers. They listened to their employees and treated them like adults. They allowed their innovative product and service "champions" long tethers. They allowed some chaos in return for quick action and regular experimentation.

The eight attributes that emerged to characterize most nearly the distinction of the excellent, innovative companies go as follows:

1. *A bias for action,* for getting on with it. Even though these companies may be analytical in their approach to decision making, they are not paralyzed by that fact (as so many others seem to be). In

many of these companies the standard operating procedure is "Do it, fix it, try it." Says a Digital Equipment Corporation senior executive, for example, "When we've got a big problem here, we grab ten senior guys and stick them in a room for a week. They come up with an answer *and* implement it." Moreover, the companies are experimenters supreme. Instead of allowing 250 engineers and marketers to work on a new product in isolation for fifteen months, they form bands of 5 to 25 and test ideas out on a customer, often with inexpensive prototypes, within a matter of weeks. What is striking is the host of practical devices the excellent companies employ, to maintain corporate fleetness of foot and counter the stultification that almost inevitably comes with size.

2. *Close to the customer.* These companies learn from the people they serve. They provide unparalleled quality, service, and reliability—things that work and last. They succeed in differentiating—*à la* Frito-Lay (potato chips), Maytag (washers), or Tupperware—the most commodity-like products. IBM's marketing vice president, Francis G. (Buck) Rodgers, says, "It's a shame that, in so many companies, whenever you get good service, it's an exception." Not so at the excellent companies. Everyone gets into the act. Many of the innovative companies got their best product ideas from customers. That comes from listening, intently and regularly.

3. *Autonomy and entrepreneurship.* The innovative companies foster many leaders and many innovators throughout the organization. They are a hive of what we've come to call champions; 3M has been described as "so intent on innovation that its essential atmosphere seems not like that of a large corporation but rather a loose network of laboratories and cubbyholes populated by feverish inventors and dauntless entrepreneurs who let their imaginations fly in all directions." They don't try to hold everyone on so short a rein that he can't be creative. They encourage practical risk taking, and support good tries. They follow Fletcher Byrom's ninth commandment: "Make sure you generate a reasonable number of mistakes."

4. *Productivity through people.* The excellent companies treat the rank and file as the root source of quality and productivity gain. They do not foster we/they labor attitudes or regard capital investment as the fundamental source of efficiency improvement. As Thomas J. Watson, Jr., said of his company, "IBM's philosophy is largely contained in three simple beliefs. I want to begin with what I think is the most important: *our respect for the individual.* This is a simple concept, but in IBM it occupies a major portion of management time." Texas Instruments' chairman Mark Shepherd talks about it in terms of every worker being "seen as a source of ideas, not just acting as a pair of hands"; each of his more than *9,000* People Involvement Program, or PIP, teams (TI's quality circles) does contribute to the company's sparkling productivity record.

5. *Hands-on, value driven.* Thomas Watson, Jr., said that "the basic philosophy of an organization has far more to do with its achievements than do technological or economic resources, organizational structure, innovation and timing." Watson and HP's William Hewlett are legendary for walking the plant floors. McDonald's Ray Kroc regularly visits stores and assesses them on the factors the company holds dear, Q.S.C. & V.

(Quality, Service, Cleanliness, and Value).

6. *Stick to the knitting.* Robert W. Johnson, former Johnson & Johnson chairman, put it this way: "Never acquire a business you don't know how to run." Or as Edward G. Harness, past chief executive at Procter & Gamble, said, "This company has never left its base. We seek to be anything but a conglomerate." While there were a few exceptions, the odds for excellent performance seem strongly to favor those companies that stay reasonably close to businesses they know.

7. *Simple form, lean staff.* As big as most of the companies we have looked at are, none when we looked at it was formally run with a matrix organization structure, and some which had tried that form had abandoned it. The underlying structural forms and systems in the excellent companies are elegantly simple. Top-level staffs are lean; it is not uncommon to find a corporate staff of fewer than 100 people running multi-billion-dollar enterprises.

8. *Simultaneous loose-tight properties.* The excellent companies are both centralized and decentralized. For the most part, as we have said, they have pushed autonomy down to the shop floor or product development team. On the other hand, they are fanatic centralists around the few core values they hold dear. 3M is marked by barely organized chaos surrounding its product champions. Yet one analyst argues, "The brainwashed members of an extremist political sect are no more conformist in their central beliefs." At Digital the chaos is so rampant that one executive noted, "Damn few people know who they work for." Yet Digital's fetish for reliability is more rigidly adhered to than any outsider could imagine.

Most of these eight attributes are not startling. Some, if not most, are "motherhoods." But as Rene McPherson says, "Almost everybody agrees, 'people are our most important asset.' Yet almost none really lives it." The excellent companies live their commitment to people, as they also do their preference for action—any action—over countless standing committees and endless 500-page studies, their fetish about quality and service standards that others, using optimization techniques, would consider pipe dreams; and their insistence on regular initiative (practical autonomy) from tens of thousands, not just 200 designated $75,000-a-year thinkers.

Above all, the *intensity itself,* stemming from strongly held beliefs, marks these companies. During our first round of interviews, we could "feel it." The language used in talking about people was different. The expectation of regular contributions was different. The love of the product and customer was palpable. And we felt different ourselves, walking around an HP or 3M facility watching groups at work and play, from the way we had in most of the more bureaucratic institutions we have had experience with. It was watching busy bands of engineers, salesmen, and manufacturers casually hammering out problems in a conference room in St. Paul in February; even a customer was there. It was seeing an HP division manager's office ($100 million unit), tiny, wall-less, on the factory floor, shared with a secretary. It was seeing Dana's new chairman, Gerald Mitchell, bearhugging a colleague in the hall after lunch in the Toledo headquarters. It was very far removed from silent board rooms marked by dim lights, somber presentations, rows of staffers lined up along the walls with calculators glowing, and the endless click of the slide projector as analysis after analysis lit up the screen.

We should note that not all eight attributes were present or conspicuous to the same degree in all of the excellent companies we studied. But in every case at least a preponderance of the eight was clearly visible, quite distinctive. We believe, moreover, that the eight are conspicuously absent in most large companies today. Or if they are not absent, they are so well disguised you'd hardly notice them, let alone pick them out as distinguishing traits. Far too many managers have lost sight of the basics, in our opinion: quick action, service to customers, practical innovation, and the fact that you can't get any of these without virtually everyone's commitment.

So, on the one hand, the traits are obvious. Presenting the material to students who have no business experience can lead to yawns. "The customer comes first, second, third," we say. "Doesn't *everyone* know that?" is the implied (or actual) response. On the other hand, seasoned audiences usually react with enthusiasm. They know that this material is important, that Buck Rodgers was right when he said good service is the

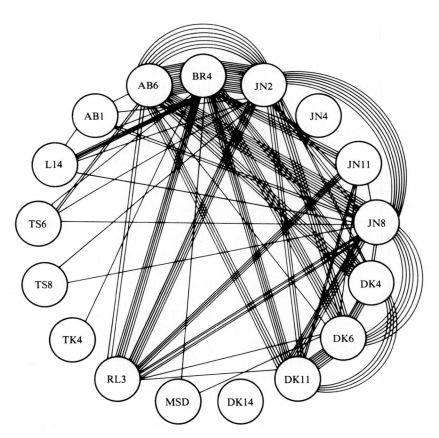

Figure 16–2
New Product Sign-Off

exception. And they are heartened that the "magic" of a P&G and IBM is simply getting the basics right, not possessing twenty more IQ points per man or woman. (We sometimes urge them not to be so heartened. The process of acquiring or sharpening the basics to anything like the excellent companies' obsessive level, after all, is a lot harder than coming up with a "strategic breakthrough" in one's head.)

American companies are being stymied not only by their staffs (about which more hereafter), but also by their structures and systems, both of which inhibit action. One of our favorite examples is shown in a diagram drawn by a manager of a would-be new venture in a moderately high technology business (Figure 16–2).

The circles in this diagram represent organizational units—for example, the one containing MSD is the Management Sciences Division—and the straight lines depict the formal linkages (standing committees) that are involved in launching a new product. There are 223 such formal linkages. Needless to say, the company is hardly first to the marketplace with any new product. The irony, and the tragedy, is that each of the 223 linkages taken by itself makes perfectly good sense. Well-meaning, rational people designed each link for a reason that made sense at the time—for example, a committee was formed to ensure that a glitch between sales and marketing, arising in the last product rollout, is not repeated. The trouble is that the total picture as it inexorably emerged, amusing as it might be to a C. Northcote Parkinson, captures action like a fly in a spider's web and drains the life out of it. The other sad fact is that when we use this diagram in presentations, we don't draw shouts of "Absurd." Instead we draw sighs, nervous laughter, and the occasional volunteer who says, "If you really want a humdinger, you should map our process."

THE RESEARCH

The sample of sixty-two companies[2] was never intended to be perfectly representative of U.S. industry as a whole, although we think we have captured a fairly broad spectrum. Nor did we try to be too precise at the beginning about what we meant by excellence or innovation. We were afraid at that point that had we tried to be too precise we would lose the essence of what we thought we were after, as in E. B. White's account of humor, which "can be dissected, as a frog, but the thing dies in the process and the innards are discouraging to any but the pure scientific mind." What we really wanted and got with our original group was a list of companies considered to be innovative and excellent by an informed group of observers of the business scene—businessmen, consultants, members of the business press, and business academics. The companies were grouped into various categories to ensure that we would have enough representation in the industry segments we were interested in. (See Table 16–1.) The industry categories include but are not limited to:

1. High-technology companies, such as Digital Equipment, Hewlett-Packard (HP), Intel, and Texas Instruments (TI)
2. Consumer goods companies, such as Procter & Gamble (P&G), Chesebrough-Pond's, and Johnson & Johnson (J&J)
3. General industrial goods companies of interest (a catch-all obviously), which included Caterpillar, Dana, and 3M (Minnesota Mining and Manufacturing)
4. Service companies such as Delta Airlines, Marriott, McDonald's, and Disney Productions
5. Project management companies such as Bechtel and Fluor
6. Resource-based companies such as At-

Table 16-1
Excellent Company Survey

Structured Interviews Plus 25-Year Literature Review					
High Technology	*Consumer Goods*	*General Industrial*	*Service*	*Project Management*	*Resource Based*
Allen-Bradley†	Blue Bell	Caterpillar Tractor*	Delta Airlines*	Bechtel†	Exxon
Amdahl*	Eastman Kodak*	Dana Corporation*	Marriott*	Boeing*	
Digital Equipment*	Frito-Lay (PepsiCo)†	Ingersoll-Rand	McDonald's*	Fluor*	
Emerson Electric*	General Foods	McDermott			
Gould	Johnson & Johnson*	Minnesota Mining &			
Hewlett-Packard*	Procter & Gamble*	Manufacturing			
International Business					
Machines*					
NCR					
Rockwell					
Schlumberger*					
Texas Instruments*					
United Technologies					
Western Electric					
Westinghouse					
Xerox					

Limited Interviews Plus 25-Year Literature Review					
High Technology	*Consumer Goods*	*General Industrial*	*Service*	*Project Management*	*Resource Based*
Data General*	Atari (Warner	General Motors	American Airlines		Arco
General Electric	Communications)†		Disney Productions*		Dow Chemical*
Hughes Aircraft†	Avon*		K mart		Du Pont*
Intel*	Bristol-Myers*		Wal-Mart*		Standard Oil
Lockheed	Chesebrough-Pond's*				(Indiana)/
National Semiconductor*	Levi Strauss*				Amoco
Raychem*	Mars†				
TRW	Maytag*				
Wang Labs*	Merck*				
	Polaroid				
	Revlon*				
	Tupperware (Dart				
	& Kraft)†				

*Passes all hurdles for "excellent" performance, 1961–1980.
†Privately held or subsidiary; no extensive public data available, but estimated to pass all hurdles for "excellent" performance.

lantic-Richfield (Arco), Dow Chemical, and Exxon

Conspicuously missing from the list were certain industries which later will be the subject of further study. Although our experience with large financial service institutions, and in particular banks, is extensive, they were thought to be too highly regulated and protected (then) to be of interest. Most chemical and drug companies were left out simply because we didn't get around to them. Finally, we didn't look extensively at small companies; our major concern was and is with how big companies stay alive, well, and innovative. Therefore, few firms in our sample had annual sales of less than $1 billion or histories shorter than twenty years.

As a next-to-last step in choosing the companies to be studied in some depth, we reasoned that no matter what prestige these companies had in the eyes of the rest of the business world, the companies were not truly excellent unless their financial performance supported their halo of esteem. Consequently, we chose and imposed six measures of long-term superiority. Three are measures of growth and long-term wealth creation over a twenty-year period. Three are measures of return on capital and sales. The six are:

1. Compound asset growth from 1961 through 1980 (a "least squares" measure that fits a curve to annual growth data).
2. Compound equity growth from 1961 through 1980 (a "least squares" measure of annual growth data).
3. The average ratio of market value to book value. "Market to book" is a standard approximation for what the economists call "wealth creation" (market value: closing share price times common shares outstanding, divided by

common book-value equity as of December 31, 1961 through 1980).
4. Average return on total capital, 1961 through 1980 (net income divided by total invested capital, where total invested capital consists of long-term debt, nonredeemable preferred stock, common equity, and minority interests).
5. Average return on equity, 1961 through 1980.
6. Average return on sales, 1961 through 1980.

In order to qualify as a top performer, a company must have been in the top half of its industry in at least four out of six of these measures over the full twenty-year period (in fact, of the thirty-six companies that qualified, seventeen ranked in the top half on all six measures, and another six ranked in the top half of five of six measures).[3] Thus, any top performer must have scored well, over the long haul, on both growth measures and absolute measures of economic health.

As a last screen, we applied a measure of innovativeness per se. We asked selected industry experts (e.g., businessmen from within the industry) to rate the companies' twenty-year record of innovation, defined as a continuous flow of industry bellwether products and services and general rapidness of response to changing markets or other external dynamics.

Imposing these criteria meant that nineteen companies dropped from our original list of sixty-two. Of the remaining forty-three, we interviewed twenty-one in depth.[4] We conducted less extensive interviews in each of the remaining twenty-two. We also conducted extensive interviews at twelve companies that we had put in a "?" category; these were ones that did not pass all the screens but had just barely missed. We also followed all sixty-two closely in the literature for the twenty-five years preceding the study.

Finally, we culled the sample in another fashion. Although we prefer to back up our conclusions with hard evidence from specific companies, we do occasionally say, "They do thus and such." In this sense, "They" is a group of exemplars which, without benefit of specific selection criteria, do seem to represent especially well both sound performance and the eight traits we have identified. They are: Bechtel, Boeing, Caterpillar Tractor, Dana, Delta Airlines, Digital Equipment, Emerson Electric, Fluor, Hewlett-Packard, IBM, Johnson & Johnson, McDonald's, Procter & Gamble, and 3M. On the surface, they have little in common; there is no universality of product line. Three are in high technology, one is in packaged goods, one principally makes medical products, two are service businesses, two are involved in project management, and five are basic industrial manufacturers. But each is a hands-on operator, not a holding company or a conglomerate. And while not every plan succeeds, in the day-to-day pursuit of their businesses these companies succeed far more often than they fail.

When we finished our interviews and research, we began to sift and codify our results. It was then, roughly six months after we had started, that we reached the conclusions which are the backbone of this book. We still had a few nagging problems, however. We had used the 7-S framework as the basic structuring device for our interviews and hence chose the same framework as a way of communicating our conclusions, with the result that, at the time, we identified twenty-two attributes of excellence. The whole thing was just too confusing and we were in danger of adding to the complexity railed at in the first place. When that was forcefully pointed out to us by several of the early consumers of our research, we went back to work, and tried to distill the essence of what we were saying in a simpler way. The result, with no material loss to the message, is the eight attributes of excellence we describe.

Several questions always come up when we are discussing our findings. First, people often challenge a few of the companies we have used on the basis of their own personal acquaintance. All big companies have their warts and blemishes; as excellent as we claim some of these companies to be, they are not without fault, and they have made plenty of well-publicized mistakes. Also, one man's excellent company is another's stock market disaster. We don't pretend to account for the perfidy of the market or the whims of investors. The companies *have* performed well over long periods, and this is good enough for us.

Second, we are asked how we know that the companies we have defined as culturally innovative will stay that way. The answer is we don't. GM looked excellent at the time and has since had serious troubles. But it will likely survive those troubles better than the rest of the American auto industry. And again, it performed so well for so long that one cannot help being impressed. So we feel about many of the excellent companies.

Third, why have we added (as the reader will soon see) examples from companies that were not on the original list, and examples from companies that do not fit our original definition of excellence? The reason is that our inquiry into corporate innovation and excellence is a continuing effort and much work has been done since 1979. For example, another team within McKinsey did a special study of excellence in the American consumer goods industry; and yet another has recently completed a study of excellent companies in Canada. A group is hard at work on the question of excellence in the medium-sized—or threshold—companies, the "so far, so good" category. Also, as the original team continues to follow up, we find more reinforcement of the early findings and more examples.

The process has been more powerful than we ever dared imagine. Since the original publication of our findings in *Business Week* in July 1980, we have given over 200 speeches, conducted more than 50 workshops—and spent a lot of time on planes. It is a rare day when we don't run into alumni (or active members) of our survey companies. At Memorex, one of us recently ran into a man who had worked directly, and for years, with Watson, Sr., at IBM. Our list of friends and acquaintances from P&G's brand-management program and IBM's sales program is as long as your arm. An acquaintance from our 3M interviews stays in touch: we have spent several long days with him talking about innovation. The corroboration at times becomes amazingly fine-grained. For instance, we laud HP's informality. Yet one of our colleagues, analyzing highly successful Tandem (founded by ex-HPers) argues that "Tandem's traditional Friday beer busts are more exuberant than HP's." We continue to learn more and more—to add comfirmation and modification at a level of detail that greatly reinforces our confidence in the findings.

Finally, we are asked, what about evolution and change? How did these companies get the way they are? Is it always a case of a strong leader at the helm? We must admit that our bias at the beginning was to discount the role of leadership heavily, if for no other reason than that everybody's answer to what's wrong (or right) with whatever organization is its leader. Our strong belief was that the excellent companies had gotten to be the way they are because of a unique set of cultural attributes that distinguish them from the rest, and if we understood those attributes well enough, we could do more than just mutter "leadership" in response to questions like "Why is J&J so good?" Unfortunately, what we found was that associated with almost every excellent company was a strong leader (or two) who seemed to have had a lot to do with making the company excellent in the first place. Many of these companies—for instance, IBM, P&G, Emerson, J&J, and Dana—seem to have taken on their basic character under the tutelage of a very special person. Moreover, they did it at a fairly early stage of their development.

But there is a caveat or two. The excellent companies seem to have developed cultures that have incorporated the values and practices of the great leaders and thus those shared values can be seen to survive for decades after the passing of the original guru. Second, going back to where we started with Chester Barnard, it appears that the real role of the chief executive is to manage the *values* of the organization. We hope that what follows, then, will illuminate just what values ought to be shaped and managed, and that we will thereby have helped to solve the leadership dilemma after all.

NOTES

1. We were hardly the first to invent a multivariable framework. Harold Leavitt's "Leavitt's Diamond," for instance (task structure, people, information and control, environment), has now influenced generations of managers. We were fortunate in enjoying good timing. Managers beset with seemingly intractable problems and years of frustration with strategy and structure shifts were finally ready for a new view by 1980. Moreover, putting the stamp of McKinsey, long known for its hard-nosed approach to

management problem solving, behind the new model added immense power.

2. There were seventy-five in the original sample. Thirteen were European. These were dropped from the analysis because they do not represent a fair cross-section of European companies.

3. "Industries" are the six categories noted previously (e.g., high-technology companies). The comparison base for each industry is a random and statistically valid sample from that industry's total population among *Fortune* 500 companies.

4. The set of forty-three includes the thirty-six mentioned above plus seven privately held companies (e.g., Mars) or subsidiaries (e.g., Frito-Lay) that we *estimate* to have passed our financial hurdles but for which verification is not wholly possible because of the absence of public data.

ARTICLE 17

Strategic Windows

Derek F. Abell

Strategic Market Planning involves the management of any business unit in the dual tasks of *anticipating* and *responding* to changes which affect the marketplace for their products. This article discusses both of these tasks. Anticipation of change and its impact can be substantially improved if an organizing framework can be used to identify sources and directions of change in a systematic fashion. Appropriate responses to change require a clear understanding of the alternative strategic options available to management as a market evolves and change takes place.

DYNAMIC ANALYSIS

When changes in the market are only incremental, firms may successfully adapt themselves to the new situation by modifying current marketing or other functional programs. Frequently, however, market changes are so far-reaching that the competence of the firm to continue to compete effectively is called into question. And it is in such situations that the concept of "strategic windows" is applicable.

The term "strategic window" is used here to focus attention on the fact that there are only limited periods during which the "fit" between the key requirements of a market and the particular competencies of a firm competing in that market is at an optimum. Investment in a product line or market area should be timed to coincide with periods in which such a strategic window is open. Conversely, disinvestment should be contemplated if what was once a good fit has been eroded—i.e., if changes in market requirements outstrip the firm's capability to adapt itself to them.

Among the most frequent questions which management has to deal with in this respect are:

Should funds be committed to a proposed new market entry? Now? Later? Or not at

Derek F. Abell, "Strategic Windows," Vol. 42 (July 1978). Reprinted from *Journal of Marketing,* published by the American Marketing Association.

all? If a commitment is to be made, how large should it be?

Should expenditures of funds of plant and equipment or marketing to support existing product lines be expanded, continued at historical levels, or diminished?

When should a decision be made to quit and throw in the towel for an unprofitable product line or business area?

Resource allocation decisions of this nature all require a careful assessment of the future evolution of the market involved and an accurate appraisal of the firm's capability to successfully meet key market requirements. The strategic window concept encourages the analysis of these questions in a dynamic rather than a static framework, and forces marketing planners to be as specific as they can about these future patterns of market evolution and the firm's capacity to adapt to them.

It is unfortunate that the heightened interest in product portfolio analysis evident in the last decade has failed to adequately encompass these issues. Many managers routinely classify their various activities as "cows," "dogs," "stars," or "question marks" based on a *static* analysis of the *current* position of the firm and its market environment.

Of key interest, however, is the question not only of where the firm is today, but of how well equipped it is to deal with *tomorrow*. Such a *dynamic* analysis may foretell non-incremental changes in the market which work to disqualify market leaders, provide opportunities for currently low share competitors, and sometimes even usher in a completely new cast of competitors into the marketplace. Familiar contemporary examples of this latter phenomenon include such products as digital watches, women's pantyhose, calculators, charter air travel, office copiers, and scientific instrumentation.

In all these cases existing competitors have been displaced by new contenders as these markets have evolved. In each case changing market requirements have resulted in a *closing* strategic window for incumbent competitors and an *opening window for new entrants*.

MARKET EVOLUTION

The evolution of a market usually embodies more far-reaching changes than the relatively systematic changes in customer behavior and marketing mix due to individual product life cycles. Four major categories of change stand out:

1. The development of new primary demand opportunities whose marketing requirements differ radically from those of existing market segments.
2. The advent of new competing technologies which cannibalize the existing ones.
3. Market redefinition caused by changes in the definition of the product itself and/or changes in the product market strategies of competing firms.
4. Channel changes.

There may be other categories of change or variants in particular industries. That doesn't matter; understanding of how such changes may qualify or disqualify different types of competitors can still be derived from a closer look at examples within each of the four categories above.

New Primary Demand
In a primary demand growth phase, decisions have to be reached by existing competitors about whether to spend the majority of the resources fighting to protect and fortify market positions that have already been established, or whether to seek new development opportunities.

In some cases, it is an original entrant who ploughs new territory—adjusting his approach to the emergent needs of the marketplace; in other cases it is a new entrant who, maybe basing his entry on expertise developed elsewhere, sees a "strategic window" and leapfrogs over the original market leader to take advantage of the new growth opportunity. Paradoxically, pioneering competitors who narrowly focus their activities in the early stages of growth may have the most difficulty in making the transition to new primary demand growth opportunities later. Emery Air Freight provides an example of a company that did face up to a challenge in such a situation.

Emery Air Freight.   This pioneer in the air freight forwarding business developed many of the early applications of air freight in the United States. In particular, Emery's efforts were focused on servicing the "emergency" segment of the market, which initially accounted for a substantial portion of all air freight business. Emery served this market via an extensive organization of regional and district offices. Among Emery's major assets in this market was a unique nationwide, and later worldwide, communications network; and the special competence of personnel located in the district offices in using scheduled carriers in the most efficient possible way to expedite deliveries.

As the market evolved, however, many new applications for air freight emerged. This included regular planned shipments of high value-low weight merchandise, shipments of perishables, "off-line" service to hard-to-reach locations, and what became known as the TCC (Total Cost Concept) market. Each of these new applications required a somewhat different approach than that demanded by the original emergency business.

TCC applications, for example, required detailed logistics planning to assess the savings and benefits to be obtained via lower inventories, quicker deliveries and fewer lost sales through the use of air freight. Customer decisions about whether or not to use air freight required substantially more analysis than had been the case for "emergency" use; furthermore, decisions which had originally been made by traffic managers now involved marketing personnel and often top management.

A decision to seek this kind of business thus implied a radical change in Emery's organization—the addition of capability to analyze complex logistics systems and to deal with upper echelons of management.

New Competing Technologies

When a fundamental change takes place in the basic technology of an industry, it again raises questions of the adaptability to new circumstances of existing firms using obsolete technology.

In many cases established competitors in an industry are challenged, not by another member of the same industry, but by a company which bases its approach on a technology developed outside that industry. Sometimes this results from forward integration of a firm that is eager to develop applications for a new component or raw material. Texas Instruments' entry into a wide variety of consumer electronic products from a base of semi-conductor manufacture is a case in point. Sometimes it results from the application by firms of a technology developed in one market to opportunities in another. Or sometimes a breakthrough in either product or process technology may remove traditional barriers to entry in an industry and attract a completely new set of competitors. Consider the following examples:

> Watchmakers have recently found that a new class of competitor is challenging their industry leadership—namely electronic firms

who are seeking end market applications for their semi-conductors, as well as a new breed of assemblers manufacturing digital watches.

Manufacturers of mechanical adjustable speed drive equipment found their markets eroded by electrical speed drives in the early 1900's. Electrical drives were based on rotating motor-generator sets and electronic controls. In the late 1950's, the advent of solid state electronics, in turn, virtually obsoleted rotating equipment. New independent competitors, basing their approach on the assembly of electronic components, joined the large electrical equipment manufacturers in the speed drive market. Today, yet another change is taking place, namely the advent of large computer controlled drive systems. This is ushering yet another class of competitors into the market—namely, companies whose basic competence is in computers.

In each of these cases, recurrent waves of new technology fundamentally changed the nature of the market and usually ushered in an entirely new class of competitors. Many firms in most markets have a limited capability to master all the technologies which might ultimately cannibalize their business. The nature of technological innovation and diffusion is such that most *major* innovations will originate outside a particular industry and not within it.

In many cases, the upheaval is not only technological; indeed the nature of competition may also change dramatically as technology changes. The advent of solid state electronics in the speed drive industry, for example, ushered in a number of small, low overhead, independent assemblers who based their approach primarily on low price. Prior to that, the market had been dominated by the large electrical equipment manufacturers basing their approach largely on applications engineering coupled with high prices and high margins.

The "strategic window" concept does not preclude adaptation when it appears feasible, but rather suggests that certain firms may be better suited to compete in certain technological waves than in others. Often the cost and the difficulty of acquiring the new technology, as well as the sunk-cost commitment to the old, argue against adaption.

MARKET REDEFINITION

Frequently, as markets evolve, the fundamental definition of the market changes in ways which increasingly disqualify some competitors while providing opportunities for others. The trend towards marketing "systems" of products as opposed to individual pieces of equipment provides many examples of this phenomenon. The situation of Docutel illustrates this point.

Docutel. This manufacturer of automatic teller machines (ATM's) supplied virtually all the ATM's in use up to late 1974. In early 1975, Docutel found itself losing market share to large computer companies such as Burroughs, Honeywell, and IBM as these manufacturers began to look at the banks' total EFTS (Electronic Funds Transfer System) needs. They offered the bank a package of equipment representing a complete system of which the ATM was only one component. In essence their success may be attributed to the fact that they redefined the market in a way which increasingly appeared to disqualify Docutel as a potential supplier.

Market redefinition is not limited to the banking industry; similar trends are underway in scientific instrumentation, process control equipment, the machine tool industry, office equipment, and electric control gear, to name but a few. In each case, manufacturers basing their approach on the marketing of individual hardware items are seeing their "strategic window" closing as computer systems producers move in to take advantage of emerging opportunities.

CHANNEL CHANGES

Changes in the channels of distribution for both consumer and industrial goods can have far reaching consequences for existing competitors and would-be entrants.

Changes take place in part because of product life-cycle phenomena—the shift as the market matures to more intensive distribution, increasing convenience, and often lower levels of channel service. Changes also frequently take place as a result of new institutional development in the channels themselves. Few sectors of American industry have changes as fast as retail and wholesale distribution, with the result that completely new types of outlets may be employed by suppliers seeking to develop competitive advantage.

Whatever the origin of the change, the effect may be to provide an opportunity for a new entrant and to raise questions about the visibility of existing competitors. Gillette's contemplated entry into the blank cassette tape market is a case in point.

Gillette. As the market for cassettes evolved due to increased penetration and new uses of equipment for automotive, study, business, letter writing, and home entertainment, so did distribution channels broaden into an increasing number of drug chains, variety stores, and large discount stores.

Presumably it was recognition of a possible "strategic window" for Gillette that encouraged executives in the Safety Razor Division to look carefully at ways in which Gillette might exploit the cassette market at this particular stage of its evolution. The question was whether Gillette's skill in marketing low-priced, frequently purchased package goods, along with its distribution channel resources, could be applied to marketing blank cassettes. Was there a place for a competitor in this market to offer a quality, branded product, broadly distributed and supported by heavy media advertising in much the same way that Gillette marketed razor blades?

Actually, Gillette decided against entry, apparently not because a "strategic window" did not exist, but because profit prospects were not favorable. They did, however, enter the cigarette lighter business based on similar analysis and reportedly have had considerable success with their *Cricket* brand.

PROBLEMS AND OPPORTUNITIES

What do all these examples indicate? *First,* they suggest that the "resource requirements" for success in a business—whether these be financial requirements, marketing requirements, engineering requirements, or whatever—may change radically with market evolution. *Second,* they appear to suggest that, by contrast, the firm's resources and key competencies often cannot be so easily adjusted. The result is a *predictable* change in the fit of the firm to its market—leading to defined periods during which a "strategic window" exists and can be exploited.

The "strategic window" concept can be useful to incumbent competitors as well as to would-be entrants into a market. For the former, it provides a way of relating future strategic moves to market evolution and of assessing how resources should be allocated to existing activities. For the latter, it provides a framework for diversification and growth.

Existing Businesses

Confronted with changes in the marketplace which potentially disqualify the firm from continued successful participation, several strategic options are available:

1. An attempt can be made to assemble the resources needed to close the gap between the new critical marketing requirements and the firm's competencies.
2. The firm may shift its efforts to selected segments, where the "fit" between requirements and resources is still acceptable.
3. The firm may shift to a "low profile" approach—cutting back severely on all further allocations of capital and deliberately "milking" the business for short-run profit.
4. A decision may be taken to exit from that particular market either through liquidation or through sale.

All too frequently, however, because the "strategic window" phenomenon is not clearly recognized, these strategic choices are not clearly articulated. Instead, "old" approaches are continued long after the market has changed with the result that market position is lost and financial losses pile up. Or, often only half-hearted attempts are made to assemble the new resources required to compete effectively; or management is simply deluded into believing that it can adapt itself to the new situation even where this is actually out of the question.

The four basic strategic choices outlined above may be viewed hierarchically in terms of *resource commitment*, with No. 1 representing the highest level of commitment. Only the company itself can decide which position on the hierarchy it should adopt in particular situations, but the following guideline questions may be helpful:

To what extent do the changes call for skills and resources completely outside the traditional competence of the firm? A careful analysis has to be made of the gap which may emerge between the evolving requirements of the market and the firm's profile.

To what extent can changes be anticipated? Often it is easier to adapt through a series of minor adjustments—a stepping stone approach to change—than it is to be confronted with a major and unexpected discontinuity in approach.

How rapid are the changes which are taking place? Is there enough time to adjust without forfeiting a major share of the market which later may be difficult to regain?

How long will realignment of the functional activities of the firm take? Is the need limited to only some functions, or are all the basic resources of the firm affected—e.g., technology, engineering, manufacturing, marketing, sales, and organization policies?

What existing commitments—e.g., technical skills, distribution channels, manufacturing approaches, etc.—constrain adaption?

Can the new resources and new approaches be developed internally or must they be acquired?

Will the changes completely obsolete existing ways of doing business or will there be a chance for coexistence? In the case of new technologies intruding from outside industry, the decision often has to be made to "join-em rather than fight-em." Not to do so is to risk complete obsolescence. In other cases, coexistence may be possible.

Are there segments of the market where the firm's existing resources can be effectively concentrated?

How large is the firm's stake in the business?

To the extent that the business represents a major source of revenues and profit, a greater commitment will probably need to be made to adapt to the changing circumstances.

Will corporate management, in the event that this is a business unit within a multibusiness corporation, be willing to accept different goals for the business in the future than it has in the past? A decision not to adapt to changes may result in high short-run returns from that particular business. Looking at the problem from the position of corporate planners interested in the welfare of the total corporation, a periodic market-by-market analysis in the terms described above would appear to be imperative prior to setting goals, agreeing on strategies, and allocating resources.

New Entrants

The "strategic window" concept has been used implicitly by many new entrants to judge the direction, timing, and scale of new entry activities. Gillette's entry into cigarette lighters, major computer manufacturers' entry into ATM's, and Procter & Gamble's entry into many consumer markets *after* pioneers have laid the groundwork for a large scale, mass market approach to the specific product areas, all are familiar examples.

Such approaches to strategic market planning require two distinctly different types of analysis:

1. Careful assessment has to be made of the firm's strengths and weaknesses. This should include audits of all the key resources of the company as well as its various existing programs of activity.

2. Attention should be directed away from the narrow focus of familiar products and markets to a search for opportunities to put unique competencies to work. This requires a broader appreciation of overall environmental, technical and

market forces and knowledge of many more markets, than is encountered in many firms today. It puts a particular burden on marketing managers, general managers, and business planners used to thinking in terms of existing activities.

Analysis of patterns of market evolution and diagnosis of critical market requirements in the future can also be of use to incumbent competitors as a forewarning of a potential new entry. In such cases, adjustments in strategy can sometimes be made in advance, which will ultimately deter would-be new competitors. Even where this is not the case, resource commitments may be adjusted to reflect the future changes in structure of industrial supply.

CONCLUSION

The "strategic window" concept suggests that fundamental changes are needed in marketing management practice, and in particular in strategic market planning activities. At the heart of these changes is the need to base marketing planning around predictions of future patterns of market evolution and to make assessments of the firm's capabilities to deal with change. Such analyses require considerably greater strategic orientation than the sales forecasting activities which underpin much marketing planning today. Users of product portfolio chart analysis, in particular, should consider the dynamic as opposed to the static implications in designating a particular business.

Entry and exit from markets is likely to occur with greater rapidity than is often the case today, as firms search for opportunities where their resources can be deployed with maximum effectiveness. Short of entry and exit, the allocation of funds to markets should be timed to coincide with the period when the fit between the firm and the market is at its optimum. Entering a market in its early stages and evolving with it until maturity may, on closer analysis, turn out to be a serious management error.

It has been said that while the life of the product is limited, a market has greater longevity and as such can provide a business with a steady and growing stream of revenue and profit if management can avoid being myopic about change. This article suggests that as far as any one firm is concerned, a market also is a temporary vehicle for growth, a vehicle which should be used and abandoned as circumstances dictate—the reason being that the firm is often slower to evolve and change than is the market in which it competes.

How Competitive Forces Shape Strategy

Michael E. Porter

The essence of strategy formulation is coping with competition. Yet it is easy to view competition too narrowly and too pessimistically. While one sometimes hears executives complaining to the contrary, intense competition in an industry is neither coincidence nor bad luck.

Moreover, in the fight for market share, competition is not manifested only in the other players. Rather, competition in an industry is rooted in its underlying economics, and competitive forces exist that go well beyond the established combatants in a particular industry. Customers, suppliers, potential entrants, and substitute products are all competitors that may be more or less prominent or active depending on the industry.

The state of competition in an industry depends on five basic forces, which are diagrammed in Exhibit 18–1. The collective

strength of these forces determines the ultimate profit potential of an industry. It ranges from *intense* in industries like tires, metal cans, and steel, where no company earns spectacular returns on investment, to *mild* in industries like oil field services and equipment, soft drinks, and toiletries, where there is room for quite high returns.

In the economists' "perfectly competitive" industry, jockeying for position is unbridled and entry to the industry very easy. This kind of industry structure, of course, offers the worst prospect for long-run profitability. The weaker the forces collectively, however, the greater the opportunity for superior performance.

Whatever their collective strength, the corporate strategist's goal is to find a position in the industry where his or her company can best defend itself against these forces or can influence them in its favor. The collective strength of the forces may be painfully apparent to all the antagonists; but to cope with them, the strategist must delve below the surface and analyze the sources of

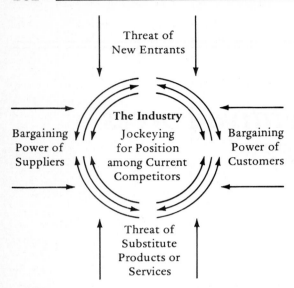

Exhibit 18–1
Forces Governing Competition in an Industry

each. For example, what makes the industry vulnerable to entry? What determines the bargaining power of suppliers?

Knowledge of these underlying sources of competitive pressure provides the groundwork for a strategic agenda of action. They highlight the critical strengths and weaknesses of the company, animate the positioning of the company in its industry, clarify the areas where strategic changes may yield the greatest payoff, and highlight the places where industry trends promise to hold the greatest significance as either opportunities or threats. Understanding these sources also proves to be of help in considering areas for diversification.

CONTENDING FORCES

The strongest competitive force or forces determine the profitability of an industry and so are of greatest importance in strategy formulation. For example, even a company

with a strong position in an industry unthreatened by potential entrants will earn low returns if it faces a superior or a lower-cost substitute product—as the leading manufacturers of vacuum tubes and coffee percolators have learned to their sorrow. In such a situation, coping with the substitute product becomes the number one strategic priority.

Different forces take on prominence, of course, in shaping competition in each industry. In the ocean-going tanker industry the key force is probably the buyers (the major oil companies), while in tires it is powerful OEM buyers coupled with tough competitors. In the steel industry the key forces are foreign competitors and substitute materials.

Every industry has an underlying structure, or a set of fundamental economic and technical characteristics, that gives rise to these competitive forces. The strategist, wanting to position his company to cope best with its industry environment or to influence that environment in the company's favor, must learn what makes the environment tick.

This view of competition pertains equally to industries dealing in services and to those selling products. To avoid monotony in this article, I refer to both products and services as "products." The same general principles apply to all types of business.

A few characteristics are critical to the strength of each competitive force. I shall discuss them in this section.

Threat of Entry

New entrants to an industry bring new capacity, the desire to gain market share, and often substantial resources. Companies diversifying through acquisition into the industry from other markets often leverage their resources to cause a shake-up, as Philip Morris did with Miller beer.

The seriousness of the threat of entry depends on the barriers present and on the reaction from existing competitors that the entrant can expect. If barriers to entry are high and a newcomer can expect sharp retaliation from the entrenched competitors, obviously he will not pose a serious threat of entering.

There are six major sources of barriers to entry:

1. *Economies of scale*—These economies deter entry by forcing the aspirant either to come in on a large scale or to accept a cost disadvantage. Scale economies in production, research, marketing, and service are probably the key barriers to entry in the mainframe computer industry, as Xerox and GE sadly discovered. Economies of scale can also act as hurdles in distribution, utilization of the sales force financing, and nearly any other part of a business.

2. *Product differentiation*—Brand identification creates a barrier by forcing entrants to spend heavily to overcome customer loyalty. Advertising, customer service, being first in the industry, and product differences are among the factors fostering brand identification. It is perhaps the most important entry barrier in soft drinks, over-the-counter drugs, cosmetics, investment banking, and public accounting. To create high fences around their businesses, brewers couple brand identification with economies of scale in production, distribution, and marketing.

3. *Capital requirements*—The need to invest large financial resources in order to compete creates a barrier to entry, particularly if the capital is required for unrecoverable expenditures in up-front advertising or R&D. Capital is necessary not only for fixed facilities but also for customer credit, inventories, and absorbing start-up losses. While major corporations have the financial resources to invade almost any industry, the huge capital requirements in certain fields, such as computer manufacturing and mineral extraction, limit the pool of likely entrants.

4. *Cost disadvantages independent of size*—Entrenched companies may have cost advantages not available to potential rivals, no matter what their size and attainable economies of scale. These advantages can stem from the effects of the learning curve (and of its first cousin, the experience curve), proprietary technology, access to the best raw materials sources, assets purchased at preinflation prices, government subsidies, or favorable locations. Sometimes cost advantages are legally enforceable, as they are through patents. (For an analysis of the much-discussed experience curve as a barrier to entry, see *Exhibit 18–2*, p. 264.

5. *Access to distribution channels*—The new boy on the block must, of course, secure distribution of his product or service. A new food product, for example, must displace others from the supermarket shelf via price breaks, promotions, intense selling efforts, or some other means. The more limited the wholesale or retail channels are and the more that existing competitors have these tied up, obviously the tougher that entry into the industry will be. Sometimes this barrier is so high that, to surmount it, a new contestant must create its own distribution channels, as Timex did in the watch industry in the 1950s.

6. *Government policy*—The government can limit or even foreclose entry to industries with such controls as license

Exhibit 18–2

THE EXPERIENCE CURVE AS AN ENTRY BARRIER

In recent years, the experience curve has become widely discussed as a key element of industry structure. According to this concept, unit costs in many manufacturing industries (some dogmatic adherents say in *all* manufacturing industries) as well as in some service industries decline with "experience," or a particular company's cumulative volume of production. (The experience curve, which encompasses many factors, is a broader concept than the better-known learning curve, which refers to the efficiency achieved over a period of time by workers through much repetition.)

The causes of the decline in unit costs are a combination of elements, including economies of scale, the learning curve for labor, and capital-labor substitution. The cost decline creates a barrier to entry because new competitors with no "experience" face higher costs than established ones, particularly the producer with the largest market share, and have difficulty catching up with the entrenched competitors.

Adherents of the experience curve concept stress the importance of achieving market leadership to maximize aggressive action to achieve it, such as price cutting in anticipation of falling costs in order to build volume. For the combatant that cannot achieve a healthy market share, the prescription is usually, "Get out."

Is the experience curve an entry barrier on which strategies should be built? The answer is: not in every industry. In fact, in some industries, building a strategy on the experience curve can be potentially disastrous. That costs decline with experience in some industries is not news to corporate executives. The significance of the experience curve for strategy depends on what factors are causing the decline.

If costs are falling because a growing company can reap economies of scale through more efficient, automated facilities and vertical integration, then the cumulative volume of production is unimportant to its relative cost position. Here the lowest-cost producer is the one with the largest, most efficient facilities.

A new entrant may well be more efficient than the more experienced competitors; if it has built the newest plant, it will face no disadvantage in having to catch up. The strategic prescription,

"You must have the largest, most efficient plant," is a lot different from, "You must produce the greatest cumulative output of the item to get your costs down."

Whether a drop in costs with cumulative (not absolute) volume erects an entry barrier also depends on the sources of the decline. If costs go down because of technical advances known generally in the industry or because of the development of improved equipment that can be copied or purchased from equipment suppliers, the experience curve is no entry barrier at all—in fact, new or less experienced competitors may actually enjoy a *cost advantage* over the leaders. Free of the legacy of heavy past investments, the newcomer or less experienced competitor can purchase or copy the newest and lower-cost equipment and technology.

If, however, experience can be kept proprietary, the leaders will maintain a cost advantage. But new entrants may require less experience to reduce their costs than the leaders needed. All this suggests that the experience curve can be a shaky entry barrier on which to build a strategy.

While space does not permit a complete treatment here, I want to mention a few other crucial elements in determining the appropriateness of a strategy built on the entry barrier provided by the experience curve:

- The height of the barrier depends on how important costs are to competition compared with other areas like marketing, selling and innovation.
- The barrier can be nullified by product or process innovations leading to a substantially new technology and thereby creating an entirely new experience curve.* New entrants can leapfrog the industry leaders and alight on the new experience curve, to which those leaders may be poorly positioned to jump.
- If more than one strong company is building its strategy on the experience curve, the consequences can be nearly fatal. By the time only one rival is left pursuing such a strategy, industry growth may have stopped and the prospects of reaping the spoils of victory long since evaporated.

---

*For an example drawn from the history of the automobile industry, see William J. Abernathy and Kenneth Wayne, "The Limits of the Learning Curve," *Harvard Business Review,* September–October 1974, p. 109.

requirements and limits on access to raw materials. Regulated industries like trucking, liquor retailing, and freight forwarding are noticeable examples; more subtle government restrictions operate in fields like ski-area development and coal mining. The government can also play a major indirect role by affecting entry barriers through controls such as air and water pollution standards and safety regulations.

The potential rival's expectations about the reaction of existing competitors also will influence its decision on whether to enter. The company is likely to have second thoughts if incumbents have previously lashed out at new entrants or if:

- The incumbents possess substantial resources to fight back, including excess cash and unused borrowing power, productive capacity, or clout with distribution channels and customers.
- The incumbents seem likely to cut prices because of a desire to keep market shares or because of industrywide excess capacity.
- Industry growth is slow, affecting its ability to absorb the new arrival and probably causing the financial performance of all the parties involved to decline.

Changing Conditions. From a strategic standpoint there are two important additional points to note about the threat of entry.

First, it changes, of course, as these conditions change. The expiration of Polaroid's basic patents on instant photography, for instance, greatly reduced its absolute cost entry barrier built by proprietary technology. It is not surprising that Kodak plunged into the market. Product differentiation in printing has all but disappeared.

Conversely, in the auto industry economies of scale increased enormously with post-World War II automation and vertical integration—virtually stopping successful new entry.

Second, strategic discussions involving a large segment of an industry can have a major impact on the conditions determining the threat of entry, For example, the actions of many U.S. wine producers in the 1960s to step up product introductions, raise advertising levels, and expand distribution nationally surely strengthened the entry roadblocks by raising economies of scale and making access to distribution channels more difficult. Similarly, decisions by members of the recreational vehicle industry to vertically integrate in order to lower costs have greatly increased the economies of scale and raised the capital cost barriers.

Powerful Suppliers and Buyers
Suppliers can exert bargaining power on participants in an industry by raising prices or reducing the quality of purchased goods and services. Powerful suppliers can thereby squeeze profitability out of an industry unable to recover cost increases in its own prices. By raising their prices, soft drink concentrate producers have contributed to the erosion of profitability of bottling companies because the bottlers, facing intense competition from powdered mixes, fruit drinks, and other beverages, have limited freedom to raise *their* prices accordingly. Customers likewise can force down prices, demand higher quality or more service, and play competitors off against each other—all at the expense of industry profits.

The power of each important supplier or buyer group depends on a number of characteristics of its market situation and on the relative importance of its sales or purchases to the industry compared with its overall business.

A *supplier* group is powerful if:

- It is dominated by a few companies and is more concentrated than the industry it sells to.
- Its product is unique or at least differentiated, or if it has built up switching costs. Switching costs are fixed costs buyers face in changing suppliers. These arise because, among other things, a buyer's product specifications tie it to particular suppliers, it has invested heavily in specialized ancillary equipment or in learning how to operate a supplier's equipment (as in computer software), or its production lines are connected to the supplier's manufacturing facilities (as in some manufacture of beverage containers).
- It is not obliged to contend with other products for sale to the industry. For instance, the competition between the steel companies and the aluminum companies to sell to the can industry checks the power of each supplier.
- It poses a credible threat of integrating forward into the industry's business. This provides a check against the industry's ability to improve the terms on which it purchases.
- The industry is not an important customer of the supplier group. If the industry *is* an important customer, suppliers' fortunes will be closely tied to the industry, and they will want to protect the industry through reasonable pricing and assistance in activities like R&D and lobbying.

A *buyer* group is powerful if:

- It is concentrated or purchases in large volumes. Large-volume buyers are particularly potent forces if heavy fixed costs characterize the industry—as they do in metal containers, corn refining, and bulk chemicals, for example—which raise the stakes to keep capacity filled.

- The products it purchases from the industry are standard or undifferentiated. The buyer, sure that they can always find alternatives suppliers, may play one company against another, as they do in aluminum extrusion.
- The products it purchases from the industry form a component of its product and represent a significant fraction of its cost. The buyers are likely to shop for a favorable price and purchase selectively. Where the product sold by the industry in question is a small fraction of buyers' cost, buyers are usually much less sensitive.
- It earns low profits, which create great incentive to lower its purchasing costs. Highly profitable buyers, however, are generally less price sensitive (that is, of course, if the item does not represent a large fraction of their costs).
- The industry's product is unimportant to the quality of the buyers' products or services. Where the quality of the buyers' products is very much affected by the industry's product, buyers are generally less price sensitive. Industries in which this situation obtains include oil field equipment, where a malfunction can lead to large losses, and enclosures for electronic medical and test instruments, where the quality of the enclosure can influence the user's impression about the quality of the equipment inside.
- The industry's product does not save the buyer money. Where the industry's product or service can pay for itself many times over, the buyer is rarely price sensitive; rather, he is interested in quality. This is true in services like investment banking and public accounting, where errors in judgment can be costly and embarrassing, and in businesses like the logging of oil wells, where an accurate survey can save thousands of dollars in drilling costs.
- The buyers pose a credible threat of integrating backward to make the industry's

product. The Big Three auto producers and major buyers of cars have often used the threat of self-manufacture as a bargaining lever. But sometimes an industry engenders a threat to buyers that its members may integrate forward.

Most of these sources of buyer power can be attributed to consumers as a group as well as to industrial and commercial buyers; only a modification of the frame of reference is necessary. Consumers tend to be more price sensitive if they are purchasing products that are undifferentiated, expensive relative to their incomes, and of a sort where quality is not particularly important.

The buying power of retailers is determined by the same rules, with one important addition. Retailers can gain significant bargaining power over manufacturers when they can influence consumers' purchasing decisions, as they do in audio components, jewelry, appliances, sporting goods, and other goods.

Strategic Action. A company's choice of suppliers to buy from or buyer groups to sell to should be viewed as a crucial strategic decision. A company can improve its strategic posture by finding suppliers or buyers who possess the least power to influence it adversely.

Most common is the situation of a company being able to choose whom it will sell to—in other words, buyer selection. Rarely do all the buyer groups a company sells to enjoy equal power. Even if a company sells to a single industry, segments usually exist within that industry that exercise less power (and that are therefore less price sensitive) than others. For example, the replacement market for most products is less price sensitive than the overall market.

As a rule, a company can sell to powerful buyers and still come away with above-average profitability only if it is a low-cost

producer in its industry or if its product enjoys some unusual, if not unique, features. In supplying large customers with electric motors, Emerson Electric earns high returns because its low cost position permits the company to meet or undercut competitors' prices.

If the company lacks a low cost position or a unique product, selling to everyone is self-defeating because the more sales it achieves, the more vulnerable it becomes. The company may have to muster the courage to turn away business and sell only to less potent customers.

Buyer selection has been a key to the success of National Can and Crown Cork & Seal. They focus on the segments of the can industry where they can create product differentiation, minimize the threat of backward integration, and otherwise mitigate the awesome power of their customers. Of course, some industries do not enjoy the luxury of selecting "good" buyers.

As the factors creating supplier and buyer power change with time or as a result of a company's strategic decisions, naturally the power of these groups rises or declines. In the ready-to-wear clothing industry, as the buyers (department stores and clothing stores) have become more concentrated and control has passed to large chains, the industry has come under increasing pressure and suffered falling margins. The industry has been unable to differentiate its product or engender switching costs that lock in its buyers enough to neutralize these trends.

Substitute Products

By placing a ceiling on prices it can charge, substitute products or services limit the potential of an industry. Unless it can upgrade the quality of the product or differentiate it somehow (as via marketing), the industry will suffer in earnings and possibly in growth.

Manifestly, the more attractive the

price-performance trade-off offered by substitute products, the firmer the lid placed on the industry's profit potential. Sugar producers confronted with the large-scale commercialization of high-fructose corn syrup, a sugar substitute, are learning this lesson today.

Substitutes not only limit profits in normal times; they also reduce the bonanza an industry can reap in boom times. In 1978 the producers of fiberglass insulation enjoyed unprecedented demand as a result of high energy costs and severe winter weather. But the industry's ability to raise prices was tempered by the plethora of insulation substitutes, including cellulose, rock wool, and styrofoam. These substitutes are bound to become an even stronger force once the current round of plant additions by fiberglass insulation producers has boosted capacity enough to meet demand (and then some).

Substitute products that deserve the most attention strategically are those that (a) are subject to trends improving their price-performance trade-off with the industry's product, or (b) are produced by industries earning high profits. Substitutes often come rapidly into play if some development increases competition in their industries and causes price reduction or performance improvement.

Jockeying for Position

Rivalry among existing competitors takes the familiar form of jockeying for position— using tactics like price competition, product introduction, and advertising slugfests. Intense rivalry is related to the presence of a number of factors:

- Competitors are numerous or are roughly equal in size and power. In many U.S. industries in recent years foreign contenders, of course, have become part of the competitive picture.

- Industry growth is slow, precipitating fights for market share that involve expansion-minded members.
- The product or service lacks differentiation or switching costs, which lock in buyers and protect one combatant from raids on its customers by another.
- Fixed costs are high or the product is perishable, creating strong temptation to cut prices. Many basic materials businesses, like paper and aluminum, suffer from this problem when demand slackens.
- Capacity is normally augmented in large increments. Such additions, as in the chlorine and vinyl chloride businesses, disrupt the industry's supply–demand balance and often lead to periods of overcapacity and price cutting.
- Exit barriers are high. Exit barriers, like very specialized assets or management's loyalty to a particular business, keep companies competing even though they may be earning low or even negative returns on investment. Excess capacity remains functioning, and the profitability of the healthy competitors suffers as the sick ones hang on.[1] If the entire industry suffers from overcapacity, it may seek government help—particularly if foreign competition is present.
- The rivals are diverse in strategies, origins, and "personalities." They have different ideas about how to compete and continually run head-on into each other in the process.

As an industry matures, its growth rate changes, resulting in declining profits and (often) a shakeout. In the booming recreational vehicle industry of the early 1970s, nearly every producer did well; but slow growth since then has eliminated the high returns, even for the strongest members, not to mention many of the weaker companies. The same profit story has been played out in industry after industry—snowmobiles, aerosol packaging, and sports equipment are just a few examples.

An acquisition can introduce a very different personality to an industry, as has been the case with Black & Decker's takeover of McCullough, the producer of chain saws. Technological innovation can boost the level of fixed costs in the production process, as it did in the shift from batch to continuous-line photo finishing in the 1960s.

While a company must live with many of these factors—because they are built into industry economics—it may have some latitude for improving matters through strategic shifts. For example, it may try to raise buyers' switching costs or increase product differentiation. A focus on selling efforts in the fastest-growing segments of the industry or on market areas with the lowest fixed costs can reduce the impact of industry rivalry. If it is feasible, a company can try to avoid confrontation with competitors having high exit barriers and can thus sidestep involvement in bitter price cutting.

FORMULATION OF STRATEGY

Once the corporate strategist has assessed the forces affecting competition in his industry and their underlying causes, he can identify his company's strengths and weaknesses. The crucial strengths and weaknesses from a strategic standpoint are the company's posture vis-à-vis the underlying causes of each force. Where does it stand against substitutes? Against the sources of entry barriers?

Then the strategist can devise a plan of action that may include (1) positioning the company so that its capabilities provide the best defense against the competitive force; and/or (2) influencing the balance of the forces through strategic moves, thereby improving the company's position; and/or (3) anticipating shifts in the factors under-lying the forces and responding to them, with the hope of exploiting change by choosing a strategy appropriate for the new competitive balance before opponents recognize it. I shall consider each strategic approach in turn.

Positioning the Company

The first approach takes the structure of the industry as given and matches the company's strengths and weaknesses to it. Strategy can be viewed as building defenses against the competitive forces or as finding positions in the industry where the forces are weakest.

Knowledge of the company's capabilities and of the causes of the competitive forces will highlight the areas where the company should confront competition and where avoid it. If the company is a low-cost producer, it may choose to confront powerful buyers while it takes care to sell them only products not vulnerable to competition from substitutes.

The success of Dr Pepper in the soft drink industry illustrates the coupling of realistic knowledge of corporate strengths with sound industry analysis to yield a superior strategy. Coca-Cola and Pepsi-Cola dominate Dr Pepper's industry, where many small concentrate producers compete for a piece of the action. Dr Pepper chose a strategy of avoiding the largest-selling drink segment, maintaining a narrow flavor line, forgoing the development of a captive bottler network, and marketing heavily. The company positioned itself so as to be least vulnerable to its competitive forces while it exploited its small size.

In the $11.5 billion soft drink industry, barriers to entry in the form of brand identification, large-scale marketing, and access to a bottler network are enormous. Rather than accept the formidable costs and scale economies in having its own bottler network—that is, following the lead of the

Big Two and of Seven-Up—Dr Pepper took advantage of the different flavor of its drink to "piggyback" on Coke and Pepsi bottlers who wanted a full line to sell to customers. Dr Pepper coped with the power of these buyers through extraordinary service and other efforts to distinguish its treatment of them from that of Coke and Pepsi.

Many small companies in the soft drink business offer cola drinks that thrust them into head-to-head competition against the majors. Dr Pepper, however, maximized product differentiation by maintaining a narrow line of beverages built around an unusual flavor.

Finally, Dr Pepper met Coke and Pepsi with an advertising onslaught emphasizing the alleged uniqueness of its single flavor. This campaign built strong brand identification and great customer loyalty. Helping its efforts was the fact that Dr Pepper's formula involved lower raw materials cost, which gave the company an absolute cost advantage over its major competitors.

There are no economies of scale in soft drink concentrate production, so Dr Pepper could prosper despite its small share of the business (6%). Thus Dr Pepper confronted competition in marketing but avoided it in product line and in distribution. This artful positioning combined with good implementation has led to an eviable record in earnings and in the stock market.

Influencing the Balance

When dealing with the forces that drive industry competition, a company can devise a strategy that takes the offensive. This posture is designed to do more than merely cope with the forces themselves; it is meant to alter their causes.

Innovations in marketing can raise brand identification or otherwise differentiate the product. Capital investments in large-scale facilities or vertical integration affect entry barriers. The balance of forces is partly a result of external factors and partly in the company's control.

Exploiting Industry Change

Industry evolution is important strategically because evolution, of course, brings with it changes in the sources of competition I have identified. In the familiar product life-cycle pattern, for example, growth rates change, product differentiation is said to decline as the business becomes more mature, and the companies tend to integrate vertically.

These trends are not so important in themselves; what is critical is whether they affect the sources of competition. Consider vertical integration. In the maturing minicomputer industry, extensive vertical integration, both in manufacturing and in software development, is taking place. This very significant trend is greatly raising economies of scale as well as the amount of capital necessary to compete in the industry. This in turn is raising barriers to entry and may drive some smaller competitors out of the industry once growth levels off.

Obviously, the trends carrying the highest priority from a strategic standpoint are those that affect the most important sources of competition in the industry and those that elevate new causes to the forefront. In contract aerosol packaging, for example, the trend toward less product differentiation is now dominant. It has increased buyers' power, lowered the barriers to entry, and intensified competition.

The framework for analyzing competition that I have described can also be used to predict the eventual profitability of an industry. In long-range planning the task is to examine each competitive force, forecast the magnitude of each underlying cause, and then construct a composite picture of the likely profit potential of the industry.

The outcome of such an exercise may differ a great deal from the existing industry structure. Today, for example, the solar heating business is populated by dozens and perhaps hundreds of companies, none with a major market position. Entry is easy, and competitors are battling to establish solar heating as a superior substitute for conventional methods.

The potential of this industry will depend largely on the shape of future barriers to entry, the improvement of the industry's position relative to substitutes, the ultimate intensity of competition, and the power captured by buyers and suppliers. These characteristics will in turn be influenced by such factors as the establishment of brand identities, significant economies of scale or experience curves in equipment manufacture wrought by technological change, the ultimate capital costs to compete, and the extent of overhead in production facilities.

The framework for analyzing industry competition has direct benefits in setting diversification strategy. It provides a road map for answering the extremely difficult question inherent in diversification decisions: "What is the potential of this business?" Combining the framework with judgment in its application, a company may be able to spot an industry with a good future before this good fortune is reflected in the prices of acquisition candidates.

MULTIFACETED RIVALRY

Corporate managers have directed a great deal of attention to defining their businesses as a crucial step in strategy formulation. Theodore Levitt, in his classic 1960 article in the *Harvard Business Review,* argued strongly for avoiding the myopia of narrow, product-oriented industry definition.[2] Numerous other authorities have also stressed

the need to look beyond product to function in defining a business, beyond national boundaries to potential international competition, and beyond the ranks of one's competitors today to those that may become competitors tomorrow. As a result of these urgings, the proper definition of a company's industry or industries has become an endlessly debated subject.

One motive behind this debate is the desire to exploit new markets. Another, perhaps more important motive is the fear of overlooking latent sources of competition that someday may threaten the industry. Many managers concentrate so single-mindedly on their direct antagonists in the fight for market share that they fail to realize that they are also competing with their customers and their suppliers for bargaining power. Meanwhile, they also neglect to keep a wary eye out for new entrants to the contest or fail to recognize the subtle threat of substitute products.

The key to growth—even survival—is to stake out a position that is less vulnerable to attack from head-to-head opponents, whether established or new, and less vulnerable to erosion for the direction of buyers, suppliers, and substitute goods. Establishing such a position can take many forms—solidifying relationships with favorable customers, differentiating the product either substantively or psychologically through marketing, integrating forward or backward, establishing technological leadership.

NOTES

1. For a more complete discussion of exit barriers and their implications for strategy, see my article, "Please Note Location of Nearest Exit," *California Management Review,* Winter 1976, p. 21.
2. Theodore Levitt, "Marketing Myopia," reprinted as a *Harvard Business Review Classic,* September-October 1975, p. 26.

A Strategic Perspective on Product Planning

George S. Day

INTRODUCTION

The past decade has seen growing recognition that the product planning function within diversified companies of all sizes involves tradeoffs among competing opportunities and strategies. During this period the combination of more complex markets, shorter product life cycles and social, legal and governmental trends puts a premium on minimizing the degree of risk in the product mix. More recently, managers have had to cope with severe resource constraints, stemming partly from weaknesses in the capital markets and a general cash shortage, and the triple traumas of the energy crisis, materials shortages and inflation.

Some of the manifestations of the new climate for product planning are skepticism toward the value of full product lines, unwillingness to accept the risks of completely new products, an emphasis on profit growth rather than volume growth and active product elimination and divestment programs.[1] Yet managements cannot afford to turn their backs on all opportunities for change and attempt to survive by doing a better job with the established products and services. Eventually all product categories become saturated or threatened by substitutes and diversification becomes essential to survival. Consumer goods companies are especially feeling this pressure as the productivity of line extensions or product adaptations directed at narrow market segments declines. Also the likelihood of regulatory actions directed at products, such as aerosols and cyclamates, points up the risks of having a closely grouped product line.[2] More than ever, long-run corporate health is going to depend on the ability of product planners to juggle those conflicting pressures of diversification and consolidation.

The pervasive nature of the resource allocation problem in product planning is the focus of this article. The emphasis is on the basic issues of the role of new and established products and markets and the choice of areas of new product development to pursue. The first issue is addressed in the context of the product portfolio, which describes the mixture of products that generate cash and in which the company can invest cash. A detailed examination of the product portfolio begins with its component parts, the product life cycle and the notion of market dominance, and then turns to the implications for strategic planning and resource allocation.

Once the role of new products has been established, the issue of where to look is addressed with an explicit statement of a search strategy. This statement defines the characteristics of desirable opportunities in terms that are meaningful to product planners.

STRATEGIC PLANNING AND PRODUCT PLANNING

There are as many concepts of strategy as writers on the subject.[3] Several of the more useful definitions for our immediate purposes are:

- Decisions today which affect the future (not future decisions)
- Major questions of resource allocation that determine a company's long-run results
- The calculated means by which the firm deploys its resources—i.e., personnel, machines and money—to accomplish its purpose under the most advantageous circumstances
- A competitive edge that allows a company to serve the customers better than its competitors
- The broad principles by which a company hopes to secure an advantage over competitors, an attractiveness to buyers and a full exploitation of company resources

Following these definitions, the desired output of the strategic planning process is a long-run plan "that will produce an attractive growth rate and a high rate of return on investment by achieving a market position so advantageous that competitors can retaliate only over an extended time period at a prohibitive cost."[4]

Most strategic planning processes and the resulting plans show a distinct family resemblance, although the specifics obviously vary greatly. These specifics usually include[5]: (1) a statement of the mission of the strategic business unit (SBU),[6] (2) the desired future position the SBU and the corporation wants to attain, comprising measurable profitability, sales, market share, efficiency and flexibility objectives, (3) the key environmental assumptions and the opportunities and threats, (4) a statement of the strengths, weaknesses and problems of the SBU and its major competitors, (5) the strategic gap between the desired and forecasted position of the SBU, (6) actions to be taken to close the gap—the strategy and (7) the required resources and where they can be obtained, including financial resources such as net cash flow, the equity base and debt capacity and management capabilities. These are the main elements of the planning process that are relevant to product planning, leaving aside the issues of detailed implementation plans, contingency plans, which state in advance what modifications will be made if key environmental or competitor assumptions turn out to be false, and the monitoring procedures.

What is lacking in the planning process just described is a systematic procedure for generating and choosing strategic alternatives. One of the greatest weaknesses of current strategic plans is the lack of viable strategy alternatives which present very different approaches and outcomes. Too frequently top management sees only one strategy which the SBU has decided is best in terms of its own and the managers' personal needs and objectives. This ignores the inter-dependency among products (the portfolio aspect)[7] and the possibility that what is best for each SBU is not necessarily best for the entire company.[8] In recognition of this prob-lem, the planning process shown in Figure 19–1 incorporates an analysis of the product portfolio. The remainder of this paper is devoted to the uses and limitations of the product portfolio and the implications for developing strategy alternates that optimize the long-run position of the firm.

THE COMPONENTS OF THE PRODUCT PORTFOLIO

Market share and stage in the product life cycle have long been regarded as important determinants of profitability. The contribu-tion of the product portfolio concept is that it permits the planner to consider these two measures simultaneously in evaluating the products of an entire company or a division or SBU.

The Value of Market Share Dominance

The belief in the benefits of a dominant market share is rooted deeply in the experi-ence of executives. It is reinforced by the facts of life in most markets:

- The market leader is usually the most profitable.
- During economic downturns, customers are likely to concentrate their purchases in suppliers with large shares, and distribu-tors and retailers will try to cut inventories by eliminating the marginal supplier.

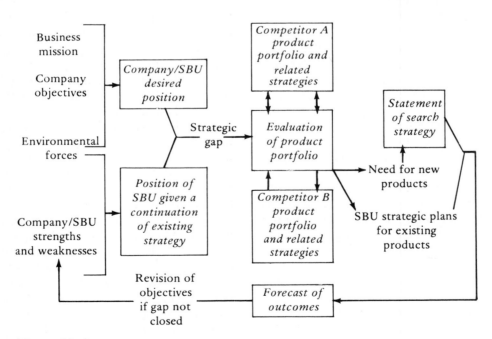

Figure 19–1
Highlighting Product Planning Activities in the Strategic Planning Process

- During periods of economic growth, there is often a bandwagon effect with a large share presenting a positive image to customers and retailers.[9]

Of course, market domination has its own pitfalls, beyond antitrust problems, ". . . monopolists flounder on their own complacency rather than on public opposition. Market domination produces tremendous internal resistance against any innovation and makes adaptation to change dangerously difficult. Also, it usually means that the enterprise has too many of its eggs in one basket and is too vulnerable to economic fluctuations."[10] The leader is also highly vulnerable to competitive actions, especially in the pricing area, since the leader establishes the basic industry price from which smaller competitors can discount.

The clearest evidence of the value of market share comes from a study of The Profit Impact of Market Strategies (PIMS) of 620 separate businesses by the Marketing Science Institute which, in turn, draws on earlier work by General Electric. Early results indicated that market share, investment intensity (ratio of total investment to sales) and product quality were the most important determinants of pretax return on investment, among a total of 37 distinct factors incorporated into a profit model.[11] On average it was found that a difference of 10 points in market share was accompanied by a difference of about 5 points in pretax ROI. As share declines from more than 40 percent to less than 10 percent, the average pretax ROI dropped from 30 percent to 9.1 percent.

The PIMS study also provided some interesting insights into the reasons for the link between market share and profitability.[12] The results point to economies of scale and, especially, the opportunities for vertical integration as the most important

explanations. Thus high-share businesses (more than 40 percent) tend to have low ratios of purchases to sales because they make rather than buy and own their distribution facilities. The ratio of purchases to sales increases from 33 percent for high-share businesses to 45 percent for low-share (less than 10 percent) businesses. But because of economies of scale in manufacturing and purchasing there is no significant relationship between manufacturing expenses or the ratio of sales to investment and the market share. To some degree these results also support the market power argument of economists; market leaders evidently are able to bargain more effectively (either through the exercise of reciprocity or greater technical marketing skills) and obtain higher prices than their competition (but largely because they produce and sell higher-quality goods and services). The fact that market leaders spend a significantly higher percentage of their sales on R and D suggests that they pursue a conscious strategy of product leadership.

Experience Curve Analysis. The importance of economies of scale in the relationship of market share and profitability is verified by the experience curve concept. Research, largely reported by the Boston Consulting Group, has found that in a wide range of businesses (including plastics, semiconductors, gas ranges and life insurance policies), the total unit costs, in constant dollars, decline by a constant percentage (usually 20 to 30 percent) with each doubling of accumulated units of output or experience.[13] Since the experience effect applies to all value added, it subsumes economies of scale and specialization effects along with the well-known learning curve which applies only to direct labor costs.

An experience curve, when plotted on a log-log scale as in Figure 19–2, appears as

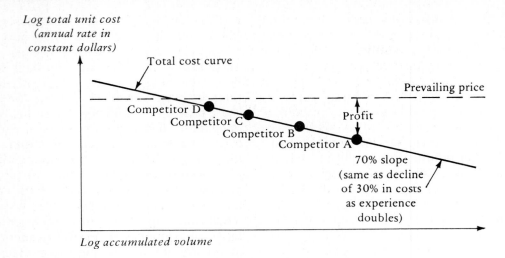

Figure 19–2
Cost Experience Curve Showing Relative Profit Levels of Competitors

a straight line. The locations of the competitors on this curve are determined approximately by their respective accumulated experience, for which relative market share is a good surrogate (this may not be true if some competitors recently have entered the market by buying experience through licenses or acquisitions). Then it follows that the competitor with the greatest accumulated experience will have the lowest relative costs and, if prices are similar between competitors, also will have the greatest profits. Of course, companies that fail to reduce costs along the product category experience curve and who are not dominant will be at an even greater competitive disadvantage.

Figure 19–2 shows a price prevailing at one point in time. Over the long run, prices also will decline at roughly the same rate as costs decline. The major exception to this rule occurs during the introduction and growth rate of the life cycle, when the innovator and/or dominant competitor, is tempted to maintain prices at a high level to recoup the development costs. The high

price umbrella usually achieves this immediate end because unit profits are high. The drawback is the incentive to higher cost competitors to enter the market and attempt to increase their market shares. In effect, the dominant competitor is trading future market share for current profits. This may be sensible if the early leader: (1) has a number of attractive new product opportunities requiring cash, (2) there are potential competitors whose basic business position will enable them eventually to enter the product category regardless of the pricing strategy[14] or (3) significant barriers to entry can be erected.

Product Life Cycle
That products pass through various stages between life and death (introduction → growth → maturity decline) is hard to deny. Equally accepted is the notion that a company should have a mix of products with representation in each of these stages.

Thus the concept of a product life cycle would appear to be an essential tool for understanding product strategies.[15] Indeed this is true, but only *if* the position of the product and the duration of the cycle can be determined. This caveat should be kept in mind when considering the following summary of the important aspects of the product life cycle:

- Volume and profit growth attract competition during the early *growth* (or takeoff) stage of the life cycle. The product market is even more attractive if the innovator lacks the capacity to satisfy demand. However, these competitors may contribute to the growth of sales by their market development expenditures and product improvements.
- Purchase patterns and distribution channels are still fluid during the rapid *growth* stage. For this reason, market shares can be increased at relatively low cost over short periods of time by capturing a disproportionate share of incremental sales (especially where these sales come from new users rather than heavier usage by existing users).
- As a product reaches *maturity* there is evidence of saturation, finer distinctions in benefits surrounding the product and appeals to special segments.
- There is often an industry shake-out to signal the *end* of the rapid growth stage. The trigger might be an excessive number of competitors who have to resort to price cutting to survive; a dominant producer who seeks to regain share; or a large competitor buying into the market (and all these effects will be accentuated by an economic slow down). The result is a period of consolidation during which marginal competitors either drop out, merge with other small competitors or sell out to larger competitors.
- During the *maturity* stage, market-share relationships tend to stabilize; distribution

patterns have been established and are difficult to change. This, in turn, contributes to inertia in purchasing relationships and selling oriented toward maintaining relationships. Any substantial increase in share of market will require a reduction in a competitor's capacity utilization which will be resisted vigorously. As a result, gains in share are both time-consuming and costly. This is not necessarily the case if the attempt to gain shares is spearheaded by a significant improvement in product value or performance which the competitor cannot easily match. A case in point is the growth in private labels, or distributor-controlled labels, in both food and general merchandising categories.

- As substitutes appear and/or sales begin to decline, the core product behaves like a commodity and is subject to intense and continuing price pressure. The result is further competitors dropping out of the market since only those with extensive accumulated experience and cost-cutting capability are able to generate reasonable profits and ROI's.
- The *decline* stage can be forestalled by vigorous promotion (plus, a new creative platform) and product improvement designed to generate more frequent usage or new users and applications.[16] Of course, if these extensions are sufficiently different, a new product life cycle is launched.

Measurement and Interpretation Problems

The concepts underlying the product portfolio are much easier to articulate than to implement.

What Is the Product-Market?   The crux of the problem is well stated by Moran:

> In our complex service society there are no more product classes—not in any meaningful

sense, only as a figment of file clerk imagination. There are only use classes—users which are more central to some products and peripheral to others—on a vast overlapping continuum. To some degree, in some circumstances almost anything can be a partial substitute for almost anything else. An eight-cent stamp substitutes to some extent for an airline ticket.[17]

Where does this leave the manager who relies on share of some (possibly ill-defined) market as a guide to performance evaluation and resource allocation. First he or she must recognize that most markets do not have neat boundaries. For example, patterns of substitution in industrial markets often look like continua, i.e., zinc, brass, aluminum and engineered plastics such as nylon and polycarbonates can be arrayed rather uniformly along dimensions of price and performance. A related complication, more pertinent to consumer product markets, is the possibility of segment differences in perceptions of product substitutability. For example, there is a timid, risk-averse segment that uses a different product for each kind of surface cleaning (i.e., surface detergents, scouring powders, floor cleaners, bleaches, lavatory cleaners and general-purpose wall cleaners). At the other extreme is the segment that uses detergent for every cleaning problem. Thirdly, product/markets may have to be defined in terms of distribution patterns. Thus, tire companies treat the OEM and replacement tire markets as separate and distinct, even though the products going through these two channels are perfect substitutes so far as the end customer is concerned.

Perhaps the most important consideration is the time frame. A long-run view, reflecting strategic planning concerns, invariably will reveal a larger product-market to account for: (1) changes in technology, price relationships and availability which may remove or reduce cost and performance limitations, e.g., the boundaries between minicomputers, programmable computers and time-sharing systems in many use situations are becoming very fuzzy; (2) the time required by present and prospective buyers to react to these changes, which includes modifying behavior patterns, production systems, etc. and (3) considerable switching among products over long periods of time to satisfy desires for variety and change, as is encountered in consumer goods with snacks, for example.

Despite these complexities, the boundaries of product markets usually are established by four-digit Standard Industrial Classification (SIC) categories and/or expert judgment. The limitations of the SIC are well known[18] but often do not outweight the benefits of data availability in a convenient form that can be broken down further to geographic markets. In short, the measure is attractive on tactical grounds (for sales force, promotional budget, etc., allocation) but potentially misleading for strategic planning purposes.

What Is Market Dominance? A measure of market share, per se, is not a good indicator of the extent to which a firm dominates a market. The value of a 30 percent share is very different in a market where the next largest competitor has 40 percent than in one where the next largest has only 20 percent. Two alternative measures which incorporate information on the structure of the competition are:

- Company share ÷ share of largest competitor
- Company share ÷ share of three largest competitors

The former measure is more consistent with the implications of the experience curve, while the latter is perhaps better suited to highly concentrated markets (where the four-firm concentration ratio is greater than 80 percent, for example). Regardless of which measure is used it is often the case that the dominant firm has to be at least 1.5 times as large as the next biggest competitor in order to ensure profitability. When there are two large firms of roughly equal shares, especially in a growth business such as nuclear power generators, the competition is likely to be severe. In this instance, both General Electric and Westinghouse have about 40 percent shares and don't expect to be profitable on new installations until after 1977. Conversely, when the two largest firms have small shares, say less than 5 percent, neither measure of market dominance is meaningful.

Return on Investment

Share Market	Infrequently Purchased (<once/mon)	Frequently Purchased (>once/mon)
Under 10%	6.9%	12.4%
10–19	14.4	13.7
20–29	17.8	17.4
30–39	24.3	23.1
Over 40	34.6	22.9

Evidence of market share dominance, no matter how it is measured, will not be equally meaningful in all product markets. Results from the PIMS study[19] suggest that importance of market share is influenced most strongly by the frequency of purchases.

While the full reasons for this difference in profitability are obscure they probably relate to differences in unit costs and prior buyer experience with the available alternatives which, in turn, determine willingness to reduce risk by buying the market leader and/or paying a premium price. Also,

the frequently purchased category is dominated by consumer goods where there is considerable proliferation of brand names through spin offs, flankers, fighting brands, etc. in highly segmented markets. Each of these brands, no matter how small, shares production facilities and will have low production and distribution costs, although they may be treated as separate businesses.[20] It is hardly surprising that the experience curve concept is difficult to apply to consumer goods. Most of the successful applications have been with infrequently purchased industrial products; relatively undifferentiated, with high value added compared to raw material costs and fairly stable rates of capacity utilization.

A further caveat regarding the experience curve concerns the extent to which costs ultimately can be reduced. The experience curve clearly does not happen according to some immutable law; it requires careful management and some degree of long-run product stability (and, ideally, standardization). These conditions cannot be taken for granted and will be threatened directly by the customer demand for product change and competitive efforts to segment the market. In effect, product innovation and cost efficiency are not compatible in the long-run.[21]

A related question concerns the relevance of the experience curve to a new competitor in an established market. It is doubtful that a new entrant with reasonable access to the relevant technology would incur the same level of initial costs as the developers of the market.

What Is the Stage in the Product Life Cycle?
It is not sufficient to simply know the current rate of growth of the product category. The strategic implications of the product life cycle often hinge on forecasting changes in the growth rate and, in particular, on estab-

lishing the end of the growth and maturity stages.

The first step in utilizing the life cycle is to ensure that the product class is identified properly. This may require a distinction between a broad product type (cigarettes) and a more specific product form (plain filter cigarettes). Secondly, the graph of product (type or form) sales needs to be adjusted for factors that might obscure the underlying life cycle, i.e., price changes, economic fluctuations and population changes. The third and most difficult step is to forecast when the product will move from one stage to another. The specific problems are beyond the scope of this article. However, the range of possibilities is illustrated by these various leading indicators of the "top-out" point.[22]

- Evidence of saturation; declining proportion of new trier versus replacement sales
- Declining prices and profits
- Increased product life
- Industry over capacity
- Appearance of new replacement product or technology
- Changes in export/import ratio
- Decline in elasticity of advertising and promotion, coupled with increasing price elasticity
- Changes in consumer preferences

These measures generally will indicate only the *timing* of the top-out point, and each is sufficiently imprecise that it is strongly advisable to use as many as possible in combination. Forecasts of the product sales *level* to be achieved at the top-out point may be obtained by astute incorporation of the leading indicators into: (1) technological forecasts, (2) similar product analysis (where sales patterns of products with analogous characteristics are used to estimate the sales pattern of the new product) or (3) epidemi-

ological models whose parameters include initial sales rates and market saturation levels estimated with marketing research methods.[23]

ANALYZING THE PRODUCT PORTFOLIO

The product life cycle highlights the desirability of a variety of products/services with different present and prospective growth rates. However, this is not a sufficient condition for a well balanced portfolio of products that will ensure profitable long-run growth. Two other factors are market share position and the need to balance cash flows within the corporation. Some products should *generate* cash (and provide acceptable reported profits) and others should *use* cash to support growth; otherwise, the company will build up unproductive cash reserves or go bankrupt.[24] These issues are clarified by jointly considering share position and market growth rate, as in the matrix of Figure 19–3. The conceptualization used here is largely attributable to the Boston Consulting Group.[25]

It must be stressed that the growth-share matrix discussed here is simply one way of conceptualizing the product portfolio. It has been useful as a device for synthesizing the analyses and judgments of the earlier steps in the planning process, especially in facilitating an approach to strategic decision making that considers the firm to be a whole that is more than the sum of its separate parts. For these purposes, the arbitrary classifications of products in the growth-share matrix are adequate to differentiate the strategy possibilities.[26]

Product Portfolio Strategies
Each of the four basic categories in the growth-share matrix implies a set of strategy

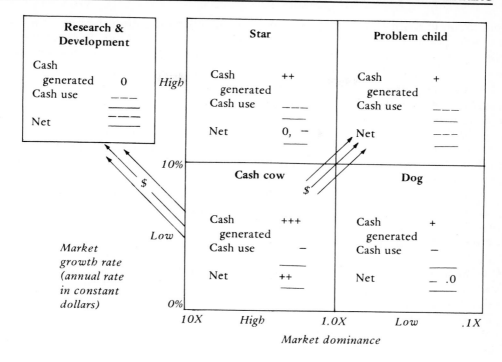

Figure 19–3
Describing the Product Portfolio in the Market Share Growth Matrix
(Arrows indicate principal cash flows.)

alternatives that generally are applicable to the portfolio entries in that category.[27]

Stars. Products that are market leaders, but also growing fast, will have substantial reported profits but need a lot of cash to finance the rate of growth. The appropriate strategies are designed primarily to protect the existing share level by reinvesting earnings in the form of price reductions, product improvement, better market coverage, production efficiency increases, etc. Particular attention must be given to obtaining a large share of the new users or new applications that are the source of growth in the market. Management may elect, instead, to maxi-

mize short-run profits and cash flow at the expense of long-run market share. This is highly risky because it usually is predicated on a continuing stream of product innovations and deprives the company of a cash cow which may be needed in the future.

Cash Cows. The combination of a slow market growth and market dominance usually spells substantial net cash flows. The amount of cash generated is far in excess of the amount required to maintain share. All strategies should be directed toward maintaining market dominance—including investments in technological leadership. Pricing decisions should be made cautiously with an eye to maintaining price leadership. Pressure to overinvest through product proliferation and market expansion should be resisted unless prospects for expanding primary demand are unusually attractive. Instead, excess cash should be used to support research activities and growth areas elsewhere in the company.

Dogs.   Since there usually can be only one market leader and because most markets are mature, the greatest number of products fall in this category.[28] Such products are usually at a cost disadvantage and have few opportunities for growth at a reasonable cost. Their markets are not growing, so there is little new business to compete for, and market share gains will be resisted strenuously by the dominant competition.

The product remains in the portfolio because it shows (or promises) a modest book profit. This accounting result is misleading because most of the cash flow must be reinvested to maintain competitive position and finance inflation.[29] Another characteristic of a dog is that individual investment projects (especially those designed to reduce production costs) show a high ROI. However, the competitive situation is such that these returns cannot be realized in surplus cash flow that can be used to fund more promising projects. In addition there are the potential hidden costs of unproductive demands on management time (and consequent missed opportunities) and low personnel morale because of a lack of achievement.

The pejorative label of dog becomes increasingly appropriate the closer the product is to the lower-right corner of the growth/ share matrix.[30] The need for positive action becomes correspondingly urgent. The search for action alternatives should begin with attempts to alleviate the problem without divesting. If these possibilities are un-

productive, attention then can shift to finding ways of making the product to be divested as attractive as possible; then to liquidation and, finally if need be, to abandonment.

- Corrective action. Naturally all reasonable cost-cutting possibilities should be examined, but, as noted above, these are not likely to be productive in the long-run. A related alternative is to find a market segment that can be dominated. The attractiveness of this alternative will depend on the extent to which the segment can be protected from competition—perhaps because of technology or distribution requirements.[31] What must be avoided is the natural-tendency of operating managers to arbitrarily redefine their markets in order to improve their share position and thus change the classification of the product when, in fact, the economics of the business are unchanged. This is highly probable when the product-market boundaries are ambiguous.

- Harvest. This is a conscious cutback of all support costs to the minimum level to maximize the product's profitability over a foreseeable lifetime, which is usually short. This cutback could include reducing advertising and sales effort, increasing delivery time, increasing the acceptable order size and eliminating all staff support activities such as marketing research.

- Value added. Opportunities may exist for reparceling a product or business that is to be divested. This may involve dividing the assets into smaller units or participating in forming a "kennel of dogs" in which the weak products of several companies are combined into a healthy package. This latter alternative is especially attractive when the market is very fractionated.

- Liquidation. This is the most prevalent solution usually involving a sale as a going concern but, perhaps, including a licensing agreement. If the business/product is to be sold as a unit, the problem is to maximize the selling price—a function of the prospective buyers need for the acquisition (which will depend on search strategy) and their overhead rate. For example, a small company may find a product attractive and be able to make money because of low overhead.

• Abandonment. The possibilities here include giveaways and bankruptcy.

Problem Children. The combination of rapid growth rate and poor profit margins creates an enormous demand for cash. If the cash is not forthcoming, the product will become a dog as growth inevitably slows. The basic strategy options are fairly clearcut; either invest heavily to get a disproportionate share of the new sales or buy existing share by acquiring competitors and thus move the product toward the star category or get out of business using some of the methods just described.

Consideration also should be given to a market segmentation strategy, but only if a defensible niche can be identified and resources are available to gain dominance. This strategy is even more attractive if the segment can provide an entree and experience base from which to push for dominance of the whole market.

Further Strategic Implications

While the product portfolio is helpful in suggesting strategies for specific products, it is equally useful for portraying the overall health of a multiproduct company. The issue is the extent to which the portfolio departs from the balanced display of Figure 19–4, both for the present and in 3 to 5 years.

Among the indicators of overall health are size and vulnerability of the cash cows (and the prospects for the stars, if any) and the number of problem children and

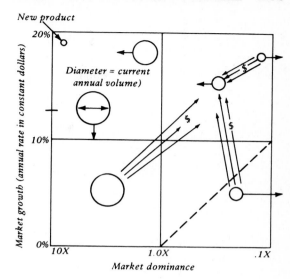

Figure 19–4
A Balanced Product Portfolio

dogs. Particular attention must be paid to those products with large cash appetites. Unless the company has abundant cash flow, it cannot afford to sponsor many such products at one time. If resources (including debt capacity) are spread too thin, the company simply will wind up with too many marginal products and suffer a reduced capacity to finance promising new product entries or acquisitions in the future. Some indication of this type of resource misallocation can be obtained from a comparison of the growth rates of the product class and the company's entrant (as illustrated in Figure 19–5). Ideally, nothing should be in the upper sector where market growth exceeds company growth—unless the product is being harvested.

Competitive Analysis. Product portfolios should be constructed for each of the major competitors. Assuming competitive management follows the logic just described, they eventually will realize that they can't do

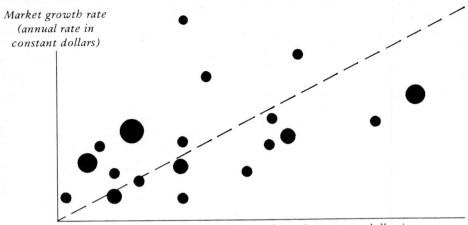

Market growth rate
(annual rate in
constant dollars)

Company growth rate (annual rate in constant dollars)

Figure 19–5
Market Industry versus Company Growth Rates (Illustrative diversified company—diameters are proportional to current annual sales volume.)

everything. The key question is which problem children will be supported aggressively and which will be eliminated. The answer obviously will be difficult to obtain, but has an important bearing on the approach the company takes to its own problem children.

Of course, a competitive position analysis has many additional dimensions which must be explored in depth before specific competitive actions and reactions within each product category can be forecast.[32] This analysis, coupled with an understanding of competitive portfolios, becomes the basis for any fundamental strategy employing the military concept of concentration which essentially means to concentrate strength against weakness.[33]

Dangers in the Pursuit of Market Share.
Tilles has suggested a number of criteria for evaluating strategy alternatives.[34] The product portfolio is a useful concept for addressing the first three: (1) environmental consistency, (2) internal consistency and (3) adequacy of resources. A fourth criteria considers whether the degree of risk is acceptable, given the overall level of risk in the portfolio.

The experience of a number of companies, such as G.E. and RCA, in the mainframe computer business, points to the particular risks inherent in the pursuit of a market share. An analysis of these "pyrrhic victories"[35] suggests that greatest risks can be avoided if the following questions can be answered affirmatively: (1) Are company financial resources adequate? (2) If the fight is stopped short for some reason, will the corporation's position be competitively viable? and (3) Will government regulations permit the corporation to follow the strategy it has chosen? The last question includes antitrust policies which now virtually preclude acquisitions made by large companies in related fields[36] and regulatory policies designed to proliferate competition, as in the airline industry.

Organizational Implications. Although this discussion has focused on the financial and market position aspects of the product portfolio, the implications encompass the deployment of all corporate resources—tangible assets as well as crucial intangibles of management skills and time.

One policy that clearly must be avoided is to apply uniform performance objectives to all products, or SBU's, as is frequently attempted in highly decentralized profit-center management approaches. The use of flexible standards, tailored to the realities of the business, logically should lead to the recognition that different kinds of businesses require very different management styles. For example, stars and problem children demand an entrepreneurial orientation, while cash cows emphasize skills in fine tuning marketing tactics and ensuring effective allocation of resources. The nature of specialist support also will differ; e.g., R and D support being important for growth products and financial personnel becoming increasingly important as growth slows.[37] Finally, since good managers, regardless of their styles are always in short supply, the portfolio notion suggests that they not be expended in potentially futile efforts to turn dogs into profitable performers. Instead they should be deployed into situations where the likelihood of achievement and, hence, of reinforcement, is high.

Other Methods of Portraying the Portfolio.

The growth-share matrix is far from a complete synthesis of the underlying analyses and judgments as to the position of the firm in each of its product-markets. The main problem of the matrix concerns the growth rate dimension. While this is an extremely useful measure in that it can have direct implications for cash flows, it is only one of many possible determinants of the attractiveness of the market. A list of other possible factors is summarized in Table 19–1. (Not all these factors will be relevant to all

Table 19-1
Factors Determining Market and Industry Attractiveness

Market	• Size (present and potential) • Growth/stage in life cycle • Diversity of user segments • Foreign opportunities • Cyclicality
Competition	• Concentration ratio • Capacity utilization • Structural changes (e.g., entries and exits) • Position changes • Vertical threats/opportunities • Sensitivity of shares and market size to price, service, etc. • Extent of "captive" business
Profitability	• Level and trend of leaders • Contribution rates • Changes/threats on key leverage factors (e.g., scale economies and pricing) • Barriers to entry
Technology	• Maturity/volatility • Complexity • Patent protection • Product/process opportunities
Other	• Social/environmental • Government/political • Unions • Human factors

markets.) The importance of each factor depends on the company's capabilities, but careful considerations will help to identify unusual threats, such as impending government regulations, that might significantly reduce future attractiveness. Similarly, market share may not provide a comprehensive indication of the company's position in each market; as in the case of a leader in a market that is rapidly fragmenting.

The qualitative aspects of overall attractiveness and position also can be incorporated into a matrix which portrays the product portfolio [see p. 286]. This matrix

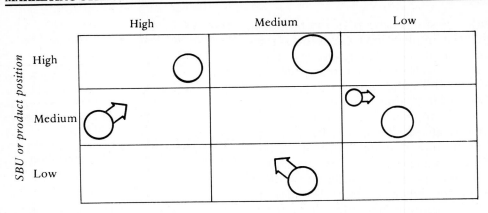

Figure 19–6
Industry or Market Attractiveness (Arrow represents forecast of change in position. Diameter [of circles] is proportional to share of company sales contributed by product.)

does not have the immediate cash flow implication of the growth-share matrix, thus, it should be used as a complementary, rather than a replacement approach.

NEW PRODUCT PLANNING

A product portfolio analysis identifies the need for new products or new markets and the probable level of available resources but does not indicate where to look. This presents management with a number of difficult questions:

- What degree of relationship to the present business is necessary and desirable?
- What are the possibilities for internal development versus acquisition?
- When is an innovation preferred to an imitation and vice versa?
- What are the characteristics of desirable new products?

These and innumerable other questions have to be answered before personnel in the product planning, corporate development or other responsible functions can pursue their tasks efficiently. In short, top management must decide how much growth is desired and feasible, the contribution of new versus established products and the broad direction as to how the growth will be achieved.

What is needed is a strategy statement that specifies those areas where development is to proceed and identifies (perhaps by exclusion) those areas that are off-limits. As Crawford notes, "the idea of putting definitive restrictions on new product activity is not novel, but use of it, especially sophisticated use, is still not widespread."[38] The major criticisms of a comprehensive statement of new product development strategy are that it will inhibit or restrict creativity and that ideas with great potential will be rejected. Experience suggests that clear guidance improves creativity by focusing energy on those areas where the payoff is likely to be greatest. Also, experience shows that significant breakthroughs outside the bounds of the product development strategy statement can be accommodated readily in an ongoing project evaluation and screening process.

The New Product Development Strategy Statement

The essential elements of this statement are the specification of the product-market scope, the basic strategies to be used for growing within that scope and the characteristics of desirable alternatives. These elements guide the search for new product ideas, acquisitions, licenses, etc., and form the basis for a formal screening procedure.

Product-Market Scope. This is an attempt to answer the basic question, "what business(es) do we want to be in" and is a specific manifestation of the mission of the SBU or company. There is no ready-made formula for developing the definition of the future business. One approach is to learn from definitions that have been useful in guiding successful strategies. For example, the General Electric Housewares SBU defines their present (circa 1973) business as "providing consumers with functional aids to increase the enjoyment or psychic fulfillment of selected lifestyles"—especially those dealing with preparation of food, care of the person, care of personal surroundings and planning assistance. In the future their business will expand to include recreation, enhancement of security and convenient care of the home.

This statement of the future business satisfied one important criteria [*sic*]: that it be linked to the present product-market scope by a clearly definable common thread. In the case of G.E. Housewares, the common threat is with generic needs being satisfied (or problems being solved, as the case may be). Ansoff argues that the linkage also can be with product characteristics, distribution capability or underlying technology—as long as the firm has distinctive competency in these areas.[39]

Other criteria for appraising the usefulness of a description of the future business opportunities are: (1) specificity—if the definition of product-market scope is too general, it won't have an impact on the organization (e.g., consider the vagueness of being in the business of supplying products with a plug on the end), (2) flexibility—the definition should be adapted constantly to recognize changing environmental conditions (e.g., Gerber no longer can say that babies are their only business), (3) attainability—can be undertaken within the firm's resources and competencies and (4) competitive advantage—it always is preferable to protect and build on these strengths and competencies that are not possessed as fully by the competition.[40]

Basic Strategies for Growth. At the broad level of a new product development strategy, the basic issues are the *growth* vector, or the direction the firm is moving within the chosen product-market scope, and the emphasis on *innovation* versus *imitation*.

There are almost an infinite number of possibilities for growth vectors. The basic alternatives are summarized in Figure 19–7.[41] there is no intention here to suggest that these strategies are mutually exclusive; indeed, various combinations can be pursued simultaneously in order to close the strategic gaps identified in the overall planning process. Furthermore, most of the strategies can be pursued either by internal development or acquisition and coupled with vertical diversification (either forward toward a business that is a customer or backward toward a business that is a supplier).

The choice of growth vector will be influenced by all the factors discussed earlier as part of the overall corporate planning

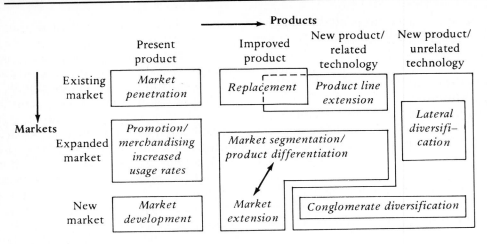

Figure 19–7
Growth Vector Alternatives

process. Underlying any choice is, by necessity, an appraisal of the risks compared with the payoffs. The essence of past experience is that growth vectors within the existing market (or, at least, closely related markets) are much more likely to be successful than ventures into new markets.[42] Therefore, diversification is the riskiest vector to follow—especially if it is attempted by means of internal development. The attractiveness of acquisitions for diversification is the chance to reduce the risks of failure by buying a known entity with (reasonably) predictable performance.

An equally crucial basic strategy choice is the degree of emphasis on innovation versus imitation. The risks of being an innovator are well known so few, if any, diversified corporations can afford to be innovators in each product-market. There are compelling advantages to being first in the market if barriers to entry (because of patent protections, capital requirements, control over distributions, etc.) can be erected, the product is difficult to copy or improve on and the introductory period is

short. The imitator, by contrast, is always put at a cost disadvantage by a successful innovator and must be prepared to invest heavily to build a strong market position. While profits over the life of the product may be lower for an imitator, the risks are much lower because the innovator has provided a full-scale market test which can be monitored to determine the probable growth in future sales. Also, the innovator may provide significant opportunities by not serving all segments or, more likely, by not implementing the introduction properly.

The conscious decision to lead or follow pervades all aspects of the firm. Some of the important differences that result can be seen from the various strategic orientations to high technology markets discussed by Ansoff and Steward:

- First to market . . . based on strong R and D, technical leadership and risk taking
- Follow the leader . . . based on strong development resources and the ability to act quickly as the market starts its growth phase

- Applications engineering . . . based on product modifications to fit needs of particular customers in mature markets
- Me-too . . . based on superior manufacturing efficiency and cost control.[43]

Characteristics of Desirable Alternatives.
Three fundamental questions have to be asked of each new product or service being sought or considered: (1) How will a strong competitive advantage be obtained? The possibilities range from superiority in underlying technology or product quality, to patent protection, to marketing requirements. Another dimension of this question is the specification of markets or competitors to be avoided on the grounds that these situations would blunt the pursuit of a competitive advantage. (2) What is the potential for synergy? This asks about joint effects, or "the mutually reinforcing impact a product-market entry has on a firm's efficiency and effectiveness."[44] Synergy can be sought for defensive reasons, in order to supply a competence that the firm lacks or to spread the risks of a highly cyclical industry, as has motivated a number of mergers in the machine tool industry. Alternatively, synergy can utilize an existing competence such as a distribution system (notable examples here are Gillette and Coca Cola), a production capability, promotional skills, etc. In addition, "financial reinforcement may occur either because of the relative pattern of funds generation and demand . . . or because the combination is more attractive to the financial community than the pieces would be separately."[45] (3) What specific operating results are required? The possibilities here usually are expressed in terms of threshold or minimum desirable levels:

- Rate of market growth

- Payback period (despite its deficiencies it is a reflection of the risk level)
- Minimum sales level. (This is a function of fixed costs and scale of operations: the danger is that a product with good long-run potential will be rejected because of modest short-run sales possibilities.)
- Profit levels, cash flow and return on assets. (Each of these financial requirements must be developed in light of the firm's product portfolio.)

SUMMARY

Too often product planning is conducted as though each established product or service, and new product opportunity being sought or evaluated were independent of the other products of the firm. The implication is that corporate performance is the sum of the contributions of individual profit centers or product strategies.[46]

This article emphasizes the need to consider the interdependencies of products as parts of a portfolio described by market share dominance and market growth rate before overall corporate performance can be optimized. Only then can decisions as to resource allocation, growth and financial objectives and specific strategies be developed for established products and the need for new products identified.

There is little doubt that the future will see increasing acceptance of a broad systems approach to overall corporate strategy, in general, and to product planning, in particular. There are already a number of successful practitioners to emulate (who have gained a competitive edge that cannot be ignored).[47] More importantly, as the business environment becomes increasingly resource-constrained there may be no other choice for most firms.

NOTES

1. "The Squeeze on Product Mix," *Business Week* (5 January 1974), pp. 50–55; "Toward Higher Margins and Less Variety," *Business Week* (14 September 1974), pp. 98–99; E. B. Weiss, "We'll See Fewer New Products in 1975—Culprit Is Shortage of Capital, Resources," *Advertising Age* (2 December 1974); "Corrective Surgery," *Newsweek* (27 January 1975), p. 50; and Jack Springer, "1975: Bad Year for New Products; Good Year for Segmentation," *Advertising Age* (10 February 1975), pp. 30–39.

2. Barry R. Linsky, "Which Way to Move with New Products," *Advertising Age* (22 July 1974), pp. 45–56.

3. George A. Steiner, *Top Management Planning* (London: Macmillan, 1969); H. Igor Ansoff, *Corporate Strategy* (New York: McGraw-Hill, 1965).

4. David T. Kollat, Roger D. Blackwell and James F. Robeson, *Strategic Marketing* (New York: Holt, Rinehart and Winston, 1972), p. 12.

5. This description of the planning process has been adapted from Kollat, et al., *Strategic Marketing;* Louis V. Gerstner, "The Practice of Business: Can Strategic Planning Pay Off?" *Business Horizons* (December 1972); Herschner Cross, "New Directions in Corporate Planning," An address to Operations Research Society of America (Milwaukee, Wisconsin: 10 May 1973).

6. The identification of "strategic business units" is a critical first step in any analysis of corporate strategy. Various definitions have been used. Their flavor is captured by the following guidelines for defining a business: (1) no more than 60 percent of the expenses should represent arbitrary allocations of joint costs, (2) no more than 60 percent of the sales should be made to a vertically integrated (downstream) subsidiary and (3) the served market should be homogeneous; i.e., segments are treated as distinct if they represent markedly different shares, competitors and growth rates.

7. E. Eugene Carter and Kalman J. Cohen, "Portfolio Aspects of Strategic Planning," *Journal of Business Policy*, 2(1972), pp. 8–30.

8. C. H. Springer, "Strategic Management in General Electric," *Operations Research* (November–December 1973), pp. 1177–1182.

9. Bernard Catry and Michel Chevalier, "Market Share Strategy and the Product Life Cycle," *Journal of Marketing*, 38 (October 1974), pp. 29–34.

10. Peter F. Drucker, *Management: Tasks, Responsibilities, Practices* (New York: Harper and Row, 1973), p. 106.

11. Sidney Schoeffler, Robert D. Buzzell and Donald F. Heany, "Impact of Strategic Planning on Profit Performance," *Harvard Business Review* (March-April 1974), pp. 137–145.

12. Robert D. Buzzell, Bradley T. Gale and Ralph G. M. Sultan, "Market Share, Profitability and Business Strategy," unpublished working paper (Marketing Science Institute, August 1974).

13. For more extended treatments and a variety of examples, see Patrick Conley, "Experience Curves as a Planning Tool," *IEEE Transactions* (June 1970); *Perspectives on Experience* (Boston: Boston Consulting Group, 1970); and "Selling Business a Theory of Economics," *Business Week* (8 September 1974).

14. "An example of this situation was DuPont's production of cyclohexane. DuPont was the first producer of the product but the manufacture of cyclohexane is so integrated with the operations of an oil refinery that oil refiners have an inherent cost advantage over companies, such as DuPont, without an oil refinery." Robert B. Stobaugh and Philip L. Townsend, "Price Forecasting and Strategic Planning: The Case of Petrochemicals," *Journal of Marketing Research*, 12 (February 1975), pp. 19–29.

15. Theodore Levitt, "Exploit the Product Life Cycle," *Harvard Business Review* (November–December 1965), pp. 81–94.

16. Harry W. McMahan, "Like Sinatra, Old

Products Can, Too, Get a New Lease on Life," *Advertising Age* (25 November 1974), p. 32.

17. Harry T. Moran, "Why New Products Fail," *Journal of Advertising Research* (April 1973).

18. See Douglas Needham, *Economic Analysis and Industrial Structure* (New York: Holt, Rinehart and Winston); Sanford Rose, "Bigness Is a Numbers Game," *Fortune* (November 1969).

19. Buzzell, Gale and Sultan, "Market Share, Profitability."

20. An extreme example is Unilever in the UK with 20 detergent brands all sharing joint costs to some degree.

21. William J. Abernathy and Kenneth Wayne, "Limit of the Learning Curve," *Harvard Business Review*, 52 (September–October 1974), pp. 109–119.

22. Aubrey Wilson, "Industrial Marketing Research in Britain," *Journal of Marketing Research*, 6 (February 1969), pp. 15–28.

23. John C. Chambers, Satinder K. Mullick and Donald D. Smith, *An Executives' Guide to Forecasting* (New York: John Wiley and Sons, 1974); Frank M. Bass, "A New Product Growth Model for Consumer Durables," *Management Science*, 15 (January 1969), pp. 215–227.

24. Of course the cash flow pattern also may be altered by changing debt and/or dividend policies. (For most companies, the likelihood of new equity funding is limited.) Limits on growth are imposed when the additional business ventures to be supported have too high a business risk for the potential reward and/or the increase in debt has too high a (financial) risk for the potential rewards.

25. Among the publications of the Boston Consulting Group that describe the portfolio are: Perspectives on Experience (1970) and the following pamphlets authored by Bruce D. Henderson in the general perspectives series; "The Product Portfolio" (1970); "The Experience Curve Reviewed: The Growth Share Matrix or the Product Portfolio" (1973); and "Cash Traps" (1972).

26. A similar matrix reportedly is used by the Mead Corporation; see John Thackray, "The Mod Matrix of Mead," *Management Today* (January 1972), pp. 50–53, 112. This application has been criticized on the grounds of oversimplification, narrow applicability and the unwarranted emphasis on investment versus new investment. Indeed the growth-share matrix is regarded by Thackray as primarily a device for achieving social control.

27. William E. Cox, Jr., "Product Portfolio Strategy: An Analysis of the Boston Consulting Group Approach to Marketing Strategies," *Proceedings of the American Marketing Association,* 1974.

28. It is also typical that the weighted ratio of average market share versus the largest competitor is greater than 1.0. This reflects the contribution of the cash cows to both sales and profits. It also accounts for the familiar pattern whereby 20 percent of the products account for 80 percent of the dollar margin (a phenomena generally described as Pareto's Law).

29. The Boston Consulting Group defines such products as cash traps when the required re-investment, including increased working capital, exceeds reported profit plus increase in permanent debt capacity: Bruce D. Henderson, "Cash Traps," *Perspectives*, Number 102 (Boston Consulting Group, 1972).

30. The label may be meaningless if the product is part of a product line, an integral component of a system or where most of the sales are internal.

31. It should be noted that full line/full service competitors may be vulnerable to this strategy if there are customer segments which do not need all the services, etc. Thus, Digital Equipment Corp. has prospered in competition with IBM by simply selling basic hardware and depending on others to do the applications programming. By contrast; IBM provides, for a price, a great deal of service backup and software for customers who are not self-sufficient. "A Minicom-

puter Tempest," *Business Week* (27 January 1975), pp. 79–80.

32. Dimensions such as product and pricing policy, geographic and distributor strength, delivery patterns, penetration by account size and probable reaction to our company initiatives need to be considered. See C. Davis Fogg, "Planning Gains in Market Share," *Journal of Marketing*, 38 (July 1974), pp. 30–38.

33. This concept is developed by Harper Boyd, "Strategy Concepts" unpublished manuscript, 1974, and is based on B. H. Liddel Hart, *Strategy: the Indirect Approach* (London: Faber and Faber, 1951).

34. Seymour Tilles, "How to Evaluate Corporate Strategy," *Harvard Business Review*, 41 (July–August 1963).

35. William E. Fruhan, "Pyrrhic Victories in Fights for Market Share," *Harvard Business Review*, 50 (September–October 1972).

36. "Is John Sherman's Antitrust Obsolete?" *Business Week* (23 March 1974).

37. Stephen Dietz, "Get More Out of Your Brand Management," *Harvard Business Review* (July–August 1973).

38. C. Merle Crawford, "Strategies for New Product Development: Guidelines for a Critical Company Problem," *Business Horizons* (December 1972), pp. 49–58.

39. H. Igor Ansoff, *Corporate Strategy*.

40. Kenneth Simmonds, "Removing the Chains from Product Policy," *Journal of Management Studies* (February 1968).

41. This strategy matrix was influenced strongly by the work of David T. Kollat, Roger D. Blackwell and James F. Robeson, *Strategic Marketing* (New York: Holt, Rinehart and Winston, 1972), pp. 21–23 which, in turn, was adapted from Samuel C. Johnson and Conrad Jones, "How to Organize for New Products," *Harvard Business Review*, 35 (May–June 1957), pp. 49–62.

42. According to the experience of A. T. Kearney, Inc., the chances of success are a direct function of how far from home the new venture is aimed. Specifically, the likelihood of success for an improved product into the present market is assessed as 0.75, declines to 0.50 for a new product with unrelated technology into the present market and to 0.25 for an existing product into a new market. The odds of success for external diversification are as low as 0.05. These numbers are mainly provocative because of the difficulties of defining what constitutes a failure (is it a product that failed in test or after national introduction, for example). See "Analyzing New Product Risk," *Marketing for Sales Executives* (The Research Institute of America, January 1974).

43. H. Igor Ansoff and John Steward, "Strategies for a Technology-Based Business," *Harvard Business Review*, 45 (November–December 1967), pp. 71–83.

44. Kollat, Blackwell and Robeson, *Strategic Marketing*, p. 24.

45. Seymour Tilles, "Making Strategy Explicit," in H. Igor Ansoff (ed.), *Business Strategy* (London: Penguin Books, 1969), p. 203.

46. Bruce D. Henderson, "Intuitive Strategy," *Perspectives*, No. 96 (The Boston Consulting Group, 1972).

47. See "Selling Business a Theory of Economics," *Business Week* (8 September 1973); "G.E.'s New Strategy for Faster Growth," *Business Week* (8 July 1972); "First Quarter and Stockholders Meeting Report" (Texas Instruments, Inc., 8 April 1973); "The Winning Strategy at Sperry Rand," *Business Week* (24 February 1973), "How American Standard Cured Its Conglomeritis," *Business Week* (28 September 1974); "G.E. Revamps Strategy: Growth through Efficiency," *Advertising Age* (3 June 1974).

Market Share—A Key to Profitability

Robert D. Buzzell, Bradley T. Gale, and Ralph G. M. Sultan

It is now widely recognized that one of the main determinants of business profitability is market share. Under most circumstances, enterprises that have achieved a high share of the markets they serve are considerably more profitable than their smaller-share rivals. This connection between market share and profitability has been recognized by corporate executives and consultants, and it is clearly demonstrated in the results of a project undertaken by the Marketing Science Institute on the Profit Impact of Market Strategies (PIMS). The PIMS project, on

Authors' note: We wish to acknowledge the contributions of our associates in the PIMS project to the results reported in this paper. Sidney Schoeffler, Donald F. Heany, and James Conlin made valuable suggestions, and Paula Nichols carried out numerous analyses very efficiently and cheerfully. The authors are, of course, solely responsible for any errors or misrepresentations that remain.

which we have been working since late 1971,[1] is aimed at identifying and measuring the major determinants of return on investment (ROI) in individual businesses. Phase II of the PIMS project, completed in late 1973, reveals 37 key profit influences, of which one of the most important is market share.

There is no doubt that market share and return on investment are strongly related. Exhibit 20–1 shows average pretax ROI figures for groups of businesses in the PIMS project that have successfully increasing shares of their markets. (For an explanation of how businesses, markets, and ROI results are defined and measured in the PIMS project, see the ruled insert on p. 316.) On the average, a difference of 10 percentage points in market share is accompanied by a difference of about 5 points in pretax ROI.

While the PIMS data base is the most extensive and detailed source of information on the profit/market-share relationship, there is additional confirming evidence of its existence. For instance, companies enjoying

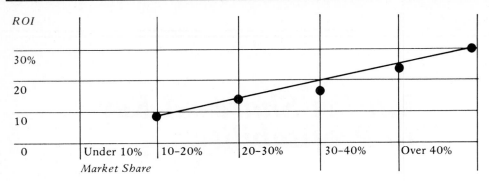

Exhibit 20–1
Relationship between Market Share and Pretax ROI

strong competitive positions in their primary product markets tend to be highly profitable. Consider, for example, such major companies as IBM, Gillette, Eastman Kodak, and Xerox, as well as smaller, more specialized corporations like Dr. Scholl (foot care products) and Hartz Mountain (pet foods and accessories).

Granted that high rates of return usually accompany high market share, it is useful to explore the relationship further. Why is market share profitable? What are the observed differences between low- and high-share businesses? Does the notion vary from industry to industry? And, what does the profitability/market-share relationship imply for strategic planning? In this article we shall attempt to provide partial answers to these questions by presenting evidence on the nature, importance, and implications of the links between market share and profit performance.

WHY MARKET SHARE IS PROFITABLE

The data shown in Exhibit 20–1 demonstrate the differences in ROI between high- and low-market-share businesses. This convinc-

ing evidence of the relationship itself, however, does not tell us why there is a link between market share and profitability. There are at least three possible explanations:

Economies of Scale. The most obvious rationale for the high rate of return enjoyed by large-share businesses is that they have achieved economies of scale in procurement, manufacturing, marketing, and other cost components. A business with a 40% share of a given market is simply twice as big as one with 20% of the same market, and it will attain, to a much greater degree, more efficient methods of operation within a particular type of technology.

Closely related to this explanation is the so-called "experience curve" phenomenon widely publicized by the Boston Consulting Group.[2] According to BCG, total unit costs of producing and distributing a product tend to decline by a more or less constant percentage with each doubling of a company's cumulative output. Since, in a given time period, businesses with large market shares generally also have larger cumulative sales than their smaller competitors, they would be expected to have lower costs and correspondingly higher profits.

Market Power. Many economists, especially among those involved in antitrust work, believe that economies of scale are of relatively little importance in most industries. These economists argue that if large-scale businesses earn higher profits than their smaller competitors, it is a result of their greater market power: their size permits them to bargain more effectively, "administer" prices, and, in the end, realize significantly higher prices for a particular product.[3]

Quality of Management. The simplest of all explanations for the market-share/profitability relationship is that both share and ROI reflect a common underlying factor: the quality of management. Good managers (including, perhaps, lucky ones!) are successful in achieving high shares of their respective markets; they are also skillful in controlling costs, getting maximum productivity from employees, and so on. Moreover, once a business achieves a leadership position—possibly by developing a new field—it is much easier for it to retain its lead than for others to catch up.

These explanations of why the market-share/profitability relationship exists are not mutually exclusive. To some degree, a large-share business may benefit from all three kinds of relative advantages. It is important, however, to understand from the available information how much of the increased profitability that accompanies high market share comes from each of these or other sources.

HOW MARKET SHARE RELATES TO ROI

Analysis of the PIMS data base sheds some light on the reasons for the observed relationship between market share and ROI.

Businesses with different market-share levels are compared as to financial and operating ratios and measures of relative prices and product quality in Exhibit 20–2. In examining these figures, remember that the PIMS sample of businesses includes a wide variety of products and industries. Consequently, when we compare businesses with market shares under 10%, say, with those having shares over 40%, we are not observing differences in costs and profits within a single industry. Each subgroup contains a diversity of industries, types of products, kinds of customers, and so on.

Differences between High- and Low-Share Businesses

The data in Exhibit 20–2 reveal four important differences between high-share businesses and those with smaller shares. The samples used are sufficiently large and balanced to ensure that the differences between them are associated primarily with variations in market share, and not with other factors. These differences are:

1. As market share rises, turnover on investment rises only somewhat, but profit margin on sales increases sharply. ROI is, of course, dependent on both the rate of net profit on sales and the amount of investment required to support a given volume of sales. Exhibit 20–2 reveals that the ratio of investment to sales declines only slightly, and irregularly, with increased market share. The data show too that capacity utilization is not systematically related to market share.

On the surface then, higher investment turnover does not appear to be a major factor contributing to higher rates of return. However, this observation is subject to some qualification. Our analysis of the PIMS data base shows that investment intensity (investment relative to sales) tends to vary directly with a business's degree of vertical integration.

Exhibit 20-2
Relationships of Market Share to Key Financial and Operating Ratios for Overall PIMS Sample of Businesses

Financial and Operating Ratios	Market Share Under 10%	10%-20%	20%-30%	30%-40%	Over 40%
Capital structure:					
Investment/sales	68.66	67.74	61.08	64.66	63.98
Receivables/sales	15.52	14.08	13.96	15.18	14.48
Inventory/sales	9.30	8.97	8.68	8.68	8.16
Operating results:					
Pretax profit/sales	−0.16	3.42	4.84	7.60	13.16
Purchases/sales	45.40	39.90	39.40	32.60	33.00
Manufacturing/sales	29.64	32.61	32.11	32.95	31.76
Marketing/sales	10.60	9.88	9.06	10.45	8.57
R&D/sales	2.60	2.40	2.83	3.18	3.55
Capacity/utilization	74.70	77.10	78.10	75.40	78.00
Product quality:					
Average of percents superior minus inferior	14.50	20.40	20.40	20.10	43.00
Relative price*	2.72	2.73	2.65	2.66	2.39
Number of businesses	156	179	105	67	87

*Average value on 5-point scale:
5 = 10% or more lower than leading competitors' average;
3 = within 3% of competition;
1 = 10% or more higher than competition.

(The degree of vertical integration is measured as the ratio of the total value added by the business to its sales. Both the numerator and denominator of the ratio are adjusted by subtracting the pretax income and adding the PIMS average ROI, multiplied by the investment.)

Vertical integration thus has a strong negative relation to the ratio of purchases to sales. Since high market-share businesses are on the average somewhat more vertically integrated than those with smaller shares, it is likely that investment turnover increases somewhat more with market share than the figures in Exhibit 20–2 suggest. In other words, as shown in Exhibit 20–3, for a given degree of vertical integration, the investment-to-sales ratio declines significantly, even though overall averages do not.

Nevertheless, Exhibit 20–2 shows that the major reason for the ROI/market-share relationship is the dramatic difference in

Exhibit 20-3
Effect of Vertical Integration on Investment/Sales Ratio

Vertical Integration	Market Share Under 10%	10%-20%	20%-30%	30%-40%	Over 40%
Low	65	61	46	58	55
High	77	76	75	70	69

pretax profit margins on sales. Businesses with market shares under 10% had average pretax losses of 0.16%. The average ROI for businesses with under 10% market share was about 9%. Obviously, no individual business can have a negative profit-to-sales ratio and still earn a positive ROI. The apparent inconsistency between the averages reflects the fact that some businesses in the sample incurred losses that were very high in relation to sales but that were much smaller in relation to investment. In the PIMS sample, the average return on sales exhibits a strong, smooth, upward trend as market share increases.

Why do profit margins on sales increase so sharply with market share? To answer this, it is necessary to look in more detail at differences in prices and operating expenses.

2. The biggest single difference in costs, as related to market share, is in the purchase-to-sales ratio. As shown in Exhibit 20–2, for large-share businesses—those with shares over 40%—purchases represent only 33% of sales, compared with 45% for businesses with shares under 10%.

How can we explain the decline in the ratio of purchases to sales as share goes up? One possibility, as mentioned earlier, is that high-share businesses tend to be more vertically integrated—they "make" rather than "buy," and often they own their own distribution facilities. The decline in the purchases-to-sales ratio is quite a bit less (see Exhibit 20–4) if we control for the level of vertical integration. A low purchases-to-sales ratio goes hand in hand with a high level of vertical integration.

Other things being equal, a greater extent of vertical integration ought to result in a rising level of manufacturing costs. (For the nonmanufacturing businesses in the PIMS sample, "manufacturing" was defined as the primary value-creating activity of the business. For example, processing transactions is the equivalent of manufacturing in a bank.) But the data in Exhibit 20-2 show little or no connection between manufacturing expense, as a percentage of sales, and market share. This could be because, despite the increase in vertical integration, costs are offset by increased efficiency.

This explanation is probably valid for some of the businesses in the sample, but we believe that, in the majority of cases, the decline in costs of purchased materials also reflects a combination of economies of scale in buying and, perhaps, bargaining power in dealing with suppliers. Economies of scale in procurement arise from lower costs of manufacturing, marketing, and distributing when suppliers sell in large quantities. For very large-scale buyers, custom-designed components and special formulations of materials that are purchased on long-term contracts may offer "order of magnitude" economies.

Still another possible explanation of the declining purchases-to-sales ratio for large-share businesses might be that they charge higher prices, thus increasing the

Exhibit 20-4
Purchase-to-Sales Ratio Corrected for Vertical Integration

Vertical Integration	Market Share Under 10%	10%–20%	20%–30%	30%–40%	Over 40%
Low	54	51	53	52	46
High	32	27	29	24	23

base on which the percentage is figured. This does not, however, appear to be the case.

In Exhibit 20–2 we give measures of price relative to competition for each group of businesses that indicate otherwise. Because of the great difficulty of computing meaningful relative price-index numbers, the measure we used here is rather crude. We asked the PIMS participants to indicate on a five-point scale whether their prices were "about the same" as major competitors, "somewhat" higher or lower, or "substantially" higher or lower for each business. The average values for this scale measure are virtually identical for each market-share group, except for those with shares over 40%.

Despite the similarity of relative prices for the first four share groups, the purchases-to-sales ratios decline in a regular, substantial fashion as share increases. In light of this, we do not believe that the decline in purchase costs is a reflection of higher price levels imposed by "market power."

3. *As market share increases, there is some tendency for marketing costs, as a percentage of sales, to decline.* The difference in marketing costs between the smallest and largest market-share groups amounts on the average to about 2% of sales. We believe that this reflects true scale economies, including the spreading of fixed marketing costs and the ability of large-share businesses to utilize more efficient media and marketing methods. In the case of industrial products, large scale permits a manufacturer to use his own sales force rather than commissioned agents and, at some point, to utilize specialized sales forces for specific product lines or markets. For consumer goods, large-scale businesses may derive an important cost advantage from their ability to utilize the most efficient mass-advertising media.

In addition, leading brands of con-

sumer products appear to benefit to some extent from a "bandwagon effect" that results from the brand's greater visibility in retail stores or greater support from retail store sales personnel. For example, Anheuser-Busch has for some time enjoyed lower advertising costs per case of beer than its smaller rivals—just as the advertising expense per car of General Motors is significantly lower than that of other competing auto manufacturers.

4. *Market leaders develop unique competitive strategies and have higher prices for their higher-quality products than do smaller-share businesses.* The figures in Exhibit 20–2 do not show smooth, continuous relationships between market share and the various components of price, cost, and investment. Indeed, it appears that one pattern operates as share increases up to 40%, but a somewhat different pattern above that figure.

Particularly, there are substantial differences in relative price and product quality between market leaders and the rest of the sample. Market leaders obtain higher prices than do businesses with smaller market shares. A principal reason for this may be that market leaders also tend to produce and sell significantly higher-quality products and services than those of their lower-share competitors.

We measured quality as follows: We asked the participating companies to judge for each business the proportions of total sales comprised of products and services that were "superior," "equivalent," and "inferior" to those of leading competitors. The figures shown in Exhibit 20–2 are averages of the differences between the superior quality and the inferior quality percentages.

The measures we used for relative price and relative quality are not, of course, directly comparable. Thus it is impossible to determine which is greater—the price premiums earned by market leaders, or the differential in the quality of their products. But it is clear that the combination of significantly higher prices and quality represents a unique competitive position for market leaders.

Market leaders, in contrast to their smaller competitors, spend significantly higher amounts on research and development, relative to sales. As shown in Exhibit 20–2, the average ratio of R&D to sales for the highest-share group of businesses was 3.55%—nearly 40% greater than the ratio for the under-10% share group. This, combined with the quality advantage enjoyed by market leaders, suggests that they typically pursue a strategy of product leadership. Certainly this is consistent with what is known about innovative leaders such as Eastman Kodak, IBM, and Proctor & Gamble.

Given that market leaders have a high market share and thus the profitability that goes with it, it is natural to question whether the share and profitability ratio shifts from industry to industry. In other words, do businesses in some kinds of industries need a higher share than others to be profitable?

Variations among Industries

While our analyses of the PIMS data base clearly demonstrates a strong general relationship between ROI and market share, they also indicate that the importance of share varies considerably from one type of industry or market situation to another. Two of the more striking variations are summarized in Exhibit 20–4. These figures show that:

1. Market share is more important for infrequently purchased products than for frequently purchased ones. For infrequently purchased products, the ROI of the average market leader is about 28 percentage points greater than the ROI of the average small-share business. For frequently purchased products (those typically bought at least

once a month), the corresponding ROI differential is approximately 10 points.

Why? Infrequently purchased products tend to be durable, higher unit-cost items such as capital goods, equipment, and consumer durables, which are often complex and difficult for buyers to evaluate. Since there is a bigger risk inherent in a wrong choice, the purchaser is often willing to pay a premium for assured quality.

Frequently purchased products are generally low unit-value items such as foods or industrial supplies. The risk in buying from a lesser-known, small-share supplier is lower in most cases, so a purchaser can feel free to shop around.

2. Market share is more important to businesses when buyers are "fragmented" rather than concentrated. As Exhibit 20–5 shows, when buyers are fragmented (i.e., no small group of consumers accounts for a significant proportion of total sales), the ROI differential is 27 percentage points for the average market leader. However, when buyers are concentrated, the leaders' average advantage in ROI is reduced to only 19 percentage points greater than that of the average small-share business.

A likely explanation for this is that when buyers are fragmented, they cannot bargain for the unit cost advantage that concentrated buyers receive, thus allowing higher profits for the large-share business. Obviously, then, the ROI differential is smaller when buyers are somewhat concentrated. In this case, powerful buyers tend to bargain away some of the seller's cost differential by holding out for low prices.

Clearly, the strategic implications of the market-share/profitability relationship vary according to the circumstances of the individual business. But there is no doubt that the relationship can be translated into dynamic strategies for all companies trying to set market goals.

A **Frequently purchased vs. infrequently purchased products**

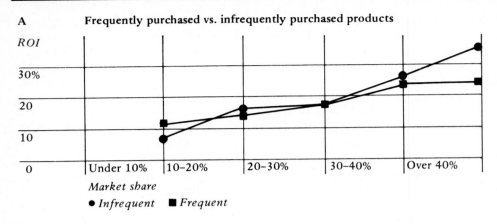

Market share
● *Infrequent* ■ *Frequent*

B **Concentrated vs. fragmented customers**

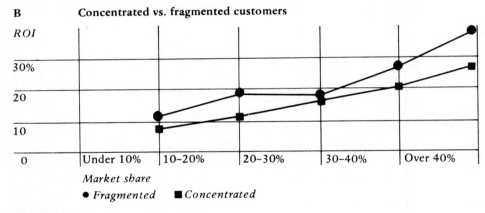

Market share
● *Fragmented* ■ *Concentrated*

Exhibit 20–5
Industry Variations in the Share/ROI Relationship

WHAT THE ROI/MARKET SHARE LINK MEANS FOR STRATEGY

Because market share is so strongly related to profitability, a basic strategic issue for top management is to establish market-share objectives. These objectives have much to do with the rate of return that can reasonably be budgeted in the short and long runs, as well as the capital requirements and cash flow of a business.

Setting Market-Share Goals
What market-share goals are feasible, or even desirable, obviously depends on many things, including the strength of competitors, the resources available to support a strategy, and the willingness of management to forgo present earnings for future results. At the risk of oversimplification, we can classify market-share strategies into three rather broad groups:

1. Building strategies are based on active efforts to increase market share by means of new product introductions, added marketing programs, and so on.
2. Holding strategies are aimed at maintaining the existing level of market share.

3. Harvesting strategies are designed to achieve high short-term earnings and cash flow by permitting market share to decline.

When does each of these market-share strategies seem most appropriate? How should each be implemented? The experiences documented in the PIMS data base provide some clues.

Building Strategies. The data presented in Exhibit 20–1 imply that, in many cases, even a marginally acceptable rate of return can be earned only by attaining some minimum level of market share. If the market share of a business falls below this minimum, its strategic choices usually boil down to two: increase share or withdraw. Of course there are exceptions to this rule.

But we are convinced that in most markets there is a minimum share that is required for viability. RCA and General Electric apparently concluded that they were below this minimum in the computer business, and they pulled out. Similarly, Motorola, with an estimated 6% to 7% share of U.S. TV-set sales, and a rumored loss of $20 million in the period from 1970 to 1973,

announced its intention early in 1974 to sell the business to Matsushita.

On the other hand, when share is not so low as to dictate withdrawal, but is still not high enough to yield satisfactory returns, managers can consider aggressive share-building strategies. They should recognize, however, that (a) big increases in share are seldom achieved quickly; and (b) expanding share is almost always expensive in the short run.

Among the 600 businesses in the PIMS sample, only about 20% enjoyed market share gains of 2 points or more from 1970 to 1972. As might be expected, successful building strategies were most common among relatively new businesses. Of those that have begun operations since 1965, over 40% achieved share increases of 2 points or more—compared with only 17% of the businesses established before 1950.

Generally speaking, businesses that are building share pay for short-run penalty for doing so. Exhibit 22–6 compares ROI results for businesses with different beginning market shares and for businesses with decreasing, steady, and increasing shares over the period 1970 to 1972. Generally, the businesses that were "building" (i.e., had

Exhibit 20-6
How ROI Is Affected by Market-Share Changes

Market-Share Strategies

Market Share 1970	Building: Up 2 Points or More	Holding: Less Than 2 Points Up or Down	Harvesting: Down 2 Points or More
Average ROI, 1970–1972			
Under 10%	7.5%	10.4%	10.0%
10%–20%	13.3	12.6	14.5
20%–30%	20.5	21.6	9.5
30%–40%	24.1	24.6	7.3
40% or over	29.6	31.9	32.6

share increases of at least 2 points) had ROI results of 1 to 2 points lower than those that maintained more or less steady ("holding") positions. The short-term cost of building was greatest for small-share businesses, but even for market leaders, ROI was significantly lower when share was rising than it was when share was stable.

Schick's campaign to build sales of the "Flexamatic" electric shaver during 1972 and 1973 dramatically illustrates the cost of increasing market share. In late 1972 Schick introduced the Flexamatic by means of a controversial national advertising campaign in which direct performance comparisons were made with its leading competitors. Trade sources have estimated that Schick spent $4.5 million in 1972 and $5.2 million in 1973 on advertising, whereas the company's advertising expenditures in 1970 and 1971 had been under $1 million annually.

In one sense the effort was successful: by late 1972 Schick's market share had doubled from 8% to 16%. But the impact on company profits was drastic. Shick's operating losses for the fiscal year ending February 28, 1974 amounted to $14.5 million on sales of $93.8 million, and it appears that although it was not the only cause, the high promotional cost of the Flexamatic campaign was a major contributing factor. Only time can tell whether Schick's short-term losses will prove to be justified by increased future cash flows.

The Schick example is, no doubt, an extreme one. Nevertheless, a realistic assessment of any share-building strategy should take into account the strong likelihood that a significant price will have to be paid—at least in the short run. Depending on how great the gains are and how long it takes to achieve them, this cost may or may not be offset by the longer-term gains.

In a recent article, William Fruhan demonstrated that there was a positive rela-

tion between market share and rate of return for automobile manufacturers and for retail food chains.[4] Yet he also cited examples of disasters stemming from overambition in the market-share dimension from the computer industry, the retail food business, and the airline companies.

The main thrust of Fruhan's article was to encourage business strategists to consider certain questions before launching an aggressive market-share expansion strategy: (1) Does the company have the necessary financial resources? (2) Will the company find itself in a viable position if its drive for expanded market share is thwarted before it reaches its market share target? (3) Will regulatory authorities permit the company to achieve its objective with the strategy it has chosen to follow? Negative responses to these questions would obviously indicate that a company should forgo market-share expansion until the right conditions are created.

It is fairly safe for us to say, therefore, that whenever the market position of a business is reasonably satisfactory, or when further building of share seems excessively costly, managers ought to follow holding strategies.

Holding Strategies. By definition, a holding strategy is designed to preserve the status quo. For established businesses in relatively mature markets—which is to say, for the majority of businesses in advanced economies—holding is undoubtedly the most common strategic goal with respect to market share.

A key question for businesses that are pursuing holding strategies is, "What is the most profitable way to maintain market position?" The answer to this question depends on many things, including the possibilities and costs of significant technological change and the strength and alertness of competitors. Because competitive conditions vary so much, few reliable generalizations can be made about profit-maximizing methods of maintaining market share.

Nevertheless, our analyses of the PIMS data base do suggest some broad relationships between ROI and competitive behavior. For example, our data indicate that large-scale businesses usually earn higher rates of return when they charge premium prices. (Recall that this pricing policy is usually accompanied by premium quality.) Also, ROI is usually greater for large-share businesses when they spend more than their major competitors, in relation to sales, on sales force effort, advertising and promotion, and research and development.

For small-share businesses, however, the most profitable holding strategy is just the opposite: on the average, ROI is highest for these businesses when their prices are somewhat below the average of leading competitors and when their rates of spending on marketing and R&D are relatively low.

Harvesting Strategies. Opposed to a share-building strategy is one of "harvesting"—deliberately permitting share to fall so that higher short-run earnings and cash flow may be secured. Harvesting is more often a matter of necessity than of strategic choice. Cash may be urgently needed to support another activity—dividends, for example, or management's earning record. Whatever the motivation, corporate management sometimes does elect to "sell off" part of a market-share position.

The experience of the businesses in the PIMS data pool, summarized in Exhibit 20-6, indicates that only large-scale businesses are generally able to harvest successfully. Market leaders enjoyed rates of return about three quarters of a point higher when they allowed market share to decline than

when they maintained it over the period 1970–1972. For the other groups of businesses shown in Exhibit 20-6, differences in ROI between "holding" and "harvesting" are irregular. Of course, these comparisons also reflect the influence of factors other than strategic choice. Market share was lost by many businesses because of intensified competition, rising costs, or other changes which hurt both their profitability and their competitive positions. For this reason, it is impossible to derive a true measure of the profitability of harvesting. Nevertheless, the PIMS data support our contention that, under proper conditions, current profits can be increased by allowing share to slide.

When does harvesting make sense, assuming it is a matter of choice? A reduction in share typically affects profits in a way directly opposite to that of building: ROI is increased in the short run but reduced in the longer term. Here again, a trade-off must be made. The net balance will depend on management's assessment of the direction and timing of future developments such as technological changes, as well as on its preference for immediate rather than deferred profits.

Balancing Costs and Benefits

Evidence from the PIMS study strongly supports the proposition that market share is positively related to the rate of return on investment earned by a business. Recognition of this relationship will affect how managers decide whether to make or buy to decrease purchasing costs, whether to advertise in certain media, or whether to alter the price or quality of a product. Also, recognizing that emphasis on market share varies considerably among industries and types of market situations, decisions concerning product and customer are likely to be influenced. For instance, a small competitor selling frequently purchased, differentiated consumer products can achieve satisfactory results with a small share of the market. Under other conditions, it would be virtually impossible to earn satisfactory profits with a small share (e.g., infrequently purchased products sold to large, powerful buyers).

Finally, choices among the three basic market share strategies also involve a careful analysis of the importance of market share in a given situation. Beyond this, strategic choice requires a balancing of short-term and long-term costs and benefits. Neither the PIMS study nor any other empirical research can lead to a "formula" for these strategic choices. But we hope that the findings presented here will at least provide some useful insights into the probable consequences of managers' choices.

THE PIMS DATA BASE

The data on which this article is based come from the unique pool of operating experience assembled in the PIMS project, now in its third year of operations at the Marketing Science Institute. During 1973, 57 major North American corporations supplied financial and other information on 620 individual "businesses" for the three-year period 1970–1972.

Each business is a division, product line, or other profit center within its parent company, selling a distinct set of *products* or *services* to an identifiable group or groups of *customers*, in competition with a well-defined set of competitors. Examples of businesses include manufacturers of TV sets; man-made fibers; and nondestructive industrial testing apparatus.

Data were compiled for individual businesses by means of special allocations of existing company data and, for some items, judgmental estimates supplied by operating managers of the companies.

For each business, the companies also provided estimates of the total sales in the market served by the business. Markets were defined, for purposes of the PIMS study, in much narrower terms than the "industries" for which sales and other figures are published by the Bureau of the Census. Thus the data used to measure market size and growth rates cover only the specific products or services, customer types, and geographic areas in which each business actually operates.

The *market share* of each business is simply its dollar sales in a given time period, expressed as a percentage of the total market sales volume. The figures shown are average market shares for the three-year period 1970–1972. (The average market share for the businesses in the PIMS sample was 22.1%.)

Return on investment was measured by relating *pretax operating profits* to the *sum of equity and long-term debt*. Operating income in a business is after deduction of allocated corporate overhead costs, but *prior* to any capital charges assigned by corporate offices. As in the case of market share data, the ROI figures shown in Exhibits 20–1, 20–5, and 20–6 are averages for 1970–1972.

As explained in the earlier HBR article, the focus of the PIMS project has been primarily on ROI because this is the performance measure most often used in strategic planning. We recognize, however, that ROI results are often not entirely comparable between businesses. When the plant and equipment used in a business have been almost fully depreciated, for example, its ROI will be inflated. Also, ROI results are affected by patents, trade secrets, and other proprietary aspects of the products or methods of operation employed in a business. These and other differences among businesses should naturally be kept in mind in evaluating the reasons for variations in ROI performance.

NOTES

1. See the earlier article on Phases I and II of the project by Sidney Schoeffler, Robert D. Buzzell, and Donald F. Heany, "Impact of Strategic Planning on Profit Performance," HBR March–April 1974.

2. Boston Consulting Group, Inc., *Perspectives on Experience* (Boston, 1968 and 1970).

3. This general argument has been made in numerous books, articles, and speeches dealing with antitrust economics, see, for example, Joe S. Bain, *Industrial Organization*, 2nd edition (New York, John Wiley & Sons, 1968), especially Chapter 6.

4. "Pyrrhic Victories in Fights for Market Share," HBR September–October 1972.

Is Market Share All That It's Cracked Up to Be?

Robert Jacobson and David A. Aaker

A most influential development in strategic management has been the emergence of market share as a pivotal key to profitability.[1] One stimulus for this view as the empirical studies of the Boston Consulting Group and others that documented experience and economies of scale effects and the associated portfolio models that suggested, at least for some business types, that resources should be withdrawn unless the firm could obtain a relatively high market share position. Another impetus was the well-known research stream based upon the PIMS data base that empirically found a consistent association between market share and profitability.

The early highly visible PIMS based article of Buzzell, Gale, and Sultan (1975) reported that a 10% point difference in market share is accompanied by a 5% point difference in ROI. Based on a model that

"Is Market Share All That It's Cracked Up to Be?" Robert Jacobson and David Aaker, Vol. 49 (Fall 1985), pp. 11–22. Reprinted from *Journal of Marketing*, published by the American Marketing Association.

also controls for concentration, Gale and Branch (1982) came to the same conclusion. Further, the multivariable PIMS Par ROI equation indicates that a 1% increase in market share leads to a .6% increase in ROI (Branch 1980; Gale, Henry, and Swire 1977).[2]

Two causal explanations are usually offered for the observed link between market share and profitability. First is the related effects of the experience curve and economies of scale. Through cumulative experience, tasks can be accomplished more efficiently by improving methods and procedures or by simple repetition. The desire to achieve cumulative experience effects can foster capital investment in operations and product redesign efforts to reduce costs. Scale economies can be achieved by larger share businesses, as plant and equipment investment and expenses such as marketing and R&D can be spread over more units.

Although experience and scale effects have been observed literally thousands of times, they are neither universal nor automatic (Aaker 1984, chapter 10). Experience effects tend to be found in industries with high levels of value added, continuous process manufacturing and high capital intensity. In other contexts, most notably service and extractive industries, experience effect strategies are rarely applied successfully. Further, experience effects are not automatic but require disciplined, effective programs in worker efficiency, product redesign, and capital utilization. In addition, economies of scale do not appear in all contexts, and, in fact, diseconomies of scale are very possible. Empirical evidence, e.g., Scherer (1980), suggests that minimum optimal scale can be achieved at output levels consistent with relatively small market shares.

A second causal explanation is that large market share can create market power over and above the cost advantage achieved by experience/scale effects. Large share firms may be able to extract favorable concessions from channel members because of their size and importance in the market. In addition, large market share may serve as an indicator of concentration, which may encourage collusive behavior and higher prices. However, this last argument is weakened by the results of Gale and Branch (1982) who find that when market share and concentration are both included in a model explaining profitability, the importance of concentration is insignificant.

There is, however, a third explanation for the observed association between market share and ROI. This explanation suggests the association is not causal but spurious, in that it is the result of both being jointly influenced by some third factor(s). One possible common causal factor is management quality. Good management may generate programs that make the marketing effort effective and the product line attractive and thereby achieve high market share. Good

management may also initiate programs that encourage cost control, productivity gains, wise product line decisions, etc., and so achieve high ROI. Thus, the high ROI would not necessarily be caused by the high market share position; rather, both would be the joint outcome of the process of good management. To illustrate the implications, consider the futility of trying to enhance ROI through promotional efforts directed at increasing market share if the causal link from market share is much less than assumed.

Perhaps of equal or more importance is another possible common factor, luck. Based on pure chance, a business may be lucky enough to stumble onto one or more products or strategies that will prove to be successful. Mancke (1974) supports this argument with a simulation in which he demonstrates that an association between market share and profitability could be the result of lucky firms obtaining higher profits that could be reinvested so as to obtain more rapid growth than their less lucky rivals.

The existence of experience, scale, or market power effects based on market share provides the motivation, as posited by neoclassical economic/marketing theory, for a firm to follow a market share strategy as a means of achieving increased profitability. The implication is that market share has some intrinsic value by its direct impact on profitability. A gain in share will cause an increase in ROI. However, if the association between market share and ROI is largely based on a common association with a third factor and is therefore spurious, this type of strategy may be inappropriate. Gain in market share need not lead to increases in profitability and in fact could result in a decrease.

These explanations of the association between market share and ROI are not mutually exclusive. Theoretically, it is reasonable to expect that all three phenomena may be at work. The crucial question and the goal of this article is to determine to what extent is the association between market share and ROI causal and to what extent is the association spurious, i.e., reflecting common associations with third factors. At issue is determining the average increase in ROI if steps are taken to increase market share by 1%. The frame of reference is the various PIMS studies that have suggested that a 1% increase in market share would generate a .5% increase in ROI.

The PIMS data base, described in the next section, is also utilized in this study. However, unlike most previous studies, the analysis makes use of both cross-sectional and time series data. As a first step, the findings of Buzzell, Gale, and Sultan (1975) are replicated using regression analysis. Efforts are then made to separate the spurious from the direct influence of market share on ROI. First, lagged values of ROI are added to the ROI model as a means of capturing factors, such as luck and management quality, that may be a source of some spurious association. Second, to reduce potential contemporaneous spurious associations, market share is seprated into two components: anticipated market share (the share explained by controllable or predetermined factors), and unanticipated market share (the share representing contemporaneous shocks). Third, additional explanatory factors, e.g., price, cost, promotion, are added to the ROI model so as to control for other influences. The result of these steps is an estimate of the market share effect with the bias caused by emitted variables substantially reduced. Our results are then contrasted with two previous studies with similar objectives. The possibility that market share might have a lagged effect or be enhanced under certain circumstances is then explored. Finally, some implications of the study are discussed.

THE DATA BASE

The data used in this analysis are drawn from the PIMS (Profit Impact of Market Strategy) data base of the Strategic Planning Institute. PIMS data are based on reports of over 2,000 business units that are components of the over 200 corporations participating in the PIMS project. A business unit is defined as a division of the firm "selling a distinct set of products to an identifiable set of customers in competition with a well-defined set of competitors." By use of a standardized form, information concerning the annual income statement, balance sheet, and other conditions such as market environment, is reported. Variables used in this study are defined in Table 21–1.

Because the data are kept confidential and participants are users of the data base, respondents are motivated to be accurate and conscientious when supplying data. In addition, the Strategic Planning Institute takes care to check any apparent inconsistencies in the data.

However, the data are not without limitations. The participating firms are not representative in that they tend to be large diversified corporations. There are very few small firms and new businesses in the project. Another limitation is that much of the data is subject to the assessment of the participant. The validity and/or consistency of subjective measures, such as relative product quality and defined market, might be subject to question. The ROI measure, based on accounting data that are often artifacts of the tax laws, e.g., depreciation, may also be a suspect indicator of the financial performance of a business (Fisher and McGowan 1983).

The PIMS project has two principal data bases. The most widely used is the SP14 data base which contains a cross-section of the four-year average of a business's report.

Table 21-1
Definition of Variables

Variable	Definition
Buyer Concentration	Number of immediate customers
Cap Util	Capacity utilization
Entry	Entry of competitors
Exit	Exit of competitors
Full Par ROI	Estimate of ROI from par equation
Mrk Int	Marketing intensity[a]
MS	Market share
MS Rank	Market share rank
MSAN	Anticipated market share
MSLAG1	Market share in previous year
MSLAG2	Market share two years ago
MSUN	Unanticipated market share
Product Importance	Importance of product to immediate customers
Product Life Cycle	Life cycle stage of product category
Real Growth	Real long-term market growth
Rel Adver	Relative media advertising expenditures
Rel Cost	Relative direct costs
Rel Image	Relative product image/company reputation
Relative Market Share	Relative market share
Rel Price	Relative price
Rel New Prod	Relative new products[b]
Rel Promo	Relative promotion expenditures
Rel Qual	Relative product quality[c]
Rel SForce	Relative salesforce expenditures
ROI	Return on investment
ROILAG1	Return on investment in previous year
ROILAG2	Return on investment two years ago
Vert Int	Vertical integration[d]

[a]marketing expenditures/revenue
[b]new products % of sales (this business)—new products % of sales (competition)
[c]% of sales from superior products—% of sales from inferior products
[d]value added/revenue

The other is the SPIYR data base that contains combined cross-sectional time series data based on the cross-sectional data for the over 2,000 business units and the time series data for the number of years the business participated in the PIMS program. This study makes use of the SPIYR data base because, unlike the SP14 data base, it offers the possibility of capturing lagged effects and examining effects that might be averaged away in the SP14 data base.

THE MARKET SHARE EFFECT

The ROI-Market Share Association

As evidenced by the regressions of equation 1 in Table 21–2, there is a significant association between market share and ROI.[3]

$$ROI = \beta_0 + \beta_1 \cdot MS + \epsilon \qquad (1)$$

The coefficient for the impact across all business units of market share on ROI of .5 is exactly in correspondence with empirical estimates reported in other studies. However, this regression does not indicate how much of the association is causal (whether it be through experience curve effects, economies of scale, or market power) and how much of it is spurious (the result of a common association with some third factor(s)). The estimate of the market share effect can be expected to be biased because there is a host of omitted factors that influence ROI and are correlated with market share.

Controlling for Lagged ROI

One way to capture some of the impact of these omitted factors is through the inclusion of previous years' ROI in the model. Previous years' ROI can act as a surrogate for firm specific factors occurring in previous periods that tend to be constant on a year-to-year basis, influence ROI, and may also influence market share. Past factors such as customer loyalty, distribution systems, advertising effectiveness, fortuitous circumstances, etc., have influenced ROI in previous periods and, if constant, may tend to influence current ROI in a similar manner. Lagged values of ROI can therefore serve to some extent as proxies for these factors.[4]

The inclusion of lagged dependent variables as explanatory factors, while rather common in time series studies, is often overlooked in cross-sectional studies. However, these terms may be able to capture some of the impact of past factors, even factors such as management quality and luck, which tend to be unobservable, on ROI and can help to reduce the potential for bias in estimates of the market share effect. In fact, ROI lagged one year is able to explain almost as much of the variation in ROI as the estimate of Full Par ROI that is generated by the PIMS Par ROI equation.[5]

A disadvantage of the inclusion of lagged ROI terms is the relative lack of dynamic variation, i.e., year-to-year movements in the data, which will not influence the consistency of coefficient estimates but

Table 21–2
ROI-Market Share Association

Coefficient Estimates	All Businesses	Consumer Goods Businesses	Capital Goods Businesses	Material, Components, and Supply Businesses
Intercept	10.16[a]	5.65[a]	4.14	13.84[a]
	(0.67)[b]	(0.94)	(2.62)	(0.69)
Market share	0.50[a]	0.74[a]	0.48[a]	0.42[a]
	(0.02)	(0.03)	(0.08)	(0.02)
R^2	0.05	0.16	0.02	0.07
Degrees of freedom	10213	2689	2011	5509

[a]significant at 99% level
[b]standard errors in parentheses

Table 21-3
ROI-Market Share Association Controlling for Past ROI

Coefficient Estimates	All Businesses	Consumer Goods Businesses	Capital Goods Businesses	Materials, Components, and Supply Businesses
Intercept	5.20[a]	1.02	8.07[a]	4.91[a]
	(0.56)[b]	(0.71)	(1.93)	(0.59)
Market share	0.22[a]	0.17[a]	0.40[a]	0.12[a]
	(0.02)	(0.03)	(0.06)	(0.02)
ROI lagged 1 year	0.54[a]	0.71[a]	0.06[c]	0.67[a]
	(0.01)	(0.02)	(0.03)	(0.02)
ROI lagged 2 years	0.06[a]	0.11[a]	0.07[a]	0.06[a]
	(0.01)	(0.02)	(0.01)	(0.02)
R^2	0.39	0.70	0.07	0.58
Degrees of freedom	6350	1640	1267	3435

[a]significant at 99% level
[b]standard errors in parentheses
[c]significant at 95% level

may not allow adequate variation to isolate the impact of the various factors. However, this lack of variation is somewhat compensated by the large sample size available in the PIMS data base.

Table 21–3 reports the results of equation 2 that regresses ROI on market share and on ROI lagged one and two years, termed ROILAG1 and ROILAG2.[6]

$$ROI = \beta_0 + \beta_1 \cdot MS + \beta_2 \cdot ROILAG1 + \beta_3 \cdot ROILAG2 + \epsilon \qquad (2)$$

Across all businesses lagged ROI was found to have a major impact and was able to substantially increase explanatory power. The relatively small standard errors for the coefficients indicate that the large sample size is able to overcome the relative lack of year-to-year variation so that the coefficients could be estimated with a relatively high level of precision. The impact of lagged ROI was very large for consumer goods and for materials, supplies, and components businesses and surprisingly small for capital goods businesses.

For each business grouping the coefficient for market share dropped from that of equation 1. For the aggregate grouping the market share effect reported in Table 21–3 is roughly half of that reported in Table 21–2, .22 versus .50. The implication is that a great deal of the association between market share and ROI is spurious and that the inclusion of lagged ROI is able to remove some of this spurious association by acting as a proxy for various third factors, such as management quality and luck.

However, there are differences between business types. The observed drop in the impact of market share was quite drastic for consumer product businesses (.74 to .17) and for materials, components, and supply businesses (.42 to .12). But the drop in capital goods businesses was relatively modest (.48 to .40). This modest drop suggests two possibilities that need to be explored further. First, the direct effect of market share may be more important in this business grouping. Second, for this grouping, lagged ROI may be an inadequate proxy for the third factor(s) and so substantial bias may still remain in the estimate of the market share effect.[7]

What specifically the lagged ROI measures are reflecting is uncertain. We do not know to what extent they represent luck, elements of management quality (e.g., ability to generate effective advertising), or other factors such as brand loyalty or distribution strength. In fact, lagged ROI undoubtedly reflects different factors for different business units. A direction for future research might well be to determine the underlying structural phenomena that account for the usefulness of lagged ROI in explaining current ROI. However, we do know that lagged ROI is not representing market share as a market share term is explicitly modeled. Possible collinearity between lagged ROI and market share will not bias either the estimate of the market share effect or its standard error but will tend to increase the standard errors of the coefficients. However, even this influence of collinearity is not especially relevant in our analysis, since the large sample size allows for the construction of relatively small confidence intervals.

The Effect of Anticipated versus Unanticipated Market Share

By including the lagged ROI terms, third factors are controlled to the extent that they appeared in a previous period. However, it is reasonable to expect that situations exist where contemporaneous shocks will effect both ROI and market share during the current year. For example, a business might run into anticipated and perhaps uncontrollable production or marketing problems affecting both ROI and market share. Sales might be greater than anticipated because of unexpected market acceptance, exit of a major competitor, or distribution success. A new management team might institute a variety of changes/shocks that simultaneously affect

both market share and ROI, but the change in ROI may not be directly influenced by the change in market share. Further, the reality is that some products do much better than others, even when they come from the same firm, have equal support, and an equal prior probability of success, just because of random shocks. By not incorporating the contemporaneous shock effect, a bias is still likely to exist in the market share coefficient reported in Table 21–3. What is needed is a means of isolating the intrinsic value of market share from that of shock that jointly influences both ROI and market share.

Towards this end, market share is separated into two components. The first component, which is termed *anticipated market share* (MSAN), is the market share that can be predicted based on controllable and/or predetermined factors. Anticipated market share is a variable that is purged of the effect of any contemporaneous shock and whose impact on ROI, as represented by β_1, equation 3, can be expected to better represent the intrinsic value of market share.

The second component, termed *unanticipated market share* (MSUN), is that market share that cannot be predicted based on the market share model. It is defined to be the difference between actual market share and anticipated market share, i.e., MS − MSAN. Unanticipated market share is to a large extent the market share that is the result of some unforeseen shock and whose impact on ROI, as represented by β_2 in equation 3, will include not only the impact of any shock but also the impact of any intrinsic value of market share.

$$\begin{aligned} \text{ROI} = \beta_0 + \beta_1 \cdot \text{MSAN} + \beta_2 \cdot \text{MSUN} \\ + \beta_3 \cdot \text{ROILAG1} + \beta_4 \cdot \text{ROILAG2} + \epsilon \end{aligned}$$
(3)

If neoclassical theory totally explains the association between market share and ROI, i.e., that the association is strictly causal, then one would expect, subject to the limitations of the PIMS data base, the impact on ROI of anticipated market share to be the same as that of unanticipated market share, i.e., $\beta_1 = \beta_2$. On the other hand, if the association of market share is solely the result of a joint dependency with some shock, then one would expect that anticipated market share would not have an impact on ROI but that unanticipated market share would have a positive impact on ROI, i.e., $\beta_1 = 0$ and $\beta_2 > 0$. If both theories are at work, then both anticipated and unanticipated market share will effect ROI. But since unanticipated market share may both reflect a common association and have a causal impact, its impact will differ from the impact of anticipated market share. The hypothesis that both views are at work but that the impact of anticipated market share is greater would imply that $\beta_1 > \beta_2 > 0$. However, the hypothesis that both views are at work but that the impact of unanticipated market share is greater would imply that $\beta_2 > \beta_1 > 0$.

The Market Share Model

In order to obtain measures of anticipated and unanticipated market share, the market share model depicted in equation 4 was developed and estimated. The model specification is very similar to that developed by Buzzell and Wiersema (1981). The most notable difference is that their analysis makes use of the average percentage change in market share over a four-year period, while we prefer to model the association of market share with previous years' market share with the use of lagged terms. Market share lagged one and two years is included in equation 4 following the similar logic that led to the inclusion of lagged ROI in the ROI model, i.e., to serve as surrogates for relevant factors not captured by other independent variables. MSAN is measured as the market share predicted by equation 4. The residual error from this equation, i.e., η, is the empirical estimate of MSUN. Table 21–4 reports the results. The R-square values in the range of .95 suggest that most of market share is anticipated, i.e., can be explained by controllable and/or predetermined variables. For each of the business groupings, the principal explanatory factor in the model is lagged market share.

$$
\begin{aligned}
MS = {} & \delta_0 + \delta_1 \cdot \text{MSLAG1} + \delta_2 \cdot \text{MSLAG2} \\
& + \delta_3 \cdot \text{Entry} + \delta_4 \cdot \text{Exit} \\
& + \delta_5 \cdot \text{MSRank} + \delta_6 \cdot \text{MrkInt} \\
& + \delta_7 \cdot \text{RelPrice} + \delta_8 \cdot \text{RelQual} \\
& + \delta_9 \cdot \text{RelNewProd} + \delta_{10} \cdot \text{RelSForce} \\
& + \delta_{11} \cdot \text{RelAdver} + \delta_{12} \cdot \text{Relpromo} \\
& + \delta_{13} \cdot \text{RelImage} + \eta
\end{aligned}
\tag{4}
$$

Other relevant factors in the model are competition entry and exit. As expected, competitor exit tends to increase share, while competitor entry does the reverse. The market share rank variable is significantly negative, perhaps because of ceiling effects; market share is more difficult to increase for larger share firms. Relative product quality and relative new product sales were both found to be positively related to market share. Of the relative marketing terms, only relative advertising was found to have a significant positive effect. A negative association was found to exist for market share with marketing intensity (except for consumer goods) and relative price.

There are two findings of Table 21–4 that warrant more detailed comment. First, the negative association found between market share and marketing intensity is consistent with an economies of scale argument discussed in Buzzell, Gale, and Sultan (1975). They suggest this is an indication

Table 21–4
Market Share Model

Coefficient Estimates	All Businesses	Consumer Goods Businesses	Capital Goods Businesses	Materials, Components, and Supply Businesses
Intercept	4.16[a] (0.51)[c]	2.71[a] (0.60)	4.32[b] (1.65)	4.22[a] (0.74)
Market share lagged 1 year	0.89[a] (0.01)	0.88[a] (0.02)	0.79[a] (0.03)	0.93[a] (0.02)
Market share lagged 2 years	0.04[a] (0.01)	0.08[a] (0.02)	0.10[a] (0.03)	−0.004 (0.02)
Entry	−0.50[a] (0.12)	−0.44[a] (0.15)	−0.71[a] (0.34)	−0.38[b] (0.17)
Exit	0.32[b] (0.13)	0.61[a] (0.16)	0.48 (0.37)	0.19 (0.19)
Market share rank	−0.89[a] (0.06)	−0.57[a] (0.08)	−1.50[a] (0.19)	−0.77[a] (0.08)
Marketing intensity	−2.35[a] (0.72)	1.19 (0.81)	−3.49 (0.19)	−5.74 (1.35)
Rel price	−0.008[b] (0.004)	−0.009[b] (0.004)	0.02 (0.01)	−0.01[b] (0.006)
Rel quality	0.01[a] (0.002)	0.004 (0.003)	0.03[a] (0.006)	0.008[b] (0.003)
Rel new products	0.03[a] (0.0005)	0.02[a] (0.006)	0.04[a] (0.009)	0.04[a] (0.007)
Rel salesforce	−0.07[b] (0.004)	−0.11 (0.07)	0.004 (0.16)	−0.08 (0.08)
Rel advertising	0.15[b] (0.06)	0.15[b] (0.07)	0.18 (0.17)	0.21[b] (0.09)
Rel promotion	0.006 (0.07)	−0.09 (0.08)	0.07 (0.20)	0.004 (0.10)
Rel image	0.14[b] (0.07)	0.19[b] (0.09)	−0.32 (0.21)	0.23[b] (0.09)
R^2	0.95	0.98	0.93	0.96
Degrees of freedom	6340	1630	1256	3425

[a]significant at 99% level
[b]significant at 95% level
[c]standard errors in parentheses

that larger share firms are in fact able to obtain lower per unit marketing costs.

Second, Table 21–4 reports a negative association between relative price and market share. Certainly economic theory would expect nothing less. However, this finding is not completely consistent with other studies making use of PIMS data. Buzzell and Wiersema (1981) do not include a measure of relative price in their model based on a lack of predictive power. Phillips, Chang, and Buzzell (1983) found a positive association between market share and price. They suggest that this finding indicates that "no lawlike connection exists between price and share." Perhaps a more realistic explanation is that the measure of relative price available in the PIMS data base is a poor indicator of the competitiveness of the price charged by the firm. However, the coefficients reported in Table 21–4 indicating a negative although relatively small association between price and share suggest that the measure has some power of detecting the workings of the price mechanism.

Separating Anticipated from Unanticipated Market Share Effects

Table 21–5 shows the results of attempting to isolate the impact of the intrinsic value of market share by regressing ROI on anticipated market share (MSAN), i.e., the market share predicted by the market share model of equation 4, and unanticipated market

(MSUN), i.e., the unexplained residual error from equation 4.[8]

The results suggest that both anticipated and unanticipated market share influence ROI. For each of the business groupings, it was found that the coeficient for unanticipated market share was far greater than that of anticipated market share. This would suggest that by not controlling for contemporaneous factors causing unexpected changes in market share, there is an upward bias in the estimate of the direct effect of market share. This bias is relatively small because unanticipated market share is a relatively minor component of market share. However, the market share impacts, as indicated by the unanticipated market share coefficients in Table 21–5, are all lower than the market share coefficients of Table 21–3 (.18 vs. .22; .15 vs. .17; .35 vs. .45; and .09 vs .12).

An alternate interpretation of the use of MSAN is that it is a means of removing

Table 21-5
ROI-Market Share Association Controlling for Past ROI and Unanticipated Market Share

Coefficient Estimates	All Businesses	Consumer Goods Businesses	Capital Goods Businesses	Materials, Components, and Supply Businesses
Intercept	5.96[a] (0.56)[c]	1.53[b] (0.70)	9.11[a] (1.91)	5.52[a] (0.59)
Anticipated market share	0.18[a] (0.02)	0.15[a] (0.03)	0.35[a] (0.06)	0.09[a] (0.02)
Unanticipated market share	0.95[a] (0.08)	1.17[a] (0.16)	.94[a] (0.21)	.74[a] (0.08)
ROI lagged 1 year	0.54[a] (0.01)	0.71[a] (0.02)	0.07[a] (0.03)	0.68[a] (0.02)
ROI lagged 2 years	0.06[a] (0.01)	0.11[a] (0.02)	0.07[a] (0.01)	0.06[a] (0.02)
R^2	0.39	0.70	0.07	0.59
Degrees of freedom	6349	1639	1266	3434

[a]significant at 99% level
[b]significant at 95% level
[c]standard errors in parentheses

Table 21–6
ROI Model

Coefficient Estimates	All Businesses	Consumer Goods Businesses	Capital Goods Businesses	Materials, Components, and Supply Businesses
Intercept	-21.52^a (3.50)[b]	-14.56^a (4.36)	-5.71 (14.46)	-22.35^a (3.66)
Anticipated market share	0.09^a (0.02)	0.13^a (0.03)	0.19^a (0.06)	0.03 (0.02)
Unanticipated market share	0.89^a (0.08)	1.04^a (0.16)	0.77^a (0.20)	0.71^a (0.08)
ROI lagged 1 year	0.50^a (0.01)	0.68^a (0.02)	$-.02$ (0.03)	$.64^a$ (0.02)
ROI lagged 2 year	0.07^a (0.01)	0.12^a (0.02)	0.06^a (0.01)	0.07^a (0.02)
Vertical integration	29.16^a (2.16)	22.21^a (3.05)	51.96^a (8.12)	22.45^a (2.19)
Marketing intensity	-36.90^a (4.81)	-18.88^a (5.34)	-116.24^a (14.88)	-18.98^c (7.10)
Capacity utilization	0.17^a (0.02)	0.11^a (0.02)	0.34^a (0.05)	0.16^a (0.02)
Rel price	0.08^c (0.03)	0.07 (0.04)	-0.02 (0.12)	0.06 (0.04)
Rel cost	-0.07^c (0.03)	-0.05 (0.05)	-0.29^c (.12)	-0.04 (0.04)
Rel quality	0.05^a (0.01)	-0.005 (0.02)	0.11^c (0.04)	0.04^a (0.01)
Rel new products	0.03 (0.03)	-0.0001 (0.04)	-0.03 (0.06)	0.04 (0.03)
Real market growth	0.14^a (0.03)	0.09^a (0.04)	0.11^a (0.07)	0.12^a (0.03)
Rel salesforce	-0.05 (0.35)	-0.46 (0.46)	0.10 (1.12)	0.39 (0.38)
Rel advertising	-0.13 (0.37)	0.98^c (0.42)	-1.60 (1.22)	-0.07 (0.43)
Rel promotion	-0.25 (0.41)	-0.21 (0.48)	1.32 (1.39)	-0.57 (0.47)
Rel image	0.90^c (0.43)	0.44 (0.58)	1.83 (1.49)	0.79 (0.44)
R^2	0.39	0.72	0.18	0.62
Degrees of freedom	6349	1627	1254	3422

[a]significant at 99% level
[b]standard errors in parentheses
[c]significant at 95% level

simultaneous equation bias from the estimate of the market share effect that might result if a feedback from ROI to market share existed. Our procedure of obtaining an estimate of MSAN from equation 4 and then utilizing this estimate in equation 3 is analogous to two-stage least squares. Given that theory exists to support positive causal influences in both directions between market share and ROI, a positive bias in the least squares estimate might be hypothesized. The reduction in the magnitude of the estimates of the market share effect reported in Table 21–5 from that of Table 21–3 may be partially or even totally caused by the removal of simultaneous equation bias from the least squares estimates.

The Role of Other Factors

Although the lagged ROI terms are able to act as surrogates for influences on ROI that do not change substantially from year to year, they are obviously imperfect measures of key factors influencing profitability. To the extent that measures of potentially relevant explanatory factors of profitability are available, it is reasonable to employ them. Further, since an increase in market share is usually assumed to be caused by expenditures in marketing, quality, etc., which may tend to depress ROI in the short run, it becomes important to control for such variables to the extent possible. Equation 5 represents such an expanded regression model, the estimation of which is reported in Table 21–6.

$$ROI = \beta_0 + \beta_1 \cdot MSAN + \beta_2 \cdot MSUN$$
$$+ \beta_3 \cdot ROILAG1 + \beta_4 \cdot ROILAG2$$
$$+ \beta_5 \cdot VertInt + \beta_6 \cdot MrkInt$$
$$+ \beta_7 \cdot CapUtil + \beta_8 \cdot RelPrice$$
$$+ \beta_9 \cdot RelCost + \beta_{10} \cdot RelQual$$
$$+ \beta_{11} \cdot RelNewProd + \beta_{12} \cdot RealGrowth$$
$$+ \beta_{13} \cdot RelSForce + \beta_{14} \cdot RelAdver$$
$$+ \beta_{15} \cdot RelPromo + \beta_{16} \cdot RelImage$$
$$+ \epsilon \tag{5}$$

The estimate of the direct effect of market share as represented by the coefficient for anticipated market share has again rather dramatically fallen. The coefficient for the aggregated grouping is .09, less than one-fifth of the commonly cited estimate of .5. The smallest and the only statistically insignificant impact (.03) is reported for materials, components, and supplies businesses. The largest impact (.19) of market share was found for capital goods businesses. However, this is about one-half the size of the effect reported in Table 21–5 and is not statistically different from the impact (.13) found for consumer products businesses.

The impacts of the other variables in the model are consistent with the findings of other PIMS studies.[9] Value added, capacity utilization, relative quality, real market growth, and relative image were all positively related to ROI. Marketing intensity had a negative relationship as did the three relative marketing variables, though not significantly. Relative cost had a negative effect, suggesting that lower costs were not entirely passed along to customers through lower prices. The positive impact of relative price perhaps indicates that businesses were, on the average, operating in an inelastic part of their demand curves. No consistent effect was found for relative new products.

PREVIOUS STUDIES FOCUSING ON THE ROLE OF THIRD FACTOR CAUSATION ON THE MARKET SHARE EFFECT

Two previous studies are particularly relevant to the findings discussed above. Gale and Branch (1982) conclude that the third factor effect exists but it is only a small part of the association between market share and ROI. In the other, Rumelt and Wensley (1980) suggest that the association between ROI and market share is solely the result of an association with a common factor. Problems relating to the experimental designs of these studies can perhaps explain the conflicting results.

Gale and Branch regress ROI on the level of market share and the change in market share, suggesting that the coefficient for the market share level represents the causal impact and the coefficient for the market share change reflects third factor effects. Both were found to be significant, but market share level had far greater explanatory power. Their finding that the third factor effect is only a small part of the explanation of the market share-ROI relationship may have been caused by a failure to adequately control for third factor effects. The inclusion of the change in market share to a large extent does control for the impact of contemporaneous shocks. However, results reported in this study make it clear that a number of other factors that are not controlled for by Gale and Branch, like management quality and luck, can also cause spurious association.

Rumelt and Wensley also explored the relative importance of the direct market share effect and stochastic (i.e., third factor) effects. They found no market share effect after market share is "cleansed" of its correlation with common third factors by use of an instrumental variable procedure. They attempted to cross-check their results by running a regression of the change in return on the growth in market share and a proxy (unanticipated growth in output) for the common third influence. They again find that the market share growth coefficient is insignificant and therefore conclude that the null hypothesis of no direct share effect on ROI cannot be rejected.[10]

This conclusion might not stem from a lack of relationship but perhaps from an ability of the approach to detect a relationship. First, as their authors note, since their instrumental variable estimate is a weak proxy for the change in market share, their tests to discern the direct market share effect will lack power, i.e., the tests will have a large Type II error in the detection of small market share effects. Second, the use of differenced data does not allow for the determination of what factors caused ROI to be at a specific level. One such factor might be market share. The change in market share, and, to a lesser extent, the change in ROI, involves an analysis of unexpected factors or shocks. The data used may well have differenced out a large amount of the underlying structural phenomenon, so that detecting possible impacts would be made more difficult. If differencing was indeed appropriate, the coefficient for ROI lagged one year should have been empirically observed to be approximately 1.00 instead of, for example, the estimate for all businesses of .50 reported in Table 21–6.

CONCLUSION

This investigation suggests that the direct impact of market share on ROI that was found using the PIMS data base is substantially lower than widely assumed. Instead of the commonly cited figure of a 1% change in market share being associated with a .5% change in ROI, we have found a 1% change in market share associated with a .1% change in ROI. The estimate of the market share effect reported in this study is 21 standard deviations less than the commonly cited estimate of .5. The discrepancy between the two estimates stems from the contention that a large amount of the correlation between ROI and market share is spurious, in the sense that they are both the joint outcome of some third factor(s).

Lagged Market Share Effects

Given the distinctly contrary nature of these findings, additional challenges would seem warranted. It could be possible that market share has delayed and/or carryover effects on ROI, in that the major impact of market share may not be contemporaneous but occur in some later periods. The activities required to generate the increase in market share could depress contemporaneous ROI but serve to increase ROI in subsequent years. The inclusion of variables such as marketing intensity and measures of the relative levels of price, quality, salesforce, advertising, and promotion in equation 5 reflect a concern to control for this possibility. However, it may be that such variables are not sufficiently sensitive to depict this effect. In addition, lagged ROI could be capturing the presence of a carryover effect via a Koyck (1954) distributed lag model.

To test the possibility that market share has a delayed/carryover effect on ROI, ROI was regressed on ROI lagged 1 and 2 years, the control variables in equation 5, current market share, and market share lagged 1, 2, 3, 4, and 5 years.[11] No such effect was detected. The sum of the coefficients involving market share was .09. The only significant impacts of market share were found contemporaneously and lagged 1 year. These impacts were exactly what would be expected, given the results of equation 5 and the high autocorrelation between market share and market share lagged 1 year.[12] The coefficients for the higher order lags were substantially smaller, insignificant, and added little explanatory power to the model. The hypothesis that the coefficients for these higher order lags were all equal to zero could not be rejected. This challenge failed to produce any evidence to indicate that market share has an impact different from that reported in Table 21–6.

Conditions under which Market Share Is More Important

Past studies, e.g., Buzzell, Gale, and Sultan (1975) and Woo and Cooper (1982), present evidence suggesting that the impact of market share differs under different circumstances. To test if our analysis averaged away a major market share effect, several variables that might be thought to interact with the market share impact were explored. ROI was regressed on market share, the control variables in Table 21–6, and dummy variables that allowed for differences in the intercept and the market share effect based on a determination of particular conditions being above or below the median. The regression coefficient for variables depicting interaction effects with market share thus provides estimates of how the market share effect differs under differing conditions.

This difference was small and insignificant for conditions relating to the product life cycle, product importance, vertical integration, and relative price. This indicates, for instance, that the market share effect was not significantly different for businesses with products early in the life cycle from businesses with products late in the life cycle. However, the market share effect did tend to be about 0.08 greater (with standard errors around .035) the more fragmented the buyer concentration, the less frequent the purchase, the higher the marketing intensity, or the higher the product quality.

The differences of impact of market share according to relative market share were large enough (.14), although insignificant (a standard error of .10), to warrant additional analysis. Following Hambrick and MacMillan (1982), who suggest that market share is more important for firms with very low or very high relative market share, the market share effect was separated by firms having a relative market share below .5, between .5 and 1.5, and above 1.5. While the difference for high relative market share firms was both relatively small and insignificant, low relative market share firms had a market share effect .13 higher than that of firms with relative market share above .5. However, the standard error of this estimate (.10) was also large so that the null hypothesis of no difference in impact could not be rejected. Still, the size of the coefficient suggests that market share growth may be more important for small share firms, perhaps because of the greater importance of economies of scale to relatively low volume producers.

Suggestions for Future Research

Obviously there are unanswered questions about the impact of market share upon financial performance. It would be useful to:

- challenge our findings by making use of other data bases.
- learn more about the structure of the process generating ROI. Clearly there are factors and lagged effects in the causal structure that are difficult to effectively model but are important to strategic decision making. Clinical research of individual industries and firms might help to reveal the nature of the third factors giving rise to an association between market share and ROI.
- identify variables that could be employed to better identify those situations where experience, scale, or market power will be

factors that will provide a substantial causal impact from market share to ROI.

Implications

The results of this study point to the conclusion that the direct impact of market share on ROI is substantially less than commonly assumed and, in fact, relatively minor. Market share would not appear to be, at least on the average, a key to profitability. Certainly this is not to suggest that market share is unimportant to the management of a business. High market share, together with high ROI, are indications that management has been following policies, whether by design or chance, that have proved to be successful. Market share can be used as an indicator of the effectiveness of current policies and suggestive of how these policies might be altered.

One implication of the conclusion that market share has been exaggerated as a causal determinant of ROI is that too much emphasis in planning and strategy development is focused on market share. Webster (1981) reports that top management view "marketing managers as unsophisticated in their understanding of the financial dimensions of marketing decisions" and tending to "focus more on sales volume and market share changes than on profit contribution and return on assets." Strategies placing strong emphasis on the attainment of high market share may be myopic and inconsistent with longer term horizons. Other fundamentals can be of equal or greater importance. More emphasis might be well-placed upon such key areas as product quality, customer satisfaction, productivity, corporate culture, product line appropriateness, and management effectiveness. In fact, situations could exist where a decline in market share may actually be an indication of good management. Efforts to keep or gain market share, for the sake of being number one or having a certain market share rank, may have a detrimental impact on ROI both in the short and long run. For example, the efforts of IBM in the 1970s to resist share erosion by aggressive price moves seem, at least in retrospect, to have been unwise.

There is no shortage of commentary in the management literature on how a smaller share competitor can achieve high returns without challenging on the basis of market share. One approach is to focus only upon part of the product line such as private labels, speciality, or high price/high quality products. Alternatively, the focus could be on a target segment, such as a regional market or those needing nonstandard products. There are numerous anecdotes about extremely successful businesses that have followed these kinds of niching strategies. Hamermesh, Anderson, and Harris (1978) studied three successful low share firms and concluded their success was due in part to good leadership, controlled growth, efficient use of R&D, and creative market segmentation.

The term *niche* has come to be associated with smallness and an inability to compete. Webster's dictionary defines niche more broadly as (i) a place, employment, or activity where an organism is best suited, or (ii) a habitat supplying the factors necessary for the existence of an organism. This view would seem to be a more insightful starting point for strategy development.

NOTES

1. Profitability is used in the sense of economic profits/rents, i.e., a rate of return more than sufficient to maintain capital investment.
2. Shepard (1972), making use of Fortune Directory data, reports two smaller estimates of the market share effect (.34 and .43).

3. The PIMS business units are identified as belonging to one of eight business types. For this study we have chosen not to analyze businesses classified as services or retail and wholesale distribution because of the relatively few number of businesses in these groups. Of the remaining businesses, analysis was done across all business types and by the groupings of (1) consumer products, (2) capital goods, and (3) materials, components, and supplies. The aggregation of the six business types into these three groupings was based on considerations of meaningful differences between regression coefficients of the various models explored. The difference between the consumer durables and consumer nondurable groupings was particularly small.
4. The use of lagged values as surrogates for other factors is, in fact, the basis for the Box and Jenkins (1970) approach to time series analysis.
5. A regression of ROI on Full Par ROI yielded an R-square of .32. The ROI on ROI lagged one year regression had an R-square of .28. Given that a regression of ROI on Full Par ROI and ROI lagged one year yielded an R-square of .45 suggests that the explanatory power of the Par ROI model can be improved by use of dynamic information.
6. The sample size is reduced from that reported in Table 21–2 because observations that did not have data for the two preceding years were deleted.
7. The relatively high year-to-year variation in ROI, and so the small impact of lagged ROI, might be explained by the fact that capital goods sales and ROI tend to be highly sensitive to fluctuations in the economy.
8. The estimates of MSAN and MSUN appear insensitive to specification changes in equation 4, e.g., attempts to model interactive and nonlinear effects, apparently because of the crucial explanatory role played by lagged market share.
9. Given that some of the same control variables appear in both equations 4 and 5, their impact in equation 5 indicates their direct

influence on ROI, i.e., an effect net of any indirect impact they might have on ROI through an influence on market share.

10. We tested the role of unanticipated output in equation 5 and found that it did not alter the impact of anticipated market share on ROI.

11. An equation involving higher order lagged terms of ROI was also tested. The estimate of the market share effect in a model involving ROI lagged 1, 2, 3, 4, and 5 years was virtually indistinguishable from that reported in Table 21–6.

12. The estimated coefficient values for current and lagged 1 year market share were .9 and −.8, respectively. To note the consistency with the estimates reported in Table 21–6, recall equation 5 models

$$ROI = \beta_1 * MSAN + \beta_2 * MSUN + \ldots$$

Since market share lagged 1 year, i.e., $MS(t-1)$, is found in Table 21–5 to provide the large percentage of explanatory power in predicting current market share, i.e., $MS(t)$, then $MSAN \cong MS(t-1)$ and so $MSUN \cong MS(t) - MS(t-1)$. Substituting these approximations in equation 5 yields:

$$ROI \cong \beta_1 * MS(t-1) + \beta_2 * (MS(t) - MS(t-1)) + \ldots$$

Upon rearranging:

$$ROI \cong (\beta_1 - \beta_2) * MS(t-1) + \beta_2 * MS(t) + \ldots$$

The estimated coefficient values reported in Table 21–6 would imply coefficient values of −.8 and .9 for $MS(t-1)$ and $MS(t)$, respectively. And, in fact, these were the values that were observed.

REFERENCES

Aaker, David A. (1984), *Strategic Market Management*, New York: Wiley.

Box, G. E. P. and G. M. Jenkins (1970), *Time Series Analysis, Forecasting and Control*, San Francisco: Holden-Day.

Branch, Ben (1980), "The Laws of the Marketplace and ROI Dynamics," *Financial Management*, 9 (Summer), 58–65.

Buzzell, Robert D., Bradley T. Gale, and Ralph G. M. Sultan (1975), "Market Share—A Key to Profitability," *Harvard Business Review*, 53 (January–February), 97–106.

Buzzell, Robert D. and Frederick D. Wiersema (1981), "Modelling Changes in Market Share: A Cross-Sectional Analysis," *Strategic Management Journal*, 2 (January–March), 27–42.

Fisher, Franklin M. and John J. McGowan (1983), "On the Misuse of Accounting Rates of Return to Infer Monopoly Profits," *American Economic Review*, 73 (March), 82–97.

Gale, Bradley T. and Ben S. Branch (1982), "Concentration versus Market Share: Which Determines Performance and Why Does It Matter?," *The Antitrust Bulletin*, 27 (Spring), 83–103.

Gale, Bradley T., Donald F. Heany, and Donald S. Swire (1977), "The Par ROI Report: Explanation and Commentary on Report," Cambridge, MA: Strategic Planning Institute.

Hambrick, Donald C. and Ian C. MacMillan (1982), "The Product Portfolio and Man's Best Friend," *California Management Review*, 24 (Fall), 84–95.

Hamermesh, R.G., M.S. Anderson, and J. E. Harris (1978), "Strategies for Low Market Share Businesses," *Harvard Business Review*, 56 (May–June), 95–102.

Koyck, L. M. (1954), *Distributed Lags and Investment Analysis*, Amsterdam: North Holland.

Mancke, Richard B. (1974), "Causes of Interfirm Profitability Differences: A New Interpretation of the Evidence," *The Quarterly Journal of Economics*, 88 (May), 181–193.

Phillips, Lynn W., Dae R. Chang, and Robert D. Buzzel (1983), "Product Quality Cost Position and Business Performance: A Test for Some Key Hypotheses," *Journal of Marketing*, 47 (Spring), 25–43.

Rumelt, Richard P. and Robin Wensley (1980), "In Search of the Market Share Effect," working paper MGL-61, University of California at Los Angeles.

Scherer, F.M. (1980), *Industrial Market Structure and Economic Performance*, Chicago: Rand McNally.

Shepard, William G. (1972), "The Elements of Market Structure," *Review of Economics and Statistics*, 54 (February), 25–37.

Webster, Frederick E. (1981), "Top Management's Concerns about Marketing: Issues for the 1980s," *Journal of Marketing*, 45 (Summer), 9–16.

Woo, Carolyn Y. and Arnold C. Cooper (1982), "The Surprising Case for Low Market Share," *Harvard Business Review*, 60 (November–December), 106–113.

Customer-Oriented Approaches to Identifying Product-Markets

George S. Day, Allan D. Shocker, and Rajendra K. Srivastava

The problems of identifying competitive product-markets pervade all levels of marketing decisions. Such strategic issues as the basic definition of the business, the assessment of opportunities presented by gaps in the market or threats posed by competitive actions, and major resource allocation decisions are strongly influenced by the breadth or narrowness of the competitive arena. Share of market is a crucial tactical tool for evaluating performance and guiding territorial advertising, sales force, and other budget allocations. The quickening pace of antitrust prosecution is a further source of demands for better definitions of relevant market boundaries that will yield a clearer understanding of the competitive consequences of acquisitions.

This paper is primarily concerned with the needs of marketing planners for

George S. Day, Allan D. Shocker, and Rajendra K. Srivastava, "Customer Oriented Approaches to Identifying Product-Markets," Vol. 43 (Fall 1979), pp. 8–19. Reprinted from *Journal of Marketing*, published by the American Marketing Association.

strategic analyses of competitive product-markets.[1] Their needs presently are served by approaches to defining product-markets which emphasize similarity of production processes, function, or raw materials used. Seldom do these approaches give a satisfactory picture of either the threats or the opportunities facing a business. In response, there has been considerable activity directed toward defining product-markets from the customers' perspective. Our objectives are first, to examine the merits of a customer perspective in the context of a defensible definition of a product-market, and second, to evaluate progress toward providing this perspective. The paper's structure corresponds to these objectives. The first two sections are concerned with the nature of the strategic problem, and the development of a customer-oriented definition of a product-market. This definition is used in the third section to help evaluate a variety of methods for identifying product-market boundaries. In this discussion, a sharp distinction is drawn between methods which rely on purchase or usage behavior and those which use customer judgments.

SOURCES OF DEMAND FOR BETTER INSIGHTS

Ultimately all product-market boundaries are arbitrary. They exist because of recurring needs to comprehend market structures and impose some order on complex market environments. But this situation could not be otherwise. One reason is the wide variety of decision contexts which dictate different definitions of boundaries.

Market and product class definitions appropriate for tactical decisions tend to be narrow, reflecting the short-run concerns of sales and product managers who regard a market as "a chunk of demand to be filled with the resources at my command." These resources are usually constrained by products in the present product line. A longer-run view, reflecting strategic planning concerns, invariably will reveal a larger product-market to account for (1) presently unserved but potential markets; (2) changes in technology, price relationships, and supply which broaden the array of potential substitute products; and (3) the time required by present and prospective buyers to react to these changes.

Of necessity, a single market definition is a compromise between the long-run and the short-run views. All too often, the resulting compromise is not consistent with customers views of the competitive alternatives to be considered for a particular usage situation or application. One consequence of these problems is the development of different definitions for different purposes. Thus, for some strategic planning purposes, General Electric treats hair dryers, hair setters, and electric brushes as parts of distinct markets while for other purposes they are part of a "personal appliance" business since they tend to compete with one another in a "gift market." General Foods has taken an even broader approach in a reorganization of its strategic business units. Each SBU now concentrates on marketing families of products made by different processing technologies but consumed by the same market segments (Hanon 1974). Thus, all desserts are in the same division whether they are frozen, powdered, or ready-to-eat.

A further reason for the inevitable arbitrariness of product-market boundaries is the frequent absence of natural discontinuities which can be readily identified—and accepted—without argument. Moran (1973) states the problem bluntly:

> In our complex service society, there are no more product classes—not in any meaningful sense, only as a figment of file clerk imagination. . . . To some degree, in some circumstances, almost anything can be a partial substitute for almost anything else. A (fifteen-cent) stamp substitutes to some extent for an airline ticket.

When a high degree of ambiguity or compromise is present in the identification of the product-market, a number of problems are created. Some will stem from inadequate and delayed understanding of emerging threats in the competitive environment. These threats may come from foreign competition, product substitution trends, shifts in price sensitivity, or changed technological possibility. Thus fiberglass and aluminum parts have displaced steel in many automotive applications due in some measure to increasing willingness to pay higher prices to obtain lower weight and consequent gas economy. Conversely, opportunities may be overlooked when the definition is drawn too narrowly for tactical purposes and the nature and size of the potential market are understated. Finally, whenever market share is used to evaluate the performance of managers or to determine resource allocations (Day 1977), there is a tendency for managers to manipulate the market boundaries to show an increasing or at least static share.

A CUSTOMER-ORIENTED CONCEPT OF A COMPETITIVE PRODUCT-MARKET

Market definitions have, in the past, focused on either the *product* (as with the following definition, ". . . products may be closely related in the sense that they are regarded as substitutes by consumers" Needham 1969, which assumes homogeneity of consumer behavior), or on the *buyers* (". . . individuals who in the past have purchased a given class of products." Sissors 1966). Neither approach is very helpful for clarifying the concept, or evaluating alternative approaches for identifying product-market boundaries.

A more productive approach can be derived from the following premises:

- People seek the benefits that products provide rather than the products per se. Specific products or brands represent the available combinations of benefits and costs.
- Consumers consider the available alternatives from the vantage point of the usage contexts with which they have experience or the specific applications they are considering (Belk 1975; Lutz and Kakkar 1976; Stout et al. (1977). It is the usage requirement which dictates the benefits being sought.[2]

From these two premises, we can define a product-market as the *set of products* judged to be substitutes, within those usage situations in which similar patterns of benefits are sought, and the *customers* for whom such usages are relevant.

This definition is *demand* or customer-oriented in that customer needs and requirements have primacy. The alternative is to take a *supply* perspective and define products by such operational criteria as similarity of manufacturing processes, raw materials, physical appearance, or function. These criteria are the basis of the Standard Industrial Classification (SIC) system—and have generally wide acceptance because they appear easy to implement. They lead to seemingly stable and clear-cut definitions, and importantly, involve factors largely controllable by the firm; implying that the definition is somehow controllable as well. They are also helpful in identifying potential competitors, because of similarities in manufacturing and distribution systems. Demand-oriented criteria, on the other hand, are less familiar and consequently appear more difficult to implement (as a consequence of the variety of methods available and the inevitable problems of empirical measurement, sampling errors, and aggregation over individual customer differences). Moreover, such definitions may be less stable over time because of changing needs and tastes. Finally, the organization must initiate a research program to collect and analyze relevant data and monitor change rather than relying on government or other external sources to make the information available. The consequence is most often a decision to use supply-oriented measures despite their questionable applicability in many circumstances (Needham 1969).

Hierarchies of Products.   The notion of a unique product category is an oversimplification in the face of the arbitrary nature of the boundaries. Substitutability is a measure of degree. Thus it is better to think in terms of the levels in a hierarchy of products within a generic product class representing all possible ways of satisfying a fundamental consumer need or want. Lunn (1972) makes the following useful distinctions between:

- Totally different *product types* or subclasses which exist to satisfy significantly different patterns of needs beyond the fundamental or generic. For example, both hot and cold cereals serve the same need for breakfast nutrition, but otherwise are different. Over the long run, product types may behave like substitutes.
- Different *product variants* are available within the same overall type, e.g., natural, nutritional, presweetened, and regular cereals. There is a high probability that some short-run substitution takes place among subsets of these variants (between natural and nutritional, for example). If there is too much substitution, then alternatives within the subset do not deserve to be distinguished.
- Different *brands* are produced within the same specific product variant. Although these brands may be subtly differentiated on many bases (color, package type, shape, texture, etc.), they are nonetheless usually direct and immediate substitutes.

There may be many or few levels in such a hierarchy, depending on the breadth and complexity of the genuine need and the variety of alternatives available to satisfy it. Thus, this typology is simply a starting point for thinking about the analytical issues.

Submarkets and Strategic Segments. The product-market definition proposed above implies submarkets composed of customers with common uses or applications of the product. These are segments according to the traditional definition of groups that have similar purchase or usage behavior or reactions to marketing efforts (Frank, Massy, and Wind 1973). For our purposes, it is more

useful to consider these as submarkets within *strategic market segments*. While each of these submarkets may serve as the focus of a positioning decision, the differences between them may not present significant strategic barriers for competitors to overcome. Such barriers may be based on factors such as differences in geography, order quantities, requirements for technical assistance and service support, price sensitivity, or perceived importance of quality and reliability. The test of strategic relevance is whether the segments defined by these or other characteristics must be served by substantially different marketing mixes. The boundaries could then be manifested by discontinuities in price structures, growth rates, share patterns, and distribution channels when going from one segment to another.

ANALYTICAL METHODS FOR CUSTOMER-ORIENTED PRODUCT-MARKET DEFINITIONS

Customer-oriented methods for identifying product-markets can be classified by whether they rely upon behavioral or judgmental data. Purchase behavior provides the best indication of what people actually do, or have done, but not necessarily what they might do under changed circumstances. As such, its value is greater as a guide to tactical planning. Judgmental data, in the form of perceptions or preferences, may give better insights into future patterns of competition and the reasons for present patterns. Consequently, it may better serve as the basis for strategic planning. In this section we will evaluate seven different analytical approaches within the two basic classes as follows:

Purchase or Usage Behavior	Customer Judgments
A1. Cross-elasticity of demand	B1. Decision sequence analysis
A2. Similarities in behavior	B2. Perceptual mapping
A3. Brand switching	B3. Technology substitution analysis
	B4. Customer judgments of substitutability

Within the broad category of customer judgments of substitutability (B4), five related approaches, using free associations, the "dollar metric," direct grouping of products, products-by-uses analysis and substitution-in-use analysis will be examined.

Analysis of Purchase or Usage Behavior

A1. *Cross elasticity of demand* is considered by most economists to be the standard against which other approaches should be compared (Scherer 1970). Despite the impressive logic of the cross-elasticity measure, it is widely criticized and infrequently used:

- The conceptual definition of this measure presumes that there is no response by one firm to the price change of another (Needham 1969). This condition is seldom satisfied in practice.
- It is a static measure, and "breaks down in the face of a market characterized by changing product composition" (Cocks and Virts 1975). This is so because a priori it is not known what all the potential substitutes or complements may be. Over time new entrants or departures from a market may affect the cross-elasticity between any two alternatives.
- Finally, "in markets where price changes

have been infrequent, or all prices change together, or where factors other than prices have also changed, there is simply not enough information contained in the data to permit valid statistical estimation of the elasticities," (Vernon 1972).

These problems may be overcome with either an experimental study, which can introduce problems of measure validity, or extensive monitoring of the factors affecting demand and use of econometric methods to control, where possible, for the effects of such factors. Not surprisingly, such studies are expensive and rather infrequently undertaken. Generally, empirical cross-elasticity studies have focused on only two goods (typically product-types as opposed to variants or brands). It is also worth noting that if simultaneous estimation of all cross-elasticities were to be attempted, some a priori determination of the limits to a product-market would be needed in order to include price change and other market data for all potential competitive brands. The estimation of any specific cross-elasticity should be sensitive to such product-market definition.

A2. *Similarities in customer usage behavior.* This approach was successfully used in a study of the ethical pharmaceutical market (Cocks and Virts 1975). The basic question was the extent to which products made up of different chemicals, but with similar therapeutic effects, could be significant substitutes. The key to answering this question was the availability of a unique set of data on physician behavior. Each of the 3,000 physicians in a panel recorded: (1) patient characteristics, (2) the diagnosis, (3) the therapeutic measures—drugs—used to treat the patient, (4) the desired action of the drugs being used, and (5) characteristics of the reporting physician.

The first step in the analysis was to estimate the percentage usage of each drug in the treatment of patients diagnosed as having the same ailment. When a drug was found to be the only one used for a certain disease, and seldom or never used in the treatment of any other diagnosis, it was assumed to represent a distinct class. Generally, it was found that several drugs were used in several diagnosis categories. The next step was to see if drugs which were used together had similar desired actions. Some drugs, such as analgesics, are frequently used along with other drugs, without being substitutes (strictly speaking, they also are not complements). Finally, drugs were classed as substitutes—and hence in the same product class—if 10% or more of the total usage of each drug was in the treatment of a specific diagnosis.

While it was not claimed that every drug in the resulting product-market competed for all uses of every other drug in that market, the data revealed a substantial amount of substitutability. The key to understanding the patterns of competition in this market was knowledge of the usage situation. As yet, few consumer panels have incorporated similar data with the usual measures of purchase behavior. The potential to conduct similar analyses suggests that usage data could be valuable when available for categories which are purchased for multiple uses.

A3. *Brand switching* measures are usually interpreted as conditional probabilities, i.e., the probability of purchasing brand A, given that brand B was purchased on the last occasion. Such measures are typically estimated from panel data where the purchases of any given respondent are represented by a sequence of indefinite length. The probabilities are computed from counts of the frequency with which each condition arises in the data (e.g., purchases of brand A are preceded by different brands in the sequence). The premise is that respondents are more likely to switch between close substitutes than distant ones and that brand switching proportions provide a measure of the probability of substitution.

As with cross-elasticity, the brand-switching measure is usable only after a set of competitive products has first been established. Since estimation of brand-switching rates is based upon a sequence of purchases, there must be some logical basis to determine which brands to include in such a sequence. Similarity of usage patterns, as discussed above, is one promising basis.

Brand switching rates as measures of degree of substitutability are flawed in several respects. (1) Applicability is typically limited to product categories having high repeat purchase rates to ensure that a sufficiently long sequence of purchases is available over a short time period for reliable estimates of switching probabilities. (2) The customer choice process, which determines switching, must be presumed stable throughout the sequence of purchases. If a long time series is used to provide reliable estimates, this assumption may be questionable. (3) Panel data, upon which switching probabilities are based, often obscure individual switching behavior since data are typically reported by only one member of a family who completes a diary of purchases. Apparent switching can result from different members of the family making consistent but different brand choices at differing points in time. A similar distortion is created by an individual who regularly purchases different brands for different usage occasions. (4) Analyses of panel data are further complicated by multiple brand purchases at the same time (does purchase of A precede B or vice versa in determining the sequence?), by lack of uniformity in package sizes across brands (since package size affects frequency of purchase), and by different sized packages of the same brand (is purchase of a large size equivalent to some sequence of purchases of smaller sizes?).

The Hendry model (Butler and Butler 1970, 1971) uses brand switching data directly to determine the market structure. Although details have been slow to appear in the literature (Kalwani and Morrison 1977; Rubison and Bass 1978) there has been a good deal of utilization of the empirical regularities uncovered by the model for marketing planning purposes.

This model does not rely solely on behavioral data, as it can also incorporate retrospective reports of switching or purchase intentions data from surveys. In essence, the model seeks an underlying structure of brand-switching maximally "consistent" with the input data. It posits a hierarchical ordering in consumer decision making: consumers are presumed to form categories within the product class (e.g., cold or hot, presweetened or regular, Kellogg's, General Mills, or Post cereals), select those classes in which they are interested, and then consider for purchase only the alternatives within the chosen class (e.g., brands within a particular type of product *or* product types within a brand name). Analysis is carried out at each submarket level. Customers may purchase brands within more than one submarket, but within any submarket all customers are considered potential purchasers of all brands. Each customer is assumed, at equilibrium, to have stable purchase probabilities.

To determine which ordering or structuring of the market best characterizes customer views, a heuristic procedure is employed. Initially, judgment is used to hypothesize a limited number of plausible partitionings of a market, i.e., *alternative* submarket definitions. For each hypothesized definition, the Hendry framework is used to predict various switching probabilities among the products/brands within each submarket and between submarkets (switching *between* submarkets should be much less than *within* any one submarket). The predictions can then be compared with the actual data. That hypothesized partitioning (market structure) yielding switching patterns in closest correspondence with actual data is selected as the appropriate definition for the structure of the market.

A procedure elaborating hierarchical partitioning concepts similar to those of Hendry, but with the ability to incorporate usage occasion has recently been discussed by Urban and Hauser (1979). As in the Hendry model, a hierarchical tree structure is specified. More switching should occur within than between branches. Individual probability estimates are derived by measuring preferences among products with a consumer interview and statistically matching these preferences to observed or reported purchase behavior using the conditional logic model (McFadden 1970). The derived trees are tested by comparing predicted with actual choices in a simulated buying situation which occurs at the end of the consumer interview.

The Hendry procedure has a substantial subjective component, depending upon the criterion used to generate the hypothetical market structure definitions to be evaluated. (The alternative to a good criterion is the testing of potentially large numbers of definitions.) It is also quite arbitrary, possessing elements of the chicken-egg controversy: the prior specification of "the market" is quite critical to the empirical determination of "market shares" for each brand but these in turn are necessary to calibrate the Hendry model (i.e., estimate its parameters). Thus the "correct" definition of the market will depend upon how well predictions of the model correspond to the actual data. The model ought to always do reasonably well in predicting switching patterns in the same market environment from which share data were taken. In other words, to use the model for purposes of selecting the superior market definition, one must presume the model valid. But to test its validity, one must already possess a valid definition of the market. Thus the Hendry model may provide a reasonable approach to market definition only if either the model itself can be independently validated or if independent criteria exist for validating the market definition it suggests.

The Hendry model presumes all customers have stable probabilities of purchasing every brand within a partition (submarket). This assumes preferences, market shares, attitudes, and all other factors of significance are stable and that learning is negligible. Such assumptions may suggest applicability of the Hendry framework only in mature product categories, where such conditions may reasonably hold. Moreover, confirmation of any a priori partitioning of a market rests solely upon analysis of the aggregate switching probabilities as these become the measures of substitutability. Since analysis is carried out on an aggregate level, individual or segment differences are largely ignored. The premise that any given brand may have a varying set of competitors depending upon intended usage and brand familiarity is assumed away by such aggregation.

Summary. Behavioral measures suffer from an endemic weakness because they are influenced by what "is" or "was" rather than what "might be." Actual switching is affected by current market factors such as the set of existing brands, their availability, current pricing structures, promotional message and expenditures, existing legislation and social mores, etc. An imported beer could be substitutable for a local brand insofar as usage is concerned, but price differences may discourage actual substitu-

tion. Similarly, a private label brand may be substitutable for a nationally distributed one, but unless the customer shops the stores in which the private label is sold, they cannot make the substitution. If data are developed over long periods of time or from a diverse set of people in differing circumstances, sufficient variability may have taken place in the determinants of demand to reveal such potential substitutability. Otherwise, if some kind of behavioral measure is desired, laboratory manipulation may be necessary.

Analyses Based upon Customer Judgments

Customers often have considerable knowledge of existing brands through personal or friends' experiences and exposure to promotion. Their perceptions may not always correspond to what manufacturers may believe about their own or competitive products. They may have purchase and consumption objectives which influence their consideration of alternatives and choices among them. They may create new uses for existing products. If such perceptual and decision making processes prove relatively stable, they may be useful for predicting which products and brands will be regarded as potential or actual substitutes and why.

B.1 *Decision Sequence Analysis* utilizes protocols of consumer decision making, which indicate the sequence in which various criteria are employed to reach a final choice (Bettman 1971; Haines 1974). The usual procedure asks individuals to verbalize what is going through their mind as they make purchase decisions in the course of a shopping trip. This verbal record is called a protocol as distinguished from retrospective questioning of subjects about their decisions. With such data, a model of the way the subject makes decisions can be developed. These models specify the *attributes* of the choice objects or situations that are considered and the *sequence* and *method* of combination of these attributes or cues. Generally, the attributes or cues are arrayed in a hierarchical structure called a decision tree. The order in which they are examined is modeled by the path structure of the tree. The branches are based merely on whether or not the level of the attribute is satisfactory or a certain condition is present "is the price too high?" "is the store out of my favorite brand?").

Analysis of protocols is at the individual level. This has the advantage of enabling individual differences in knowledge and beliefs about alternative products and choice criteria to be recognized. Individuals may, in principle, be grouped into segments on the basis of similar decision procedures. Measures of the extent of competition between brands can be obtained from protocols of different segments by noting which alternatives are even considered and when they are eliminated from further consideration by criteria used at each stage of the decision process (alternatives eliminated at later stages should be more competitive than those eliminated earlier).

Applications of decision sequence analysis have focused on choices at the brand level. Yet the real benefits of this approach would seem to be better insights into the hierarchy of product types and variants within a generic product class. Thus in understanding patterns of competition in the vegetable market, it is important to know whether buyers first decide on the type of vegetable (corn, beans, peas, etc.) or the form (fresh, frozen, or canned). Proposals for a similar kind of study have been made by economists in connection with the concept of a "utility tree" (Strotz 1957) and are similar in intent to the Hendry procedure.

There are numerous empirical problems to be considered in any effort to collect protocols of choice hierarchies. The typical representations of decision sequences appear quite complex and pose serious difficulties for aggregation of the individual models into any small number of segments. Aggregation requires some definition of "similarity" in order to group different decision structures. Further, since it is generally expensive to develop protocols, a representative sample of customers may be unrealizable. Customers are not used to reporting their decision processes so explicitly. A trained interviewer is needed to coax information which is specific enough to be meaningful (e.g., what is too high a price or a satisfactory level of preference?) and yet not unduly bias the process. Since customer decision making for some product categories may take place over prolonged periods of time, it may be necessary for the length of the interviewing to be similarly extended or to rely on respondent's recall of certain events. Finally, since protocol data are collected in the context of the purchase situation, factors associated with that situation may assume greater importance than factors of intended usage. This could place misleading emphasis on in-store factors as determinants of competition.

B.2. *Perceptual mapping* includes a large family of techniques used to create a geometric representation of customer's perceptions of the qualities possessed by products/brands comprising a previously defined product-market (Green 1975). Brands are represented by locations (points or, possibly, regions) in the space. The dimensions of this space distinguish the competitive alternatives and represent benefits or costs perceived important to the purchase. Thus any product/brand might be located in such a space according to a set of coordinates which represent the extent to which the product is believed to possess each benefit or cost attribute. Relative "distances" between product alternatives may be loosely interpreted as measures of perceived substitutability of each alternative for any other.

There are several different techniques which can be used to create perceptual configurations of product-markets (e.g., direct scaling, factor analysis, multiple discriminant analysis, multidimensional scaling). Analysis may be based upon measures of perceived overall similarity/dissimilarity, perceived appropriateness to common usage situations, and correlations between attribute levels for pairs of products. Unfortunately such diversity of criteria and method can lead to somewhat different perceptual maps and possibly different product-market definitions. Much empirical research is still needed to compare the alternatives and assess which produce definitions that are more valid for particular purposes (Shocker and Srinivasan 1979).

When perceptual maps can be represented in two or three dimensions without destroying the data, there is a great improvement in the understanding of the competitive structure. Further, to the extent that substitutability in such a representation corresponds in some straightforward way to interproduct distance, analytic techniques such as cluster analysis (or simply looking for "open spaces" in the map) could prove useful in identifying product-market boundaries. The eventual decision must necessarily be judgmental, with the geometric representation simply facilitating that judgment. Customers or segments may also be represented in such a space by the location of their "most preferred" combination of attribute levels—termed their ideal point.

The major advantage offered by perceptual mapping methods is versatility. Maps can be created for each major usage situation. When care is taken to control for customer knowledge of available product/brand alternatives, perceptual homogeneity

may be sufficient to permit the modeling of preference and choice for different user segments within a common perceptual representation (Pessemier 1977). Moreover, perceptual maps can be created for different levels of product competition to explore competitive relations at the level of product types, variants, or brands. For example, Jain and Etgar (1975) have used multidimensional scaling to provide a geometric representation of the beverage market which incorporates all these different levels in the same configuration. These analyses become cumbersome when it is not possible to assume perceptual homogeneity (Day, Deutscher, and Ryans 1976). Then it is necessary to cluster the respondents into homogeneous "points-of-view" groups, based on the commonality in their perceptions, and conduct a separate analysis for each group. Alternatively, one can assume that respondents use the same perceptual dimensions, but differ with respect to the weights they attach to the various dimensions.

In principle, new product concepts can be positioned in the space, or existing brands repositioned or deleted, and the effects on the individual or segment choice behavior predicted. Unfortunately, the relation between interproduct distances in the perceptual space and substitutability is not rigorously established. Stefflre (1972) has argued that a perceptual space contains only labeled regions and hence that gaps may simply represent discontinuities. The question is not whether such discontinuities in fact exist, but rather whether a preference model based upon distances from ideal-points to products remains a reasonable predictor of individual or segment behavior. If so, the decision framework of a common perceptual space coupled with models of individual/segment decision making can be used to assess the relative substitutability of different brands for each segment. These measures can then be aggregated over segments to estimate patterns of competition for the broader market.

B.3. *Technology substitution analysis* adapts the idea of preference related to distance in a multiattribute space to the problem of forecasting the substitution of one material, process, or product for another—aluminum for copper in electrical applications and polyvinyl for glass in liquor bottles, for example. Each successful substitution tends to follow an S-shaped or "logistic" curve representing a slow start as initial problems and resistance to change have to be overcome, followed by more rapid progress as acceptance is gained and applications can be publicized, and finally a slowing in the pace of substitution as saturation is reached.

A simple approach to forecasting the course and speed of the substitution process is to project a function having the appropriate logistics curve, using historical data to determine its parameters (Lenz and Lanford 1972). This curve-fitting method overlooks many potential influences on the process, such as: the age, condition, and rate of obsolescence of the capital equipment used in the old technology; the price elasticity of demand; and the "utility-in-use" or relative performance advantage. Recent efforts to model substitution rates have focused on relative "utility" as the basis for improvements in forecasting ability (Stern, Ayres, and Shapanko 1975). The procedure for assessing "utility-in-use" involves: first, identifying the relevant attributes and performance characteristics of each of the competing products or technologies, followed by ratings by experts of the extent to which each alternative possesses each attribute and the perceived importance of each attribute in each end-use market. Finally, an overall utility for each product in each usage situation is obtained by multiplying the attribute possession score by the importance ratings, summing the resulting products, and adjusting for differences in unit price. While criticism can be made of the model structure and the seeming reliance on measurable physical properties to specify the attributes, the value of the basic approach should not be discounted. The outcome is a highly useful quantitative measure of utility which can be used to estimate substitutability among competing products or technologies in specific usage situations.

B.4. *Customer judgments of substitutability* may be obtained in a variety of ways. The simplest is to ask a sample of customers to indicate the degree of substitutability between possible pairs of brands on a rating scale such as: none, low, some, or substantial substitutability. Beyond this familiar approach, several methods of utilizing customer judgments have recently been developed which provide far greater diagnostic insights into patterns of competition.

1. *The free response approach* (Green, Wind, and Jain 1973). Respondents are presented with various brands and asked to free-associate the names of similar or substitute brands. Two kinds of data are obtained. One is the *frequency* of mention of one brand as a substitute for another, which could be used as a measure of similarity of the two brands in order to establish a perceptual space. Secondly, the *order of mention* of substitute brands can be treated as rank-order data (Wind 1977). These data represent an aggregate judgment across situations, and leave it to the respondent to decide how similar two brands must be before they become substitutes.

A useful variant of the free-response question asks respondents what they would do if they were unable to buy their preferred brand. One advantage of this question is that it can realistically be tailored to specific situations. For example, one study asked scotch drinkers what they would do if scotch were not available in a variety of situations, such as a large cocktail party in the early evening. Evidently, there were some situations where white wine was the preferred alternative.

2. *The dollar metric approach* (Pessemier et al. 1970/71). Respondents first are presented with all possible pairs of brands, each of the brands being marked with their regular prices. In each case, the respondent selects the brand he/she would buy in a forced choice purchase. They are then asked the price to which the preferred brand must rise before they would switch their original preference. Strength of preference is measured in terms of this price increment. Such data must be further "processed" to compute aggregated preference measures.

This procedure is somewhat analogous to a laboratory measurement of cross-elasticity of demand. The set of potentially competitive brands must be again identified in advance. The procedure is reasonably easy to administer and analyze; although the simplicity may be eroded if considerations of intended usage, brand familiarity, and market segmentation are incorporated. It appears that respondents are able to reveal their preferences for different alternatives in the forced-choice situation. Whether they can relate validly how they arrived at the preference—by estimating the minimum price change that would cause a switch—remains an open question (Huber and James 1977).

3. *Direct grouping into product categories*. Bourgeois, Haines, and Sommers (1979) have taken broadly related sets of brands and asked samples of customers to: (1) divide the set into as many groups as they consider meaningful, (2) explain the criteria used for each grouping, and (3) judge the similarity of the brands within each group. A measure of the similarity of brands is created by summing across customers to find the frequency with which pairs of brands are assigned to the same group. These data are analyzed by nonmetric, multidimensional scaling programs to obtain interval-scaled measures of brand similarity (according to their proximity in a reduced space). These are input to a cluster analysis routine to obtain groupings of brands regarded as "customer product types." Products are assigned to one type only. An application of this procedure to the generic "personal care" market yielded intuitively appealing groups of brands. However the data were reported to be quite "noisy," which is not surprising in view of the wide latitude given the respondents. Potentially, respondents could differ both in the frame of reference for the task (the intended application or usage) and the criterion for grouping. Some, for example, might emphasize physical similarity while others might elect appropriateness-in-use or similarity of price as the criterion.

4. *Products-by-uses analysis*. In the procedure developed by Stefflre (1979; Myers and Tauber 1977), a sample of customers is given a list of target products or brands and asked to conjecture as many uses for them as possible. They are then asked to suggest additional products or brands appropriate to these same uses and additional uses appropriate to these new products. This sequence of free response questions generates large lists of products/brands and potential uses. An independent sample is then asked to judge the appropriateness of each product for each use. In one study of proprietary medicines, for example, respondents were asked to judge the acceptability of each of 52 medicines for 52 conditions of use ranging from "when you have a stuffy nose" to "when the children have a fever."

Two assumptions underlie analyses of the products-by-uses matrix: (1) the set of products constitutes a representative sample of the benefits sought by customers and (2) two usage situations are similar if similar benefits are desired in both situations. If these assumptions are valid, then grouping usage situations according to similarity of products judged appropriate should be equivalent to grouping them explicitly by the benefits desired. The net result is a somewhat circular procedure:

Similar Usage Situations = those in which similar product alternatives are judged appropriate	⟳	Competitive Products = those judged appropriate in similar usage situations

The merits of the Stefflre (1972, 1979) procedure are first, that the introduction of specific situations gives respondents frames of reference for their judgments of substitutability or appropriateness and second, that the criteria can be modified to reflect greater concern with *potential* competition (respondents are asked which existing products or descriptions of concepts would be appropriate to specified uses) or with *actual* competition (which products they would consider for purchase in the situation.) This ability to use descriptions of concepts greatly extends the flexibility of the approach to provide data relevant to actual or proposed changes in the product-market. A further advantage, shared with the direct grouping approach, is an ability to cope with large numbers of alternatives if necessary, without a requirement for large numbers of respondents because of a high degree of homogeneity in perceptual judgments.

These advantages are seemingly offset by the evident impracticability of the demands on respondents to complete a matrix with as many as 2,500 cells. For many purposes, however, it is not necessary that each respondent complete the entire matrix. A related problem is the lack of a sound basis for deciding how many situations and at what level of specificity, to include in the matrix.

5. *Substitution-in-use analysis.* This extends the Stefflre procedure in two directions (Srivastava, Shocker, and Day 1977). First, a separate analysis step is introduced to ensure that the set of usage situations is parsimonious and representative. If the latter condition is not met, it is likely there will be too many of one "type" of situation, with consequent distortion in the grouping of products. Secondly, the measure of appropriateness-in-use is modified to measure the degree of suitability. This is feasible as the number of situations the respondents are given is significantly smaller than in the Stefflre procedure. The result is a three-stage procedure:

1. The *exploratory* stage uses free response plus repertory grid and focused group methods to elicit usage situations associated with a generic need.
2. A *typology* of usage situations is then developed from a principal components analysis of the products-by-uses matrix (after a check for perceptual homogeneity). Both uses and products can be plotted in the reduced space described by the first two or three principal components. A typology of uses may be derived from factorial combinations of different levels of the independent dimensions of this space.
3. A new sample is employed to obtain a measure of the suitability or appropriateness of each brand or product for each of the usage situations in the typology. Each alternative can be rated separately, or all alternatives can be ranked, within each situation.

There are several ways to analyze the resulting matrix. Insights into a firm's competitive position within distinct situational submarkets can be obtained from a principal components analysis similar to stage 2 of the procedure described above. Experience with breath fresheners and banking services (Srivastava and Shocker 1979) indicates that ideas for new products or product positions can come from the identification of inadequately served usage situations. A useful test of the effectiveness of a company's positioning efforts is the extent of variability of customer perceptions of the appropriateness of a specific brand for a distinct usage submarket. The analysis can also help assess the possibility of cannibalization. If two or more products or brands of a single manufacturer are seen as appropriate for the same usage submarket, then efforts to promote one may be at the expense of a loss in sales of the other.

The data can also be analyzed with categorical conjoint or similar procedures, as long as the factorial combinations of usage situations are properly balanced. Here the focus would be on both the patterns of competition within a usage situation and the elements of the situation which have the greatest influence on these patterns. Wind (1977) used this approach to study the relative positions of finance companies. Automobile dealers were given 16 different financing situations and asked to assign each to one of five possible financing alternatives. The situations represented combinations of six different factors including customer's credit rating, familiarity with customer, amount to finance, and length of term. The estimated utility functions suggested the degree of appropriateness of each source of financing for each level of the six factors. It was found, for example, that the client (a finance company associated with an automobile dealer) faced quite different competition depending on the amount to be financed.

Many of the advantages of the substi-tution-in-use approach derive from the consistency of the approach with the conceptual definition of a product-market. Despite these potential advantages, the procedure produces only a relative measure of substitutability. Managerial judgment must still decide the level of judged appropriateness that permits each product/brand to be considered as part of a situational submarket.

SUMMARY AND CONCLUSIONS

The questions of how to identify product-market boundaries cannot be separated from the ways results are to be used. Strategic or long-run definitions of market structure inevitably hold more significance even though they are mainly obtainable from customer judgments rather than behavior. Very narrowly defined boundaries appear adequate for short-run, tactical decisions in most product categories. The value of a valid and strategically relevant product-market definition lies in "stretching" the company's perceptions appropriately far enough so that significant threats and opportunities are not missed, but not so far as to dissipate information gathering and analysis efforts on "long shots." This is a difficult balance to achieve given the myriad of present and potential competitors faced by most companies.

The principal conclusions from the analysis of the nature of boundaries and the various empirical methods for identifying competitive product-markets are:

- Boundaries are seldom clear-cut—ultimately, all boundaries are arbitrary,
- The suitability of different empirical methods is strongly influenced by the character of the market environment,
- On balance, those empirical methods which explicitly recognize the variety of usage situations have widest applicability

and yield maximum insights. The concept of usage situation appears to be the most prevalent common denominator of market environments which can be used as the basis for empirical methods,
- Most methods, particularly those based upon behavioral measures are static and have difficulty coping with changes in preferences or additions and deletions of choice alternatives in the market,
- Regardless of method, the most persistent problem is the lack of defensible criteria for recognizing boundaries.

These conclusions add up to a situation where the state of knowledge has not kept abreast of either the present need to understand, or the changing technological, social, and economic factors which are constantly reshaping market environments. To redress this situation, there is a clear need for a strategically oriented program of research in a variety of market situations. Research in each market should be characterized by the use of multiple techniques to seek confirmation through cross validation and longitudinal approaches in which judgmental methods are followed by behavioral methods which can validate inferences. As we have noted, different methods have different strengths and weaknesses, and more needs to be learned about the sensitivity of results to the shortcomings of each method. Also there will inevitably be points of contradition and consistency in the insights gained from boundaries established by different methods. The process of resolution should be most revealing, both in terms of understanding a firm's competitive position and suggesting strategy alternatives.

NOTES

1. Many of the same issues are encountered during efforts to define the relevant product-market for antitrust purposes. Here the question is whether a company so dominates a market that effective competition is precluded, or that a past or prospective merger has lessened competition. The conceptual approach to this question is very similar to the one developed in this paper (Day, Massy, and Shocker 1978). However, because of the adversarial nature of the proceedings and the existence of prior hypotheses of separation to be tested, the treatment of "relevant market" issues is otherwise quite different.
2. This premise was directly tested, and supported, in a study of the variation of judged importance of various fast food restaurant attributes across eating occasions (Miller and Ginter 1979). This study and others also have found that some needs, and benefits sought, are reasonably stable across situations. Thus it is usually productive to segment a market on the basis of both people and occasions (Goldman and McDonald 1979).

REFERENCES

Belk, Russell (1975), "Situational Variables and Consumer Behavior," *Journal of Consumer Research*, 2 (December), 157–164.

Bettman, James R. (1971), "The Structure of Consumer Choice Processes," *Journal of Marketing Research*, 8 (November), 465–471.

Bourgeois, Jacques D., George H. Haines, and Montrose S. Sommers (1979), "Defining an Industry," paper presented to the TIM/ORSA Special Interest Conference on Market Measurement and Analysis, Stanford, CA, March 26.

Butler, Ben Jr. and David H. Butler (1970 and 1971), "Hendrodynamics: Fundamental Laws of Consumer Dynamics," Hendry Corp., Croton-on-Hudson, NY, Chapter 1 (1970) and Chapter 2 (1971).

Cocks, Douglas L. and John R. Virts (1975), "Market Definition and Concentration in the Ethical Pharmaceutical Industry," Internal publication of Eli Lilly and Co., Indianapolis.

Day, George S. (1977), "Diagnosing the Product Portfolio," *Journal of Marketing*, 41 (April), 29–38.

———, Terry Deutscher, and Adrian Ryans (1976), "Data Quality, Level of Aggregation and Nonmetric Multidimensional Scaling Solutions," *Journal of Marketing Research*, 13 (February), 92–97.

———, William F. Massy, and Allan D. Shocker (1978), "The Public Policy Context of the Relevant Market Question," in *Public Policy Issues in Marketing*, John F. Cady, ed., Cambridge, MA: Marketing Science Institute, 51–67.

Frank, Ronald, William F. Massy, and Yoram Wind (1973), *Market Segmentation*, Englewood Cliffs, NJ: Prentice-Hall, Inc.

Goldman, Alfred and Susan S. McDonald (1979), "Occasion Segmentation," paper presented to American Marketing Association Attitude Research Conference, Hilton Head, S.C., February 25–28.

Green, Paul E. (1975), "Marketing Applications of MDS: Assessment and Outlook," *Journal of Marketing*, 39 (January), 24–31.

———, Yoram Wind, and Arun K. Jain (1973), "Analyzing Free Response Data in Marketing Research," *Journal of Marketing Research*, 10 (February), 45–52.

Haines, George H. (1974), "Process Models of Consumer Decision-Making," in *Buyer/Consumer Information Processing*, G. D. Hughes and M. L. Ray, eds., Chapel Hill, NC: University of North Carolina Press.

Hanon, Mack (1974), "Reorganize Your Company around Its Markets," *Harvard Business Review*, 79 (November–December), 63–74.

Huber, Joel and Bill James (1977), "The Monetary Worth of Physical Attributes: A Dollarmetric Approach," in *Moving A Head with Attitude Research*, Yoram Wind and Marshall Greenberg, eds., Chicago: American Marketing Association.

Jain, Arun K. and Michael Etgar (1975), "How to Improve Antitrust Policies with Marketing Research Tools," in *1975 Combined Proceedings of the American Marketing Association*, Edward M. Mazze, ed., Chicago: American Marketing Association, 72–75.

Kalwani, Manohar U. and Donald G. Morrison (1977), "A Parsimonious Description of the Hendry System," *Management Science*, 23 (January), 476–477.

Lenz, Ralph C. Jr. and H. W. Lanford (1972), "The Substitution Phenomena," *Business Horizons*, 15 (February), 63–68.

Luhn, Tony (1972), "Segmenting and Constructing Markets," in *Consumer Market Research Handbook*, R. M. Worcester, ed. Maindenhead, Berkshire: McGraw-Hill.

Lutz, Richard J. and Pradeep Kakkar (1976), "Situational Influence in Interpersonal Persuasion," in *Advances in Consumer Research*, Vol. III, Beverlee B. Anderson, ed., Atlanta: Association for Consumer Research, 370–378.

McFadden, Daniel (1970), "Conditional Logit Analysis of Qualitative Choice Behavior" in *Frontiers in Econometrics*, P. Zarembka, ed., New York: Academic Press, 105–142.

Miller, Kenneth E. and James L. Ginter (1979), "An Investigation of Situational Variation in Brand Choice Behavior and Attitude," *Journal of Marketing Research*, 16 (February), 111–123.

Moran, William R. (1973), "Why New Products Fail," *Journal of Advertising Research*, 13 (April), 5–13.

Myers, James H. and Edward Tauber (1977), *Market Structure Analysis*, Chicago: American Marketing Association.

Needham, Douglas (1969), *Economic Analysis of Industrial Structure*, New York: Holt, Rinehart, and Winston, Chapter 2.

Pessemier, Edgar A. (1977), *Product Management: Strategy and Organization*, Santa Barbara, CA: Wiley/Hamilton, 203–254.

———, Philip Burger, Richard Teach, and Douglas Tigert (1970/71), "Using Laboratory Brand Preference Scales to Predict Consumer Brand Purchases," *Management Science*, 17 (February), 371–385.

Rubison, Joel R. and Frank M. Bass (1978), "A Note on 'A Parsimonious Description of the Hendry System,'" paper 658, West Lafayette, IN: Krannert School, Purdue, March.

Scherer, Frederic (1970), *Industrial Market Structure and Economic Performance*, Chicago: Rand McNally.

Shocker, Allan D. and V. Srinivasan (1979), "MultiAttribute Applications for Product Concept Evaluation and Generation: A Critical Review," *Journal of Marketing Research*, 16 (May), 159–180.

Sissors, Jack Z. (1966), "What is a Market?" *Journal of Marketing*, 30 (July), 17–21.

Srivastava, Rajendra and Allan D. Shocker (1979), "The Validity/Reliability of a Method for Developing Product-Specific Usage Situational Taxonomies," working paper, Pittsburgh: University of Pittsburgh, Graduate School of Business (September).

————,————, and George S. day (1978), "An Exploratory Study of Situational Effects on Product Market Definition," in *Advances in Consumer Research*, Vol. V., H. Keith Hunt, ed., Ann Arbor: Association for Consumer Research, 32–38.

Stefflre, Volney (1972), "Some Applications of Multidimensional Scaling to Social Science Problems," in *Multidimensional Scaling: Theory and Applications in the Behavioral Sciences*, Vol. III, A. K. Romney, R. N. Shepard, and S. B. Nerlove, eds., New York: Seminar Press.

————(1979), "New Products: Organizational and Technical Problems and Opportunities," in *Analytic Approaches to Product and Marketing Planning*, A. D. Shocker, ed., Cambridge, MA: Marketing Science Institute, April Report 79–104, 415–480.

Stern, M. O., R. V. Ayres, and A. Shapanko (1975), "A Model for Forecasting the Substitution of One Technology for Another," *Technological Forecasting and Social Change*, 7 (February), 57–79.

Stout, Roy G., Raymond H. S. Suh, Marshall G. Greenberg, and Joel S. Dubow (1977), "Usage Incidents as a Basis for Segmentation," in *Moving Ahead with Attitude Research*, Yoram Wind and Marshall Greenberg, eds., Chicago: American Marketing Association.

Strotz, Robert H. (1957), "The Empirical Implications of a Utility Tree," *Econometrica*, 25 (April), 269–280.

————, and John R. Hauser (1979), "Market Definition" in *Design and Marketing of New Products and Services*, Cambridge, MA: MIT, Sloan School of Management, Ch. 5.

Vernon, John (1972), *Market Structure and Industrial Performance*, Boston: Allyn and Bacon.

Wind, Yoram (1977), "The Perception of a Firm's Competitive Position," in *Behavioral Models for Market Analysis*, F. M. Nicosia and Y. Wind, eds., New York: The Dryden Press, 163–181.

Toward Strategic Intelligence Systems

David B. Montgomery and Charles B. Weinberg

In the past 10 years, there has been a dramatic increase in the use of strategic planning tools such as BCG's growth/share matrix, AD Little's life cycle strategy, Shell's Directional Policy Matrix, and GE's stoplight strategy matrix. This has resulted from the much-needed perception by management that projecting yesteryear's trends into the future and then concentrating on day-to-day operating decisions is not enough for success. Strategic planning is rapidly being included in the definition of essential managerial tasks, and a tremendous amount of managerial interest has been focused on the techniques outlined above.

While this focus has been and should continue to be of great value, a critical point is often overlooked. *A strategic plan can be no better than the information on which it is based.* There has been little focus on strate-

gic intelligence systems, the selection, gathering, and analysis of information needed for strategic planning. Yet it is obvious that without good market share information, a growth/share matrix will be unreliable, or that knowledge of a competitor's intentions can be the key determinant of a strategy.

This paper is designed first to present an overview of strategic intelligence systems (SIS)—their purpose and the kinds of information they gather. The second section discusses the collection of strategic intelligence. The final section provides a brief discussion of the analysis and processing of strategic intelligence.

Examples are provided describing different companies' approaches to SIS, based on a research project in which, in addition to an extensive literature review, more than 100 executives in over 30 companies were interviewed. Although corporate names need to be disguised, the firms interviewed come from a broad range of industries and in most cases had sales in excess of $100 million. These examples are not intended to add up

David B. Montogmery and Charles B. Weinberg, "Toward Strategic Intelligence Systems," Vol. 43 (Fall 1979). Reprinted from *Journal of Marketing,* published by the American Marketing Association.

to "the" one complete, integrated approach to be copied, but rather are illustrations and stimuli for thought.

STRATEGIC INTELLIGENCE SYSTEMS—AN OVERVIEW

Purposes

It is important that the design of a SIS consider the purposes for which it is intended. Some method is needed to avoid collecting vast quantities of meaningless data, while simultaneously preventing a focus so narrow that crucial information is missed. An understanding of the purposes of a SIS is helpful in achieving this aim.

Defensive intelligence is oriented towards avoiding surprises. A company plans and manages itself on the basis of certain implicit and explicit assumptions about the world. A properly designed SIS should monitor the world to make certain that these assumptions continue to hold and to send up a flag if a major change (usually a threat) occurs. In one company which desired to implement this mode of thinking, a policy was made that unanticipated "surprises" would not be accepted as a reason for not meeting a strategic business unit's (SBU) targets. The view taken was that if an event was potentially so important, the manager should have a SIS watching for it and would therefore be able to prepare contingency plans.

Passive intelligence is designed to provide benchmark data for objective evaluation. An example of this is Dayton-Hudson's gathering of competitive retailer performance in order to reward management performance on a basis relative to competition.

Offensive intelligence is designed to identify opportunities. Often opportunities that would not otherwise be discovered can be identified through a SIS. For example,

one company's strategic intelligence indicated that a major competitor was laying off R&D people of a certain type during a recession. From this, the company knew that the competitor would be unable to respond on a timely basis to a certain class of research-generated product improvements. The company used this knowledge to justify current R&D expenditures which enabled it to capture market position when the competitor was weakest. Another example was when a company's intelligence system indicated that a competitor had a serious service problem. From its own previous experience, the company recognized this as an inventory investment problem and knew that it would take the competitor about two years to straighten out its problems. Armed with this knowledge, the company substantially increased its market share.

Areas of Focus

In order to accomplish the three purposes of defensive, passive, and offensive intelligence, a SIS should focus on the following environments.

Competitive

The competitive environment is of critical importance. However, a firm should not simply monitor its current competitors, but should scan the environment for potential competitors. The price of ignoring potential competitors and neglecting to take proactive steps to avoid or blunt their effect can be extremely high. For example, Scott Paper's preoccupation with acquisitions apparently diverted its attention from the threat posed by Proctor and Gamble's potential and actual emergence as a substantial force in Scott's major paper markets (Hyatt and Coonly 1971).

Customers may also be potential competitors. One company which was heavily dependent upon a large customer analyzed that customer's incentives for backward integration. This analysis, triggered by an explicit requirement for contingency plans, suggested that, from the customer's viewpoint, backward integration was not in the customer's best interest. The next year, when the company's intelligence agents—its salespeople—learned about the customer's plans to integrate backward, the previous analysis was used to dissuade the customer from that course of action.

Technological
The technological environment is crucial not only because of its evolutionary impact on existing products but also because many innovations are introduced from outside a traditional industry—e.g., ball point pens, xerography, instant photography. Cooper and Schendel's (1976) study of 22 companies in seven industries (locomotives, vacuum receiving tubes, fountain pens, safety razors, fossil fuel boilers, propellers, and leather) found the first commercial introduction of an innovation occurred from outside the industry in four out of seven industries. The study further found that the old technologies did not decline immediately, but continued to expand in four out of the seven cases. In fact, it took anywhere from five to 14 years for the dollar volume of the new technology to exceed that of the old technology. The mode of penetration of the new technology tended to be the capturing of a series of submarkets. This study suggests that replacement technologies may emerge and develop even while companies engaged in the old technology are lulled into complacency by near term prosperity. From a strategic perspective, long-run survival requires at least a monitoring of emerging technology. In one company interviewed in our study, the corporate planning staff provides a list of emerging technologies and division managers then are required in their strategic plans to indicate the likely impact of these technologies upon their division. The purpose is not only to sensitize division managers, but the corporation as a whole to coming opportunities and threats.

Customer
Thorough analysis of a firm's customers and noncustomers is possibly the most valuable and most neglected area of strategic intelligence. Customer analysis means more than figuring out how to get Customer X to repeat or expand an order. Good customer and noncustomer analysis should reveal emerging technologies, competitive advantages and disadvantages and new product ideas. Von Hippel's (1977) study of technological innovation in two industries found that in 74% of the 137 innovations studied, the source of the innovation was the supplier's customers. In these two industries, customers provided about three times as many new ideas as the company research departments.

Economic
The economic environment is of overriding importance to a company's future. Issues such as GNP, inflation, the money market, and interest rates are of obvious importance. Changes in the price of raw materials (e.g., oil) significantly affect most companies. It is also important to try to determine the secondary implications of these benchmark indicators. For example, a move towards balancing the federal budget may lower the amount of government-sponsored R&D forthcoming in a particular field. Government responses to continuing inflation, such as price and wage guidelines, should be anticipated and contingency plans prepared.

Examination of the effects of these issues on suppliers is also crucial. For example, many institutional food services on long-term, fixed price contracts have had profits severely hurt due to very sharp increases which their suppliers have imposed on certain products due to worldwide shortages.

Political and Regulatory

The political and regulatory environment is a difficult one as international companies are particularly aware. However, the increasing number of federal and state agencies which seek to impact on corporate policies, often with conflicting objectives, affects virtually all companies. In a recent survey of CEOs of the 1975 Fortune 500, government was cited as the number one area of concern (Burk 1976). Several companies such as Mobil and General Electric have adopted a proactive stance to try to improve the political climate within which private corporations must function (Ross 1976).

The fact that government agencies often do not correctly anticipate either the impact or the response to regulatory actions indicates the opportunity for a broadening of business/government contact. A recent example would be the FTC's de facto voiding (by unacceptable restrictions) the Bic purchase of American Safety Razor from Phillip Morris. The FTC rejected this acquisition on the grounds that it would be anticompetitive. This FTC action has been considered a remote possibility, and was apparently a surprise to the companies involved. Perhaps better intelligence would have identified the FTC as a potential major problem. Extensive advance briefing could have conceivably altered the outcome, or else the effort could have been abandoned before significant amounts of managerial time were expended.

Social

The final environment to be reviewed here relates to the rapidly changing social environment which has led to concerns with such issues as pollution control, conserva-

tion, and the rights of minorities. Again, appropriate intelligence may enable corporations to anticipate and react to such shifts in a more functional manner than has been typical of the past. As a case in point, GE claims that its environmental system led it to anticipate the emerging women's movement which enabled it to produce guidelines for women's employment one year ahead of the government (Wilson 1975). Anticipating social concerns generates a time advantage in which companies can provide positive, helpful input to government policy makers charged with establishing guidelines and regulations.

STRATEGIC INTELLIGENCE SYSTEMS IN THE STRATEGIC INTELLIGENCE CYCLE

Strategic intelligence systems can be seen as being part of the strategic intelligence cycle (see Figure 23–1). As mentioned above, most current work has been concerned with the latter stages of this cycle—processing and analysis, dissemination, and use. A SIS is essentially the feeder process to the analysis and use segments of the strategic intelligence cycle. The SIS performs two crucial functions, directing the intelligence function and collecting the information. This section will focus on these tasks.

Directing the Intelligence Function

This first stage of the intelligence cycle is concerned with establishing parameters for what information is needed, what priorities should be established, and what indicators should be monitored. Since a specific corporate application must account for idiosyncracies in the company's situation and its management style, the discussion in this section will not prescribe a formula, but

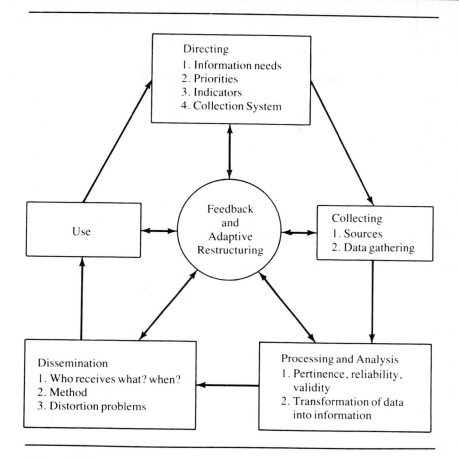

Figure 23–1
The Intelligence Cycle

rather will provide a broad outline of the issues and offer several specific illustrations.

Needs
There has been a substantial and praiseworthy increase in management's desires for environmental information. However, a word of caution is in order. The problem is not to generate data, but to determine what information is relevant and actionable. The emerging tools of strategic planning and analysis—product portfolios, competitive audits, etc.—provide a framework for ascertaining what information is needed and how it might be used if obtained. As the USE portion of the strategic intelligence cycle has become more sophisticated, the need for focused information also has increased.

A potentially useful framework for specifying information needs can be generated from the tripartite military paradigm of (1) areas of influence, (2) immediate zone, and (3) area of interest. The areas of influence would be the product/market segments in which the company is currently engaged. The immediate zone represents areas of competitive activity which are close to, but not directly competitive with, the company's current operations. The area of interest represents areas of potential opportunities or threats in the longer term. Generally there is less need for detail and a longer time horizon as the focus shifts outward from areas of influence.

Many companies fail to utilize available opportunities due to their exclusive concentration on their areas of influence and consequent lack of attention to their immediate zone and areas of interest. As an example of this kind of opportunity, Gillette noted that Bic, which had been a formidable competitor in the disposable lighter market, had pioneered disposable razors in Europe in 1975 (*Business Week* Feb. 28, 1977). When Gillette learned that Bic had introduced the disposable razor in Canada in early 1976, it became clear that a major potential competitor was drawing near to the U.S. market. In response, Gillette rushed its "Good News" disposable razor into production and onto the national market in early 1976. Bic followed with U.S. test markets in mid-1976, but Gilette had apparently already paved the way for its dominance of this market. It is clear that by paying attention to its immediate zone and area of interest, Gillette was able to capitalize on an opportunity it would have lost had it only focused on its domestic markets.

Priorities

A useful conceptual approach to establishing priorities may be stated as follows:

Importance of becoming aware of an event of interest =
1. Importance of event to the organization.
2. Speed with which the event can impact the organization.

3. Speed with which the organization can react to the event.

Intelligence priorities should be established based upon (1) the importance of becoming aware of an event, (2) the likelihood the event will occur, and (3) the costs of anticipation and reaction. A SIS is justified if the costs of reacting to events exceed the costs of anticipating them and responding proactively. We believe that if companies were to carefully make such evaluations and tradeoffs, then far more companies would attend to the development and nurturing of strategic intelligence systems.

Indicators

While a company might like to have some direct measures of a competitor's intentions, such measures are usually lacking. Hence firms must resort to using indicators or surrogate measures. For example, content analysis of corporate annual reports might be used in order to assess the extent to which a competitor's management is proactive or reactive in its approach to the world.

An indicator need not be unambiguous in its potential impact on the company. For example, if a competitor should make an unexpectedly low bid on a contract, this could be an indicator of one or more conditions such as: (1) the competitor's backlog is running dangerously low and he is getting desperate for work, (2) the persons in charge of the bid erred, or (3) the competitor has leap frogged existing technology. The indicator—an unusually low bid—may therefore relate to a variety of true states, each of which has substantially different strategic implications for the company.

Collecting Intelligence

Intelligence collection entails the notion of scanning the environments of a company in search of data which individually or collectively will provide decision relevant inputs to the firm.

Scanning can be subdivided into two subcomponents: surveillance and search. Surveillance is a viewing and monitoring function which does not focus upon a single target or objective, but rather observes multiple aspects of the environment being scanned in an effort to detect relevant changes. In contrast, search implies deliberate investigation and research. The detection of significant events in the environment by surveillance will often trigger a search for further answers. To illustrate, one of the companies interviewed learned, through its conventional competitive surveillance activities (e.g., attending to articles and announcements concerning competitors in the business press), that a major competitor had sold a particular manufacturing operation. Since the company knew from its own operations that this manufacturing activity was the most profitable portion of its own vertically integrated chain of activities, the question arose as to why the competitor had sold this operation. Two potential reasons seemed apparent: (1) the competitor, a closely held company, was in a serious cash bind and was forced to sell this profitable operation in order to improve its financial position or (2) the competitor had made a breakthrough that would render the sold technology either obsolete or at least substantially less valuable. Set against the background of data the company had, both answers seemed plausible. Learning the true answer had important strategic significance. If done for financial reasons, this could signal either competitor vulnerability or a reduction in his vulnerability depending upon the results of a further investigation. On the other hand, if the competitor had made some technological breakthroughs, then the company could no longer assume a stable environment. Clearly, early resolution of these uncertainties was required. This example illustrates how a signal detected by the surveillance function of scanning can lead to questions which require search to answer.

There is some empirical evidence indicating that scanning can be beneficial. In his analysis of a contingency theory of strategy formulation, Miller (1975) concludes that successful firms tend to use more scanning. Or, to view the situation conversely, Schendel, Patten, and Riggs's (1976) study of corporate turn-around strategies in some 54 companies concluded that the original downturn typically resulted from the failure of the firm's scanning or management control procedure to identify more than one or two of the major problems confronting the firm. Thus, there can be both upscale reward and downside risk attached to environmental scanning. These results are consistent with Grinyer and Norburn's (1975) study which found that higher financial performance was positively associated with the use of more informal channels of communication and with the number of items of information used in reaching decisions.

Sources of Intelligence

Legitimate sources of intelligence are in abundant supply for the manager and company willing to apply imagination and effort in structuring a strategic intelligence system. Table 23-1 illustrates primary sources of intelligence along with selected examples of each. While it would be of doubtful value for any given company to pursue all sources on a continuing basis, a company should review a wide range of potential sources before choosing which one to use. The text will highlight some of the sources in Table 23-1 and examples of their use. Hopefully this will suggest the possibilities available to management.

Federal Government. A significant recent development has been the emergence of the

Table 23-1
Sources of Intelligence

Source	Examples	Comment
Government	Freedom of Information Act	1974 amendments have led to accelerating use.
	Government Contract Administration	Examination of competitor's bids and documentation may reveal competitor's technology and indicate his costs and bidding philosophy.
	Patent filings	Belgium and Italy publish patent applications shortly after they are filed. Some companies (e.g., pharmaceutical) patent their mistakes in order to confuse their competitors.
Competitors	Annual reports and 10Ks	FTC and SEC line of business reporting requirements will render this source more useful in the future.
	Speeches and public announcements of competitor's officers	Reveal management philosophy, priorites, and self-evaluation systems.
	Products	Systematic analysis of a competitor's products via back engineering may reveal the competitor's technology and enable the company to monitor changes in the competitor's engineering and assembly operations. Forecasts of a competitor's sales may often be made from observing his serial numbers over time.
	Employment ads	May suggest the technical and marketing directions in which a competitor is headed.
	Consultants	For example, if a competitor has retained Boston Consulting, then portfolio management strategies become more likely.
Suppliers	Banks, advertising agencies, public relations firms, and direct mailers and catalogers, as well as hard goods suppliers	Have a tendency to be more talkative than competitors since the information transmitted may enhance supplier's business. Can be effective sources of information on such items as competitor's equipment installations and on what retail competitors are already carrying certain product lines. Suppliers biases can usually be recognized.
Customers	Purchasing agents	Generally regarded as self serving. Low reliability as a source.
	Customer engineers and corporate officers	Valued sources of intelligence. One company taught its salespersons to perform elementary service for customers in order to get the salespersons past the purchasing agent and on to the more valued sources of intelligence.
Professional Associations and Meetings	Scientific and technical society meetings, management association meetings	Examine competitor's products, research and development, and management approach as revealed in displays, brochures, scientific papers, and speeches.

Table 23-1
Sources of Intelligence (continued)

Source	Examples	Comment
Company Personnel	Executives, sales force, engineers and scientists, purchasing agents	Sensitize them to the need for intelligence and train them to recognize and transmit to the proper organizational location relevant intelligence which comes to their attention.
Other Sources	Consultants, management service companies, and the media	Wide variety of special purpose and syndicated reports available.

federal government as a source of strategic intelligence.[1] While the government has long been a source of commercially relevant information, recent amendments to the Freedom of Information Act (FOIA) have greatly expanded the potential role of the government as an intelligence source. The 1966 FOIA was amended in 1974 in order to give it greater force. The amended Act provides that any person has the right of access to and can obtain copies of any document, file, or other record in the possession of any federal agency or department. To limit noncompliance by delay, the amended FOIA provides that requests must either be granted or denied within 10 working days in most cases. Nine specific discretionary exemptions are provided in the amended Act; exemption 4, which exempts "trade secrets and commercial or financial information obtained from a person and privileged or confidential," is of the greatest interest from the standpoint of corporate FOIA use.

It should be emphasized that the exemptions may be used at the discretion of the agency in question. Further, if the government is to use the exemptions to protect information, it must prove, if challenged, that the requested information is confidential and that its disclosure would result in substantial competitive injury to the company which originally supplied the information or would impair the agency's ability to obtain future information. Recent practice

illustrates reluctance by some agencies to invoke the discretionary exemptions. For example, in response to FOIA requests, the Securities and Exchange Commission plans to release illegal or dubious payments information which had been voluntarily supplied by companies after a promise of confidentiality. Another example of this tendency to release information is the FTC's decision to make material submitted by a defendant publicly available whenever hearings are held on proposed consent degrees in antitrust or consumer protection actions.

In the years since FOIA amendments have taken effect, business has made increasing use of the FOIA as an intelligence source. The experience of Air Cruisers Co. illustrates both the threats and opportunities provided by the amended FOIA. In August 1975, Air Cruisers received Federal Aviation Administration (FAA) approval of its design for a 42-person inflatable life raft for commercial aircraft. As the largest raft ever to gain FAA approval, it constituted a substantial competitive advantage to Air Cruisers. Six months later, Air Cruisers learned that the FAA was about to release an 18-inch high stack of confidential technical documents to a competitor, Switlik Parachute Company, which had made an FOIA request for the documents. The material included results of performance tests and construction designs, which would enable Switlik to shortcut costly design, testing, and certification procedures. While Air Cruisers was able to block the FAA from releasing all of the data, it had to accept the release of some documents. This information helped Switlik design its own large raft with which it defeated Air Cruisers in a contest for an important European contract.

Additional examples abound. Consider the following which provide some notion of the breadth and type of competitive information potentially available from government agencies and departments under FOIA requests:

- A Washington, D.C. lawyer, presumably on behalf of a rival drug company, obtained an FDA inspector's report on conditions in the Midwestern plant of a larger pharmaceutical company. It included such useful trade secrets as a description of proposed new products, manufacturing capabilities, and sterilization procedures at the inspected plant.
- Crown Zellerbach requested all FTC information on the Proctor & Gamble announcement that "New White Cloud bathroom tissue is the softest bathroom tissue on earth. We have been called on to prove this claim by the United States Government and have."
- Westinghouse received from the Department of Commerce 10 reports which had been paid for and submitted by other corporations on how Japanese nontariff barriers hurt sales in Japan.
- Both Honeywell and Burroughs requested details of an $8 million Interior Department contract with Control Data Corporation.

Further evidence of substantial business use of FOIA may be found at the FTC and the FDA. In the nearly eight years between the July 1967 effective date of the original FOIA and the February 1975 effective date for the amendments, the FTC is estimated to have received less than 1,000 FOIA requests with 10% coming from business. Requests reached this same level, in the first 18 months after the amendments took effect, with almost 20% coming from business. To be sure, these figures understate total business use of FOIA because the original source of a request can often be masked by having attorneys and FOIA service companies make the direct request of a government agency. Nevertheless, the above usage data underscore the impact of the 1974 amendments on the functioning of the FOIA.

The agency with one of the largest volumes of FOIA requests and a substantial share from business is the FDA. In 1974, 2,000 FOIA requests were received by the FDA. The volume exploded to 13,052 in 1975, the year in which the amendments took effect, and doubled in 1976 to nearly 22,000. Over 70% of all requests were from industry or FOI service companies. One reason for this rapid growth has been this agency's liberal interpretation of the FOIA.

While a substantial amount of business use has been made of the FOIA, the potential has just begun to be realized. Although corporate attorneys often claim that their managers know about the operation of the Act (usually because the attorneys had circulated a memo about it), field research indicated that only a tiny minority of managers were at all well informed about the Act and its managerial significance. Managers must be made aware of both the opportunities and inherent threats in the FOIA. The opportunities for learning about competitors are amply illustrated in the above examples. On the other hand, it is imperative that managers become aware of just how vulnerable their own confidential data are when in the hands of the government. Companies should plan in advance, as part of any submission of confidential data to the government, for the defense of such data against a FOIA request from a competitor for these data. Not to do so will increasingly expose a company to the prospect of meeting a 10 working day deadline in which it must convince an agency not to release the company's data. So whether for offensive or defensive purposes, companies must learn to live with and utilize for FOIA as a source of strategic intelligence.

The amended FOIA along with the Sunshine Laws which took effect in March 1977 have broader strategic implications than competitive intelligence. Together they have the potential to reduce the uncertainty which plagues business and government relations by more fully opening government decision processes to outside scrutiny. As discussed earlier, this potential is particularly important because the CEOs of Fortune's 500 indicated that government is their most troublesome area.

Competitors. A second major source of strategic intelligence is competitors themselves. Use of strategic planning tools such as one of the variants of product portfolio analysis helps management focus on critical strategy issues. Some of the most important of these issues relate to the incentives and opportunities facing various competitors and their financial and managerial capacities for carrying out alternative strategies. In a very real sense, the introduction of these strategic planning tools has raised a host of questions relating to competitive response and reaction. A variety of intelligence sources are available for addressing such questions. Annual reports and 10Ks may provide considerable insight into the philosophy and management capability of a competitor as well as his financial capabilities and technological and product plans. For example, GE was stimulated to take a careful look at solid state controls on wash-ers and dryers as a result of having seen both Whirlpool and Hitachi mention these devices in their annual reports (Allen 1978). The FTC and SEC requirements for line of business reporting should greatly enrich annual reports and 10Ks as a source of intelligence. Further, a careful perusal of the footnote to a competitor's annual report may reveal, for example, pension obligations which will drastically impact the ability of a competitor to respond flexibly.

The priorities and self-evaluation systems of a competitor may also be revealed by public announcements and speeches as well as in 10Ks and annual reports. Presidents often cannot resist the opportunity to "brag," and in so doing may reveal much about the firm's growth objectives, investment strategy, trade-offs between long-term and short-term results, and product/market policies. The advantage of knowing a competitor's personality was underlined in the field study at one company. This company knew that one of its major competitors tended to be extremely inconsistent in its marketing activities. This knowledge enabled the company to avoid overaction to any one of the competitor's scattered moves.

Much valuable competitive intelligence may be gleaned from scanning a competitor's personnel activities. For example, if technical personnel of a given type are being laid off, this can be indicative of the competitor's intentions and capabilities in that technical area. A company who observes a competitor taking such action may have an excellent opportunity to gain a technical and marketing edge on that competitor, as was discussed earlier. On the other hand, analysis of a competitor's employment ads may tell a great deal about that competitor's future plans. There is some evidence that such an approach may be valuable. In one case, an outside team was assigned to monitor the personnel ads of a company for one month. At the end of the month, the team reported on what they thought was going on. Not only were they accurate in most cases, but they spotted three problems in production and quality control which the firm's own top management didn't even know existed.

Own Personnel.   A company's own personnel can be invaluable sources of intelligence if they have been trained to be receptive to intelligence and if they are encouraged to transmit the intelligence to appropriate organizational locations. Sales call reports which explicitly encourage reporting of intelligence and debriefing reports submitted by scientists and engineers upon return from professional meetings are two of the more common methods used. In many instances, a firm's purchasing agents may play a key role in intelligence acquisition. The key issue in tapping this internal source is to sensitize personnel to the need for intelligence, train them to recognize it, and reward them for transmitting it. In this area, the firm should bear in mind Pasteur's statement that ". . . chance favors the prepared mind."

In summary, most firms have a large number of potential intelligence sources. Some of these are common and widely used, such as trade association data, but others, such as studies of competitor's want ads, may be less so. The proper choice of intelligence sources depends not only upon the data that it provides, but also how it interrelates with other aspects of the company's strategic intelligence system.

ANALYSIS AND PROCESSING OF STRATEGIC INTELLIGENCE

A firm and its managers use a variety of approaches to combine, sort, and process the environmental *data* in order to produce timely and relevant *information* for forming, monitoring, evaluating, and modifying strategy. The strategic data management problem is complicated by the considerable emphasis placed on personal communications by senior managers. For example, Rohlf and Wish (1974) found that managers spend an average of six hours a day in personal or telephone communications. Further, the unstructured nature of many strategic decisions, especially in the problem finding state, increases the difficulty of transforming data into strategic information.

Despite these difficulties, the process of intelligence derivation is a critical one in the formulation of strategies. After data are generated or enter the system, they should be evaluated. The formal evaluation of data, although frequently carried out in military intelligence systems, appears to be rarely done by business.

Evaluation of Data

Evaluation includes determining the pertinence, reliability, and validity (accuracy) of data obtained. Evaluation of pertinence can include pertinence to a number of people in the organization and specifically determines if the data are relevant to the company, if needed immediately, and, if so, by whom.

Reliability is an evaluation of the source or agency by which the data are gathered or transmitted. The principal basis for judging reliability is previous experience with a source. This is particularly relevant for businesses which use such recurrent sources as the sales force, security analysts, and suppliers. Although it would seem that a "track record" of these sources can be built up over time, for example, to identify the biases of salesmen in reporting only certain events or in being overly optimistic, such practices were rarely observed in the field interviews. It should be noted that suppliers recognize that they are being used as a source of data and try to draw a line between "providing something of value, but not too much."

Validity or accuracy means the probable truth of the data itself. Methods for assessing validity include comparison with other data which may be available from other sources, searching for associated indicators, and face validity. For example in a long-term policy study for the Environmental Protection Agency, 16 different futures studies were reviewed in a fixed format as one approach to convergent validity (Elgin, MacMichael, and Schwartz 1975).

Transformation of Data into Information

The six transformation functions—transmission, accumulation, aggregation, analysis, pattern recognition, and mixing—by which data can become information vary considerably in complexity (See Table 23–2). Although the six functions overlap, each has at its core a distinctive transformation. Obviously, the functions do not necessarily occur sequentially and can occur at several levels in an organization.

Transmission

Transmission, conceptually a very simple notion, is the movement of data from one point or person in the organization to another. Transmission can also occur simultaneously with some of the other processing functions. However, data which are received through many corporate entry points are often not communicated to those who can use them most effectively. In consequence, transmission should be at least conceptually considered as a separate function. Companies need to develop methods to facilitate ("force") the transmission of information by providing incentives for the reporting of certain types of information or by providing

ways for a manager to know the information needs of others.

Accumulation

Accumulation is the storage of data in such a way that it can be retrieved by the managers in a company. A substantial data base provides a source from which the organization can learn about itself and its environment. This is particularly true when attempting to resolve unstructured strategic problems, for which information needs are difficult to define beforehand.

The field interviews revealed limited amounts of accumulation of strategic environmental data. Several reasons explain why this accumulation does not take place. First, because the data often originate from the personal sources of a manager, the effort required to record it and enter it into a more formal and permanent system may not seem worthwhile, especially for "soft data." The remedies would seem to be easing the transmission process and increasing the rewards. In one company, the central collector receives data varying from rumors to documented facts by telephone or in person. The central collector then alerts line managers on an individual basis of particularly significant events, publishes a weekly newsletter, prepares special reports, and maintains files on competitors. There are substantial behavioral advantages to this system. The managers do not fill out forms, they input data verbally and are rewarded, in turn, by receiving pertinent information.

Second, information accumulation may not take place because managers do not think the system works well. For instance, computer-based systems often concentrate on the easily quantified factors in formats which reflect the needs of accounting systems rather than those of operating or strategy managers.

Third, managers may have incentives

Table 23-2
Six Transformation Functions

Name	Description	Brief Examples
1. Transmission	1. Moving data from one point to another	1a) Manager in one company who receives information personally or by telephone from line managers and distributes information personally or by weekly newsletter 1b) Highly mechanized interactive computer system to make data base reachable by numerous managers
2. Accumulation	2. Storing data in one place; implies some notion of retrievability	2a) Corporate libraries or computer systems 2b) Not frequently observed in practice, managers tend to keep data in their heads or in individualized data bases ("little black book")
3. Aggregation	3. Many data points brought together into a smaller set which is usually more easily accessed	3a) Use of computer program to reduce thick Nielsen reports to much shorter documents 3b) Page length limitation on planning documents
4. Analysis	4. The analysis, usually formal, of data in order to seek and measure relations	4a) Use of econometric consulting firms to provide forecasts of the economy 4b) Use of Shell's Directional Policy Matrix to locate businesses for a portfolio analysis
5. Mix	5. Passing of data around to a variety of managers looking for possible links. The data is often not well ordered	5a) CEO insists on plans which show multiple inputs at each phase 5b) Open planning meetings in which managers must give and defend plans before colleagues
6. Pattern Recognition	6. A more informal, less analytic process than analysis (4) in which patterns or relations are sought. Can be a result of the other five functions described	6a) Combining plant closing, financial and product change information to recognize a competitor is short of cash 6b) Special purpose competitor studies & role playing or the use of adversary teams

for not wanting others to have their full data set. In a corporate budgeting system, a manager may be able to present plans which maximize his or her capital allocation or limit his or her performance goals based on his or her unique knowledge of the data.

One consumer durables manufacturer has a particularly interesting central collection system based on a substantial disaggregated data base which includes such factors as factory shipments, survey data on consumer habits, and construction reports. The system is unique because rather than distribution of a large number of reports (as had been done in the past), the main way to use it is for managers to visit the central facility, which is located in the marketing department. The location was chosen to provide user access and the overall style is casual and user oriented to create an environment "painless and pleasant for the harried marketing executive" (from a company brochure).

Aggregation

Aggregation is the function in which many data points are collapsed into a smaller set of pertinent information. It is the first of the functions in which something is done to the data beyond making it available to managers. Summarization of environmental data occurs in virtually all companies, although with various degrees of care and attention. Given the massive amounts of data potentially available and a manager's limited time for reviewing information, aggregation is a vital function.

Corporate staff groups are often responsible for the summarization of economic trends. In a relatively smaller number of companies, social, political, and regulatory factors are summarized as well. Thus, on a macro or corporate level, summarization or aggregation of data takes place. However, only limited aggregation of environmental data, especially competitive data, was observed on a SBU or product-market basis except as part of the annual planning process or, in a few cases, when special purpose competitive assessment reports were made.

Analysis

The analysis of data is a formal process which attempts to find and measure relations among variables. Although at times it may draw heavily on mathematics and numeric procedures, it is a logical and not a mathematical process. A number of companies employ econometric consulting firms and others do similar work on their own. Many consumer goods companies employ analytical approaches to measure relationships between sales and marketing mix variables. In several companies, the main focus of analysis is on predicting industry capacity.

The level of analysis of environmental data varies extensively across companies. For example, in some companies, competitive balance sheets are used primarily as a benchmark or "scoreboard" to rate the company as compared to its competition. In others, it is used more aggressively to anticipate threats or provide opportunities. As an illustration, when one company noticed that a competitor was highly leveraged and consequently would be unable to finance new product development, it gained considerable market share by improving its own product.

Pattern Recognition

Pattern recognition, although not as structured or formal as the analysis process just discussed, also attempts to find patterns or relations among variables. Human abilities to perceive and determine patterns among disparate sets of information and data are the critical distinctive elements in the process of pattern recognition. Although computerized systems can be of great assistance, in strategic analysis the "lack of simple alpha-numeric indicators, combined with enormous textural complexity, suggests that [pattern recognition] . . . will not be trivial or automatic in the foreseeable future" (Webb 1969, p. 10). An example of pattern recognition occurred in one company when the information that a competitor was closing a plant and changing his product line was combined with balance sheet analysis to realize that the competitor was short of cash. This, of course, left the competitor vulnerable to a number of aggressive strategies. The generation and use of indepth competitive assessment reports, the preparation of strategy documents from the viewpoint of a major competitor, and the formation of inhouse competitor teams exemplify different organizational approaches to pattern recognition.

Mixing

The unstructured and often unstable nature of strategic problems requires that an additional transformation function be defined which brings together the apparently unrelated data spread throughout an organization in order to identify linkages. This function is termed "mixing."

A somewhat analogous notion is Cohen, March, and Olsen's (1972) garbage can model. In that conceptualization, an organization is conceived of as a collection of problems and solutions in which organizational members find ways either to enrich the collection of problems and solutions or to find links between the problems and solutions. The approach formulated here emphasizes two major factors. First, problems and solutions are viewed as being dynamic so that "windows" as to when linkages can be established are limited. Thus, problems and opportunities should be viewed as moving through a container rather than residing in a collection. Second, an active approach can be taken to ensure that problems and solutions are actively interchanged or mixed within an organization.

Companies appear to use a variety of techniques to force mixing including participative planning meetings across divisions and organizational levels, weekly senior executive sessions with invited presentations, and rejection of plans which do not reflect mixing. For example, in one company, the CEO rejected divisional plans out of hand because they did not show any evidence of interaction across divisions. In another, marketing managers were asked to write the finance plan, financial managers were asked to write the production plan, etc. In large companies, facing a broad variety of strategic options, mixing can help the company to become aware of the range of opportunities and threats facing it and to develop synergistic responses.

SUMMARY AND PERSPECTIVES

As more organizations implement strategic planning and management activities, there will be an increasing need for strategic intelligence systems which can help managers to learn about the important environments with which their organization interrelates and to become aware of threats and opportunities that are posed.

The construction of viable strategic intelligence systems is exceedingly complex because of the unstructured nature of strategic decisions, the difficulty of separating out important and relevant information from the vast amounts of data accessible to the manager, and the reliance of managers on personal information sources. As would be expected, in most of the companies interviewed tactical information systems were better articulated than strategic ones. On the other hand, a number of companies have developed effective means of learning about their environments and, most importantly, have implemented strategic decision systems which allow them to capitalize on opportunities and to defend themselves against threats. This article has developed a framework for examining intelligence systems which is sensitive to the character of the strategic process.

For a strategic intelligence system to be useful, a company must have a real commitment to strategic planning. Otherwise, the planning process, if carried out at all, becomes only an exercise and managers appear to place limited effort towards gathering and communicating accurate, relevant intelligence. There are a number of different organizational policies which can be utilized to promote the transformation of data into information and the utilization of this information. Elaboration on this issue is beyond the scope of this article. However, only in rare circumstances do effective intelligence systems emerge without organizational incentives to encourage their operation.

There appear to be a number of asymmetries in managers' perceptions about information collection. Four, in particular, stand out. (1) Companies tend to believe that their competitors nearly always detect and rapidly decide how to respond to company actions such as a price change. This perception persists in spite of knowledge of substantial delays in their own detection and response decision time in reacting to the competitors. This can lead a company to rescind prematurely an effort to lead a price increase based upon a belief competitors won't follow, when in fact the lack of response by the competitor may merely be symptomatic of a poor and slow intelligence system. (2) The government is viewed as an extensive collector of information, but not as a source; the discussion of the FOIA indicated how companies could access data held by the government. (3) Conversely, to the case of the government, suppliers are more often viewed as a source of information about competitors than as a source to the competitors. (4) Companies send engineers and managers to meeting with instructions to gather more information than they reveal; it would seem unlikely for this outcome to occur for all companies involved. These asymmetries, which obviously are not shared by all managers, suggest some of the potential available from a review of an organization's procedures to gather and process strategic data.

Information systems are a means to an end—decision making which leads to more profitable results. The concepts and structures for strategic intelligence systems discussed in this article are designed to help organizations make more profitable strategic decisions.

NOTE

1. The following discussion of the Freedom of Information Act is based on Montgomery, Peters, and Weinberg (1978).

REFERENCES

Allen, Michael G. (1978), "Strategic Planning with a Competitive Focus," *The McKinsey Quarterly* (Autumn), 2–13.

Burk, Charles G. (1976), "A Group Profile of the Fortune 500 Chief Executives," *Fortune*, 19 (May), 173.

Business Week (1977), "Gillette: after the Diversification that Failed," (February 28), 58.

Cohen, Michael D., James G. March, and Johan P. Olsen (1972), "A Garbage Can Model of Organizational Choice," *Administrative Science Quarterly* (March), 1.

Cooper, A. C. and D. Schendel (1976), "Strategic Responses to Technological Threats," *Business Horizons*, 19 (February), 61.

Elgin, D. S., D. C. MacMichael, and P. Schwartz (1975), "Alternative Futures for Environmental Policy Planning: 1975–2000," Environmental Protection Agency (October).

Grinyer, P. H. and D. Norburn (1975), "Planning for Existing Markets: Perceptions of Executives and Financial Performance," *Journal of the Royal Statistical Society A*, 138 (Part 1), 70.

Hyatt, J. and J. Coonly (1971), "How Proctor & Gamble Put the Big Squeeze on Scott Paper Company," *The Wall Street Journal* (October 20), 1.

Miller, D. (1975), "Toward a Contingency Theory of Strategy Formulation," paper presented at 35th annual Academy of Management Meeting (August).

Montgomery, David B., Anne H. Peters, and Charles B. Weinberg (1978), "The Freedom of Information Act: Strategic Opportunities and Threats," *Sloan Management Review*, 19 (Winter), 1–13.

Rohlf, J. and M. Wish (1974), "Analysis of Demand for Video Communication," Telecommunication Policy Research Conference, Airlie, Virginia (April 18).

Ross, I. (1976), "Public Relations Isn't Kid Gloves Stuff at Mobil," *Fortune*, 93 (September), 106.

Schendel, D. E., G. R. Patten, and J. Riggs (1976), "Corporate Turnaround Strategies: A Study of Profit, Decline, and Recovery," *Journal of General Management*, 3 (Spring), 3.

von Hippel, E. (1977), "Has a Customer Already Developed Your Next Product?" *Sloan Management Review*, 18 (Winter), 63.

Webb, Eugene J. (1969), "Individual and Organizational Forces Influencing the Interpretation of Indicators," unpublished working paper, Stanford: Graduate School of Business, Stanford University (April), 10.

Wilson, I. (1975), "Does GE Really Plan Better," *MBA*, 9 (November), 42.

The Marketing Program

After buying behavior has been analyzed and basic strategy formulated, the marketing manager must operationalize that strategy by combining many different elements of marketing decision-making. In marketing parlance, the elements are combined into a marketing program. Part Four begins with Borden's seminal statement of the combination of elements to form "the marketing mix." The remaining papers in this part focus on classic expositions of the elements.

The product life cycle (PLC) is one of the discipline's key managerial frameworks. Smallwood reviews the PLC and shows how it relates to other mix elements. The Booz, Allen and Hamilton report is a systematic review of factors influencing new product development during the 1980s. Berry's paper contends that too much of marketers' thinking about products is restricted to tangible goods; he calls for a broader conception of the nature of benefits available to customers, emphasizing the intangible nature of many such benefits.

The distribution area is represented by two classic papers. Bucklin connects retail institutions to the types of goods that they market; his paper thus not only addresses distribution but also reviews the standard convenience/shopping/speciality good taxonomy first introduced to the discipline in 1923 by Melvin Copeland. The second distribution paper is the masterful synthesis by Stern and Reve of the concept of the channel of distribution (an idea unique to marketing thinking) and the vast literature on the sociopolitical environment of marketing.

Pricing is an area of considerable significance to marketing decision-making. Most of the literature here is derived from price theory in economics, an area that assumes certainty of knowledge. Oxenfeldt provides a classic decision-making structure for managers involved in pricing decision. Tellis's more recent paper integrates the many factors involved in pricing decisions.

The area of promotion in marketing is broad and diverse. Two papers explore aspects of promotion. Lavidge and Steiner present the definitive statement of the "hierarchy of effects"—the thinking stages through which a buyer must pass—and associated advertising objectives. Ryans and Weinberg do a masterful job of synthetizing knowledge in sales force management.

The Concept of the Marketing Mix

Neil H. Borden

I have always found it interesting to observe how an apt or colorful term may catch on, gain wide usage, and help to further understanding of a concept that has already been expressed in less appealing and communicative terms. Such has been true of the phrase "marketing mix," which I began to use in my teaching and writing some 15 years ago. In a relatively short time it has come to have wide usage. This note tells of the evolution of the marketing mix concept.

The phrase was suggested to me by a paragraph in a research bulletin on the management of marketing costs, written by my associate, Professor James Culliton.[1] In this study of manufacturers' marketing costs he described the business executive as a

> "decider," and "artist"— a "mixer of ingredients," who sometimes follows a recipe as he goes along, sometimes adapts a recipe to the

ingredients immediately available, and sometimes experiments with or invents ingredients no one else has tried.

I liked his idea of calling a marketing executive a "mixer of ingredients," one who is constantly engaged in fashioning creatively a mix of marketing procedures and policies in his efforts to produce a profitable enterprise.

For many years previous to Culliton's cost study the wide variations in the procedures and policies employed by managements of manufacturing firms in their marketing programs and the correspondingly wide variation in the costs of these marketing functions, which Culliton aptly ascribed to the varied "mixing of ingredients," had become increasingly evident as we had gathered marketing cases at the Harvard Business School. The marked differences in the patterns or formulae of the marketing programs not only were evident through facts disclosed in case histories, but also were reflected clearly in the figures of a cost study

Reprinted from *Journal of Advertising Research*, © Advertising Research Foundation, Inc. (June, 1964), pp. 2–7.

of food manufacturers made by the Harvard Bureau of Business Research in 1929. The primary objective of this study was to determine common figures of expenses for various marketing functions among food manufacturing companies, similar to the common cost figures which had been determined in previous years for various kinds of retail and wholesale businesses. In this manufacturer's study we were unable, however, with the data gathered to determine common expense figures that had much significance as standards by which to guide management, such as had been possible in the studies of retail and wholesale trades, where the methods of operation tended toward uniformity. Instead, among food manufacturers the ratios of sales devoted to the various functions of marketing such as advertising, personal selling, packaging, and so on, were found to be widely divergent, no matter how we grouped our respondents. Each respondent gave data that tended to uniqueness.

Culliton's study of marketing costs in 1947–48 was a second effort to find out, among other objectives, whether a bigger sample and a more careful classification of companies would produce evidence of operating uniformities that would give helpful common expense figures. But the result was the same as in our early study: there was wide diversity in cost ratios among any classifications of firms which were set up, and no common figures were found that had much value. This was true whether companies were grouped according to similarity in product lines, amount of sales, territorial extent of operations, or other bases of classification.

Relatively early in my study of advertising, it had become evident that understanding of advertising usage by manufacturers in any case had to come from an analysis of advertising's place as one element in the total marketing program of the firm. I came to realize that it is essential always to ask: what overall marketing strategy has been or might be employed to bring about a profitable operation in light of the circumstances faced by the management? What combination of marketing procedures and policies has been or might be adopted to bring about desired behavior of trade and consumers at costs that will permit a profit? Specifically, how can advertising, personal selling, pricing, packaging, channels, warehousing, and the other elements of a marketing program be manipulated and fitted together in a way that will give a profitable operation? In short, I saw that every advertising management case called for a consideration of the strategy to be adopted for the total marketing program, with advertising recognized as only one element whose form and extent depended on its careful adjustment to the other parts of the program.

The soundness of this viewpoint was supported by case histories throughout my volume, *The Economic Effects of Advertising*.[2] In the chapters devoted to the utilization of advertising by business, I had pointed out the innumerable combinations of marketing methods and policies that might be adopted by a manager in arriving at a marketing plan. For instance, in the area of branding, he might elect to adopt an individualized brand or a family brand. Or he might decide to sell his product unbranded or under private label. Any decision in the area of brand policy in turn has immediate implications that bear on his selection of channels of distribution, sales force methods, packaging, promotional procedure, and advertising. Throughout the volume the case materials cited show that the way in which any marketing function is designed and the burden placed upon the function are determined largely by the overall marketing strategy adopted by managements to meet the market conditions under which they operate. The forces met by different firms vary widely. Accordingly, the programs fashioned differ widely.

Regarding advertising, which was the function under forces in the economic effects volume, I said at one point:

> In all the above illustrative situations it should be recognized that advertising is not an operating method to be considered as something apart, as something whose profit value is to be judged alone. An able management does not ask, "Shall we use or not use advertising," without consideration of the product and of other management procedures to be employed. Rather the question is always one of finding a management formula giving advertising its due place in the combination of manufacturing methods, product form, pricing, promotion and selling methods, and distribution methods. As previously pointed out different formulae, i.e., different combinations of methods, may be profitably employed by competing manufacturers.

From the above it can be seen why Culliton's description of a marketing manager as a "mixer of ingredients" immediately appealed to me as an apt and easily understandable phrase, far better than my previous references to the marketing man as an empiricist seeking in any situation to devise a profitable "pattern" or "formula" of marketing operations from among the many procedures and policies that were open to him. If he was a "mixer of ingredients," what he designed was a "marketing mix."

It was logical to proceed from a realization of the existence of a variety of "marketing mixes" to the development of a concept that would comprehend not only this variety, but also the market forces that cause management to produce a variety of mixes. It is the problems raised by these forces that lead marketing managers to exercise their wits in devising mixes or programs which they hope will give a profitable business operation.

To portray this broadened concept in a visual presentation requires merely:

1. A list of the important elements or ingredients that make up marketing programs.
2. A list of the forces that bear on the marketing operation of a firm and to which the marketing manager must adjust in his search for a mix or program that can be successful.

The list of elements of the marketing mix in such a visual presentation can be long or short, depending on how far one wishes to go in his classification and sub-classification of the marketing procedures and policies with which marketing managements deal when devising marketing programs. The list of elements which I have employed in my teaching consulting work covers the principal areas of marketing activities which call for management decisions as revealed by case histories. I realize others might build a different list. Mine is as follows:

Elements of the Marketing Mix of Manufacturers

1. *Product Planning*—policies and procedures relating to:
   a. Product lines to be offered—qualities, design, etc.
   b. Markets to sell—whom, where, when, and in what quantity.
   c. New product policy—research and development program.
2. *Pricing*—policies and procedures relating to:
   a. Price level to adopt.
   b. Specific prices to adopt—odd-even, etc.

c. Price policy—one price or varying price, price maintenance, use of list prices, etc.

d. Margins to adopt—for company, for the trade.

3. *Branding*—policies and procedures relating to:

   a. Selection of trade marks.

   b. Brand policy—individualized or family brand.

   c. Sale under private label or unbranded.

4. *Channels of Distribution*—policies and procedures relating to:

   a. Channels to use between plant and consumer.

   b. Degree of selectivity among wholesalers and retailers.

   c. Efforts to gain cooperation of the trade.

5. *Personal Selling*—policies and procedures relating to:

   a. Burden to be placed on personal selling and the methods to be employed in:

      1. Manufacturer's organization.

      2. Wholesale segment of the trade.

      3. Retail segment of the trade.

6. *Advertising*—policies and procedures relating to:

   a. Amount to spend—i.e., the burden to be placed on advertising.

   b. Copy platform to adopt:

      1. Product image desired.

      2. Corporate image desired.

   c. Mix of advertising—to the trade, through the trade, to consumers.

7. *Promotions*—policies and procedures relating to:

   a. Burden to place on special selling plans or devices directed at or through the trade.

   b. Form of these devices for consumer promotions, for trade promotions.

8. *Packaging*—policies and procedures relating to:

   a. Formulation of package and label.

9. *Display*—policies and procedures relating to:

   a. Burden to be put on display to help effect sale.

   b. Methods to adopt to secure display.

10. *Servicing*—policies and procedures relating to:

    a. Providing service needed.

11. *Physical Handling*—policies and procedures relating to:

    a. Warehousing.

    b. Transportation.

    c. Inventories.

12. *Fact Finding and Analysis*—policies and procedures relating to:

    a. Securing, analysis, and the use of facts in marketing operations.

Also, if one were to make a list of all the forces which managements weigh at one time or another when formulating their marketing mixes, it would be very long indeed, for the behavior of individuals and groups in all spheres of life has a bearing, first, on what goods and services are produced and consumed, and second, on the procedures that may be employed in bringing about exchange of these goods and services. However, the important forces which bear on marketers, all arising from the behavior of individuals or groups, may readily be listed under four heads, namely, the behavior of consumers, the trade, competitors, and government.

The next outline contains these four behavior forces with notations of some of the important behavioral determinants within each force. These must be studied and understood by the marketer, if his marketing mix is to be successful. The great quest of marketing management is to understand the behavior of humans in response to the stimuli to which they are subjected. The skillful marketer is one who is a perceptive and practical psychologist and sociologist, who has keen insight into individual and group behavior, who can foresee changes in behavior that develop in a dynamic world, who has creative ability for building well-knit programs because he has the capacity to visualize the probable response of consumers, trade, and competitors to his moves. His skill in forecasting response to his marketing moves should well be supplemented by a further skill in devising and using tests and measurements to check consumer or trade response to his program or parts thereof, for no marketer has so much prescience that he can proceed without empirical check.

Here, then, is the suggested outline of forces which govern the mixing of marketing elements. This list and that of the elements taken together provide a visual presentation of the concept of the marketing mix.

Market Forces Bearing on the Marketing Mix

1. *Consumers' Buying Behavior*—as determined by their:
   a. Motivation in purchasing.
   b. Buying habits.
   c. Living habits.
   d. Environment (present and future, as revealed by trends, for environment influences consumers' attitudes toward products and their use of them).
   e. Buying power.
   f. Number (i.e., how many).
2. *The Trade's Behavior*—wholesalers' and retailers' behavior, as influenced by:
   a. Their motivations.
   b. Their structure, practices, and attitudes.

   c. Trends in structure and procedures that portend change.
3. *Competitors' Position and Behavior*—as influenced by:
   a. Industry structure and the firm's relation thereto.
      1. Size and strength of competitors.
      2. Number of competitors and degree of industry concentration.
      3. Indirect competition—i.e., from other products.
   b. Relation of supply to demand—over-supply or undersupply.
   c. Product choices offered consumers by the industry—i.e., quality, price, service.
   d. Degree to which competitors compete on price vs. nonprice bases.
   e. Competitors' motivations and attitudes—their likely response to the actions of other firms.
   f. Trends technological and social, portending change in supply and demand.
4. *Government Behavior*—controls over marketing:
   a. Regulations over products.
   b. Regulations over pricing.
   c. Regulations over competitive practices.
   d. Regulations over advertising and promotion.

When building a marketing program to fit the needs of his firm, the marketing manager has to weigh the behavioral forces and then juggle marketing elements in his mix with a keen eye on the resources with which he has to work. His firm is but one small organism in a large universe of complex forces. His firm is only a part of an industry that is competing with many other industries. What does the firm have in terms of money, product line, organization, and reputation with which to work? The manager must devise a mix of procedures that fit these resources. If his firm is small, he must judge the response of consumers, trade, and competition in light of his position and resources and the influence that he can exert in the market. He must look for special opportunities in product or method of operation. The small firm cannot employ the procedures of the big firm. Though he may sell the same kind of product as the big firm, his marketing strategy is likely to be widely different in many respects. Innumerable instances of this fact might be cited. For example, in the industrial goods field, small firms often seek to build sales on a limited and highly specialized line, whereas industry leaders seek patronage for full lines. Small firms often elect to go in for regional sales rather than attempt the national distribution practiced by larger companies. Again, the company of limited resources often elects to limit its production and sales to products whose potential is too small to attract the big fellows. Still again, companies with small resources in the cosmetic field not infrequently have set up introductory marketing programs employing aggressive personal selling and a "push" strategy with distribution limited to leading department stores. Their initially small advertising funds have been directed through these selected retail outlets, with the offering of the products and their story told over the signatures of the stores. The strategy has been to borrow kudos for their products from the leading stores' reputations and to gain a gradual radiation of distribution to smaller stores in all types of channels, such as often comes from the trade's follow-the-leader behavior. Only after resources have grown from mounting sales has a dense retail distribution been aggressively sought and a shift made to place the selling burden more and more on company-signed advertising.

The above strategy was employed for Toni products and Stoppette deodorant in their early marketing stages when the resources of their producers were limited (cf. case of Jules Montenier, Inc. in Borden and Marshall).[3] In contrast, cosmetic manufacturers with large resources have generally followed a "pull" strategy for the introduction of new products, relying on heavy campaigns of advertising in a rapid succession of area introductions to induce a hoped-for, complete retail coverage from the start (cf. case of Bristol-Myers Company in Borden and Marshall).[4] These introductory campaigns have been undertaken only after careful programs of product development and test marketing have given assurance that product and selling plans had high promise of success.

Many additional instances of the varying strategy employed by small versus large enterprises might be cited. But those given serve to illustrate the point that managements must fashion their mixes to fit their resources. Their objectives must be realistic.

LONG VS. SHORT TERM ASPECTS OF MARKETING MIX

The marketing mix of a firm in a large part is the product of the evolution that comes from day-to-day marketing. At any time the mix represents the program that a management has evolved to meet the problems with which it is constantly faced in an ever-changing, ever-challenging market. There are continuous tactical maneuvers: a new product, aggressive promotion, or price-change initiated by a competitor must be considered and met; the failure of the trade to provide adequate market coverage or display must be remedied; a faltering sales force must be reorganized and stimulated; a decline in sales share must be diagnosed and remedied; an advertising approach that has lost effectiveness must be replaced; a general business decline must be countered. All such problems call for a management's maintaining effective channels of information relative to its own operations and to the day-to-day behavior of consumers, competitors, and the trade. Thus, we may observe that short-range forces play a large part in the fashioning of the mix to be used at any time and in determining the allocation of expenditures among the various functional accounts of the operating statement.

But the overall strategy employed in a marketing mix is the product of longer-range plans and procedures dictated in part by past empiricism and in part, if the management is a good one, by management foresight as to what needs to be done to keep the firm successful in a changing world. As the world has become more and more dynamic, blessed is that corporation which has managers who have foresight, who can study trends of all kinds—natural, economic, social, and technological—and, guided by these, devise long-range plans that give promise of keeping their corporations afloat and successful in the turbulent sea of market change. Accordingly, when we think of the marketing mix, we need to give particular heed today to devising a mix based on long-range planning that promises to fit the world of five or ten or more years hence. Provision for effective long-range planning in corporate organization and procedure has become more and more recognized as the earmark of good management in a world that has become increasingly subject to rapid change.

To cite an instance among American marketing organizations which have shown foresight in adjusting the marketing mix to meet social and economic change, I look upon Sears Roebuck and Company as an outstanding example. After building an unusually successful mail order business to meet the needs of a rural America, Sears management foresaw the need to depart from its marketing pattern as a mail order company catering primarily to farmers. The trend from a rural to an urban United States was going on apace. The automobile and good roads promised to make town and city stores increasingly available to those who continued to be farmers. Relatively early, Sears launched a chain of stores across the land, each easily accessible by highway to both farmer and city resident, and with adequate parking space for customers. In time there followed the remarkable telephone and mail order plan directed at urban residents to make buying easy for Americans when congested city streets and highways made shopping increasingly distasteful. Similarly, in the areas of planning products which would meet the desires of consumers in a fast-changing world, of shaping its servicing to meet the needs of a wide variety of mechanical products, of pricing procedures to meet the challenging competition that came with the advent of discount retailers, the Sears organization has shown a foresight, adaptability, and creative ability worthy of emulation. The amazing growth and profitability of the company attest to the foresight and skill of its managements. Its history shows the wisdom of careful attention to market forces and their impending change in devising marketing mixes that may assure growth.

USE OF THE MARKETING MIX CONCEPT

Like many concepts, the marketing mix concept seems relatively simple, once it has been expressed. I know that before they were ever tagged with the nomenclature of "concept," the ideas involved were widely understood among marketers as a result of the growing knowledge about marketing and marketing procedures that came during the preceding half century. But I have found for myself that once the ideas were reduced to a formal statement with an accompanying visual presentation, the concept of the mix has proved a helpful advice in teaching, in business problem solving, and, generally, as an aid to thinking about marketing. First of all, it is helpful in giving an answer to the question often raised as to "what is marketing?" A chart which shows the elements of the mix and the forces that bear on the mix helps to bring understanding of what marketing is. It helps to explain why in our dynamic world the thinking of management in all functional areas must be oriented to the market.

In recent years I have kept an abbreviated chart showing the elements and the forces of the marketing mix in front of my classes at all times. In case discussion it has proved a handy device by which to raise queries as to whether the student has recognized the implications of any recommendation he might have made in the areas of the several elements of the mix. Or, referring to the forces, we can question whether all the pertinent market forces have been given due consideration. Continual reference to the mix chart leads me to feel that the students' understanding of "what marketing is" is strengthened. The constant presence and use of the chart leaves a deeper understanding that marketing is the devising of programs that successfully meet the forces of the market.

In problem solving the marketing mix chart is a constant reminder of:

1. The fact that a problem seemingly lying in one segment of the mix must be deliberated with constant thought regarding the effect of any change in that sector on the other areas of marketing operations. The necessity of integration in marketing thinking is ever present.
2. The need of careful study of the market

forces as they might bear on problems in hand.

In short, the mix chart provides an ever-ready checklist as to areas into which to guide thinking when considering marketing questions or dealing with marketing problems.

MARKETING: SCIENCE OR ART?

The quest for a "science of marketing" is hard upon us. If science is in part a systematic formulation and arrangement of facts in a way to help understanding, then the concept of the marketing mix may possibly be considered a small contribution in the search for a science of marketing. If we think of a marketing science as involving the observation and classification of facts and the establishment of verifiable laws that can be used by the marketer as a guide to action with assurance that predicted results will ensue, then we cannot be said to have gotten far toward establishing a science. The concept of the mix lays out the areas in which facts should be assembled, these to serve as a guide to management judgment in building marketing mixes. In the last few decades American marketers have made substantial progress in adopting the scientific method in assembling facts. They have sharpened the tools of fact finding—both those arising within the business and those external to it. Aided by these facts and by the skills developed through careful observation and experience, marketers are better fitted to practice the art of designing marketing mixes than would be the case had not the techniques of gathering facts been advanced as they have been in recent decades. Moreover, marketers have made progress in the use of the scientific method in designing tests whereby the results from mixes or parts of mixes can be measured. Thereby marketers have been learning how to subject the hypotheses of their mix artists to empirical check.

With continued improvement in the search for and the recording of facts pertinent to marketing, with further application of the controlled experiment, and with an extension and careful recording of case histories, we may hope for a gradual formulation of clearly defined and helpful marketing laws. Until then, and even then, marketing and the building of marketing mixes will largely lie in the realm of art.

NOTES

1. James W. Culliton, *The Management of Marketing Costs* (Boston: Division of Research, Graduate School of Business Administration, Harvard University, 1948).
2. Neil H. Borden, *The Economic Effects of Advertising* (Homewood, Illinois: Richard D. Irwin, 1942).
3. Neil H. Borden and M. V. Marshall, *Advertising Management: Text and Cases* (Homewood, Illinois: Richard D. Irwin, 1959), pp. 498–518.
4. *Ibid.*, pp. 518–33.

The Product Life Cycle: A Key to Strategic Marketing Planning

John E. Smallwood

Modern marketing management today increasingly is being supported by marketing information services of growing sophistication and improving accuracy. Yet the task remains for the marketing manager to translate information into insights, insights into ideas, ideas into plans, and plans into reality and satisfactory programs and profits. Among marketing managers there is a growing realization of the need for concepts, perspectives, and for constructs that are useful in translating information into profits. While information flow can be mechanized and the screening of ideas routinized, no alternative to managerial creativity has yet been found to generate valuable marketing ideas upon which whole marketing programs can be based. The concept of the product life cycle has been extremely useful in focusing this creative process.

The product life cycle concept in many ways may be considered to be the marketing equivalent of the periodic table of the elements concept in the physical sciences; like the periodic table, it provides a framework for grouping products into families for easier predictions of reactions to various stimuli. With chemicals—it is a question of oxidation temperature and melting point; with products—it is marketing channel acceptance and advertising budgets. Just as like chemicals react in similar ways, so do like products. The product life cycle helps to group these products into homogeneous families.

The product life cycle can be the key to successful and profitable product management, from the introduction of new products to profitable disposal of obsolescent products. The fundamental concept of the product life cycle (PLC) is illustrated in Figure 25–1.

In application, the vertical scale often is measured in saturation of the product (percentage of customer units using), while the horizontal scale is calibrated to represent the passage of time. Months or years are

Reprinted from *MSU Business Topics* (Winter 1973), pp. 29–35.

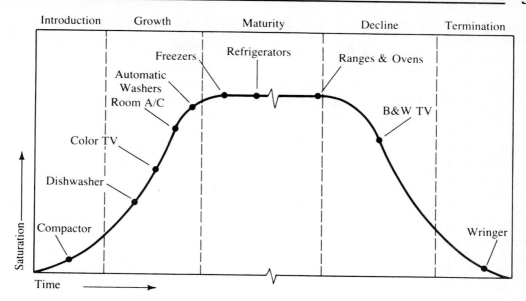

Figure 25–1
Life Cycle Stages of Various Products

usually the units of time used in calibration, although theoretically, an application along the same concept of much shorter or longer durations (milliseconds in physical sciences, millenia in archaeology) might be found. In Figure 25–1 the breakdown in the time scale is shown by stages in the maturity of product life. The saturation scale, however, is a guide only and must be used accordingly. When comparing one product with another, it is sometimes best treated by use of qualitative terms, not quantitative units. It is important to the user of the product life cycle concept that this limitation be recognized and conceptual provisions be made to handle it. For example, if the basic marketing unit chosen is "occupied U.S. households," one cannot expect a product such as room air conditioners to attain 100 percent saturation. This is because many households already have been fitted with central air conditioning; thus, the potential saturation attainment falls well

short of 100 percent of the marketing measurement chosen.

To overcome this difficulty, marketing managers have two basic options. They can choose a more restrictive, specific marketing unit such as "all occupied U.S. households that do not have forced air heating"; homes without forced air heating are unlikely candidates for central air conditioning. It can be anticipated that room air conditioners will saturate not only *that* market, but portions of other markets as well. On the other hand, on the basis of informed judgment, management can determine the *potential* saturation of total households and convert the PLC growth scale to a measurement representing the degree of attainment of potential saturation in U.S. households. The author has found the latter approach to be the more useful one. By this device, automatic washers are considered to be at 100 percent saturation when they are at their full potential of an arbitrarily chosen 80 percent.

Consider Figure 25–1, where various products are shown positioned by life cycle stages: the potential saturations permit the grouping of products into like stages of life cycle, even when their actual saturation attainments are dissimilar. One can note that in Figure 25–1 automatic washers (which are estimated at 58 percent saturation) and room air conditioners (30 percent) are positioned in the same growth stage in Figure 25–1; freezers (29 percent) and refrigerators (99 percent), on the other hand, are in the maturity stage. This occurs because, *in our judgment,* freezers have a potential of only about one-third of "occupied households" and thus have attained almost 90 percent of that market. Automatic clothes washers, however, have a potential of about four-fifths of the occupied households and at about 70 percent of their potential still show

some of the characteristics of the growth stage of the PLC. General characteristics of the products and their markets are summarized in Table 25–1.

The product life cycle concept is illustrated as a convenient scheme of product classification. The PLC permits management to assign given products to the appropriate stages of acceptance by a given market: *introduction, growth, maturity, decline,* and *termination.* The actual classification of products by appropriate stages, however, is more art than science. The whole process is quite imprecise; but unsatisfactory as this may be, a useful classification can be achieved with management benefits that are clearly of value. This can be illustrated by examining the contribution of the PLC concept in the following marketing activities: sales forecasting, advertising, pricing, and marketing planning.

Table 25–1
Product Life Cycle

	Introduction	Growth	Maturity	Decline	Termination
		Marketing			
Customers	Innovative/ High income	High income/ Mass market	Mass market	Laggards/ Special	Few
Channels	Few	Many	Many	Few	Few
Approach	Product	Label	Label	Specialized	Availability
Advertising	Awareness	Label superiority	Lowest price	Psychographic	Sparse
Competitors	Few	Many	Many	Few	Few
		Pricing			
Price	High	Lower	Lowest	Rising	High
Gross margins	High	Lower	Lowest	Low	Rising
Cost Reductions	Few	Many	Slower	None	None
Incentives	Channel	Channel/ Consumer	Consumer/ Channel	Channel	Channel
		Product			
Configuration	Basic	Second generation	Segmented/ Sophisticated	Basic	Stripped
Quality	Poor	Good	Superior	Spotty	Minimal
Capacity	Over	Under	Optimum	Over	Over

APPLICATIONS OF THE PLC TO SALES FORECASTING

One of the most dramatic uses of the PLC in sales forecasting was its application in explaining the violent decline in sales of color TV during the credit crunch recession of 1969–70. This occurred after the experience of the 1966–67 mini-recession which had almost no effect on color TV sales that could be discerned through the usual "noise" of the available product flow data. A similar apparent insensitivity was demonstrated in 1958,

in 1961, and again in 1966–67, with sales of portable dishwashers. However, it too was followed by a noticeable sales reduction in the 1969–71 period, with annual factory shipments as shown in Figure 25–2.

In early 1972 sales of both portable dishwashers and color TV sets showed a positive response to an improving economic climate, raising the question as to why both products had become vulnerable to economic contractions after having shown a great degree of independence of the business cycle during previous years. The answer to

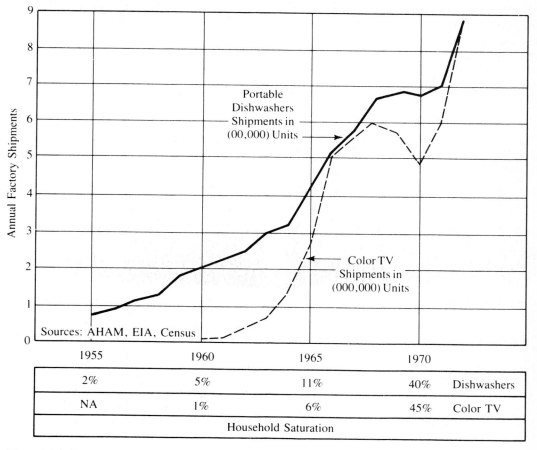

Figure 25–2
Effect of Recession on Product Sales

the question seems to lie in their stage in the product life cycle. In comparing the saturation of color TV and dishwashers, as shown in Figure 25–2, consider first the case of color TV sales.

We can ascertain that as late as 1966, saturation of color TV was approximately 8 percent. By late in 1969, however, saturation had swiftly increased to nearly 40 percent.

The same observation is true in the case of dishwashers—considered a mass market appliance only since 1965. This is the key to the explanation of both situations. At the early, introductory stages of their life cycles, both appliances were making large sales gains as the result of being adopted by consumers with high incomes. Later, when sales growth depended more upon adoption by the less affluent members of the mass market whose spending plans are modified

by general economic conditions, the product sales began to correlate markedly to general economic circumstances.

It appears that big ticket consumer durables such as television sets and portable dishwashers tend to saturate as a function of customer income. This fact is illustrated by the data displayed in Figure 25–3, concerning refrigerators and compactors, where one can note the logical relationship between the two products as to the economic status of their most important customers and as to their position in the product life cycle. The refrigerator is a mature product while the compactor is the newest product in the major appliance family.

The refrigerator once was in the introduction stage and had marketing attributes similar to the compactor. The refrigerator's present marketing characteristics

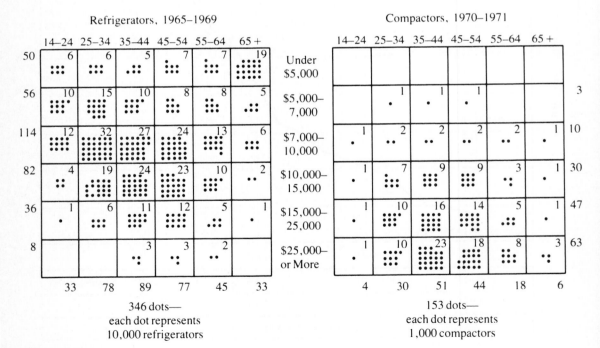

Figure 25–3
Purchase Patterns by Age and Income of Households

are a good guide to proper expectations for the compactor as it matures from the *introductory* stage through *growth* to *maturity*. One can anticipate that the compactor, the microwave oven, and even nondurables such as good quality wines will someday be included in the middle income consumption patterns, and we will find their sales to be much more coincident with general economic cycles.

PRODUCT LIFE STAGES AND ADVERTISING

The concept of a new product filtering through income classes, combined with long-respected precepts of advertising, can result in new perspectives for marketing managers. The resulting observations are both strategic and tactical. New advertising objectives and new insights for copy points and media selection may be realized. Consider the advertising tasks by the following phases:

Phase 1. Introduction
The first objective is to make the best customer prospects aware that the new product or service is now available; to tell him what it does, what are the benefits, why claims are to be believed, and what will be the conditions of consumption.

Phase 2. Growth
The next objective is to saturate the mass market with the same selling points as used in Phase 1. In addition, it is to recognize that a particular brand of the product is clearly superior to other "inferior" substitutes while, at the same time, to provide a rationalization that this purchase is not merely a wasteful, luxury indulging activity, but that it will make the consumer a better *something*, a

better husband, mother, accountant, driver, and so forth.

Phase 3. Maturity
A new rationalization, respectability, is added, besides an intensification of brand superiority ("don't buy substitutes; get the real XYZ original, which incidentally, is *new* and *improved...*"). To a great extent, the *product* registration is dropped. Respectability is a strong requisite of the American lower class, which in this phase is the economic stratum containing the most important opportunities for sales gains. Companies do not abandon higher income customers, but they now match advertising to a variety of market segments instead of concentrating on only one theme for the market. Several distinct advertising programs are used. All elements of the marketing mix—product, price, sales promotion, advertising, trading and physical distribution channels—are focused on specific market segments.

Phase 4. Decline
Superior substitutes for a product generally will be adopted first by the people who before were the first to adopt the product in consideration. These people usually are from the upper economic and social classes. Advertising themes reflect this situation when they concentrate on special market segments such as West Coast families or "consumption societies" such as beer drinkers or apartment dwellers.

PRODUCT LIFE STAGES AND PRICING

As a product progresses through all five stages of the life cycle shown in Figure 25–1, the price elasticity can be expected to undergo dramatic changes. Generally speaking, price elasticity of a relatively simple product will be low at first. Thus, when customers are drawn from the higher income classes, demand is relatively inelastic. Later, when most customers are in the lower income categories, greater price elasticity will exist.

Of course, increased price elasticity will not automatically lower prices during the growth stage of the PLC. It is in this growth stage, however, that per unit costs *are* most dramatically reduced because of the effect of the learning curve in engineering, production, and marketing. Rising volume and, more important, the *forecasts* of higher volumes, justifies increased capital investments and higher fixed costs, which when spread over a larger number of units thereby reduce unit costs markedly. New competitors surface with great rapidity in this stage as profits tend to increase dramatically.

Pricing in the mature phase of the PLC usually is found to be unsatisfactory, with no one's profit margins as satisfactory as before. Price competition is keener within the distribution channel in spite of the fact that relatively small price differences seldom translate into any change in aggregate consumer activity.

PRODUCT PLANNING AND THE PLC

Curiously enough, the very configuration of the product takes on a classical pattern of evolution as it advances through the PLC. At first, the new device is designed for function alone; the initial design is sometimes crude by standards that will be applied in the future. As the product maturation process continues, performance sophistication increases. Eventually the product develops to the point where competitors are hard-pressed to make meaningful differences which are perceptible to consumers.

As the product progresses through the product life cycle these modifications tend to describe a pattern of metamorphosis from "the ugly box" to a number of options. The adjustment cycle includes:

Part of house: the built-in look and function. Light fixtures, cooking stoves, wall safes, and furnaces are examples.

Furniture: a blending of the product into the home decor. This includes television, hi-fi consoles, radios, clocks, musical instruments, game tables, and so forth.

Portability: a provision for increased *presence* of the product through provisions for easier movement (rollers or compactness), or multiple unit ownership (wall clocks, radios, even refrigerators), or miniaturization for portability. Portability and *personalization*, such as the pocket knife and the wristwatch, can occur.

System: a combination of components into one unit with compatible uses and/or common parts for increased convenience, lower cost, or less space. Home entertainment centers including television, radio, hi-fi, refrigerator-freezers, combination clothes washers-dryers, clock radios, pocket knife-can-and-bottle openers are illustrative.

Similar changes can also be observed in the distribution channel. Products often progress from specialty outlets in the introductory stage to mass distribution outlets such as discount houses and contract buyers during the "maturity" and "decline" phases of the PLC. Interestingly enough, the process eventually is reversed. Buggy whips can still be found in some specialty stores and premium prices are paid for replicas of very old products.

CONCLUSION

The product life cycle is a useful concept. It is the equivalent of the periodic table of the elements in the physical sciences. The maturation of production technology and product configuration along with marketing programs proceeds in an orderly, somewhat predictable course over time with the merchandising nature and marketing environment noticeably similar between products that are in the same stage of their life cycle. Its use as a concept in forecasting, pricing, advertising, product planning, and other aspects of marketing management can make it a valuable concept, although considerable amounts of judgment must be used in its application.

New Product Management for the 1980s

Booz, Allen & Hamilton, Inc.

THE NEW PRODUCT MANAGEMENT CHALLENGE

During the 1980s, managers in all industries expect new products to fuel industry sales and profit growth. Indeed, the contribution made by new products to sales growth is expected to increase by one-third, while the portion of total company profits generated by new products is expected to increase by 40 percent over the next 5 years. These higher expectations exist in all industries, including the information processing industry, which had over the last 5 years the highest profit contribution from new products of all industry groups surveyed.

To support these new product targets, companies expect to double the number of new products introduced over the next 5 years. From 1976 to 1981, the companies we surveyed introduced from zero to over 100 new products; the median number of new products introduced was 5. Over the next 5 years, that number is expected to double.

This trend towards increased development and introduction of new products is supported by a number of factors. Technology advances, changing market requirements, and world market competition are expected to increase the number of new products introduced over the next 5 years. On the other hand, several factors could impede new product development in the coming decade. The increased cost of capital, in particular, is expected to have a negative impact on the number of new products, introduced over the next 5 years.

A short-term orientation by management is viewed as the principal *internal* obstacle to successful new product development. Inadequate market research, delays in decision-making, lack of a new product strategy, and ineffective communication between functions and departments are other major internal obstacles.

Despite these obstacles, many new products will be selected for development and brought to the marketplace by the mid-

Reprinted with permission by Booz, Allen & Hamilton, 1982.

1980s. How well-prepared U.S. companies are to meet the challenge is suggested by our major survey findings:

Most companies use a formal new product process, usually beginning with identifying the new product strategy. According to our survey results, companies that have successfully launched new products are more likely to have had a formal new product process in place for a longer period of time. They are also more likely to have a strategic plan, and be committed to growing through internally developed new products.

The new product strategy links corporate objectives to the new product effort, and provides direction for the new product process. The step identifies the strategic roles to be played by new products—roles that depend on the type of product itself and the industry. It also helps set the formal financial criteria to be used in measuring new product performance and in screening and evaluating new product ideas.

The more sophisticated new product process has dramatically reduced the number of new product ideas considered for every successful new product introduced—from an average of 58 in 1968 to 7 in 1981. Again, our survey results indicate that companies with a strong record of successful new product introductions consider fewer ideas per successful new launch, and do more and better screening of ideas.

More management attention and more financial resources are given to the early steps in the new product process than was the case a decade ago. In 1968, roughly one-half of all new product expenditures was made during the commercialization stage. Today, commercialization accounts for only one-fourth of all new product expenditures. Conversely, the portion of expenditures in the first three steps more than doubled during the same period, from 10 percent in 1968 to 21 percent in 1981.

*The percent of total new product expen-*ditures allocated to products that are ultimately successful has increased—from 30 percent in 1968 to 54 percent today. The probable causes are the reduction in the number of ideas considered and the increase in resource allocations to early process steps.

Almost half the companies surveyed use more than one type of organization structure to guide new product programs. Over three-fourths of these companies tie the choice of structure used to product-specific requirements.

Experience in introducing new products enables companies to improve new product performance. With increased new product experience, companies improve profitability by reducing the cost per introduction. For the 13,000 new product introductions between 1976 and 1981 in the 700 companies we surveyed, at each doubling of the number of new products introduced, the cost of each introduction declined by 29 percent.

Two-thirds of all companies surveyed formally measure new product performance. The three most commonly used criteria are profit contribution, return on investment, and sales volume.

The success rate of commercialized new products has not improved, on average, over the last two decades. In the period from 1963 to 1968, 67 percent of all new products introduced were successful—that is, they met company-specific financial and strategic criteria. From 1976 to 1981, a 65 percent rate of success was achieved.

The dichotomy of the major findings is obvious. More companies are using a more sophisticated new product process, thereby reducing the number of new ideas needed to generate a successful product and increasing the portion of total resources spent on market "winners." And more companies are fitting the organizational structures used to their product-specific requirements. Yet, there has been virtually no change in the *rate* of successful introductions.

New product managers are thus faced with the important challenge in the coming decade of improving new product performance to meet their higher new product objectives. To that end, and based on our findings from the survey and our in-depth interviews with new product executives, Booz-Allen concludes:

- A company-specific, implementation-oriented approach is the key to improving new product performance.
- A well-defined new product strategy should be at the core of the company-specific approach.
- The new product effort should be guided by a formal, seven-step process.
- Consistent management commitment to new product development for extended periods of time allows a company to accumulate the new product experience crucial to achieving and maintaining competitive advantage.
- The entire new product program should be carried out in an environment conducive to achieving company-specific new product and corporate objectives.

These summary results and their implications for new product management in the 1980s are expanded on in the following sections.

CURRENT PRACTICES AND TRENDS

Our analysis of the survey findings identified four key new product practices and trends. They relate to: (1) the mix of new products introduced; (2) changes in the new product process; (3) the types of organization structures used to guide new product programs; and (4) the impact of improved new product processes on new products development.

Mix of New Product Introductions

In our survey, we identified six categories of new products in terms of their newness to the company and to the marketplace.

- *New-to-the-world products:* New products that create an entirely new market (10 percent of total new introductions).
- *New product lines:* New products that, for the first time, allow a company to enter an established market (20 percent of total).
- *Additions to existing product lines:* New products that supplement a company's established product lines (26 percent of total).
- *Improvements in/revisions to existing products:* New products that provide improved performance or greater perceived value, and replace existing products (26 percent of total).
- *Repositionings:* Existing products that are targeted to new markets or market segments (7 percent of total).
- *Cost reductions:* New products that provide similar performance at lower cost (11 percent of total).

The results of the survey indicate that, typically, a company's new product program includes a mix of these new products. Additions to existing product lines and improvements in or revisions to existing products have accounted for 52 percent of all new product introductions over the last 5 years. Another 30 percent of introductions are new-to-the-world products and new product lines, which often become a firm's most successful new products. Indeed, they account for 60 percent of new products viewed as most successful.

Despite the obvious attractiveness of these two new product categories, many new product managers are reluctant to introduce these types of new products because their variability of return is greater. As a result, over 50 percent of the companies surveyed introduced *no* new-to-the-world products over the last 5 years, and 25 percent of the companies introduced *no* new product lines, thus supporting the notion that few innovative new products were introduced over the 5-year period.

This broad mix of new product introductions is consistent across all industries, although rapidly changing technology has fostered more truly innovative new products in high technology or growth industries. For example, although only 10 percent of all new products introduced over the last 5 years were new-to-the-world products, advances in electronics technology prompted a larger percentage of new-to-the-world product introductions in the information processing industry (over 20 percent of total) and in the instruments and controls industry (15 percent).

Changes in New Product Process

The new products introduced over the last 5 years have been selected for development through a seven-step new product process. [Exhibit 26–1.] A new step, developing an explicit new product strategy, is the major addition to the process developed by Booz-Allen-Hamilton in the 1950s, with 77 percent of the companies surveyed using it in their new product process.

The addition of this step has changed the nature of the beginning of the process. The first three steps—developing a new product strategy, generating ideas and concepts, and screening and evaluating those ideas and concepts—are now more closely linked to each other and have become more iterative. The new product strategy develop-

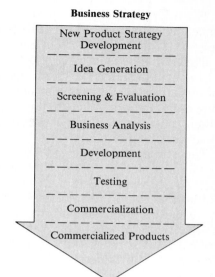

Business Strategy

New Product Strategy Development

Idea Generation

Screening & Evaluation

Business Analysis

Development

Testing

Commercialization

Commercialized Products

Exhibit 26–1
New Product Process in the 1980s

ment step provides a focus for the idea-generation step in that the ideas and concepts generated are developed to meet strategic objectives. In addition, screening criteria used during the screening and evaluation step are tied to the same strategic objectives.

The purpose of the step to develop new product strategy is to identify the strategic business requirements that new products should satisfy. The requirements, which can be both market and company driven, determine the roles to be played by new products. For example, over the past 5 years, defending a market share position and maintaining position as a product innovator were the two most common new product roles. As a consumer nondurable company executive told us: "We have different uses and roles for new products. Some are developed to meet earnings growth objectives; others are introduced to maintain distribution leverage or to combat a competitive entry."

The roles played by new products are influenced by individual industry needs. For example, industrial goods companies are more likely to have developed their most successful new products to satisfy technological objectives, while customer nondurable companies are more likely to have developed their most successful new products to satisfy market requirements.

The strategic role played by a new product is linked also to the *type* of new product. To maintain a position as a product innovator or to exploit technology in a new way, for example, more companies develop a new-to-the-world product than any other type. To defend a market share position, more companies introduce an addition to an existing line or a revision of an existing product.

Once a new product strategy has been developed and new product idea selected on the basis of the roles they can play in achieving strategic objectives, financial performance criteria can be established. Nearly two-thirds of the companies surveyed formally measure new product performance, using, on the average, more than one performance criterion. The three most commonly used are profit contribution, sales volume, and return on investment.

A consumer packaged goods company illustrates how performance criteria are tied to the strategic roles played by new products. This company set a higher return-on-investment threshold for products used to enter a new geographic market (25 percent) than for products designed to increase (15 percent). The higher performance standard in the former situation reflects the higher investment level and higher probability of failure associated with entering a new geographic market.

The increased attention given a new product strategy development reflects a general increase in management attention to the early steps in the new product process. Companies that have excellent records of successful new product introductions are more likely to develop specific new product strategies. They conduct more analyses early in the process and focus their idea and concept generation. And they conduct more rigorous screening and evaluation of the ideas generated. However, in comparing product development in the United States with that in Japan, we found that the Japanese invest even more time in and give more attention to these early steps in the new product process. In particular, the Japanese carry out extensive analyses and more carefully define the roles of their new products in corporate strategy.

Over the last decade, U.S. companies also have increased the share of total new product expenditures spent on analysis, screening, and development, and have reduced the share of the total expended on commercialization. In 1968, roughly one-half of all new product expenditures was made during the commercialization stage. Today, commercialization accounts for only one-fourth.

Consistent with reduced commercialization expenditures and the reality of the high cost of capital, capital expenditures in support of new product projects declined from 46 percent of total new product expenditures in 1968 to 26 percent today.

The steps up to and including development benefited most from this reapportionment of new product dollars. Expenditures during the development step increased from 28 percent of total in 1968 to 37 percent today. The portion of expenditures in the first three steps more than doubled during the same period, from 10 percent in 1968 to 21 percent in 1981.

Although the early steps in the process of developing new products are generally viewed as the most critical, different industries emphasize different steps, depending on industry dynamics. Industries with rapidly changing markets, such as information processing, instruments and controls, consumer nondurables, and textiles, place greater emphasis on developing a new product strategy. Companies in industries with more stable markets, like chemicals, industrial machinery, OEM components, and power-generating equipment, focus more on business analysis.

Types of New Product Organization and Management

The organization structures used to guide new product programs fall into two general categories: free-standing or autonomous units, like interdisciplinary teams, separate new product departments, and venture groups; and functionally based units that are part of existing planning, marketing, R & D, or engineering departments.

Almost half the companies surveyed use *more* than one type of structure, and over three-fourths of these companies tie the choice of organization structure used to product-specific requirements. For example, a manager in an information processing company told us: "New products related to one of our existing businesses are developed within an existing division. New products that represent a shift in direction for the company are developed by a separate venture group."

Heading these new product units are managers who need and use a range of general and functional management skills to develop new products. Almost half the companies surveyed encourage "product champions" to promote and shepherd new product concepts through the development process.

The tenure of senior new product managers, who usually are functional department heads, increased from 2.5 years to 8.0 years over the last 15 years, suggesting top management is providing for greater continuity in new product development.

There are no standard compensation practices for new product executives. Fifty-seven percent of all companies surveyed tie compensation for new product managers to general performance. Thirty-eight percent use base salary alone. Only 5 percent tie compensation *directly* to new product performance. But the results of our interviews suggest compensation for new product managers is an important and unresolved issue within many companies. As an industrial components company executive told us: "Compensation for new product managers is one of the hottest issues within our company. This year, for the first time, we have implemented a bonus system tied to long-term new product objectives."

Impact of Refined Process on New Product Development

The more sophisticated new product process has had a profound effect on the number of ideas considered in developing one successful new product. The "mortality curve" for new product ideas has changed dramatically. In 1968, on average, 58 new product ideas were considered for every successful new product. Today, only seven ideas are required to generate one successful new product.

However, there are variations by industry. Consumer nondurable companies consider more than twice as many new product ideas to generate one successful new product as industrial or consumer durable manufacturers.

Companies have reduced the number of new ideas needed to produce one successful new product, in part, by increasing their attention to the market and to potential new applications of available technologies. A consumer durable company executive told us: "One thing that has changed is the level of sophistication in segmenting the market. Ideas generated today are more clearly defined and better focused than they were 5 to 10 years ago." And a high-technology company executive told us: "In our company, technology advances drive idea generation, limiting new product concepts to the application of these technologies.

Industries also differ in the allocation of time to the various steps in the new product process. Industrial goods companies devote 47 percent of their total time to the development step, compared with 30 percent spent by consumer nondurable companies and 36 percent spent by consumer durable companies. On the other hand, consumer durable and nondurable companies devote a higher percentage of total time to commercialization—26 percent and 29 percent, respectively, versus 18 percent for industrial goods companies.

The net result of the improved process has been better expenditure allocations. By reducing the number of ideas considered to develop one successful new product, companies have been able to increase the portion of total new product expenditures going to products that are ultimately successful. Thus, the overall percentage of new product expenditures attributable to successful products increased from 30 percent in 1968 to 54 percent today.

But despite the increased sophistication of the process and improved effectiveness of allocations, there has been, as we have cited, no improvement in the percentage of successful new product introductions. It remains at about 65 percent. This suggests greater process sophistication does not necessarily lead to improved new product performance. Rather, various other factors are also at work.

KEY FACTORS IN IMPROVING NEW PRODUCT PERFORMANCE

To determine the keys to improved new product performance, we examined successful new product introductions as well as companies that had successfully launched new products. We learned that the two most important factors in successful new product introductions are how well the product fits market needs and the functional strengths of the company. *However,* the relative importance of the several factors cited varies significantly by industry and by type of product being introduced.

In addition, successful companies appear to have developed a corporate philosophy, a strategic approach, and a management style that encourage successful new product development. In particular, they maintain commitment to growing through internally developed new products, and select management styles that foster the kind of environment needed to satisfy company-specific new product objectives.

Factors Contributing to the Introduction of Successful New Products

The two most important factors in successful new product introductions are the fit of the product with market needs and with internal functional strengths. Having a technologically superior product, receiving support from top management, and using a multiple-step new product process are additional factors contributing to new product success.

The relative importance of each factor does vary, however, by industry. Although fit of the product with market needs is cited as the most important factor by the sample as a whole, technological superiority is considered more important by industrial goods companies, and top-management support is more important in consumer durable and nondurable companies.

Factor importance varies also by the type of new product being developed. Overall, as in the industry rankings of factors responsible for successful new product introductions, the fit of the product with market needs is the most important factor for every type of product being introduced. Technological superiority of the product is important in developing new-to-the-world products. As an executive of a major chemicals company told us: "We are trying to develop innovations that will reach the market in 5–10 years. Our new product development executives understand today's marketplace, but they emphasize technology to generate new product ideas since they have no mechanism to identify the market requirements 5–10 years from now."

In the development of new product lines and additions to existing lines, how well the product fits with internal functional strengths is important. In developing this type of product, a company is trying to enter existing markets in which production, distribution, and selling requirements are known and can be assessed relative to company capabilities. In the development of improvements to/revisions in existing products, technological superiority is important because in this case a company is trying to improve its position within an existing market, which depends more on developing a technologically-based competitive advantage. And top-management support is cited as one of the three most important factors to the successful introduction of new product lines and of additions to existing lines.

Characteristics of Companies with Successful New Products

To determine the existence of common characteristics in companies that had success-fully launched new products, we divided our sample into two groups: companies achieving greater than 90 percent success in all new product introductions (i.e., 90 percent of all new product introductions met company-set performance criteria); and companies achieving less than 50 percent success for their new products.

In many ways, companies successful in new product introductions look like their less successful counterparts. They introduce about the same mix of new products. They spend about the same amount of money (as a percent of sales) on R & D and promotion in support of new products. Both groups are as likely to use a formal new product process or formally measure new product performance. And both groups spend about the same proportion of total time and expense on the various steps in the new product process. These similarities strongly suggest that successful new product management is a delicate and subtle process, not subject to broad generalizations or universal guidelines.

Important differences as well as similarities exist between the two groups. These differences are related to operating philosophy, organization structures, extent of experience with new product introductions, and management styles.

Operating Philosophy. Successful companies in our survey are more committed to growth through new products developed internally. They are more likely to have a formal new product process in place for a longer period of time. They are more likely to have a strategic plan that includes a certain portion of company growth from new products. They are also more likely to prescreen new product ideas thoroughly, considering almost 10 times fewer new product ideas per successful new product as unsuccessful companies.

Probably as a result of this philosophy and commitment, successful companies report fewer major obstacles to successful new product development. Short-term-oriented management, lack of a new product strategy, and organizational issues are considered less of an obstacle by successful companies than by unsuccessful ones.

Organization Structures. From an organizational standpoint, successful companies are more likely to house the new product organization in R & D or engineering, and are more likely to allow the marketing and R & D functions to have greater influence on the new product process. They are also more likely to keep the senior new product executive in place for a longer period of time.

The Experience Effect. We also found that experience in introducing products enables companies to improve new product performance. Specifically, with increased new product experience, companies improve new product profitability by reducing the cost per introduction.

The concept at work is the experience curve—that is, the more you do something, the more efficient you become at doing it. More precisely, in this situation, with each doubling of the number of new product introductions, the cost of each introduction declines at a predictable and constant rate.

New product development costs conform to this concept. For the 13,000 new product introductions between 1976 and 1981 in the 700 companies we surveyed, the experience effect yields a 71 percent cost curve. At each doubling of the number of new products introduced, the cost of each introduction declines by 29 percent.

Companies that adroitly exploit the benefits of experience can achieve competitive advantage. For example, if Company A and Company B introduce two new products and are equally effective in managing them, they incur the same cost per introduction. But if Company B continues to devote resources to the introduction of new products and thus gains greater experience than Company A, Company B will achieve a sizeable and sustainable advantage in the cost per new product introduction.

Much of the advantage stems from having acquired a knowledge of the market and of the steps required to develop a new product. This knowledge, accumulated over time, enables the experienced company to move more efficiently through the development process.

The positive effects of accumulated experience do not imply, however, that companies should introduce as many new products as possible for the sole purpose of gaining experience. Maintaining competitive advantage requires a consistent commitment to new product development. Theoretically, a firm that cuts back on its new product program may put itself at a competitive disadvantage from which it may never recover. As an executive of a consumer durable company stated: "While our company has been successful in new products over the last 10 years, top management has recently narrowed the new product pipeline due to current business pressure. What will it take to get back up to speed once the valve is turned on again?" In actual practice, our survey results show that successful companies remain committed to new product efforts for extended periods of time, thereby improving effectiveness and reducing the cost per introduction.

Management Styles. Successful companies appear not only to select a management style appropriate to immediate new product development needs, but also to revise and tailor that approach to *changing* new product opportunities. For example, a major instruments and controls company that historically had used an entrepreneurial management approach to new product development is moving to a more structured, top-down managerial style as it finds some of its high-technology market segments maturing. A major industrial components company is moving to a less structured, more entrepreneurial style as it positions itself to enter emerging high-technology growth segments. Both companies report these management style changes are enabling them to meet new product objectives more effectively.

In general, the companies we surveyed use some form of one to three approaches to managing new product development:

- An entrepreneurial approach, associated primarily with developing new-to-the-world products.
- A collegial approach, associated primarily with entering new business and adding products to existing product lines.
- A managerial approach, most closely associated with developing new products that are closely linked to existing businesses.

In the entrepreneurial approach, an autonomous new product group is established, reporting to a general manager. It consists of an interdisciplinary venture team, headed by an entrepreneurial new product manager capable of integrating diverse functional skills. Top management is strongly committed to and involved in the effort to develop new products. But less attention is paid to formal business planning than in either of the other two approaches, and there is less dependence on formal financial criteria to evaluate new product opportunities.

This less restrictive approach supports entrepreneurial behavior, thus creating a positive environment for risk-taking. Moreover, new product managers in this environment enjoy incentive systems that

reward success. As a result, they want to remain in the new product development function, which provides greater continuity and accumulation of new product experience.

The collegial approach is characterized by strong senior management participation in new product decision-making, strong top-management support of risk-taking, commitment to and support for a new product effort, and a formal new product process to guide the effort and ensure discipline. It is characterized also by a clear commitment across functional lines to provide whatever is necessary for success and to make decisions quickly.

The managerial approach is characterized by a hierarchical management structure that involves many levels of management and provides strong top-down direction to new product efforts. Such companies stress functional leadership, have a strong business planning orientation, use a formal and often inflexible new product process, and rely heavily on formal financial criteria to evaluate new product opportunities.

This approach is suitable for managing ongoing business because it rewards successful new product managers with quick promotions. However, it tends to restrict new product endeavors to variations on existing products, and provides less continuity than in the other two approaches because new product managers are promoted to other functions.

A "BEST PRACTICES" PRESCRIPTION FOR MANAGING NEW PRODUCTS IN THE 1980s

New product management will not be easy in the 1980s. In the rapidly changing and financially constrained environment envisioned, companies will be increasingly challenged to improve new product performance.

Although the similarities among successful companies may seem to imply a set of common factors for success, the differences suggest that effective management of new product development is very complex and highly company-specific.

Based on our survey results, the companies most likely to meet this challenge successfully will be those that develop new products internally as their primary means of growth, that have well-defined new product efforts, and that consistently commit the necessary resources to these efforts. They have in place and in use overall approaches carefully tailored to the specific goals and needs of their respective companies. In particular, at the core of their company-specific approaches are clearly defined new product strategies that allow management to generate and select new products that fulfill specific internal strategic and external market needs. They focus on opportunities for which they have the requisite internal strengths, and in which they enjoy competitive advantage, either cost or effectiveness, gained through cumulative experience. Finally, successful companies in the turbulent decade ahead will be those that tailor their organizational structures and management styles to the type of new product opportunities they pursue.

Making the Long-Term Commitment

Between the end of World War II and the late 1970s, U.S. business and industry enjoyed almost uninterrupted overall success in new product introductions both at home and abroad. Our management expertise, our technological know-how, and our design, production, and distribution superiority allowed us to introduce and market new products almost at will. At home, we found ready markets in an expanding economy charac-terized by stable, low inflation rates. Abroad, we marketed a range of mass-produced quality goods eagerly sought after by a world recovering from the devastation of a worldwide conflict.

Today, U.S. business faces a far different set of circumstances. The major industrial nations of the world have regained their footing not only at home but also in the United States and in many of the growth markets elsewhere. The competition is now world-scale competition. Technology advances occur more rapidly, with high-technology products or their components enjoying ever-shortening life cycles. And the increased cost of capital in this country has escalated the cost of every new product introduced, whether or not it is successful.

In such an environment, companies cannot be satisfied with an average performance. Rather, they must commit themselves to achieving and sustaining outstanding results.

They must look inward for their future product opportunities, and be committed to internal development of new products as the major means of growth. They must be willing to mount well-defined new product efforts that are driven by corporate objectives and strategies, and that conclude with the development and introduction of specific new products that fulfill internal strategic and external market needs. They must support these efforts with consistent commitments of the necessary funds and of the requisite managerial and technical know-how. In short, successful corporate practitioners will be those who marry corporate needs to customer needs, and pledge the resources necessary to a successful marriage.

Developing a New Product Strategy

At the core of a company-specific approach to a sound new product program is a well-

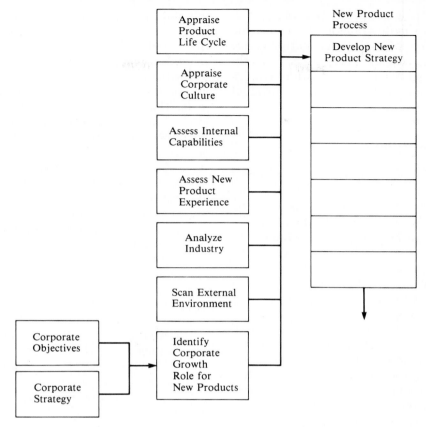

Exhibit 26–2
Strategic Approach to New Product Planning

defined new product strategy. [Exhibit 26–2.] A new product strategy links the new product process to company objectives, and provides focus for idea/concept generation and guidelines for establishing appropriate screening criteria.

The purpose of developing a new product strategy is to identify the strategic roles new products will play to fulfill corporate objectives.

That identification is a complex analytical process in which the role new products will play in the company's growth determines the level of new product activity. In the analytical process, industries are evalu-

ated to determine the growth potential of existing markets, and the external environment is scrutinized to identify emerging product opportunities. Internal capabilities are assessed to identify relevant company strengths and weaknesses, and existing management style and new product experience are evaluated to determine their impact on the new product effort.

The outcome of this analysis is a set of strategic roles, used *not* to generate specific new product ideas, but to help identify markets for which new products will be developed. These market opportunities provide the set of product and market requirements from which new product ideas are generated. In addition, strategic roles provide guidelines for new product performance measurement criteria. Performance thresholds tied to strategic roles provide a more precise means of screening new product ideas.

Capitalizing on the Experience Advantage

As part of the new product effort, internal capabilities are assessed to determine specific strengths and weaknesses vis à vis the strategic goals to be accomplished and the competitors in the marketplace. One of the capabilities most closely scrutinized is the depth of experience a company enjoys in new product introductions, as new product performance can be improved with experience by reducing the cost per introduction.

Companies that refuse to recognize or choose to ignore the importance of the experience effect in long-term success run the risk of placing themselves at a serious, perhaps fatal, competitive disadvantage. Winning companies in the 80s, however, will take a very hard look at their own—and their competition's—pluses and minuses, and ruthlessly weed out those new product ideas that, while popular, glamorous, or ego-satisfying, offer little if any real potential for success for their corporations. They will focus, instead, on those opportunities in which they enjoy, by reason of solid, cumulative experience, a premier position or a competitive advantage. Chronic failure to "see things as they really are," and not as we would like them to be can, and all too often does, lead to debilitating failures.

Establishing an Appropriate Environment

Any new product program should be carried out in an environment conducive to achieving both new product and corporate objectives.

Once the types of new products required to meet strategic objectives have been identified, an environment must be created to support the development of these products. The elements of this environment are organization structure, management style, management responsibility, and top-management support.

In creating this supportive environment, the important consideration is matching the new product opportunities to these various elements. For example, in general, riskier ventures or those with a longer payback period, such as the development and launching of new product lines or new-to-the-world products, require a relatively unstructured, entrepreneurial management approach. A highly creative venture team headed by a general manager eager to take substantial risks and strongly supported by top management, is one such approach.

However, new product opportunities change over time, and many companies fail to change their environments accordingly. To avoid the problems that will inevitably result from the mismatch, companies must periodically and systematically evaluate the new product process environment, and tailor their approaches to support emerging new product objectives. Sensitivity and appropriate response to the need for change produce environments that directly support new product programs—programs that will allow companies and corporations to realize their goals rather than merely to fantasize about them.

American business and industry will face serious challenges from within and without in the coming decade. One of the most serious is the need to improve new product performance. Consequently, new product managers of ability, vision, and conviction are needed now, perhaps more than ever before. They must be able to confront the issues vital to corporate growth, profitability, and survival; seize the appropriate and promising opportunities; and solve the problems that impede progress toward achieving long-term corporate and strategic goals. To these ends, they must implement the requisite techniques, such as the seven-step new product process, and they must capitalize on whatever experience advantage they enjoy. For corporate management's part, it must be obviously committed to creating a corporate environment conducive to carrying out the tasks at hand successfully, and it must be willing to pledge the resources needed for the length of time required. Without this total commitment, we risk giving up the industrial leadership role we have played around the world for the past several decades.

Services Marketing Is Different

Leonard L. Berry

In 1978 $600 billion was spent by Americans for services—for airline tickets, electricity, rent, medical care, college tuition, sports entertainment, automobile repair, and so forth. Today, in excess of 45% of the average family's budget is spent on services.[1]

Despite the importance of the services sector in the American economy, services marketing has only recently attracted the attention of academic marketers. As a result, far more research has been done on how to market goods than on how to market services. This would not really matter if the problems encountered in services marketing were identical to those encountered in goods and marketing, but such is not the case. This article examines some of the special characteristics of services and suggests some of the marketing strategy implications that arise from them.

Reprinted by permission from *Business Magazine.* "Service Marketing Is Different," by Leonard L. Berry, May–June 1980.

CHARACTERISTICS OF SERVICES

Although service industries are themselves quite heterogeneous (ranging from beauty salons to electric utilities), there are some characteristics of services about which it is useful to generalize. Three of the most important of these characteristics are discussed here.

More Intangible than Tangible. A good is an object, a device, a thing; a service is a deed, a performance, an effort. When a good is purchased, something tangible is acquired; something that can be seen, touched, perhaps smelled or worn or placed on a mantel. When a service is purchased, there is generally nothing tangible to show for it. Money has been spent, but there are no additional clothes to hang in the closet and nothing to place on the mantel.

Services are consumed but not possessed. Although the performance of most services is supported by tangibles—for instance, the automobile in the case of a taxi service—the essence of what is being bought is a performance rendered by one party for another.

Most market offerings are a combination of tangible and intangible elements.[2] It is whether the essence of what is being bought is tangible or intangible that determines its classification as a good or a service. In a restaurant the acquisition of supplies, the preparation and serving of meals, and the after-meal cleanup (or some combination thereof) is performed for the consumer by another party. Hence, we think of the restaurant industry as a service industry. This is so even though there are tangibles involved—for example, the building, interior decor, kitchen equipment, and food.

The concept of intangibility has two meanings, both of which present challenges for marketing—

- That which cannot be touched, impalpable.
- That which cannot be easily defined, formulated, or grasped mentally.[3]

Addressing the marketing problems that intangibility presents is generally a matter of far more concern to the services marketer than to the goods marketer.

Simultaneous Production and Consumption.
Services are generally produced and consumed in the same time frame. The college professor produces an educational service while the student consumes it. The telephone company produces telephone service while the telephone user consumes it. The babysitter produces a babysitting service while the children and parents consume it.

Generally, goods are produced, then sold, then consumed. Services on the other hand are usually sold first, then produced and consumed simultaneously.

Simultaneous production and consumption means that the service provider is often physically present when consumption takes place. Whereas a washing machine might be manufactured in Michigan and consumed in Virginia, the dentist is present when examining a patient; the singer is present when performing a concert; the airline stewardess is present when serving an in-flight meal.

What is important to recognize about the presence of the service provider is that the "how" of service distribution becomes important. In the marketing discipline, great stress is placed on distributing goods where and when customer-prospects desire them to be distributed—that is, to the "right place" and at the "right time." With services, it often is important to distribute them in the "right way" as well. How automobile mechanics, physicians, lawyers, teachers, and bank tellers conduct themselves in the presence of the customer can influence future patronage decisions. Washing machines can't be rude or careless or thoughtless, but people providing services can be and sometimes are. And when they are, the result may be a search for a new service supplier.

Less Standardized and Uniform.
Service industries tend to differ on the extent to which they are "people-based" or "equipment-based."[4] That is, there is a larger human component involved in performing some services (for example, plumbing) than others (for example, telephone communications). One of the implications of this distinction is that the "outcomes" of people-based service operations tend to be less standardized and uniform than the outcomes of equipment-based service- or goods-producing operations. Stated differently, the extensive involvement of people in the production of a service introduces a degree of variability in the outcome that is

not present when machines dominate. This is an important consideration, given the vast number of service industries that are labor-intensive.

The ever-present potential for variability in a labor-intensive service situation is well known in the marketplace. Whereas consumers expect their favorite breakfast cereal to always taste the same, and to almost always hear a dial tone when picking up a telephone receiver, expectations are far less certain on the occasion of getting a haircut. This is why consumers look at their hair in a mirror before the hair-cutting service is concluded. The outcome is uncertain and more service production may be needed, even when the barber or beautician has had long experience with the consumer.

The growing use of automatic-teller machines (ATMs) by the financial-services industry makes the point. The net effect of the ATM is to transform the delivery of certain traditional banking services from a human delivery mode to a machine delivery mode. This transformation does not mean that all consumers will like or use these machines. It does mean, however, that those who do use ATMs will find far less variability in the services rendered than if human tellers were used. A banker can paint a smile on an ATM and call it Tillie; except when not working properly, the machine will perform uniformly for all customers regardless of how these customers are dressed, the time of day, or the length of the queue waiting for service. Such is not the case with the human teller who may have a bad day, get tired, or become angry with a supervisor, co-worker, or customer. Moreover, human tellers differ among themselves in their customer-relation and technical skills, their personalities, and their attitudes toward their work. In short, bankers cannot paint a smile on a human being.

MARKETING SERVICES

The special characteristics of services present a number of implications concerning their marketing. Although many marketing concepts and tools are applicable to both goods and services, the relative importance of these concepts and tools, and how they are used, are often different. This section suggests a number of strategic marketing opportunities of particular importance to the service industries.

Internal Marketing

In what Richard Chase calls "high-contact" service businesses, the quality of the service is inseparable from the quality of the service provider.[5] High-contact businesses are ones in which there is considerable contact between the service provider and the customer, e.g., health care, financial services, and restaurants. Human performance materially shapes the service outcome and hence becomes part of the "product."

Just as goods marketers need to be concerned with product quality, so do services marketers need to be concerned with service quality, which means—in labor-intensive situations—special attention to employee quality and performance. It follows that in high-contact service industries, marketers need to be concerned with internal, not just external, marketing.

Internal marketing means applying the philosophy and practices of marketing to the people that serve the external customer so that (1) the best possible people can be employed and retained and (2) they will do the best possible work. (Technically the phrase "internal marketing" can be applied to any form of marketing inside an organization, for example, marketing an idea to a superior. In this article, the phrase concerns marketing to employees.) More specifically, internal marketing is viewing employees as internal customers, viewing jobs as internal products, and (just as with external marketing) endeavoring to design these products to better meet the needs of these customers.[6]

Although most executives are not accustomed to thinking of marketing in this way, the fact is that people do buy jobs from employers, and employers can and do use marketing to sell these jobs on an initial and on-going basis. To the extent that high-contact service firms use the concepts and tools of marketing to offer better, more satisfying jobs, they upgrade their capabilities for being more effective service marketers.

The relevance of marketing thinking to personnel management is very real. The banks and insurance companies (among others) adopting flexible working hours are redesigning jobs to better accommodate individual differences, which is market segmentation.[7] The Marriott Corporation is noted for its commitment to employee attitude monitoring, but what it really is doing is marketing research.[8] Indiana National Bank's recent "Person-to-Person" advertising campaign featuring its own personnel was designed to motivate employees as well as external customers and prospects. Aggressive investment in behalf of employee quality and performance is a hallmark of many of American's most successful service companies, including Delta Airlines,[9] Bank of America,[10] and Walt Disney.[11]

Importantly, the crucial matter is not that the phrase "internal marketing" come into widespread use, but that the implication of the phrase be understood; i.e., by satisfying the needs of its internal customers, an organization upgrades its capability for satisfying the needs of its external customers. This is true for most organizations and is certainly true for high-contact service organizations. As one recent article pointed out,

"the successful service company must first sell the job to employees before it can sell its services to customers.[12]

Customizing Service

The simultaneous production and consumption characteristic of services frequently provides opportunities to "customize" service. Some service organizations take full advantage of this opportunity within the boundary of productivity requirements, but many do not.

Since a fundamental marketing objective is to effect a good fit between what the customer-prospect wants to buy and what the organization has to sell, the potential for tailoring service to meet the precise desires of individual customers should not be taken lightly. The possibilities for service customization are far greater than first meet the eye. Free Spirit Travel Agency, headquartered in Boulder, Colorado, completes information forms for first-time customers indicating travel patterns and preferences. The marketing potential of such a customer-information system is significant—for example, automatically sending notices on travel specials to Japan to those customers expressing an interest in that country. Automotive Systems, a Decatur, Georgia, automotive repair and maintenance firm, provides explicit notes on its customer bills indicating what still needs to be done with the car and the degree of priority. A growing number of financial institutions have implemented training and incentive programs to encourage tellers to refer to customers by name during transactions. Wendy's designed its hamburger production line to accommodate individual preferences in the makeup of a hamburger and, in the process, to capitalize on the limited flexibility of the McDonald's system.

One of the key strategic issues for

many service marketers is to determine the circumstances under which customization should apply and the circumstances under which standardization should apply. This issue is at the heart of an interesting trend in the banking industry toward the use of "personal bankers." Banks fully implementing personal banking assign to each retail customer a specific banker who opens new accounts and compiles information for future reference, makes loans and provides financial consultation, cuts red tape when problems arise, and in general is available when service of a non-routine nature is needed. In short, personal bankers function on a client basis in much the same way as public accountants or attorneys function.[13]

Banks that have adopted a personal-banker mode of organization have, in effect, established a system in which customers can on appropriate occasions get individualized service from a trained banker with whom they have dealt before. For routine transactions, the customer continues to use the teller station or ATMs that provide more standardized services. Although neither inexpensive nor easy to implement, personal banking is growing because it facilitates the custom packaging and hence the cross-selling of financial services; because it helps banks attract more affluent customers who value personalized and competent service; and because it is a way for larger institutions—a Wachovia, Harris Bank, or Irving Trust, for example—to *credibly* position themselves in the market as personalized institutions.[14]

Managing Evidence

Because goods are tangible and can be seen and touched, they are generally easier to evaluate than services. The intangibility of service prompts customer-prospects to be attentive to tangibles associated with the service for clues of the service's nature and quality.

A prime responsibility for the service marketer is to manage these tangibles so that the proper signals are conveyed about the service. As one author convincingly writes on this subject:

> Product marketing tends to give first emphasis to creating *abstract* associations. *Service* marketers, on the other hand, should be focused on enhancing and differentiating "realities" through manipulation of *tangible* clues. The management of evidence comes first for service marketers.[15]

There are a number of ways service marketers can manage evidence, as the following sections indicate.

Physical Services Environment. The physical environment in which services are purchased generally provides an important opportunity to tell the "right" story about a given service. Fortunately, service marketers are frequently in a position to shape the environment to their specifications because they distribute the service they produce.

There are many examples of service marketers capitalizing on this opportunity to manage evidence. A Richmond, Virginia, pediatrician decorated his office with bright, multicolored carpeting, pictures of Disney characters on the walls, a huge balloon Superman suspended from the ceiling in one of the examining rooms, a play area in a corner of the waiting room, and an after-visit toybox from which each child could select an inexpensive toy to take home. Braniff Airlines not only painted the exteriors of its planes a variety of bright colors but also furnished the interior with leather seats and wall murals. Hyatt with its daring hotel designs, Walt Disney with its spectacular theme parks, and TransAmerica with its pyramid-like headquarters building are three service companies that have succeeded notably in making architecture a centerpiece of their marketing strategy.

Appearance of Service Providers. The appearance of service providers is another tangible that can be managed. Fitness consultants at Cosmopolitan Health Spas often wear white "doctor" smocks and are rarely flabby. The Richmond pediatrician referred to earlier wore bright shirts and oversized bow ties rather than the traditional smock, which would have signaled "doctor" to the child. Braniff stewardesses wear designer outfits to complement the striking decor of the planes. Disney goes to great lengths to assure that theme park employees appear "freshly scrubbed," neatly groomed, and unfailingly cheerful.

Service Pricing. The tendency for customer-prospects to use the price of a product as an indicator of its quality is well known. Some researchers suggest that this tendency is even more pronounced for services. They argue that the relative absence of material data with which to appraise services makes price a potentially important index of quality.[16]

It follows that setting the right price is especially critical in circumstances where there is reason to expect differences in service quality from one supplier to another, and where the personal risk of buying a lower quality service is high. Lawyers, accountants, investment counselors, consultants, convention speakers, and even hair stylists can contradict signals they wish to communicate about quality by setting their prices too low. In short, a price can be a confidence builder; price is a clue.

Tying Services Marketing to Goods Marketing. Sometimes increased credibility concerning a service's quality can be gained by distributing it through a goods-marketing organization that already has credibility. The automobile-service and insurance business lines at Sears have undoubtedly benefited greatly from the association with the Sears' name and reputation.

A recent paper illustrates the potential benefits of tying services marketing into a goods-marketing organization with a hypothetical scenario involving an established department store adding a health spa.

> The store's strengths include a loyal market of middle age, upper middle class, upper income customers . . . a reputation for quality; and an image of progressive merchandising. . . . The health spa industry, in general, has a poor image which includes high pressure selling tactics, poor quality personnel, and inattention once the sale has been made. The new offering's intangibility allows the store to use its positive image to reduce the uncertainty and perceived risks for potential users of the spa. In addition to revenues generated from the spa services, there are many possibilities for cross-selling other store lines such as sporting goods, sportswear, and health food products.[17]

Interestingly, the process can work the other way with well-known and well-regarded service companies moving into the goods marketing. The key of course is where the credibility and access to the customer-prospect lies. In the preceding scenario, it lies with the department store. In the case of service enterprises like American Express and TWA, it lies with them.

Making the Service Tangible

Earlier it was indicated that intangibility has two meanings: that which cannot be touched; that which cannot be easily grasped mentally. Marketing advantage usually is to be gained if the service can be made more "touchable" and more easily grasped mentally. This involves attempting to make the service more tangible.[18]

Sometimes it is possible to make a service more palpable by creating a tangible representation of it. This is what has occurred with the development of the bank credit card. By representing the service with a specially encoded plastic card that, when used, triggers the service, Visa and others have been able to overcome many of the handicaps normally associated with marketing an intangible. The existence of the plastic card has allowed Visa to physically differentiate the service through color and graphics and to build and even extend a potent brand name, e.g., Visa travelers checks. Moreover, institutions distributing bank charge cards can extend their trading areas because once the card is obtained by consumers (often by mail), credit purchases can be made without going to the bank.

Just as service marketers should consider whether there are opportunities to develop a tangible representation of the service, so should they look for opportunities to make the service more easily grasped mentally. For example, the insurance industry has made it easier for consumers to perceive what is being sold by associating the intangible of insurance with relevant tangible objects. Consider the following:

- "You are in good *hands* with Allstate."
- "I've got a piece of the *rock*."
- "Under the Traveler's *umbrella*."
- "The Nationwide *blanket* of protection."

Hands, rocks, umbrellas, and blankets are used to more effectively communicate what insurance can provide people; they are devices used to make the service more easily grasped mentally.

Synchronizing Supply and Demand

Because services are performances, they cannot be inventoried. This is a significant fact of life in a service business because demand peaks cannot be accommodated simply by taking goods off a shelf. If an airline has 40 more flight-reservation requests than capacity permits, some business will likely be lost. Conversely, if an airliner takes off with 40 empty seats, the revenue that those 40 seats could have produced, had they been filled, is lost forever. One of the crucial challenges in many service industries is to find ways to better synchronize supply and demand as an alternative to recurring conditions of severe overdemand and underdemand. This is easier said than done. Demand peaks can occur during certain times of the day (airlines, restaurants), during certain days of the week (movies, hair styling), and during certain months of the year (income tax services, beach resorts).[19]

The service marketer interested in better synchronizing supply and demand may attempt to reshape demand and/or supply patterns for the service.

Reshaping Demand. All elements of the marketing mix are potentially available to help bring demand more in line with supply constraints. Delta Airlines, for example, has used pricing incentives to encourage travelers to fly during the early morning hours ("Early Bird" flights) and late evening ("Owly Bird" flights). Differential pricing to encourage demand during nonpeak periods is also commonly used by rental-car companies, movie theatres, and bars, among others. Through intensive promotion, the U.S. Postal Service has persuaded many customers that it is beneficial to them and their addressees to mail Christmas cards and packages early.[21] By adding a breakfast product line, McDonald's and other fast-food companies have been able to make productive use of previously underutilized facilities. Many banks have been able to lessen lobby traffic during peak hours by the use of automatic teller machines.

Importantly, demand-altering marketing actions can only have an impact when customer-prospects have control over their demand patterns. One recent article discusses the failure of the Boston bus system to attract significant numbers of new riders between 10:00 A.M. and 2:00 P.M. by reducing the normal $.25 fare to $.10 (promoted as "Dime Time"). A key problem was that most rush-hour riders were commuting to and from work and had little control over work schedules. More recent efforts by the bus system have centered on helping area employers understand the benefits of staggered and flexible working hours and how to implement them.[22]

Reshaping Supply. Another option available to the service marketer is to attempt to alter supply capacities to better match demand patterns. The possibilities are many and include the following:

* Using part-time employees and performing only essential tasks during peak demand periods.
* Training employees to perform multiple jobs so they can switch from one to another as demand dictates.
* Using paraprofessionals so that professionals can concentrate on duties requiring their expertise, e.g., parabankers who do legwork, solve routine problems, and handle clerical duties.
* Substituting equipment for human labor to make the service system more productive, e.g., automated car washes and computer-prepared income tax returns.

Obviously there are limits to how much supply capacity can be modified to fit demand requirements. The use of part-time personnel may be a variable cost, but the space they use when they come to work is a fixed cost. Nevertheless, the bottom-line potential from finding new ways to mesh supply capacity with demand is significant, and we can expect considerable innovation in this area during the 1980s. The same should be true for demand management as well. Indeed, America's best-managed service firms can be expected to vigorously work both sides of the street by seeking ways to reshape demand *and* supply patterns.

SUMMARY

Services differ from goods in some very important ways, and these differences present special challenges to the services marketer. The importance of the services sector in the American economy suggests the advisability of learning more about these differences and their marketing implications.

Services are more intangible than tangible, are produced and consumed simultaneously, and in many cases are less standardized and uniform than goods. These characteristics heighten the importance of certain marketing approaches that are usually not considered priorities or even applicable in goods marketing. These important services-marketing approaches include internal marketing, service customization, managing evidence, making the service tangible, and synchronizing supply and demand patterns.

In the academic discipline, services marketing has long been a stepchild to goods marketing, although progress has been made in recent years. It is time to do some serious catching up in terms of marketing thought. Perhaps the 1980s will be the decade in which this occurs.

NOTES

1. Fabian Linden, "Service, Please," *Across the Board* (August 1978), p. 42.
2. For a good discussion of this point see G. Lynn Shostack, "Breaking Free from Product Marketing," *Journal of Marketing* (April 1977), pp. 73–80.
3. *New World Dictionary of the American Language* (1974), p. 731.
4. Dan R. E. Thomas, "Strategy Is Different in Service Businesses," *Harvard Business Review* (July–August 1978), pp. 158–65.
5. Richard B. Chase, "Where Does the Customer Fit in a Service Operation?" *Harvard Business Review* (November–December 1978), pp. 137–42.
6. Thomas W. Thompson, Leonard L. Berry, and Phillip H. Davidson, *Banking Tomorrow—Managing Markets through Planning* (New York: Van Nostrand Reinhold, 1978), p. 243.
7. See, for example, Warren Magoon and Larry Schnicker, "Flexible Hours at State Street Bank of Boston: A Case Study," *Personnel Administrator* (October 1977), pp. 34–37; and Charles A. Cottrell and J. Mark Walker, "Flexible Work Days: Philosophy and Bank Implementation," *Journal of Retail Banking* (December 1979), pp. 72–80.
8. See G. M. Hostage, "Quality Control in a Service Business," *Harvard Business Review* (July–August 1975), pp. 104–05.
9. See "Delta's Flying Money Machine," *Business Week* (May 9, 1977), pp. 84–89.
10. See "Listening and Responding to Employee Concerns—An Interview with A. W. Clause," *Harvard Business Review* (January–February 1980), pp. 101–14.
11. See N. W. Pope, "Mickey Mouse Marketing," *American Banker* (July 25, 1979), pp. 4 and 14; and N. W. Pope, "More Mickey Mouse Marketing," *American Banker* (September 12, 1979), pp. 4–14.
12. W. Earl Sasser and Stephen P. Arbeit, "Selling Jobs in the Service Sector," *Business Horizons* (June 1976), p. 64.
13. Leonard L. Berry, "The Personal Banker," *Bankers Magazine* (January–February 1978), pp. 54–55.
14. See Thomas J. Stanley, Leonard L. Berry, and William D. Danko, "Personal Service Versus Convenience: Perceptions of the High-Income Customer," *Journal of Retail Banking* (June 1979), pp. 54–61.
15. Shostack, "Breaking Free from Product Marketing," p. 78.
16. Pierre Eiglier and Eric Langeard, "A New Approach to Service Marketing," in Eiglier, et al., *Marketing Consumer Services: New Insights* (Cambridge, Mass.: Marketing Science Institute, 1977), p. 41.
17. William R. George, "The Retailing of Services—A Challenging Future," *Journal of Retailing* (Fall 1977), pp. 88–89.
18. This section draws heavily from James H. Donnelly, Jr., "Service Delivery Strategies in the 1980s—Academic Perspective," in Leonard L. Berry and James H. Donnelly, Jr., eds., *Financial Institution Marketing: Strategies in the 1980s* (Washington, D.C.: Consumer Banker Association, 1980), pp. 143–150.
19. W. Earl Sasser, "Match Supply and Demand in Service Industries," *Harvard Business Review* (November–December 1976), p. 138.
20. *Ibid.*, pp. 137–40.
21. Christopher H. Lovelock and Robert F. Young, "Look to Consumers to Increase Productivity," *Harvard Business Review* (May–June 1979), p. 176.
22. *Ibid.*, p. 173.

Retail Strategy and the Classification of Consumer Goods

Louis P. Bucklin

When Melvin T. Copeland published his famous discussion of the classification of consumer goods, shopping, convenience, and specialty goods, his intent was clearly to create a guide for the development of marketing strategies by manufacturers.[1] Although his discussion involved retailers and retailing, his purpose was to show how consumer buying habits affected the type of channel of distribution and promotional strategy that a manufacturer should adopt. Despite the controversy which still surrounds his classification, his success in creating such a guide may be judged by the fact that through the years few marketing texts have failed to make use of his ideas.

The purpose of this article is to attempt to clarify some of the issues that exist with respect to the classification, and to extend the concept to include the retailer and the study of retail strategy.

Reprinted from *Journal of Marketing,* published by the American Marketing Association (January, 1963), pp. 51–56.

CONTROVERSY OVER THE CLASSIFICATION SYSTEM

The starting point for the discussion lies with the definitions adopted by the American Marketing Association's Committee on Definitions for the classification system in 1948.[2] These are:

Convenience Goods: Those consumers' goods which the customer purchases frequently, immediately, and with the minimum of effort.

Shopping Goods: Those consumers' goods which the customer in the process of selection and purchase characteristically compares on such bases as suitability, quality, price and style.

Specialty Goods: Those consumers' goods on which a significant group of buyers are habitually willing to make a special purchasing effort.

This set of definitions was retained in virtually the same form by the Committee on Definitions in its latest publication.[3]

401

Opposing these accepted definitions stands a critique by Richard H. Holton.[4] Finding the Committee's definitions too imprecise to be able to measure consumer buying behavior, he suggested that the following definitions not only would represent the essence of Copeland's original idea, but be operationally more useful as well.

Convenience Goods: Those goods for which the consumer regards the probable gain from making price and quality comparisons as small compared to the cost of making such comparisons.

Shopping Goods: Those goods for which the consumer regards the probable gain from making price and quality comparisons as large relative to the cost of making such comparisons.

Specialty Goods: Those convenience or shopping goods, which have such a limited market as to require the consumer to make a special effort to purchase them.

Holton's definitions have particular merit because they make explicit the underlying conditions that control the extent of a consumer's shopping activities. They show that a consumer's buying behavior will be determined not only by the strength of his desire to secure some good, but by his perception of the cost of shopping to obtain it. In other words, the consumer continues to shop for *all goods* so long as he feels that the additional satisfaction from further comparisons are at least equal to the cost of making the additional effort. The distinction between shopping and convenience goods lies principally in the degree of satisfaction to be secured from further comparisons.

The Specialty Good Issue
While Holton's conceptualization makes an important contribution, he has sacrificed some of the richness of Copeland's original ideas. This is essentially David J. Luck's complaint in a criticism of Holton's proposal.[5] Luck objected to the abandonment of the *willingness* of consumers to make a special effort to buy as the rationale for the concept of specialty goods. He regarded this type of consumer behavior as based upon unique consumer attitudes toward certain goods and not the density of distribution of those goods. Holten, in a reply, rejected Luck's point; he remained convinced that the real meaning of specialty goods could be derived from his convenience goods, shopping goods continuum, and market conditions.[6]

The root of the matter appears to be that insufficient attention has been paid to the fact that the consumer, once embarked upon some buying expedition, may have only one of two possible objectives in mind. A discussion of this aspect of consumer behavior will make possible a closer synthesis of Holton's contributions with the more traditional point of view.

A Forgotten Idea
The basis for this discussion is afforded by certain statements, which the marketing profession has largely ignored over the years, in Copeland's original presentation of his ideas. These have regard to the extent of the consumer's awareness of the precise nature of the item he wished to buy, *before* he starts his shopping trip. Copeland stated that the consumer, in both the case of convenience goods and specialty goods, has full knowledge of the particular good, or its acceptable substitutes, that he will buy before he commences his buying trip. The consumer, however, lacks this knowledge in the case of a shopping good.[7] This means that the buying trip must not only serve the objective of purchasing the good, but must enable the consumer to discover which item he wants to buy.

The behavior of the consumer during any shopping expedition may, as a result, be regarded as heavily dependent upon the state of his decision as to what he wants to buy. If the consumer knows precisely what he wants, he needs only to undertake communication activities sufficient to take title to the desired product. He may also undertake ancillary physical activities involving the handling of the product and delivery. If the consumer is uncertain as to what he wants to buy, then an additional activity will have to be performed. This involves the work of making comparisons between possible alternative purchases, or simply search.

There would be little point, with respect to the problem of classifying consumer goods, in distinguishing between the activity of search and that of making a commitment to buy, if a consumer always performed both before purchasing a good. The crucial point is that he does not. While most of the items that a consumer buys have probably been subjected to comparison at some point in his life, he does not make a search before each purchase. Instead, a past solution to the need is frequently remembered and, if satisfactory, is implemented.[8] Use of these past decisions for many products quickly moves the consumer past any perceived necessity of undertaking new comparisons and leaves only the task of exchange to be discharged.

REDEFINITION OF THE SYSTEM

Use of the concept of problem solving permits one to classify consumer buying efforts into two broad categories which may be called shopping and nonshopping goods.

Shopping Goods

Shopping goods are those for which the consumer *regularly* formulates a new solu-tion to his need each time it is aroused. They are goods whose suitability is determined through search before the consumer commits himself to each purchase.

The motivation behind this behavior stems from circumstances which tend to perpetuate a lack of complete consumer knowledge about the nature of the product that he would like to buy.[9] Frequent changes in price, style, or product technology cause consumer information to become obsolete. The greater the time lapse between purchases, the more obsolete will his information be. The consumer's needs are also subject to change, or he may seek variety in his purchases as an actual goal. These forces will tend to make past information inappropriate. New search, due to forces internal and external to the consumer, is continuously required for products with purchase determinants which the consumer regards as both important and subject to change.[10]

The number of comparisons that the consumer will make in purchasing a shopping good may be determined by use of Holton's hypothesis on effort. The consumer, in other words, will undertake search for a product until the perceived value to be secured through additional comparisons is less than the estimated cost of making those comparisons. Thus, shopping effort will vary according to the intensity of the desire of the consumer to find the right product, the type of product and availability of retail facilities. Whether the consumer searches diligently, superficially, or even buys at the first opportunity, however, does not alter the shopping nature of the product.

Nonshopping Goods

Turning now to nonshopping goods, one may define these as products for which the consumer is both willing and able to use stored solutions to the problem of finding a product to answer a need. From the remarks on shopping goods it may be generalized that nonshopping goods have purchase determinants which do not change, or which are perceived as changing inconsequentially, between purchases.[11] The consumer, for example, may assume that price for some product never changes or that price is unimportant. It may be unimportant because either the price is low, or the consumer is very wealthy.

Nonshopping goods may be divided into convenience and specialty goods by means of the concept of a preference map. Bayton introduces this concept as the means to show how the consumer stores information about products.[12] It is a rough ranking of the relative desirability of the different kinds of products that the consumer sees as possible satisfiers for his needs. For present purposes, two basic types of preference maps may be envisaged. One type ranks all known product alternatives equally in terms of desirability. The other ranks one particular product as so superior to all others that the consumer, in effect, believes this product is the only answer to his need.

Distinguishing the Specialty Good

This distinction in preference maps creates the basis for discriminating between a convenience good and a specialty good. Clearly, where the consumer is indifferent to the precise item among a number of substitutes which he could buy, he will purchase the most accessible one and look no further. This is a convenience good. On the other hand, where the consumer recognizes only one brand of a product as capable of satisfying his needs, he will be willing to bypass more readily accessible substitutes in order to secure the wanted item. This is a specialty good.

However, most nonshopping goods will probably fall in between these two polar extremes. Preference maps will exist where the differences between the relative desirability of substitutes may range from the slim to the well marked. In order to distinguish between convenience goods and specialty goods in these cases, Holton's hypothesis regarding consumer effort may be employed again. A convenience good, in these terms, becomes one for which the consumer has such little preference among his perceived choices that he buys the item which is most readily available. A specialty good is one for which consumer preference is so strong that he bypasses, or would be willing to bypass, the purchase of more accessible substitutes in order to secure his most wanted item.

It should be noted that this decision on the part of the consumer as to how much effort he should expend takes place under somewhat different conditions than the one for shopping goods. In the nonshopping good instance the consumer has a reasonably good estimate of the additional value to be achieved by purchasing his preferred item. The estimate of the additional cost required to make this purchase may also be made fairly accurately. Consequently, the consumer will be in a much better position to justify the expenditure of additional effort here than in the case of shopping goods where much uncertainty must exist with regard to both of these factors.

THE NEW CLASSIFICATION

The classification of consumer goods that results from the analysis is as follows:

Convenience Goods: Those goods for which the consumer, before his need arises, possesses a preference map that indicates a willingness to purchase any of a number of known substitutes rather than to make the additional effort required to buy a particular item.

Shopping Goods: Those goods for which the consumer has not developed a complete preference map before the need arises, requiring him to undertake search to construct such a map before purchase.

Specialty Goods: Those goods for which the consumer, before his need arises, possesses a preference map that indicates a willingness to expend the additional effort required to purchase the most preferred item rather than to buy a more readily accessible substitute.

EXTENSION TO RETAILING

The classification of the goods concept developed above may now be extended to retailing. As the concept now stands, it is derived from consumer attitudes or motives toward a *product*. These attitudes, or product motives, are based upon the consumer's interpretation of a product's styling, special features, quality, and social status of its brand name, if any. Occasionally the price may also be closely associated with the product by the consumer.

Classification of Patronage Motives

The extension of the concept to retailing may be made through the notion of patronage motives, a term long used in marketing. Patronage motives are derived from consumer attitudes concerning the retail establishment. They are related to factors which the consumer is likely to regard as controlled by the retailer. These will include assortment, credit, service, guarantee, shopping ease and enjoyment, and usually price. Patronage motives, however, have never been systematically categorized. It is proposed that the procedure developed above to discriminate among product motives be used to classify consumer buying motives with respect to retail stores as well.

This will provide the basis for the consideration of retail marketing strategy and will aid in clearing up certain ambiguities that would otherwise exist if consumer buying motives were solely classified by product factors. These ambiguities appear, for example, when the consumer has a strong affinity for some particular brand of a product, but little interest in where he buys it. The manufacturer of the product, as a result, would be correct in defining the product as a specialty item if the consumer's preferences were so strong as to cause him to eschew more readily available substitutes. The retailer may regard it as a convenience good, however, since the consumer will make no special effort to purchase the good from any particular store. This problem is clearly avoided by separately classifying product and patronage motives.

The categorization of patronage motives by the above procedure results in the following three definitions. These are:

Convenience Stores: Those stores for which the consumer, before his need for some product arises, possesses a preference map that indicates a willingness to buy from the most accessible store.

Shopping Stores: Those stores for which the consumer has not developed a complete preference map relative to the product he wishes to buy, requiring him to undertake a search to construct such a map before purchase.

Specialty Stores: Those stores for which the consumer, before his need for some product arises, possesses a preference map that indicates a willingness to buy the item from a particular establishment even though it may not be the most accessible.

The Product-Patronage Matrix

Although this basis will not afford the retailer a means to consider alternative strategies, a finer classification system may be obtained by relating consumer product motives to consumer patronage motives. By cross-classifying each product motive with each patronage motive, one creates a three-by-three matrix, representing nine possible types of consumer buying behavior. Each of the nine cells in the matrix may be described as follows:

1. *Convenience Store—Convenience Good:* The consumer, represented by this category, prefers to buy the most readily available brand of product at the most accessible store.
2. *Convenience Store—Shopping Good:* The consumer selects his purchase from among the assortment carried by the most accessible store.
3. *Convenience Store—Specialty Good:* The consumer purchases his favored brand from the most accessible store which has item in stock.
4. *Shopping Store—Convenience Good:* The consumer is indifferent to the brand of product he buys, but shops among different stores in order to secure better retail service and/or lower retail price.
5. *Shopping Store—Shopping Good:* The consumer makes comparisons among both retail controlled factors and factors associated with the product (brand).
6. *Shopping Store—Specialty Good:* The consumer has a strong preference with respect to the brand of the product, but shops among a number of stores in order to secure the best retail and/or price for this brand.
7. *Specialty Store—Convenience Good:* The consumer prefers to trade at a specific store, but is indifferent to the brand of product purchased.
8. *Specialty Store—Shopping Good:* The consumer prefers to trade at a certain store, but is uncertain as to which product he wishes to buy and examines the store's assortment for the best purchase.
9. *Specialty Store—Specialty Good:* The consumer has both a preference for a particular store and a specific brand.

Conceivably, each of these nine types of behavior might characterize the buying patterns of some consumers for a given product. It seems more likely, however, that the behavior of consumers toward a product could be represented by only three or four of the categories. The remaining cells would be empty, indicating that no consumers bought the product by these methods. Different cells, of course, would be empty for different products.

THE FORMATION OF RETAIL STRATEGY

The extended classification system developed above clearly provides additional information important to the manufacturer in the planning of his marketing strategy. Of principal interest here, however, is the means by which the retailer might use the classification system in planning his marketing strategy.

Three Basic Steps

The procedure involves three steps. The first is the classification of the retailer's potential customers for some product by market segment, using the nine categories in the consumer buying habit matrix to define the principal segments. The second requires the retailer to determine the nature of the marketing strategies necessary to appeal to each market segment. The final step is the retailer's selection of the market segment, and the strategy associated with it, to which he will sell. A simplified, hypothetical example may help to clarify this process.

A former buyer of dresses for a department store decided to open her own dress shop. She rented a small store in the downtown area of a city of 50,000, ten miles distant from a metropolitan center of several hundred thousand population. In contemplating her marketing strategy, she was certain that the different incomes, educational backgrounds, and tastes of the potential customers in her city meant that various groups of these women were using sharply different buying methods for dresses. Her initial problem was to determine, by use of the consumer buying habit matrix, what proportion of her potential market bought dresses in what manner.

By drawing on her own experience, discussions with other retailers in the area, census and other market data, the former buyer estimated that her potential market was divided, according to the matrix, in the proportions [shown in Table 28–1].

This analysis revealed four market segments that she believed were worth further consideration. (In an actual situation,

Table 28–1
Proportion of Potential Dress Market in Each Matrix Cell

Buying Habit	% of Market
Convenience store—convenience good	0
Convenience store—shopping good	3
Convenience store—specialty good	20
Shopping store—convenience good	0
Shopping store—shopping good	35
Shopping store—specialty good	2
Specialty store—convenience good	0
Specialty store—shopping good	25
Specialty store—specialty good	15
	100

each of these four should be further divided into submarket segments according to other possible factors such as age, income, dress size required, location of residence, etc.) Her next task was to determine the type of marketing mix which would most effectively appeal to each of these segments. The information for these decisions was derived from the characteristics of consumer behavior associated with each of the defined segments. The following is a brief description of her assessment of how elements of the marketing mix ought to be weighted in order to formulate a strategy for each segment.

A Strategy for Each Segment
To appeal to the convenience store—specialty good segment she felt that the two most important elements in the mix should be a highly accessible location and selection of widely-accepted brand merchandise. Of somewhat lesser importance, she found, were depth of assortment, personal selling and price. Minimal emphasis should be given to store promotion and facilities.

She reasoned that the shopping store—shopping good requires a good central location, emphasis on price, and a broad assortment. She ranked store promotion, accepted brand names and personal selling as secondary. Store facilities would, once again, receive minor emphasis.

The specialty store—shopping good market would, she believed, have to be catered to with an exceptionally strong assortment, a high level of personal selling and more elaborate store facilities. Less emphasis would be needed upon prominent brand names, store promotions, and price. Location was of minor importance.

The specialty store—specialty good category, she thought, would require a marketing mix heavily emphasizing personal selling and highly elaborate store facilities and service. She also felt that prominent brand names would be required, but that these would probably have to include the top names in fashion, including labels from Paris. Depth of assortment would be secondary, while least emphasis would be placed upon store promotion, price, and location.

Evaluation of Alternatives

The final step in the analysis required the former dress buyer to assess her abilities to implement any one of these strategies, given the degree of competition existing in each segment. Her considerations were as follows. With regard to the specialty store—specialty good market, she was unprepared to make the investment in store facilities and services that she felt would be necessary. She also thought, since a considerable period of time would probably be required for her to build up the necessary reputation, that this strategy involved substantial risk. Lastly, she believed that her experience in buying high fashion was somewhat limited and that trips to European fashion centers would prove burdensome.

She also doubted her ability to cater to the specialty store—shopping good market, principally because she knew that her store would not be large enough to carry the necessary assortment depth. She felt that this same factor would limit her in attempting to sell to the shopping store—shopping good market as well. Despite the presence of the large market in this segment, she believed that she would not be able to create sufficient volume in her proposed quarters to enable her to compete effectively with the local department store and several large department stores in the neighboring city.

The former buyer believed her best opportunity was in selling to the convenience store—specialty good segment. While there were already two other stores in her city which were serving this segment, she believed that a number of important brands were still not represented. Her past contacts with resources led her to believe that she would stand an excellent chance of securing a number of these lines. By stocking these brands, she thought that she could capture a considerable number of local customers who currently were purchasing them in the large city. In this way, she believed, she would avoid the full force of local competition.

Decision

The conclusion of the former buyer to use her store to appeal to the convenience store—specialty good segment represents the culmination to the process of analysis suggested here. It shows how the use of the three-by-three matrix of consumer buying habits may aid the retailer in developing his marketing strategy. It is a device which can isolate the important market segments. It provides further help in enabling the retailer to associate the various types of consumer behavior with those elements of the marketing mix to which they are sensitive. Finally, the analysis forces the retailer to assess the probability of his success in attempting to use the necessary strategy in order to sell each possible market.

NOTES

1. Melvin T. Copeland, "Relation of Consumers' Buying Habits to Marketing Methods," *Harvard Business Review* (April, 1923), pp. 282–289.
2. Definitions Committee, American Marketing Association, "Report of the Definitions Committee," *Journal of Marketing* (October, 1948), pp. 202–217, at p. 206, p. 215.
3. Definitions Committee, American Marketing Association, *Marketing Definitions*, (Chicago: American Marketing Association, 1960), pp. 11, 21, 22.

4. Richard H. Holton, "The Distinction between Convenience Goods, Shopping Goods, and Specialty Goods," *Journal of Marketing* (July, 1958), pp. 53–56.

5. David J. Luck, "On the Nature of Specialty Goods," *Journal of Marketing* (July, 1959), pp. 61–64.

6. Richard H. Holton, "What Is Really Meant by 'Specialty Goods'?" *Journal of Marketing* (July, 1959), pp. 64–67.

7. Melvin T. Copeland, same reference as footnote 1, pp. 283–284.

8. George Katona, *Psychological Analysis of Economic Behavior* (New York: McGraw-Hill Book Co., Inc., 1951), p. 47

9. Same reference, pp. 67–68.

10. George Katona and Eva Mueller, "A Study of Purchase Decisions in Consumer Behavior," Lincoln Clark, editor, *Consumer Behavior* (New York: University Press, 1954), pp. 30–87.

11. Katona, same reference as footnote 8, p. 68.

12. James A. Bayton, "Motivation, Cognition, Learning—Basic Factors in Consumer Behavior," *Journal of Marketing* (January, 1958), pp. 282–289, at p. 287.

Distribution Channels as Political Economies: A Framework for Comparative Analysis

Louis W. Stern and Torger Reve

Published studies related to distribution channels present, collectively, a rather disjointed collage. This is due, in part, to the absence of a framework which can accommodate the various paradigms and orientations employed in performing research on distribution channel phenomena. What is needed is a comprehensive mapping of the field which depicts the various paths one could follow, the likely places where one might end up, and the boundaries of the various places within the entire conceptual space. If this mapping were successfully accomplished, then those individuals already within the field would have a better understanding of where their work stood relative to others' and would, hopefully, be encouraged to seek out complementary paradigms to those which they have adopted. The mapping would also indicate to many of

those who perceive themselves as standing outside the field that much of what they are doing could easily have relevance to the substance of the field. They might even be motivated to advance the field themselves. And, most importantly, the mapping would be helpful to prospective scholars who, to a large extent, do not have a very solid understanding of the research opportunities available within the field. While no single article is ever likely to accomplish such a comprehensive mapping, there is clearly a strong need to make a beginning. If a meaningful start at ordering the field can be undertaken, then this will likely encourage others to pursue the completion and refinement of the ordering process.

Despite the centrality of distribution channels in marketing, there exist three major deficiencies in the current status of distribution channel theory and research. *First*, analyses of distribution channels have largely focused on the technologies (e.g., sales force incentive systems, pricing procedures, and the like) employed by individual

Louis W. Stern and Torger Reve, "Distribution Channels as Political Economies: A Framework for Comparative Analysis," Vol. 44 (Summer 1980). Reprinted from *Journal of Marketing*, published by the American Marketing Association.

organizations in their efforts to structure and control channel activities (cf., Gattorna 1978; McCammon and Little 1965; McCammon, Bates and Guiltinan 1971). These analyses have adopted a *micro* orientation in keeping with traditional problem-solving approaches in marketing management. Little attention has been given to questions of the maintenance, adaptation, and evolution of marketing channels as competitive entities.

Second, channel theory is fragmented into two seemingly disparate disciplinary orientations: an *economic* approach and a *behavioral* approach. The former attempts to apply microeconomic theory and industrial organization analysis to the study of distribution systems and has been essentially "efficiency" oriented, focusing on costs, functional differentiation, and channel design (cf., Baligh and Richartz 1967; Bucklin 1966; Bucklin and Carman 1974; Cox, Goodman, and Fichandler 1965). The latter borrows heavily from social psychology and organization theory and has been essentially "socially" oriented, focusing on power and conflict phenomena (cf., Alderson 1957; Stern 1969). Rarely have there been attempts to integrate these two perspectives. Indeed, they should be viewed as complementary, because the former deals mainly with economic "outputs" while the latter is concerned with behavioral "processes."

Third, empirical studies of distribution networks have been extremely limited in their scope and methodological sophistication. The vast majority of empirical works in the channels area has been purely descriptive in nature, with little or no testing of formal hypotheses derived from theory (cf., McCammon and Little 1965). Although more recent studies evidence a trend toward more systematic testing of theoretical relationships, these investigations have typically been confined to an analysis of a single distribution channel within a particular in-

dustry (exceptions include Etgar 1976a, 1978; Hunt and Nevin 1974; Porter 1974; Weik 1972).[1] Future channel research must focus on making systematic *comparisons* of different distribution networks within and between various environmental conditions, irrespective of whether the different networks are found in the same industry or across industries.

A promising framework for addressing these issues is provided by the *political economy* approach to the study of social systems (Benson 1975; Wamsley and Zald 1973, 1976; Zald 1970a, 1970b). Basically, the *political economy approach views a social system as comprising interacting sets of major economic and sociopolitical forces which affect collective behavior and performance.* The purpose of this article, therefore, is to present a political economy framework which can be applied to gain deeper understanding of the *internal* functioning of a distribution channel. Such a framework also permits comprehension of the processes where distribution channels are influenced by and adapt to environmental conditions. It is, however, recognized that this framework is only one of many that might be suggested. It has been selected because of its strong potential for comprehensively mapping this area of marketing inquiry.

The political economy framework outlined here should be viewed as the first step in the direction of identifying and dimensionalizing the major variables influencing and ordering channel structure and behavior. A premise of the framework as initially formulated is that complex socioeconomic interrelations involve multilateral interactions as opposed to "simple" cause-effect mechanisms, such as those between power use and conflict or between channel design and costs. Given the present state of channel theory development, the initial task to be performed in accomplishing methodological and interpretive rigor is to lay out the relevant channel dimensions in terms of "fields," e.g., external-internal, economic-sociopolitical; structural-process. Otherwise, theoretical research in the area will continue to suffer from ad hoc operationalizations, where researchers select independent measures and globally hypothesize some dependent outcome without indicating or even being aware of which other interacting variables are being held or assumed constant. Hence, the political economy framework should be seen as an attempt to *chart out* or classify the total field of channel interaction. The political economy perspective as an organizing framework impels the generation of significant research questions and, therefore, has the potential for producing new theoretical insights.

As an aid to exploring the promise of the framework, a number of *illustrative* propositions have been generated throughout this article. They should be helpful in stimulating future research because they provide some insights into the kinds of meaningful relationships among core concepts which are motivated by employing the framework. However, it should be noted that there has been no attempt to specify re-

search designs to "test" the propositions. This is because the propositions can be operationalized in a variety of ways. Given the existing state of knowledge in the channels area, it might be misleading for us to suggest specific operationalizations and would, almost certainly, deflect attention from the main purpose of the article due to the controversy they might evoke. As an aid to the reader, we have provided an appendix which conceptually defines a few of the key constructs used. This "glossary" only serves to suggest the conceptual boundaries of the constructs; it is not intended to provide operation allegations.

In the following section, the full political economy framework is broadly outlined. Then, the remainder of the paper explores, in considerable detail, the *intra*-channel variables included in the framework.

THE POLITICAL ECONOMY FRAMEWORK

The political economy framework is capsulized in Figure 29–1. As indicated, there are two major systems: (I) the *internal political economy,* i.e., the internal structuring and

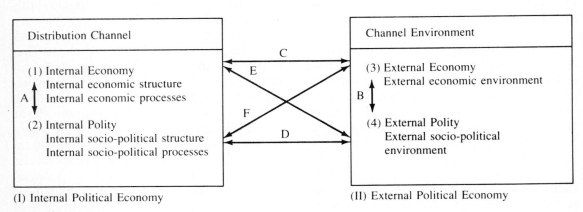

(I) Internal Political Economy   (II) External Political Economy

Figure 29–1
A Political Economy Framework for Distribution Channel Analysis

functioning of the distribution channel, and (II) the *external political economy*, i.e., the channel's task environment. Both systems are divided into two component parts: an *economy* and a *polity*. The major relationships which need to be explored are indicated by arrows with capital letter notations (see Figure 29–1).

The Internal Political Economy

Distribution channels are interorganizational "collectives" of institutions and actors simultaneously pursuing self-interest and collective goals (Reve and Stern 1979; Van de Ven, Emmett, and Koenig 1974). As such, the actors interact in a socioeconomic setting of their own, called an internal political economy. To comprehend fully the relevant internal dimensions and interactions, the framework suggests that a channel be analyzed in relation to its (1) *internal economy*, i.e., the internal economic structure and processes and its (2) *internal polity*, i.e., the internal sociopolitical structure and processes.

The internal economic structure is described by the type of transactional form linking channel members, i.e., the vertical economic arrangement within the marketing channel, while the internal economic processes refer to the nature of the decision mechanisms employed to determine the terms of trade among the members. On the other hand, the internal sociopolitical structure is defined by the pattern of power-dependence relations which exist among channel members, while the internal sociopolitical processes are described in terms of the dominant sentiments (i.e., cooperation and/or conflict) within the channel.

Identifying that marketing channels consist of an internal economy and an internal polity is not a major departure from prior approaches to channel research. The contribution of the political economy framework is the explicit insistence that economic and sociopolitical forces not be analyzed in isolation. By considering the interactions between the economy and the polity, it is possible to understand and explain the internal structuring and functioning of distribution systems and to derive a number of illustrative propositions for channel research.

The 'External' Political Economy

Organizations always operate within an environment. The environment of a distribution channel is a complex of economic, physical, cultural, demographic, psychological, political, and technological forces. In the political economy framework, such as forces are, as shown in Figure 29–1, incorporated in (3) *the external economy*, i.e., the prevailing and prospective economic environment and (4) *the external polity*, i.e., the external sociopolitical system in which the channel operates. The external economy of a distribution channel can be described by the nature of its vertical (input and output) and horizontal markets. The external polity can be described by the distribution and use of power resources among external actors (e.g., competitors, regulatory agencies, and trade associations) (cf., Palamountain 1955; Pfeffer and Salancik 1978; Thompson 1967; Yuchtman and Seashore 1967). An analysis of the external sociopolitical environment entails specification of the type of actors exercising power in the environment (Evan 1965), the power relations and means of control used between the external actors and the focal channel (Thompson 1967), the power relations between external actors (Terreberry 1968), and the extent to which the activities of channel members are actually controlled by environmental forces (Benson 1975).

The external economic and sociopolitical forces interact and define environmental conditions for the channel. The external political economy thus influences the internal political economy through adaptation and interaction processes (Aldrich 1979). Furthermore, channels not only adapt to their environments, but also influence and shape them (Pfeffer and Salancik 1978). The arrows in Figure 29–1 which indicate interactions between the component systems therefore point in both directions.

Attention is now turned to an elaboration of the internal political economy of distribution channels. The focus on intrachannel variables is a natural starting point, given that virtually all existing channel research has dealt with internal channel phenomena. Knowledge of environmental variables and their impact is fragmentary at best (Etgar 1977). Future examinations of the political economy framework must, however, focus on environmental variables and on the interactions between the internal and external economies.

THE INTERNAL POLITICAL ECONOMY OF DISTRIBUTION CHANNELS: AN ELABORATION OF THE FRAMEWORK

In this section the major internal economic and sociopolitical forces at work in distribution channels are described. These forces interact in shaping channel arrangements and in affecting marketing channel behavior and performance.

Internal Economy of Distribution Channels

Distribution channels are primarily set up to perform a set of essential *economic* functions in society, bridging the gap between production and consumption. Thus, it is no surprise that a substantial proportion of channel research, especially the earlier stud-

ies, has focused on an analysis of the *internal economy* of distribution channels (see Gattorna 1978; McCammon and Little 1965 for reviews).

As already indicated, the internal economy of a distribution channel may be divided into two components. The *internal economic structure* refers to the vertical economic arrangements or the transactional form in the channel. These arrangements range from a series of independently owned and managed specialized units which transact exchanges across markets to complete vertical integration where exchanges between wholly-owned units are conducted within a hierarchy (Williamson 1975). Whereas market transactions primarily on the use of the price mechanism, hierarchial transactions rely on administrative mechanisms. Between the two extreme economic arrangements lies a wide variety of structures in which the market mechanism is modified through some kine of formal or informal contractual arrangements between the parties involved (Blois 1972; Liebeler 1976).

Operating within each internal economic structure of a channel are certain *internal economic processes* or decision mechanisms. Thus, agreement on the terms of trade and the division of marketing functions among channel members may be reached in impersonal, routine, or habitual ways; through bargaining; or via centralized planning processes. The type of processes used to allocate resources in any given channel is likely to conform to or, at least, be constrained by the transactional form of the channel. Typically, competitive, price-mediated mechanisms are dominant in those market transactions where information is relatively complete and products are undifferentiated, as in soybean trading, while centralized planning is dominant in most hierarchical transactions. But competitive, price-mediated mechanisms have also been simulated in hierarchical structures through mathematical programming models using computed shadow prices as terms of transfer (Jennergren 1979). For other transactions which fall in between the two structural extremes, the allocation of many marketing activities is largely determined through bargaining among the parties.

Of critical importance for channel analysis is the need to compare the efficiency and effectiveness of various transactional forms of structures across each of the three decision making mechanisms. It is also important to consider cases where a specific economic process is employed across economic structures. For example, an illustrative proposition dealing with centralized planning processes might be:

P1. The more centralized planning processes predominate, irrespective of the transactional form, the more efficient and effective the marketing channel for a product or service is likely to be.

In this sense, efficiency could be defined in terms of output to input ratios (e.g., sales per square foot) and effectiveness could be some external market referent (e.g., market share). A number of theoretical rationales underlie P1: (1) the likely constraints on suboptimization within the channel derived from joint decision making, (2) the exploitation of potential scale economics, (3) the possible cost advantages gained via increased programming of distributive functions, and (4) the reduction of transaction costs due to reduced uncertainties and lessened opportunism (cf., Etgar 1976a, Grønhaug and Reve 1979).

There are, however, a number of rationales working against P1's central premise: (1) the satisficing modes which operate when centralized planning processes pre-

dominate, (2) the danger of bureaucratization and loss of cost consciousness, and (3) the curbing of initiative at "lower" levels. Therefore, P1 demands investigation in concert with a second, counter proposition.

P.2 The more centralized planning processes predominate, irrespective of the transactional form, the less likely is the marketing channel to be able to react quickly to external threats.

This proposition has its roots in the criticism which has often been directed at vertically integrated systems (cf., Arndt and Reve 1979; Sturdivant 1966). However, it may also apply to market transactions, because the more that the exchange process among channel members is organized, the more severe become trade-offs between efficiency and adaptiveness. On the other hand, while fast and specific adaptation to localized threats will likely be slow when centralized planning processes are prevalent, the adoption of such processes may permit better environmental scanning, more opportunities to influence external actors, and more ability to absorb shocks over the long run than those channels which are typified by bargaining or by routine or habitual decision making.

Analysis is also required within transactional forms across the various decision making mechanisms. Especially significant are the issues which Williamson (1975) raises in his markets and hierarchies framework. He shows how market transactions may become very costly due to human factors, such as bounded rationality and opportunism, coupled with environmental factors, such as uncertainty and economically concentrated input or output markets (i.e., small number bargaining). When information is unequally possessed, opportunistic behavior is likely to prevail, and exchange may be commercially hazardous. An illustrative proposition drawn from this line of reasoning is:

P3. Market transactions in oligopsonistic situations are likely to lead to information imbalances, opportunistic behavior, and high transaction costs. Impersonal, routine, or habitual decision making mechanisms in such situations will not suffice to overcome opportunistic behavior within the channel.

For example, when the members of atomistic industries, such as those found in the manufacture of maintenance, operating, and repair items, rely on open market forces to determine the terms of trade between themselves and the members of oligopolies, such as in the aerospace or automative industries, the latter may withhold relevant information regarding demand projections and manipulate the exchange process by distorting any information passed along in order to achieve inequitable advantages from their fragmented suppliers. Extensive theoretical rationales underlying P3 are provided by Williamson (1975), Arrow (1974), and Lindblom (1977). Empirical research, using this internal economy perspective, is required to test the large number of Williamsonian hypotheses dealing with why channel structuring based on market transactions may tend to fail.

Internal Polity of Distribution Channels

As has been noted by several channel analysts (e.g., Alderson, Palamountain), distribution channels are not only economic systems but also social systems.[2] This observation has led to research on the behavioral aspects of distribution channels and the intrachannel sociopolitical factors (Stern 1969; Stern and El-Ansary 1977). In a political economy framework, these forces are referred to as the *internal polity* of distribution channels. The economy and the polity of channels are basically allocation systems, allocating scarce economic resources and power or authority, respectively. Both the economy and polity of channels can also be viewed as coordination systems (Hernes 1978) or ways of managing the economics and politics of interorganizational systems.

The polity of a marketing channel might be seen as oriented to the allocation and use of authority and power within the system. Similar to the internal economy, there are also structured and process variables which describe the working of the internal polity. Adopting Emerson's (1962, 1972) notion of power relationships as the inverse of the existing dependency relationships between the system's actors, the *internal sociopolitical structure* is given by the initial pattern of power-dependence relations within the channel. The limiting cases of dependence are minimal power and completely centralized power. Power is a relational concept inherent in exchange between social actors (Emerson 1962, 1972). There will always be *some* power existing within channels due to mutual dependencies which exist among channel members, even though that power may be very low (El-Ansary and Stern 1972). However, power can also be fully concentrated in a single organization which then appears as the undisputed channel administrator (e.g., Lusch 1976). Such a power constellation can be referred to as a unilateral power system (Bonoma 1976). Because of the numerous marketing flows which tie the channel members together, the more common case is a mixed power situation where different firms exercise control over different flows, functions, or marketing activities (e.g., Etgar 1976b). The latter can be referred to as a mixed power system (Bonoma 1976).[3] Careful analysis is required to assess correctly the power-dependency patterns in a marketing channel (cf., El-Ansary and Stern 1972; Etgar 1976b; Frazier and Brown 1978; Hunt and Nevin 1974; Wilkinson 1973), because sociopolitical structures alter over time. Changing bases of power, coalition formations, and evolving linkages with external actors are among the factors causing such dynamism and creating measurement problems.

The various patterns of power-dependency relationships in a distribution channel are thought to be associated with various *sociopolitical processes*. The sociopolitical processes primarily refer to the dominant sentiments and behaviors which characterize the interactions between channel members. Although channel sentiments and behaviors are multidimensional constructs, two major dimensions in channel analysis are cooperation and conflict. Cooperation can be represented as joint striving towards an object (Stern 1971)—the process of coalescing with others for a good, goal, or value of mutual benefit. Cooperation involves a combination of object- and collaborator-centered activity which is based on a compatibility of goals, aims, or values. It is an activity in which the potential collaborator is viewed as providing the means by which a divisible goal or object desired by the parties may be obtained and shared. Conflict, on the other hand, is opponent-centered behavior (Stern 1971) because in a conflict situation, the object is controlled by the opponent while incompatibility of goals, aims, or values exist. The major concern in such situations is to overcome the opponent or counterpart as a means of securing the object. Conflict is characterized by mutual interference or blocking behavior.[4]

While they are highly interrelated, cooperation and conflict are separate, distinguishable processes. Exchange between social actors generally contains a certain dialect varying between conflictual and cooperative behavior (Guetzkow 1966). A common example is found in customer-supplier relationships ordered by long-term contracts. They reflect basically cooperative sentiments, but conflicts regularly take place regarding the interpretation of contractual details and problem-solving approaches.

At one extreme, dysfunctional conflict processes—those aimed at injuring or destroying another party—will severely impede any existing or potential cooperative behaviors among the parties. However, the absence of confrontation will not necessarily produce maximal joint-striving, because the complacency and passivity which may be present in the relationship may cause the parties to overlook salient opportunities for coalescing (cf., Coser 1956; Thomas 1976). Indeed, because of the mutual dependencies which exist in channels, it is likely that conflict, in some form, will always be present (Schmidt and Kochan 1972; Stern and El-Ansary 1977; Stern and Gorman 1969). In addition, channels cannot exist without a minimum level of cooperation among the parties. Thus, conflictual and cooperative processes will exist simultaneously in all channels.

Having specified major structure and process variables in the internal polity, it now is possible to examine their interactions for illustrative propositions. For instance, there exists a relatively large number of situations in distribution where power is somewhat balanced, e.g., when department store chains deal with well-known cosmetic manufacturers, when large plumbing and heating wholesalers deal with major manufacturers of air conditioning equipment, and when supermarket chains deal with large grocery manufactuers. Drawing from political science theory, it can be proposed that:

P4. In marketing channels typified by balanced power relationships, interactions will be predominantly cooperative as long as the balance of strength is preserved (e.g., Kaplan 1957). However, the potential for dysfunctional conflict is higher than it would be if power were imbalanced (Gurr 1970).

The first part of P4 is primarily drawn from balance of power theories of international politics which predict peaceful coexistence as long as balance of strength remains. This position is congruent with the insights offered by bilateral oligopoly and duopoly theories in economics (Scherer 1970) which forecast the development of informal or formal interfirm agreements regarding pricing and competitive actions. The second part of P4 draws on relative deprivation theories of collective conflict (Gurr 1970) which predict that conflict potential and the magnitude of manifest dysfunctional conflict will be highest in balanced power situations.

Even though P4 is intuitively appealing, counter propositions can be offered which indicate that empirical verification is required. For example, Korpi (1974), a political scientist, argues that conflict potential is higher in slightly imbalanced than in balanced power constellations while Williamson (1975), an economist, posits that a centralized power pattern—the extreme form of imbalanced power—will tend to exhibit predominantly cooperative modes of exchange when compared to a more balanced pattern. Furthermore, in an imbalanced situation, ideology is often used as a unifying and cooperation-inducing force by the more powerful party. The seeming cooperation in a balanced power constellation may be of a deterrent nature. Thus, there is a need to distinguish between detente-type cooperation and ideologically induced cooperation.

As with the variables specified for the internal economy, there is clearly a need to compare structural sociopolitical conditions across processes and vice versa in order to generate propositions which can permit predictions for channel management. At the same time, it is important to understand that conflict and cooperation processes are activities conducive to some economic end; they are not ends in themselves. Furthermore, the way in which power is used within a channel will clearly affect the sociopolitical processes. For example, it may be proposed that:

P5. In marketing channels characterized by imbalanced power, the use of coercive power will produce a dysfunctional level of conflict.

Additionally,

P6. Marketing channels characterized by imbalanced power and dominated by coercive influence strategies will be inherently unstable, resulting in decreased competitive viability.

To some extent, the works of Raven and Kruglanski (1970); Stern, Schulz, and Grabner (1973); and Lusch (1976) examining the relation between bases of power and resulting conflict point in the direction of these propositions.

Alternatively, in line with findings generated by Wittreich (1962), Kriesberg (1952), and Weik (1972), it is possible to propose that:

P7. Marketing channels characterized by minimal power will exhibit low levels of cooperation.

This is supported by McCammon (1970) who has argued that conventional marketing channels, comprised of isolated and autonomous decision making units, are unable to program distribution activities successfully. If power is low, so is dependence. Thus, two or more relatively independent entities may not be motivated to cooperate.

The above propositions indicate a few of the expected relations within the internal polity of distribution channels. As mentioned, they are merely illustrative of the meaningful insights for channel theory and management available in this kind of analysis.

Interaction between Internal Economy and Internal Polity of Distribution Channels

The essence of the political economy framework for the analysis of marketing systems is that economic and sociopolitical forces are not analyzed in isolation. Therefore, it is imperative to examine the interactions between the economy and the polity. To illustrate the potency of the combination, it is again possible to generate a series of propositions. Each of these propositions draws upon the variables enumerated previously.

The constellation of a given economic structure with a certain sociopolitical structure within a marketing channel will influence the economic and sociopolitical processes which take place. Considered first is the intersection between various power structures and economic structures typified by market transactions.

P8. In marketing channels in which market transactions are the predominant mode of exchange and in which power is centralized, centralized planning processes will emerge.

A relative power advantage within a channel is often used to program channel activities, and in such situations, decision making with respect to at least certain functions (e.g., promotion, physical distribution) tends to be centralized. Indicative of these types of channel arrangements are those found in the food industry where manufacturers, such as Nabisco and Kraft, develop shelf or dairy case management plans for supermarket chains; in the automotive aftermarket where warehouse distributors, such as Genuine Parts Company, evoke inventory management programs for jobbers (e.g., NAPA); in lawn care products where manufacturers, such as O.M. Scott, engage in detailed merchandise programming with the various retailers of their products; and in general merchandise retailing where retailers, such as Sears, Wards, and Penneys, preprogram the activities of their private label suppliers.

In addition to economic efficiency considerations, several behavioral considerations underlie P8. Thus, following Williamson (1975), some form of organizing process (in this case, centralized planning or programming) is required in order to overcome the tendencies toward opportunistic behavior present in market transactions and to cope with the bounded rationality of each channel member. The means to achieve centralized planning may be centralized power, although this is not always likely to be the case. For example, even in cases where there are balanced power structures in channels, centralized planning processes have emerged. This was the case when the Universal Product Code was developed jointly by retailers and manufacturers operating through their food industry trade associations.

P8 can be elaborated by considering the sociopolitical processes which are likely to prevail in market transactions with centralized planning.

P9. Under the conditions specified by P8, marketing channels will exhibit a relatively high level of conflict, but they will also exhibit highly cooperative processes. Such channels will tend to be more competitively effective than others where market transactions are also the predominant mode of exchange.

Following Korpi's (1974) reasoning, P9 predicts that conflict potential will be high due to the imbalanced power situation. The expectation with respect to cooperation is based on the ability of the channel administrator to mitigate the opportunistic tendencies among the units in the channel and to establish superordinate goals. The overall effect of the combination of interacting variables in P9 will be to produce effective channel systems in which programmed merchandising is likely to be the rule rather than the exception. Such channels are likely to be more successful in improving their market shares relative to other channels typified by market transactions.

Anecdotal evidence supporting P8 and P9 can be found in the construction and farm equipment industries. In these industries, market transactions are the predominant means of exchange between the various manufacturers and their dealers. However, Caterpillar and Deere have gained sizable leads over their rivals by developing highly efficient and effective systems of distribution through the use of their considerable power in their channels. They have achieved an unusual amount of success by programming their networks and by managing conflict within them.

Another proposition in line with the discussion above is that:

P10. In marketing channels in which hierarchical transactions are the predominant mode of exchange and in which power is centralized, conflict processes are more likely to be effectively managed, superordinate goals are more likely to be established, and efficiency is more likely to be achieved relative to any other marketing channel.

The underlying rationale for this proposition is supplied by Williamson (1975):

> Unlike autonomous contractors, internal divisions that trade with one another in a vertical integration relationship do not ordinarily have pre-emptive claims on their respective profit streams. Even though the divisions in question may have profit center standing, this is apt to be exercised in a restrained way. For one thing, the terms under which internal trading occurs are likely to be circumscribed. Cost-plus pricing rules, and variants thereof, preclude supplier divisions from seeking the monopolistic prices to which their sole supply position might otherwise entitle them. In addition, the managements of the trading divisions are more susceptible to appeals for cooperation. Since the aggressive pursuit of individual interests redounds to the disadvantage of the system and as present and prospective compensation (including promotions) can be easily varied by the general office to reflect noncooperation, simple requests to adopt a cooperative mode are more apt to be heeded. Altogether, a more nearly joint profit maximizing attitude and result is to be expected. (p. 29)

However, it should be noted that, even within a vertically integrated channel, opportunism and bounded rationality may still be found. In addition, the large size of many vertically integrated organizations often creates problems of bureaucratization and inflexibility. Thus, P10 isolates centralized, as opposed to decentralized, power. For example, the power which Sears' field operations held with regard to inventory levels within its stores was one of the major reasons for the disastrous inventory situation the company faced in 1974. In order to reduce the opportunistic behavior which existed among Sears' various divisions (e.g., the retail stores refused to hold their rightful share of the inventories which were building to abnormal levels in Sears' distribution centers), the entire company was reorganized and power was centralized more firmly in its Chicago headquarters. Now it remains to be seen whether Sears' management is equal to the task of successfully controlling the organization. Clearly, the advantages of such an internal political economy can dissipate as increasing degrees of vertical integration lead to more complex organization, more impersonal relationships, less perception of the relationships between actions and results, less moral involvement, generally more self-serving behavior, and greater toleration for substandard performance.

It should be noted that the political economy framework also encourages the examination of more narrowly focused propositions than those already stated. Given the difficulties associated with researching channel issues (due primarily to the lack of accessibility to and the sensitivity of the data involved), it is likely that research using the political economy framework should start with relatively manageable tasks. Illustrative of such propositions are:

P11. The more that relationships between channel members are characterized by cooperative behavior, the greater the level of profits attainable to the channel as a whole.

P.12 The greater the proportion of relative power possessed by any channel member, the greater the proportion of the channel's profits that member will receive.

Central issues in political economies are (1) how surpluses are generated and (2) how they are distributed among the members.

These "processes" provide critical links between the "political" and "economic" aspects of the system. P11 suggests a positive relationship between the level of cooperation within the channel and the joint profits obtained by it. The rationale is that cooperative behavior facilitates coordination and programming of activities within the channel which, in turn, provides potential cost advantages and improved competitive strength. In some cases, cooperation is likely to be informal, requiring a minimum of interaction. In these cases, environmental factors such as professional or trade norms, the role of trade associations, and the impact of government regulations may play significant roles in encouraging joint striving behavior. In other cases, cooperation may take the form of ad hoc consultations, the formation of committees, the establishment of federative coordination bodies, or the construction of bilateral contracts, joint ventures, or other types of formal long-term agreements (Pfeffer and Salancik 1978).

P12 addresses the critical issue of the allocation of joint profits within the marketing channel. The division of returns clearly is a matter of relative power and bargaining skill. Thus, the benefits obtained in the economic arena are divided in the political arena, a situation which is analogous to the income reallocation problem in welfare economics. Porter (1974) has found some empirical support for P12 using mainly secondary data.

Focusing on the interaction between the economy and polity of marketing channels may also produce insights into the evolution and adaptation of channel institutions. Innovative distributive institutions, such as limited line-limited service grocery stores (e.g., Aldi) and catalogue showrooms (e.g., McDade), may emerge due to differential cost advantages achieved by improved logistical systems or sharper positioning relative to specific consumer segments. The initative for such innovations often comes from "outsiders" who are at odds with traditional channel norms and practices (Kriesberg 1955; McCammon and Bates 1965). Thus, the innovations result, at least in part, because of functional conflicts within existing channels. As the new institutions mature, they tend to hire personnel from competitors, thereby gradually changing their professional orientation. At the same time, they become preoccupied with quality, add services, and begin to cater to broader market segments, thus moving towards the same practices as their competitors. The functional conflicts with other channel members tend to disappear, and opportunities for new outsiders to innovate emerge. Such scenarios as the "wheel of retailing" simply illustrate how sociopolitical circumstances often influence economic activities within a marketing channel. In turn, the economic form influences the sociopolitical sentiments surrounding the emerging transactions which lead, in turn, to further changes in economic activities.

CONCLUSION

Analysis of distribution channels as political economies provides a framework in which to incorporate and integrate the variety of approaches and findings found in the existing channel literature. More importantly, the emergent framework provides a basis for future research by isolating the critical dimension determining transactional effectiveness and efficiency in distribution. It also provides a conceptual mapping which may be useful to anyone with an interest in channel relationships.

The framework, including the illustrative propositions developed from it, presents a preliminary, general look at distribution channel structuring and functioning. In particular, the propositions advanced above serve to underscore the caveat that the economy and the polity of such systems are inseparably linked and cannot be studied in isolation (Frey 1978; Lindblom 1977; Thorelli 1965; Tivey 1978). Choosing an internal economic structure for a channel seems to have clear implications for the internal sociopolitical structure involved. The constellations formed by the intersection of the various economic and sociopolitical structures also have implications for the type of sociopolitical processes to be expected within channels. An internal economic structure may have certain benefits in terms of economic performance and the competitive effectiveness of the channel. On the other hand, the sociopolitical processes associated with a given internal economy may vary both in transaction costs and in the rationality of decision making for the channel as a whole. All of these factors directly influence channel performance. Another general implication which may be drawn from this type of analysis is that the various political economies of channels require different interorganizational management strategies for maintaining and expanding channel operations and for dealing with channel conflicts.

Clearly, factors in the external political economy will have a profound influence on a channel's internal political economy. Any propositions generated by adopting the political economy framework, including those outlined here, need to be modified by circumstances in the external economy and polity. A description of the impact of external forces and internal-external interactions then emerges as a topic for future work. However, this directive must be kept in proper perspective. In the only published empirical research focusing directly on the latter topic, Etgar (1977) has indicated that certain aspects of the internal political economy of channels can be expected to explain more of the variance in channel behavior than environmental factors. Following his findings, the strongest emphasis in future research should probably remain focused on achieving a deeper understanding of the internal political economy. The framework provided in this article should, hopefully, be of some assistance in this respect.

APPENDIX

Definitions of Key Concepts in the Political Framework

(See Fig. 29–A–1)

Political economy = collectively comprised of an economic system (polity) which jointly influence collective behavior and performance.

I. *Internal political economy* = the internal structuring and functioning of an organized collectivity (e.g., marketing channel) analyzed in terms of an internal economy and in internal polity and their interactions.

II. *External political economy* = the task environment of an organized collectivity (e.g., marketing channel) analyzed in terms of an external economy and an external polity and their interactions.

I.1. *Internal economy* = the internal economic allocation system analyzed in terms of the internal economic structure and processes.

I.2. *Internal polity* = the internal sociopolitical allocation system analyzed in terms of the internal sociopolitical structure and processes.

II.1. *External economy* = the economic

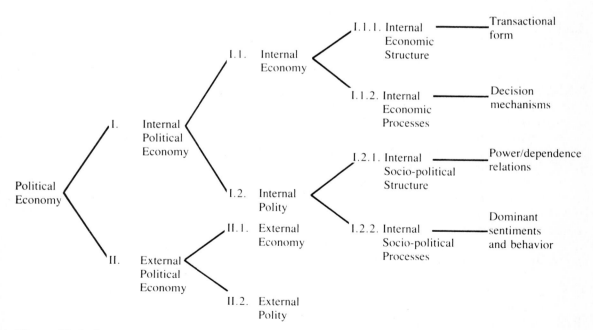

Figure 29–A–1
Key Concepts in the Political Economy Framework

task environment of an organized collectivity (e.g., marketing channel) described by the nature of its vertical (input and output) and horizontal markets.

II.2. *External polity* = the sociopolitical task environment of an organized collectivity (e.g., marketing channel) described by the distribution and use of power resources among external actors and their prevailing sentiments.

I.1.1. *Internal economic structure* = the economic arrangements or transactional form within an organized collectivity (e.g., marketing channel) set up to complete internal exchanges.

I.1.2. *Internal economic processes* = the decision making processes within an organized collectivity (e.g., marketing channel) which determine the terms of trade and the division of labor, functions, and activities among the internal actors.

I.2.1. *Internal sociopolitical structure* = the pattern of power/dependence relations within an organized collectivity (e.g., marketing channel).

I.2.2. *Internal sociopolitical processes* = the dominant sentiments and behaviors which characterize the interactions between actors within an organized collectivity (e.g., marketing channel).

I.1.1. *Transactional form* = internal economic arrangements ranging from markets to hierarchies (e.g., vertical integration).

I.1.2. *Decision making processes* = internal collective choice processes ranging from impersonal determination of terms of trade through the price mechanism, through bargaining processes, to centralized planning processes.

I.2.1. *Power/dependence relations* = internal power/dependence pattern ranging from minimal power (low depen-

dence), through mixed power constellations of balanced and imbalanced power (mutual dependence), to centralized power (unilateral dependence).

I.2.2. *Dominant sentiments and behaviors* = internal sentiments and behaviors of cooperation and functional or dysfunctional conflict characterizing internal exchange, ranging from minimal cooperation, high dysfunctional conflict to maximal cooperation, functional conflict.

NOTES

1. Methodologically, many of the studies fall short due to the incorrect use of informant methodologies as well as insufficent and often single-item operationalizations of constructs, thus not allowing for reliability checks and construct validation. For an excellent critique, see Phillips (1980). Thus, more emphasis needs to be given to careful research designs and improved measurement.

2. Simply observing that many marketing channels are loosely aligned (e.g., McVey 1960) does not invalidate their systemic nature. For argumentation supporting the perspective that channels are social action systems, see Reve and Stern (1979).

3. Bonoma (1976) also proposes a third power constellation—the bilateral power system—in which the interactants are in a unit relation jointly determining unit policy for individual and group action. Such systems, which are held together by social altruism, have not yet been examined in distribution channel settings.

4. In the social sciences in general and the conflict literature in particular, there has been a considerable amount of controversy surrounding the distinction between conflict and competition. We believe that competition is distinguishable from conflict.

Competition can be viewed as a form of opposition which is object-centered; conflict is opponent-centered behavior. Competition is indirect and impersonal; conflict is very direct and highly personal. In competition, a third party controls the goal or object; in conflict, the goal or object is controlled by the opponent. A swim meet is competition; a football game is conflict. For a discussion of the distinction between the two terms in a distribution channel context, see Stern (1971). For an excellent comprehensive review of the controversy, see Fink (1968).

REFERENCES

Alderson, W. (1957), *Marketing Behavior and Executive Action*, Homewood, IL: Irwin.

Aldrich, H. A. (1979), *Organizations and Environments*, Englewood Cliffs, NJ: Prentice-Hall, Inc.

Arndt, J. and T. Reve (1979), "Innovations in Vertical Marketing Systems," in *Proceedings of Fourth Macro Marketing Conference*, P. White & G. Fisk, eds., Boulder, CO: University of Colorado Press.

Arrow, K. J. (1974), *Limits of Organizations*, New York: John Wiley and Sons.

Baligh, H. H. and L. E. Richartz (1967), *Vertical Market Structures*, Boston: Allyn and Bacon.

Benson, J. K. (1975), "The Interorganizational Network as a Political Economy," *Administrative Science Quarterly*, 20 (June), 229–249.

Blois, K. (1972), "Vertical Quasi-Integration," *Journal of Industrial Economics*, 20 (July), 253–260.

Bonoma, T. V. (1976), "Conflict, Cooperation and Trust in Three Power Systems," *Behavioral Science*, 21 (November), 499–514.

Bucklin, L. P. (1966), *A Theory of Distribution Channel Structure*, Berkeley, CA: Institute of Business and Economic Research, University of California.

———, and J. M. Carman (1974), "Vertical Market Structure Theory and the Health Care Delivery System," in *Marketing Analysis of Societal Problems*, J. N. Sheth and P. L. Wright, eds., Urbana-Champaign, IL: Bureau of Economic and Business Research, 7–41.

Coser, L. A. (1956), *The Functions of Social Conflict*, Glencoe, IL: Free Press.

Cox, R., C. Goodman and T. Fichandler (1965), *Distribution in a High Level Economy*, Englewood Cliffs, NJ: Prentice-Hall, Inc.

El-Ansary, A. and L. W. Stern (1972), "Power Measurement in the Distribution Channel," *Journal of Marketing Research*, 9 (February), 47–52.

Emerson, R. M. (1962), "Power-Dependence Relations," *American Sociological Review*, 27 (February), 31–41.

———, (1972), "Exchange Theory, Part II: Exchange Relations and Network Structures," in *Sociological Theories in Progress*, J. Berger, M. Zelditch Jr., and A. Anderson, eds., Boston: Houghton Mifflin.

Etgar, M. (1976a), "The Effect of Administrative Control on Efficiency of Vertical Marketing Systems," *Journal of Market Research*, 13 (February), 12–24.

———, (1976b), "Channel Domination and Countervailing Power in Distribution Channels," *Journal of Marketing Research*, 13 (August), 254–262.

———(1977), "Channel Environment and Channel Leadership," *Journal of Marketing Research*, 14 (February), 69–76.

———(1978), "Differences in the Use of Manufacturer Power in Conventional and Contractual Channels," *Journal of Retailing*, 54 (Winter), 49–62.

Evan, W. M. (1965), "Toward a Theory of Inter-Organizational Relations," *Management Science*, 11 (August), B–217–230.

Fink, C. F. (1968), "Some Conceptual Difficulties in the Theory of Social Conflict," *Journal of Conflict Resolution*, 12 (December), 412–460.

Frazier, G. L. and J. R. Brown (1978), "Use of Power in the Interfirm Influence Process," in *Proceedings*, Eighth Annual Albert Haring Symposium, Indiana University, 6–30.

Frey, B. S. (1978), *Modern Political Economy*, Oxford, England: Martin Robertson.

Gattorna, J. (1978), "Channels of Distribution," *European Journal of Marketing*, 12, 7, 471–512.

Grønhaug, K. and T. Reve (1979), "Economic Performance in Vertical Marketing Systems," *Proceedings of Fourth Macro Meeting Conference*, P. White and G. Fisk, eds., Boulder, University of Colorado Press.

Guetzkow, H. (1966). "Relations among Organizations," in *Studies in Organizations*, R. V. Bowers, ed., Athens, GA: University of Georgia Press, 13–44.

Gurr, T. R. (1970), *Why Men Rebel*, Princeton, NJ: Princeton University Press.

Hernes, G., editor (1978), *Forhandlingsøkonomi og Blandingsadministrasjon*, Bergen, Norway: Universitetsforlaget.

Hunt, S. D. and J. R. Nevin (1974), "Power in a Channel of Distribution: Sources and Consequences," *Journal of Marketing Research*, 11 (May), 186–193.

Jennergren, L. P. (1979), "Decentralization in Organizations," to appear in *Handbook of Organizational Design*, P. G. Nystrom and W. H. Starbuck, eds., Amsterdam: Elsevier.

Kaplan, M. A. (1957), "Balance of Power, Bipolar and Other Models of International Systems," *American Political Science Review*, 51 (September), 684–695.

Korpi, W. (1974), "Conflict and the Balance of Power," *Acta Sociologica*, 17, 2, 99–114.

Kriesberg, L. (1952), "The Retail Furrier: Concepts of Security and Success," *American Journal of Sociology*, 58 (March), 478–485.

———(1955), "Occupational Control among Steel Distributors," *American Journal of Sociology*, 61 (November), 203–212.

Liebeler, W. J. (1976), "Integration and Competition," in *Vertical Integration in the U.S. Oil Industry*, E. Mitchell, ed., Washington DC: American Enterprise Institute for Public Policy Research, 5–34.

Lindblom, C. E. (1977), *Politics and Markets*, New York: Basic Books.

Lusch, R. F. (1976), "Sources of Power: Their Impact on Intrachannel Conflict," *Journal of Marketing Research*, 13 (November), 382–390.

McCammon, B. C. Jr. (1970), "Perspectives for Distribution Programming," in *Vertical Market Systems*, L. P. Bucklin, ed., Glenview, IL: Scott, Foresman, 32–51.

———, and A. D. Bates (1965), "The Emergence and Growth of Contractually Integrated Channels in the American Economy," in *Economic Growth, Competition, and World Markets*, P. D. Bennett, ed., Chicago: American Marketing Association, 496–515.

———, and R. W. Little (1965), "Marketing Channels: Analytical Systems and Approaches," in *Science in Marketing*, G. Schwartz, ed., New York: John Wiley and Sons, 321–384.

———, A. D. Bates and J. D. Guiltinan (1971), "Alternative Model for Programming Vertical Marketing Networks," in *New Essays in Marketing Theory*, G. Fisk, ed., Boston: Allyn and Bacon, 333–358.

McVey, P. (1960), "Are Channels of Distribution What the Textbooks Say?" *Journal of Marketing*, 24 (January), 61–65.

Palamountain, J. C. Jr. (1955), *The Politics of Distribution*, Cambridge, MA: Harvard University Press.

Pfeffer, J. and G. R. Salancik (1978), *The External Control of Organizations*, New York: Harper & Row.

Phillips, L. (1980), *The Study of Collection Behavior in Marketing: Methodological Issues in the Use of Key Informants*, unpublished doctoral dissertation, Evanston, IL: Northwestern University.

Porter, M. (1974), "Consumer Behavior, Retailer Power, and Market Performance in Consumer Goods Industries," *Review of Economics and Statistics*, 56 (November), 419–436.

Raven, B. H. and A. W. Kruglanski (1970), "Conflict and Power," in *The Structure of Conflict*, P. Swingle, ed., New York: Academic Press, 69–109.

Reve, T. and L. W. Stern (1979), "Interorganizational Relations in Marketing Channels," *Academy of Management Review*, 4 (July), 405–416.

Scherer, F. M. (1970), *Industrial Market Structure and Economic Performance*, Skokie, IL: Rand McNally.

Schmidt, S. M. and T. A. Kochan (1972), "Conflict: Toward Conceptual Clarity," *Administrative Science Quarterly*, 17 (September), 359–370.

Stern, L. W., editor (1969), *Distribution Channels: Behavioral Dimensions,* Boston: Houghton Mifflin.

——— (1971), "Antitrust Implications of a Sociological Interpretation of Competition, Conflict, and Cooperation in the Marketplace," *The Antitrust Bulletin,* 16 (Fall), 509–530.

———, and A. I. El-Ansary (1977), *Marketing Channels,* Englewood Cliffs, NJ: Prentice-Hall, Inc.

———and R. H. Gorman (1969), "Conflict in Distribution Channels: An Exploration," in *Distribution Channels: Behavioral Dimensions,* L. W. Stern, ed., Boston, Houghton Mifflin, 156–175.

———, R. A. Schulz and J. R. Grabner (1973), "The Power Base-Conflict Relationship: Preliminary Findings," *Social Science Quarterly,* 54 (September), 412–419.

Sturdivant, F. D. (1966), "Determinants of Vertical Integration in Channel Systems," in *Science, Technology and Marketing,* R. H. Haas, ed., Chicago: American Marketing Association, 472–479.

Terreberry, S. (1968), "The Evolution of Organizational Environments," *Administrative Science Quarterly,* (March), 590–613.

Thomas, K. (1976), "Conflict and Conflict Management," in *Handbook of Industrial and Organizational Psychology,* M. D. Dunnette, ed., Chicago: Rand McNally, 889–935.

Thompson, J. D. (1967), *Organizations in Action,* New York: McGraw Hill.

Thorelli, H. B. (1965), "The Political Economy of the Firm: Basis for a New Theory of Competition?" *Schweizerische Zeitschrift fur Volkwirtschaft und Statistik,* 101, 3, 248–262.

Tivey, L. (1978), *The Politics of the Firm,* Oxford: Martin Robertson.

Van de Ven, A., D. Emmett and R. Koenig, Jr. (1974), "Framework for Interorganizational Analysis," *Organization and Administrative Sciences,* 5 (Spring), 113–129.

Wamsley, G. and M. Zald (1973), "The Political Economy of Public Organizations," *Public Administration Review,* 33 (January–February), 62–73.

———, and ——— (1976), *The Political Economy of Public Organizations,* Bloomington, IN: Indiana University Press.

Weik, J. (1972), "Discrepant Perceptions in Vertical Marketing Systems," in *1971 Combined Preceedings,* F. Allvine, ed., Chicago: American Marketing Association, 181–188.

Wilkinson, I. (1973), "Power in Distribution Channels," *Cranfield Research Papers in Marketing and Logistics,* Cranfield, England: Cranfield School of Management.

Williamson, O. E. (1975), *Markets and Hierarchies: Analysis and Antitrust Implications,* New York: Free Press.

Wittreich, W. (1962), "Misunderstanding the Retailer," *Harvard Business Review,* 40 (May–June), 147–155.

Yuchtman, E. and S. Seashore (1967), "A System Resources Approach to Organizational Effectiveness," *American Sociological Review,* 33 (December), 891–903.

Zald, M. (1970a), "Political Economy: A Framework for Comparative Analysis," in *Power in Organizations,* M. Zald, ed., Nashville: Vanderbilt University Press, 221–261.

——— (1970b), *Organizational Change: The Political Economy of the YMCA,* Chicago: University of Chicago Press.

A Decision-Making Structure for Price Decisions

Alfred R. Oxenfeldt

Until recently, almost all pricing decisions have either been highly intuitive, as in the case of new product introductions, or based on routine procedures, as in cost-plus or imitative pricing. The proportion of price decisions representing these extreme approaches seems to have declined substantially; yet, many business executives have not altered their pricing methods substantially.[1]

Research continues on how businesses should set prices. Most of these studies attempt to uncover the best methods rather than those in current practice. No researcher has completely overcome the enormous difficulties of learning the basis on which group decisions are made and the "sensitive" reasons underlying many price decisions.[2] This article examines some trends in pricing and the apparent gulf be-

tween pricing theory and practice. A pricing framework is presented to aid practitioners structure their important pricing decisions.

THE GAP BETWEEN PRICING THEORY AND APPLICATION

The current pricing literature has produced few new insights or exciting new approaches that would interest most businessmen enough to change their present methods. Those executives who follow the business literature have no doubt broadened their viewpoint and become more explicit and systematic about their pricing decisions; however, few, if any, actually employ new and different goals, concepts, or techniques.

The gap between pricing literature and practice may exist because the authors lack extensive personal experience with the practical problems facing executives in a highly competitive and complex business environment. Other explanatory factors include: the number of products for which

Alfred R. Oxenfeldt, "A Decision-Making Structure for Price Decisions," Vol. 37 (January 1973). Reprinted with permission from *Journal of Marketing*, published by the American Marketing Association.

executives are responsible, the lack of reliable information on product demand, the dynamic nature of technology, and the unpredictable responses from competitors. Because of the large number of highly uncertain and variable factors, executives responsible for pricing closely adhere to methods that they have found to be effective in the past. Economists and practitioners have long recognized that price is a dangerously explosive and complex marketing variable.

This discussion does not suggest that those responsible for pricing should always adhere to traditional methods of setting price, or that those writing about pricing have contributed little of value. The point is that a significant gap exists between two areas and that this gap must be closed if pricing is to continue to develop as a crucially important area of marketing theory and practice. Pricing specialists have suggested many helpful methods that have not been implemented in practice even after they have been demonstrated to be valid.

LITERATURE TRENDS: A CRITIQUE

The field of pricing remains largely the domain of economic theorists who discuss price primarily in relation to the analyses of specific market structures.

Much of the pricing literature deals with tactics and stratagems for particular kinds of firms—wholesalers, manufacturers, franchises, or joblot shops. Special corporate situations such as new product introductions, inflation, declining products, product-line pricing, price-structure problems, and price-cutting are also popular topics in the pricing literature.[3] The current literature on pricing, like that in most other areas of marketing, draws heavily on the behavioral sciences, quantitative tools, and

detailed empirical research. Present-day writers employ simulation techniques and other computer applications much more than in the past, and are often concerned with cost computation and demand estimation. Pricing receives far more attention from marketing specialists today than it did when managerial economists such as Joel Dean, Jules Bachman, Arthur R. Burns, Donald Wallace, Edward Mason, Edwin Nourse, Walton Hamilton, Walter Adams, and Morris A. Adelman were the chief contributors to the field.

Recently, pricing specialists have channeled much of their research efforts into the development of approaches designed to aid the accuracy and efficiency of the decision-maker. The most promising methods are: use of the computer;[4] simulation as a method for anticipating the effect of price changes on sales and for testing complex strategies;[5] research techniques for obtaining more reliable information about prospective customer responses to price change;[6] and the nature and determinants of price perception.[7]

Nevertheless, large gaps still remain in the pricing literature. Very little is said about reconciling the various price-optima; i.e., the prices that are best vis-à-vis costs, the ultimate customer, resellers, and rivals. Most authors deal with pricing problems unidimensionally, whereas businessmen must generally deal with price as one element in a multidimensional marketing program. Price is often dealt with as if it were completely separated from the other elements in the marketing mix. These authors tend to concentrate on the effect of price on immediate marketwide sales without adequately considering long-run or individual market effects. The writers dealing with pricing decisions typically identify variables that are sometimes not considered and suggest conceptual errors that are commonly made, but they typically treat only small, isolated parts of the problem faced by a business executive. Little has been written on innovative approaches to pricing—approaches designed to *increase* demand, rather than *adapt to existing* demand. This failing has been most common in writings that employ quantitative techniques. A price-setter must not merely view his responsibility as that of determining the various demand elasticities (price, promotion, assortment, quality, design, and place) and finding the price that best adapts to them. Attention must be given to measures that alter these elasticities in his firm's favor.

The setting of any price involves: (1) values that particular segments of customers place on a firm's offering; (2) consumer responses to price changes of the product; (3) competitive responses to any price changes; and (4) reseller's sensitivity to price changes. No one has yet developed a completely reliable method to measure the price elasticity of demand for a particular brand. Similarly, little is known about resellers' responses to margin changes or the sales support a brand will receive from distributors and retailers. The specific responses of competitors to both price and nonprice actions is still a matter of great uncertainty in almost all industries.

Pricing should be regarded as a field where the essential elements are quite clear and well known and where the concepts that need to be applied also are widely recognized and within reach of all executives. Practitioners face the problem of measuring a multitude of factors in many different specific situations; that is, they must attempt to quantify the response functions (elasticities) so they can be compared. One of the major problems in pricing is obtaining the data required to measure each of these response functions in different market contexts. Pricing specialists have made very

few contributions to the solution of this problem.

CONSTRAINTS ON PRICING DECISIONS

Many vital price-related decisions made by top management deal with the following issues: Are we willing to drive competitors from business if we can? Should we inflict serious injury upon them when they have been struck by misfortune? Are we willing to violate the spirit or letter of the law to increase sales? At a different level of concern, pricing decisions are related to price strategy and general competitive policy by questions such as: Should we seek price leadership for ourselves or foster a pattern of price leadership with some other firm as leader? Should we try to shake out the weak firms in the industry to achieve price stability and higher profitability? Should we foster a spirit of cooperativeness among rivals by an avoidance of price competition?

These decisions are properly made by top executives and do not require a frequent revision. When they are not made explicitly, the executive responsible for pricing decision implicitly makes many of these decisions by default. A complete discussion of these constraints goes beyond the scope of this article.

To manage the complex nature of price-setting, practitioners need an effective, multidimensional model to guide their analysis. Such a pricing model would not only explicitly encourage systemized thinking, but also underscore the differential advantage available to the firm which strategically sets the prices of all of its products.

A FRAMEWORK FOR PRICING DECISIONS

The following discussion of price decisions employs a decision-making framework which identifies the following stages:

1. *Recognize the need for a pricing decision.*
2. *Price determination.*
3. *Develop a model.*
4. *Identify and anticipate pricing problems.*
5. *Develop feasible courses of action.*
6. *Forecast the outcome of each alternative.*
7. *Monitor and review the outcome of each action.*

These seven stages overlap somewhat and are not strictly sequential.

Recognize the Need for a Pricing Decision

A firm's pricing difficulties and opportunities are related to its overall objectives. Only when a firm is explicit in defining its corporate objectives can the executive specifically evaluate the obstacles and opportunities confronting him. Exhibit 30–1 provides a partial list of feasible pricing objectives. It is important to note that objectives of profitability and growth constitute only a small part of this list. The pricing objectives of many different firms are listed below; however, *each firm* must evaluate and determine the priority of these objectives as they relate to the individual firm.

From this list of objectives, some of the pricing problems that firms face can readily be inferred. Among the more important are:

1. A decline in sales.
2. Prices are too high—relative to those charges by rivals, relative to the benefits of the product. (Prices might be too high in a few regional markets and very appropriate elsewhere.)
3. Price is too low, again in certain markets and not in others.
4. The company is regarded as exploitative of customers and not to be trusted.

Exhibit 30-1
Potential Pricing Objectives

1. Maximum long-run profits
2. Maximum short-run profits
3. Growth
4. Stabilize market
5. Desensitize customers to price
6. Maintain price-leadership arrangement
7. Discourage entrants
8. Speed exit of marginal firms
9. Avoid government investigation and control
10. Maintain loyalty of middlemen and get their sales support
11. Avoid demands for "more" from suppliers—labor in particular
12. Enhance image of firm and its offerings
13. Be regarded as "fair" by customers (ultimate)
14. Create interest and excitement about the item
15. Be considered trustworthy and reliable by rivals
16. Help in the sale of weak items in the line
17. Discourage others from cutting prices
18. Make a product "visible"
19. "Spoil market" to obtain high price for sale of business
20. Build traffic

5. The firm places excessive financial burdens on its resellers.
6. The price differentials among items in the line are objectionable or unintelligible.
7. Its price changes are too frequent—or do not take account of major changes in market circumstances.
8. The firm's price reflects negatively on itself and on its products.
9. The price is unstabilizing the market which had finally become stabilized after great difficulty.
10. The firm is offering its customers too

many price choices and confusing its customers and resellers.

11. The firm's prices seem higher to customers than they really are.
12. The firm's price policy attracts undesirable kinds of customers which have no loyalty to any seller.
13. The firm's pricing behavior makes customers unduly price sensitive and unappreciative of quality differences.
14. The company has fostered a decline in market discipline among sellers in the industry.

The list of pricing objectives in Exhibit 30–1 and the illustrative list of pricing difficulties above suggest that prices and price changes do not simply affect current sales, but have more far-reaching effects.

To identify the problems listed, a firm requires a monitoring system or a means of empirically determining the existence of potential problems and opportunities. Exhibit 30–2 presents indicators a firm might use to suggest the existence of pricing problems.

It is evident that some of these indicators are very difficult to measure with accuracy.

Price Determination

A warning system will detect pricing problems and allow the manager to decide how much attention to give to each potential price problem and to whom to assign it. In assigning a problem for study, a decision-maker must determine whether to use his own staff or call upon outside resources. Some price problems are self-correcting, in which case the price setter should ignore the warning.

Develop a Model

The primary question that must be addressed here is: What models would help

Exhibit 30–2
Data That Might Be Used to Design a Price Monitoring System

1. Sales—in units and in dollars
   a. Previous year comparisons
   b. Different markets/channels comparisons
2. Rivals' prices
3. Inquiries from potential customers about the line
4. Company's sales at "off list" price
   a. Measured as a % of total sales
   b. Revenue as % of sales at full price
5. Types of customers getting the most and largest price reductions
6. Market shares—in individual markets
7. Marketing costs; production cost; production costs at nearly output
8. Price complaints
   a. From customers
   b. From salesmen
9. Inventories of finished goods at different levels
10. Customers' attitudes toward firm, prices, etc.
11. Number of lost customers (brand-switching)
12. Inquiries—and subsequent purchases
13. Marketing costs

businessmen to best cope with pricing responsibilities? Models developed by economic theorists rarely direct a pricing executive's attention to the key variables. Behavioral science offers far more insight into the factors that determine how price changes will be perceived and reacted to by consumers. The influence of price extends far beyond current sales figures, and behavioral science helps us more fully understand the extensive effect of price decisions.

Some mathematical models deserve a brief mention, even though they are not widely used in practice. The multiple regression model is familiar to most economists and marketing specialists. Based on historical data, this technique determines a linear functional relationship between sales and factors such as price, advertising, personal selling, relative product quality, product design, distribution arrangements, and customer services.

Another technique is the experimental approach to pricing strategy. One type of experimental approach, which may be based on regression analysis, is simulation. Such models allow the pricing specialist to combine wide varieties of inputs (including price) to achieve desired results such as short- and long-run sales together with the costs incurred. The relative merits of different factor combinations can be tested and compared.

A third type of mathematical model emphasizes the situation-specific parameters of a strategy. This approach is referred to as adaptive modeling and combines historical analysis with different environmental situations. A given input mix may have widely divergent results for each situation. This type of approach is particularly helpful in assessing the merits of market expansion, segmentation analysis, and other decisions where contextual analysis is important.

These last two models deal with some fundamental characteristics of price. First, the interdependence and synergy of related model components become key issues in their effective use. Second, the proper mix of variables will differ from occasion to occasion, even for the same product or brand. Third, the outcome of any combination of marketing actions may be perceived differently by different consumers.

To completely understand how and when price works, an executive must understand how potential customers perceive, interpret, and evaluate price changes in making their purchase decisions. These decisions vary with the individual; therefore, an executive must also consider different market segments.

Identify and Anticipate Pricing Problems

When a firm encounters a pricing problem, its manifestations are generally not subtle and obscure; however, executives still have difficulty obtaining information that identifies the source of the problem. Information about customer reactions to a product are extremely difficult to interpret because the responses must be related to their particular market segments. A seller primarily seeks the opinions of those customer segments he wishes to serve, rather than of all prospective customers. Most research data, however, do not match customer responses with the corresponding market segment to which they belong.

Price-setters require an information system to monitor the effects of their pricing arrangements and thus to help make prompt and specific adaptive action in a fast changing market environment. Salemen's reports, current sales experience, and individual favorite customers are the primary sources of information available to most firms.

Develop Feasible Courses of Action

Traditionally, price setters have considered only a very limited number of alternatives when faced with pricing difficulties. If their price seemed high, they would lower it, and if it was too low, they would simply raise it. Much more complex behaviors are available to most pricers which provide opportunities for novel approaches. In addition to varying the price level, the executive responsible for pricing may also change the following factors: (1) the timing of the price change; (2) the number of price changes (he is not limited to a single change); (3) the time interval to which the price change applies; and (4) the number of items whose price he changes (he could raise some prices while lowering others). In addition, the executive can combine a price change with other marketing actions. For example, he might change the product's package, advertising, quality, apearance, or the after-sale customer service. Even more important, he can change price in some markets and not in others, or change them in different ways. The price-setter may even modify his discount arrangements in such a way as to increase the effectiveness of the price change.

A price-setter must not regard his actions as simply shifting prices on individual product offerings. He must recognize that his firm sells a line of products in a wide variety of geographic markets, and that its offerings embrace many benefits of varying importance to customers. Price is only one of those consumer benefits. A firm rarely makes its very best reaction to a pricing problem or opportunity by simply altering price.

Forecast the Outcome of Each Alternative Action

Once a price-setter has selected the most feasible actions available, he must forcast their consequences to determine which will best achieve his goals. At this stage, the price-setter must be as specific as possible about the expected short- and long-term consequences of his decision.

Successful management of pricing information requires an understanding of the possible consequences of price changes. The more important of these include the effect of price changes on: the customer's ability to buy; the brand image and customer's evaluations of a product's quality; the value of inventories held by resellers; the willingness of resellers to hold inventory; the attitude of ultimate customers and resellers who recently purchased the product at a different price; the company's cash flow; and the need to borrow capital. Price changes can also disrupt or improve market discipline; foster

or retard the growth and power of a trade association; instill the trust or suspicion of competitors in the integrity of one's business practices; or increase or reduce the probability of government investigation and criminal prosecution.

The effects of most business actions are extremely difficult to forecast, but an executive must attempt to forecast them. Before selecting an alternative, the executive should consciously consider all possible effects.

If the concept of price elasticity of demand has any value to price-setters, it is in forecasting the effect of price changes. Therefore, the following questions should be asked: Can price elasticity of demand be measured accurately? How much do such measurements cost? How long are such measurements valid? Does price elasticity apply to all geographic markets or only represent an average of all regions? Do elasticity measurements apply equally to all items in a firm's line of products? Is the elasticity of demand the same for all brands of the same product? The emphatic answer is that it is impossible to measure accurately the price elasticity of demand for any brand or product. However, executives responsible for pricing must continue to improve their understanding of the effects of price changes on sales.

Can a measure of demand be developed that is a better indicator than the price elasticity of demand? As implied above, past experience is an unreliable guide to present relationships. Rather than seek a quantitative measure of price elasticity, perhaps a different concept is needed. Businessmen will rarely change price alone, but ordinarily adopt a marketing program coordinated around the proposed price change. A marketing executive wishes to forecast the effects of the total marketing program, rather than the effect of price change alone.

Since most markets are highly dynamic and extremely complex, one cannot expect to develop reliable quantitative measures of the effects of different marketing programs on unit sales. How can a marketing executive forecast the results of alternative price strategies and marketing programs? He must intuitively estimate the effects of the program; however, he will rarely find precisely comparable circumstances in either his own firm's experience or in that of other firms. Specifically, the executive should consider the extent to which his price change will be perceived; the possible interpretations that customers and resellers can attribute to his price change; and the effects of customers' reactions to the price changes.

Select among Alternative Outcomes

When a price-setter forecasts the outcomes of alternative actions, he selects that alternative which best achieves his objectives. As indicated earlier, an executive actually pursues many objectives; therefore, the selection among alternatives is quite difficult in practice, although it is simple in principle. An index should be developed to indicate the extent to which any set of outcomes achieves the executive's multiple goals—weighing each one according to its importance. Various outcomes of each feasible course of action can then be forecast by assigning probabilities to each one. The action selected should represent the alternative that best realizes product, department, and corporate goals, while reflecting an acceptable amount of risk.

SUMMARY

Pricing involves far more than arriving at a dollar and cents figure for a single product. A price-setter is responsible for managing a complex function, even though pricing in- volves relatively little effort for the implementation of decisions. To manage the pricing function, a firm must develop a detailed hierarchy of objectives; a monitor system; explicit mathematical models; and, most importantly, new approaches to pricing management.

The corporate pricing function within a decision-making structure is a very complex process. Many components must be integrated and managed as a unit if the firm is quickly to capitalize on its pricing opportunities.

NOTES

1. Professor F. E. Gillis writes in 1969, "Joel Dean opines that cost-plus pricing is the most common technique in the United States. The statement is too weak; it is almost universal." See his *Managerial Economics* (Reading, Mass.: Addison-Wesley, 1969), p. 254.
2. A. A. Fitzpatrick, *Pricing Methods of Industry* (Boulder, Colo.: Pruett Press, Inc., 1964); *Decision Making in Marketing—A Description of Decision Making Processes and Its Application to Pricing*, 1971, Report No. 525, National Industrial Conference Board; Kaplan, Dirlam, and Lanziolotti, *Pricing in Big Business* (Washington, D.C.: The Brookings Institution, 1958); B. Fog, *Industrial Pricing Policies* (Amsterdam, Holland: North Holland Publishing Co., 1960); W. W. Haynes, *Pricing Decisions in Small Business* (Lexington, Ky.: University of Kentucky Press, 1962); and J. Fred Wested has been reported as directing a major study of this subject. See "The Myths and Realities of Corporate Pricing," *Fortune*, 85 (April 1972), p. 85.
3. The best of these writings are to be found in several collections of articles and talks about pricing. These are: Elizabeth Marting, ed., *Creative Pricing* (New York: American Marketing Association, 1968); Almarin Phillips and O. E. Williamson, eds., *Prices: Issues in Theory, Practice and Public Policy* (Philadelphia: University of Pennsylvania

Press, 1967); D. F. Mulvihill and S. Paranka, eds., *Price, Policies and Practices: A Source Book of Readings* (New York: John Wiley, 1967); American Management Association, *Competitive Pricing: Policies, Practices and Legal Considerations*, Management Report No. 17 (1958); American Management Association, *Pricing: The Critical Decision*, Management Report No. 66 (1961): Donald Watson, ed., *Price Theory in Action: A Book of Readings* (Boston: Houghton Mifflin, 1965); and B. Taylor and G. Wills, eds., *Pricing Strategy* (London: 1969).

4. R. E. Good, "Using the Computer in Pricing," in *Creative Pricing*, Elizabeth Marting, ed. (New York: American Marketing Association, 1968), pp. 182–94.

5. Arnold E. Amstutz, *Computer Simulation of Competitive Market Response* (Cambridge, Mass.: M.I.T. Press, 1967); and D. Kollat, R. Blackwell, and J. Robeson, *Strategic Marketing* (New York: Holt, Rinehart and Winston, 1972), Chapter 19.

6. A. Gabor and C. W. J. Granger, "On the Price Consciousness of Consumers," *Applied Statistics*, 10 (1961), pp. 170–88; Gabor and Granger, "Price as an Indicator of Quality: Report on an Enquiry," *Economica*, 33 (1966), pp. 43–70; and Gabor and Granger, "The Pricing of New Products," *Scientific Business*, 3 (1965), pp. 141–50.

7. Nystrom, *Retail Pricing: An Integrated Economic and Psychological Approach* (Stockholm: Economic Research Institute of Stockholm School of Economics, 1970), especially Chapters 7 and 8; Brown and Oxenfeldt, *Misperceptions of Economic Phenomena* (New York: Sperr and Douth, 1972).

Beyond the Many Faces of Price: An Integration of Pricing Strategies

Gerald J. Tellis

In the last two decades the field of pricing strategy has made great progress in the form of better theoretical explanations, more precise models, and innovative pricing strategies (see Nagle 1984 for one review). However, the rich variety of pricing models and strategies developed in different time periods and contexts has resulted in a multiplicity of labels, several overlapping descriptions of strategies, and partially obsolete typologies. Some pricing strategies are not yet presented adequately in the marketing literature (e.g., price bundling, Stigler 1968; random discounting, Varian 1980; or price signaling, Cooper and Ross 1984) and others have not been developed formally (e.g., price skimming and penetration pricing, Dean 1951). A more pressing issue, however, is that because the principles underlying each strategy have not been presented together, it

has not been possible to develop a unifying taxonomy of strategies that shows their relatedness or differences and immediately suggests the circumstances under which each can be adopted. Thus there is a need to compare, rationalize, and reclassify the various pricing strategies in the literature.

The first objective of this article is to present a number of pricing strategies, some of which are simplifications and others elaborations of strategies described in the literature. A second objective is to state their underlying principles in comparable terms and thus demonstrate their relationship to each other and their practical applications. A third objective is to propose a classification of these strategies that is parsimonious, logically derived, and enlightening to the user. Such a taxonomy could stimulate alternate schemes or general theoretical models or new applications of empirical models or new strategies (Hunt 1983, pp. 348–60).

These objectives are carried out in the following order. First the classification is presented (though it can be fully appreciated

"Beyond the Many Faces of Price: An Integration of Pricing Strategies," Gerald J. Tellis, Vol. 50 (October 1986), pp. 146–160. Reprinted from *Journal of Marketing*, published by the American Marketing Association.

only at the end of the article). Then each strategy is discussed in terms of a pricing problem presented in simple numerical form. A particular pricing strategy is shown to be the only one that can resolve the problem, given the demand, cost, competitive, and legal environment. The theoretical and welfare aspects of the strategy are summarized and applications discussed. Finally, the relationship among strategies is explained.

This article describes a set of normative pricing strategies. A pricing strategy is a reasoned choice from a set of alternative prices (or price schedules) that aim at profit maximization within a planning period in response to a given scenario. Thus, the article describes a set of ideal options one may choose and outcomes that result from such choices, assuming profit maximization by the strategist. Several important pricing topics are necessarily excluded from this discussion: managerial pricing approaches, price implementation, and price, cost, and demand estimation (see Monroe 1979 or Rao 1984 for excellent reviews).

In the case of consumer behavior, however, allowances are made for non-optimal behavior. Its most important cause is incomplete information, which leads to three types of behavior: consumers may purchase randomly, consumers may use a surrogate for an unknown attribute (e.g., price as a surrogate for quality), or consumers may evaluate choices incorrectly with resultant intransitivity in preferences. On the basis of this hypothesis, Kahneman and Tversky (1979) developed prospect theory as an alternative to traditional utility theory and Thaler (1980, 1985) extended that work. Their work has important implications for pricing strategy. This article shows the impact of all three types of information deficiencies on pricing strategies.

A CLASSIFICATION OF PRICING STRATEGIES

The underlying principle in all the strategies discussed here is that the best strategy in certain circumstances is not apparent until certain shared economies or cross-subsidies are taken into account. In a shared economy, one consumer segment or product bears more of the average costs than another, but the average price still reflects cost plus acceptable profit. The use of such economies may be triggered by heterogeneity among consumers, firms, or elements of the product mix. The pricing strategies can be broadly classified into three groups based on which of these three factors affects a firm's use of shared economies: differential pricing, whereby the same brand is sold at different prices to consumers; competitive pricing, whereby prices are set to exploit competitive position; and product line pricing, whereby related brands are sold at prices that exploit mutual dependencies. The pricing objective of the firm thus constitutes the first dimension on which this classification scheme is constructed.

The second dimension is the characteristics of consumers. Again there are three categories of interest. First, at least some consumers are assumed to have search costs. That is, consumers do not know exactly which firm sells the product they want and they have to search for it. Further, for some of them the opportunity cost of time exceeds the benefit of search, so that they are willing to purchase without full information. Second, at least some consumers have a low reservation price for the product. That is, some consumers are price sensitive or do not need the product urgently enough to pay the high price other consumers pay. Third, all consumers have certain transaction costs other than search costs—for example, traveling costs, the risk of investment, the cost of money, or switching costs.

The two dimensions—firm objectives and consumer characteristics—each with three categories yield nine cells into which the strategies discussed here are classified (see Table 31–1). Table 31–2 further compares and contrasts these strategies on several dimensions and is discussed in the concluding section. The real world, however, is more complex and several of the conditions listed (search costs, transaction costs, or demand heterogeneity) may occur jointly. Accordingly, in reality a firm may adopt a combination of these strategies. What is demonstrated in the proposed classification is the necessary conditions for each strategy, conditions that are jointly sufficient to classify them conveniently. Similarly, in the following discussion the problems define fairly simple scenarios where "other things are assumed constant" and only factors affecting the choice of a strategy are allowed to vary.

The list of available strategies also is affected by the legal environment. Because of the potential for pricing abuses, especially against weak competitors or weak or uninformed buyers, Congress and the states have passed laws that regulate the pricing strategies firms can adopt. These laws generally ensure that there is no collusion among competitors, no deception of consumers, no explicit discrimination among industrial buyers, or no attempt to manipulate the competitive structure. Some of these laws rule out certain pricing options whereas others include new possibilities, and these effects are discussed in the appropriate place. The laws are not always fully explicit, but the general motivation of the laws and the spirit in which they have been interpreted by the courts indicate that no strategy should reduce the impact of competitive forces unless it is to the benefit of consumers (Areeda 1974; Scherer 1980).

DIFFERENTIAL PRICING STRATEGIES

The price strategies discussed here all arise primarily because of consumer heterogeneity, so that the same product can be sold to consumers under a variety of prices. The three strategies discussed refer to consumer heterogeneity along three dimensions: transaction costs that motivate second market

Table 31–1
Taxonomy of Pricing Strategies

	Objective of Firm		
Characteristics of Consumers	Vary Prices Among Consumer Segments	Exploit Competitive Position	Balance Pricing over Product Line
Some have high search costs	Random discounting	Price signaling	Image pricing
Some have low reservation price	Periodic discounting	Penetration pricing Experience curve pricing	Price bundling Premium pricing
All have special transaction costs	Second market discounting	Geographic pricing	Complementary pricing

Table 31-2
Comparison of Pricing Strategies

Criteria	Differential Pricing			Competitive Pricing			Product Line Pricing		
	Second Market Discounting	Periodic Discounts	Random Discounts	Penetration and Experience Curve Pricing	Price Signaling	Geographic Pricing	Price Bundling	Premium Pricing	Complementary Pricing
Characteristic of price strategy varies systematically over:									
Consumer segments	Yes	Yes	Yes	No	No	No	No	No	No
Competitors in market	No	No	No	Yes	Yes	Yes	No	No	No
Product mix	No	No	No	No	No	No	Yes	Yes	Yes
Characteristics of consumers	High transaction costs: physically separated segments	Only some with low reservation price: sensitive segment	High search costs: some uninformed about price	Some with low reservation price: price sensitive segment	High search costs: some uninformed on quality; uninformed prefer high quality	High transportation costs: geographically distinct markets	Some prefer one product, others, another: asymmetric demand	Only some prefer basic products at low prices	High transaction costs: risk averseness or store or brand loyalty

440

Product and cost characteristics	Unused capacity	Economies of scale or unused capacity	Economies of scale or unused capacity	Economies of scale or experience, or unused capacity	Signaling firm has higher costs or suboptimizes or cheats on quality	Higher production costs in adjacent market; economies of scale or unused capacity	Perishable product or purchase occasion	Joint economies of scale across products; features with low cost increase relative to price increase	Patents, superior technology
Variants	Generic pricing, dumping	Price skimming, peak-load pricing, price discrimination, priority pricing	Variable price merchandising, cents-off, coupons	Limit pricing	Reference pricing	FOB, base point, uniform, zone, and freight pricing	Mixed bundling, pure components, pure bundling	—	Captive pricing, two-part pricing, loss leadership
Relevant legal constraints	Explicit price discrimination illegal	Explicit price discrimination illegal	Explicit price discrimination illegal	Predatory pricing illegal	—	Price collusion, explicit price discrimination, predatory pricing illegal	Explicit price discrimination, pure bundling illegal	—	(Minimum) retail price maintenance illegal, tie-ins illegal

discounting, demand that motivates periodic discounting, and search costs that motivate random discounting.[1] These conditions enable a firm to discriminate implicitly in the prices it charges its consumers. In industrial and wholesale markets, explicit price discrimination whereby a firm charges different prices to two competing buyers under identical circumstances is illegal under the Robinson-Patman Act's (1936) amendment of the Clayton Act (1914), unless the price-cutting firm can meet specific defenses (Scherer 1980, p. 572; Werner 1982). In the consumer market, explicit price discrimination would lead to the ill-will of consumers. Aside from the special motivations for each type of discounting to be discussed hereafter, discounting in general has a sales enhancing effect, probably because consumers overweight the saving on a deal ("the silver lining," Thaler 1985) in relation to the cost still incurred in buying the product at the discounted price. If the product were regularly at the discounted price, many of these consumers may not buy it at all!

Second Market Discounting

> Consider a competitive firm that sells 100,000 units of a product at $10 each, when variable costs are $1 and fixed costs are $500,000 for a capacity of 200,000 units. The firm gets a request to sell in a new market such that there will be a negligible loss of sales in the first market and a negligible increase in fixed or variable costs. What is the minimum selling price the firm should accept?

This is a classic problem in incremental costing and the solution is well known. The minimum acceptable price would be anything over $1, because any price over variable costs would make a contribution to this ongoing business. Generics, secondary demographic segments, and some foreign markets provide opportunities for profitable use of this strategy. Often pioneering drugs are faced with competition from identical but much lower priced generics after the expiry of the patent. The pioneering firm has the options of either maintaining its price and losing share or dropping price and losing margin. The relevant strategy would be to enter the generic market segment with an unbranded product and arrest loss of sales to that segment without foregoing either margin or position in the branded segment. The same principle also holds for a firm changing to a mixed brand strategy after selling under a manufacturer brand only or a private label brand only. A second illustration of this strategy is the discounts to secondary demographic markets such as students, children, or new members.

Similarly, for some countries the foreign market represents an opportunity rather than a threat if the same theory is applied. Often a firm's selling price or even current average cost in the home market may be higher than the selling price in the foreign market. However, if its variable costs are sufficiently below the selling price in the foreign market, the firm can export profitably at a price somewhere between the selling price in the foreign market and its variable costs. The term "dumping" is sometimes used to describe the latter strategy if the firm's selling price in the foreign market is below its average costs.

The essential requirements for this strategy are that the firm have unused capacity and consumers have transaction costs so there is no perfect arbitrage between the two markets. In terms of profitability, additional revenues from the second market should exceed all increases in variable and fixed costs and loss of profits from the first market. Note here that the first market provides an external economy to the second, because the latter market gets goods at a lower price than it would otherwise. (For this reason some economists are not critical of dumping. Others, however, stress that there may be long-term damage to the foreign economy from lost wages and production facilities.) The second market provides neither an economy nor a diseconomy to the first in the short run.

Periodic Discounting

> Consider a firm faced with the following pricing problem. Average economic costs[2] are $55 at 20 units and $40 at 40 units. There are 40 consumers per period that are interested in its product. Half of them are fussy and want the product only at the beginning of each period even if they have to pay $50 per unit. The other half are price sensitive and would take the product at any time but will pay no more than $30 per unit. At what price should the firm sell its product?

Initially it may seem that the firm cannot bring the product to market profitably because costs exceed acceptable prices for each segment. However, in effect, the firm can produce and sell profitably if it exploits the consumers' heterogeneity of demand by a strategy of periodic discounting. It should produce at the level of 40 units per period at a cost of $40 per unit, price at $50 at the beginning of each period, and systematically discount the product at the end of the period to $30. In this way it would sell to the fussy consumers at the beginning and to the rest at the end of each period. Note that its average selling price is $40, which equals its average economic cost.

This is the principle often involved in the temporal markdowns and periodic discounting of off-season fashion goods, off-season travel fares, matinee tickets, and happy hour drinks, as well as peak-load-pricing for utilities (Hirshleifer 1958; Houthakker 1951; Steiner 1957; Williamson 1966). Similarly, this is the principle involved in the discounting of older models (Stokey 1981), the priority pricing of scarce products (Harris and Raviv 1981), and the strategy of price skimming, first suggested as one alternative for new products by Dean (1950a). Because of the circumstances in which this discounting strategy has been used, it often is referred to by different names. However, a more general label would be "periodic discounting," because of the essential principle underlying this strategy: the manner of discounting is predictable over time and not necessarily unknown to consumers (unlike random discounting discussed next) and the discount can be used by all consumers (unlike second market discounting).

An interesting issue in periodic discounting is that both segments of the market provide an external economy to each other.[3] The first segment that pays the higher price can be viewed as providing a sort of "venture" price to the firm to produce the product, whereas the second segment can be viewed as providing a "salvage" price to the firm for unsold items at the period's end. This intuition suggests that, even if the demand for the product is not exactly known, a strategy of pricing high and systematically discounting with time is likely to ensure that the firm covers its costs and makes a reasonable profit. However, the first segment provides a greater external economy than the second, because it bears more of the production costs.

Random Discounting

> Consider a firm that has a minimum average economic cost of production of $30. Assume a distribution of prices for the same product between $30 and $50 because there are several other firms with other cost structures

and $50 is the maximum consumers will pay for it. It takes one hour to search for the lowest price, $30. If a consumer does not search but buys from the first seller, he/she may if lucky get a $30 seller but if unlucky may get a $50 seller. Further, assume consumers' opportunity cost of time ranges from $0 to well over $20 per hour. What is the best shopping strategy for consumers and the best pricing strategy for firms? For consumers, the problem is fairly simple. Let us assume that the distribution of prices is such that on average a consumer who does not search and is uninformed about prices pays $40 for the product. Then on average a consumer who searches and is informed saves $10 (40 − 30). Hence consumers whose opportunity cost of time is more than $10 should not shop and the rest should. Let us assume that at least some consumers search and others buy randomly. What strategy should the firm with an average economic cost of $30 adopt?

The answer is a stratgey of random discounts, which involves maintaining a high price of $50 regularly and discounting to $30. However, the manner of discounting is crucial. It should be undiscernible or "random" to the uninformed consumers and infrequent, so that these consumers do not get lucky too often. The uninformed consumers will not be able to second guess the price; they will buy randomly, usually at the high price. In contrast, the informed will look around or wait until they can buy at the low price. In this way the firm tries to maximize the number of informed at its low price instead of at a competitor's low price, while maximizing the number of uninformed at its high rather than its low price. Research on the intransitivity of preferences indicates some interesting twists to the appeal of discounts and coupons. First, searchers are likely to oversearch. They spend more time shopping than is justified by their gains, the result of what Thaler (1980) calls

the "endowment effect." The real saving from the discounts is overweighted in relation to the opportunity cost of time. In contrast, nonsearchers are likely to undersearch for high cost products. This behavior can be explained by the psychophysics of pricing (Thaler 1980). Consumers relate the benefits of search to the cost of the good rather than to the cost of the time it takes to search.

Most discounting today by specialty stores, department stores, services, and especially supermarkets is of this type (referred to as "variable price merchandising" by Nelson and Preston 1966; Preston 1970). Out-of-store coupons or features are of this type unless motivated by periodic discounting, inventory buildup, or damaged goods.

The vast volume of business in this category has increased the importance of understanding the issues involved. A static model of interfirm price variation due to consumer search costs first was developed by Salop and Stiglitz (1977) in their well-known piece, "Bargains and Ripoffs." Varian (1980) developed a dynamic model of random price variation by each firm, similar to the mechanism described in the last example. Since then a whole body of literature has developed pursuing various ramifications of this strategy. The basic condition for this strategy is heterogeneity of perceived search costs, which enables firms to attract informed consumers by discounting. All consumers know there is a distribution of prices and have the same reservation price. However, for high income individuals hunting for the lowest price may not be worth their time. For others the opposite holds.

The individual firm should adopt a strategy of random discounts if the increased profit from new informed consumers at the discounted price exceeds the cost arising from the uninformed buying at the discounted price plus the cost of administering the discount (see McAlister 1983 and Neslin and Shoemaker 1983 for profitability models).

It is interesting to examine the implications of this strategy. First, note that the uninformed consumers provide a diseconomy to other uninformed consumers and to informed consumers. Inefficient firms that produce above $30 or efficient firms that price above $30 can exist because some consumers do not search. As a result, prices vary, so that the informed must search for the lowest price. Similarly, the average price paid by the uninformed increases. In contrast, the informed provide an external economy to the uninformed by encouraging the existence of low price firms, thus lowering the average price the uninformed pay. From a public policy perspective, all consumers as well as the efficient firms would benefit if some mechanism could be provided to disseminate price information in the market at relatively low cost.

COMPETITIVE PRICING

This category covers a group of pricing strategies based primarily on a firm's competitive position. Penetration pricing and experience curve pricing attempt to exploit scale[4] or experience[5] economies, respectively, by currently pricing below competitors in the same market and thus driving them out. Predatory pricing is a strategy of pricing low to hold out competition with the sole objective of establishing monopolistic conditions and subsequently raising price; this practice is illegal under Section 2 of the Sherman Act and the Robinson-Patman Act of 1936. Many states also have laws that forbid a firm from pricing below cost for extended periods of time. A third strategy is price signaling,[6] whereby a firm exploits consumer trust in the price mechanism de-veloped by other firms. A fourth strategy, geographic pricing, involves competitive pricing for adjacent market segments.

Penetration Pricing

Consider the periodic discounting example with the following two modifications: the economic cost price at 40 units is $30 and other competitors can freely enter the market with the same cost structure. How should the firm price now?

The firm could still adopt a strategy of periodic discounting, producing 40 units a period at $30 each and selling to the first set of consumers at $50 and to the second at $30. Now, however, because its average cost price is $30, it would make an excess profit of $10 per unit. Given this scenario, any other firm would be willing to come in and sell the same product for an average price that is less than $40 but more than $30. To preempt competition and stay in business, the firm would have to sell at $30 to all consumers.

The same logic underlies penetration pricing, a strategy first proposed for new products by Dean (1950a,b, 1951) as an alternative to periodic discounting (or price skimming in Dean's terminology). Periodic discounting is obviously preferable for a firm, even if its costs are lower than demand prices (as in the modified example here), as long as there is no immediate threat of competitive entry. Besides being used for new products, penetration pricing can be observed in the growth of discount stores and in the consolidation of manufacturers during the "shake out" phase of the life cycle. A variation of penetration pricing that has been closely studied in the economics literature is limit pricing (Scherer 1980), whereby a firm prices above costs but just low enough to keep out new entrants.

Penetration pricing is relevant only when the average selling price can or does exceed the minimum average cost. Other essentials for penetration pricing strategy are price sensitivity on the part of some consumers and the threat of competitive entry. In penetration pricing, unlike periodic discounting, the presence of the price sensitive consumers and of competition provides a benefit to the price insensitive segment, who can now buy the product at a price lower than they were willing to pay.

Experience Curve Pricing

Assume a competitive market with experience effects as shown in Figure 31–1. There are four firms (A, B, C, and D), each with

per period volume of 2000 units but the first having the most experience and average costs of $3.75 per unit. Current prices are $5 per unit. Consumers are price sensitive and react immediately to price changes. What would be a good pricing strategy for firm A?

Note that currently firm A makes more profit than the others and that, given the projections, cost declines will be less prominent after year 6. A good strategy for firm A would be to price aggressively, even below current costs, at $3.75. This strategy has two advantages. First, it will be uneconomical for firms B, C, and D, which may have to leave the market. Firm A is then faced with less rivalry. Second, firm A can benefit from the share of the others and gain experience more rapidly. Indeed, it would

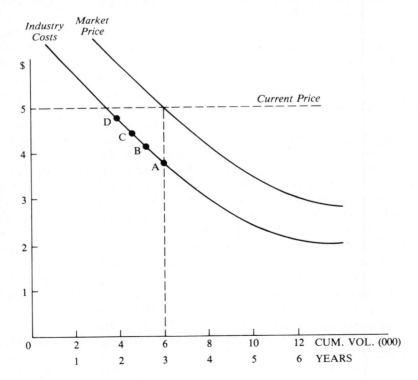

Figure 31–1
Effect of Experience Economies on Pricing Strategy

sell a cumulative volume of 12,000 units as early as year 6 and its costs would have dropped by then to $2 per unit. In addition, the low price is likely to encourage more consumers to enter the market, giving firm A an opportunity to exploit economies of scale. As a result the firm will soon be profitable again and total revenue and profits could be much higher in the future. The strategy for the other firms is less clear. In general, unless there are other competitive advantages, it is inadvisable for the others to start a price war as they have a cost disadvantage to firm A.

Experience curve pricing, like penetration pricing, is an alternative strategy to periodic discounting. In this strategy the consumers who buy the product early in the life cycle gain an external economy from late buyers, as they buy the product at a lower price than they were willing to pay. They get this discount, however, because of economies of experience and active or potential competition that forces prices down.

The essential requirements for adopting an experience curve pricing strategy are that experience effects are strong, the firm has more experience than competitors, and that consumers are price sensitive. Typically, these conditions occur for nonessential durable goods in the early or growth stage, when a relatively large number of competitors are striving for a strong long-run position. The different sources of economies for penetration pricing and experience curve pricing must be clearly understood, because the circumstances in which they are applicable are often very similar but the mechanisms for tracking costs and pricing products are very different.

Price Signaling

Consider a market in which firms can produce products at two different quality levels, under the constraint that the minimum aver-

age economic cost is $30 for the low quality product and $50 for the high quality product. Assume that, to avoid image conflicts, each firm chooses to produce only one quality but may sell at either price, $30 or $50. Let us assume for convenience that there are at least a few firms selling the high quality product for $50 and the low quality product for $30. Consumers can easily find the lowest price (in negligible time), say by a phone call or consulting a price list. They generally prefer high quality, but it takes them 1 hour of study and consulting manuals to tell quality differences. Let these consumers have a distribution of opportunity costs of time as in the random discounting example. What are consumers' shopping strategies and firms' pricing strategies?

Firms can choose among three pricing strategies (no firm would sell the high quality product at less than $50). First, they could produce the low quality product and sell it at $30. Second, they could produce the high quality product and sell it at $50. Third, they could sell the low quality product at $50, with the intention that some consumers who cannot tell high quality but want it will be fooled. The latter strategy is called "price signaling." Consumers also have three strategies. Those with low costs of time could study quality and buy the high quality product at $50. Those with high costs of time could adopt a risk aversive strategy and always buy the low priced product, or could buy the high priced product with the hope of getting a high quality product.

Extensive research in marketing has indicated that consumers may use price to infer quality (Monroe and Petroshius 1981; Olson 1977), but the equilibrium properties of such behavior in real markets have only recently been worked out (Cooper and Ross 1984; Tellis 1985). Three underlying conditions are necessary for price signaling to be an equilibrium strategy. First, consumers must be able to get information about price more easily than information about quality. Second, they must want the high quality enough to risk buying the high priced product even without a certainty of high quality. This motive is especially necessary because consumers underweight the value of uncertain events (the "certainty effect," Kahneman and Tversky 1979). Third, there must be a sufficiently large number of informed consumers who can understand quality and will pay the high price only for the high quality product. This third condition ensures a sufficiently positive correlation between price and quality so that those uninformed consumers who infer quality from price find it worthwhile to do so on average.

The issue of pricing in the presence of quality variation and asymmetric consumer information is typical of durable goods, though not uncommon for services and nondurable goods where it may involve less risk. For durables, quality is an important attribute yet consumer information on quality is low because of the difficulty of determining quality by inspection, the large number of brands, and the high innovation rate relative to repurchase time (Thorelli and Thorelli 1977). One result is the possibility of consumers using price to infer quality. However, another result is that the correlation between price and quality is low (Tellis and Wernerfelt 1985) and consumers may often be mistaken. Price signaling is probably most common for new or amateur consumers in a market, who do not know the quality of competitive brands but find quality important. The purchase of a high priced wine by the casual buyer is a good example. The success of several high priced, inferior quality brands, as reported by *Consumer Reports*, is another illustration of consumers either buying randomly or using price to infer quality.

There are some other variations of price signaling that firms can adopt to exploit consumer behavior in other circumstances. Image pricing, discussed subsequently, and reference pricing are two common examples. In reference pricing, a firm places a high priced model next to a much higher priced version of the same product, so that the former may seem more attractive to risk aversive uninformed consumers. The latter model serves primarily as a reference point, though consumers who infer quality may buy it. Monroe and Petroshius (1981) document empirical support for consumers' use of reference prices. Kahneman and Tversky (1979) provide the rationale for this behavior in what they call the "isolation effect": a choice looks more attractive next to a costly alternative than it does in insolation. The strategy is sometimes adopted by retailers of durable goods. A more common variation is for firms to state that a product is on sale, with the "regular" sticker price adjacent, when actually the regular price is on for less than half the time. To minimize deception on the part of firms, several states now define minimum time periods for the regular price.

In this context it is worthwhile to consider the welfare aspects of such strategy. The most important point is that all consumers would be better off if a mechanism could be devised to provide information on quality to the market at low cost. Second, those firms that sell the low quality product for the low price and those that sell the high quality product for the high price would also be better off if information on quality were disseminated, because they would not lose customers to firms that sell the low quality product at the high price. The last category of firms would vanish. Therefore, heterogeneous search costs on quality create benefits for some firms at the expense of others. Third, there could be many reasons for firms to sell the low quality product at the high price. Some could adopt such a strategy accidentally, others because they are inefficient producers, and still others because they intentionally cheat. Fourth, consumers who use price to infer quality may not necessarily be worse off. To the extent that obtaining information on quality is difficult for them, the correlation between price and quality is positive, and they prefer the high quality product, they may profitably use the high price to infer quality. In such a situation there is an external economy from the informed to the uninformed who gather information via the price mechanism.

Note that price signaling is independent of the strategy of random discounting. Both are used in situations in which consumers have heterogeneous search costs, but differ on other dimensions. For price signaling, there must be quality differences among products, information on quality must be more scarce than that on price, and quality must be important to consumers; further, each firm need adopt only one price level always and at least some efficient firms are necessary to establish consumer trust in the price mechanism.

Geographic Pricing

Consider two adjacent markets X and Y, of 20 consumers each, where all consumers have a reservation price of $50 for the product and incur a cost of more than $10 for purchasing the product in the adjacent market. A firm operating in market X is faced with free competitive entry and the following cost structure: the economic cost price for the product is $40 at 20 units and $30 at 40 units, with an added cost of $10 per unit to ship the product to the adjacent market. The cost of production is higher in market Y. What pricing strategy should the firm adopt?

The firm should produce 40 units and sell to both markets at an average economic cost price of $35 ($30 + $10 × 20 ÷ 40). To avoid competitive entry, the firm must set the average selling price over both markets at $35. However, the firm has several options

for pricing the product to the two markets, called "geographic pricing strategies," depending on the competitive condition in market Y.

If the competitive price in market Y is above $40, the firm can sell the product at $30 in market X and $40 in market Y to reflect the transportation costs of $10 per unit to the latter market. Because price equals average costs, the price would be profitable yet ward off entry. This strategy is called "FOB." If the competitive price in market Y is a little over $35, the firm could sell at $35 in both markets and still achieve the same competitive effect. This strategy is called "uniform delivered price." Zone pricing is a strategy between the two when more markets are involved. When using zone pricing, the firm would charge different prices for different zones depending on the transportation costs to each, but within each zone it would charge one price, the average of all costs to all points in that zone. Basing point is still another variation of uniform delivered price; the firm chooses a base point for transportation costs to points other than the point of production.

If the competitive price is a little over $30 in market Y, the firm could sell profitably to both markets by pricing at $30 in market Y and $40 in market X. This strategy is called "freight absorption cost," because market Y bears none of the transportation cost it incurs for the product. In a monopolistic situation, the firm may absorb the transportation cost or pass it on to consumers in market X. However, in a competitive market such as this one, all the transportation costs are borne by market X.

Geographic pricing strategies can be thought of as being between price penetration and second market discounting (see Table 31–1). As in price penetration, in geographic pricing the firm seeks to exploit economies of scale by pricing below competitors in a second market segment. As a result, the second market generally provides a benefit to the first. However, in geographic pricing the two segments are separated by transportation costs rather than by reservation prices. In this respect, geographic pricing is similar to the strategy of second market discounting, where two markets are also separated by transaction costs. In second market discounting, however, the firm explicitly attempts to exploit the differences between the two segments, providing considerable savings to the second market. By contrast, in geographic pricing the firm attempts to minimize differences between the two markets by sharing or "absorbing" the transportation costs between them. In spite of these transportation costs and because of economies of scale, the second market does not provide a diseconomy and generally provides an economy to the first.

Some of the geographic pricing strategies discussed may be illegal in certain circumstances. Three general principles can be used to guide policy in this respect. First, a firm should not discriminate between competing buyers in the same region (especially in zone pricing for buyers on either side of a zonal boundary) because such action may violate the Robinson-Patman Act of 1936. Second, the firm's strategy should not appear to be predatory, especially in freight absorption pricing, because such a strategy would violate Section 2 of the Sherman Act of 1890. Third, in choosing the basing point of zone pricing the firm should not attempt to fix prices among competitors because such action would violate Section 1 of the Sherman Act.

PRODUCT LINE PRICING STRATEGIES

Product line pricing strategies are relevant when a firm has a set of related products. In all of the cases considered, the firm seeks to maximize profit by pricing its products to match consumer demand. However, in each of these strategies, the nature of either the demand or the cross-subsidies varies among the firm's products. A firm uses price bundling when it faces heterogeneity of demand for nonsubstitute, perishable products. A firm uses premium pricing when it faces heterogeneity of demand for substitute products with joint economies of scale. Image pricing is used when consumers infer quality from prices of substitute models. Complementary pricing (including captive pricing, two-part pricing, and loss leadership) is used when a firm faces consumers with higher transaction costs for one or more of its products.

Price Bundling

Assume a distributor of two films, "Romancing the Stone" and "Places in the Heart," is faced by the following demand for these films from two movie houses, Astro and Classic Theatres, that serve the same market.

	Maximum Prices ($'000) Paid By:	
For:	Classic Theatres	Astro
"Romancing the Stone"	12	18
"Places in the Heart"	25	10

What is the best pricing strategy for the distributor to adopt if we assume it cannot explicitly discriminate in price or use tying contracts (force a theatre to buy both movies)?

An explicit price discriminating strategy, charging each distributor the most it will pay for each movie, would yield a total revenue of $65K, but this practice is illegal. Assume the buyers are sufficiently informed and the products perishable so that differential pricing by periodic or random discounting is not possible. A penetration strategy is to price the first movie at $12K and the second at $10K, but in that case total revenue is only $44K from both theatres $(2 \times (12 + 10))$. A "pure components" strategy is to price the first at $18K and the second at $25K, for a total revenue of $43K.

The best solution is to price the first movie at $18K, the second at $25K, and offer both at $28K for a total revenue of $56K. Note that Classic Theatres will take both movies at no more than $37K and Astro at no more than $28K. Thus both theatres will accept the package for $28K, which is the profit maximizing strategy. This strategy is called "mixed bundling" to contrast it with a pure bundling alternative in which case only the package is available for $28K. Pure bundling may be illegal as a tying contract (Scherer 1980; Werner 1982). The mixed bundling strategy has the added advantage of creating the reference price effect: the package is offered at a much lower price than the sum of the parts.

The economics of price bundling was first analyzed by Stigler (1968) and further developed by Adams and Yellen (1976), Telser 1979, Spence (1980), Paroush and Peles (1981), Phillips (1981), and Schmalensee (1984). Examples of such a strategy are the lower prices for season tickets, buffet dinners, packages of stereo equipment, and packages of options on automobiles. The basic requirement for mixed bundling is nonsubstitute (i.e., complementary or independent), perishable products with an asymmetric demand structure. Because the products are not perfect substitutes, it is possible to get consumers to buy both (or all). Because the products are perishable, the differential pricing strategies of periodic or random discounting are not feasible. The perishability of food items or seats for shows is apparent. The perishability in the purchase of durable goods is the purchase occasion, at which time it is in the interest of sellers to maximize revenues within consumers' demand schedule by price bundling. For example, consumers may buy automobiles once in 3 or 5 years. Each of those times is an opportunity for a firm to sell a maximum number of options by appropriate pricing.

The strategy of price bundling must not be confused with that of "trading up," in which consumers are persuaded to buy more or higher priced models than they originally intended. As the numerical example shows, a passive strategy of correctly bundling the prices of related items is all that is needed to maximize profit. It is also in the interest of consumers to buy at the price bundle. Thus, all consumers and sellers are better off with the mixed bundling strategy than with the pure components strategy.[7]

Premium Pricing

Consider a firm faced with the following pricing problem. There is free entry and average economic costs (for production and marketing) are $50 at 20 units and $35 at 40 units. At any volume, it costs the firm an additional $10 per unit to produce and market a superior version of the product. Assume that any fixed costs of marketing two products instead of one are negligible. Forty consumers per period are interested in its product. Half of them are price insensitive and want the superior version of the product even if they have to pay $50 per unit. The other half are price sensitive and want the basic version of the product but will pay no more than $30 per unit. In what version and at what price should the firm sell the product?

As in the periodic discounting example, costs seem to exceed prices if the firm chooses to sell to only one segment or at only one price. However, it can solve its problem by a premium pricing strategy that exploits consumer heterogeneity in demand. It should produce at 40 units, half of which will be of the superior version, for an average economic cost of $40. It should sell the basic product for $30 and the premium for $40, for an average selling price of $40, at which price it is profitable and wards off entry. Relative to its costs, the firm takes a premium on its higher priced version and a loss on its lower priced version. However, by exploiting joint economies of scale and the heterogeneity of demand, it can profitably produce and sell the product.

Premiun pricing applies in a large number of circumstances in markets today. It is used in the pricing of durable goods, typically appliances, for which multiple versions differing in price and features cater to different consumer segments. It also could apply for the pricing of some nondurable goods such as basic and specialty breads or common and exclusive perfumes. A similar strategy is used for the pricing of alternate service plans such as term and preferred insurance policies, front and rear auditorium seating, and deluxe and basic hotel rooms. As is well known in the case of autos, firms do not find their lower priced models "very profitable," but typically make their profits on the premium versions. Often these premium versions differ from the basic only by features and options, whose production costs generally are not high enough to justify the higher markup. Why does the firm produce the lower priced version and why do other firms not enter the market with only the higher priced version? The preceding explanation is based on heterogeneity in demand and joint economies of scale. Notice that the firm, by using a premium strategy, sells at exactly its economic cost price, which is compatible with a competitive market with free entry.[8] No firm could enter and

profitably produce only for the price insensitive segment.

Premium pricing also is used in retail, where it enables retailers to carry some otherwise unprofitable products desired only by select segments. The pricing of byproducts, though generally considered different from premium pricing, involves the same principle. A byproduct may carry a cost of disposal to the firm, and this may add to the price of the main product. In some cases a byproduct may be worth much more than it costs the firm to produce, and this advantage can be used to subsidize the price of the main product.

The essential difference between premium pricing and price bundling is that the former applies to substitutes and the latter to complementary products. Both require heterogeneity in demand, but in using premium pricing the firm tries to emphasize segment differences by pricing substitutes differently, whereas in using price bundling the firm seeks to bridge segment differences by selling at the lowest common package price. The difference between premium pricing and price signaling is that in the latter each firm produces only one type of product, which is sold at different prices to differently informed consumers. In the former, a firm produces two types of products to exploit joint economies of scale and markets them to heterogeneous but fully informed consumers.

The welfare aspects of premium pricing parallel those of periodic discounting. The main difference is in the fact that in periodic discounting the strategy is carried out for any one brand and the price variation is over time; in premium pricing, the strategy holds for any one time and the price variation is over related models. As in the periodic discounting example, each segment here provides an external economy to the other; however, the advantage to the price sensitive segment is greater because they buy a product below its average cost.

Image Pricing
By image pricing, a firm brings out an identical version of its current product with a different name (or model number) and a higher price. The intention is to signal quality. This strategy is between price signaling and premium pricing in that the demand characteristics are similar to those of price signaling and the cost aspects are similar to those of premium pricing (see Table 31–1). Thus the firm uses the higher priced version to signal quality to uninformed consumers and uses the profit it makes on the higher priced version to subsidize the price on the lower priced version. Image pricing differs from price signaling in that the prices are varied over different brands of the same firm's product line. It differs from premium pricing in that differences between brands are not real but only in the images or positions adopted. This strategy may account for some of the variation in prices of alternative brands of cosmetics, soaps, wines, and dresses that differ only in brand names.

Complementary Pricing
Complementary pricing includes three related strategies—captive pricing, two-part pricing, and loss leadership.

> Captive pricing: Consider a firm that produces a durable good whose economic cost price is $100 and life span is 3 years. During that time the product needs supplies that have an economic cost price of $.50 a month. All consumers are willing to pay at most $50 for the product and $2 per month for supplies. Assuming all buyers will keep on purchasing supplies regularly and the discount rate for future earnings is zero, what pricing strategy should the firm adopt?

Under the given assumptions, the firm would do well to price the basic product at $50 and the supplies at $2. The accumulated premium over the life of the product would equal $54 (3 × 12 × $1.5) and would more than compensate for the loss at the time of selling the basic product. In actually computing the minimum price of the product, the firm would have to include as costs a discount for future earnings and the risk that consumers would not purchase supplies. The firm also needs to consider the potential gains from this strategy. For example, consumers may not view the basic product they purchased as a sunk cost, and may try to "recover" their investment by buying the accessories and using it (the "sunk cost effect," Thaler 1980). Alternatively, they may get involved in the product and use it more than expected. This possibility has led some authors to label this strategy "captive pricing" (e.g., Kotler 1984, p. 529).

An interesting question is whether consumers would buy the package with the product at $100 and the accessories at $.50 if they were informed they were incurring the same cost the other way around. Probably they would not. A consumer may be reluctant to incur a big immediate investment (a certain loss) for an uncertain future satisfaction ("the certainty effect," Kahneman and Tversky 1979), or may not have the funds for the purchase. In either case, the consumer has a "transaction cost," which the firm apparently absorbs.

The chief restraint on the use of captive pricing for durable goods and accessories is that there are often no major shared economies in the manufacture of the basic product and its accessories. Thus, if the premium on the accessories is too high, marginal producers of the accessories may enter the market and drive down prices. In some circumstances, as in the automobile industry, the accessories are themselves produced by smaller firms. Consequently this strategy has limited importance unless consumers are source loyal and would like to buy supplies from the original source even at a higher price. In other circumstances, manufacturers hold patents or are the only source of the technology for the production of the supplies. In this case captive pricing is crucial for the success of the product. Bain (1956) refers to the superior position of these firms as "absolute cost advantages." In no circumstances may the firm bind the buyer to purchase the supplies from it. Such a strategy of tying contracts may be illegal under the Sherman Act of 1890 or the Clayton Act of 1914 (Burstein 1960; Scherer 1980; Werner 1982).

The well-known examples of captive pricing are razors and blades, cameras and films, autos and spare parts, and videos or computers and software packages. In the case of services, this strategy is referred to as "two-part pricing" because the service price is broken into a fixed fee plus variable usage fees (e.g., the pricing by telephone companies, libraries, health or entertainment clubs, amusement parks, and various rental agencies). The economics of two-part pricing has been studied by several researchers, more recently by Schmalensee (1982).

In retailing, the corresponding strategy is called "loss leadership," and involves dropping the price on a well-known brand to generate store traffic. The drop in price should be large enough to compensate consumers for the transaction cost involved in making the extra trip, switching from their normal place of purchase, or foregoing the cheaper basket of prices they pay at the alternative store. However, in many cases the drop in price may not be exactly that high, primarily because consumers may see the price drop as a real gain while underestimating the transaction costs (Thaler 1985). Nevertheless, to ensure a success in this strategy, retailers normally feature several "super buys," nationally branded products sold below cost.

Manufacturers of nationally branded products have always disapproved of loss leadership for two reasons. First, a product that is often available on discount may give consumers the impression that the quality is inferior. Second, specialty stores that depend on the branded products for their source of income may lose sales to discount stores and therefore cease to distribute the product. Manufacturers have sought to restrain loss leadership by a strategy of retail price maintenance. However, (minimum) retail price maintenance is now illegal under a federal statute, the Consumer Goods Pricing Act of 1975 (Scammon 1985; Scherer 1980; Werner 1982).

The reverse case, maintaining maximum retail prices, is not illegal (Scammon 1985). This situation occurs when a retailer charges too high a price for a branded product over which it has exclusive or selective distributorship. In such a case the retailer may suboptimize the manufacturer's profits (Machlup and Taber 1960). The manufacturer can control this practice by advertising the "suggested (maximum) retail price" and then enforcing such a price during the advertising period. High priced durable goods such as appliances and automobiles are examples of products for which this strategy is used.

Complementary pricing is similar to premium pricing in that the loss in the sale of a product is covered by the profit from the sale of a related product. However, there are two important distinctions. First, premium pricing applies to substitutes and complementary pricing to complements. Second, complementary pricing requires variation in transaction costs over the products whereas premium pricing requires variation in preferences over consumer groups. As a result there is no sharing of economies among customer groups in complementary pricing.

AN INTEGRATION AND COMPARISON OF STRATEGIES

The preceding discussion demonstrates the variety of pricing strategies available to a firm. The theory underlying some of them has only recently been analyzed in the economics literature, though they all have been discussed in some form in the marketing discipline. A major contribution of this article is that all these strategies are discussed on the same basis and are compared in a manner that is theoretically rich yet typologically simple. The most important contribution is that the strategies are shown to have a common denominator—shared economies. This proposition makes possible an enlightening classification of the strategies and a summarization of their underlying principles. The classification is based on two dimensions: the objective of the firm in exploiting these shared economies and the consumer characteristics necessary for each strategy (see Table 31–1).

The relevance of the central idea of shared economies is summarized here with respect to Table 31–1. A more detailed explanation is given in the description of the welfare aspects of each strategy. In the class of differential pricing strategies, one product is sold to two segments at different prices. By this means the firm exploits economies of scale and each segment provides an economy to the other. In addition, in second market discounting and periodic discounting, one segment buys the product at a higher price and in so doing incurs more of the production costs so that the product can be made available to the other segment at its lower acceptable price. In random discount-

ing, the searchers ensure that the product is available at a lower price at random periods, thus providing a lower average price to the nonsearchers.

In the class of competitive pricing strategies, firms sell one product to one or more market segments at the same price, but the pattern of shared economies is more complex. In price signaling, the searchers provide an economy to nonsearchers, who can get the quality they desire (either high or low) at an acceptable risk of an error just by observing prices. In penetration, experience curve, and geographic pricing, the two segments provide a simple cost economy to each other, enabling the firm to exploit economies of scale or experience. In addition, in penetration and experience curve pricing the common price is that of the more price sensitive segment, which therefore confers a great economy to the price insensitive segment. In geographic pricing, the lower the competitive price in the adjacent market, the higher the price and hence the greater the diseconomy borne by the home market.

In the class of product line pricing strategies, the shared economies are primarily over the production or marketing of the products in the line. In image pricing, premium pricing, and complementary pricing, one product is sold at a "loss" which is then recovered from the higher price of a complementary product sold to the same segment or of a substitute product sold to a less price sensitive segment. In price bundling, there is an asymmetric demand by two consumer segments over two nonsubstitute products. A firm using the optimum price sells both products at the lower of the joint reservation prices. In this way the firm sells one product below the acceptable price of one segment, but compensates by selling both products to both segments. In all of these cases the creative dimension of pricing is to identify the source and pattern of shared economies that can be exploited for the benefit of the individual firm and its consumers.

Besides delineating the classification scheme, this article compares and contrasts the various strategies with closely related alternatives. In addition, a summary comparison based on five criteria is presented in Table 31–2. These criteria are the characteristics of the strategy; the necessary consumer, product, and cost characteristics; the relevant legal constraints; and the variants of this strategy. The table demonstrates that the multiplicity of names distracts from the essential similarity among the strategies and the common principles that unify them. A small, theoretically based set of labels, like the one suggested here, enhances understanding and communication of the issues.

Besides the pedagogical and managerial benefits from this presentation of pricing strategies, the theoretical presentation suggests certain research avenues. One would be to review and further develop pricing models based on this classification scheme. Different models then could be usefully compared, new uses for older models identified, and newer models developed. Another avenue would be to determine to what extent these different strategies are carried out in practice, the types of firms that use particular strategies, and the factors that determine empirical success. A third avenue is to determine whether the principle of shared economies is in fact the main explanation for these strategies, as is proposed here.

NOTES

1. There are also other motivations for discounting, the most common being damaged goods, overstocking, or quantity purchases. These discounts are not considered pricing strategies because they are merely adjustments for costs, often of an *ad hoc* nature. The term "price discrimination" has been used in the literature very broadly to mean charging different customer groups prices not proportionate to costs for the same or related products. It would cover almost all the strategies discussed here (Cassady 1946a,b; Monroe 1979; Scherer 1980).

2. The term "average economic cost" is used to mean all costs, production and marketing, fixed and variable, plus acceptable profit divided by number of units.

3. The discussion of welfare applies only to the competitive case as in the example described. Some of the applications of this strategy cited above have been to the monopolistic case, in which situation the price sensitive buyers are the primary beneficiaries. However, as the example illustrates, *monopoly is not a necessary condition for periodic discounting*, though some authors mistakenly say so.

4. "Economies of scale" refers to the decline in average total costs with scale. This effect is generally attributed to superior technology or more efficient organization or cheaper purchases (Mansfield 1983; Palda 1969). Average total costs also are believed to increase beyond a certain point because of the difficulty of managing very large operations.

5. "Experience curve" or "experience economies" refers to the decline in average total costs in constant dollars with *cumulative* volume (see Figure 1). Define C_1 as average costs at volume V_1, let V_1 hold for n_1 periods; define C_2 as average costs at volume V_2, let V_2 hold for n_2 periods. Then economies of scale are captured by the elasticity ϵ_s defined by

$$\frac{C_2}{C_1} = \left(\frac{V_2}{V_1} \right)^{\epsilon_2}, \ V_2 \neq V_1 \qquad (1)$$

and economies of experience by the elasticity ϵ_e defined by

$$\frac{C_2}{C_1} = \left[\frac{\sum\limits_{j=1}^{n_2} V_{2j} + \sum\limits_{i=1}^{n_1} V_{1i}}{\sum\limits_{i=1}^{n_1} V_{1i}}\right]^{\epsilon_s} \quad (2)$$

$$= \left(\frac{n_2 V_2 + n_1 V_1}{n_1 V_1}\right)^{\epsilon_s} = \left(1 + \frac{n_2 V_2}{n_1 V_1}\right)^{\epsilon_s}$$

Note that change in the scale of operation, measured by V_2/V_1, affects the value of ϵ_s and ϵ_e, which are therefore related. However, ϵ_s does not *cause* ϵ_e or vice versa. Moreover, unlike ϵ_s, ϵ_e is defined even if $V_2 = V_1$, and when $V_2 = V_1$ may still be dependent primarily on n_2/n_1, the time parameters. The strategic implications of the experience curve were best documented and popularized by the Boston Consulting Group (1972), though the issue was addressed in the literature earlier (e.g., Alchian 1959; Arrow 1962; Hirsch 1952; Preston and Keachie 1964). More recent theoretical contributions were made by Robinson and Lakhani (1975), Dolan and Jeuland (1981), and Kalish (1983). The decline in costs due to experience could be caused by a number of factors, most importantly labor efficiency and newer process technology (see Abell and Hammond 1979 and Porter 1980 for a complete list). Two important issues to be kept in mind when pricing are that economies of experience *can occur independently of scale* (as shown above) and that their decline generally takes place fairly constantly with cumulative volume. Because cumulative volume increases at a faster rate in the first few years of a product's production history, experience effects are most noticeable at that time period. Because of competitive pressures, prices also decline with costs.

6. The term is used here to mean firms signaling quality to consumers by price. It must be distinguished from various interfirm signaling strategies that firms may use to "implicitly collude" (Scherer 1980).

7. In this example all cost issues are ignored, which could lead to at least three scenarios. One is a monopolistic situation in which the costs are sufficiently low that any of the pricing options would be profitable. The second is a cost situation in which only the mixed bundling option would be profitable. This then would hold either for monopoly or pure competition. The third is a situation in which costs are sufficiently low that any option would be profitable, but there is free entry so firms would use only the penetration pricing strategy ($10 for the first and $12 for the second movie) which is always the preferable option for consumers.

8. In some markets oligopolistic or monopolistic situations exist, in which case a firm can market profitably only to the premium segment. However, there are several reasons for marketing to both segments. First, dealers, especially of high priced durables, are more likely to accept an exclusive dealing strategy if the manufacturer has a complete line of products. Second, with a complete line it is easier to develop brand loyalty, especially as consumers tend to buy better versions of durables with each subsequent purchase. Third, a low priced basic version may be used to attract consumers into stores, and then motivate them to buy the higher priced versions. Since an early note by Dean (1950b), there is an extensive literature on alternative theoretical models for premium pricing. However, without formal empirical analysis it is not possible to determine which model is relevant or what alternatives need to be developed (Katz 1984).

REFERENCES

Abell, Derek F. and John S. Hammond (1979), *Strategic Market Planning: Problems and Analytical Approaches*. Englewood Cliffs, NJ: Prentice-Hall, Inc.

Adams, W. J. and J. L. Yellen (1976), "Commodity Bundling and the Burden of Monopoly," *Quarterly Journal of Economics*, 90 (August), 475–98.

Alchian, A. (1959), "Costs and Outputs," in *The Allocation of Economic Resources*, M. Abramovitz et al., eds. Stanford, CA: Stanford University Press, 23–40.

Areeda, Phillip (1974), *Antitrust Analysis*. Boston: Little, Brown & Company.

Arrow, K. J. (1962), "The Economic Implications of Learning by Doing," *Review of Economic Studies*, 29 (June), 155–73.

Bain, Joe S. (1956), *Barriers to New Competition*. Cambridge, MA: Harvard University Press.

Boston Consulting Group (1972), *Perspectives on Experience*. Boston, MA: Boston Consulting Group, Inc.

Burstein, M. L. (1960), "The Economics of Tie-In Sales," *Review of Economics and Statistics*, 27 (February), 68–73.

Cassady, Ralph, Jr. (1946a), "Some Economic Aspects of Price Discrimination Under Nonperfect Market Conditions, *Journal of Marketing*, 11 (July), 7–20.

——— (1946b), "Techniques and Purposes of Price Discrimination," *Journal of Marketing*, 11 (October), 135–58.

Cooper, R. and T. W. Ross (1984), "Prices, Product Qualities and Asymmetric Information: The Competitive Case," *Review of Economic Studies*, 51, 197–207.

Dean, Joel (1950a), "Pricing Policies for New Products," *Harvard Business Review*, 28 (November–December), 45–53.

——— (1950b), "Problems of Product-Line Pricing," *Journal of Marketing*, 14 (4), 518–28.

——— (1951), *Managerial Economics*. Englewood Cliffs, NJ: Prentice-Hall, Inc.

Dolan, Robert, and Abel Jeuland (1981), "Experience Curves and Dynamic Demand Models: Implications for Optimal Pricing Strategies," *Journal of Marketing*, 45 (Winter), 52–62.

Harris, Milton and Arthur Raviv (1981), "A Theory of Monopoly Pricing Schemes with Demand Uncertainty," *American Economic Review*, 71 (June), 347–65.

Hirsch, W. (1952), "Manufacturing Progress Functions," *Review of Economics and Statistics*, 34 (May), 143–55.

Hirshleifer, Jack (1958), "Peak Loads and Efficient Pricing: Comment," *Quarterly Journal of Economics*, 72 (August), 451–62.

Houthakker, Hendrik (1951), "Electricity Tariffs in Theory and Practice," *Economic Journal*, 61 (March), 1–25.

Hunt, Shelby D. (1983), *Marketing Theory, The Philosophy of Marketing Science*. Homewood, IL: Richard D. Irwin, Inc.

Kahneman, Daniel and Amos Tversky (1979), "Prospect Theory: An Analysis of Decision Under Risk," *Econometrica*, 47 (March), 263–91.

Kalish, Shlomo (1983), "Monopolist Pricing with Dynamic Demand and Production Cost," *Marketing Science*, 2 (Spring), 135–60.

Katz, Michael L. (1984), "Firm-Specific Differentiation and Competition Among Multiproduct Firms," *Journal of Business*, 57, 1, 2, S149–S166.

Kotler, P. (1984), *Marketing Management*. Englewood Cliffs, NJ: Prentice-Hall, Inc.

Machlup, Fritz and Martha Taber (1960), "Bilateral Monopoly, Successive Monopoly, and Vertical Integration," *Economica*, 27 (May), 101–19.

Mansfield, Edwin (1983), *Principles of Microeconomics*, 4th ed. New York: W. W. Norton & Company.

McAlister, Leigh (1983), "A Theory of Consumer Promotions: The Model," Sloan School Working Paper #1457–83, Massachusetts Institute of Technology.

Monroe, Kent B. (1979), *Pricing: Making Profitable Decisions*. New York: McGraw-Hill Book Company.

——— and S. M. Petroshius (1981), "Buyers' Perceptions of Price: An Update of the Evidence," in *Perspectives in Consumer Behavior*, H. H. Kassarjian and T. S. Robertson, eds. Glenview, IL: Scott, Foresman and Company, 43–5.

Nagle, Thomas (1984), "Economic Foundations for Pricing," *Journal of Business*, 57, 1, 2, S3–S26.

Nelson, Paul E. and Lee E. Preston (1966), *Price Merchandising in Food Retailing: A Case Study*. Berkeley, CA: The Special Publications.

Neslin, Scott A. and Robert W. Shoemaker (1983), "A Model for Evaluating the Profitability of Coupon Promotions," *Marketing Science*, 2 (Fall), 361–88.

Olson, J. C. (1977), "Price as an Informational

Cue: Effects on Product Evaluations," in *Consumer and Industrial Buying Behavior,* A. G. Woodside et al., eds. New York: North-Holland Publishing Company, 267–86.

Oren, Shmuel S. (1984), "Comments on Pricing Research in Marketing: The State of the Art," *Journal of Business,* 57, 1, 2, 561–4.

Palda, Kristian S. (1969), *Economic Analysis for Marketing Decisions.* Englewood Cliffs, NJ: Prentice-Hall, Inc.

Paroush, J. and Y. C. Peles (1981), "A Combined Monopoly and Optimal Packaging Model," *European Economic Review,* 15 (March), 373–83.

Phillips, O. R. (1981), "Product Bundles, Price Discrimination and the Two Product Firm," working paper, Texas A&M University.

Porter, M. E. (1980), *Competitive Strategy, Techniques for Analyzing Industries and Competitions.* New York: The Free Press.

Preston, Lee E. (1970), *Markets and Marketing.* Glenview, IL: Scott, Foresman and Company.

——— and E. C. Keachie (1964), "Cost Functions and Progress Functions: An Integration," *American Economic Review,* 54 (March), 100–7.

Rao, Vithala R. (1984), "Pricing Research in Marketing: The State of the Art," *Journal of Business,* 57, 1, 2, S39–S60.

Robinson, Bruce and Chet Lakhani (1975), "Dynamic Price Models for New Product Planning," *Management Science,* 21 (June), 1113–22.

Salop, Steven and Joseph Stiglitz (1977), "Bargains and Ripoffs: A Model of Monopolistically Competitive Price Dispersion," *Review of Economic Studies,* 493–510.

Scammon, Debra (1985), "Price Control (Minimum and Maximum)," *Journal of Marketing,* 49 (Spring), 147.

Scherer, F. M. (1980), *Industrial Market Structure and Economic Performance.* Chicago: Rand McNally College Publishing Company.

Schmalensee, Richard (1982), "Commodity Bundling by Single-Product Monopolies," *Journal of Law and Economics,* 25 (April), 67–72.

——— (1984), "Gaussian Demand and Commodity Bundling," *Journal of Business,* 57, 1, 2, S211–S230.

Spence, A. M. (1980), "Multi-Product Quantity-Dependent Prices and Profitability Constraints," *Review of Economic Studies,* 47 (October), 821–42.

Steiner, Peter O. (1957), "Peak Loads and Efficient Pricing," *Quarterly Journal of Economics,* 71 (November), 585–610.

Stigler, G. J. (1968), "A Note on Block Booking," reprinted in *The Organization of Industry,* G.J. Stigler, ed. Homewood, IL: Richard D. Irwin, Inc.

Stokey, Nancy L. (1981), "Rational Expectations and Durable Goods Pricing," *Bell Journal of Economics,* 12 (Spring), 112–28.

Tellis, Gerard J. (1985), "Do Prices Signal Quality: Theory, Measurement and Evidence," Working Paper #85–53, College of Business Administration, The University of Iowa.

——— and Birger Wernerfelt (1985), "The Price of Quality," Working Paper #85–52, College of Business Administration, The University of Iowa.

Telser, L. G. (1979), "A Theory of Monopoly of Complementary Goods," *Journal of Business,* 52 (April), 211–30.

Thaler, Richard (1980), "Toward a Positive Theory of Consumer Choice," *Journal of Economic Behavior and Organization,* 1 (March), 39–60.

——— (1985), "Mental Accounting and Consumer Choice," *Marketing Science,* 4 (Summer), 199–214.

Thorelli, Hans B. and Sarah V. Thorelli (1977), *Consumer Information Systems and Consumer Policy.* Cambridge, MA: Ballinger Publishing Company.

Tversky, Amos (1969), "Intransitivity of Preferences," *Psychological Bulletin,* 76, 31–48.

Varian, Hal (1980), "A Model of Sales," *The American Economic Review* (September), 651–9.

Werner, Ray O. (1982), "Marketing and the United States Supreme Court, 1975–1981," *Journal of Marketing,* 46 (Spring), 73–81.

Williamson, Oliver E. (1966), "Peak-Load Pricing and Optimal Capacity Under Indivisibility Constraints," *American Economic Review,* 56 (September), 810–27.

A Model for Predictive Measurements of Advertising Effectiveness

Robert J. Lavidge and Gary A. Steiner

What are the functions of advertising? Obviously the ultimate function is to help product sales. But all advertising is not, should not, and cannot be designed to produce immediate purchases on the part of all who are exposed to it. Immediate sales results (even if measurable) are, at best, an incomplete criterion of advertising effectiveness.

In other words, the effects of much advertising are "long-term." This is sometimes taken to imply that all one can really do is wait and see—ultimately the campaign will or will not produce.

However, if something is to happen in the long run, something must be happening in the short run, something that will ultimately lead to eventual sales results. And this process must be measured in order to provide anything approaching a comprehensive evaluation of the effectiveness of the advertising.

Ultimate consumers normally do not switch from disinterested individuals to convinced purchasers in one instantaneous step. Rather, they approach the ultimate purchase through a process or series of steps in which the actual purchase is but the final threshold.

SEVEN STEPS

Advertising may be thought of as a force, which must move people up a series of steps:

1. Near the bottom of the steps stand potential purchases who are completely *unaware of the existence* of the product or service in question.
2. Closer to purchasing, but still a long way from the cash register, are those who are merely *aware of its existence*.
3. Up a step are prospects who *know what the product has to offer*.

Reprinted from *Journal of Marketing*, published by the American Marketing Association (October 1961), pp. 59–62.

4. Still closer to purchasing are those who have favorable attitudes toward the product—those who *like the product.*

5. Those whose favorable attitudes have developed to the point of *preference over all other possibilities are up still another step.*

6. Even closer to purchasing are consumers who couple preference with a desire to buy and the *conviction* that the purchase would be wise.

7. Finally, of course, is the step which translates this attitude into actual *purchase.*

Research to evaluate the effectiveness of advertisements can be designed to provide measures of movement on such a flight of steps.

The various steps are not necessarily equidistant. In some instances the "distance" from awareness to preference may be very slight, while the distance to purchase is extremely large. In other cases, the reverse may be true. Furthermore, a potential purchaser sometimes may move up several steps simultaneously.

Consider the following hypotheses. The greater the psychological and/or economic commitment involved in the purchase of a particular product, the longer it will take to bring consumers up these steps, and the more important the individual steps will be. Contrariwise, the less serious the commitment, the more likely it is that some consumers will go almost "immediately" to the top of the steps.

An impulse purchase might be consummated with no previous awareness, knowledge, liking, or conviction with respect to the product. On the other hand, an industrial good or an important consumer product ordinarily will not be purchased in such a manner.

DIFFERENT OBJECTIVES

Products differ markedly in terms of the role of advertising as related to the various positions on the steps. A great deal of advertising is designed to move people up the final steps toward purchase. At an extreme is the "Buy Now" ad, designed to stimulate immediate overt action. Contrast this with industrial advertising, much of which is not intended to stimulate immediate purchase in and of itself. Instead, it is designed to help pave the way for the salesman by making the prospects aware of his company and products, thus giving them knowledge and favorable attitudes about the ways in which those products or services might be of value. This, of course, involves movement up the lower and intermediate steps.

Even within a particular product category, or with a specific product, different advertisements or campaigns may be aimed primarily at different steps in the purchase process—and rightly so. For example, advertising for new automobiles is likely to place considerable emphasis on the lower steps when new models are first brought out. The advertiser recognizes that his first job is to make the potential customer aware of the new product, and to give him knowledge and favorable attitudes about the product. As the year progresses, advertising emphasis tends to move up the steps. Finally, at the end of the "model year" much emphasis is placed on the final step—the attempt to stimulate immediate purchase among prospects who are assumed, by then, to have information about the car.

The simple model assumes that potential purchasers all "start from scratch." However, some may have developed negative attitudes about the product, which place them even further from purchasing the product than those completely unaware of it.

The first job, then, is to get them off the negative steps—before they can move up the additional steps which lead to purchase.

THREE FUNCTIONS OF ADVERTISING

The six steps outlined, beginning with "aware," indicate three major functions of advertising. The first two, awareness and knowledge, relate to *information or ideas*. The second two steps, liking and preference, have to do with favorable *attitudes or feelings* toward the product. The final two steps, conviction and purchase, are to produce *action*—the acquisition of the product.

These three advertising functions are directly related to a classic psychological model which divides behavior into three components or dimensions:

1. The *cognitive* component—the intellectual, mental, or "rational" states.
2. The *affective* component—the "emotional" or "feeling" states.
3. The *conative* or *motivational* component—the "striving" states, relating to the tendency to treat objects as positive or negative goals.

This is more than a semantic issue, because the actions that need to be taken to stimulate or channel motivation may be quite different from those that produce knowledge. And these, in turn, may differ from actions designed to produce favorable attitudes toward something.

FUNCTIONS OF ADVERTISING RESEARCH

Among the first problems in any advertising evaluation program are to:

1. Determine what steps are most critical in a particular case, that is, what the steps leading to purchase are for most consumers.
2. Determine how many people are, at the moment, on which steps.
3. Determine which people on which steps it is most important to reach.

Advertising research can then be designed to evaluate the extent to which the advertising succeeds in moving the specified "target" audience(s) up the critical purchase steps.

Table 32–1 summarizes the stair-step model, and illustrates how several common advertising and research approaches may be organized according to their various "functions."

Over-All and Component Measurements

With regard to almost any product there are an infinite number of additional "subflights" which can be helpful in moving a prospect up the main steps. For example, awareness, knowledge and development of favorable attitudes toward a specific product feature may be helpful in building a preference for the line of products. This leads to the concept of other steps, subdividing or "feeding" into the purchase steps, but concerned solely with more specific product features or attitudes.

Advertising effectiveness measurements may, then, be categorized into:

1. Over-all or "global" measurements, concerned with measuring the results—the consumers' positions and movement on the purchase steps.
2. Segment or component measurements, concerned with measuring the relative effectiveness of various means of moving people up the purchase steps—the

Table 32–1
Advertising and Advertising Research Related to the Model

Related Behavioral Dimensions	Movement toward Purchase	Examples of Types of Promotion or Advertising Relevant to Various Steps	Examples of Research Approaches Related to Steps of Greatest Applicability
Conative —the realm of motives. Ads stimulate or direct desires	PURCHASE ↑ | | | | CONVICTION	Point-of-purchase Retail store ads Deals "Last-chance" offers Price appeals Testimonials	Market or sales test Split-run tests Intention to purchase Projective techniques
Affective —the realm of emotions. Ads change attitudes and feelings	↑ PREFERENCE ↑ | | | | LIKING	Competitive ads Argumentative copy "Image" ads Status, glamour appeals	Rank order of preference for brands Rating scales Image measurements including check lists and semantic differentials Projective techniques
Cognitive —the realm of thoughts. Ads provide information and facts	↑ KNOWLEDGE ↑ | | | | AWARENESS	Announcements Descriptive copy Classified ads Slogans Jingles Sky writing Teaser campaigns	Information questions Play-back analyses Brand awareness surveys Aided recall

consumers' positions on ancillary flights of steps, and the relative importance of these flights.

Measuring Movement on the Steps

Many common measurements of advertising effectiveness have been concerned with movement up either the first steps or the final step on the primary purchase flight. Examples include surveys to determine the extent of brand awareness and information and measures of purchase and repeat purchase among "exposed" versus "unexposed" groups.

Self-administered instruments, such as adaptations of the "semantic differential" and adjective check lists, are particularly helpful in providing the desired measurements of movement up or down the middle steps. The semantic differential provides a means of scaling attitudes with regard to a number of different issues in a manner which facilitates gathering the information on an efficient quantitative basis. Adjective lists, used in various ways, serve the same general purpose.

Such devices can provide relatively spontaneous, rather than "considered," responses. They are also quickly administered and can contain enough elements to make recall of specific responses by the test participant difficult, especially if the order of items is changed. This helps in minimizing "consistency" biases in various comparative uses of such measurement tools.

Efficiency of these self-administered devices makes it practical to obtain responses to large numbers of items. This facilitates measurement of elements or components differing only slightly, though importantly, from each other.

Carefully constructed adjective check lists, for example, have shown remarkable discrimination between terms differing only in subtle shades of meaning. One product may be seen as "rich," "plush," and "expensive," while another one is "plush," "gaudy," and "cheap."

Such instruments make it possible to secure simultaneous measurements of both *global* attitudes and *specific* image components. These can be correlated with each other and directly related to the content of the advertising messages tested.

Does the advertising change the thinking of the respondents with regard to specific product attributes, characteristics or features, including not only physical characteristics but also various image elements such as "status"? Are these changes commercially significant?

The measuring instruments mentioned are helpful in answering these questions. They provide a means for correlating changes in specific attitudes concerning image components with changes in global attitudes or position on the primary purchase steps.

Testing the Model

When groups of consumers are studied over time, do those who show more movement on the measured steps eventually purchase the product in greater proportions or quantities? Accumulation of data utilizing the stair-step model provides an opportunity to test the assumptions underlying the model by measuring this question.

THREE CONCEPTS

This approach to the measurement of advertising has evolved from these concepts:

1. Realistic measurements of advertising effectiveness must be related to an understanding of the functions of advertising. It is helpful to think in terms of a model where advertising is likened to a force which, if successful, moves people up a series of steps toward purchase.
2. Measurements of the effectiveness of the advertising should provide measurements of changes at all levels on these steps—not just at the levels of the development of product or feature awareness and the stimulation of actual purchase.
3. Changes in attitudes as to specific image components can be evaluated together with changes in over-all images, to determine the extent to which changes in the image components are related to movement on the primary purchase steps.

Sales Force Management: Integrating Research Advances

Adrian B. Ryans and Charles B. Weinberg

Nearly half of the marketing expenses of industrial marketing companies are direct selling expenses. For most of these firms, selling expenditures exceed 5 percent of sales revenues.[1] In spite of this heavy commitment of marketing resources to personal selling, researchers have only recently given this area the attention it warrants. The surge of research in this area has been accompanied by the development of a number of models to provide conceptual frameworks for the research. As might be expected, the variety of research approaches and perspectives has resulted in a plethora of specialized models, each being well suited to the needs of the particular researchers, but integrating poorly with the models and conceptual frameworks developed by others. Even the most general of these conceptual models, the one proposed by Orville Walker, Gilbert Churchill, and Neil Ford, appears to empha-

size psychological elements at the expense of organizational and situational factors.[2]

This fragmentation makes it difficult to determine the state of knowledge in the personal selling area, to integrate different research efforts, and, perhaps most importantly, to identify where the major gaps in knowledge lie. The specialized nature of the models used in much sales force research, and the lack of managerial perspective in many of the models, calls into question, at least for managers, the relevance of many of the research results achieved. In addition, when a model provides low explanatory power because of the omission of some intuitively important variables, managers may be skeptical about the reasonableness of the results. A major objective of this article is to help managers understand and interrelate different research directions in sales force management.

A three-stage conceptual model of personal selling and the management of the personal selling function is proposed. This multilevel framework incorporates factors

Reprinted with permission from *California Management Review*, Vol. 24 (Fall 1981).

ranging from the specification of the role of personal selling in the marketing mix to individual salesperson factors such as role perceptions and motivation. The three stages of the framework reflect the major decision-making levels—strategic tactical, and operational (or implementation)—in the management of the personal selling function.

Other decision-oriented models of personal selling are available (David Montgomery and Glen Urban's and Kenneth Davis and Frederick Webster's are two early examples).[3] However, we believe that the proposed model goes further than these by providing a means to integrate current empirical results, behavioral science theories, and marketing models into a decision-oriented framework.

Much of the empirical research to date has focused on the operational level and has not fully considered the impact of decisions at the strategic and tactical levels on the situation at the operational level. We will review carefully the types of decisions that are made at the two prior levels and the factors that are important in making these strategic and tactical decisions. As limited empirical evidence is available about these two levels, this review will be largely expository; relevant empirical research will be cited at all three levels.

THE THREE-LEVEL MODEL

Conceptually, a model of personal selling and the management of the personal selling function can be viewed as being comprised of the three stages shown in Figure 33–1: a strategic, a tactical, and an operational or implementation level. A multilevel model is appropriate because sales force and personal selling decisions are made at several different levels in the marketing organiza-

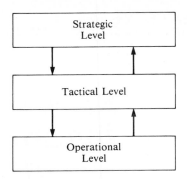

Figure 33–1
Structure of Conceptual Model

tion. The decisions at each level are made within guidelines set by the levels above it in the organization. The results and feedback obtained from the lower levels in the organization provide one basis for modifying the policies and plans at higher levels. From a research strategy perspective, it is usually necessary to focus on one part of the sales management system at a time, otherwise the problems encouraged in conducting research can become unmanageable.

Three stages are specified because this number seems to best capture the levels of sales force decision making, and the decisions at each stage tend to be the responsibility of, or to involve, different persons. At the strategic level, decisions are made by the top management of the company or business unit. At the tactical level, decisions are typically made by senior sales management but are frequently implemented by managers lower in the sales organization. At the operational or implementation level, the focus is on the salesperson, although many of the decisions are made or influenced by field sales management.

Strategic Level
The name of a firm's personal selling program and the contribution it makes to the

achievement of the firm's objectives are ultimately determined by the firm's or business unit's marketing strategy and the plans developed to implement this strategy. In the briefest possible terms, as Figure 33–2 indicates, a well-formulated marketing strategy is based on a thorough analysis and understanding of the company's internal and external environment. The analysis of the internal environment involves a careful review of the company's mission and objectives and a critical assessment of its resources and capabilities. The analysis of the external environment includes analyses of the company's customers, channel members, competitors and markets, and the likely impact of political, regulatory, economic, social, and technological trends on these groups and on the company. From the possible marketing strategies that might be adopted to achieve the company's objectives, top management selects the strategy that appears most likely to capitalize on the oppor-

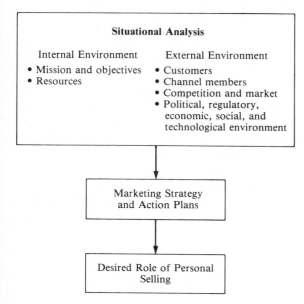

Figure 33–2
The Strategy Level

tunities and solve the problems uncovered by these analyses. The marketing strategy selected can imply very different roles for personal selling. The role assigned to personal selling has two major dimensions: the emphasis on personal selling relative to the other elements of the marketing communication mix (advertising, sales promotion, and publicity); and the particular set of objectives that the personal selling function is expected to accomplish. This role of personal selling in the marketing strategy (the desired role) is the major influence on the tactical decisions made by senior managers in the sales force.

Researchers have recently begun to examine empirically the relationship of expenditures on personal selling activities to product-market characteristics and factors related to the firm's strategy. The ADVISOR project includes an analysis of the marketing budgeting practices of a number of major U.S. industrial marketers for a large number of products.[4] Two of the models estimated in the project provide some guidance on the norms for marketing expenditures and the advertising/marketing expenditure ratio (and conversely some indication of the sales force/marketing expenditure ratio) given the characteristics of the product-market. Robert Buzzell and Paul Farris have also looked directly at the variables associated with the sales force/sales revenue ratio for three types of businesses using the PIMS data base.[5] While it is obviously difficult to infer a causal relationship for many of the independent variables, these models may be useful to managers charged with setting general levels for budgets for new or existing products given a particular strategy and particular market conditions.

Tactical Level
Typically, the top sales executive in the company and his or her staff are responsible for

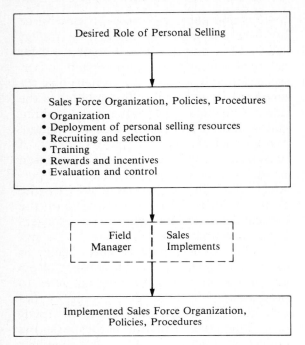

Figure 33–3
The Tactical Level

Deployment of Personal Selling Resources.
Once the basic sales organization is determined, decisions must next be made about how the sales resources of the company should be deployed. The issues include the assignment of accounts to salespersons—the territory design problem—and allocation of sales force time to accounts, product lines, and activities, such as opening new accounts versus servicing existing accounts. While a company's sales management usually develops general policy guidelines on deployment issues, the implementation of deployment policies are generally made by the field sales manager and the salesperson. Deployment is one aspect of the management of the personal selling function that lends itself quite well to quantitative modeling. A number of models have been proposed and several have been used to deal with deployment problems. Thomas Glaze and Charles Weinberg, Sidney Hess and Stuart Samuels, Leonard Lodish, and Roy Shanker, Ronald Turner, and Andris Zoltners have all proposed models to help with the territory design problem.[6] Zoltners and Kathy Gardner have recently reviewed the available sales force decision models.[7]

developing an organization and a set of policies and procedures (the tactical decisions) so that the sales force can achieve its desired role in the company's marketing strategy. Figure 33–3 indicates the main decision areas that must be considered.

Organization. The major organizational decision is whether the sales force should be organized on a geographic, product, or market basis, or some combination of these. Many companies find it more effective to deal with their major or national accounts with a special sales force. Other organizational decisions include the number of levels of sales management, the number of people who will report to each type of manager (the span of each manager's control in the organization), and whether staff specialists, such as sales trainers, are needed.

Recruiting and Selection. The desired role of personal selling and the tasks the salesperson is expected to carry out help suggest the types of salespersons needed in the sales force, likely sources of these salespersons, and the criteria that should be used in the selection process. For example, corporate resources, the size of the sales force, and job requirements often determine whether the company should try to hire experienced or inexperienced people.

Training. Almost all companies must do some training. For newly hired salespersons, training might provide selling skills, detailed understanding of the customers and their needs, extensive knowledge of products and services, and company policies and procedures. Besides this initial training, additional training for experienced salespersons is often needed in order to improve selling skills, to inform them about new products and policies, or to prepare them for new or more responsible positions within the sales organization.

Rewards and Incentives.

Rewards and incentives include both financial and nonfinancial elements. Rewards can be subdivided into two main categories, intrinsic and extrinsic rewards. Intrinsic rewards, which are linked to the carrying out of the job, include such intangibles as feelings of competence, completion, and self-actualization. Managers and researchers are paying increasing attention to intrinsic rewards as part of the overall incentive system, but the relative importance and interrelationship of these rewards as compared to extrinsic ones are still controversial.[8]

Extrinsic rewards, tangible, external factors that are controlled by the organization, include financial and other benefits. The compensation systems should be designed to encourage the types of behavior desired by the company. The relative importance of salary, commissions, and bonuses can have a significant effect on the behavior and performance of the salesperson. A heavy emphasis on commissions often focuses the salesperson on the short term, sometimes causing him or her to pay insufficient attention to building long-term account relationships. Because a heavy emphasis on commissions lessens the roles of salary and bonuses, it also reduces the control the field sales manager has over the salespersons. The field sales manager usually has a good deal of influence over these latter forms of compensation and can use them to help guide the salesperson's efforts in directions that

are important to the company's long-term needs. The compensation system also serves to attract and retain qualified people for the sales force.

Evaluation and Control.

The evaluation and control procedures in a sales force allow the sales executives to monitor the performance of the individual salespersons and units in the sales force against certain standards. This information can then be fed back to the involved parties so that corrective action can be taken if it is necessary. The standards can be in the form of measures of input—such as the number of sales calls to be made, number of new accounts to be contacted, and level of salesperson's knowledge—or output—such as sales quotas, perhaps by product line. Performance against some of these standards can be measured quite objectively, while performance against others must often rely on the subjective judgment of the field sales manager. Clearly, a good evaluation and control system can be an important management tool providing the field sales manager and the salesperson with an opportunity to identify areas of strength and weakness and to develop programs to correct any deficiencies that are identified.

Field Sales Manager.

Limited empirical research, along with much folklore, suggests that the first-level field sales manager is a major factor in the success of a sales force.[9] Figure 33–3 positions the field sales manager as the critically important implementer of the policies and procedures developed by the senior sales executive. The field sales manager's responsibilities can include the deployment of sales resources, the final selection of salespersons, salesperson training, the setting of salaries and bonuses, the setting of quotas, and the evaluation and motivation of the salespersons. He or she must also be skilled in dealing with problem salespersons, including dismissing them when necessary. In addition, the field sales manager is responsible for tailoring the personal selling program in response to the particular environmental factors that obtain in his or her territories. The role of the field sales manager as an implementer requires that in empirical studies of a sales force, measurement should be based on the value of variables as implemented by the manager, which are not necessarily the same as those suggested by senior sales management.

Implementation or Operational Level

The model's third level, the implementation or operational level, focuses on the individual salesperson as the unit of analysis. As illustrated in Figure 33–4, this level consists of three types of constructs: situational characteristics and exogenous factors; the sales predisposition of the salesperson—motivation, knowledge and skills, and selling strategy; and salesperson-customer interactions and outcomes, including the salesperson's job performance and job satisfaction.

In developing the model at the salesperson level, we are using the term *implementation* in two senses. First, it represents the fact that we are examining the effect of exogenous variables as implemented by the field sales manager in particular and the company in general for that particular salesperson. To choose an obvious example, when examining the impact of span of con-

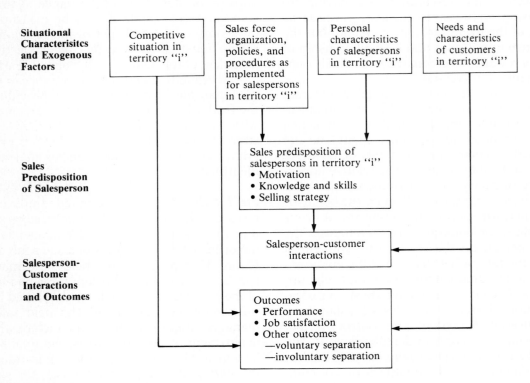

Figure 33–4
The Implementation or Operational Level

trol, the value to use is the one that the particular salesperson is supervised under, not the average for the organization as a whole. Second, the term is used to refer to whether (and how) the assigned selling tasks (the desired selling job) are carried out. In advertising, implementation concerns essentially cease once the advertisement is designed and placed in the media; however, a salesperson may not consistently carry out the assigned tasks and role. Does the salesperson allocate time across accounts, products, and selling activities in a manner consistent with the policies and procedures developed at the tactical level? The actions of the salespersons are influenced by the actual and anticipated reactions of customers. Most prior conceptualizations of the sales response model have been postulated at the individual salesperson level.[10]

Exogenous Factors and Situational Constructs

The four groups of exogenous factors and situational constructs are: sales force organization, policies, and procedures, as implemented for the salesperson; personal, enduring characteristics of the salesperson; competitive situation in the salesperson's territory; and characteristics of the customers in the salesperson's territory. The first group of variables is situational and is comprised of variables under the control of the company, whereas the last three groups are best regarded as exogenous, since the company has only very limited control over them in the short run. Thus, while the four groups are treated as exogenous with regard to analysis at the individual salesperson level, these variables are not necessarily exogenous at previous levels of the model.[11] For example, at the sales management level, the sales executive decides what the span of control will be. Furthermore, in the long run, the company's recruitment and selection

programs will partially determine the personal characteristics of the salespersons, or at least the range of personal characteristics that are present in the sales force. The competitive situation in the territory can be most clearly classified as exogenous, but even here the company's actions with regard to territory design may influence the level of competitive activity encountered in any given territory. Similarly, the company's actions can influence which customers are actually served.

Personal Characteristics. This set of constructs includes all characteristics which are defined as being part of the individual and are not contingent on organization and other factors. We would include such variables as verbal intelligence and age as personal characteristics, but we would not include the salesperson's perceived role ambiguity because it is a consequence of organizational as well as personal factors. We would also exclude measures of the salesperson's motivation, since it can be modified as a result of such things as the firm's compensation plan. We think it is important to identify constructs that are both individual-specific and not contingent on organizational factors. As Walker, Churchill, and Ford point out, one of the major failings in models of salesperson performance is the failure to recognize that some "determinants are *not* independent; there are substantial interaction effects among them."[12] Our approach attempts to identify exogenous and contingent variables a priori and classify them separately.

Personal characteristics include:

- physical factors, such as physical appearance, posture, sex, and age;
- historical factors, such as educational background, previous occupations, and previous sales experience;
- personality factors, such as interpersonal

style, social sensitivity, locus of control, and risk taking;

- mental factors, such as general intelligence, verbal ability, quantitative ability, and cognitive style.

In the past few years there has been a growing realization among personality researchers that situational factors are at least as important as personality traits in understanding why individuals behave the way they do.[13] Thus, relationships found in personal selling contexts may have only limited generalizability. Similarly, findings from other settings must be used with careful attention to the situational contingencies present in a personal selling situation. An individual who exhibits a certain style of risk-taking behavior in his or her personal life may exhibit a different pattern at work.

Organization, Policies, and Procedures. This set of constructs includes those variables which are set for the sales force as a whole at the sales management (or tactical) level, but which are implemented at the level of the individual salesperson. Some of these variables may be set uniformly for the sales force, while others may vary. A company may rigidly adhere to a certain span of control in the field sales organization while allowing wide variations in the market potential of the individual sales territories. Special focus needs to be placed on the implementation of the organizational, policy, and procedures variables for the individual salesperson, particularly, as transmitted by the field sales manager. The salesperson's understanding of the specific selling tasks to be performed is dependent on how well the field sales manager interprets and explains those tasks. This clearly raises some difficult measurement issues with regard to what the assigned tasks are and what the field sales manager communicates to the salesperson.

Among the constructs we would include here are span of control (the number of salespersons that report to the first-level sales manager); territory characteristics, including potential, concentration of potential among accounts, and geographic dispersion of customers; type and level of marketing support provided to the territory, including direct mail effort, marketing support personnel, and seminars and advertising; salesperson training programs; salesperson's assigned tasks; and the compensation program as implemented for the individual salespersons. Although many organizations have undoubtedly made formal or informal assessments of the impact of these factors on performance, only limited published, empirical research exists. The most well-developed literature concerns territory characteristics, where several studies have indicated the relationships between territory potential and sales performance.[14]

Competitive Situation. Depending on the nature of the market the company is in, the competitive variables of concern may vary. These variables can include product and service attributes, the competitive equivalent of any type of marketing support that the company can provide for its own sales force, and finally, the nature and intensity of the competitor's personal selling efforts.

Characteristics of Customer. This is again largely an exogenous set of variables. As will be discussed later, there is evidence in the personal selling literature that indicates that the performance outcomes from the salesperson-customer interaction depend on the characteristics of both members of the dyad.

Sales Predisposition of the Salesperson

The performance of an individual salesperson can be viewed as being a function of three classes of factors: motivation, knowledge and skills, and selling strategy.[15] This classification, while consistent with the one proposed by Walker, Churchill, and Ford in which motivation, aptitude, and role perceptions are used, is more general and can be used to incorporate and categorize more of the research that has been conducted on sales performance and its antecedents.[16]

As Figure 33–4 indicates, the sales predisposition of the salesperson is viewed as being largely a function of the enduring personal characteristics of the salesperson (which are in part a result of the organization's recruiting and selection policies), and the sales force organization, policies, and procedures. In contrast to the enduring personal characteristics, sales predisposition is mediated by the tactical levers under the control of sales management.

Motivation. Motivation in the personal selling context has been defined as "the amount of effort the salesman desires to expend on each of the activities and tasks associated with his job, such as calling on potential new accounts, planning sales presentations and filling out reports."[17] As Terence Mitchell has noted, theoretical research in motivation can be viewed as being focused on three problem areas: individual needs and motives, classification systems of needs and motives, and the motivational process itself.[18] Theories dealing with the first two of these areas are termed *content theories of motivation* since they are concerned with the factors that lead to motivational arousal. The third area involving process theories focuses directly on the mental processes underlying the behavioral choice —in the personal selling area, on the decision to devote effort to certain tasks.

Richard Bagozzi, in his study on sales force performance, approaches the motivational question largely from the first

orientation using the theory of need for achievement.[19] Examples of the second orientation—the use of classification schemes in motivation research—includes Maslow's hierarchy of needs and the controversial dual factor theory of Frederick Herzberg, Bernard Mausner, and Barbara Snyderman, where potential organizational rewards are broken into two groups—the hygienes and the motivators.[20] Basically, Herzberg and his colleagues view the hygienes (monetary rewards and working conditions) as merely maintaining employees in a neutral state of satisfaction, whereas the motivators (advancement and recognition) can be used to generate high job satisfaction. While there appears to have been no formal research in the sales area on this theory, the approach has undoubtedly influenced the design of motivational policies in some sales organizations.

Process theories of motivation, as suggested above, are concerned with the process by which people decide to work hard and to allocate their efforts over the possible activities open to them. Expectancy theory has been the most widely used theoretical approach to motivation in personal selling research.[21] However, expectancy theory has been difficult to test in the personal selling area due to methodological problems. The results obtained to date, which are not particularly strong, have been summarized by Walker, Churchill, and Ford.[22]

Most managers would support the hypothesis that a salesperson's motivation is a function of both enduring personal characteristics and the full range of organizational, policy, and procedures factors. Span of control (an organizational factor), deployment policies, recruiting and selection policies, training, the evaluation and control system, and the incentive system all can clearly affect the motivation of a salesperson. The particular theoretical orientation to motivation adopted by the researcher would probably suggest a somewhat different emphasis on these factors if the motivational level of the salespersons is to be improved. For example, a need-for-achievement orientation might result in attention being paid to recruiting and selection policies and, to a lesser extent, training,[23] whereas other orientations might place greater emphasis on the incentive system. In spite of the obvious importance of motivation in sales performance, almost no empirical research has been conducted on how various organizational practices and sales force policies and procedures affect the motivation of salespersons.

Knowledge and Skills. The performance of a salesperson can be viewed as being a function of the following types of knowledge and skills:

- Product knowledge: this includes not only knowledge of the product line and its features, but knowledge of the benefits associated with each feature, the ability to handle common product-related objections, and a detailed understanding of the product line strengths and weaknesses relative to competitive products or services.
- Customer knowledge: this includes knowledge of the customer's business, how the product or service fits into the customer's operations, and a thorough understanding of the customer's decision-making process.
- Knowledge of company policy and procedures: this can be particularly critical in some industrial selling situations, where the salesperson's role is largely one of marshalling his or her company's resources and specialist talents to solve the customer's problems. It is essential to have a good in-depth knowledge of the company's organization and the location of specialist talent.

- Interpersonal and communication skills: this includes skills in establishing rapport with members of a customer decision-making unit, probing and questioning skills to uncover needs, communication and persuasion techniques, and skills in reading a customer's reactions to ideas and proposals. One persuasion technique that has received considerable attention is "foot-in-the-door": start with a small request (asking a retailer to place a manufacturer's sign in his store window) before going on to the large request (asking the retailer to attend a sales presentation at the manufacturer's office).[24] A considerable amount of empirical research (largely in nonmarketing contexts) has been conducted on foot-in-the-door and other compliance-gaining techniques.[25] However, as Richard Yalch points out in his excellent review, "There has been no published research adequately evaluating what happens when an individual is involved in a series of compliance-gaining strategies."[26] Recent research is also beginning to clarify other situational contingencies under which these techniques are likely to be effective.[27]

The knowledge and skills of the salespersons are largely the result of the recruiting and selection policies of the sales organization and the types of training programs it offers to the salespersons. The span of control in the organization and the level of sales manager-salesperson interaction it encourages undoubtedly also indirectly influence the knowledge and skills of the salespersons.

Selling Strategy. Selling strategy subsumes the role perceptions component that plays a central role in the Walker, Churchill, and Ford model.[28] It involves: allocation of effort across the salesperson's accounts and products; a perception of the role the salesperson is to play; and a strategy for dealing with each individual account. The first and third elements of the selling strategy are expected to change over time as a result of the feedback the salesperson receives from his or her interactions with the individual customers.

Little is known about how salespersons decide to allocate effort (particularly time) across their accounts, yet this appears to be a very important decision and is closely related to the salesperson's performance. Lodish, who developed the CALLPLAN model to help allocate salespersons' time across customers and prospects,[29] has reported that a salesperson using the model had, on average, sales 8 percent higher than a matched colleague who did not have access to the model.[30] Some companies influence the time and effort allocations for their salespersons by establishing rigid call policies—a certain number of calls per day, or a required number of calls per effort period for each type or size of account.

Walker, Churchill, and Ford have developed the role perceptions component most fully in the personal selling area, and we follow their discussion of this component.[31] The role attached to the position of salesperson in any firm represents the set of activities or behaviors to be performed by any person occupying that position. This role is defined largely through the expectations, demands, and pressures communicated to the salesperson by his or her role partners—persons inside and outside the firm who have a vested interest in how the salesperson's job is performed, such as top management, the sales manager, customers, and family members. The salesperson's perceptions of these role partners' expectations and demands strongly influence his or her understanding of the job and the kinds of behavior necessary to perform it well.

It is clear from the above discussion

that the elements of the role perceptions component are partly a function of the sales force organization, policies, and procedures. Training, in particular, can do a great deal to resolve issues of role accuracy and perceived role ambiguity. Recruiting and selection policies can also help seek out persons capable of handling the inevitable role conflict and who are less likely to experience serious perceived role ambiguity. While some research has been conducted on the relationship between aspects of role perceptions and such outcomes as job performance and job satisfaction,[32] only a very limited amount of research has been conducted on the antecedents of aspects of role perceptions. Walker, Churchill, and Ford found a significant negative relationship between salesperson experience and both role conflict and role ambiguity, and between both span of control and the salesperson's influence over supervisory standards and role ambiguity.[33]

The development of a strategy for dealing with the decision-making unit at each individual account is an important area that has received little research attention. Barton Weitz has done perhaps the most interesting and innovative research in this area.[34] He proposes a five-stage model of the sales process: developing an impression of the customer; formulating a strategy; transmitting the selected communication; evaluating the effect of the communication; and making appropriate adjustments in the strategy. While this five-step model clearly involves and requires the various types of knowledge and skills discussed in the earlier section, it requires more than them. It involves taking the information gathered, synthesizing and organizing it, developing alternative selling strategies for given situations, and selecting one, which must then be implemented. In many respects, effective interpersonal and communication skills of the type alluded to earlier are necessary, but not sufficient, skills in developing an effective strategy. In the empirical part of his study, Weitz demonstrated that there was a significant positive relationship between a salesperson's performance and understanding of the customer's choice decision process. Since Weitz only studies the first two stages of the model in a relatively simple selling environment (well-known product, single decision maker in the customer organization), much remains to be done in this area.

A salesperson's ability to develop effective strategies is likely to be largely the result of the salesperson's experience, the knowledge and skills he or she possesses to develop the necessary base of information about the customer, and the training the salesperson has received. A particularly important aspect of the training in more complicated selling situations where experiential learning may be very important is the coaching provided by the field sales manager. The degree to which this interaction can occur will be influenced by the span of control.

The Salesperson and the Customer

The ultimate success of the strategic and tactical decision made with respect to a company's personal selling program depends on the individual interactions of salespersons and customers. The inputs to this interaction process can, to a large extent, be controlled, but the interaction process itself contains a significant set of uncontrollable elements as well. Researchers have attempted to probe aspects of this interaction process to gain a better understanding of what influences the productivity of a given salesperson-customer dyad. Early research by Franklin Evans and M. S. Gadel relates sales performance in a life insurance company to the similarity of the buyer-seller dyad.[35] However, a reanalysis of Evans's data by Noel Capon, Morris Holbrook, and

James Hulbert suggests that given the number of variables studied, a significant correlation would be expected on a chance basis.[36] More recent research attempts to establish what types of similarity, or in more formal terms, bases of power in social exchanges, are the major sources of the relationship between similarity and performance.[37] The results to date have been inconclusive, and this research approach may not be as productive in the long term as research of the type conducted by Weitz.

The interrelationships between the various outcomes at the implementation level are only now beginning to receive attention from marketing scholars. It has been generally assumed that high job satisfaction leads to improved performance, but the relationship between the two constructs is proving to be a surprisingly weak one. Mitchell, in summarizing the industrial psychology literature on this point, reports that the average correlation between job satisfaction and performance is about .15. Bagozzi, in a further analysis of the data in his 1978 paper (he omits the territory potential variable) concludes that performance is an antecedent of satisfaction.[38] Other research in industrial psychology, such as Edwin Locke's, tends to support this finding.[39] As might be expected, this relationship appears to be contingent on individual difference factors and other situational factors. Finally, the relationship between job satisfaction and other outcomes, such as turnover and absenteeism, while an intuitively appealing one which has received support in other occupational groups, has not yet received much empirical support in marketing. Again, any relationship is likely to be a highly contingent one.

Unanswered Questions

The conceptual model proposed in this article is not intended to be a general theory, but a framework sufficiently comprehensive so that the major research streams in personal selling can be interrelated. It also suggests areas which might be productively explored in future resarch. Particularly from the manager's perspective, the model links the research and researchable issues in personal selling with the levels of decision making in the sales force and the types of decisions that must be made at each level. We now turn to some of the unanswered questions that the three-level model suggests are important areas warranting further research.

At the strategic level, the ADVISOR and PIMS data bases are being used to address a critical sales management issue—the budgeting decision. Both data bases are not adequate for the task. The ADVISOR project is focused on advertising issues and only tangentially touches on the personal selling expenditure issue, and the PIMS project has a much broader strategic marketing focus. Both lack the specific sales force data necessary for a more complete examination of the strategic sales issues. In particular, major tactical variables, such as the type of sales organization, the span of control, and the compensation system, need to be investigated in models designed to explain the sales force expenditures/sales ratio, the profitability of a product, and the like. This would begin to give some insight into the effectiveness of different tactical approaches in various product-market environments. A strategic issue that has received no attention in the literature to date is the decision to use manufacturers' representatives versus a direct sales force. The markets and hierarchies approach espoused by Oliver Williamson might suggest some useful hypotheses about when the use of sales representatives would be the most productive approach.[40]

Only limited empirical research has focused on the tactical levers available to sales management, probably because of the difficulties involved in conducting such research. Few of the relevant variables show any variation within a given sales force—compensation systems are usually uniform throughout the sales force.[41] This area does not lend itself well to laboratory experimentation and field experimentation will likely meet a great deal of managerial resistance given the risks involved and the difficulty of developing research designs with strong internal and external validity. Empirical research must usually follow one of two directions: cross-sectional studies involving a number of different sales forces; or longitudinal studies within one or more companies covering a period when a significant change in policies and procedures occurs. Even in the latter case, variables may be confounded since a change in one variable, such as the organization, frequently occurs simultaneously with a change in other variables, such as the compensation system. Despite the difficulties involved, quasi-experimental research may be the best hope for establishing the direction of causality which is so frequently ambiguous in observational studies in the personal selling area.[42] Rene Darmon's investigation of a change in sales compensation system in a company is one of the few examples of longitudinal research on these types of sales force policies.[43]

The operational level has received the most attention from marketing researchers. Much of the research has focused on the "selling knowledge and skills" and "salesperson-customer interactions" constructs included in Figure 33–4. As Capon, Holbrook, and Hulbert point out, a number of studies have implicitly or explicitly used the source-message-receiver model from mass communications to study the effects of the personal characteristics of the salesperson, the needs and characteristics of the customer, and the content of the message on some output measure of interest. As was pointed out earlier, few of these studies have viewed the salesperson and customer as an interacting dyad. Most of these studies do not explicitly recognize situational characteristics and exogenous factors on which the findings may be contingent. Furthermore, researchers have just begun to grapple with the fact that from a sales force perspective many customer decision-making units are multiperson and that many salesperson-customer interactions are part of an ongoing process, not a one-shot meeting. These raise important, but complex, research questions.

Other researchers have approached the study of the operational level differently. These researchers have shown less interest in the results of the individual interactions between salespersons and customers and have focused on long-run, aggregate outcome measures of sales performance and job satisfaction. This research has generally involved a more comprehensive set of the constructs from Figure 33–4 than do models that emphasize the interaction level. It is useful to distinguish two approaches that have been followed in this type of research.

Walker, Churchill, and Ford's work, which exemplifies such research, is an attempt to develop a theory of motivation and performance in the industrial sales force.[44] Much of their empirical research to date has involved the testing of hypotheses from their theory in a number of sales forces. As a result of this systematic program of research, an improved understanding of many of the links of their model is emerging. Because a great deal of their attention is devoted to psychological variables and the relationships between these variables, and because, to this point, their research has focused on dependent variables not closely related to sales performance (usually the variable of most direct managerial interest), the payoff in terms of results of high managerial relevance is likely to occur in the long run. Furthermore, as this research program proceeds and the contingent nature of many of the relationships in the model becomes apparent, their model will probably become more complex in order to incorporate these contingencies. In fact, this may already be occurring, as can be seen by comparing the model as originally conceived by Walker, Churchill, and Ford in 1977 with the 1978 version.[45]

The territory sales response models of Henry Lucas, Charles Weinberg, and Kenneth Clowes, Charles Beswick and David Cravens, Bagozzi, and Adrian Ryans and Charles Weinberg represent a second type of comprehensive model at the operational level.[46] Here, the focus has been on the relationship between an objective measure of sales performance and observable, readily measured factors that are believed to influence sales performance. These models, when set in the context of clear conceptual frameworks, can lead to greater understanding of the personal selling process through identification of important factors and measurement of their relationships. Moreover, such models can be tailored to the needs of, and readily estimated for, the individual sales force. In the four studies cited, the dependent variable is sales, which is the variable generally of most direct interest to sales management. This choice of dependent variable, combined with the operational nature of the independent variables, can have direct managerial impact.[47]

Using the Results

Although substantial gaps in knowledge exist, substantive findings of interest are available at all three levels of the model. However, a manager must be cautious in attempting to apply these findings to a specific setting for several reasons.

First, the research findings may have been developed in selling environments quite different than his or her own environment. As was pointed out above, much of the research on compliance-gaining strategies has been conducted in one-time selling situations. Even findings that seem quite robust, such as the foot-in-the-door strategy (demonstrated in field studies by Jacob Varella and Alice Tybout)[48] may not be effective if used on a continuing basis by a particular salesperson with a particular customer, or if the requested behavior is viewed as being very costly by the customer. As these findings are verified in richer, more externally valid settings (from the point of view of the individual manager), then the manager can have more confidence in applying the results.

Most importantly, as the three-stage model highlights, many relationships are likely to be contingent ones. The manager must try to determine if variables that were not considered in a particular study might not mediate the results. A general conceptual model such as the one proposed here provides the manager with a structure for reviewing these contingencies. If a manager finds it necessary to verify the relationships and findings for his or her own sales force, then the three-stage model will help to indicate which variables need to be studied. For example, the three-stage model can be used in conjunction with the emerging literature in the territory sales response area to provide a framework for developing such a function and to offer some guidelines on how particular variables might be put into operation.

Studies which rely heavily on attitudinal and other psychological variables will be difficult to verify in individual company settings. With increasing attention to invasion-of-privacy issues among the management of many companies, there may be serious concern about gathering much of this information.[49] Furthermore, for some variables, employees might be reluctant to give honest responses. Respondents who are asked for the valence of various rewards might attempt to "game" the researcher rather than provide honest responses. One potential tactical area where many of the findings from this stream of research might be valuable is the selection area, but it is in this area where it is difficult and expensive to demonstrate that psychological tests or other types of information do not unfairly discriminate against members of minority groups.[50]

One value of the three-stage model proposed here is that it provides a way for the manager to structure the different aspects of sales force decision making. The model emphasizes that the sales manager has a mix of tactical levers to implement a desired strategic sales force role, and that these levers should not be treated in isolation.

Conclusions

The three-stage sales force model developed in this article emphasizes the relationship between sales force management decision making and the empirical research being conducted in the personal selling area should not be underestimated. Moreover, the situational contingencies upon which research findings depend need to be specified clearly. Current research has provided a base of knowledge for researchers who wish to work in the field, but no area of personal selling is so well understood that further research is foreclosed. In conclusion, we believe that the conceptual model provided in this article provides a useful way to summarize present knowledge, to approach personal selling decisions, and to identify areas for further study.

NOTES

1. Sales and Marketing Management, "Survey of Selling Costs" (26 February 1979), p. 57.
2. Orville C. Walker, Jr., Gilbert A. Churchill,

Jr., and Neil M. Ford, "Motivation and Performance in Industrial Selling: Present Knowledge and Needed Research," *Journal of Marketing Research*, Vol. 14 (May 1977), pp. 156–168.

3. David B. Montgomery and Glen L. Urban, *Management Science in Marketing* (Englewood Cliffs, New Jersey: Prentice-Hall, Inc., 1969); Kenneth R. Davis and Frederick E. Webster, Jr., *Sales Force Management* (New York: Ronald Press Company, 1968).

4. Gary L. Lilien, "ADVISOR 2: Modeling the Marketing Mix Decision for Industrial Products," *Management Science*, Vol. 25 (February 1979), pp. 191–204.

5. Robert D. Buzzell and Paul W. Farris, "Industrial Marketing Costs: An Analysis of Variations in Manufacturers' Marketing Expenditures," Report Number 76-118 (Cambridge, Massachusetts: Marketing Science Institute, 1976).

6. Thomas A. Glaze and Charles B. Weinberg, "A Sales Territory Alignment Program and Account Planning System," in Richard Bagozzi (ed.), *Sales Management: New Developments from Behavioral and Decision Model Research* (Cambridge, Massachusetts: Marketing Science Institute, 1979); Sidney W. Hess and Stuart A. Samuels, "Experiences with a Sales Districting Model: Criteria and Implementation," *Management Science*, Part II, Vol. 18 (December 1971), pp. 41–54; Leonard Lodish, " 'Vaguely Right' Approach to Sales Force Allocation," *Harvard Business Review*, Vol. 52 (January–February 1974), pp. 119–124; Roy J. Shanker, Ronald E. Turner, and Andris A. Zoltners, "Sales Territory Design: An Integrated Approach," *Management Science*, Vol. 22 (November 1975), pp. 309–320.

7. Andris A. Zoltners and Kathy S. Gardner, "A Review of Salesforce Decision Models," unpublished working paper (Evanston, Illinois: Northwestern University, 1980).

8. Terence R. Mitchell, *People in Organizations: Understanding Their Behavior* (New York: McGraw-Hill, 1978).

9. Robert T. Davis, "Sales Management in the Field," *Harvard Business Review*, Vol. 36 (January–February 1958), pp. 91–98; idem, "A Sales Manager in Action," in H. W. Boyd, Jr., and R. T. Davis (eds), *Readings in Sales Management* (Homewood, Illinois: Richard D. Irwin, 1970); J. S. Livingston, "Pygmalion in Management," *Harvard Business Review*, Vol. 47 (July–August 1969), pp. 81–89.

10. Richard P. Bagozzi, "Towards a General Theory for the Explanation of the Performance of Salespeople," unpublished doctoral dissertation (Northwestern University, 1976); Adrian B. Ryans and Charles B. Weinberg, "Sales Territory Response," *Journal of Marketing Research*, Vol. 16 (November 1979), pp. 453–465; Walker, Churchill, and Ford, op. cit.

11. Researchers attempting to estimate the effect of exogenous and situational factors on outcomes such as performance or job satisfaction must be concerned about whether the implemented sales force organization, policies, and procedures have suppressed the effects of interest. If the sales force's management has a policy of assigning territories of equal potential, then it would make little sense to include this variable in a research study designed to relate territory sales performance to territory characteristics. However, it would be incorrect to assume that territory potential has no effect on sales performance.

12. Orville C. Walker, Jr., Gilbert A. Churchill, Jr., and Neil M. Ford, "Where Do We Go From Here?—Selected Conceptual and Empirical Issues Concerning the Motivation and Performance of the Industrial Sales Force," paper presented at the American Institute for Decision Sciences, St. Louis (1978), p. 4.

13. Mitchell, op. cit.

14. Adrian B. Ryans and Charles B. Weinberg, "Managerial Implications of Models of Territory Sales Response," in Neil Beckwith et al. (eds.), *1979 Educators' Conference Proceedings* (Chicago, Illinois: American Marketing Association, 1979), pp. 426–430; Ryans and Weinberg, op. cit.

15. This is similar to the conceptualization used by J. Richard Hackman and Charles G.

Morris in their discussion of the performance of task groups. See J. Richard Hackman and Charles G. Morris, "Group Tasks, Group Interaction Process, and Group Performance Effectiveness," in L. Berkowitz (ed.), *Advances in Experimental Social Psychology*, Vol. 7 (New York: Academic Press, 1975).

16. Walker, Churchill, and Ford, "Motivation and Performance."

17. Ibid., p. 162.

18. Mitchell, op. cit.

19. Bagozzi, op. cit.

20. Frederick Herzberg, Bernard Mausner, and Barbara B. Snyderman, *The Motivation to Work* (New York: John Wiley and Sons, 1975).

21. Walker, Churchill, and Ford, "Motivation and Performance."

22. Walker, Churchill, and Ford, "Where Do We Go?"

23. David McClelland, the originator of the need-for-achievement theory, has reported some success in increasing the level of need for achievement in adults through training. See David C. McClelland, *The Achieving Society* (Princeton, New Jersey: Van Nostrand, 1961).

24. Alice M. Tybout, "The Relative Effectiveness of Three Behavioral Influence Strategies as Supplements to Persuasion in a Marketing Context," *Journal of Marketing Research*, Vol. 15 (May 1978), pp. 229–242; Jacob A. Varella, *Psychological Solutions to Social Problems* (New York: Academic Press, 1971).

25. William DeJong, "An Examination of Self-Perception Mediation of the Foot-in-the-Door Effect," *Journal of Personality and Social Psychology*, Vol. 37 (December 1979), pp. 2221–2239; Richard F. Yalch, "Closing Sales: Compliance-Gaining Strategies for Personal Selling," in Bagozzi (ed.), op. cit. (Cambridge, Massachusetts: Marketing Science Institute, 1979).

26. Yalch, op. cit., p. 197.

27. Robert D. Foss and Carolyn B. Dempsey, "Blood Donation and the Foot-in-the-Door Technique: A Limiting Case," *Journal of*

Personality and Social Psychology, Vol. 37 (1979), pp. 580–590; Yalch, op. cit.

28. Walker, Churchill, and Ford, "Motivation and Performance."

29. Leonard Lodish, "CALLPLAN: An Interactive Salesman's Call Planning System," *Management Science*, Part II, Vol. 18 (December 1971), pp. 25–40.

30. William K. Fudge and Leonard M. Lodish, "Evaluation of the Effectiveness of a Model Based Salesman's Call Planning System by Field Experimentation," *Interfaces*, Part II, Vol. 8 (November 1977), pp. 97–106.

31. Walker, Churchill, and Ford, "Motivation and Performance," and "Where Do We Go?"

32. Gilbert A. Churchill, Jr., Neil M. Ford, and Orville C. Walker, Jr., "Organizational Climate and Job Satisfaction in the Salesforce," *Journal of Marketing Research*, Vol. 13 (November 1976), pp. 323–332; and Bagozzi, op. cit.

33. Orville C. Walker, Jr., Gilbert A. Churchill, and Neil M. Ford, "Organizational Determinants of the Industrial Salesman's Role Conflict and Ambiguity," *Journal of Marketing*, Vol. 39 (January 1975), pp. 32–39.

34. Barton A. Weitz, "Relationship Between Salesperson Performance and Understanding of Customer Decision-Making," *Journal of Marketing Research*, Vol. 15 (November 1978), pp. 501–516.

35. Franklin Evans, "Selling as a Dyadic Relationship—A New Approach," *American Behavioral Scientist*, Vol. 6 (May 1963), pp. 76–79; M.S. Gadel, "Concentration by Salesmen on Congenial Prospects," *Journal of Marketing*, Vol. 28 (January 1964), pp. 64–66.

36. Noel Capon, Morris B. Holbrook, and James M. Hubert, "Selling Processes and Buying Behavior: Theoretical Implications of Recent Research," in Arch G. Woodside, Jagdish N. Sheth, and Peter D. Bennett (eds.), *Consumer and Industrial Buying Behavior* (New York: Elsevier North-Holland, 1977), pp. 323–332.

37. Timothy C. Brock, "Communicator-Recipient Similarity and Decision Change," *Journal of Personality and Social Psychology*, Vol.

1 (June 1965), pp. 650–654; Paul Busch and David T. Wilson, "An Experimental Analysis of a Salesman's Expert and Referent Bases of Social Power in the Buyer-Seller Dyad," *Journal of Marketing Research*, Vol. 13 (February 1976), pp. 3–11.

38. Richard P. Bagozzi, "Salesperson Performance and Satisfaction as a Function of Individual Difference, Interpersonal, and Situational Factors," *Journal of Marketing Research*, Vol. 15 (November 1978), pp. 517–531; idem, "Performance and Satisfaction in an Industrial Sales Force: An Examination of Their Antecedents and Simultaneity," *Journal of Marketing*, Vol. 44 (Spring 1980), pp. 65–77. The omission of territory potential from the Bagozzi 1980 model is surprising given the highly significant correlation between it and both performance and job satisfaction in his earlier paper. The framework proposed here emphasizes the need to include relevant precursors.

39. Edwin A. Locke, "The Nature and Causes of Job Satisfaction," in M. D. Dunnette (ed.), *Handbook of Industrial and Organizational Psychology* (Chicago, Illinois: Rand McNally, 1976), pp. 1297–1349.

40. Oliver E. Williamson, *Markets and Hierarchies: Analysis and Antitrust Implications* (New York: The Free Press, 1975).

41. However, considerable theoretical attention has been devoted to the design of optimal compensation systems under assumptions about the salesperson's objective function and constraints under which the salesperson operates. See John U. Farley, "Optimal Plan for Salesmen's Compensation," *Journal of Marketing Resarch*, Vol. 1 (May 1964), pp. 39–43; Venkataraman Srinivasan, "The Non-optimality of Equal Commission Rates in Multi-Product Sales Force Compensation Schemes," Working Paper No. 529 (Stanford, California: Graduate School of Business, 1979); and Charles B. Weinberg, "Jointly Optimal Sales Commissions for Non-Income Maximizing Sales Force," *Management Science*, Vol. 24 (August 1978), pp. 1252–1258.

42. Territory sales response models could be used in some situations to increase the statistical precision of the experiment.

43. Rene Y. Darmon, "Salesmen's Response to Financial Incentives: An Empirical Study," *Journal of Marketing Research*, Vol. 11 (November 1974), pp. 418–426.

44. Walker, Churchill, and Ford, "Motivation and Performance," and "Where Do We Go?"

45. Ibid.

46. Bagozzi's research can be viewed as straddling both types of models, as it, for example, also examines some motivational components. See Bagozzi, "Salesperson Performance"; Charles A. Beswick and David W. Cravens, "A Multistage Decision Model for Sales Force Management," *Journal of Marketing Research*, Vol. 14 (May 1977); Henry C. Lucas, Jr., Charles B. Weinberg, and Kenneth Clowes, "Sales Response as a Function of Territorial Potential and Sales Representative Workload," *Journal of Marketing Research*, Vol. 12 (August 1975), pp. 298–305; and Ryans and Weinberg, "Sales Territory."

47. Ryans and Weinberg, "Managerial Implications."

48. Varella, op. cit.; Tybout, op. cit.

49. Frank T. Cary, "IBM's Guidelines to Employee Privacy," *Harvard Business Review*, Vol. 54 (September–October, 1976), pp. 82–90.

50. William C. Byham and Morton E. Spitzer, "Personal Testing: The Law and Its Implications," *Personnel*, Vol. 48 (September–October 1971), pp. 8–19.

PART FIVE

Implementing and Extending Marketing

A new section in this edition highlights the importance of two emerging trends in the discipline. First, marketing implementation is receiving increased attention. Strategies and programs will not be successful unless they are competently implemented. Walker and Ruekert emphasize this point in a comprehensive review article which offers a nice framework for implementation. Kotler, Gregor and Rogers pioneered the concept of the marketing audit, a fundamental tool in marketing implementation.

The second trend is the extension of the marketing discipline beyond geographic and subject matter boundaries. There is no question that marketing is now a global endeavor; it is no longer sufficient for companies to have a "international division." Levitt provides an overview of the globalization of markets. Douglas and Dubois emphasize the importance of the cultural environment in implementing the marketing strategies. Finally, the broadening of marketing which Kotler and Levy promised in one of the early articles in this book is becoming a reality. But it is an extension of the discipline not without problems and challenges, as discussed by Bloom and Novelli.

Marketing's Role in the Implementation of Business Strategies: A Critical Review and Conceptual Framework

Orville C. Walker, Jr. & Robert W. Ruekert

Consultants used to counter criticism of their concepts with what might be termed "the implementation problem." The strategy was perfectly good, they would say, the client just couldn't implement it. . . . For some folks, including some consultants, a small, disturbing voice began to whisper, "Doesn't the fact that hardly anyone can carry it out say something about the value of the strategy?" (Kiechel 1982, pp. 37–8)

During the decade of the 1970s many marketing managers and consultants fervently embraced the processes and tools of strategic planning. Though some evidence suggests many firms have benefited from formal strategic planning (Armstrong 1982), doubts have been expressed about the effectiveness of the strategies flowing from the strategic planning process (Kiechel 1981, 1982). Part

"Marketing's Role in the Implementation of Business Strategies: A Critical Review and Conceptual Framework," Orville C. Walker and Robert W. Ruekert, Vol. 51 (July 1987), pp. 15–33. Reprinted from the *Journal of Marketing*, published by the American Marketing Association.

of the dissatisfaction may stem from weaknesses in some of the popular planning tools and processes. However, recognition is growing both within the academic literature and in the business press that *implementation* of strategy is a key factor in determining business and marketing performance (Bonoma 1984, 1985a).

We integrate into one conceptual framework various theoretical views, normative statements, and pieces of empirical evidence about contingent relationships between business-level strategies and organizational structures and processes, particularly those structures and processes involved in the conduct of marketing activities. The essential question addressed is: Given a specific type of strategy, what marketing structures, policies, procedures, and programs are likely to distinguish high performing business units from those that are relatively less effective, efficient, or adaptable? An improved understanding of the organizational contingencies that influence the effective implementation of different business strategies should be useful in addressing several important marketing management questions, including the identification of the most appropriate kinds of marketing programs, the most promising sources of marketing synergy, and the most effective mechanisms for coordinating marketing activities with other functional departments within businesses pursuing different types of strategy.

We first discuss alternative definitions and typologies of business strategy and propose a hybrid marketing-oriented typology of business-level strategy. Then we develop a conceptual framework relating specific organizational structures, policies, and programs to the successful implementation of different business-level strategies. Finally, we discuss the rationale for several research propositions.

TYPOLOGIES OF BUSINESS-LEVEL STRATEGY

One reason for the lack of a detailed framework linking internal structures and processes to the successful implementation of different business strategies is that there is no generally accepted typology of business-level strategy to provide the foundation for such a framework. Wrigley (1970) and Rumelt (1974) led the way more than a decade ago in developing useful, replicable operationalizations of corporate-level strategies, but similar progress has been made only recently at the business-unit level.

Whereas corporate strategy typically is concerned with the question of what business(es) a firm should be involved in and how its priorities and resources should be allocated across those businesses, business-level strategies focus on *how a business unit or division of a company chooses to compete*

in an industry.[1] Many attempts have been made to define and categorize such strategies over the years, but most of the resulting taxonomies have been conceptual rather than empirically based and they differ greatly in generalizability (see Hambrick 1980 for a thorough review).

Empirical Typologies

Recently there have been several notable attempts to derive more generalizable typologies of business-level strategy through empirical observation. Two important typologies that have emerged from such efforts are those of Porter (1980, 1985) and Miles and Snow (1978).

Porter (1980) distinguishes three types of strategy based on how a business attempts to gain and maintain a competitive advantage: (1) "overall cost leadership," (2) "differentiation" based on building customer perceptions of superior product quality, design, brand name, or service, and (3) a "focus" strategy whereby the business concentrates on a narrowly defined market niche and uses either a cost leadership or differentiation approach. Porter's typology is drawn from individual case observations of a variety of businesses. He concentrates on discussing the appropriate fit between the three strategies and aspects of a business environment—particularly the forces driving industry competition. However, he has relatively little to say about the kinds of organizational structures, processes, or programs necessary to implement each strategy effectively. Also, Porter's three categories are defined largely in terms of competitive actions actually undertaken by a business, rather than the kinds of actions management *intended* to be taken. This feature can be a major limitation if one wants to explain factors related to the successful implementation of strategies, because differences between "intended" strategies and "realized" strategies are sometimes due to ineffective implementation of the intended strategy.

Miles and Snow's (1978) strategic typology overcomes at least some of the preceding criticisms. The primary variable underlying their schema is a business' intended rate of product-market change (e.g., new product development, share growth, etc.). They classify business units into four strategic types: (1) prospectors, (2) analyzers, (3) defenders, and (4) reactors.[2] Their typology provides a useful framework for studying the successful implementation of different strategies because it classifies businesses according to management's strategic *intentions* and it suggests several propositions about how various aspects of structure, processes, and management style should fit together under each type of strategy. Miles and Snow emphasize a strategic dimension—the desired rate of product-market development—that is particularly meaningful in determining the appropriate role of marketing within different business strategies.

However, Miles and Snow's focus on businesses' intended growth rates causes some of their categories to be rather broadly defined and heterogeneous in terms of other aspects of strategy. For example, their defender category combines businesses that attempt to maintain their positions in mature markets by offering low cost with those that compete by providing high product quality or superior service. Successful implementation of such different competitive strategies seems likely to require very different processes, programs, and personnel.

A Hybrid Typology of Business Strategy

Both the Porter and Miles-Snow typologies have received popular acceptance and at least some empirical support, but both have shortcomings. To establish a more comprehensive foundation for our discussion of the implementation of different strategies, we combine the two frameworks to form a hybrid typology.

As shown in Figure 34–1, the hybrid

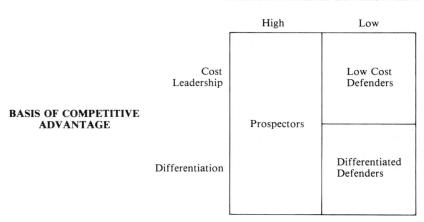

Figure 34–1
A Hybrid Typology of Business Unit Strategy

typology defines business strategies in terms of two major dimensions: (1) the unit's desired rate of new product-market development (consistent with the prospector, analyzer, and defender categories of Miles and Snow) and (2) the unit's intended method of competing in its core business or established product markets (either through maintaining a low cost position or by differentiating itself by offering higher quality or better service, as suggested by Porter). This framework divides business unit strategy in terms of the polar opposites suggested by both Porter and Miles and Snow. As a consequence, some of the intermediate and outlier strategic types included in the other typologies are ignored in both our framework and our subsequent discussion. We believe that this focus on polar types is justified because of space limitations and the fact that inclusion of additional strategic categories would add little to our understanding of the organizational contingencies related to the successful implementation of different strategies. For example, the reactor strategy in Miles and Snow's typology is not represented here because reactors tend not to have well-defined or consistent approaches to *either* new product-market development *or* ways of competing in established markets. Similarly, though implementation of analyzer strategies presents some unique problems, they are essentially an intermediate type between the prospector strategy at one extreme and the defender strategies at the other.

Each of our three strategic categories could be subdivided according to whether a business applies the strategy across a broadly defined market domain or set of market segments or chooses to focus on a narrowly defined segment to avoid direct confrontation with major competitors (i.e., the focus strategy of Porter). This distinction is useful in determining whether a business'

strategy fits its capabilities and its external competitive environment, but it is somewhat less germane to the questions we explore. The kinds of organizational structure, processes, and programs most appropriate for successfully implementing each of the strategies described in Figure 34–1 are not likely to vary much whether the strategy is applied within a broad or narrow market domain.

Finally, prospectors are grouped into a single category in our framework because the desire for rapid new product or market development is the overriding aspect of their strategy. A prospector has relatively little need to consider how it will compete in the new product markets it develops because it often faces little or no competition until those markets become established. Consequently, our hybrid typology represents three types of business strategy: (1) prospectors, (2) differentiated defenders, and (3) low cost defenders.

Strategic Fit and the External Environment

Though the purpose of our article is to examine the fit between generic competitive strategies and the internal structures, programs, and procedures used to implement those strategies effectively, a second and related issue is the fit between business-level strategy and the external environment in which it is used. Among the many kinds of empirical studies pertaining to the proper match between a business and its environment are (1) studies of strategic groups that stress the need to formulate differential strategies according to the conditions imposed by the strategic group to which a business belongs as well as the conditions of its industry (Hatten and Schendel 1976; Schendel and Patton 1978), (2) research on the fit between different strategies and broad macroenvironmental variables such as product life cycle stage of the business (Anderson and Zeithaml 1984) or environmental uncertainty (for an extensive review, see Jauch and Kraft 1986), and (3) studies based on business or product portfolio models suggesting that strategies should be aligned with the market growth rates and the relative market share of the business (Hambrick 1983; Hambrick, MacMillan, and Day 1982). Underlying most of this research is the rather deterministic assumption that the organization must react to external conditions by aligning both its strategy and its structure.

Recently some strategic management theorists have begun to challenge this assumption and have taken a more proactive approach to achieving an environment-strategy fit (Bourgeois 1984). Instead of viewing the external environment as uncontrollable, they argue that a business can "enact" environments to fit a desired strategy (Weick 1979), either through choosing the markets in which to compete and those to avoid or by taking actions to alter the structure of the environment, such as erecting new barriers to entry in the industry (Yip 1982).

Other theorists argue that the generic strategy adopted by a business unit is impossible to adjust radically in the short run. Quinn (1981), for example, argues that strategy development occurs in small, incremental steps where actions are observed to precede goals, solutions are invented before problems are identified, and formal strategies and plans are devised after the real "strategies and plans" have been accomplished. Miller and Freisen (1984), in contrast, suggest that the organization can adapt effectively to changes in the external environment only through radical, "quantum" shifts.

Thus, in the current literature, the fit between external environments and internal strategies and structures is argued to be a reactive, deterministic relationship on one extreme and a proactive, enactment position on the other. Interestingly, however, both Porter and Miles and Snow suggest that the selection and implementation of generic business unit strategies are not necessarily contingent on the external environment. That is, across different environmental contexts, one can find business units effectively pursuing each of the strategies described by those authors.

Though the question of external environmental fit with business-level strategy is important, very little empirical evidence is available on which environmental variables are key and how business unit strategies and structures must coalign for successful implementation. As Galbraith and Nathanson (1978, p. 266) lament, "although the concept of fit is a useful one, it lacks the precise definition needed to test and recognize whether an organization has it or not." Thus, though we recognize that the fit between strategy and environmental variables may be significant in determining the ultimate success of that strategy, we limit our discussion to the internal fit between a strategy and the structure, policies, and procedures that are best suited for implementing that strategy. Our rationale is that *regardless* of how well a strategy fits the external environment, it will be implemented more effectively when there is an appropriate fit between the strategy and the internal characteristics of the business (Bonoma 1984).

A CONCEPTUAL FRAMEWORK FOR EXAMINING THE IMPLEMENTATION OF BUSINESS STRATEGIES

Authors have attempted to relate—either theoretically or empirically—a great variety of organizational variables to the successful implementation of one or more strategies. One source of confusion in the literature, however, is that the contingent variables have been drawn from a jumble of different organizational levels: some reflect the structure of the overall corporation, others represent the structure, processes, or programs within separate functional or work units (such as marketing or R&D), and still others involve the characteristics of individual employees and their roles within the business. Ignored in this mixture of variables is the fact that units at different levels of a corporation constitute distinct organizational subsystems, each with different—though interdependent—subgoals, unique tasks and functions to be performed, different structures and processes for organizing their activities, and different evaluation and reward systems (Van de Ven and Morgan 1980). Consequently, we consider the impact on strategy implementation of three separate sets of organizational contingency variables representing three different levels of analysis.[3]

1. *Corporate–business unit relationships.* These variables are related to the business unit's role within the overall organization and to the resources and flexibility it has in pursuing its individual strategy. These variables include, for example, the corporate structure, the allocation of resources across business units, the amount of decentralization and the autonomy of the business unit's managers, the amounts and types of synergy across businesses, and the criteria and systems the corporation uses to evaluate, control, and reward the business unit's performance.

2. *Interfunctional structure and processes.* These variables are related to the division and coordination of activities among functional departments and work groups within the business unit. These variables include the allocation of financial and personnel resources across departments, competencies in relation to competitors, relative influence on decisions made within the business unit, coordination structures and conflict resolution mechanisms, and the systems used to control and reward the performance of the various departments.

3. *Marketing policies and processes.* Though there should be consistency between all functional departments' policies and programs and the business unit's strategic objectives, we primarily examine marketing's role in strategy implementation. Therefore this category consists of variables related to the structure, budgets, and competitive strengths and weaknesses of marketing activities within the business unit.

Performance Dimensions

In the following sections we review conceptual arguments and some limited empirical evidence about the influence of the three categories of organizational variables on the likely performance of businesses pursuing either prospector, differentiated defender, or low cost defender strategy. The question is: What criteria should be used to define "good" performance under each of the three strategies?

A business unit's performance can be measured and judged on a variety of dimensions, the relevance and importance of which vary (1) across "stakeholder" groups (e.g., investors vs. employees vs. customers) and (2) with whether one takes a long-term or short-term view of the business' outcomes. We limit our discussion to three performance dimensions of primary importance to top corporate and business unit managers.

1. *Effectiveness* is the success of a business' products and programs in relation to

those of its competitors in the market. Effectiveness commonly is measured by such items as sales growth in comparison with that of competitors or *changes in market share.*

2. *Efficiency* is the outcome of a business' programs in relation to the resources employed in implementing them. Common measures of efficiency are profitability as a percentage of sales and *return on investment* (ROI).

3. *Adaptability* is the business' success in responding over time to changing conditions and opportunities in the environment. Adaptability can be measured in a variety of ways, but the most common measures are the number of successful new product introductions in relation to those of competitors or *the percentage of sales accounted for by products introduced within some recent time period (often operationally defined as the past five years).*

The problem with attempting to compare performance across business units on even this limited number of dimensions is that they involve substantial tradeoffs; good performance on one dimension often means sacrificing performance on another (Donaldson 1984). No single strategy can be expected to perform well on all three dimen-

sions no matter how well it is implemented. Consequently, the three types of strategy we consider are expected on average to perform differently on the three performance dimensions, as shown in Table 34–1. Prospector businesses should outperform both types of defenders in new product development and attaining market share growth, whereas both defender strategies should lead to better returns on investment.[4] Differentiated defenders are likely to produce higher returns than low cost defenders if the greater expenses involved in maintaining their differentiated positions can be more than offset by the higher margins gained by avoiding the kind of intense price competition low cost competitors often face.

Because different strategies are expected to perform well on different dimensions, the effectiveness with which a particular strategy is implemented should strongly affect performance on dimensions on which the strategy is expected to do well, but may have little effect on other aspects of performance. A well-implemented prospector strategy, for example, should substantially outperform a poorly implemented one in generating successful new products and increases in market share, but there may be little difference between the two strategies' returns on investment. Consequently, in the following discussion of the impacts of orga-

Table 34-1
Relative Performance of Prospectors Versus Defenders

Type of Strategy	Performance Dimensions		
	Adaptability (new product success)	Effectiveness (increase in market share)	Efficiency (ROI)
Prospectors	++	+	−
Low cost defenders	−−	−	+
Differentiated defenders	−	−	++

nizational variables on the implementation of different types of strategy, we examine the likely effects of each variable on those performance dimensions most relevant under each type of strategy—new product success and market share growth under prospector strategies and return on investment under the two types of defender strategies.

A Caveat

Before suggesting how the implementation of marketing activities might be related systematically to business-level strategies, we must recognize a basic limitation inherent in any conceptual model of organizational performance. Historically, in much of the strategic management literature, a strategy-structure-performance model has been used to explain organizational functioning. One could argue that this tradition dates back to classical economic approaches to the study of industrial organization.

Though such a theoretical model may be useful for organizing and integrating the diverse sets of factors operating on organizations, empirical tests often fail to uncover such linear and predictable relationships. Our concern is how the implementation of a given strategy is related to the performance of the business unit. We do not assume strict causal direction in our propositions; that is, we do not subscribe to the strict strategy-structure-performance model. It is entirely possible that internal structures, policies, procedures, and personnel may constrain the type of strategy an organization can pursue. Further, performance outcomes in one time period may influence the manner in which strategies are implemented in future periods, thereby reversing the logical order of the traditional approach.

Our position is that the traditional strategy-structure-performance paradigm is an overly simplistic and at times misleading view of organizational functioning. We believe this position is shared by both Porter and Miles and Snow, on whose work the hybrid typology is based. Those authors argue that business unit strategy forms a gestalt of purpose, practice, and performance, which are inextricably linked. Thus, though the direction of causation may not be linear, they agree that there are common, observable relationships among strategy, internal structure, and process and performance. It is this set of relationships we attempt to describe in the following sections.

CORPORATE–BUSINESS UNIT RELATIONSHIPS AND THE IMPLEMENTATION OF BUSINESS STRATEGIES

When a business is but one unit of a larger organization, its managers' ability to implement different strategies successfully is influenced by the administrative relationships between the unit and headquarters. The theoretical and empirical work on these administrative ties suggests that three aspects of the corporate–business unit relationship are especially likely to affect a unit's success in implementing a particular strategy: (1) the degree to which the unit's managers have the *autonomy* to make decisions independently of other parts of the company, especially the corporate head office, (2) the degree to which the unit *shares functional programs and facilities* with other units in a search for corporate synergies, and (3) the manner in which corporate officers *evaluate and reward* the performance of the business unit's managers.

Business Unit Autonomy

Decision-making autonomy enables the business unit to be flexible and adaptable. It frees managers from the restrictions of standard rules and procedures imposed from above, allows decisions to be made with few consultations and participants, and disperses power. Hence, the business unit can produce quick and innovative responses to unique opportunities or threats in its environment (cf. Lawrence and Lorsch 1967; Mintzberg 1979; Thompson 1969). Such autonomous responses are likely to fit the characteristics of the business unit's environment because the unit's managers are closer than corporate managers to their customers and competitors. As the successful implementation of a prospector strategy requires timely and innovative responses to changing environmental conditions, we expect the relationship between business unit autonomy and the performance of prospector business units to be positive.

P$_{1a}$: Prospector business units should perform better on the critical dimensions of new product success and increased sales volume and market share when decision making within the corporation is decentralized and the unit's managers hold substantial autonomy.

In contrast, the search for operating efficiencies necessitates close attention to operational details, including the relentless pursuit of cost economies and productivity improvements through standardization of components and processes, routinization of procedures, and the integration of functional activities across units. Such efficiencies are more likely to be attained when decision making and control are relatively centralized at the highest managerial levels. Thus, for low cost defender business units where operating efficiency is a major key to success, we expect the following relationship.

P$_{1b}$: Low cost defender business units should perform better on the critical dimension of ROI when

unit managers have relatively little decision-making autonomy.

The relationship between autonomy and the ROI performance of differentiated defenders is more difficult to predict. Because such businesses are defending current positions in established—and perhaps stable and mature—markets and their primary objective is ROI rather than volume growth, one could argue that the increased efficiency and tighter control associated with relatively low autonomy should lead to better performance. However, such units can maintain their profitability only if they continue to differentiate themselves from competitors by offering superior products, service, or other advantages. As customers' tastes change and new competitive threats emerge, the greater flexibility and market focus that accrue with increased autonomy may enable these businesses to maintain their differentiated positions—and higher levels of ROI—more successfully over time. These arguments suggest the following relationship between autonomy and performance for units attempting to defend a differentiated market position.

P$_{1c}$: Differentiated defender business units should perform better on the critical dimensions of market share maintenance and ROI when unit managers have moderate levels of decision-making autonomy.

Evidence. A recent review of studies of the relationship between decentralization and innovativeness suggests that the evidence is mixed (Miller and Friesen 1984, p. 158). Some studies show that decentralized organizations are more innovative, but a nearly equal number of studies indicate that centralized organizations are more innovative, perhaps because a powerful, autocratic leader can overcome resistance to change and make bold innovations (Thompson 1969).

A possible explanation for the inconsistent findings is simply that the studies examined decentralization across all levels of the organization rather than the degree of autonomy of individual business units. Also, their measures of "innovation" include major reorientations of strategy and organizational structure as well as the more specific kinds of new product and market development that are of greatest interest in assessing the performance of prospector business units. Consequently, those studies do not provide a "fair" test of the specific propositions.

In a recent study, however, Hamermesh and White (1984) directly examined differences in decision-making autonomy across 69 different business units and related them to variations in the units' rates of sales growth and ROI. For the total sample, businesses with relatively high autonomy had significantly greater rates of sales growth than less autonomous units. In addition, when competing in dynamic environments, autonomous units had average sales growth rates more than double those of more tightly controlled businesses. These findings seem consistent with the proposition that autonomy is related positively to the sales and market share performance of prospector business units.

Hamermesh and White also found that businesses with low autonomy had significantly higher average ROI percentages than more autonomous units. Moreover, among businesses pursuing low cost strategies, those with low autonomy had ROI percentages more than twice as high as those of units with greater autonomy. These findings appear to support the proposition that greater autonomy is related negatively to the ROI performance of low cost defenders.

Finally, Hamermesh and White found that business units pursuing differentiation strategies had slightly higher ROIs when they had higher levels of autonomy. However, as these authors' "differentiation" classification may have included some businesses pursuing what we would call a prospector strategy, and as the differences in ROI across units with high and low autonomy were not great, the relationship between autonomy and the performance of differentiated defenders is still open to question.

Shared Programs and Synergy across SBUs

Companies face a tradeoff when designing strategic business units (SBUs). An SBU should be large enough to afford and maintain critical resources and to operate on an efficient scale, but not so large that its market scope is too broad or that "it is inflexible and does not respond quickly to customer needs, to the tactics of competition, and to its unique market opportunities" (Corey and Star 1971, p. 9). Some firms attempt to avoid this tradeoff between adaptability and efficiency by designing relatively small, narrowly focused business units, but having two or more units share functional programs or facilities such as common manufacturing plants, R&D programs, or a single salesforce. These firms anticipate that the managers of such narrowly defined units can stay in close contact with their customers and competitive environments while the shared programs increase economies of scale and synergy across units.

Unfortunately, though shared programs and facilities can lead to increased operating efficiency, they also can have a negative impact on the innovativeness of the business units involved (Woo 1984, p. 53). Shared programs and facilities can increase the centralization of decision making and decrease the specialization within each participating business unit. As pointed out in the preceding section, such factors are likely to have an adverse effect on a business' innovativeness and adaptability. Consequently, we hypothesize a negative relationship between the sharing of functional programs and resources and the performance of businesses pursuing prospector strategies.

P$_{2a}$: The success[5] of prospector business units is related negatively to the sharing of programs and resources (e.g., product and process R&D programs, manufacturing facilities, a salesforce, distribution channels, advertising and promotion programs) with other business units.

In contrast, the increased economies of scale gained through the sharing of programs and facilities should have a positive effect on the profitability and ROI performance of units pursuing low cost defender stategies. The inflexibility inherent in shared programs should not be a major problem to such defenders.

P$_{2b}$: The performance of low cost defender business units is related positively to the sharing of programs and resources with other business units.

Sharing functions and resources with other business units can either improve or hinder the performance of differentiated defender business units, depending on which functions and resources are shared. In areas central to the unit's differential advantage, such as marketing, programs and functions should remain separate to preserve flexibility and maintain quality. In noncentral functions, some sharing may be useful for improving efficiency.

P$_{2c}$: The performance of differentiated defender business units is related negatively to the sharing of programs and functions related to the units' source of differential advantage, but positively to the sharing of other functional programs and resources.

Evidence. Few empirical studies have examined the multiple sources and impacts of synergy at the business unit level. Hamermesh and White (1984) found that, among units pursuing low cost strategies, those businesses that shared line responsibility with other units for at least some key functions (e.g., sales, marketing, manufacturing, R&D) attained ROI percentages twice as large as those achieved by businesses that were entirely self-contained. The relationship between shared functions and ROI was exactly the opposite among business units pursuing differentiated strategies. Also, when results were examined across the entire sample, self-contained businesses achieved significantly higher rates of real sales growth than units that shared one or more key functions. These findings seem consistent with our propositions.

To confuse matters, however, Hamermesh and White also found that businesses operating in "dynamic" market environments had equal sales growth but higher ROI when they shared functions than when they were self-contained. Alternatively, in "stable" market environments, sales growth and ROI percentages were higher for self-contained units than for those sharing functions. If one assumes that more businesses in dynamic environments are likely to pursue prospector or differentiated strategies, whereas those in stable environments are more likely to be low cost defenders, these results appear inconsistent with the propositions.

A possible reason for the somewhat ambiguous findings of Hamermesh and White is the "all or nothing" nature of the measure of shared programs. Comparisons were made only between units that were totally self-contained and those having some degree of sharing. The negative impact of shared programs on the adaptability, innovativeness, and sales growth of a business may vary with the number and type of shared programs and with the relative degree of sharing. Some support for this view is provided by Woo's (1984) study of 112 business units that were the market share leaders in their industries. Though many of the units in her sample shared marketing and sales programs, she found a relationship between the *degree* of sharing and average ROI. She divided the sample in half according to four-year average ROI and found a higher proportion of shared marketing programs and distribution channels among low return business units than among those with higher returns. Other information in the article suggests that many of the business units in Woo's sample were pursuing differentiated defender strategies, in which case the findings are consistent with at least one of our propositions. However, Woo did not explicitly examine the impact of shared marketing programs on performance across businesses pursuing different types of strategies. Consequently, as neither study provides a complete or unambiguous examination of the conceptual propositions, further empirical work on the sources and effects of synergy across business units—particularly in terms of the impact of shared marketing programs on innovativeness and profitability—appears both necessary and important.

Control and Reward Systems

Regardless of how much or how little autonomy an SBU's managers are given, the complexity of coordinating diverse businesses and the long lines of communication from boardroom to operating managers often force corporate executives to rely on periodic comparisons of SBU performance with planned objectives as a primary method of control. The unit's managers, in turn, commonly are motivated to achieve those planned objectives through bonuses or other financial incentives. It seems reasonable to suppose, then, that a business unit will perform better when the criteria used by corporate managers to evaluate and reward the unit's managers are consistent with the business unit strategy.

Profitability criteria for evaluating and rewarding business unit performance—such as meeting specified ROI objectives—encourage managers to use assets wisely, be cautious in their investment in plant and equipment, and control costs tightly. Because such actions are most consistent with the thrust of the two defender strategies, a reward system that strongly emphasizes business unit profitability or ROI is likely to have a positive relationship with the performance of businesses pursuing such strategies.

P_{3a}: The greater the proportion of rewards received by a business unit's managers that is determined by short-term profitability or ROI criteria, the greater the performance of low cost defender and differentiated defender business units.

Profitability-based reward systems discourage risk taking and entrepreneurial efforts by business unit managers because the payoffs associated with such actions are uncertain and may occur only in the longer term. In contrast, incentives based on volume criteria such as a unit's sales or market share growth encourage managers to be more innovative and to take the risks necessary to spur growth. Therefore, volume-based reward systems are more consistent with a prospector business unit's strategy (Norburn and Miller 1981; Rappaport 1978).

P$_{3b}$: The greater the proportion of rewards received by a business unit's managers that is based on sales or market share growth criteria, the greater the performance of prospector business units.

Evidence. Several studies have investigated the relationship between profit-based management incentive systems and the decision-making behaviors of managers. These studies have consistently found positive relationship between the magnitude of such incentives and the level of risk aversion and short-term orientation apparent in managerial decisions. However, as most of the studies did not include broader measures of the performance of the business units being managed (Bower 1970; Lawler 1976), none of them provides an adequate test of the propositions.

We conclude that the propositions about the impact of different kinds of reward systems on the performance of businesses pursuing different kinds of strategies are a fertile field for further research, both because they suggest important managerial implications and because they have yet to be tested rigorously.

INTERFUNCTIONAL RELATIONSHIPS AND THE IMPLEMENTATION OF BUSINESS STRATEGIES

Implementing any business strategy requires the performance and coordination of a variety of tasks and activities across many functional departments and work units within the SBU. However, conceptual arguments for various taxonomies of business strategy (cf. Miles and Snow 1978; Porter 1980) suggest that different functional activities have crucial roles in the successful implementation of different kinds of strategies. We therefore hypothesize that (1) the SBU's relative level of *competence* on specific functional dimensions, (2) the *amount of resources* it allocates to those functional areas in relation to its major competitors, (3) the amount of *participation and influence* each functional area has in making decisions about the SBU's products and policies, and (4) the specific mechanisms for *coordinating activities across functional departments and resolving conflicts between departments* have differential effects on the critical performance outcomes attained by business units pursuing different strategies.

Functional Competencies

The term "distinctive competence" refers to what a business does particularly well in comparison with its competitors operating within a similar environment (Selznick 1957). The number of specific activities in which a business may have distinctive competence is vast, but we aggregate those activities into broad categories that roughly correspond to the tasks of different functional departments or work groups commonly found across business units.

Though some minimum level of competence on a full range of functional activities is necessary for the long-run survival of the business unit regardless of its strategy, the three business strategies have somewhat different requirements for competing successfully. Because prospector business units attempt to generate new business opportunities and to grow rapidly, those functions closest to the customer are of crucial importance. Competence in marketing, sales, and product R&D and engineering is the impetus for growth and therefore should be related positively to the success of such a strategy.

P$_{4a}$: The greater the competence in marketing, personal selling, and product R&D and engineering, relative to competitors, the greater the performance of prospector business units.

Low cost defenders primarily pursue profitability objectives through efficient operations and by competing on price. Such units must carefully monitor and control costs associated with producing and distributing their products. Consequently, we expect that competence in the areas of process engineering, production, distribution, and financial management and control are critical to the ROI performance of low cost defenders.

P$_{4b}$: The greater the competence in process engineering, production, distribution, and financial management and control, the greater the performance of low cost defenders.

Differentiated defenders require perhaps the broadest range of functional competencies. Such units must pay close attention to customer demands to maintain market share, but also must monitor costs carefully to protect profit margins. Therefore, we expect that high competence in the areas of sales and financial management and control, as well as on the specific functions central to the unit's differential advantage, is critical to the success of differentiated defenders.

P$_{4c}$: The greater the competence in sales, financial management and control, and those functions on which the unit maintains a differential advantage over competitors, the greater the performance of differentiated defenders.

Evidence. Snow and Hrebiniak (1980) examined the perceptions of 247 top-level managers of 88 businesses in four different industries about (1) the strategy being pursued by their unit and (2) the relative competence of the various functional areas within their organization. Managers of defender businesses in all four industries perceived their units to be particularly competent in the areas of general management, production, financial management, and applied engineering/process R&D. In contrast, managers of prospector businesses perceived their units to be highly competent in the area of general management in all four industries; marketing, sales, financial management, and basic engineering in three of the industries; product R&D in two of the industries; and market research in none. These findings have some interesting anomalies, but are largely consistent with the propositions. However, they do not represent an adequate test of the propositions for two reasons: (1) low cost and differentiated defenders were combined in a single category and (2) the study did not explore the relationship between perceived variations in functional competence and actual differences in performance across businesses pursuing similar strategies. Thus, the question of what kinds of functional competence are important for enabling a business to *implement a particular strategy most successfully* remains open for future research.

Allocation of Resources

To implement a particular type of strategy successfully a business not only must have the necessary functional competencies, but also must support the critical functions with needed resources and ensure that those resources are utilized effectively. Therefore, we expect that the allocation of resources within the business unit corresponds to the functional competencies the unit needs to develop. Prospector business units should support marketing, personal selling, and product R&D at higher levels than do competitors. Low cost defenders should invest a greater proportion of resources in process engineering, production, distribution, and financial management and control. Differentiated defender business units require higher levels of resources in personal selling, financial management and control, and functions that create differential advantage for the business unit.

P$_{5a}$: The greater the allocation of resources to marketing, personal selling, and product R&D and engineering, relative to competitors, the greater the performance of prospector business units.

P$_{5b}$: The greater the allocation of resources to process engineering, production, distribution, and financial management and control, relative to competitors, the greater the performance of low cost defender business units.

P$_{5c}$: The greater the allocation of resources to sales, financial management and control, and functions that differentiate the unit from competitors, the greater the performance of differentiated defender business units.

Evidence.   In a comparison of 201 prospector with 649 defender business units with data drawn from the PIMS data base, Hambrick (1983) found that both product R&D and marketing/selling expenses as a percentage of sales were higher for prospector businesses than for defender businesses. Defenders had significantly higher gross fixed assets and value added per employee than did prospectors. Defenders also had somewhat higher levels of capacity utilization and process R&D expenditures than prospectors, though these differences were not statistically significant.

In general, Hambrick's findings are consistent with the propositions. Again, though, the evidence does not provide an adequate test of our propositions because Hambrick grouped both types of defender businesses into a single category and did not examine the relationship of the various allocation variables to differences in performance outcomes across businesses pursuing the same type of strategy.

Decision-Making Participation and Influence

Given that it is important for an SBU to have competence in, and to devote adequate resources to, those functional departments most critical to the success of its chosen strategy, it seems reasonable to conclude that a business will be most successful when managers of those "critical" functional departments are relatively active and influential in making strategic and administrative decisions within the business unit. Hence prospector business units should perform better on share growth and new product success dimensions when executives in marketing, sales, and R&D have a relatively large influence in making strategic decisions about the unit's products, capital investments, and other policies.

We expect low cost defender business units to perform best in terms of ROI when production or finance executives have a dominant role in decision making because their careful attention to operating efficiencies and expense controls is essential for satisfactory financial performance under such a strategy.

Finally, we expect relatively greater influence by sales executives to be related positively to the ROI performance of differentiated defenders over the long term because of the critical role of that "boundary-spanning" department in maintaining a differentiated position in the market. Similarly, the influence of financial managers may be related positively to the performance of such businesses because intelligent control of expenses and investments should have a direct effect on ROI, at least in the short run. The likely relationship between the decision-making influence of marketing, R&D, and production executives and the performance of such business units, however, depends on the source of the unit's differential advantage.

P$_{6a}$: The greater the participation and influence of marketing, sales, and product R&D and engineering managers in the strategic and administrative decisions within the business unit, the greater the performance of prospector units.

P$_{6b}$: The greater the participation and influence of production, process engineering, distribution, and financial management and control managers in the strategic and administrative decisions within the business unit, the greater the performance of low cost defender units.

P$_{6c}$: The greater the participation and influence of sales and financial management and control managers, and those functions on which the unit differentiates itself from competitors, in the strategic and

administrative decisions within the business unit, the greater the performance of differentiated defender units.

Evidence.   The preceding propositions have received little empirical attention. Miles and Snow (1978), however, concluded from an examination of case studies of firms in the publishing industry that defenders tended to emphasize efficient production and strong financial controls and that finance and production executives tended to have important roles in the "dominant coalition," of decision makers within such businesses. In contrast, they found that prospectors tended to emphasize the exploitation of new market opportunities and technological flexibility and that marketing and R&D executives were prominent members of the dominant coalition of top managers in such businesses. Miles and Snow's findings are largely consistent with our propositions, but they are based on a qualitative assessment of a small number of cases drawn from a single industry and therefore should be treated with some caution. In addition, the impact of the relative decision-making influence of managers in different functional areas on variations in performance across business units pursuing similar strategies has yet to be examined.

Interfunctional Conflict and Coordination

Several authors attribute variations in the conflict between functional departments to the strains produced by different resource and workflow interdependencies between departments, differences in their short-term objectives, and their desires for autonomy (Dutton and Walton 1966; McCann and Galbraith 1981; Van de Ven and Ferry 1980). However, the strategy being pursued by a business unit also may mediate the degree of interfunctional conflict within that unit. Because of their broad product-market domains and their emphasis on new product and market development, prospector businesses often have a high degree of complexity and uncertainty in their operations. Consequently, functional managers face unfamiliar decision situations without standing rules or operating procedures. Such complex and unfamiliar situations can result in substantial interfunctional conflict, particularly among departments that have interdependent roles in helping the business adapt to new market and technological opportunities, such as marketing, sales, R&D, and production. We therefore expect prospector businesses to have higher levels of interfunctional conflict than defender businesses.

P_{7a}: Prospector business units will have higher levels of interfunctional conflict than defender business units.

Low cost defenders commonly operate in more narrowly defined domains and in more mature, stable markets. They also tend to have clearly defined objectives and well-established operating procedures for holding down costs through routinization. Consequently, though the functional managers may chafe under the restrictions imposed by top management, low cost defender businesses are likely to have less interfunctional conflict across departments than businesses pursuing other types of strategy.

P_{7b}: Low cost defender business units should have the lowest level of interfunctional conflict of the three business unit types considered.

Resolution Mechanisms. Regardless of the type of strategy being pursued, every business has some degree of conflict across functional departments. Many researchers have examined the mechanisms firms use to resolve those conflicts (e.g., Blake and Mouton 1964; Lawrence and Lorsch 1967; McCann and Galbraith 1981). There are many variations, but the mechanisms fit into two basic categories: (1) hierarchical approaches whereby top management imposes a solution, either by requiring adherence to formal rules and operating procedures or by serving as judge on a case-by-case basis and (2) participative approaches in which the parties themselves are expected to work out a mutually acceptable solution.

Hierarchical resolution mechanisms tend to be efficient because they reduce the amount of time and human resources necessary to reach a decision and they help ensure consistency in the relations across functional departments over time. Such routinization and efficiency should be particularly beneficial to low cost defenders operating in relatively mature and stable markets.

P_{8a}: The greater the use of hierarchical conflict resolution mechanisms, the greater the performance of low cost defender business units.

Participative resolution mechanisms, as McCann and Galbraith (1981) point out, often lead to a fuller understanding of, and more innovative solutions to, problems that cut across and cause conflict among functional departments. They argue that participative approaches are particularly appropriate for highly uncertain situations in which innovative, adaptive actions are necessary. Prospector businesses commonly face such situations.

P_{8b}: The greater the use of participative conflict resolution mechanisms, the greater the performance of prospector business units.

Differentiated defenders need a combination of conflict resolution mechanisms both to maintain efficiency and be responsive to market conditions.

P_{8c}: The performance of differentiated defenders is greatest when moderate use is made of participative conflict resolution mechanisms, particularly when such mechanisms are used for resolving conflicts relevant to the basis of the business' differential advantage (e.g., customer service policies, product quality).

Evidence.   Miles and Snow (1978), in their qualitative study of businesses within the publishing industry, found that prospector businesses were much more likely to use administrative structures conducive to participative forms of interfunctional coordination and conflict resolution, such as the creation of "liaison" positions and the use of new product development teams. However, they did not test explicitly whether prospectors relied more heavily than defenders on participative mechanisms or whether prospectors who relied most heavily on participative approaches outperformed those using hierarchical methods. As Miles and Snow's case studies represent the only empirical evidence about variations in interfunctional conflict resolution mechanisms across businesses pursuing different strategies, more research in this area obviously is needed. This need has been recognized in the marketing literature (Anderson 1982; Wind 1981; Wind and Robertson 1983), but empirical research has not been forthcoming.

MARKETING STRUCTURE AND POLICIES AND THE IMPLEMENTATION OF BUSINESS STRATEGIES

In defining marketing's role in the effective implementation of business strategies, one critical question is whether different types of marketing organization, policies, and programs work better under different strategies. Miles and Snow (1978) speculated only briefly about the functional policies and competitive devices (e.g., product quality, customer service, advertising) that might most effectively accompany different strategies. However, more recent work in both the strategic management and marketing literature suggests that both (1) the way in which *decision-making and coordination processes are organized within the marketing department* and (2) the *marketing policies and programs* pursued within the business unit affect the performance of different business strategies in different ways.

Decision-Making and Coordination Structures in the Marketing Department

Three structural constructs—formalization, centralization, and specialization—seem particularly important in shaping an organization's or department's performance. *Formalization* is the degree to which decisions and working relationships are governed by formal rules and standard policies and procedures. *Centralization* refers to the locus of decision authority and control within an organizational entity. In highly centralized organizations only one or a few top managers hold most decision-making authority, whereas in more decentralized firms, middle and lower level managers have more autonomy and participate in a wider range of decisions. Finally, *specialization* refers to the division of tasks and activities across positions within the system. As the term implies, highly specialized organizations have a greater number of "specialist" employees who direct their efforts to a relatively narrowly defined set of activities.

As Ruekert et al. (1985) point out, high levels of formalization and centralization together with low levels of specialization are likely to be associated with relatively efficient performance within marketing departments. In such departments, the top marketing manager can use his or her centralized decision-making authority to set a common direction for the department and keep overt conflicts to a minimum. The formal rules and procedures help routinize activities and hold down risks and administrative costs. Hence, higher levels of centralization and formalization and lower levels of specialization in the marketing department should be related positively to the ROI performance of low cost defender business units.

P_{9a}: The greater the formalization and centralization and the lower the specialization of the marketing organization, the greater the performance of low cost defender business units.

Such highly structured marketing departments, however, are unlikely to be very innovative or quick to adapt to new market opportunities or changing environmental conditions. Adaptiveness and innovation are enhanced when (1) decision-making authority is extended down to or at least shared with lower-level managers within the department, (2) rigid rules and policies are supplanted by discretion and informal coordination mechanisms, and (3) more specialists with more detailed knowledge about particular techniques, products, or customers are incorporated within the department. Such organizational structures are especially well suited for prospector business units.

P_{9b}: The lower the formalization and centralization and the greater the specialization of the marketing organization, the greater the performance of prospector business units.

Because differential defenders must maintain both efficiency and innovativeness, we expect moderate levels of the three variables to be most appropriate for marketing departments in businesses pursuing such a strategy.

P_{9c}: Moderate levels of formalization, centralization, and specialization are related positively to the performance of differentiated defender business units.

Evidence. The relationships between the structural dimensions of centralization, formalization, and specialization and organizational performance under different environmental circumstances have been investigated empirically within a variety of organizational contexts (Baldridge and Burnham 1975; Burns and Stalker 1961; Dalton et al. 1980; Pugh et al. 1968). The preponderance, though not all, of the evidence supports the contention that centralized, formalized, and nonspecialized organizations tend to be more efficient but less innovative and adaptive than those with the opposite structural characteristics. However, with the exception of the case analyses of Corey and Star (1971), the relationship of organization structure variables to performance has not been examined explicitly in a marketing context. Also, no studies have related structural differences in marketing departments to variations in performance across businesses pursuing similar strategies. The specific propositions we discuss are unexplored and warrant future research.

Marketing Policies and Programs

Any attempt to draw broad generalizations about how specific marketing program elements might fit within different business strategies involves "level of analysis" problems. Though a business strategy is a general statement about how the unit chooses to compete in an industry, that unit may encompass a large number of different products, each facing somewhat different competitive situations in different markets. There is likely to be considerable variation in marketing programs across products within the same business unit. Nevertheless, because a business strategy *does set a general direction* for how the unit will compete, it should at least have some impact on broad marketing policies that cut across products and product lines. The more consistent those marketing policies are with the overall strategy, and the more successful the unit is in adhering to those policies, the more likely it is that the strategy will be effective.

Product Policies.   One set of such marketing policies broadly defines the *nature of the products* the business will offer to the market. These policies cover (1) the *breadth or diversity* of the product line, (2) the general *level of technical sophistication* of those products, and (3) the target *level of product quality* in relation to that of competitors. Because prospector businesses rely heavily on the continuing development of unique new products and the penetration of new markets as a primary competitive strategy, their adherence to policies encouraging

broad and technically advanced product lines should be related positively to their performance on the critical dimension of share growth. Whether those products should also be of "higher quality" than competitors' products is open to question, primarily because of the problem of defining quality. As Hambrick (1983, p. 23) suggests, in those product markets where technical features or up-to-the-minute styling are key attributes in customers' definitions of quality, high quality products may have a positive role in determining the success of a prospector strategy. In markets where the critical determinants of quality are reliability or brand familiarity, the maintenance of relatively high product quality is likely to be related more strongly to the successful performance of defender businesses, particularly those following a differentiated defender strategy.

As differential defenders compete by offering more or "better" choices to customers than do their competitors, success in developing relatively broad and technically sophisticated product lines also should be related positively to the long-term ROI performance of those businesses. However, such policies are inconsistent with the efficiency requirements of the low cost defender strategy. Broad and complex product lines lead to short production runs and large inventories. Maintaining technical sophistication in products requires continuing investments in product and process R&D. Consequently, the adoption of such policies is expected to be related negatively to the ROI performance of low cost defender businesses.

Service Policies.   Instead of or in addition to competing on the basis of product characteristics, businesses can distinguish themselves from competitors on the *quality of service* they offer. Service can take many forms, including engineering and design services, alterations, installation, training of customer personnel, and maintenance and repair services. Adherence to a policy of high service quality seems particularly appropriate for differentiated defenders because it offers a means of maintaining a competitive advantage in well-established markets. The appropriateness of such a policy for low cost defenders, though, is questionable. The customer satisfaction benefits of high quality service may be offset by higher operating and administrative costs. Such a policy could detract from the low cost defender's ability to maintain the low prices that are the critical element of its strategy and also could lower ROI. Similarly, the higher costs and greater administrative effort of a high quality service policy raise questions about the appropriateness of such a policy for prospector businesses. Efforts to improve service to current customers may divert resources and attention from the more critical objective of new product and market development.

Price Policies. Successful adherence to a policy of offering *low prices* in relation to those of competitors should be related positively to the performance of low cost defender businesses because low price is the primary competitive weapon in such a strategy. However, a policy of "meeting or beating" competitors' prices is inconsistent with both differentiated defender and prospector strategies. The higher costs involved in differentiating a business' products on either a quality or a service basis (1) necessitate higher prices to maintain profitability and (2) provide customers with additional value for which higher prices can be charged. Similarly, the costs and benefits of new product and market development by prospector businesses require and justify relatively high prices. We therefore expect adherence to a policy of low competitive prices

to be related negatively to the critical performance outcomes of differentiated defenders and prospectors.

Distribution Policies. Both Miles and Snow (1978) and Hambrick (1983) argue that prospector businesses should show a greater degree of *forward vertical integration* than defender businesses. In their view, the prospector's focus on new product development requires superior market intelligence, as well as frequent reeducation and motivation of members of the distribution channel. They argue that these tasks can be accomplished best through tight bureaucratic control of company-owned channels. However, these arguments seem entirely inconsistent with the prospector's need for flexibility in constructing new channels for new products and markets. Tight control over channel member behavior seems a much more appropriate policy for defenders who are trying to maintain strong positions in established markets, particularly when they rely on good customer service to differentiate themselves from competitors. Consequently, we hypothesize that a relatively high degree of forward vertical integration is related positively to the ROI performance of differentiated defender businesses, but negatively to the new product and share growth success of prospectors.

Marketing Communications Policies. Extensive marketing communications should be important in the successful implementation of both prospector and differentiated defender strategies. The form of that communication, however, may be different under the two strategies. As prospectors must work constantly to generate awareness, stimulate trial, and build primary demand for new and unfamiliar products, a policy of *high advertising and sales promotion expenditures* in relation to those of competitors seems likely to bear a positive relationship to the new product and share growth success of such businesses. Differentiated defenders, in contrast, are concerned primarily with maintaining the loyalty of established customers by adapting to their needs and providing good service, tasks that can be accomplished best by an extensive, well-trained, well-supported salesforce. Therefore, a policy of *high salesforce expenditures* in relation to those of competitors should be related positively to the financial performance of differentiated defenders. Finally, because low cost defenders appeal to their customers primarily on a price basis, high expenditures in relation to those of competitors on either advertising or the salesforce would detract from their basic strategy and could have a negative impact on their ROI performance.

In summary, the marketing program elements most appropriate for each of the three business unit strategies can be stated as follows.

P_{10a}: The performance of prospector business units is related positively to:
  • relatively broad, technically sophisticated product lines,
  • relatively high quality of service,
  • relatively higher prices,
  • relatively less forward vertical integration, and
  • relatively high advertising and sales promotion expenditures.

P_{10b}: The performance of low cost defender business units is related positively to:
  • relatively narrow, less technically sophisticated product lines,
  • relatively low quality of service,
  • relatively lower prices,
  • relatively greater forward vertical integration, and

  • relatively low advertising and sales promotion expenditures.

P_{10c}: The performance of differentiated defender business units is related positively to:
  • relatively narrow, higher quality product lines,
  • relatively high quality of service,
  • relatively high prices,
  • relatively greater forward vertical integration, and
  • relatively high salesforce expenditures.

Evidence. In several recent studies the PIMS data base has been used to examine differences in marketing policies and expenditures (as well as other functional and strategic variables) across businesses operating at different stages in the product life cycle (Anderson and Zeithaml 1984; Hambrick, MacMillan, and Day 1982). Unfortunately, none of these studies included the generic business strategy pursued by a business as either an independent or a moderating variable. If, however, we assume that most businesses pursue strategies that fit their environments appropriately, perhaps we can argue that businesses operating in growth industries are more likely to be prospectors and those in mature or declining industries are apt to be defenders.

In view of such logic, it is interesting that the relationships observed between marketing policies and market share performance among businesses in growth industries are consistent with the propositions relevant to prospectors. In general, regression analyses in the PIMS-based studies show significant positive relationships between market share and (1) relative product line breadth, (2) relative product quality, (3) relative service quality, and (4) relative advertising expenses among businesses in growth industries. The same studies found no significant relationships between market share and (1) relative prices, (2) forward vertical integration, or (3) relative salesforce expenses.

The same set of studies also found some relationships between marketing policies and ROI performance among businesses in mature and declining industries that are generally consistent with our propositions about defenders, particularly those for differentiated defenders. In such industries, significant positive relationships were found between ROI performance and (1) relative product quality and (2) relative service quality. No significant relationship with ROI performance was found for (1) product line breadth, (2) relative prices, (3) forward vertical integration, (4) relative salesforce expenses, and (4) relative advertising expenses.

Though these findings do suggest some reason for optimism about the validity of our research propositions, they obviously do not provide an adequate test of those propositions. The studies did examine relationships between differences in marketing policies and various performance outcomes across businesses operating at a particular stage in the industry life cycle, but to assume that all businesses at a given life cycle stage are pursuing the same type of strategy is clearly tenuous. Because the studies did not measure explicitly the type of strategy being pursued by units in their samples, it is impossible to tell whether particular marketing policies are related to variations in performance across businesses pursuing the same strategy under similar environmental conditions.

One other recent study did explicitly relate differences in some general marketing policies to the type of generic strategy being pursued by a sample of 850 SBUs drawn from the PIMS data base (Hambrick 1983). Prospector businesses were found to have significantly higher marketing expenses as a percentage of sales but less forward vertical integration and lower service quality than defender businesses. No significant differences were found between the two types of strategy on relative product quality or relative prices. These findings seem generally consistent with our propositions, but Hambrick's failure to include specific performance measures precludes comparisons of the relationship between various marketing policies and the performance of businesses pursuing similar types of strategy.

SUMMARY AND CONCLUSIONS

Research Implications
We derive and discuss the conceptual rationale for a set of propositions about the impact of (1) corporate–business unit relationships, (2) interfunctional structures and coordination processes, and (3) marketing policies on the performance of business units pursuing either prospector, low cost defender, or differentiated defender strategies. This set of propositions is summarized in Table 34–2.

One obvious conclusion to be drawn from the review of empirical evidence germane to our propositions is that in every case evidence is sparse and riddled with limitations. This finding suggests a variety of interesting opportunities for future research, but those opportunities present some substantial methodological challenges. There are several good reasons why more research has not been done on factors related to the effective implementation of strategy. One of the most imposing is the fact that the appropriate unit of analysis for studying the implementation of business strategies is the

Table 34-2
Factors Related to the Successful Implementation of Business Unit Strategies

Organizational Variable	Prospectors	Differentiated Defenders	Low Cost Defenders
Corporate-Business Unit Relationships			
Business unit autonomy	High levels of autonomy	Moderate levels of autonomy	Low levels of autonomy
Shared programs and synergy	Low levels of synergy	Low levels in areas related to differential advantage; high levels in other areas	High levels of synergy
Control and reward systems	Sales- or market-share-based systems	Profitability-based systems	Profitablity-based systems
Interfunctional Relationships			
Functional competencies	Marketing, sales, product R&D, and engineering	Sales, financial management and control, and those functions related to differential advantage	Process engineering, production, distribution, financial management and control
Allocation of resources	Marketing, sales, product R&D, and engineering	Sales, financial management and control, and those functions related to differential advantage	Process engineering, production, distribution, financial management and control
Decision-making influence and participation	Marketing, sales, product R&D, and engineering	Sales, financial management and control, and those functions related to differential advantage	Process engineering, production, distribution, financial management and control
Interfunctional conflict	High levels	Moderate levels	Low levels
Conflict resolution mechanisms	Participative	Participative for issues related to differential advantage, hierarchical for others	Hierarchical
Marketing Structure and Policies			
Decision-making and coordination structures	Low levels of formalization and centralization; high levels of specialization	Moderate levels of formalization, centralization, and specialization	High levels of formalization and centralization, low levels of specialization
Marketing policies and programs	• Broad, technically sophisticated product lines • High quality of service • High prices • Less forward vertical integration • High advertising and sales promotion expenditures	• Narrow, high-quality product lines • High quality of service • High prices • Greater forward vertical integration • High salesforce expenditures	• Narrow, less technically sophisticated product lines • Lower quality of service • Lower prices • Greater forward vertical integration • Low advertising and sales promotion expenditures

business unit iself. As a result, strategy researchers are faced with two problems: (1) to obtain a sufficient number of observations, substantial time and money are needed to gather data from many firms and business units and (2) researchers must either gain access to the kinds of information necessary to provide objective measures of structure, process, and performance variables or cope with the much-discussed shortcomings of self-report and key informant data (Phillips 1981). Such problems help to explain why much of the implementation research has drawn on the PIMS data base in spite of its widely recognized limitations (Ramanujam and Venkatraman 1984).

Despite such problems, however, the relevance and importance of the unanswered questions about marketing and the implementation of strategy should motivate uncommon efforts to answer them. Indeed, there has been renewed interest in more qualitative research methods in both the strategic management and marketing literatures (cf. Bonoma 1985b; Harrigan 1983). Such approaches may be better suited for the complex and interactive research problems in the strategy area.

Managerial Implications

Many of the specific managerial implications of our propositions are straightforward and require little elaboration. However, when viewed as a whole, the propositions seem to imply an interesting conclusion: it is not always appropriate for marketers and their activities to have a primary role in implementing a business' strategy. We believe organizations should *always* be market driven in the sense of being responsive to customer needs, but individual business units should not always be "market*ing* driven" in the sense of comparatively large marketing budgets or primary control by marketing managers over strategic and op-

erational decisions within the unit. This conclusion raises the possibility that marketers may have different roles across different units within the same corporation. Such a possibility, in turn, raises intriguing questions about the role of corporate-level marketing units in coordinating disparate marketing programs across business units, about the possible synergies and limitations of sharing marketing programs across units, and about the appropriate career paths for marketing managers in such organizations (e.g., how to keep morale high among marketing managers who are transferred from a prospector unit to a defender unit where their influence and budgets may be restricted). Though we suspect some marketers may find such a "contingency" view of marketing's appropriate role in the strategic scheme of things to be a bit heretical and deserving of debate, sparking such a debate—one that will lead to a marshalling of more empirical evidence—is a major purpose of our review.

NOTES

1. Business strategy generally is discussed in the context of a large, multidivisional firm. However, the concept of business-level strategy also applies to smaller firms operating within a single industry.

2. As defined by Miles and Snow, *prospector* business units take an aggressive new product-market position within broadly defined markets and tend to be industry pioneers in the creation and development of new technologies. *Defender* business units take a conservative view of new product development and attempt to maintain a secure market position in a narrower segment of the market. Defenders often compete on price or quality and rarely introduce new technologies to the market. *Analyzer* business units represent an intermediate form of strategy,

sharing elements of both the prospector and defender strategies. Analyzer business units maintain a secure market position within a core market, much like the defender, but also seek new market positions through product development as do prospectors. The fourth business unit strategy, a *reactor* strategy, is characterized by the absence of any well-developed plan for competing within an industry.

3. A fourth set of variables at the individual level of analysis also might be considered. *Personal characteristics* related to the background, experience, training, values, and perceptions of a business unit's personnel have been hypothesized to mediate the unit's ability to implement different strategies successfully (Hambrick and Mason 1984; Szilagyi and Schweiger 1984). Such relationships suggest some interesting implications for the appropriate training and career development of marketing personnel across businesses pursuing different strategies, but space limitations preclude our explicit examination of them.

4. These expectations are consistent with the very limited theoretical (Donaldson 1984) and empirical (Hambrick 1983) evidence currently available.

5. Again, because different strategies are expected to perform well on different dimensions, "success" for prospector businesses refers to their performance on new product development and market share growth, whereas successful performance of businesses pursuing either of the two defender strategies is shown by relatively high ROI. However, this and all subsequent propositions refer simply to "successful performance" without reiterating the critical dimensions on which that performance is expected to occur under each type of strategy.

REFERENCES

Anderson, Carl R. and Carl P. Zeithaml (1984), "Stages of the Product Life Cycle, Business Strategy, and Business Performance," *Academy of Management Journal*, 27, 5–24.

Anderson, Paul F. (1982), "Marketing, Strategic Planning and the Theory of the Firm," *Journal of Marketing*, 46 (Spring), 15–26.

Armstrong, J. Scott (1982), "The Value of Formal Planning for Strategic Decisions: Review of Empirical Research," *Stratetic Management Journal*, 3, 197–211.

Baldridge, J. Victor and Robert A. Burnham (1975), "Organizational Innovation: Individual, Organizational, and Environmental Impacts," *Administrative Science Quarterly*, 20, 165–75.

Blake, Robert R. and Jane S. Mouton (1964), *The Managerial Grid*. Houston, TX: Gulf Publishing Company.

Bonoma, Thomas V. (1984), "Making Your Marketing Strategy Work," *Harvard Business Review*, 62 (March/April), 69–76.

———(1985a), *The Marketing Edge: Making Strategies Work*. New York: The Free Press.

———(1985b) "Case Research in Marketing: Opportunities, Problems, and a Process," *Journal of Marketing Research*, 22 (May), 199–208.

Bourgeois, Louis J., III (1984), "Strategic Management and Determinism," *Academy of Management Review*, 9 (4), 586–96.

Bower, Joseph L. (1970), *Managing the Resource Allocation Process: A Study of Corporate Planning and Investment*. Cambridge, MA: Graduate School of Business Administration, Harvard University.

Burns, Tom and G. M. Stalker (1961), *The Management of Innovation*. London: Tavistock Publications.

Corey, E. Raymond and Steven H. Star (1971), *Organization Strategy: A Marketing Approach*. Cambridge, MA: Division of Research, Graduate School of Business Administration, Harvard University.

Dalton, Dan R., William D. Todor, Michael J. Spendolini, Gordon J. Fielding, and Lyman W. Porter (1980), "Organizational Structure and Performance: A Critical Review," *Academy of Management Review*, 5 (1), 49–64.

Donaldson, Gordon (1984), *Managing Corporate Wealth*. New York: Praeger, Inc.

Dutton, John M. and Ray E. Walton (1966), "Interdepartmental Conflict and Cooperation: Two Contrasting Studies," *Human Organization*, 25, 207–20.

Galbraith, Jay and Daniel Nathanson (1978),

Strategy Implementation: The Role of Structure and Process. St. Paul, MN: West Publishing Company.

Hambrick, Donald C. (1980), "Operationalizing the Concept of Business-Level Strategy," *Academy of Management Review*, 5, 567–75.

———(1983), "Some Tests of the Effectiveness and Functional Attributes of Miles and Snow's Strategic Types," *Academy of Management Journal*, 26, 5–26.

———, Ian MacMillan, and Diana L. Day (1982), "Strategic Attributes and Performance in the BCG Matrix—A PIMS-Based Analysis of Industrial Product Businesses," *Academy of Management Journal*, 25, 510–31.

———and Phyllis A. Mason (1984), "The Organization as a Reflection of Its Top Managers," *Academy of Management Review*, 9, 193–206.

Hamermesh, Richard G. and Roderick E. White (1984), "Manage Beyond Portfolio Analysis," *Harvard Business Review*, 62 (January–February), 103–9.

Harrigan, Kathyrn (1883), "Research Methodologies for Contingency Approaches to Business Strategy," *Academy of Management Review*, 8 (3), 398–405.

Hatten, Kenneth J. and Dan E. Schendel (1976), "Heterogeneity Within an Industry: Firm Conduct in the U.S. Brewing Industry, 1952–1971." West Lafayette, IN: Institute for Research in the Behavioral, Economics and Management Sciences.

Jauch, Lawrence J. and Kenneth L. Kraft (1986), "Strategic Management of Uncertainty," *Academy of Management Review*, 11 (4), 777–90.

Kiechel, Water, III (1981), "The Decline of the Experience Curve," *Fortune* (October 4), 139–42.

———(1982), "Corporate Strategists Under Fire," *Fortune* (December 27), 33–9.

Lawler, Edward E., III (1976), "Control Systems in Organizations," in *Handbook of Industrial and Organizational Psychology*, M. D. Dunnette, ed. Chicago: Rand McNally, Inc., 1247–91.

Lawrence, R. Paul and Jay W. Lorsch (1967), "Differentiation and Integration in Complex Organizations," *Administrative Science Quarterly*, 12, 1–47.

MacMillan, Ian C., Donald C. Hambrick, and D. L. Day (1982), "The Product Portfolio and Profitability—A PIMS-Based Analysis of Industrial Products Businesses," *Academy of Management Journal*, 25, 733–55.

McCann, John and Jay R. Galbraith (1981), "Interdepartmental Relations," *Handbook of Organizational Design*, Vol. 2, Paul C. Nystrom and William Starbuck, eds. New York: Oxford University Press, 60–84.

Miles, Raymond E. and Charles C. Snow (1978), *Organizational Strategy, Structure and Process*. New York: McGraw-Hill Book Company.

Miller, Danny and Peter H. Freisen (1984), *Organizations: A Quantum View*. Englewood Cliffs, NJ: Prentice-Hall, Inc.

Mintzberg, Henry (1979), *The Structuring of Organizations*. Englewood Cliffs, NJ: Prentice-Hall, Inc.

Norburn, David and Paul Miller (1981), "Strategy and Executive Reward: The Mis-Match in the Strategic Process," *Journal of General Management*, 6, 17–27.

Phillips, Lynn W. (1981), "Assessing Measurement Error in Key Informant Reports: A Methodological Note on Organizational Analysis in Marketing," *Journal of Marketing Research*, 18 (November), 395–415.

Porter, Michael E. (1980), *Competitive Strategy*. New York: The Free Press.

———(1985), *Competitive Advantage: Creating and Sustaining Superior Performance*. New York: The Free Press.

Pugh, Derek S., David J. Hickson, C. Robert Hinings, and Christopher Turner (1968), "Dimensions of Organization Structure," *Administrative Science Quarterly*, 13, 65–105.

Quinn, James Brian (1981), "Formulating Strategy One Step at a Time," *Journal of Business Strategy*, 1 (Winter), 42–63.

Ramanujam, Vasu and N. Venkatraman (1984), "An Inventory and Critique of Strategy Research Using the PIMS Database," *Academy of Management Review*, 9, 138–51.

Rappaport, Alfred (1978), "Executive Incentives vs. Corporate Growth," *Harvard Business Review*, 56 (July–August), 81–8.

Ruekert, Robert W., Orville C. Walker, Jr., and Kenneth J. Roeing (1985), "The Organization of Marketing Activities: A Contingency Theory of Structure and Performance," *Journal of Marketing*, 49 (Winter), 13–25.

Rumelt, Richard (1974), *Strategy, Structure and Economic Performance*, Cambridge, MA: Harvard University Press.

Schendel, Dan and G. Richard Patton (1978), "A Simultaneous Equation Model of Corporate Strategy," *Management Science*, 24, 1611–21.

Selznick, P. (1957), *Leadership in Administration*. New York: Harper & Row Publishers, Inc.

Snow, Charles C. and Lawrence C. Hrebiniak (1980), "Strategy, Distinctive Competence and Organizational Performance," *Administrative Science Quarterly*, 25, 317–35.

Szilagyi, Andrew D. and David M. Schweiger (1984), "Matching Managers to Strategies: A Review and Suggested Framework," *Academy of Management Review*, 9, 626–37.

Thompson, Victor (1969), *Bureaucracy and Innovation*. University of Alabama Press.

Van de Ven, Andrew H. and Diane L. Ferry (1980), *Measuring and Assessing Organizations*. New York: John Wiley & Sons, Inc.

———and Marilyn A. Morgan (1980), "A Revised Framework for Organization Assessment," in *Organizational Assessment*, E. E. Lawler, III, D. A. Nadler, and C. Cammann, eds. New York: Wiley-Interscience, 216–60.

Weick, Karl (1979), *The Social Psychology of Organizing*, 2nd ed. Reading, MA: Addison-Wesley Publishing Company.

Wind, Yoram (1981), "Marketing and the Other Business Functions," in *Research in Marketing*, J. N. Sheth, ed. Greenwich, CT: JAI Press, Inc., 237–64.

———and Thomas S. Robertson (1983), "Marketing Strategy: New Directions for Theory and Research," *Journal of Marketing*, 47 (Spring), 12–25.

Wood, Carolyn Y. (1984), "Market Share Leadership—Not Always So Good," *Harvard Business Review*, 62 (January–February), 50–4.

Wrigley, Leonard (1970), *Divisional Autonomy and Diversification*, unpublished doctoral dissertation, Graduate School of Business Administration, Harvard University.

Yip, George (1982), *Barriers to Entry*. Lexington, MA: D.C. Heath and Company.

The Marketing Audit Comes of Age

Philip Kotler, William Gregor, and William Rogers

Comparing the marketing strategies and tactics of business units today versus ten years ago, the most striking impression is one of marketing strategy obsolescence. Ten years ago U.S. automobile companies were gearing up for their second postwar race to produce the largest car with the highest horsepower. Today companies are selling increasing numbers of small and medium-size cars and fuel economy is a major selling point. Ten years ago computer companies were introducing ever-more powerful hardware for more sophisticated uses. Today they emphasize mini- and micro-computers and software.

It is not even necessary to take a ten-year-period to show the rapid obsolescence of marketing strategies. The growth economy of 1950–1970 has been superseded by a volatile economy which produces new strategic surprises almost monthly. Competitors launch new products, customers switch their business, distributors lose their effectiveness, advertising costs skyrocket, government regulations are announced, and consumer groups attack. These changes represent both opportunities and problems and may demand periodic reorientations of the company's marketing operations.

Many companies feel that their marketing operations need regular reviews and overhauls but do not know how to proceed. Some companies simply make many small changes that are economically and politically feasible, but fail to get to the heart of the matter. True, the company develops an annual marketing plan but management normally does not take a deep and objective look at the marketing strategies, policies, organizations, and operations on a recurrent basis. At the other extreme, companies install aggressive new top marketing management hoping to shake down the marketing cobwebs. In between there must be more orderly ways to reorient marketing operations to changed environments and opportunities.

ENTER THE MARKETING AUDIT

One hears more talk today about the *marketing audit* as being the answer to evaluating marketing practice just as the public accounting audit is the tool for evaluating company accounting practice. This might lead one to conclude that the marketing audit is a new idea and also a very distinct methodology. Neither of these conclusions is true.

The marketing audit as an idea dates back to the early fifties. Rudolph Dallmeyer, a former executive in Booz-Allen-Hamilton, remembers conducting marketing audits as early as 1952. Robert J. Lavidge, President of Elrick and Lavidge, dates his firm's performance of marketing audits to over two decades ago. In 1959, the American Management Association published an excellent set of papers on the marketing audit under the title *Analyzing and Improving Marketing Performance*, Report No. 32, 1959. During the 1960s, the marketing audit received increasing mention in the lists of marketing services of management consultant firms. It was not until the turbulent seventies, however, that it began to penetrate management awareness as a possible answer to its needs.

As for whether the marketing audit has reached a high degree of methodological sophistication, the answer is generally no. Whereas two certified public accountants will handle an audit assignment using approximately the same methodology, two marketing auditors are likely to bring different conceptions of the auditing process to their task. However, a growing consensus on the major characteristics of a marketing audit is emerging and we can expect considerable progress to occur in the next few years.

In its fullest form and concept, a marketing audit has four basic characteristics. The first and most important is that it is *broad* rather than narrow in focus. The term "marketing audit" should be reserved for a *horizontal (or comprehensive) audit* covering the company's marketing environment, objectives, strategies, organization, and systems. In contrast a *vertical(or indepth) audit* occurs when management decides to take a deep look into some key marketing function, such as sales force management. A vertical audit should properly be called by the function that is being audited, such as a sales force audit, an advertising audit, or a pricing audit.

A second characteristic feature of a marketing audit is that it is conducted by someone who is *independent* of the operation that is being evaluated. There is some loose talk about self-audits, where a manager follows a checklist of questions concerning his own operation to make sure that he is touching all the bases.[1] Most experts would agree, however, that the self-audit, while it is always a useful step that a manager should take, does not constitute a *bona fide* audit because it lacks objectivity and independence. Independence can be achieved in two ways. The audit could be an *inside audit* conducted by a person or group inside the company but outside of the operation being evaluated. Or it could be an *outside audit* conducted by a management consulting firm or practitioner.

The third characteristic of a marketing audit is that it is *systematic*. The marketing auditor who decides to interview people inside and outside the firm at random, asking questions as they occur to him, is a "visceral" auditor without a method. This does not mean that he will not come up with very useful findings and recommendations; he may be very insightful. However, the effectiveness of the marketing audit will normally increase to the extent that it incorporates an orderly sequence of diagnostic steps, such as there are in the conduct of a public accounting audit.

A final characteristic that is less intrinsic to a marketing audit but nevertheless desirable is that it be conducted *periodically*. Typically, evaluations of company marketing efforts are commissioned when sales have turned down sharply, sales force morale has fallen, or other problems have occurred at the company. The fact is, however, that companies are thrown into a crisis partly because they have failed to review their assumptions and to change them during good times. A marketing audit conducted when things are going well can often help make a good situation even better and also indicate changes needed to prevent things from turning sour.

The above ideas on a marketing audit can be brought together into a single definition:

> A marketing audit is a *comprehensive, systematic, independent,* and *periodic* examination of a company's—or business unit's—marketing environment, objectives, strategies, and activities with a view of determining problem areas and opportunities and recommending a plan of action to improve the company's marketing performance.

WHAT IS THE MARKETING AUDIT PROCESS?

How is a marketing audit performed? Marketing auditing follows the simple three-step procedure shown in Figure 35–1.

Setting the Objectives and Scope
The first step calls for a meeting between the company officer(s) and a potential auditor to explore the nature of the marketing operations and the potential value of a marketing audit. If the company officer is convinced of the potential benefits of a marketing audit, he and the auditor have to work out an agreement on the objectives, coverage, depth, data sources, report format, and the time period for the audit.

Consider the following actual case. A plumbing and heating supplies wholesaler with three branches invited a marketing consultant to prepare an audit of its overall marketing policies and operations. Four major objectives were set for the audit:

- determine how the market views the company and its competitors,
- recommend a pricing policy,
- develop a product evaluation system,
- determine how to improve the sales activity in terms of the deployment of the sales force, the level and type of compensation, the measurement of performance, and the addition of new salesmen.

Furthermore, the audit would cover the marketing operations of the company as a whole and the operations of each of the three branches, with particular attention to one of the branches. The audit would focus on the marketing operations but also include a review of the purchasing and inventory systems since they intimately affect marketing performance.

The company would furnish the auditor with published and private data on the industry. In addition, the auditor would contact suppliers of manufactured plumbing supplies for additional market data and contact wholesalers outside the company's market area to gain further information on wholesale plumbing and heating operations. The auditor would interview all the key corporate and branch management, sales and purchasing personnel, and would ride

Figure 35–1
Steps in a Marketing Audit

with several of those salesmen on their calls. Finally, the auditor would interview a sample of the major plumbing and heating contractor customers in the market areas of the two largest branches.

It was decided that the report format would consist of a draft report of conclusions and recommendations to be reviewed by the president and vice-president of marketing, and then delivered to the executive committee which included the three branch managers. Finally, it was decided that the audit findings would be ready to present within six to eight weeks.

Gathering the Data

The bulk of an auditor's time is spent in gathering data. Although we talk of a single auditor, an audit team is usually involved when the project is large. A detailed plan as to who is to be interviewed by whom, the questions to be asked, the time and place of contact, and so on, has to be carefully prepared so that auditing time and cost are kept to a minimum. Daily reports of the interviews are to be written up and reviewed so that the individual or team can spot new areas requiring exploration, while data are still being gathered.

The cardinal rule in data collection is not to rely solely for data and opinion on those being audited. Customers often turn out to be the key group to interview. Many companies do not really understand how their customers see them and their competitors, nor do they fully understand customer needs. This is vividly demonstrated in Table 35–1, which shows the results of asking end users, company salesmen, and company marketing personnel for their views of the importance of different factors affecting the user's selection of a manufacturer. According to the table, customers look first and foremost at the quality of technical support services, followed by prompt delivery, followed by quick response to customer needs. Company salesmen think that company reputation, however, is the most important factor in customer choice, followed by quick response to customer needs and technical support services. Those who plan marketing strategy have a different opinion. They see company price and product quality as the two major factors in buyer choice, followed by quick response to customer needs. Clearly, there is lack of consonance between what buyers say they want, what company salesmen are responding to, and what company marketing planners are emphasizing. One of the major contributions of marketing auditors is to expose those discrepancies and suggest ways to improve marketing consensus.

Preparing and Presenting the Report

The marketing auditor will be developing tentative conclusions as the data come in. It is a sound procedure for him to meet once or twice with the company officer before the data collection ends to outline some initial findings to see what reactions and suggestions they produce.

When the data gathering phase is

Table 35-1
Factors in the Selection of a Manufacturer

Factor	All Users Rank	Company Salesmen Rank	Company Nonsales Personnel Rank
Reputation	5	①	4
Extension of Credit	9	11	9
Sales Representatives	8	5	7
Technical Support Services	①	△3	6
Literature and Manuals	11	10	11
Prompt Delivery	□2	4	5
Quick Response to Customer Needs	△3	□2	△3
Product Price	6	6	①
Personal Relationships	10	7	8
Complete Product Line	7	9	10
Product Quality	4	8	□2

Source: Marketing and Distribution Audit, A Service of Decision Sciences Corporation, p. 32. Used with permission of the Decision Sciences Corporation.

over, the marketing auditor prepares notes for a visual and verbal presentation to the company officer or small group who hired him. The presentation consists of restating the objectives, showing the main findings, and presenting the major recommendations. Then, the auditor is ready to write the final report, which is largely a matter of putting the visual and verbal material into a good written communication. The company officer(s) will usually ask the auditor to present the report to other groups in the company. If the report calls for deep debate and action, the various groups hearing the report should organize into subcommittees to do follow-up work with another meeting to take place some weeks later. The most valuable part of the marketing audit often lies not so much in the auditor's specific recommendations but in the process that the managers of the company begin to go through to assimilate, debate, and develop their own concept of the needed marketing action.

MARKETING AUDIT PROCEDURES FOR AN INSIDE AUDIT

Companies that conduct internal marketing audits show interesting variations from the procedures just outlined. International Telephone and Telelgraph, for example, has a history of forming corporate teams and sending them into weak divisions to do a complete business audit, with a heavy emphasis on the marketing component. Some teams stay on the job, often taking over the management.

General Electric's corporate consulting division offers help to various divisions on their marketing problems. One of its services is a marketing audit in the sense of a broad, independent, systematic look at the marketing picture in a division. However, the corporate consulting division gets few requests for a marketing audit as such. Most of the requests are for specific marketing studies or problem-solving assistance.

The 3M Company uses a very interesting and unusual internal marketing plan audit procedure. A marketing plan audit office with a small staff is located at corporate headquarters. The main purpose of the 3M marketing plan audit is to help the divisional marketing manager improve the marketing planning function, as well as come up with better strategies and tactics. A divisional marketing manager phones the marketing plan audit office and invites an audit. There is an agreement that only he will see the results and it is up to him whether he wants wider distribution.

The audit centers around a marketing plan for a product or product line that the marketing manager is preparing for the coming year. This plan is reviewed at a personal presentation by a special team of six company marketing executives invited by the marketing plan audit office. A new team is formed for each new audit. An effort is made to seek out those persons within 3M (but not in the audited division) who can bring the best experience to bear on the particular plans' problems and opportunities. A team typically consists of a marketing manager from another division, a national salesmanager, a marketing executive with a technical background, a few others close to the type of problems found in the audited plan, and another person who is totally unfamiliar with the market, the product, or the major marketing techniques being used in the plan. This person usually raises some important points others forget to raise, or do not ask because "everyone probably knows about that anyway."

The six auditors are supplied with a summary of the marketing manager's plan about ten days before an official meeting is held to review the plan. On the audit day, the six auditors, the head of the audit office, and the divisional marketing manager gather at 8:30 A.M. The marketing manager makes a presentation for about an hour describing the division's competitive situation, the long-run strategy, and the planned tactics. The auditors proceed to ask hard questions and debate certain points with the marketing manager and each other. Before the meeting ends that day, the auditors are each asked to fill out a marketing plan evaluation form consisting of questions that are accompanied by numerical rating scales and room for comments.

These evaluations are analyzed and summarized after the meeting. Then the head of the audit office arranges a meeting with the divisional marketing manager and presents the highlights of the auditor's findings and recommendations. It is then up to the marketing manager to take the next steps.

COMPONENTS OF THE MARKETING AUDIT

A major principle in marketing audits is to start with the marketplace first and explore the changes that are taking place and what they imply in the way of problems and opportunities. Then the auditor moves to examine the company's marketing objectives and strategies, organization, and systems. Finally he may move to examine one or two key functions in more detail that are central to the marketing performance of that company. However, some companies ask for less than the full range of auditing steps in order to obtain initial results before commissioning further work. The company may ask for a marketing environment audit, and if satisfied, then ask for a marketing strategy audit. Or it might ask for a marketing organization audit first, and later ask for a marketing environment audit.

We view a full marketing audit as having six major components, each having a semiautonomous status if a company wants less than a full marketing audit. The six components and their logical diagnostic sequence are discussed below. The major auditing questions connected with these components are gathered together in Appendix A at the end of this article.

Marketing Environment Audit

By marketing environment, we mean both the *macro-environment* surrounding the industry and the *task environment* in which the organization intimately operates. The macro-environment consists of the large-scale forces and factors influencing the company's future over which the company has very little control. These forces are normally divided into economic-demographic factors, technological factors, political-legal factors, and social-cultural factors. The marketing auditor's task is to assess the key trends and their implications for company marketing action. However, if the company has a good long-range forecasting department, then there is less of a need for a macro-environment audit.

The marketing auditor may play a more critical role in auditing the company's task environment. The task environment consists of markets, customers, competitors, distributors and dealers, suppliers, and marketing facilitators. The marketing auditor can make a contribution by going out into the field and interviewing various parties to assess their current thinking and attitudes and bringing them to the attention of management.

Marketing Strategy Audit

The marketing auditor then proceeds to consider whether the company's marketing strategy is well-postured in the light of the opportunities and problems facing the company. The starting point for the marketing strategy audit is the corporate goals and objectives followed by the marketing objectives. The auditor may find the objectives to be poorly stated, or he may find them to be well-stated but inappropriate given the company's resources and opportunities. For example, a chemical company had set a sales growth objective for a particular product line at 15 percent. However, the total market showed no growth and competition was fierce. Here the author questioned the basic sales growth objective for that product line. He proposed that the product line be reconsidered for a maintenance or harvest objective at best and that the company should look for growth elsewhere.

Even when a growth objective is warranted, the auditor will want to consider whether management has chosen the best strategy to achieve that growth.

Marketing Organization Audit

A complete marketing audit would have to cover the question of the effectiveness of the marketing and sales organization, as well as the quality of interaction between marketing and other key management functions such as manufacturing, finance, purchasing, and research and development.

At critical times, a company's marketing organization must be reviwed to achieve greater effectiveness within the company and in the marketplace. Companies without product management systems will want to consider introducing them, companies with these systems may want to consider dropping them, or trying product teams instead. Companies may want to redefine the role concept of a product manager from being a promotional manager (concerned primarily with volume) to a business manager (concerned primarily with profit). There is the issue of whether decision-making responsibility should be moved up from the brand level to the product level. There is the perennial question of how to make the organization more market-responsive including the possibility of replacing product divisions with market-centered divisions. Finally, sales organizations often do not fully understand marketing. In the words of one vice-president of marketing: "It takes about five years for us to train sales managers to think marketing."

Marketing Systems Audit

A full marketing audit then turns to examine the various systems being used by marketing management to gather information, plan, and control the marketing operation. The issue is not the company's marketing strategy or organization per se but rather the procedures used in some or all of the following systems: sales forecasting, sales goal and quota setting, marketing planning, marketing control, inventory control, order processing, physical distribution, new products development, and product pruning.

The marketing audit may reveal that marketing is being carried on without adequate systems of planning, implementation, and control. An audit of a consumer products division of a large company revealed that decisions about which products to carry and which to eliminate were made by the head of the division on the basis of his intuitive feeling with little information or analysis to guide the decisions. The auditor recommended the introduction of a new product screening system for new products and an improved sales control system for existing products. He also observed that the division prepared budgets but did not carry out formal marketing planning and hardly any research into the market. He recommended that the division establish a formal marketing planning system as soon as possible.

Marketing Productivity Audit

A full marketing audit also includes an effort to examine key accounting data to determine where the company is making its real profits and what, if any, marketing costs could be trimmed. Decision Sciences Corporation, for example, starts its marketing audit by looking at the accounting figures on sales and associated costs of sales. Using marketing cost accounting principles,[2] it seeks to measure the marginal profit contribution of different products, end user segments, marketing channels, and sales territories.

We might argue that the firm's own controller or accountant should do the job of providing management with the results of marketing cost analysis. A handful of firms have created the job position of marketing controllers who report to financial controllers and spend their time looking at the productivity and validity of various marketing costs. Where an organization is doing a good job of marketing cost analysis, it does not need a marketing auditor to study the same. But most companies do not do careful marketing cost analysis. Here a marketing auditor can pay his way by simply exposing certain economic and cost relations which indicate waste or conceal unexploited marketing opportunities.

Zero-based budgeting[3] is another tool for investigating and improving marketing productivity. In normal budgeting, top management allots to each business unit a percentage increase (or decrease) of what it got last time. The question is not raised whether that basic budget level still makes sense. The manager of an operation should be asked what he would basically need if he started his operation from scratch and what it would cost? What would he need next and what would it cost? In this way, a budget is built from the ground up reflecting the true needs of the operation. When this was applied to a technical sales group within a large industrial goods company, it became clear that the company had three or four extra technical salesmen on its payroll. The manager admitted to the redundancy but argued if a business upturn came, these men would be needed to tap the potential. In the meantime, they were carried on the payroll for two years in the expectation of a business upturn.

Marketing Function Audit
The work done to this point might begin to point to certain key marketing functions which are performing poorly. The auditor might spot, for example, sales force problems that go very deep. Or he might observe that advertising budgets are prepared in an arbitrary fashion and such things as advertising themes, media, and timing are not evaluated for their effectiveness. In these and other cases, the issue becomes one of notifying management of the desirability of one or more marketing function audits if management agrees.

WHICH COMPANIES CAN BENEFIT MOST FROM A MARKETING AUDIT?

All companies can benefit from a competent audit of their marketing operations. However, a marketing audit is likely to yield the highest payoff in the following companies and situations:

Production-Oriented and Technical-Oriented Companies. Many manufacturing companies have their start in a love affair with a certain product. Further products are added that appeal to the technical inter-ests of management, usually with insufficient attention paid to their market potential. The feeling in these companies is that marketing is paid to sell what the company decides to make. After some failures with its "better mousetraps," management starts getting interested in shifting to a market orientation. But this calls for more than a simple declaration by top management to study and serve the customer's needs. It calls for a great number of organizational and attitudinal changes that must be introduced carefully and convincingly. An auditor can perform an important service in recognizing that a company's problem lies in its production orientation, and in guiding management toward a market orientation.

Troubled Divisions. Multidivision companies usually have some troubled divisions. Top management may decide to use an auditor to assess the situation in a troubled division rather than rely solely on the division management's interpretation of the problem.

High Performing Divisions. Multidivision companies might want an audit of their top dollar divisions to make sure that they are reaching their highest potential, and are not on the verge of a sudden reversal. Such an audit may also yield insights into how to improve marketing in other divisions.

Young Companies. Marketing audits of emerging small companies or young divisions of large companies can help to lay down a solid marketing approach at a time when management faces a great degree of market inexperience.

Nonprofit Organizations. Administrators of colleges, museums, hospitals, social agencies, and churches are beginning to think in marketing terms, and the marketing audit can serve a useful educational as well as diagnostic purpose.

WHAT ARE THE PROBLEMS AND PITFALLS OF MARKETING AUDITS?

While the foregoing has stressed the positive aspects of marketing audits and their utility in a variety of situations, it is important to note some of the problems and pitfalls of the marketing audit process. Problems can occur in the objective-setting step, the data collection step, or the report presentation step.

Setting Objectives

When the marketing audit effort is being designed by the auditor and the company officer who commissioned the audit, several problems will be encountered. For one thing, the objectives set for the audit are based upon the company officer's and auditor's best *a priori* notions of what the key problem areas are for the audit to highlight. However, new problem areas may emerge once the auditor begins to learn more about the company. The original set of objectives should not constrain the auditor from shifting his priorities of investigation.

Similarly, it may be necessary for the auditor to use different sources of information than envisioned at the start of the audit. In some cases this may be because some information sources he had counted on became unavailable. In one marketing audit, the auditor had planned to speak to a sample of customers for the company's electro-mechanical devices, but the company officer who hired him would not permit him to do so. In other cases, a valuable new source of information may arise that was not recognized at the start of the audit. For example, the auditor for an air brake system manufacturer found as a valuable source of market intelligence a long-established manufacturers' representatives firm that approached the company after the audit had begun.

Another consideration at the objective-setting stage of the audit is that the management most affected by the audit must have full knowledge of the purposes and scope of the audit. Audits go much more smoothly when the executive who calls in the auditor either brings the affected management into the design stage, or at least has a general introductory meeting where the auditor explains his procedures and answers questions from the people in the affected business.

Data Collection

Despite reassurances by the auditor and the executive who brought him in, there will still be some managers in the affected business who will feel threatened by the auditor. The auditor must expect this, and realize that an individual's fears and biases may color his statements in an interview.

From the onset of the audit, the auditor must guarantee and maintain confidentiality of each individual's comments. In many audits, personnel in the company will see the audit as a vehicle for unloading their negative feelings about the company or other individuals. The auditor can learn a lot from these comments, but he must protect the individuals who make them. The auditor must question interviewees in a highly professional manner to build their confidence in him, or else they will not be entirely honest in their statements.

Another area of concern during the information collection step is the degree to which the company executive who brought in the auditor will try to guide the audit. It will be necessary for this officer and the auditor to strike a balance in which the executive provides some direction, but not too much. While overcontrol is the more likely excess of the executive, it is possible to undercontrol. When the auditor and the company executive do not have open and frequent lines of communication during the audit, it is possible that the auditor may place more emphasis on some areas and less on others than the executive might have desired. Therefore, it is the responsibility of both the auditor and the executive who brought him in to communicate frequently during the audit.

Report Presentation

One of the biggest problems in marketing auditing is that the executive who brings in the auditor, or the people in the business being audited, may have higher expectations about what the audit will do for the company than the actual report seems to offer. In only the most extreme circumstances will the auditor develop surprising panaceas or propose startling new opportunities for the company. More likely, the main value of his report will be that it places priorities on ideas and directions for the company, many of which have already been considered by some people within the audited organization. In most successful audits, the auditor, in his recommendations, makes a skillful combination of his general and technical marketing background (e.g., designs of salesman's compensation systems, his ability to measure the size and potential of markets) with some opportunistic ideas that people in the audited organization have already considered, but do not know how much importance to place upon them. However, it is only in the company's implementation of the recommendations that the payoff to the company will come.

Another problem at the conclusion of the audit stems from the fact that most audits seem to result in organizational changes. Organizational changes are a common outcome because the audit usually identifies new tasks to be accomplished and new tasks demand people to do them. One thing the auditor and the executive who

brought him in must recognize, however, is that organizational promotions and demotions are exclusively the executive's decision. It is the executive who has to live with the changes once the auditor has gone, not the auditor. Therefore, the executive should not be lulled into thinking that organizational moves are any easier because the auditor may have recommended them.

The final problem, and this is one facing the auditor, is that important parts of an audit may be implemented incorrectly, or not implemented at all, by the executive who commissioned the audit. Non-implementation of key parts of the audit undermines the whole effectiveness of the audit.

SUMMARY

The marketing audit is one important answer to the problem of evaluating the marketing performance of a company or one of its business units. Marketing audits are distinguished from other marketing exercises in being *comprehensive*, *independent*, *systematic*, and *periodic*. A full marketing audit would cover the company's (or division's) external environment objectives, strategies, organization, systems, and functions. If the audit covers only one function, such as sales management or advertising, it is best described as a marketing function audit rather than a marketing audit. If the exercise is to solve a current problem, such as entering a market, setting a price, or developing a package, then it is not an audit at all.

The marketing audit is carried out in three steps: developing an agreement as to objectives and scope; collecting the data; and presenting the report. The audit can be performed by a competent outside consultant or by a company auditing office at headquarters.

The possible findings of an audit include detecting unclear or inappropriate marketing objectives, inappropriate strategies, inappropriate levels of marketing expenditures, needed improvements in organization, and needed improvements in systems for marketing information, planning, and control. Companies that are most likely to benefit from a marketing audit include production-oriented companies, companies with troubled or highly vulnerable divisions, young companies, and nonprofit organizations.

Many companies today are finding that their premises for marketing strategy are growing obsolete in the face of a rapidly changing environment. This is happening to company giants such as General Motors and Sears as well as smaller firms that have not provided a mechanism for recycling their marketing strategy. The marketing audit is not the full answer to marketing strategy recycling but does offer one major mechanism for pursuing this desirable and necessary task.

APPENDIX A—COMPONENTS OF A MARKETING AUDIT

The Marketing Environment Audit

I. *Macro-Environment*

Economic-demographic

1. What does the company expect in the way of inflation, material shortages, unemployment, and credit availability in the short run, intermediate run, and long run?
2. What effect will forecasted trends in the size, age distribution, and regional distribution of population have on the business?

Technology

1. What major changes are occurring in product technology? In process technology?
2. What are the major generic substitutes that might replace this product?

Political-legal

1. What laws are being proposed that may affect marketing strategy and tactics?
2. What federal, state, and local agency actions should be watched? What is happening in the areas of pollution control, equal employment opportunity, product safety, advertising, price control, etc., that is relevant to marketing planning?

Social-cultural

1. What attitudes is the public taking toward business and toward products such as those produced by the company?
2. What changes are occurring in consumer life-styles and values that have a bearing on the company's target markets and marketing methods?

II. *Task Environment*

Markets

1. What is happening to market size, growth, geographical distribution, and profits?
2. What are the major market segments? What are their expected rates of growth? Which are high opportunity and low opportunity segments?

Customers

1. How do current customers and prospects rate the company and its com-

petitors, particularly with respect to reputation, product quality, service, sales force, and price?

2. How do different classes of customers make their buying decisions?

3. What are the evolving needs and satisfactions being sought by the buyers in this market?

Competitors

1. Who are the major competitors? What are the objectives and strategies of each major competitor? What are their strengths and weaknesses? What are the sizes and trends in market shares?

2. What trends can be foreseen in future competition and substitutes for this product?

Distribution and dealers

1. What are the main trade channels bringing products to customers?

2. What are the efficiency levels and growth potentials of the different trade channels?

Suppliers

1. What is the outlook for the availability of different key resources used in production.

2. What trends are occurring among suppliers in their pattern of selling?

Facilitators

1. What is the outlook for the cost and availability of transportation services?

2. What is the outlook for the cost and availability of warehousing facilities?

3. What is the outlook for the cost and availability of financial resources?

4. How effectively is the advertising agency performing? What trends are occurring in advertising agency services?

Marketing Strategy Audit

Marketing objectives

1. Are the corporate objectives clearly stated and do they lead logically to the marketing objectives?

2. Are the marketing objectives stated in a clear form to guide marketing planning and subsequent performance measurement?

3. Are the marketing objectives appropriate, given the company's competitive position, resources, and opportunities? Is the appropriate strategic objective to build, hold, harvest, or terminate this business?

Strategy

1. What is the core marketing strategy for achieving the objectives? Is it a sound marketing strategy?

2. Are enough resources (or too much resources) budgeted to accomplish the marketing objectives?

3. Are the marketing resources allocated optimally to prime market segments, territories, and products of the organization?

4. Are the marketing resources allocated optimally to the major elements of the marketing mix, i.e., product quality, service, sales force, advertising, promotion, and distribution?

Marketing Organization Audit

Formal structure

1. Is there a high-level marketing officer with adequate authority and responsibility over those company activities

that affect the customer's satisfaction?

2. Are the marketing responsibilities optimally structured along functional product, end user, and territorial lines?

Functional Efficiency

1. Are there good communication and working relations between marketing and sales?
2. Is the product management system working effectively? Are the product managers able to plan profits or only sales volume?
3. Are there any groups in marketing that need more training, motivation, supervision, or evaluation?

Interface Efficiency

1. Are there any problems between marketing and manufacturing that need attention?
2. What about marketing and R&D?
3. What about marketing and financial management?
4. What about marketing and purchasing?

Marketing Systems Audit

Marketing information system

1. Is the marketing intelligence system producing accurate, sufficient, and timely information about developments in the marketplace?
2. Is marketing research being adequately used by company decision makers?

Marketing planning system

1. Is the marketing planning system well-conceived and effective?
2. Is sales forecasting and market potential measurement soundly carried out?
3. Are sales quotas set on a proper basis?

Marketing control system

1. Are the control procedures (monthly, quarterly, etc.) adequate to insure that the annual plan objectives are being achieved?
2. Is provision made to analyze periodically the profitability of different products, markets, territories, and channels of distribution?
3. Is provision made to examine and validate periodically various marketing costs?

New product development system

1. Is the company well-organized to gather, generate, and screen new product ideas?
2. Does the company do adequate concept research and business analysis before investing heavily in a new idea?
3. Does the company carry out adequate product and market testing before launching a new product?

Marketing Productivity Audit

Profitability analysis

1. What is the profitability of the company's different products, served markets, territories, and channels of distribution?
2. Should the company enter, expand, contract, or withdraw from any business segments and what would be the short- and long-run profit consequences?

Cost-effectiveness analysis

1. Do any marketing activities seem to have excessive costs? Are these costs

valid? Can cost-reducing steps be taken?

Marketing Function Audit

Products

1. What are the product line objectives? Are these objectives sound? Is the current product line meeting these objectives?
2. Are there particular products that should be phased out?
3. Are there new products that are worth adding?
4. Are any products able to benefit from quality, feature, or style improvements?

Price

1. What are the pricing objectives, policies, strategies, and procedures? To what extent are prices set on sound cost, demand, and competitive criteria?
2. Do the customers see the company's prices as being in line or out of line with the perceived value of its offer?
3. Does the company use price promotions effectively?

Distribution

1. What are the distribution objectives and strategies?
2. Is there adequate market coverage and service?
3. Should the company consider changing its degree of reliance on distributors, sales reps, and direct selling?

Sales force

1. What are the organization's sales force objectives?

2. Is the sales force large enough to accomplish the company's objectives?
3. Is the sales force organized along the proper principle(s) of specialization (territory, market, product)?
4. Does the sales force show high morale, ability, and effort? Are they sufficiently trained and incentivized?
5. Are the procedures adequate for setting quotas and evaluating performances?
6. How is the company's sales force perceived in relation to competitors' sales forces?

Advertising, promotion, and publicity

1. What are the organization's advertising objectives? Are they sound?
2. Is the right amount being spent on advertising? How is the budget determined?
3. Are the ad themes and copy effective? What do customers and the public think about the advertising?
4. Are the advertising media well chosen?
5. Is sales promotion used effectively?
6. Is there a well-conceived publicity program?

NOTES

1. Many useful checklist questions for marketers are found in C. Eldridge, *The Management of the Marketing Function* (New York: Association of National Advertisers, 1967).
2. See P. Kotler, *Marketing Management Analysis Planning and Control* (Englewood Cliffs, N.J.: Prentice-Hall, Inc., 1976), pp. 457–462.
3. See P. J. Stonich, "Zero-Base Planning—A Management Tool," *Managerial Planning*, July–August 1976, pp. 1–4.

The Globalization of Markets

Theodore Levitt

A powerful force drives the world toward a converging commonality, and that force is technology. It has proletarianized communication, transport, and travel. It has made isolated places and impoverished peoples eager for modernity's allurements. Almost everyone everywhere wants all the things they have heard about, seen, or experienced via the new technologies.

The result is a new commercial reality—the emergence of global markets for standardized consumer products on a previously unimagined scale of magnitude. Corporations geared to this new reality benefit from enormous economies of scale in production, distribution, marketing, and management. By translating these benefits into reduced world prices, they can decimate competitors that still live in the disabling grip of old assumptions about how the world works.

Gone are accustomed differences in national or regional preference. Gone are the days when a company could sell last year's models—or lesser versions of advanced products—in the less-developed world. And gone are the days when prices, margins, and profits abroad were generally higher than at home.

The globalization of markets is at hand. With that, the multinational commercial world nears its end, and so does the multinational corporation.

The multinational and the global corporation are not the same thing. The multinational corporation operates in a number of countries, and adjusts its products and practices in each—at high relative costs. The global corporation operates with resolute constancy—at low relative cost—as if the entire world (or major regions of it) were a single entity; it sells the same things in the same way everywhere.

Which strategy is better is not a matter of opinion but of necessity. Worldwide communications carry everywhere the constant drumbeat of modern possibilities to lighten and enhance work, raise living standards, divert, and entertain. The same countries that ask the world to recognize and respect the individuality of their cultures insist on the wholesale transfer to them of modern goods, services, and technologies. Modernity is not just a wish but also a widespread practice among those who cling, with unyielding passion or religious fervor, to ancient attitudes and heritages.

Who can forget the televised scenes during the 1979 Iranian uprisings of young men in fashionable French-cut trousers and silky body shirts thirsting with raised modern weapons for blood in the name of Islamic fundamentalism?

In Brazil, thousands swarm daily from pre-industrial Bahian darkness into exploding coastal cities, there quickly to install television sets in crowded corrugated huts and, next to battered Volkswagens, make sacrificial offerings of fruit and fresh-killed chickens to Macumban spirits by candlelight.

During Biafra's fratricidal war against the Ibos, daily televised reports showed soldiers carrying bloodstained swords and listening to transistor radios while drinking Coca-Cola.

In the isolated Siberian city of Krasnoyarsk, with no paved streets and censored news, occasional Western travelers are stealthily propositioned for cigarettes, digital watches, and even the clothes off their backs.

The organized smuggling of electronic equipment, used automobiles, western clothing, cosmetics, and pirated movies into primitive places exceeds even the thriving underground trade in modern weapons and their military mercenaries.

A thousand suggestive ways attest to the uniquity of the desire for the most advanced things that the world makes and sells—goods of the best quality and reliability at the lowest price. The world's needs and desires have been irrevocably homogenized. This makes the multinational corporation obsolete and the global corporation absolute.

LIVING IN THE REPUBLIC OF TECHNOLOGY

Daniel J. Boorstin, author of the monumental trilogy *The Americans*, characterized our age as driven by "the Republic of Technology [whose] supreme law . . . is convergence, the tendency for everything to become more like everything else."

In business, this trend has pushed markets toward global commonality. Corporations sell standardized products in the same way everywhere—autos, steel, chemicals, petroleum, cement, agricultural commodities and equipment, industrial and commercial construction, banking and insurance services, computers, semiconductors, transport, electronic instruments, pharmaceuticals, and telecommunications, to mention some of the obvious.

Nor is the sweeping gale of globalization confirmed to these raw material or high-tech products, where the universal language of customers and users facilitates standardization. The transforming winds whipped up by the proletarianization of communication and travel enter every crevice of life.

Commercially, nothing confirms this as much as the success of McDonald's from the Champs Elysées to the Ginza, of Coca-Cola in Bahrain and Pepsi-Cola in Moscow, and of rock music, Greek salad, Hollywood movies, Revlon cosmetics, Sony televisions, and Levi jeans everywhere. "High-touch" products are as ubiquitous as high-tech.

Starting from opposing sides, the

high-tech and the high-touch ends of the commercial spectrum gradually consume the undistributed middle in their cosmopolitan orbit. No one is exempt and nothing can stop the process. Everywhere everything gets more and more like everything else as the world's preference structure is relentlessly homogenized.

Consider the cases of Coca-Cola and Pepsi-Cola, which are globally standardized products sold everywhere and welcomed by everyone. Both successfully cross multitudes of national, regional, and ethnic taste buds trained to a variety of deeply ingrained local preferences of taste, flavor, consistency, effervescence, and aftertaste. Everywhere both sell well. Cigarettes, too, especially American-made, make year-to-year global inroads on territories previously held in the firm grip of other, mostly local, blends.

These are not exceptional examples. (Indeed their global reach would be even greater were it not for artificial trade barriers.) They exemplify a general drift toward the homogenization of the world and how companies distribute, finance, and price products.[1] Nothing is exempt. The products and methods of the industrialized world play a single tune for all the world, and all the world eagerly dances to it.

Ancient differences in national tastes or modes of doing business disappear. The commonality of preferences leads inescapably to the standardization of products, manufacturing, and the institutions of trade and commerce. Small nation-based markets transmogrify and expand. Success in world competition turns on efficiency in production, distribution, marketing, and management, and inevitably becomes focused on price.

The most effective world competitors incorporate superior quality and reliability into their cost structures. They sell in all national markets the same kind of products sold at home or in their largest export market. They compete on the basis of appropriate value—the best combinations of price, quality, reliability, and delivery for products that are globally identical with respect to design, function, and even fashion.

That, and little else, explains the surging success of Japanese companies dealing worldwide in a vast variety of products—both tangible products like steel, cars, motorcycles, hi-fi equipment, farm machinery, robots, microprocessors, carbon fibers, and now even textiles, and intangibles like banking, shipping, general contracting, and soon computer software. Nor are high-quality and low-cost operations incompatible, as a host of consulting organizations and data engineers argue with vigorous vacuity. The reported data are incomplete, wrongly analyzed, and contradictory. The truth is that low-cost operations are the hallmark of corporate cultures that require and produce quality in all that they do. High quality and low costs are not opposing postures. They are compatible, twin identities of superior practice.[2]

To say that Japan's companies are not global because they export cars with left-side drives to the United States and the European continent, while those in Japan have right-side drives, or because they sell office machines through distributors in the United States but directly at home, or speak Portuguese in Brazil is to mistake a difference for a distinction. The same is true of Safeway and Southland retail chains operating effectively in the Middle East, and to not only native but also imported populations from Korea, the Philippines, Pakistan, India, Thailand, Britain, and the United States. National rules of the road differ, and so do distribution channels and languages. Japan's distinction is its unrelenting push for economy and value enhancement. That translates into a drive for standardization at high quality levels.

Vindication of the Model T

If a company forces costs and prices down and pushes quality and reliability up—while maintaining reasonable concern for suitability—customers will prefer its world-standardized products. The theory holds, at this stage in the evolution of globalization, no matter what conventional market research and even common sense may suggest about different national and regional tastes, preferences, needs, and institutions. The Japanese have repeatedly vindicated this theory, as did Henry Ford with the Model T. Most important, so have their imitators, including companies from South Korea (television sets and heavy construction), Malaysia (personal calculators and microcomputers), Brazil (auto parts and tools), Colombia (apparel), Singapore (optical equipment), and, yes, even from the United States (office copiers, computers, bicycles, castings), Western Europe (automatic washing machines), Rumania (housewares), Hungary (apparel), Yugoslavia (furniture), and Israel (pagination equipment).

Of course, large companies operating in a single nation or even a single city don't standardize everything they make, sell, or do. They have product lines instead of a single product version, and multiple distribution channels. There are neighborhood, local, regional, ethnic, and institutional differences, even within metropolitan areas. But although companies customize products for particular market segments, they know that success in a world with homogenized demand requires a search for sales opportunities in similar segments across the globe in order to achieve the economies of scale necessary to compete.

Such a search works because a market segment in one country is seldom unique; it has close cousins everywhere precisely because technology has homogenized the globe. Even small local segments have their global equivalents everywhere and become subject to global competition, especially on price.

The global competitor will seek constantly to standardize his offering everywhere. He will digress from this standardization only after exhausting all possibilities to retain it, and he will push for reinstatement of standardization whenever digression and divergence have occurred. He will never assume that the customer is a king who knows his own wishes.

Trouble increasingly stalks companies that lack clarified global focus and remain inattentive to the economics of simplicity and standardization. The most endangered companies in the rapidly evolving world tend to be those that dominate rather small domestic markets with high value-added products for which there are smaller markets elsewhere. With transportation costs proportionately low, distant competitors will enter the now-sheltered markets of those companies with goods produced more cheaply under scale-efficient conditions. Global competition spells the end of domestic territoriality, no matter how diminutive the territory may be.

When the global producer offers his lower costs internationally, his patronage expands exponentially. He not only reaches into distant markets, but also attracts customers who previously held to local preferences and now capitulate to the attractions of lesser prices. The strategy of standardization not only responds to worldwide homogenized markets but also expands those markets with aggressive low pricing. The new technological juggernaut taps an ancient motivation—to make one's money go as far as possible. This is universal—not simply a motivation but actually a need.

THE HEDGEHOG KNOWS

The difference between the hedgehog and the fox, wrote Sir Isaiah Berlin in distinguishing between Dostoevski and Tolstoy, is that the fox knows a lot about a great many things, but the hedgehog knows everything about one great thing. The multinational corporation knows a lot about a great many countries and congenially adapts to supposed differences. It willingly accepts vestigial national differences, not questioning the possibility of their transformation, not recognizing how the world is ready and eager for the benefit of modernity, especially when the price is right. The multinational corporation's accommodating mode to visible national differences is medieval.

By contrast, the global corporation knows everything about one great thing. It knows about the absolute need to be competitive on a worldwide basis as well as nationally and seeks constantly to drive down prices by standardizing what it sells and how it operates. It treats the world as composed of few standardized markets rather than many customized markets. It actively seeks and vigorously works toward global convergence. Its mission is modernity and its mode, price competition, even when it sells top-of-the line, high-end products. It knows about the one great thing all nations and people have in common: scarcity.

Nobody takes scarcity lying down; everyone wants more. This in part explains division of labor and specialization of production. They enable people and nations to optimize their conditions through trade. The median is usually money.

Experience teaches that money has three special qualities: scarcity, difficulty of acquisition, and transcience. People understandably treat it with respect. Everyone in the increasingly homogenized world market wants products and features that everybody else wants. If the price is low enough, they will take highly standardized world products, even if these aren't exactly what mother said was suitable, what immemorial custom decreed was right, or what market-research fabulists asserted was preferred.

The implacable truth of all modern production—whether of tangible or intangible goods—is that large-scale production of standardized items is generally cheaper within a wide range of volume than small-size production. Some argue that CAD/CAM will allow companies to manufacture customized products on a small scale—but cheaply. But the argument misses the point. (For a more detailed discussion, see the insert, "Economies of Scope.") If a company treats the world as one or two distinctive product markets, it can serve the world more economically than if it treats it as three, four, or five product markets.

Why Remaining Differences?

Different cultural preferences, national tastes and standards, and business institutions are vestiges of the past. Some inheritances die gradually; others prosper and expand into mainstream global preferences. So-called ethnic markets are a good example. Chinese food, pita bread, country and western music, pizza, and jazz are everywhere. They are market segments that exist in worldwide proportions. They don't deny or contradict global homogenization but confirm it.

Many of today's differences among nations as to products and their features actually reflect the respectful accommodation of multinational corporations to what they believe are fixed local preferences. They *believe* preferences are fixed, not because they are but because of rigid habits of thinking about what actually is. Most executives in multinational corporations are thoughtlessly accommodating. They falsely presume that marketing means giving the customer what he says he wants rather than trying to understand exactly what he'd like. So they persist with high-cost, customized multinational products and practices instead of pressing hard and pressing properly for global standardization.

I do not advocate the systematic disregard of local or national differences. But a company's sensitivity to such differences does not require that it ignore the possibilities of doing things differently or better.

There are, for example, enormous differences among Middle East countries. Some are socialist, some monarchies, some republics. Some take their legal heritage from the Napleonic Code, some from the Ottoman Empire, and some from the British common law; except for Israel, all are influenced by Islam. Doing business means personalizing the business relationship in an obsessively intimate fashion. During the month of Ramadan, business discussions can start only after 10 o'clock at night, when people are tired and full of food after a day of fasting. A company must almost certainly have a local partner; a local lawyer is required (as, say, in New York), and irrevocable letters of credit are essential. Yet, as Coca-Cola's Senior Vice Presedent Sam Ayoub noted, "Arabs are much more capable of making distinctions between cultural and religious purposes on the one hand and economic realities on the other than is generally assumed. Islam is compatible with science and modern times."

Barriers to globalization are not confined to the Middle East. The free transfer of technology and data across the boundaries of the European Common Market countries

ECONOMIES OF SCOPE

One argument that opposes globalization says that flexible factory automation will enable plants of massive size to change products and product features quickly, without stopping the manufacturing process. These factories of the future could thus produce broad lines of customized products without sacrificing the scale economies that come from long production runs of standardized items. Computer-aided design and manufacturing (CAD/CAM), combined with robotics, will create a new equipment and process technology (EPT) that will make small plants located close to their markets as efficient as large ones located distantly. Economies of scale will not dominate, but rather economies of scope—the ability of either large or small plants to produce great varieties of relatively customized products at remarkably low costs. If that happens, customers will have no need to abandon special preferences.

I will not deny the power of these possibilities. But possibilities do not make probabilities. There is no conceivable way in which flexible factory automation can achieve the scale economies of a modernized plant dedicated to mass production of standardized lines. The new digitized equipment and process technologies are available to all. Manufacturers with minimal customization and narrow product-line breadth will have costs far below those with more customization and wider lines.

are hampered by legal and financial impediments. And there is resistance to radio and television interference ("pollution") among neighboring European countries.

But the past is a good guide to the future. With persistence and appropriate means, barriers against superior technologies and economics have always fallen. There is no recorded exception where reasonable effort has been made to overcome them. It is very much a matter of time and effort.

A FAILURE IN GLOBAL IMAGINATION

Many companies have tried to standardize world practice by exporting domestic products and processes without accommodation or change—and have failed miserably. Their deficiencies have been seized on as evidence of bovine stupidity in the face of abject impossibility. Advocates of global standardization see them as examples of failures in execution.

In fact, poor execution is often an important cause. More important, however, is failure of nerve—failure of imagination.

Consider the case for the introduction of fully automatic home laundry equipment in Western Europe at a time when few homes had even semiautomatic machines. Hoover, Ltd., whose parent company was headquartered in North Canton, Ohio, had a prominent presence in Britain as a producer of vacuum cleaners and washing machines. Due to insufficient demand in the home market and low exports to the European continent, the large washing machine plant in England operated far below capacity. The company needed to sell more of its semiautomatic or automatic machines.

Because it had a "proper" marketing orientiation, Hoover conducted consumer preference studies in Britain and each major continental country. The results showed feature preferences clearly enough among several countries (see *Exhibit 36–1*).

The incremental unit variable costs (in pounds sterling) of customizing to meet just a few of the national preferences were:

	£	s	d
Stainless steel vs. enamel drum	1	0	0
Porthole window		10	0
Spin speed of 800 rpm vs. 700 rpm		15	0
Water heater	2	15	0
6 vs. 5 kilos capacity	1	10	0
	£6	10 s	0 d
	$18.20 at the exchange rate of that time.		

Considerable plant investment was needed to meet other preferences.

The lowest retail prices (in pounds sterling) of leading locally produced brands in the various countries were approximately:

U.K.	£110
France	114
West Germany	113
Sweden	134
Italy	57

Product customization in each country would have put Hoover in a poor competitive position on the basis of price, mostly due to the higher manufacturing costs incurred by short production runs for separate features. Because Common Market tariff reduction programs were then incomplete, Hoover also paid tariff duties in each continental country.

How to Make a Creative Analysis
In the Hoover case, an imaginative analysis of automatic washing machine sales in each

Exhibit 36-1
Consumer Preferences as to Automatic Washing Machine Features in the 1960s

Features	Great Britain	Italy	West Germany	France	Sweden
Shell dimensions*	34"and narrow	Low and narrow	34" and wide	34" and narrow	34" and wide
Drum material	Enamel	Enamel	Stainless steel	Enamel	Stainless steel
Loading	Top	Front	Front	Front	Front
Front porthole	Yes/no	Yes	Yes	Yes	Yes
Capacity	5 kilos	4 kilos	6 kilos	5 kilos	6 kilos
Spin speed	700 rpm	400 rpm	850 rpm	600 rpm	800 rpm
Water-heating system	No†	Yes	Yes††	Yes	No†
Washing action	Agitator	Tumble	Tumble	Agitator	Tumble
Styling features	Inconspicuous appearance	Brightly colored	Indestructible appearance	Elegant appearance	Strong appearance

*34" height was (in the process of being adopted as) a standard work-surface height in Europe.
†Most British and Swedish homes had centrally heated hot water.
††West Germans preferred to launder at temperatures higher than generally provided centrally.

country would have revealed that:

1. Italian automatics, small in capacity and size, low-powered, without built-in heaters, with porcelain enamel tubs, were priced aggressively low and were gaining large market shares in all countries, including West Germany.
2. The best-selling automatics in West Germany were heavily advertised (three times more than the next most promoted brand), were ideally suited to national tastes, and were also by far the highest priced machines available in that country.
3. Italy, with the lowest penetration of washing machines of any kind (manual, semiautomatic, or automatic) was rapidly going directly to automatics, skipping the pattern of first buying hand-wringer, manually assisted machines and then semiautomatics.
4. Detergent manufacturers were just be-

ginning to promote the technique of cold-water and tepid-water laundering then used in the United States.

The growing success of small, low-powered, low-speed, low-capacity, low-priced Italian machines, even against the preferred but highly priced and highly promoted brand in West Germany, was significant. It contained a powerful message that was lost on managers confidently wedded to a distorted version of the marketing concept according to which you give the customer what he says he wants. In fact the customers *said* they wanted certain features, but their behavior demonstrated they'd take other features provided the price and the promotion were right.

In this case it was obvious that, under prevailing conditions, people preferred a low-priced automatic over any kind of manual or semiautomatic machine and certainly over higher priced automatics, even though the low-priced automatics failed to fulfill all their expressed preferences. The supposedly meticulous and demanding German consumers violated all expectations by buying the simple, low-priced Italian machines.

It was equally clear that people were profoundly influenced by promotions of automatic washers; in West Germany, the most heavily promoted ideal machine also had the largest market share despite its high price. Two things clearly influenced customers to buy: low price regardless of feature preferences and heavy promotion regardless of price. Both factors helped homemakers get what they most wanted—the superior benefits bestowed by fully automatic machines.

Hoover should have aggressively sold a simple, standardized high-quality machine at a low price (afforded by the 17% variable cost reduction that the elimination of £6-10–0 worth of extra features made possible). The suggested retail prices could have been somewhat less than £100. The extra funds "saved" by avoiding unnecessary plant modifications would have supported an extended service network and aggressive media promotions.

Hoover's media message should have been: *this* is the machine that you, the homemaker, *deserve* to have to reduce the repetitive heavy daily household burdens, so that *you* may have more constructive time to spend with your children and your husband. The promotion should also have targeted the husband to give him, preferably in the presence of his wife, a sense of obligation to provide an automatic washer for her even before he bought an automobile for himself. An aggressively low price, combined with heavy promotion of this kind, would have overcome previously expressed preferences for particular features.

The Hoover case illustrates how the perverse practice of the marketing concept and the absence of any kind of marketing

imagination let multinational attitudes survive when customers actually want the benefits of global standardization. The whole project got off on the wrong foot. It asked people what features they wanted in a washing machine rather than what they wanted out of life. Selling a line of products individually tailored to each nation is thoughtless. Managers who took pride in practicing the marketing concept to the fullest did not, in fact, practice it at all. Hoover asked the wrong questions, then applied neither thought nor imagination to the answers. Such companies are like the ethnocentricists in the Middle Ages who saw with everyday clarity the sun revolving around the earth and offered it as Truth. With no additional data but a more searching mind, Copernicus, like the hedgehog, interpreted a more compelling and accurate reality. Data do not yield information except with the intervention of the mind. Information does not yield meaning except with the intervention of imagination.

ACCEPTING THE INEVITABLE

The global corporation accepts for better or for worse that technology drives consumers relentlessly toward the same common goals—alleviation of life's burdens and the expansion of discretionary time and spending power. Its role is profoundly different from what it has been for the ordinary corporation during its brief, turbulent, and remarkably protean history. It orchestrates the twin vectors of technology and globalization for the world's benefit. Neither fate, nor nature, nor God but rather the necessity of commerce created this role.

In the United States two industries became global long before they were consciously aware of it. After over a generation of persistent and acrimonious labor shutdowns, the United Steelworkers of America have not called an industrywide strike since 1959; the United Auto Workers have not shut down General Motors since 1970. Both unions realize that they have become global—shutting down all or most of U.S. manufacturing would not shut out U.S. customers. Overseas suppliers are there to supply the market.

Cracking the Code of Western Markets

Since the theory of the marketing concept emerged a quarter of a century ago, the more managerially advanced corporations have been eager to offer what customers clearly wanted rather than what was merely convenient. They have created marketing departments supported by professional market researchers of awesome and often costly proportions. And they have proliferated extraordinary numbers of operations and product lines—highly tailored product and delivery systems for many different markets, market segments, and nations.

Significantly, Japanese companies operate almost entirely without marketing departments or market research of the kind so prevalent in the West. Yet, in the colorful words of General Electric's chairman John F. Welch, Jr., the Japanese, coming from a small cluster of resource-poor islands, with an entirely alien culture and an almost impenetrably complex language, have cracked the code of Western markets. They have done it not by looking with mechanistic thoroughness at the way markets are different but rather by searching for meaning with a deeper wisdom. They have discovered the one great thing all markets have in common—an overwhelming desire for dependable, world-standard modernity in all things, at aggressively low prices. In response, they deliver irresistible value everywhere, attracting people with products that market-research technocrats described with superficial certainty as being unsuitable and uncompetitive.

The wider a company's global reach, the greater the number of regional and national preferences it will encounter for certain product features, distribution systems, or promotional media. There will always need to be some accommodation to differences. But the widely prevailing and often unthinking belief in the immutability of these differences is generally mistaken. Evidence of business failure because of lack of accommodation is often evidence of other shortcomings.

Take the case of Revlon in Japan. The company unnecessarily alienated retailers and confused customers by selling world-standardized cosmetics only in elite outlets; then it tried to recover with low-priced world-standardized products in broader distribution, followed by a change in the company president and cutbacks in distribution as costs rose faster than sales. The problem was not that Revlon didn't understand the Japanese market; it didn't do the job right, wavered in its programs, and was impatient to boot.

By contrast, the Outboard Marine Corporation, with imagination, push, and persistence, collapsed long-established three-tiered distribution channels in Europe into a more focused and controllable two-step system—and did so despite the vociferous warnings of local trade groups. It also reduced the number and types of retail outlets. The result was greater improvement in credit and product-installation service to customers, major cost reductions, and sales advances.

In its highly successful introduction of Contac 600 (the timed-release decongestant) into Japan, SmithKline Corporation used 35 wholesalers instead of the 1,000-plus that established practice required. Daily contacts with the wholesalers and key retailers, also in violation of established practice, supplemented the plan, and it worked.

Denied access to established distribution institutions in the United States, Komatsu, the Japanese manufacturer of lightweight farm machinery, entered the market through over-the-road construction equipment dealers in rural areas of the Sunbelt, where farms are smaller, the soil sandier and easier to work. Here inexperienced distributors were able to attract customers on the basis of Komatsu's product and price appropriateness.

In cases of successful challenge to prevailing institutions and practices, a combination of product reliability and quality, strong and sustained support systems, aggressively low prices, and sales-compensation packages, as well as audacity and implacability, circumvented, shattered, and transformed very different distribution systems. Instead of resentment, there was admiration.

Still, some differences between nations are unyielding, even in a world of microprocessors. In the United States almost all manufacturers of microprocessors check them for reliability through a so-called parallel system of testing. Japan prefers the totally different sequential testing system. So Teradyne Corporation, the world's largest producer of microprocessor test equipment, makes one line for the United States and one for Japan. That's easy.

What's not so easy for Teradyne is to know how best to organize and manage, in this instance, its marketing effort. Companies can organize by product, region, function, or by using some combination of these. A company can have separate marketing organizations for Japan and for the United States, or it can have separate product groups, one working largely in Japan and the other in the United States. A single manufacturing facility or marketing operation might service both markets, or a company might use separate marketing operations for each.

Questions arise if the company organizes by product. In the case of Teradyne, should the group handling the parallel system, whose major market is the United States, sell in Japan and compete with the group focused on the Japanese market? If the company organizes regionally, how do regional groups divide their efforts between promoting the parallel vs. the sequential system? If the company organizes in terms of function, how does it get commitment in marketing, for example, for one line instead of the other?

There is no one reliably right answer—no one formula by which to get it. There isn't even a satisfactory contingent answer.[3] What works well for one company or one place may fail for another in precisely the same place, depending on the capabilities, histories, reputations, resources, and even the cultures of both.

THE EARTH IS FLAT

The differences that persist throughout the world despite its globalization affirm an ancient dictum of economics—that things are driven by what happens at the margin, not at the core. Thus, in ordinary competitive analysis, what's important is not the average price but the marginal price; what happens not in the usual case but at the interface of newly erupting conditions. What counts in commercial affairs is what happens at the cutting edge. What is most striking today is the underlying similarities of what is happening now to national preferences at the margin. These similarities at the cutting edge cumulatively form an overwhelming, predominant commonality everywhere.

To refer to the persistence of economic nationalism (protective and subsidized trade practices, special tax aids, or restrictions for home market producers) as a barrier to the globalization of markets is to make a valid point. Economic nationalism does have a powerful persistence. But, as with the present almost totally smooth internationalization of investment capital, the past alone does not shape or predict the future. (For reflections on the internationalization of capital, see the insert, "The Shortening of Japanese Horizons.")

Reality is not a fixed paradigm, dominated by immemorial customs and derived attitudes, heedless of powerful and abundant new forms. The world is becoming increasingly informed about the liberating and enhancing possibilities of modernity. The persistence of the inherited varieties of national preferences rests uneasily on increasing evidence of, and restlessness regarding, their inefficiency, costliness, and confinement. The historic past, and the national differences respecting commerce and industry it spawned and fostered everywhere, is now subject to relatively easy transformation.

Cosmopolitanism is no longer the monopoly of the intellectual and leisure classes; it is becoming the established property and defining characteristic of all sectors everywhere in the world. Gradually and irresistibly it breaks down the walls of economic insularity, nationalism, and chauvinism. What we see today as escalating commercial nationalism is simply the last violent death rattle of an obsolete institution.

Companies that adapt to and capitalize on economic convergence can still make distinctions and adjustments in different markets. Persistent differences in the world are consistent with fundamental underlying commonalities; they often complement rather than oppose each other—in business as they do in physics. There is, in physics,

THE SHORTENING OF JAPANESE HORIZONS

One of the most powerful yet least celebrated forces driving commerce toward global standardization is the monetary system, along with the international investment process.

Today money is simply electronic impulses. With the speed of light it moves effortlessly between distant centers (and even lesser places). A change of ten basis points in the price of a bond causes an instant and massive shift of money from London to Tokyo. The system has profound impact on the way companies operate throughout the world.

Take Japan, where high debt-to-equity balance sheets are "guaranteed" by various societal presumptions about the virtue of "a long view," or by government policy in other ways. Even here, upward shifts in interest rates in other parts of the world attract capital out of the country in powerful proportions. In recent years more and more Japanese global corporations have gone to the world's equity markets for funds. Debt is too remunerative in high-yielding countries to keep capital at home to feed the Japanese need. As interest rates rise, equity becomes a more attractive option for the issuer.

The long-term impact on Japanese enterprise will be transforming. As the equity proportion of Japanse corporate capitalization rises, companies will respond to the shorter-term investment horizons of the equity markets. Thus the much-vaunted Japanese corporate practice of taking the long view will gradually disappear.

simultaneously matter and anti-matter working in symbiotic harmony.

The earth is round, but for most purposes it's sensible to treat it as flat. Space is curved, but not much for everyday life here on earth.

Divergence from established practice happens all the time. But the multinational mind, warped into circumspection and timidity by years of stumbles and transnational troubles, now rarely challenges existing overseas practices. More often it considers any departure from inherited domestic routines as mindless, disrespectful, or impossible. It is the mind of a bygone day.

The successful global corporation does not abjure customization or differentiation for the requirements of markets that differ in product preferences, spending patterns, shopping preferences, and institutional or legal arrangements. But the global corporation accepts and adjusts to these differences only reluctantly, only after relentlessly testing their immutability, after trying in various ways to circumvent and reshape them as we saw in the cases of Outboard Marine in Europe, SmithKline in Japan, and Komatsu in the United States.

There is only one significant respect in which a company's activities around the world are important, and this is in what it produces and how it sells. Everything else derives from, and is subsidiary to, these activities.

The purpose of business is to get and keep a customer. Or, to use Peter Drucker's more refined construction, to *create* and keep a customer. A company must be wedded to the ideal of innovation—offering better or more preferred products in such combinations of ways, means, places, and at such prices that prospects *prefer* doing business with the company rather than with others.

Preferences are constantly shaped and reshaped. Within our global commonality enormous variety constantly asserts itself and thrives, as can be seen within the world's single largest domestic market, the United States. But in the process of world homogenization, modern markets expand to reach cost-reducing global proportions. With better and cheaper communication and transport, even small local market segments hitherto protected from distant competitors now feel the pressure of their presence. Nobody is safe from global reach and the irresistible economies of scale.

Two vectors shape the world—technology and globalization. The first helps determine human preferences; the second, economic realities. Regardless of how much preferences evolve and diverge, they also gradually converge and form markets where economies of scale lead to reduction of costs and prices.

The modern global corporation contrasts powerfully with the aging multinational corporation. Instead of adapting to superficial and even entrenched differences within and between nations, it will seek sensibly to force suitably standardized products and practices on the entire globe. They are exactly what the world will take, if they come also with low prices, high quality, and blessed reliability. The global company will operate, in this regard, precisely as Henry Kissinger wrote in *Years of Upheaval* about the continuing Japanese economic success—"voracious in its collection of information, impervious to pressure, and implacable in execution."

Given what is everywhere the purpose of commerce, the global company will shape the vectors of technology and globalization into its great strategic fecundity. It will systematically push these vectors toward their own convergence, offering everyone simultaneously high-quality, more or less standardized products at optimally low prices, thereby achieving for itself vastly expanded markets and profits. Companies that do not adapt to the new global realities will become victims of those that do.

NOTES

1. In a landmark article, Robert D. Muzzell pointed out the rapidity with which barriers to standardization were falling. In all cases they succumbed to more and cheaper advanced ways of doing things. See "Can You Standardize Multination Marketing?" *HBR* November–December 1968, p. 102.

2. There is powerful new evidence for this, even though the opposite has been urged by analysis of PIMS data for nearly a decade. See "Product Quality Cost Production and Business Performance—A Test of Some Key Hypotheses" by Lynn W. Phillips, Dae Chang, and Robert D. Buzzell, Harvard Business School Working Paper No. 83–13.

3. For a discussion of multinational reorganization, see Christopher A. Bartlett, "MNCs Get off the Reorganization Merry-Go-Round," *HBR* March-April 1983, p. 138.

Looking at the Cultural Environment for International Marketing Opportunities

Susan Douglas and Bernard Dubois

The fast foods formula, one of the success stories of United States business, has met with a variety of responses in Europe. Wimpy has been highly profitable in the United Kingdom, but a dismal flop in France. McDonald's has achieved only moderate success in the French market and currently is watching the performance of its pilot outlets before opening sixty others as originally planned. Colonel Sanders' Kentucky Fried Chicken, on the other hand, has flourished in France, Germany, and the United Kingdom.[1]

What accounts for these differences? Why did hamburgers fail in France, and fried chicken, using essentially the same sales formula, succeed? Geographic, demographic, and economic factors are no doubt partly responsible, but they are by no means the total explanation. It could be said that hamburgers are unsuccessful in France because they are priced higher than their local competitor—*le sandwich jambon*—thinly sliced ham in a crusty French roll. But why does the Colonel Sanders formula work so well? It is more expensive than its competition—barbecued chicken roasted on a spit.

Underlying the varying fate of fast foods in Europe are the special characteristics of their respective consumer markets—distinctive living patterns, habits, and values—in other words, cultural influences. The importance of cultural influences in product positioning, packaging, communication, and distribution decisions is nothing new to marketers.[2] Attention has already been given to the role of culture on consumer behavior.[3] Yet, despite recognition of such factors, little attention has been paid to examining their implications for the development of marketing strategies, especially in international markets.

This neglect appears little justified, given the increasing interest in entering and

The authors wish to acknowledge the financial support of the Centre d'Enseignement Superieur des Affaires, Jouy-en-Josas, France, and the Marketing Science Institute, Cambridge, MA. Reprinted with permission from *Columbia Journal of World Business* (Winter, 1977).

expanding international markets. These current trends suggest the potential for market segmentation on a cross-national basis. In addition, further probing of cultural influences may provide ideas for international market development, product positioning, communication, and distribution.

The purpose of this paper is to highlight some of the ways in which cultural factors can influence consumer response patterns, and to illustrate, thereby, the need to consider cultural factors in planning international marketing strategies. First, some key elements of the cultural setting are outlined. Then, decision areas and examples of situations in which these play an important role are discussed. Finally, the potential advantages and insights to be gained from looking at cultural factors are summarized.

THE CULTURAL SETTING OF MARKET BEHAVIOR

At present there is no consistent theoretical perspective on the impact of cultural forces on behavior in general. Although cultural influence has been the subject of study in many of the social sciences from anthropology to cross-cultural psychology, each discipline adopts a different viewpoint, and often different definitions of cultural factors.[4] Consequently, the theoretical work in these fields offers no clearcut guidelines for investigation of cultural influences in relation to consumer behavior.

It is not our intention to examine and compare the different approaches. Instead, we will identify a number of recurring themes emerging from the various social sciences that have specific relevance for developing international marketing strategies and briefly outline them here.

Central to any culture or society is a common *set of values*, shared by its members

which determine what is considered socially acceptable behavior. In U.S. middle-class culture, for example, cleanliness is considered "next to godliness." Time and effort are devoted to activities such as taking daily baths or showers, brushing teeth, and washing clothes.[5] The success of Mr. Clean is a direct reflection of the potency of the cleanliness appeal in influencing consumer behavior.

Cultural values also determine the forms of *social organization*, such as the family, the education system, or the social class system which characterize a society. For example, the spirit of individualism and equality is an important factor in the emphasis on mass education and liberal child-rearing in the United States.[6] By contrast, in the United Kingdom, a child's right to independence and freedom of choice is less well-recognized. In England, breakfast cereal marketed in a package showing a grinning freckled youngster saying "Gee, Mom, it's great" was left on supermarket shelves, since British housewives rejected the direct appeal to children.[7]

The network of social organizations generates different overlapping *roles and status positions*.[8] In a family, a female can be a wife, mother, grandparent, or child. In a local neighborhood, she can be a community leader or inhabitant. Rules for appropriate behavior in each role are clearly established and often are important in attitudes toward products and their uses. The Swiss housewife, for example, considers the performance of household chores such as washing dishes or cleaning floors central to the housewife's role. She finds it difficult to accept the idea of labor-saving machines or commercial products, and she rejects commercial appeals emphasizing time and effort saved in performing household tasks.[9]

Social institutions also develop *conventions, rituals, and practices* governing behavior at different times, such as when entertaining family or friends, at graduation, or during holidays.[10] Rules relating to the exchange of gifts are closely governed by local conventions. Thus, while in the United States bringing a bottle of wine for the host at a dinner party is likely to please, in France such a gift would be considered an insult to the host's choice of wine, and a bouquet of flowers for the hostess is considered more appropriate.

All such values, behavioral norms, role expectations, and social conventions are transmitted to individuals through the *communication system* and language of their society or subgroup. Furthermore, communication occurs not only through words and language, but also through gestures, expressions and other body movements.[11] The door-to-door salesman takes the cue for his sales argument not only from the verbal response of the housewife, but also from the warmth of her smile and manner, and the rigidity of her stance and posture.[12]

The inherent values, social institutional arrangements, and behavior conventions conveyed through communication and language systems lead to the establishment of characteristic *daily-life routines and rhythms*. These provide the temporal setting in which consumption and purchasing activities and interchange between buyer and seller take place.

At the same time, the values, behavior, and life patterns of a society are not static and unchanging. Rather, they adapt and change over time as the physical, technological, and social environments change and new problems arise.[13] Industrialization, urbanization, and social mobility have all helped introduce new cultural patterns and values. Today dehydrated and frozen foods, supersonic airplanes, and oral contraceptives are all aspects of daily life unheard of fifty or sixty years ago.

The cultural setting thus provides a basic framework for social interaction. Founded on a core of common values and behavioral norms, it forms an important cohesive element among individual members of a society.

IMPLICATIONS FOR INTERNATIONAL MARKETING STRATEGY DECISIONS

The pervasive influence of cultural factors makes them an important consideration both in drawing up international marketing strategies and in planning the international marketing mix. Cultural factors not only provide opportunities and ideas at the strategic level, but they can operate as constraints in strategy formulation, as well.

In marketing products internationally, understanding cultural practices can be useful in assessing whether a single strategy can be effective in different national environments, or whether several strategies should be adopted, each geared to the distinctive cultural setting.

The development of blood donor programs provides an interesting example from the field of social marketing. Cultural differences in the significance of this gift and its role in the network of human relationships make the development of different approaches in different countries an absolute necessity.[14]

Among the Bantu of South Africa, for example, blood is an inviolable property which if taken away weakens the body for life. The white man's proposal to "take the blood" of the black is viewed as an aggression and is regarded with considerable suspicion and anxiety. Since there is widespread ignorance and fear of blood donations, attempts to recruit donors outside of "forced" institutional settings are largely unsuccessful.

In Western societies, educational programs have reduced similar fears and anxieties concerning blood donation by positioning the giving of blood within the system of social exchange as a means of redistributing scarce resources in society. In the United Kingdom sense of duty is strong, and donorship is viewed as a moral obligation to the community. Consequently, it has been possible to establish an almost entirely voluntary donor system, based on "free" gifts, unassociated with any exchange of money or with the guarantee of a future return in kind.

In other countries, giving blood is closely tied to community or social obligations. Financial incentives or personal and family interests have to be brought into play. In the USSR and other Eastern bloc countries, paid donors are recruited principally through institutions such as the armed forces at moderate rates of remuneration. In the United States family insurance plans have been developed which guarantee a regular blood supply for future family blood needs. These methods supplement blood obtained from paid donors, which is often of poor quality.

As the differences in blood donorship programs illustrate, there is a close link between attitudes toward giving blood and a society's value system. Appreciation of these complex forces is important in planning an effective program to produce adequate supplies of blood.

Investigation of cultural influences can also provide insights into international market segmentation. While at times, as in the blood donor case, specific national needs, tastes, or market response patterns merit specific marketing strategies, opportunities do exist for cross-national segmentation. Within different countries similar subculture groups—businessmen, senior citizens, teenagers, working wives—may possess similar consumption patterns because of shared problems and outlooks. In this case management may prefer to segment to subgroups *across* national boundaries.[15] For example, members of the teen cult throughout the world may provide an appropriate target for Coke, college teeshirts and blue jeans, pop records, fan magazines, and motorcycle accessories, as well as for beauty and grooming products for their specific complexion needs.[16]

Similarly, the Omega watch company selected an international business elite as the target market for its quartz digital watches. The product benefits this group sought were considered sufficiently homogeneous to justify a global marketing strategy. Two major themes with universal appeal to the target group were identified and used in a worldwide sales campaign. One was a "rational" appeal focusing on the mechanism of the watch and emphasizing the technology, reputation, and prestige of the Omega brand. The other was an "emotional" appeal, highlighting visual aspects and emphasizing the finish and beauty of the Omega Quartz.

The selection of appropriate bases for segmentation is no simple matter, however. The boundaries of cultural influence are not clearly marked out and are often overlapping.[17] A young French-Canadian, for example, may belong to the universal teenage cult and at the same time be influenced by his French-Canadian background. In some cases, he may behave like any other teenager. In others, his behavior may be typically French-Canadian as in showing resistance to "U.S. made" products.[18] In such cases management must weigh the advantages of focusing on common elements across national frontiers against those of concentrating on the particular characteristics of each national setting.

In addition, opportunities exist for transferring products and marketing ideas from one country to another even when the success of the transfer may, for cultural reasons, initially appear quite remote. Despite apparent incompatibility with cultural traditions, a product may be successfully marketed by an astute positioning strategy.

For instance, an English company was recently able to launch a mint chocolate candy with considerable success in France. While popular in the United Kingdom, the mint and chocolate flavor combination is alien to French food habits and evoked negative consumer reaction. As a consequence of this response, the product was positioned as an exclusive and expensive chocolate to be eaten after dinner as in the best British social circles. These traditions of the British upper class are valued in France and provided an appropriate platform for marketing the product.[19]

The "match" of a product or service with existing social practices and cultural conventions may, therefore, be subtle. As the mint chocolate example illustrates, much depends on the strategy used to launch the product or service and on a detailed planning of the marketing mix. Examples of how this can be done and of constraints imposed by cultural factors are more fully explored below.

PRODUCT POSITIONING

Understanding the significance and social symbolism of products in different cultural settings is often crucial in designing positioning strategies for foreign markets and for related decisions such as pricing or packaging.[20]

When Renault, one of the three major French automobile companies, launched the Renault 5, their latest entry in the European small car market, they were unable to use the same positioning strategy in all countries. The prototype campaign developed for the French market was based on an amusing "fun" image of a little "Supercar" adapted both to urban and highway driving. The

copy platform took the form of a cartoon strip, showing a bouncy chatty car with eyes and mouth drawn in on the headlights and bumper.

In some other European countries the same humorous image could not be used. The purchase of an automobile was perceived as a serious affair, so technical superiority had to be emphasized. In the German campaign the key features were the safety in the Renault 5 and its modern engineering and interior comfort. In Finland the emphasis was on solid construction and reliability. In Italy, where importance is attached to road performance, the advertising campaign focused on mechanical features, road handling capacity, and acceleration. The importance of creating an individual personality for the car dropped to second place, and the term "Little Supercar" was transformed into "la Cittadina del Mondo"—the citizen of the world.

In Holland, the product line policy had to be modified. The Renault 5 was positioned as a small, high quality, expensive automobile, but to the Dutch public the idea that a small automobile is cheap and mechanically inferior is deeply entrenched. Consequently management decided to go into the market first with the Renault 5TL, its top luxury model which has several options as standard equipment. Only later was a standard "stripped" model introduced.

DISTRIBUTION POLICY

The choice of distribution channels open to management in international markets can be restricted by cultural conventions. Rules concerning the admission of strangers and friends into the home, and a strict separation of business and social activities, can limit the effectiveness of door-to-door sales or other direct sales methods. In the U.S. the success of the Avon company stems in large measure from the use of housewives as sales ladies. These women organize sales meetings for Avon beauty products in their homes. In markets overseas, this formula has been less well received. In Europe it proved highly unsuccessful.[21] European women regard at-home sales calls, even by other housewives, as an instrusion of privacy. Equally, they are reluctant to sell to friends at a profit.

Organization of sales activities can be affected by the existence of different cultural entities and influences. A large French manufacturer ran into problems when management decided to use in various African countries the same organizational principles employed in Europe. Selling zones with equivalent market potential were marked out respecting local administrative boundaries. These failed to recognize that the countries contained a number of tribes, each with a particular individual responsible for buying in the community. The sales zones set up by the company overlapped with these tribal areas and caused much confusion in the assignment of salesmen's responsibilities.

COMMUNICATION POLICY

Of all the elements involved in marketing mix decisions, communication policy is the one where the impact of culture is often most keenly felt.

The choice of advertising themes and copy platform for international markets, in particular, gives rise to questions of appropriateness in different cultural environments. Even if a product is desired for similar target markets and serves the same needs, cultural differences in each national environment can render a universal appeal virtually useless.

The manufacturer of a product designed to soothe stomach pain, headaches,

and hangover symptoms found it necessary to emphasize different consumer benefits in various European countries, since the social acceptability of admitting to these symptoms varied.[22] In one group of countries, a certain pride in "hangover" life-style was apparent, and hence the product could be described as suitable "for the morning after." In another group, the occasional hangover was acceptable, so the product was marketed as appropriate for headaches and upset stomachs. For the third group, however, suffering from a hangover was unthinkable and the product had to be sold as a remedy for stomach upsets.

The connotations of words and symbols may require careful attention also. In its European advertising campaign, Chrysler-France translated the phrase "the Original," used in the U.K. market, by "the Example" in Germany. In Germany "Die Original" carries the connotation of being "peculiar." Equally, in Holland the slogan was turned into "Ahead of the Pack."

Similarly, awareness of the ways pictorial conventions are interpreted can be critical. An advertisement for brandy was tested in the South Bantu market. The advertisement showed a well-to-do couple in conversation, with a liquor bottle superimposed on the scene. The bottle was perceived by many Bantus as placed on the wife's head symbolizing her in her traditional domestic role. As a result, the advertisement failed to transmit the desired association of the brand with prosperous modern family life.[23]

Media choices must also be sensitive to cultural differences in the effectiveness of various modes of communication. BEA, the British airline, for example, found sufficient common ground among European air travellers to develop a pan-European advertising campaign. It used a reliability theme built around the reassuring image of a British pilot.[24] Initially, print media were emphasized in all countries, with considerable success throughout Europe with the exception of Italy. Investigation revealed that print media diminished considerably the campaign's impact in Italy because of the greater importance of verbal communication to Italians. A number of changes in media scheduling resulted in a dramatic increase in effectiveness.

CONCLUSION

The investigation of cultural influences on market behavior can provide insights and opportunities for international market development and segmentation strategies, as well as clues concerning the pitfalls in positioning, distribution, and communication policies. In particular, exploration of culture and the dynamics of cultural change can aid in these ways:

- Identifying opportunities for the transfer of products, services, and marketing strategies developed in one national culture or segment to another by comparing and examining similarities in needs and problems in each environment and projecting their evolutionary trends.
- Designing the most effective strategies for various national cultures and assessing the need to tailor those strategies to particular cultural factors.

Despite this rich potential, the study of cultural influences and the subtle ways in which they channel and pattern market behavior has been largely neglected. Yet, in an age of growing involvement in foreign markets, examination and mastery of these factors should command increased attention from management in designing strategies for the international marketplace.

NOTES

1. "Disaster Hits Euorpe—also Wimpy," *Advertising Age* (June 4, 1973), pp. 22, 33.

2. Maneck S. Wadia, "The Concept of Culture," *Journal of Retailing*, 4, No. 1 (Spring 1965), pp. 21–29; and Charles Winick, "Anthropology's Contributions to Marketing," *Journal of Marketing*, 25, No. 5 (July 1961), pp. 53–60.

3. S. H. Britt, "Standardizing Marketing for the International Market," *The Columbia Journal of World Business*, 9, No. 1 (Winter 1974), pp. 39–45; Susan P. Douglas, "Cross-Cultural Comparisons and Consumer Stereotypes," *Journal of Consumer Research*, 3, No. 1 (June 1976), pp. 12–20; Walter A. Henry, "Cultural Values Do Correlate with Consumer Behavior," *Journal of Marketing Research*, 13 (May 1976), pp. 121–27; Sidney J. Levy, "Social Class and Consumer Behavior," in *On Knowing the Consumer*, Joseph W. Newman, ed. (New York: John Wiley, 1966); Montrose Sommers and Jerome Kernan, "Why Products Flourish Here, Fizzle There," *Columbia Journal of World Business*, 2, No. 2 (March–April 1967), pp. 89–97; and Donald E. Vinson, Jerome E. Scott, and Lawrence M. Lamont, "The Role of Personal Values in Marketing and 'Consumer Behavior'," *Journal of Marketing*, 41, No. 2 (April 1977), pp. 44–50.

4. Kroeber and Kluckhohn (1952) in their landmark study identified 164 definitions and were sufficiently dissatisfied with all of them to add a 165th. Alfred L. Kroeber and Clyde Kluckhohn, *Culture: A Critical Review of Concepts and Definitions*, Anthropological Papers, Peabody Museum, No. 4 (1952).

5. James P. Spradley and David W. McCurdy, *Anthropology: The Culture Perspective* (New York: John Wiley, 1975).

6. D. Yankelovich, "What New Life-Style Means to Market Planners," *Marketing Communications*, 299, No. 6 (June 1971), pp. 38–45; and Cora Dubois, "The Dominant Value Profile of American Culture," *American Anthropologist*, 57, No. 6 (December 1955), pp. 1232–39.

7. David A. Ricks, Jeffrey S. Arpan, and Marilyn J. Fu, "Pitfalls in Advertising Overseas," *Journal of Advertising Research*, 14, No. 6 (December 1974), pp. 47–51.

8. Ralph Linton, *The Cultural Background of Personality* (New York: Appleton-Century-Crofts, Inc., 1945); and Theodore R. Sarbin and Vernon L. Allen, "Role Theory," in *The Handbook of Social Psychology*, Gardner Lindzey and Elliot Aronson, eds. (Reading, Mass.: Addison Wesley, 1969).

9. Similar examples can be found in Ernest Dichter, "The World Customer," *Harvard Business Review*, 40, No. 4 (July–August 1962), pp. 113–22.

10. Claude Levi-Strauss, "The Principle of Reciprocity," in *Sociological Theory*, Lewis A. Coser and Bernard Rosenberg, eds. (New York: Macmillan Co., 1965); Marcel Mauss, *The Gift* (London: Cohen & West, 1954); and Barry Schwarz, "The Social Psychology of the Gift," *American Journal of Sociology*, 7, No. 1 (July 1967), pp. 1–11.

11. Ray L. Birdwhistell, *Kinesics and Control* (Philadelphia: University of Pennsylvania, 1970).

12. Lynn M. Buller, "The Encyclopedia Game," in *Life Styles—Diversity in American Society*, Saul D. Feldman and Gerald W. Thielbar, eds. (Boston, Mass.: Little, Brown & Co., 1975), pp. 74–86.

13. E. Hagen, *On the Theory of Social Change* (Homewood, Ill: Dorsey Press, 1962); and Everett M. Rogers and F. Floyd Shoemaker, *Communication of Innovations* (New York: Free Press, 1971).

14. Richard M. Titmuss, *The Gift Relationship* (New York: Allen and Unwin, 1971).

15. Yoram Wind and Susan Douglas, "Segmenting International Markets," *European Journal of Marketing*, 6, No. 1 (Spring 1972), pp. 17–25.

16. Melvin Helitzer and Carl Hegel, *The Youth Market: Its Dimensions, Influence, and Opportunities for You* (New York: Media Books, 1970).

17. Al Kroeber, *Anthropology* (New York: Harcourt, Brace and World, 1948); and Frederick D. Sturdivant, "Subculture Theory: Poverty, Minorities, and Marketing," in *Consumer Behavior: Theoretical Sources*, Scott Ward and Thomas S. Robertson, eds. (Englewood Cliffs, N.J.: Prentice-Hall, 1973).

18. M. A. Bouraoni, "Living Next Door to an Elephant: Canadian Reactions to the American Ethos," in *Life Styles—Diversity in American Society*, Saul Feldman and Gerald W. Thielbar, eds. (Boston, Mass.: Little, Brown & Co., 1975).

19. Peter M. Kraushar, "The Cost Effectiveness of Market Research with Particular Applications to Search for New Product Ideas in Fast Moving Consumer Goods," *Proceedings of ESOMAR Congress, Main Sessions*, Hamburg, ESOMAR, 1974.

20. S. J. Levy, "Symbols for Sale," *Harvard Business Review*, 37, No. 4 (July–August 1959), pp. 117–24; and S. J. Levy, "Myth and Meaning in Marketing," in *New Marketing for Social and Economic Progress, Marketing's Contributions to the Firm and to Society: Combined Proceedings*, Ronald C. Curhan, ed. (Chicago: American Marketing Association, 1974), pp. 555–58.

21. "Avon on Products: Is Its Beauty Only Skin Deep?" *Forbes* (July 1, 1973), pp. 20–27; and "German Cosmetics Thrive: Avon Hikes Budget 70%," *Advertising Age* (June 27, 1977), p. 2.

22. M.R.C. Lovell, "Examining the Multi-National Consumer," *Developments in Consumer Psychology*, ESOMAR Seminar, Maidenhead, ESOMAR, 1973.

23. A. P. Van der Reis, *Some Aspects of the Acceptability of Particular Photographic Models to the Bantu* (Pretoria: Bureau of Market Research, University of South Africa, 1972).

24. Lovell, *op. cit.*

Problems and Challenges in Social Marketing

Paul N. Bloom and William D. Novelli

INTRODUCTION

Much has been written about social marketing since Kotler and Zaltman (1971) introduced the concept a decade ago. The literature has contained extended discussions about the definition of social marketing (Lazer and Kelley 1973, Sheth and Wright 1974), the ethics of social marketing (Laczniak, Lusch, and Murphy 1979), the appropriateness of broadening the marketing discipline to include social marketing (Luck 1974), and the potential of applying various social science theories in social marketing contexts (Swinyard and Ray 1977). In addition, several case studies of social marketing efforts have been reported (Blakely, Schutz, and Harvey 1977, Gutman 1978). However, there have been few attempts (Rothschild 1979) to move beyond the reporting of case

studies toward the development of general knowledge about social marketing, including knowledge about the problems most organizations tend to find in applying conventional marketing approaches in social programs.

This article identifies a set of general problems that confront practitioners who attempt to transfer the marketing approaches used to sell toothpaste and soap to promote concepts like smoking cessation, safe driving, and breast self-examination. An awareness of these problems should allow social agency administrators or their marketing advisors to formulate more workable and effective social marketing programs. While the authors believe strongly in the contribution marketing can make to social programs, they feel compelled to temper the enthusiasm that may have been shown for social marketing by pointing out the difficulties and challenges associated with its practice.

Note that the term "social marketing" is used throughout this article to mean "the design, implementation, and control of pro-

"Problems and Challenges in Social Marketing," Paul N. Bloom and William D. Novelli, Vol. 45 (Spring 1981), pp. 79–88. Reprinted from *Journal of Marketing*, published by the American Marketing Association.

grams seeking to increase the acceptability of a social idea or practice in a target group(s)" (Kotler 1975, p. 283). Consequently, social marketing is treated as an endeavor that can be engaged in by profit making organizations (e.g., a liquor company program encouraging responsible drinking), as well as by nonprofit and public organizations. It is also treated as an endeavor that generally encourages people to do something that will be beneficial to more than just themselves (Lovelock 1979). For example, responsible drinking, safe driving, and smoking cessation can all reduce health hazards for others or lower the insurance premiums of others. This article is concerned with the marketing of social ideas and behaviors by any organization to any target group.

The problems discussed here have come to the attention of the authors through work they have done with numerous social agencies and organizations. Problems are identified in eight basic decision making areas: market analysis, market segmentation, product strategy development, pricing strategy development, channel strategy development, communications strategy development, organizational design and planning, and evaluation. In each area an effort has been made to point out several problems encountered by social marketers that typically do not face the large commercial marketers who are the focus of most textbook examples. Admittedly, many of the cited problems may also confront small businesses and other less conventional marketers. But the discussion here will concentrate on how these problems manifest themselves for social marketers.

MARKET ANALYSIS PROBLEMS

A basic tenet of marketing is that an organization builds its marketing program using research it has gathered on the wants, needs, perceptions, attitudes, habits, and satisfaction levels of its markets. The good marketer is supposed to examine previous research on his or her consumers and, if necessary, conduct original consumer research in order to design maximally effective marketing strategies. Although large commercial marketers surely have difficulty accumulating valid, reliable, and relevant data about their consumers, the data gathering problems facing the social marketer tend to be far more serious. Social marketers typically find that:

• *They have less good, secondary data available about their consumers.* Social marketers can rarely go to the shelf to get fast, inexpensive guidance from reports on previous consumer studies. Most social organizations have done little consumer research, and what has been done has been weakened by small budgets and, consequently, poor samples and simplistic analysis procedures. Moreover, there are no syndicated services or panels available that can provide reasonably priced data on health behavior, safety behavior, conservation behavior, etc. Perhaps the best source of secondary data is the academic or scholarly literature. Journals such as the *Journal of Health and Social Behavior, American Journal of Public Health, Health and Society,* and *Social Service Review* can sometimes be helpful. But many academic works tend to be narrowly focused and hard to tap for actionable marketing ideas (especially by people with limited research backgrounds). Unfortunately, marketing academics—who have the capability of producing consumer studies that could be more readily used by social marketing planners—have given only limited attention to how consumers deal with social ideas and behaviors (Rothschild 1979, Swinyard and Ray 1977).

- *They have more difficulty obtaining valid, reliable measures of salient variables.* In doing primary data collection, social marketers must ask people questions about topics such as smoking, sickness, sex, and charity—topics that touch people's deepest fears, anxieties, and values. While people are generally willing to be interviewed about these topics, they are more likely to give inaccurate, self-serving, or socially desirable answers to such questions than to questions about cake mixes, soft drinks, or cereals. A recent study on how to ask questions about drinking and sex suggests that "threatening questions requiring quantified answers are best asked in open-ended, long questions with respondent-familiar wording" (Blair et al. 1977, p. 316). Using such methods can be extremely time-consuming and expensive.

- *They have more difficulty sorting out the relative influence of identified determinants of consumer behavior.* Social behaviors tend to be extremely complex and usually hinge on more than just one or two variables. The reasons patients drop out of antihypertensive drug therapy, for instance, may be related to an individual's limited self-discipline, lack of family support, drug side effects, physician/patient miscommunication, or any combination of these and other factors. It is extremely difficult for respondents to sort out these contributing variables in their own minds, and articulate them to a researcher in such a way that they can be recorded and analyzed for marketing planning. Furthermore, asking physicians to untangle patient behavior is often no more enlightening than asking the patients themselves. A recent study of physicians revealed, for example, that the reason patients were not on antihypertensive therapy was because they were not following the regimen that had been prescribed for them (U.S. Department of Health, Education, and Welfare 1979). This may be logical, in a self-evident sort of way, but not very helpful to the marketing planner.

- *They have more difficulty getting consumer research studies funded, approved, and completed in a timely fashion.* Social agencies typically have very limited funds, and the intangible output of a research study is often more difficult to justify to donors (e.g., Congress) than the more tangible output of a new program or publication. Furthermore, if the federal government is involved in some way in the proposed research, lengthy delays often will occur while the questionnaire and research design are approved by the agency doing the study, its Department, the Office of Management and Budget, and other parties. For example, the Office of Cancer Communications of the National Cancer Institute began the paperwork on a straightforward three stage study of knowledge, attitudes, and reported behavior related to breast cancer in April 1977. Red tape and the system delayed the completion of the analysis of the full study until July, 1980.

As a final comment on market analysis problems, it should be pointed out that the red tape that chokes and delays consumer studies can lead to some very unsound but highly original research tactics. One ploy is to conduct focus groups, always with fewer than nine respondents. This gets around the letter, if not the spirit, of the OMB clearance regulations concerning what constitutes a survey. However, this tactic, while it may provide some useful research hypotheses, can lead to misleading conclusions and poor planning. This is because the focus groups are often not followed by larger scale studies to quantify the preliminary findings and assess the hypotheses. The misuse of qualitative research as a substitute, rather than a precursor, to more definitive research appears to be a common problem among many social agencies.

MARKET SEGMENTATION PROBLEMS

The process of dividing up the market into homogeneous segments and then developing unique marketing programs for individual target segments (while perhaps ignoring certain segments) is fundamental to modern marketing. Market segmentation is generally viewed as being more productive than treating the entire market in an undifferentiated manner. Although market segmentation is widely utilized and accepted by most profit making and many nonprofit (e.g., universities, hospitals) marketers, social marketers find that:

• *They face pressure against segmentation, in general, and especially against segmentation that leads to the ignoring of certain segments.* The notion of treating certain groups differently or with special attention while perhaps ignoring other groups completely, is not consistent with the egalitarian and antidiscriminatory philosophies that pervade many social agencies (particularly those within government). The social marketer is, therefore, frequently asked to avoid segmenting or to try to reach an unreasonably large number of segments (Lovelock and Weinberg 1975). If a marketing plan has only a few target markets identified, requests will be made to add to the list of targets until, with the limited funds that usually are available, only a very broad and very shallow marketing effort is authorized. This will produce the opposite of the rifle approach the marketer normally attempts to bring to bear.

• An example of this problem occurred in a multiagency federal effort in 1978–79 to increase public understanding of the health risks of exposure to asbestos, and to persuade those exposed to get regular medical checkups, stop smoking, and seek prompt medical treatment for respiratory illness. The serious diseases associated with asbestos take from 15 to 35 years to develop, and workers exposed during World War II (especially ship yard workers) were identified as the primary target segment for the program. However, due to the mandates of some of the agencies involved, it became necessary also to target the effort to current workers. The characteristics of this segment differed substantially from the other, and throughout the planning and implementation of the program, there was a constant problem about whether to divide limited resources or simply take a general audience route.

• *They frequently do not have accurate behavioral data to use in identifying segments.* The data collection problems alluded to earlier impede segmentation attempts by making it difficult to separate users from nonusers. Utilizing self reports on behaviors like breast self-examination and contraceptive usage can be very misleading, and it may be impossible to obtain other behavioral measures (e.g., observational data).

• *Their target segments must often consist of those consumers who are the most negatively predisposed to their offerings.* Social marketers often segment on the basis of risk to the consumer. They will target their efforts at drivers who tend to avoid using seat belts, sexually active teenagers who tend to avoid using contraceptives, heavy smokers, etc. They may sometimes even target their efforts at segments facing greater legal risk, such as in a program recently formulated by William Novelli to persuade sheet metal contractors to recruit and accept more women into their field. This segmentation approach creates situations where social marketers face target markets having the strongest negative dispositions toward their offerings—the exact opposite of the situation faced by most commercial marketers. Moreover, as Rothschild (1979) has pointed out, these target markets are frequently highly involved with their negative feelings, making them much more resistant to changing their views than people who have negative attitudes toward low involved products like soap or bread.

PRODUCT STRATEGY PROBLEMS

Once the marketer has analyzed the market and determined target segments, he or she should then develop an offering that conforms closely to the desires of the target segments. Conventional marketers will typically adjust product characteristics, packaging, the product name, the product concept, and the product position to increase the likelihood of a sale to the target segments. However, social marketers find:

- *They tend to have less flexibility in shaping their products or offerings (Kotler 1975, Lovelock and Weinberg 1975).* They often find themselves locked into marketing a given social behavior that cannot be modified or changed. This could occur because the government might approve of only one way of doing the behavior. For example, social marketers may be able to market only one way to get a home insured against floods or one way to get a child immunized. On the other hand, they may be able to market several ways of quitting smok-

ing, getting physically fit, or conserving energy.

- *They have more difficulty formulating product concepts.* They frequently find that the product they are selling is a complex behavior which may, in some cases, have to be repeated over a considerable period of time. It therefore becomes difficult to formulate a simple, meaningful product concept around which a marketing and communications program can be built. Effective concepts like a squeezably soft toilet paper and an extra thick and zesty spaghetti sauce do not come readily to mind when thinking about selling behaviors such as drug therapy maintenance or use of an in-home colon-rectal cancer detection test (i.e., the hemocult test). In addition, the problems associated with doing consumer research (discussed above) tend to hinder product concept development.

- *They have more difficulty selecting and implementing long-term positioning strategies.* Assuming the social marketer has some ability to shape the offering and to formulate a relatively simple product concept, he or she may still have major problems selecting a product position that will be attractive and/or acceptable to the extremely diverse publics that impact on the typical social agency. The current dilemma of the Asthma and Allergy Foundation of America (AAFA) illustrates this problem. The new executive director wants to revitalize the agency at the national headquarters level, to strengthen the existing 13 chapters, and to add new chapters throughout the country. She sees several positioning options open to help AAFA achieve these objectives, including presenting AAFA as a service organization, a research organization, or a public education organization.

The best positioning approach is not clear, as each position has a positive appeal for some publics and a negative appeal for other publics. For instance, projecting a service position will probably help AAFA in its exchange relationships with patients and local chapter volunteers and personnel (who apparently favor this stance), but it might not be the best approach for attracting funds from donors or for generating public clamor for more congressional funding of research and public education.

Even if the social marketer can settle on a preferred positioning strategy, the implementation of this strategy over a lengthy period of time may be impossible. Social marketers frequently do not have the ability to communicate persistently and present a position—like Avis did with "We Try Harder"—for more than a few months. The result is often consumer confusion about what it is an agency or program is trying to accomplish. The short life of many positioning strategies is caused (in government agencies at least) by frequent budget shifts, sudden personnel changes, a desire to show that something new and different is being tried, and other forces. For example, the government rarely concentrates funds and effort on a single problem for an extended period, producing instead what seems like a disease of the month approach. A notable exception is the National High Blood Pressure Education Program, which has been unerring in its positioning for eight years and has made substantial progress in contributing to hypertension control in the United States (Ward 1978).

Because doing anything in the product strategy is difficult for social marketers, many will ignore this aspect of marketing planning and, instead, concentrate their efforts on developing advertising and promotion strategies for the product they have been told to sell. However, social marketers should recognize that although they may be unable to adjust the performance characteristics of their products, they may be able to adjust the perception characteristics of their products and achieve significant results. Through minimal amount of product testing research with consumers, and some creative concept development and positioning, social marketers can gain confidence that the signals being transmitted by their offerings are favorable. They can also avoid making the kind of product strategy mistake made by the Agency for International Development in a program designed to persuade Nicaraguan mothers to give their babies the proper treatment for diarrhea (a major cause of infant mortality). Problems occurred with this program because of lack of in-home product testing of the super lemonade (a rehydration solution) the program promoted. It was discovered after the program had begun, that the solution may not have been administered in some cases because some mothers who sampled it before giving it to their babies, thought it tasted bad. In addition, there was evidence that some women had difficulty measuring the ingredients and concocting the solution. The solution also caused the diarrhea to increase for a short time after first being administered, providing mothers with a potential signal that the product was ineffective or perhaps even harmful. In a new program in Honduras, extensive formative research, including product testing, is being applied (Smith 1980).

PRICING STRATEGY PROBLEMS

Marketers of most products and services find that the development of a pricing strategy involves primarily the determination of an appropriate (i.e., goal satisfying) monetary price to charge for an offering. On the other hand:

• *Social marketers find that the development of a pricing strategy primarily involves trying to reduce the monetary, psychic, energy, and time costs incurred by consumers when engaging in a desired social behavior.* Social marketers generally have much more complex objective functions than commercial marketers. They are primarily concerned with shifting birth rates, death rates, pollution levels, and the like, and are concerned with the financial consequences of their actions only to the extent that they want to insure their organization's financial viability. They do not price their offerings to maximize financial returns but instead try to price offerings to minimize any barriers that might be preventing consumers from taking desired actions. This task is made difficult because consumer research data are often not available to provide social marketers with information about the psychic, energy, and time costs consumers perceive as being associated with a particular action. In other words:

• *Social marketers have difficulties measuring their prices (Rothschild 1979).* In addition, the pricing task is made difficult because:

• *Social marketers tend to have less control over consumer costs.* Unlike commercial marketers who can readily change consumer costs by essentially adjusting monetary prices, social marketers often can do little to change the time costs involved with carpooling, the embarrassment costs involved with getting an examination for cervical cancer, or other nonmonetary costs. In some cases, all the social marketer can do is try to make sure that consumers perceive the various costs accurately and do not inflate them in their minds. In other

cases, however, the social marketer may at least be able to cut some red tape or eliminate other inconveniences to lower the price. This last strategy is being employed in the food stamp program of New York state. They have made it easier to become enrolled and have eliminated the necessity of putting up any money with food stamps in the retail stores. Additional strategies for lowering time costs are discussed in a recent paper by Fox (1980).

CHANNELS STRATEGY PROBLEMS

Developing a channels strategy usually gets an organization involved with selecting appropriate intermediaries through which to distribute its products or offerings, and formulating ways to control these intermediaries to make sure they behave in a supportive manner. Social marketers typically must distribute the idea of engaging in a social behavior and/or a place to engage in such behavior, rather than a tangible product. However, they find that, relative to more conventional marketers:

• *They have more difficulty utilizing and controlling desired intermediaries.* Social marketers often find that they cannot convince desired intermediaries, such as doctors or the television news media, to pass along and support an idea, nor can they control effectively what these intermediaries might say if they choose to cooperate. Control over clinics, community centers, government field offices, or other places where a social behavior might be performed or encouraged is also frequently lacking. Unfortunately, social marketers usually cannot provide incentives to desired intermediaries to get cooperation, as a business marketer would do, and they generally cannot afford to build their own distribution channels. To achieve a smoothly functioning distribution system of basically volunteers, they must rely primarily on the attractiveness of their offerings, the creativity of their appeals for assistance, and the quality of their intermediary training programs.

The problems associated with establishing, utilizing, and controlling distribution channels produce a major difference between social and more conventional forms of marketing. The following two examples illustrate just how serious these problems can be.

- The federal flood insurance program has had difficulty getting insurance companies' agents to add flood insurance to their product line. The agents have seen this insurance as being hard to learn about, hard to sell (with government forms and regulations to worry about), and low in profitability.

- A program designed to motivate physicians to teach their patients how to quit smoking ran up against the problem that, although the physicians wanted to cooperate, they did not know the most effective quitting skills, or benefits, or how to communicate them. It, therefore, became necessary to teach physicians how to teach patients—a task that was complicated by the beliefs held by many physicians that they are adept at all facets of patient management.

COMMUNICATIONS STRATEGY PROBLEMS

There are several approaches that marketers use to communicate with their target markets. These include advertising, public relations, sales promotion, personal contact,

and atmospherics. Social marketers, however, often find that their communications options are somewhat limited. As discussed in the previous section, social marketers sometimes find channels of distribution for their ideas unavailable or difficult to control. For instance:

- *They usually find paid advertising impossible to use.* This problem may arise because of advertising's cost or because of media fears of offending certain advertisers or audiences by carrying messages about controversial social issues. In addition, many voluntary organizations may see paid advertising as impossible to use because they fear the effects on all voluntary organizations. If the American Cancer Society pays for an antismoking campaign, then the media might ask the American Lung Association and others to pay for their campaigns also. Furthermore, government agencies may see paid advertising as impossible to use because they fear criticism about wasting taxpayer money and about having the media overly populated with government sponsored advertisements (e.g., military recruitment). Questions could arise about who controls the media if the government became the largest total advertiser.

- An inability to use paid advertising restricts many social marketers to the use of public service announcements. Since the competition for PSA time and space is heated, social marketers often find they cannot control the reach and frequency of their messages among their target segments. Audience coverage, therefore, becomes much more uncertain.

Social marketers face several other communications problems:

- *They often face pressure not to use certain types of appeals in their messages (Houston and Homans 1977, Lovelock and Weinberg 1975).* Donors and other influential parties may not want to see a social change organization cheapened by the use of hard sell, fear, or humor appeals. The use of hard sell and fear appeals may also be unwise when target audiences are strongly predisposed against a social behavior. These appeals could backfire and solidify a person's feelings against behaviors such as seat belt usage, smoking cessation, or responsible drinking. In general, an audience reaction of "they can't tell me how to run my life" is much more likely to confront a social marketer than a more conventional marketer.

- *They usually must communicate relatively large amounts of information in their messages.* Social marketers typically need to say more to consumers in a media message than commercial marketers. A complex social behavior may need to be described, along with the benefits of the behavior (i.e., a reason why) and a time and a place for acting. Particular emphasis must be given to presenting benefits, since the benefits of behaviors like reducing salt in the diet or lowering one's thermostat might not be as obvious or personal to people as the benefits of buying a new car or piece of clothing (Rothschild 1979). Equally important is a message conclusion, which tells in specific terms what (and where and when) the consumer should do next. The social marketer cannot be like most commercial marketers and assume that consumers know this (e.g., pick up a six pack at the store and drink it). Unfortunately, the need to provide large amounts of information forces many social marketing messages to close with the old standby, For more information, please call or write. . . .

- The need to communicate large amounts of information makes it imperative for social marketers to look beyond the use of public service announcements toward the use of nonadvertising channels of communication (Rothschild 1979, Mendelsohn 1973). One program that has clearly recognized this necessity is the breast cancer education program of the National Cancer Institute. They have recognized that communicating the benefits of doing breast self-examination is very problematical, since unlike many other preventive health behaviors (e.g., exercise, taking blood pressure medication), the payoff is perceived by many women as the discovery of sickness rather than the improvement of one's health. This program has, therefore, shifted its emphasis away from media messages toward more personal forms of communication using health care professionals and other credible intermediaries.

- *They have difficulty conducting meaningful pretests of messages.* Given the problems social marketers tend to have with selecting appeals and communicating desired behaviors, it would seem essential for careful pretesting to be done on social media messages. However, pretests of social messages run up against the same funding and measurement problems discussed earlier. For example, in a recent test of a message on the need to take mental patients out of institutions and accept them into our communities, few respondents gave expected (but socially unacceptable) comments such as: "I don't like the message. These people are dangerous and unpredictable and I don't want them in my neighborhood."

  Pretesting is also made less meaningful by the lack of any norms or standards against which newly tested social messages can be compared. Clearly, it would be instructive to the social marketer to know how his/her message performed compared to previously tested messages on measures of comprehension, recall, believability, personal relevance, etc. Fortunately, social marketers working in the health area can now get comparison data on pretest performances by using the newly established Health Message Testing Service. This service, funded and administered by the National Heart, Lung, and Blood Institute, National Cancer Institute, and several other federal agencies, has now tested more than thirty-five television and radio messages with samples of up to 300 individuals. The service invites randomly selected subjects from specified target audiences to view pilot television programs that have health messages and other commercials appearing within them. During an experimental period that is still underway, the service has been conducting pretests for public and nonprofit organizations at no charge. The data accumulated by the service are also available at no charge. A print testing capability is now being added to the service (Novelli 1978, Bratic and Greenberg 1980).[1]

ORGANIZATIONAL DESIGN AND PLANNING PROBLEMS

The well-managed marketing organization has a marketing person in a key position at the top of the organization chart and numerous well-trained marketing individuals throughout the organization. This organization has a carefully drawn marketing plan developed annually, with procedures set up to make sure the plan is implemented and monitored. However, social marketers typically find that while social organizations usually know something about management and organizational design, they rarely have an interest in setting up responsive marketing organizations with marketing planning and control procedures. Social marketers typically find that:

- *They must function in organizations where marketing activities are poorly understood, weakly appreciated, and inappropriately located.* Social organizations have a tendency to adopt marketing in small doses. The management may decide to try marketing by hiring a few employees or consultants with marketing backgrounds. These persons are generally assigned to work with public affairs or public information offices because management generally equates marketing with communications or promotion. The results the marketers achieve in these positions are quite limited, since they have little influence over program development and administration and must restrict themselves primarily to informing the public about the features of the program. Thus, social marketers are often programmed for mediocre performance from the very beginning. They cannot convince management to give marketing the prominence it needs to be effective, and they cannot earn their way to prominence through outstanding performance. This dilemma may continue to confront social marketers as long as physicians, lawyers, scientists, law enforcement specialists, social workers, and others who often dominate social agencies and organizations feel uncomfortable and unfamiliar with marketing.

- *They must function in organizations where plans (if any are developed) are treated as archival rather than action documents.* Social organizations (particularly those in government) do not feel the competitive pressures that the business world feels. Employees do not lose their jobs or gain promotions based on how well the organization does. Consequently, it is more difficult to get them to take the time and effort needed to formulate and follow plans. This, of course, can seriously impede the social marketing effort.

- *They must function in organizations that suffer from institutional amnesia.* In trying to put together a comprehensive marketing plan for a social organization, it often is impossible to get guidance for present efforts from information on how past strategies worked. Unlike many commercial organizations, social organizations frequently do not have information about the past results of using free samples, contests, price cuts, and so on. This kind of forgetting occurs in social organizations because they tend to keep poor records and have high employee turnover.

- Two individuals involved in the high intensity national antismoking efforts of the late 1960's and early 70s recently remarked to the authors that none of the experience or lessons learned then seem to be applied to current programs. "They're starting from zero," remarked one official, "as if the earlier programs never existed."

- *They must predict how both friendly and unfriendly competitors will behave.* Marketing planning is made difficult in all organizations by the need to predict how competitors will behave over a planning horizon. Social marketers face this difficulty as much as anyone. The marketer of a smoking cessation program must assess what the tobacco companies and their trade association are likely to do, while the marketer of a nutrition program must give thought to the future activities of the grocery manufacturers and their associations. But social marketers must also be concerned about the impact of a type of competition that commercial marketers rarely face—the friendly competition provided by other social organizations fighting for the same cause. Thus, in developing a marketing plan for the smoking cessation program of the National Cancer Institute, it becomes necessary to consider the poten-

tial actions of the National Heart, Lung, and Blood Institute, the U.S. Office of Smoking and Health, the American Cancer Society, the American Lung Association, the American Heart Association, and a host of others. Friendly competitors can help the social marketer in many ways, but they can also create fragmented efforts, funding problems, and other difficulties.

EVALUATION PROBLEMS

Evaluating the effectiveness of a marketing program is difficult for all marketers. One must determine measures of effectiveness and then develop a research design capable of isolating the role the marketing program has had in shifting those effectiveness measures. Naturally, social marketers face the same problems in doing evaluation studies as in doing market analysis studies (see above). They have serious problems with measurement and with getting support and approval for the research. In addition, social marketers find that:

- *They frequently face difficulties trying to define effectiveness measures.* Unlike business firms having quantitative objectives stated in terms of profitability, sales, or market share, social organizations may merely have vaguely stated mission or goal statements from which measures of effectiveness are difficult to extract (Houston and Homans 1977). Even after lengthy discussions with management, social marketers often have difficulty deciding whether a program is designed to create awareness of an issue, change people's behavior, save lives, or do something else. Beyond this it is hard to identify constructs or variables that should be monitored to indicate whether program objectives are being achieved. Should one examine, for example, smoking quitting rates or cigarette sales to evaluate the success of a smoking cessation program? Should one examine measures that indicate something about the secondary or unintended effects of such a program, such as data on the consumption of junk food and alcohol by people who are persuaded to quit smoking?

• *They often find it difficult to estimate the contribution their marketing program has made toward the achievement of certain objectives.* Although the field of evaluation research has become increasingly sophisticated and precise (for reviews see Rossi and Wright 1977, Phillips 1978, Bloom and Ford 1979), social marketing programs do not typically lend themselves to evaluation using the more interpretable research designs that have been identified in the literature. Using randomized experiments or quasi-experiments is hard to do in social marketing, not only because they tend to be expensive but also because social marketing programs are hard to compress into neat packages that can be delivered to some people or regions and not to others. It is easy, for example, for a press release intended for an experimental group to be picked up by the media serving a control group.

• As a result, much of the evaluation activity that has occurred with social marketing programs (see Bloom 1980 for a review) has taken the form of after only or before and after with no control group studies. While these types of studies can help to identify clearly ineffective programs and can provide management with an indicator that a program might be working, they cannot show an unambiguous cause and effect relationship between a program and an outcome. For instance, before and after studies have not been able to show that the sharp decline in hypertension related

deaths that have taken place during the course of the National High Blood Pressure Education Program can be definitely attributed to the program. However, to discover the true impact of this program might cost more money and trouble than it would be worth.

CONCLUSION

The relationship between social marketing and more conventional commercial marketing may be somewhat like the relationship between football and rugby. The two marketing games have much in common and require similar training, but each has its own set of rules, constraints, and required skills. The good player of one game may not necessarily be a good player of the other.

In this article we have attempted to document why social marketing is the more difficult game to master. While success in the battles over market share in industries like detergents or automobiles may call for equal or even greater stamina and perseverance, success in the social marketing arena requires greater ingenuity and imagination. In spite of this, social marketing efforts can succeed, particularly if the problems cited in this article are anticipated and dealt with in a creative and logical manner. Social marketing clearly provides a difficult but potentially rewarding challenge for members of the marketing profession.

NOTES

1. For further information about this service contact Health Message Testing Service, Office of Cancer Communications, National Cancer Institute, Bethesda, Maryland 20205.

REFERENCES

Blair, Ed et al. (1977), "How to Ask Questions About Drinking and Sex: Response Effects in

Measuring Consumer Behavior," *Journal of Marketing Research,* 14 (August), 316–21.

Blakely, Edward J., Howard Schutz, and Peter Harvey (1977), "Public Marketing: Policy Planning for Community Development in the City," *Social Indicators Research,* 4, 163–184.

Bloom, Paul N. (1980), "Evaluating Social Marketing Programs: Problems and Prospects," in *Marketing in the 80's: Changes and Challenges,* Richard P. Bagozzi et al., eds. , Chicago: American Marketing Association, 460–463.

———, and Gary T. Ford (1970), "Evaluation of Consumer Education Programs," *Journal of Consumer Research,* 6 (December), 270–279.

Bratic, Elaine and Rachel H. Greenberg (1980), "An Approach to the Standardization of Pretesting Health Public Service Announcements," paper presented at the 30th annual conference of the International Communication Association, Acapulco, Mexico (May 19).

Fox, Karen F. A. (1980), "Time as a Component of Price in Social Marketing," in *Marketing in the 80's: Changes and Challenges,* Richard P. Bagozzi et al., eds., Chicago: American Marketing Association, 464–467.

Gutman, Evelyn (1978), "Effective Marketing of a Cancer Screening Program," in *Marketing in Nonprofit Organizations,* Patrick J. Montana, ed., New York: Amacom, 133–147.

Houston, Franklin S. and Richard E. Homans (1977), "Public Agency Marketing: Pitfalls and Problems," *MSU Business Topics,* 25 (Summer), 37–40.

Kotler, Philip (1975), *Marketing for Nonprofit Organizations,* Englewood Cliffs, NJ: Prentice-Hall.

———, and Gerald Zaltman (1971), "Social Marketing: An Approach to Planned Social Change," *Journal of Marketing,* 35 (July), 3–12.

Laczniak, Gene R., Robert F. Lusch, and Patrick E. Murphy (1979), "Social Marketing: Its Ethical Dimensions," *Journal of Marketing,* 43 (Spring), 29–36.

Lazer, William and Eugene J. Kelley, eds. (1973), *Social Marketing: Perspectives and Viewpoints,* Homewood, IL: Richard D. Irwin, Inc.

Lovelock, Christopher H. (1979), "Theoretical Contributions from Services and Nonbusiness Marketing," working paper 79–16, Harvard Business School.

———, and Charles B. Weinberg (1975), "Contrasting Private and Public Sector Marketing," in *1974 Combined Proceedings,* Ronald C. Curhan, ed., Chicago: American Marketing Association, 242–247.

Luck, David J. (1974), "Social Marketing: Confusion Compounded," *Journal of Marketing,* 38 (October), 70–72.

Mendelsohn, H. (1973), "Some Reasons Why Information Campaigns Can Succeed," *Public Opinion Quarterly,* 37 (Spring), 50–61.

Novelli, William D. (1978), "Health Messages: Milk Duds, Sunburns and Other Consumer Perspectives," working paper, Porter, Novelli and Associates, Inc., Washington, D.C.

Phillips, Lynn W. (1978), "Threats to Validity in Quasi-Experimental Evaluations of Consumer Protection Reforms: A Critical Review of Extant Research," technical report 78–102, Marketing Science Institute, Cambridge, Mass.

Rossi, Peter H. and Sonia R. Wright (1977), "Evaluation Research: An Assessment of Theory, Practice and Politics," *Evaluation Quarterly,* 1, 5–52.

Rothschild, Michael L. (1979), "Marketing Communications in Nonbusiness Situations or Why It's So Hard to Sell Brotherhood Like Soap," *Journal of Marketing,* 43 (Spring), 11–20.

Sheth, Jagdish and Peter Wright, eds. (1974), *Marketing Analysis for Societal Problems,* Champaign, IL: University of Illinois Press.

Smith, William A. (1980), "Mass Media and Health Practices-Implementation: Description of Field Activity in Honduras," working paper, Academy for Educational Development, Inc., Washington, D.C.

Swinyard, William R. and Michael L. Ray (1977), "Advertising-Selling Interactions: An Attribution Theory Experiment," *Journal of Marketing Research,* 14 (November), 509–516.

U.S. Department of Health, Education, and Welfare (1979), *Diagnosis and Management of Hypertension: A Nationwide Survey of Physicians' Knowledge, Attitudes, and Reported Behavior,* DHEW Publication No. (NIH) 79–1056.

Ward, Graham W. (1978), "Changing Trends in Control of Hypertension," *Public Health Reports,* 93 (January–February), 31–34.

INDEX